D0217867

FOURTH EDITION

EXPERIMENTAL PSYCHOLOGY

UNDERSTANDING PSYCHOLOGICAL RESEARCH

FOURTH EDITION

EXPERIMENTAL PSYCHOLOGY

UNDERSTANDING PSYCHOLOGICAL RESEARCH

BARRY H. KANTOWITZ
BATTELLE MEMORIAL INSTITUTE, SEATTLE

HENRY L. ROEDIGER III
RICE UNIVERSITY

DAVID G. ELMES
WASHINGTON AND LEE UNIVERSITY

WEST PUBLISHING COMPANY
ST. PAUL   NEW YORK   LOS ANGELES   SAN FRANCISCO

Copyediting: Kathleen Rae Pruno
Text Design: Paula Schlosser Design
Composition: Parkwood Composition Services, Inc.

Cover Image: Orion, FPG International

COPYRIGHT © 1978   By Rand McNally
COPYRIGHT © 1984   By WEST PUBLISHING COMPANY
COPYRIGHT © 1988   By WEST PUBLISHING COMPANY
COPYRIGHT © 1991   By WEST PUBLISHING COMPANY
                    50 W. Kellogg Boulevard
                    P.O. Box 64526
                    St. Paul, MN 55164-1003

All rights reserved

Printed in the United States of America

98 97 96 95 94 93 92 91   8 7 6 5 4 3 2 1 0

Library of Congress Cataloging-in-Publication Data

Kantowitz, Barry H.
    Experimental psychology: understanding psychological research
Barry H. Kantowitz; Henry L. Roediger, III; David G. Elmes.—4th ed.
        p.   cm.
    Includes bibliographical references and index.
    ISBN 0-314-79995-8 (hard)
        1. Psychology, Experimental.   2. Psychology—Research.
I. Roediger, Henry L.   II. Elmes, David G.   III. Title.
BF181.K35   1991
150'.724—dc20   90-47054
                                            ∞ CIP

Photo/Figure Credits
Fig. 2–1. From *The Intelligent Eye* by R. L. Gregory. Copyright © 1970 R. L. Gregory. Used with permission of McGraw-Hill Book Company. **Fig. 2–2.** From L. C. Drickamer and S. H. Vessey, *Animal Behavior: Concepts, Processes, and Methods.* Copyright © 1982 by PWS Publishers. Used with permission of Willard Grant Press. All rights reserved. **Fig. 2–5.** Eron, Huesman, Lefkowitz, & Walder. Copyright © 1972 by The American Psychological Association. Reprinted by permission of the author. **Figs. 3–1, 3–2, and 3–3.** Piliavin, Piliavin, & Rodin. *Costs, Diffusion and the Stigmatized Victim,* Journal of Personality and Social Psychology, 32, 1975. Copyright © 1975 by The American Psychological Association. Reprinted by permission of the

Photo/Figure Credits continue following index

CONTENTS

PART TWO ▨ PRINCIPLES AND PRACTICES OF EXPERIMENTAL PSYCHOLOGY 152

Experimental Topics	6	7	8	9	10	11	12	13	14	15
Confounding			X							
Converging operations		X							X	
Counterbalancing				X						
Demand characteristics								X		
Ethical issues								X		
Experimental control/ extraneous variables						X		X		
Experimenter effects								X		
Field research								X		X
Generalization of results					X				X	
Interaction effects			X		X					
Measurement scales	X									
Operational definition	X						X			
Regression artifacts							X			
Reliability of measures							X			
Replication						X				
Scale attenuation					X					
Selection of dependent variable			X							
Small-*n* design	X			X						X
Verbal report		X				X				
Within- and between- subjects designs				X						

Organization of the Book

We have chosen to organize our book topically, for reasons described in the Preface. However, the subjects discussed in a topically organized book are included in our text. The table above lists important methodological topics covered in chapters 6 through 15 and the specific chapters in which they are discussed. (Many of these same concepts are introduced briefly in Part One of the book, the first five chapters.) The table should be useful for those who prefer an alternate organization to the one we have used in writing the text.

PREFACE

T HIS TEXTBOOK IS THE fourth edition of a book first published in 1978. Each successive edition has seen both major and minor changes, and this edition is no exception. One chapter is entirely new to this edition, another is essentially new (having been completely revised and given a new title), and a third chapter has been so radically changed that it, too, is essentially new. Most of the remaining chapters have also been improved in response to readers' comments, with many old examples deleted and new ones added. We have tried to blend the best aspects of the previous three editions with new features to make the book even more appealing. (We describe the changes in more detail below.) We are pleased that the continued popularity of this text has permitted us to produce this new edition, because we think we have been able to improve it and we have enjoyed working on it again.

The title *Experimental Psychology* has appeared on many textbooks that have lasted to become classics, beginning with E. B. Titchener's pair in the early 1900s, through Woodworth's (1928) text and its revision (Woodworth & Schlossberg, 1954), and finally to those books by Osgood (1953) and Underwood (1966). All these books provided an introduction to research methodology, but they did so in the context of fundamental research in experimental psychology. The books were primarily about the content of experimental psychology, with an emphasis on the research methods used to acquire the knowledge. We see our textbook as firmly within this tradition, even if much less encyclopedic than the great books mentioned above.

Today this approach is unique; during the 1970s, many "research methods" texts appeared that organize the subject matter quite differently. Instead of providing methodology in the context in which it is used, these books treat methodological topics (e.g., between-subjects designs, small-n designs) as chapter titles and introduce content examples to flesh out the discussion of the methods. This is certainly a defensible approach, and we have produced another text that embodies this method (*Research Methods in Psy-*

chology, by Elmes, Kantowitz, and Roediger, also published by West Publishing Co.). However, *Experimental Psychology* seeks to provide an integrated blend of content and methodology, with methods discussed in the context of actual research. A primary difference between our text and those of our predecessors in this tradition is that our approach is to select particular examples that best illustrate the methodological point under consideration, and that our book is intended mostly for an undergraduate audience with only a first course in psychology as a background.

Text Organization

The philosophy of the text remains unchanged. As with the first three editions, we have striven to achieve an integrated treatment of experimental psychology with a seamless link binding methodology and content. The book includes two main parts. The first five chapters constitute Part One, Fundamentals of Research, and discuss some basic methodological preliminaries that students need. In these chapters we describe some general aspects of science and theory construction; features of and differences among observational, correlational, and experimental methods (with an emphasis on the latter); ethical issues in research; and how to read and write research reports.

In the remaining ten chapters, which make up Part Two, Principles and Practices of Research, we flesh out the bare bones provided in Part One by illustrating experimental topics in the context of actual research problems. The chapters are provided with content titles (for example, Perception) and some content is covered in its own right, but the main purpose of the chapters is to present methodological topics in the context of actual research. This organization reflects our belief that the best way to provide students with an understanding of methodology is to embed it in the context of real problems that occur in conducting research. Methodology does not exist in a vacuum, but is devised to solved concrete research problems. We hope that presenting methods in the context of important content issues will help students to see the importance of considering research methods.

Chapter Format

The chapters in Part Two all share a common format. This parallel structure should help orient students to important features of the text that facilitate learning.

Chapter opening. The chapters begin with an outline and a quotation. Following a brief orientation to the content area explored in the chapter, the student will come across the first of several boxed inserts, which readers of the previous editions have found to be helpful and which have therefore been carried over to the fourth edition.

Introducing the Variables quickly orients the student to those independent, dependent, and control variables commonly used in particular research areas. Our coverage of these variables does not exhaust the possibilities, but it does include some of the most common ones.

Experimental Topics and Research Illustrations represents the main part of the chapter, in which two or three methodology issues are presented in the context of an actual research problem. Thus, for example, in chapter 10 we discuss the difficulty of ceiling and floor effects in the context of a memory experiment in which this problem actually arose. Many of these experimental topics have been introduced in Part One and are covered in more detail in Part Two. Some crucial topics are even covered more than once in Part Two to insure better comprehension. The content topics were chosen to be good vehicles for discussing the particular methodological point under consideration. Thus, the content topics may not represent the most important topics in the subject under discussion; nor do we intend our chapters to represent a complete summary of contemporary work in the area. To reiterate, our intent is to illustrate issues of methods in the context of actual research problems that are of interest. Two other unique features appear toward the end of each chapter in Part Two.

From Problem to Experiment: The Nuts and Bolts presents the rationale behind experimental-design decisions—how many subjects should be used, why variable X is selected instead of variable Y, and so on—when hypotheses are taken from a general form to the specifics of an experiment. These decisions are the "nuts and bolts" of experimental research. They are second nature to practicing experimenters and hence seldom articulated in journal articles, but they may represent puzzles to those new to research.

Psychology in Action suggests safe and simple experimental demonstrations that require little or no equipment and that can be used in or out of class. For example, chapter 7 includes a demonstration of the Stroop effect and chapter 14 presents methods to measure one's personal territory or "space bubble."

End-of-Chapter Features. Finally, each chapter contains a *Summary* in which the main points of the chapter are reviewed, a set of *Key Terms* for review and study, and several *Discussion Questions*.

Chapter Sequence

Although students will be best served by reading Part One in correct serial order, (especially the first three chapters), those professors and students more interested in methodology than in content can ignore the chapter numbers in Part Two. The table that cross-lists chapter numbers and experimental topics (to be found at the end of the Table of Contents) can be used to determine the order in which chapters in Part Two are assigned. Thus, the teacher has the option of following a more or less traditional order, or of creating a unique ordering better suited to his or her educational goals. Two lesser-used chapters which, however, may be quite necessary for some, are located in appendixes. Appendix A provides a brief sketch of the history of experimental psychology, and appendix B contains a review of basic statistics.

Changes in the Fourth Edition

Users of the third edition will note many changes in the fourth edition. We have added an entirely new chapter, chapter 4, on ethics in research. This addition was suggested by several reviewers and adopters. Chapter 15, Human Factors, is also new. It replaces the chapter in the third edition called "Applications of learning and attention theory: Methodology outside the laboratory." Reviewers justifiably complained about the rather cumbersome nature (and title) of this chapter spanning, as it did, rather disparate fields. The new chapter concentrates on human factors psychology while still fulfilling the goal of illustrating research methodology in applied settings. A third major change has been the complete revision of chapter 5, "How to read and write research reports," complete with new examples of articles. Students should find these new examples easier to follow, and they should prove a more useful aid for students when preparing their own papers in the format required by the American Psychological Association.

In addition to these major changes, most of the other chapters have been revised to include better examples of research topics or to provide more up-to-date coverage. For example, in chapter 12 we discuss how psychologists might define intelligence in a computer in terms of specific operations and criteria. In chapter 10, we use research about the levels of processing approach to memory in discussing the issue of generality and generalizability of research. Because the levels of processing approach to memory has engendered such a great amount of research, with investigators asking whether the basic effects hold over a wide array of conditions, this topic serves as a particularly useful focus to ask about generalizability. These two additions are only samples of how we have tried to pick particularly cogent pieces of research to illustrate methodological points. As always, these changes in examples still serve to illustrate some important methodological topic. The items above provide only a selection of the numerous improvements in the fourth edition.

Ancillaries

The fourth edition is accompanied by two outstanding ancillary features. The Study Guide for students was prepared by David G. Payne of the State University of New York at Binghamton. A number of useful study aids are included for each chapter: a summary; a key terms list; a programmed review; an experimental project that requires little equipment; an experimental dilemma for discussion; three types of sample questions for tests. The Study Guide is keyed for the text and permits review and study opportunities that should prove invaluable for students. We hope you will consider adopting it.

Bradford H. Challis of the University of Toronto has prepared an Instructor's Manual that contains many aids for teaching a course on experimental psychology and research methods. Included are a selection of test questions for each chapter (both multiple choice and essay) and suggestions for lectures and demonstrations.

Acknowledgments

It takes many more people than authors to create a text, and we are pleased to acknowledge with gratitude the assistance of numerous others. Our greatest debt is to the users of previous editions. Without their helpful suggestions, this new edition would not exist. We thank our editor, Mary Schiller, for motivating us to do a fourth edition and for her many helpful suggestions along the way. Although many teachers offered useful suggestions, we would be remiss not to thank specifically John B. Best, David del Castillo, John Ceraso, Wendy Domjan, Jerome Friedman, E. Rae Harcum, Richard Haude, John Jahnke, Janet McDonald, Kenneth McIntire, Gary Meunier, Douglas Mook, Renee Neely, Gregg Oden, Charles Peyser, James Pomerantz, Robert Proctor, Albert Silverstein, Lois Tepper, Harriet Wall, and Mary Susan Weldon for cogent reviews and sage advice. Amy Adamson and Heather Turner helped in tracking down references and in numerous other ways, and we appreciate their hard work and good humor. The staff at West Publishing Co. offered expert professional assistance and turned a manuscript into a book with remarkable speed and efficiency. Emily Autumn, our production editor, deserves special praise for her masterful efforts on our behalf. We would like to acknowledge the help of several authors and publishers who permitted us to reprint some of their work, and we are grateful to the Literary Executor of the late Sir Ronald A. Fisher, F.R.S. and to the Longman Group Ltd. of London, for permission to reprint from their book *Statistical Tables for Biological, Agricultural, and Medical Research.* Finally, our deepest gratitude and affection go to our families, who tolerated our absence during the long period it took to complete this revision.

Barry H. Kantowitz
Henry L. Roediger III
David G. Elmes

ABOUT THE AUTHORS

BARRY H. KANTOWITZ is a Senior Staff Research Scientist at Battelle Memorial Institute, Seattle, in the Center for Human Factors and Organizational Effectiveness. He received the Ph.D. degree in Experimental Psychology from the University of Wisconsin in 1969. From 1969 to 1987 he held positions as Assistant, Associate, and Professor of Psychological Sciences, at Purdue University, West Lafayette, Indiana. Dr. Kantowitz was elected a Fellow of the American Psychological Association in 1974. He has been a National Institute of Mental Health Postdoctoral Fellow at the University of Oregon, a Senior Lecturer in Ergonomics at the Norwegian Institute of Technology, Trondheim, Norway, and a Visiting Professor of Technical Psychology at the University of Lulea, Sweden. He has written and edited more than one dozen books. His research on human attention, mental workload, reaction time, human-machine interaction, and human factors has been supported by the Office of Education, the National Institute of Mental Health, the National Aeronautics and Space Administration, and the Air Force Office of Scientific Research. He served a five-year term on the editorial board of *Organizational Behavior and Human Performance*. He has published over seventy scientific articles and book chapters.

HENRY L. ROEDIGER III is the Lynette S. Autrey Professor of Psychology at Rice University, where he has taught since 1988. He received a B.A. degree in psychology from Washington and Lee University in 1969 and a Ph.D. in cognitive psychology from Yale University in 1973. He has previously been on the faculty at Purdue University (1973–1988) and spent three years as a visiting professor at the University of Toronto. His research interests lie in cognitive psychology, particularly in human learning and memory. He has published over seventy chapters, articles, and reviews as well as two other textbooks: *Psychology* (coauthored with E. D. Capaldi, S. G. Paris, and J. Polivy) and *Research Methods in Psychology* (with D. G. Elmes and B. H. Kantowitz). He also edited (with F. I. M. Craik) *Varieties of Memory and Consciousness: Essays in Honour of Endel Tulving.* Roediger serves as a Consulting editor for *Contemporary Psychology; Journal of Experimental Psychology: Learning, Memory, and Cognition;* and *Journal of Memory and Language.* He served as Editor of the *Journal of Experimental Psychology: Learning, Memory, and Cognition* from 1985–1989 and as its Associate Editor from 1981 to 1984. He is a member of the Governing Board of the Psychonomics Society (Chair, 1989–1990) and is Secretary-Treasurer of the Midwestern Psychological Association.

DAVID G. ELMES is a Professor of Psychology and Head of the Department of Psychology at Washington and Lee University, where he has taught since 1967. He earned his B.A. with high honors from the University of Virginia and continued on to complete the M.A. and Ph.D. degrees there. Elmes has also taught at Hampden-Sydney College, was a research associate for a year in the Human Performance Center of the University of Michigan, and was a Visiting Fellow of University College at the University of Oxford. At Washington and Lee he is codirector of the Cognitive Science Program. Professor Elmes edited *Readings in Experimental Psychology* and is coauthor of the third edition of *Research Methods in Psychology* (with B. H. Kantowitz and H. L. Roediger III). He has published numerous articles concerned with human and animal learning and memory in the *Journal of Comparative and Physiological Psychology, Memory & Cognition, Physiological Psychology,* and *Journal of Experimental Psychology: Learning, Memory, and Cognition,* among others. He frequently referees papers submitted to technical journals and was a Consulting Editor for the *Journal of Experimental Psychology: Learning, Memory and Cognition* for several years.

PART ONE

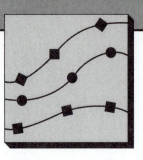

Fundamentals of Research

AS STATED IN THE PREFACE, this text uses an integrated approach, blending content and methodology. Part One, "Fundamentals of Research," builds the foundation by explaining basic concepts that are required for an understanding of the meld of content and methodology presented in the chapters of part two.

We first discuss some general issues pertinent to all the sciences, and then show how these general issues apply in particular to the science of psychology. As with any science, psychology centers about two crucial concepts: theory and data. Acquiring useful data is a primary challenge for experimental psychologists. Thus, there is extensive discussion of the research techniques that psychologists use to acquire meaningful data. We divide these techniques into two broad classifications: (1) observation and correlation, and (2) experiments. Part one provides an introduction to these topics; part two elaborates and provides many concrete illustrations of the concepts introduced in part one.

Scientists are guided not only by techniques of practice, but also by ethical principles. Ethical issues in psychological research are examined in chapter 4. Before undertaking a research project, you must understand the type of ethical dilemmas that you will face and the ethical principles that should influence your behavior.

Finished research is usually reported in technical journal articles in a wide variety of psychology journals. The style required for these journals is quite distinctive and may be unlike any you have experienced in reading magazine articles or term papers. In chapter 5, we provide a set of guidelines that will help you to read articles in psychology journals, and also to write in the technical style required. If you have a laboratory component to your course, you may be required to write reports of this form.

The first five chapters introduce many crucial concepts for an understanding of research in experimental psychology. In part one, these concepts are often presented abstractly. In part two, we will provide many concrete examples of how these concepts are used in research.

1

Explanation in Scientific Psychology

Ask any scientist what he conceives the scientific method to be, and he will adopt an expression that is at once solemn and shifty-eyed; solemn, because he feels he ought to declare an opinion, shifty-eyed because he is wondering how to conceal the fact that he has no opinion to declare. If taunted he would probably mumble something about "Induction" and "Establishing the Laws of Nature," but if anyone working in a laboratory professed to be trying to establish Laws of Nature by induction we should begin to think he was overdue for leave.

—P. B. MEDAWAR

THE GOAL OF SCIENTIFIC PSYCHOLOGY is to understand why people think and act as they do. In contrast to the informal and secondary sources of knowledge relied on by nonscientists, psychologists use a variety of well-developed techniques to gather information and develop theoretical explanations. As one example of this scientific approach to understanding, consider the following case study of the research process.

Making Sense of the World

Social Loafing

A common observation—one you probably have made yourself on many occasions—is that people working in a group often seem to "slack off" in their effort. Many people in groups seem willing to let a few do the work. Bibb Latané, a social psychologist, noticed this tendency and decided to study it experimentally. Initially, Latané examined the research literature to see if there were any evidence for this phenomenon of people's working less hard in groups, which he named *social loafing*. One of the earliest studies of social loafing was conducted by a French Agricultural Engineer (Ringelmann, 1913; Kravitz and Martin, 1986), who asked people to pull on a rope as hard as they could. The subjects pulled by themselves or with one, two, or seven others. A sensitive gauge was used to measure how strongly they pulled the rope. If people exert as much effort in groups as when alone, then the group performance should be the sum of the efforts of all individuals. Ringelmann discovered that groups of two pulled at only 95 percent of their capacity, and groups of three and eight sank to 85 percent and 49 percent, respectively. So, it is probably not just our imaginations when we notice others (and ourselves?) seeming to put forth less effort when working in groups: Ringelmann's research provides us with a good example of social loafing.

Latané and his colleagues went on to perform a systematic series of experiments on the phenomenon of social loafing (Latané, 1981; Latané, Williams, and Harkins, 1979). They first showed that the phenomenon could be obtained in other experimental situations besides that of rope pulling. They have also demonstrated that social loafing occurs in several different cultures (Gabrenya, Latané, and Wang, 1983), and even holds for young children. Thus social loafing seems to be a pervasive characteristic of working in groups.

Latané has related this work to a more general theory of human social behavior (Latané, 1981). The evidence from the experimental studies points to *diffusion of responsibility* as a possible reason for social loafing. People working by themselves think they are responsible for completing the task; when they work in groups, however, this feeling of responsibility diffuses to others. The same idea accounts for behavior in other group situations: if one of your professors asked a question in a class containing only two other people, you would probably feel responsible for trying to answer. However, if there were two hundred other people in the class, you would likely feel much less responsible for answering. Similarly, people are more likely to help in an emergency when they feel the burden of responsibility than when there are several others about who could help.

One possible benefit of such basic research into a phenomenon is that the findings may be applied later to solve some practical problem. A great problem in American society is the declining productivity of the work force. Although social loafing is, at best, only one factor involved in this complicated issue, Marriott (1949) showed that factory workers working in large groups produce less per individual than do those working in small groups. Thus, basic research that would show a way to overcome the problem of social loafing may be of great practical import. In fact, Williams, Harkins, and Latané (1981) did find conditions that eliminated the effect of social loafing in their experimental situation. When individual performance (rather than just performance of the entire group) could be monitored within the group situation, the individuals worked just as hard as they did when they worked alone. Certainly more research must be done, but it may be that simply measuring individual performance in group situations could help eliminate social loafing and increase productivity. The proposed solution may seem simple, but in many jobs only group performance is measured: individual performance is ignored.

We have taken the trouble to discuss Latané's studies of social loafing as an example of psychological research to illustrate how an interesting problem can be brought into a laboratory setting and studied in a controlled manner. The experiments performed will, when carefully conducted, promote a better understanding of the phenomenon of interest than will simple observation of events and reflection about them. This book is largely about the proper conduct of such experimental studies—how to develop hypotheses, arrange experimental conditions to test the hypotheses, collect observations (data) within an experiment, and then analyze and interpret the data collected. In short, in this book we try to cover the fundamentals of scientific inquiry as applied to psychology.

Before examining the specifics of research, we will discuss some general issues in the remainder of this chapter. The research on social loafing will be used to illustrate several aspects of psychological science—its purposes, its sources, and its nature.

Curiosity: The Wellspring of Science

A scientist wants to discover how and why things work. In this desire he or she is not different from a child or anyone else who also is curious about the world we inhabit. The casual observer may not feel terribly frustrated if some observation (for example, that water always goes down a sink drain counterclockwise, or that individual effort in a group is low) cannot be explained. However, the professional scientist has a strong desire to pursue an observation until an explanation is at hand or a problem is solved. It is not so much that scientists are more curious than other people as that they are willing to go to much greater lengths to satisfy their curiosity than are nonscientists. This unwillingness to tolerate unanswered questions and unsolved problems has led science to develop several techniques for obtaining relief from curiosity. It is the careful application of these techniques that distinguishes scientific curiosity from everyday curiosity.

Of what use is scientific curiosity? What purpose does it serve? We have stated that psychologists try to determine why people think and act as they do. Let us explore what this means in more detail.

Sources of Knowledge

Fixation of Belief

Science and scientific psychology in particular are valid ways to acquire knowledge about the world around us. What characteristics of the scientific approach make it a desirable way to learn about and arrive at beliefs about the nature of things? Perhaps the best way to answer this question is to contrast science with other modes of fixing belief, since science is only one way that beliefs are formed.

More than a hundred years ago, the American philosopher Charles Sanders Peirce (1877) compared the scientific way of knowing with three other methods of developing beliefs. He called these the *authority, tenacity,* and *a priori* methods. According to Peirce, the simplest way of fixing belief is to take someone else's word on faith. A trusted authority tells you what is true and what is false. Young children believe what their parents tell them simply because Mommy and Daddy are always right. As children get older they may discover, unhappily, that Mom and Dad are not always correct when it comes to astrophysics, macroeconomics, computer technology, and other specialized fields of knowledge. Although this may cause children to doubt some of their parents' earlier proclamations, it may not result in utter rejection of this method of fixing belief. Instead, some other authority may be sought. Religious beliefs are formed by the method of authority. Long after children have rejected their parents as the source of all knowledge, they may still believe that the pope is infallible insofar as religious doctrine is concerned. Believing the evening news means that one accepts Dan Rather or some other news commentator as authority. You may believe your professors because they are authorities. Since people lack the resources to investigate everything they learn, much knowledge and many beliefs are fixed by the method of authority. Provided nothing happens to raise doubts about the competence of the authority setting the beliefs, this method offers the great advantages of minimum effort and substantial security. It is most pleasant in a troubled world to have complete faith in beliefs handed down to you.

Another method of fixing belief is one in which a person steadfastly refuses to alter acquired knowledge, regardless of evidence to the contrary. The method of tenacity, as it was termed by Peirce, is commonly seen in racial bigots who rigidly cling to a stereotype even in the presence of a good counterexample. Although this method of maintaining a belief may not be entirely rational, we cannot say it is completely without value. Bigots are still around and somehow manage to find a few others to share their beliefs. The method of tenacity allows people to maintain a uniform and constant outlook on things, so it may relieve them from a certain amount of stress and psychological discomfort. For people who have difficulty handling stress, the method of tenacity may be a reasonable way to fix belief.

The third nonscientific method discussed by Peirce fixes belief a priori. In this context the term *a priori* refers to something that is believed without prior study or examination. Propositions that seem reasonable are believed. This is an extension of the method of authority. However, there is no one particular authority being followed blindly in this method. The general cultural outlook is what seems to fix belief a priori. People once believed the world was flat; and it did seem reasonable to suppose that the sun revolved around the earth as does the moon. Indeed, the world does look flat if you are not in a spacecraft.

The last of Peirce's methods, the *scientific* one, fixes belief on the basis of experience. If we define scientific psychology (as well as science in general) as a repeatable, self-correcting undertaking that seeks to understand phenomena on the basis of empirical observation, then we can see several advantages to science over the methods just outlined. Let us see what we mean by *empirical* and *self-correcting*, and examine the advantages associated with those aspects of science. First, none of those other methods relies on data (observations of the world) obtained by systematic observation. In other words, there is no empirical basis for fixing belief. The word *empirical* is derived from an old Greek word meaning *experience*. Having an empirical basis for beliefs means that experience rather than faith is the source of knowledge. Having one's beliefs fixed by authority carries no guarantee that the authority obtained data before forming an opinion. By definition, the method of tenacity refuses to consider data, as does the a priori method. Facts that are considered in these other modes of fixing belief are not ordinarily obtained by systematic procedures. For example, casual observation was the "method" that led to the ideas that the world was flat and that frogs spontaneously generated from the mud each spring, as Aristotle believed.

The second advantage of science is that it offers procedures for establishing the superiority of one belief over another. Persons holding different beliefs will find it difficult to reconcile their opinions. Science overcomes this problem. In principle, anyone can make an empirical observation, which means that scientific data can be public and can be repeatedly obtained. Through public observations, new beliefs are compared with old beliefs, and old beliefs are discarded if they do not fit the empirical facts. This does not imply that each and every scientist instantaneously drops outmoded beliefs in favor of new opinions. Changing scientific beliefs is usually a slow process, but eventually incorrect ideas are weeded out. Empirical, public observations are the cornerstone of the scientific method, because they make science a *self-correcting* endeavor.

Scientific Procedures

The remainder of this book details appropriate ways to make empirical observations. Here we will outline the nature of the scientific procedures used to gather empirical data.

Science usually begins with analysis: the breaking down of a complex problem into its elements. Psychological analysis of thought and behavior involves *description, prediction,* and *explanation.* With regard to social loafing, description refers to what social loafing entails and when and where it occurs. Prediction in this case specifies relationships, such as the one relating group and social loafing. How things covary allows the psychologist to predict future behaviors. But ultimately psychologists want to be able to explain the behavior. Explanation here means that the psychologist can determine some of the conditions under which social loafing occurs—put another way, the causes of social loafing.

The analytic activities of *description, prediction,* and *explanation* correspond to the three major classes of research techniques used in scientific psychology: *observation, correlation,* and *experimentation. Observation* procedures include naturalistic observation. Latané's initial views about social loafing were shaped by his observations in natural settings. Another way of obtaining descriptive data is by means of surveys, in which substantial numbers of people are systematically interviewed about some aspect of behavior. The case study is another observation technique. In a case study, one person (or, perhaps, a few people) are interrogated in detail to obtain a descriptive history of that individual.

Very often the results from these observation procedures allow further research. A *correlation* technique might be used for prediction or selection. Even though you may not have been aware of it, you probably were selected by your college admissions office on the results of correlation research. College admissions offices correlate such things as high-school grades with freshman college grades so that they can predict who will succeed (at least in the freshman year). Thereafter, students with certain high-school credentials are selected on the basis of the previous correlation, and the admissions office can then predict that the selected students have a particular chance of success.

If the goal is, for example, to explain or determine the causes of social loafing, then the psychologist will have to engage in *experimentation.* Experimentation involves manipulating or changing some aspect of the situation and observing the effect this has on some thought or behavior. In a laboratory setting, an experimenter might vary the number of other people in a group (from zero to seven) and note the differences in effort that result from changes in group size.

A type of research that is not quite an experiment, the *quasi-experiment,* uses natural manipulations rather than ones imposed by the researcher. In a quasi-experiment, the "manipulation" could be ethnic group (social loafing in Chinese people contrasted to that in Americans), or it could be any other naturally occurring attribute or event, such as age, intelligence, the occurrence of a strike in industry, and so on. Quasi-experiments do not allow as much control as true ones do; therefore the conclusions drawn from a quasi-experiment usually cannot be as strong as the explanations derived from a true experiment with a controlled manipulation.

The appropriate use of these research techniques and an adequate analysis of the data obtained from them provide the backbone of scientific psychology. Before considering the details of these procedures, we will examine the nature of the scientific explanation.

The Nature of the Scientific Explanation

Empirical observation and self-correction are the hallmarks of the scientific method. In this section we will examine how these work in science and scientific psychology.

Let us first step back and look at the social loafing research in a general way. Casual observation and some applied work suggested the problem area to be investigated. Laboratory experiments indicated some characteristics of social loafing and tested some predictions about its nature. Eventually, the data from the experiments suggested a solution to the practical aspects of social loafing, and the same data were related to diffusion of responsibility, a more general theory in social psychology. This summary seems to capture how science typically works: empirical observations made on the basis of either casual observations or more formal theories reveal something about those theories, which in turn can lead to further empirical work.

According to Harré (1983), this cyclical and self-correcting nature of science was first recognized by Francis Bacon (1561–1626), who has been credited with being the leading force in the scientific revolution that began in the seventeenth century (Jones, 1982). Although Bacon's analysis might today be seen as somewhat primitive, he anticipated several important aspects of modern science that we will explore in detail.

Induction and Deduction

Certain basic elements are shared by all approaches to science. The most important of these are *data* (empirical observations) and *theory* (organization of concepts that permit prediction of data). Science needs and uses both data and theory, and our outline of research on social loafing indicates that they can be interlinked in a complex way. However, in the history of science, individual scientists have differed about which is more important and which comes first. Trying to decide this is a little like trying to decide whether the chicken or the egg comes first. Science attempts to understand why things work the way they do, and, as we will argue, understanding involves both data and theory.

Although Bacon recognized the importance of both data and theory, he believed in the primacy of empirical observations; modern scientists also emphasize data and view progress in science as working from data to theory. Such an approach is an example of *induction*, in which reasoning proceeds from particular data to a general theory. The converse approach, which emphasizes theory predicting data, is called *deduction;* here, reasoning proceeds from a general theory to particular data. Because many scientists and philosophers of science have argued for the primacy of one form of reasoning over the other, we will examine induction and deduction in some detail.

Since empirical observations distinguish science from other modes of fixing belief, many have argued that induction must be the way that science should work. As Harré (1983) states it, "observations and the results of experiments are said to be 'data,' which provide a sound and solid base for the erection of the fragile edifice of scientific thought" (p. 6). In the case of social loafing, the argument would be that the facts of social loafing derived from experimentation produced the theory of diffusion of responsibility.

One problem with a purely inductive approach has to do with the finality of empirical observations. Scientific observations are tied to the circumstances under which they are made, which means that the laws or theories that are induced from them must also be limited in scope. Subsequent experiments in different contexts may suggest another theory or modifications to an existing one, so our theories that are induced on the basis of particular observations can (and usually do) change when other observations are made. This, of course, is a problem only if one takes an authoritarian view of ideas and believes in clinging tenaciously to a particular theory. Thus, theories induced from observations are tentative ideas not final truths, and the theoretical changes that occur as a result of continued empirical work exemplify the self-correcting nature of science.

According to the deductive view, which emphasizes the primacy of theory, the important scientific aspect of the social loafing research is the empirical guidance provided by the formal theory of social loafing. Further, the more general theory, diffusion of responsibility, provides understanding of social loafing. The deductive approach holds well-developed theories in high regard. Casual observations, informal theories, and data take second place to broad theories that describe and predict a substantial number of observations.

From the standpoint of the deductive approach, scientific understanding means, in part, that a theory will predict that certain kinds of empirical observations should occur. In the case of social loafing, the theory of diffusion of responsibility suggests that monitoring individual performance in a group should reduce the diffusion of responsibility, which in turn will reduce the amount of social loafing that is observed. This prediction, as we have seen, proves to be correct.

But what do correct predictions reveal? If a theory is verified by the results of experiments, a deductive scientist might have increased confidence in the veracity of the theory. However, since empirical observations are not final and can change, something other than verification may be essential for acceptance or rejection of a theory. Popper (1961), a philosopher of science, has suggested that good theories must be fallible. That is, the empirical predictions must be capable of tests that could show them to be false. This suggestion of Popper's has been called the *falsifiability view*. According to the falsifiability view, the temporary nature of induction makes negative evidence more important than positive support. If a prediction is supported by data, one cannot say that the theory is true. However, if a theory leads to a prediction that is not supported by the data, then Popper would argue that the theory must be false, and it should be rejected. According to Popper, a theory can never be proven; it can only be disproven.

One problem with the deductive approach has to do with the theories themselves. Most theories include many assumptions about the world that are difficult to test and that may be wrong. In Latané's work one assumption underlying the general theory is that measuring a person's behavior in an experimental context does not change the behavior in question. Although this often is a reasonable assumption, we will show later that people can react to being observed in unusual ways, which means that this assumption is sometimes wrong. If the untested assumptions are wrong, then a particular experiment that falsifies a theory may have falsified it for the wrong reasons. That is, the test of the theory may not have been fair or appropriate. It can be concluded, therefore, that the deductive approach by itself cannot lead to scientific understanding.

At this point you may be wondering whether scientific understanding is possible if both induction and deduction are not infallible. Do not despair. Science is self-correcting, and it can provide answers to problems, however temporary those answers may be. Scientific understanding changes as scientists ply their trade. We have a better understanding of social loafing now than we did before Latané and his coworkers undertook their research. Through a combination of induction and deduction (see figure 1–1), science progresses toward a more thorough understanding of its problems.

By way of concluding this section, let us reexamine social loafing. Initially, positive experimental results bolstered our confidence in the general notion of social loafing. These results, in turn, suggested hypotheses about the nature of social loafing. Is it a general phenomenon that would influence even group-oriented individuals? Does it occur in the workplace as well as the laboratory? Positive answers to these questions are consistent with a diffusion-of-responsibility interpretation of social loafing.

In the next phase of the research, Latané and his colleagues attempted to eliminate other explanations of social loafing by falsifying predictions made by these alternative theories. In their earlier work, Latané and his colleagues tested a particular person's effort both when alone and when in a group. They subsequently reasoned that under these conditions a person might rest during the group test so that greater effort could be allocated to the task when he or she was tested alone. To eliminate the possibility that allocation of effort rather than diffusion of responsibility accounted for social loafing, they conducted additional experiments in which a person was tested either alone or in a group—but not

FIGURE 1–1.

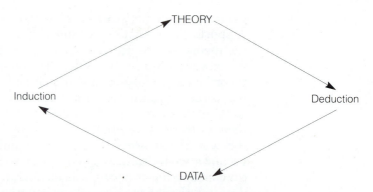

A theory organizes and predicts data. By means of deduction, particular observations (data) may be predicted. By means of induction, the data suggest organizing principles (theories). This circular relationship indicates that theories are tentative pictures of how data are organized.

in both situations. Contrary to the allocation-of-effort hypothesis, the results indicated that social loafing occurred when a person was tested in just that one condition of being in a group (Harkins, Latané, and Williams, 1980). Therefore, it was concluded that diffusion of responsibility was a more appropriate account of social loafing than was allocation of effort.

Note the course of events here. Successive experiments pitted two possible outcomes against each other in the hopes that one possibility would be eliminated and one supported by the outcome of the research. As Platt (1964) has noted, this eliminative procedure, which he calls *strong inference,* should, in the ideal case, yield one remaining theory (if the procedure of strong inference is used repeatedly). Of course, subsequent tests of the diffusion-of-responsibility theory probably will contradict it or add to it in some way. Thus, the theory might be revised or, with enough contradictions, rejected for an alternative explanation, itself supported by empirical observations. In any event, where we stand now is that we have constructed a reasonable view of what social loafing entails and what seems to cause it. It is the mixture of hypotheses induced from data and experimental tests deduced from theory that resulted in the theory that diffusion of responsibility leads to social loafing.

What Is a Theory?

Thus far we have argued that scientific understanding is tentative: incorrect theories are modified and additional information is gathered through empirical tests about the problem at hand. In this section we will focus on explaining theories.

A theory can be crudely defined as a set of related statements that explains a variety of occurrences. The more the occurrences, and the fewer the statements, the better the theory. The law of gravity explains falling apples, the behavior of roller coasters, and the position of bodies within the solar system. With a small number of statements about the mutual attraction of bodies, it explains a large number of events. It is therefore a powerful theory. (This does not necessarily mean it is a correct theory, since there are some events it cannot explain.)

Theory in psychology performs two major functions. First, it provides a framework for the systematic and orderly display of data—that is, it serves as a convenient way for the scientist to *organize* data. Even the most dedicated inductive scientist will eventually have difficulty remembering the outcomes of dozens of experiments. Theory can be used as a kind of filing system to help experimenters organize results. Second, it allows the scientist to generate *predictions* for situations in which no data have been obtained. The greater the degree of precision of these predictions, the better the theory. With the best of intentions, scientists who claim to be testing the same theory often derive from the theory different predictions about the same situation. This unfortunate circumstance is relatively more common in psychology, where many theories are stated in a loose verbal fashion, than in physics, where theories are more formal and better quantified through the use of mathematics. Although psychologists are rapidly becoming equipped to state their theories more precisely through such formal mechanisms as mathematics and computer simulations, the typical psychological theory still is not as precise as theories in more established, older sciences.

Let us see how the theory devised by Latané to account for social loafing stacks up with regard to organization and prediction. The theory of diffusion of responsibility organizes a substantial amount of data about social loafing. More important, the theory seems to account for a remarkable variety of other observations. For example, Latané (1981) notes that the size of a tip left at a restaurant table is inversely related to the number of people in the dinner party. Likewise, proportionately more people committed themselves to Christ at smaller Billy Graham crusades than at larger ones. Finally, work by Latané and Darley (1970), which is discussed in detail later in this book, shows that the willingness of people to help in a crisis is inversely related to the number of other bystanders present. The entire pattern of results can be subsumed under the notion of diffusion of responsibility, which asserts that people feel less responsibility for their own actions when they are in a group than when they are alone—so, they are less likely to help in an emergency, they are less likely to leave a large tip, and so on. Latané's theory also makes rather precise predictions about the impact of the presence of other people on a person's actions. In fact, one version of the theory (Latané, 1981) presents its major assumptions in terms of mathematical equations.

Theories are devised to organize concepts and facts into a coherent pattern and to predict additional observations. Sometimes the two functions of theory—organization and prediction—are called *description* and *explanation*, respectively. Unfortunately, formulating the roles of theory in this manner often leads to an argument about the relative superiority of deductive or inductive approaches to science—a discussion we have already dismissed as fruitless. According to the deductive scientist, the inductive scientist is concerned only with description. The inductive scientist defends against this charge by retorting that description is explanation—if a psychologist could correctly predict and control all behavior by referring to properly organized sets of results, then that psychologist would also be explaining behavior. The argument is futile because both views are correct. If all the necessary data were properly organized, predictions could be made without recourse to a formal body of theoretical statements. Since all the data are not properly organized as yet, and perhaps never will be, theories are required to bridge the gap between knowledge and ignorance. Remember, however, that theories will never be complete, because all the data will never be in. So, we have merely recast the argument between inductive and deductive views about which approach will more quickly and surely lead to truth. Ultimately, description and explanation may be equivalent. The two terms describe the path taken more than the eventual theoretical outcome. So, to avoid this pitfall, we shall refer to the two major functions of theory as *organization* and *prediction* rather than as description and explanation.

Intervening Variables

Theories often use constructs that summarize the effects of several variables. Variables are discussed at greater length in chapter 3. For now, we will only briefly describe two different kinds of variables. Independent variables are those manipulated by the experimenter. For example, not allowing rats to have any water for several hours would create an independent variable called hours of deprivation. Dependent variables are those observed by the experimenter. For example, one could observe how much water a rat drinks.

Science tries to explain the world by relating independent and dependent variables. *Intervening variables* are abstract concepts that link independent variables to dependent variables. Gravity is a familiar construct that accomplishes this goal. It can relate an independent variable, how many feet of height an object is dropped, to a dependent variable, the speed of the object when it hits the ground. Gravity also summarizes the effects of height on speed for all manner of objects. Gravity explains falling apples as well as falling baseballs. Science progresses when a single construct, such as gravity, explains outcomes in many different environments.

Miller (1959) has explained how a single intervening variable, thirst, organizes experimental results efficiently. Figure 1–2 shows a direct and an indirect way to relate an independent variable,

FIGURE 1–2.

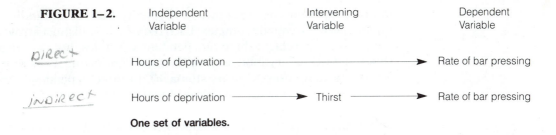

DiRect

iNDiRect

One set of variables.

hours of deprivation, to a dependent variable, rate of bar pressing. The dependent variable is obtained by placing a rat into a small chamber where it can press a bar to obtain drinking water. The experimenter observes the rate (how many presses per minute) at which the rat presses the bar to get water. The direct relationship uses only one arrow to link hours of deprivation to rate of bar pressing. After doing the experiment, we could build a mathematical formula that directly related hours of deprivation to rate of bar pressing. The indirect method uses two arrows. The first arrow relates hours of deprivation to thirst, an intervening variable. The second arrow relates the intervening variable, thirst, to the rate of bar pressing. Since the indirect method is more complicated, requiring an extra arrow, you might expect the scientist to prefer the direct method of explanation. Indeed, if the only scientific goal were to relate hours of deprivation to rate of bar pressing, you would be correct because science prefers simple explanations to complex explanations. However, as we shall explain, the scientific goal is more general.

Figure 1–3 relates two independent variables, hours of deprivation and feeding dry food, to two dependent variables, rate of bar pressing and volume of water drunk. Again both direct and

FIGURE 1–3.

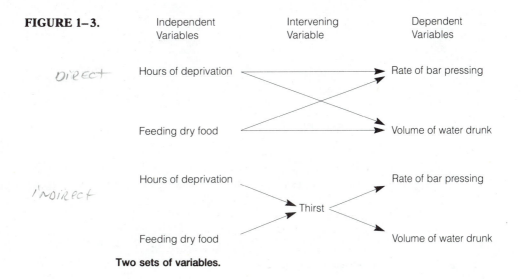

DiRect

iNDiRect

Two sets of variables.

indirect explanations are shown. In figure 1–3 direct and indirect explanations are equally complex. Each requires four distinct arrows.

Figure 1–4 relates three independent variables, hours of deprivation, feeding dry food, and saline injection (giving a rat water through a tube inserted in its stomach), to three dependent variables, rate of bar pressing, volume of water drunk, and amount of quinine required to stop the rat from drinking. Again both direct and indirect explanations are shown. Now it is obvious that the indirect method is less complicated. It requires six distinct arrows whereas the direct method requires nine arrows. So as science tries to relate more independent and dependent variables, intervening variables become more efficient.

There is yet another advantage of intervening variables. Thirst, no matter how produced, should have the same effect on all dependent variables. This can be tested in experiments. If it is not true, we can reject the idea of a single intervening variable. Later chapters discuss this under the topic of converging operations.

Evaluating Theories

The sophisticated scientist does not try to determine if a particular theory is true or false in an absolute sense. There is no black-and-white approach to theory evaluation. A theory may be known to

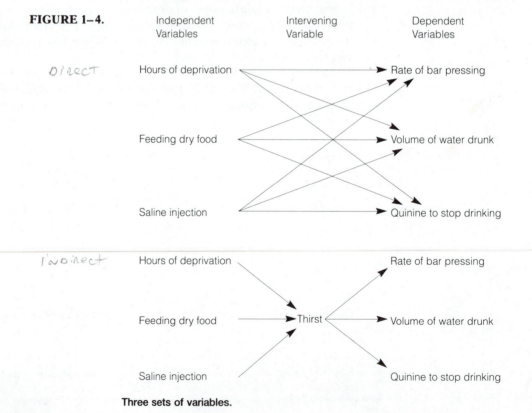

FIGURE 1–4.

Direct

Indirect

Three sets of variables.

be incorrect in some portion and yet continue to be used. In modern physics, light is represented, according to the theory chosen, either as discrete particles called quanta or as continuous waves. Logically, light cannot be both at the same time. Thus, you might think that at least one of these two theoretical views must necessarily be false. The physicist tolerates this ambiguity (although perhaps not cheerfully) and uses whichever representation—quantum or wave—is more appropriate. Instead of flatly stating that a theory is true, the scientist is much more likely to state that it is supported substantially by data, thereby leaving open the possibility that new data may not support the theory. Although scientists do not state that a theory is true, they must often decide which of several theories is best. As noted earlier, explanations are tentative; nevertheless, the scientist still needs to decide which theory is best for now. To do so, there must be explicit criteria for evaluating a theory. Three such criteria are *parsimony*, *precision*, and *testability*.

One important criterion was hinted at earlier when it was stated that the fewer the statements in a theory, the better the theory. This criterion is called *parsimony*, or sometimes Occam's razor, after William of Occam. If a theory needs a separate statement for every result it must explain, clearly no economy has been gained by the theory. Theories gain power when they can explain many results with few explanatory concepts. Thus, if two theories have the same number of concepts, the one that can explain more results is a better theory. If two theories can explain the same number of results, the one with fewer explanatory concepts is to be preferred.

Precision is another important criterion, especially in psychology (where it is often lacking). Theories that involve mathematical equations or computer programs are generally more precise, and hence better, than those that use loose verbal statements (all other things being equal, of course). Unless a theory is sufficiently precise so that different investigators can agree about its predictions, it is for all intents and purposes useless.

Testability goes beyond precision. A theory can be very precise and yet not able to be tested. For example, when Einstein proposed the equivalence of matter and energy ($E = MC^2$), nuclear technology was not able to directly test this relationship. The scientist places a very high value on the criterion of testability, because a theory that cannot be tested can never be disproved. At first you might think this would be a good quality since it would be impossible to demonstrate that such a theory was incorrect. The scientist takes the opposite view. For example, consider ESP (extrasensory perception). Some believers in ESP claim that the presence of a disbeliever is sufficient to prevent a person gifted with ESP from performing, because the disbeliever puts out "bad vibes" that disrupt ESP. This means that ESP cannot be evaluated, because only believers can be present when it is demonstrated. The scientist takes a dim view of this logic, and most scientists, especially psychologists, are skeptical about ESP. Belief in a theory increases as it survives tests that could reject it. Since it is logically possible

FIGURE 1–5.

Reprinted by permission of UFS, Inc.

From Lucy's standpoint the theory may be a perfect one, but since it cannot be tested it is a poor scientific theory. ·

that some future test may find a flaw, belief in a theory is never absolute. If it is not logically possible to test a theory, it cannot be evaluated; hence, it is useless to the scientist. If it is logically possible but not yet technically feasible, as was once the case with Einstein's theory, then evaluation of a theory is deferred.

The Science of Psychology

Some students find it difficult to think of psychology as a science in the same sense that physics and chemistry are sciences. They believe that there are aspects of human experience, such as the arts, literature, and religion, that defy scientific analysis. How can the beauty of a Klee lithograph, a Beethoven sonata, a Cartier-Bresson photograph be reduced to cold scientific equations? How can the tender feelings of a first romance, the thrill of driving a sports car at 100 miles per hour, and the agony of a defeated football team be captured in the objective, disinterested fashion required by science?

Some psychologists, known as humanists, would answer these questions in the negative. These humanists, most often clinical and counseling psychologists, claim that it is impossible objectively to evaluate and test much of human feelings and experience by traditional scientific methods. Even tough, "brass-instrument" experimental psychologists concur that the domain of science is limited. We cannot establish or refute the existence of God by scientific means any more than we could test gravity by theological methods. Science operates where its tools are appropriate (see chapter 14). This does not imply that knowledge cannot be gained wherever science fears to tread—that is, by nonscientific means. Many important fields of human endeavor have yet to benefit from extensive scientific analysis—ethics, morals, law, to name but a few.

However, most scientists would hold out the hope that scientific analysis eventually might be usefully applied to many such areas. Much of contemporary psychology was regarded as the sole property of philosophy at one time. As psychological techniques improved, these aspects of human expertise and behavior moved into the realm of science. And now most psychologists believe that virtually all facets of human experience are fair game for the science of psychology. Deriding scientific progress in psychology, as did one United States senator who criticized the National Science Foundation for supporting research on romantic love, will not halt efforts to expand psychological knowledge. Although concern for the proper and ethical use of such knowledge is valid and important, ignorance is no solution.

Hard Science as a Model for Experimental Psychology

Psychologists can be arranged along a continuum according to how well they think physics and chemistry serve as a model for psychology to emulate. The "hard-shelled" psychologists think these older sciences are perfect models whereas the "soft-shelled" psychologists believe that social sciences must find another model. Since we are experimental psychologists by trade, and since this book is intended as an experimental-psychology test, we tend to sample more from the hard-boiled end of the continuum.

All science has data and theory. What distinguishes among the different sciences, and among the subspecialties within a science like psychology, is the different techniques used. Astronomers do not need Skinner boxes any more than animal-learning psychologists need telescopes. Yet both practice science. A learning theorist's memory drum is not intrinsically superior to a social psychologist's "aggression machine" (see chapter 13). Even the modern microcomputer of an information-processing psychologist does not guarantee better science, although it may improve the odds. Most of this text is devoted to explaining the techniques needed in psychological research today. While the hard-shelled psychologist does have more refined techniques, this is in part because of selection of problems that are amenable to sophisticated analysis. As psychology subjects more and more of human experience and behavior to scientific analysis, it is only natural that initial techniques may be crude. At one time this was true of hard-shelled psychology, too. Having a hard shell should not preclude one from having an open mind.

Psychology and the Real World

Scientists in general, and psychologists in particular, have many reasons for pursuing their profession. Although we think it rather easy to prove that psychological research does serve mankind, we would like to stress that we do not find this the only, or necessarily the major, justification for a career as a research psychologist. Many scientists investigate certain problems simply because they find them interesting. We have complete sympathy with a colleague who might state that he or she studies gerbils just because gerbils provoke his or her curiosity. It is true that certain studies are performed on animals because they are unethical or impractical to perform on humans—for example, studies of long-term crowding, punishment, drugs, and so on—but it is equally true that the behavior of animals is interesting in its own right.

Scientific research is often divided into two categories: basic and applied. *Applied research* aims at solving a specific problem—such as how to cure bedwetting—whereas *basic research* has no immediate practical goal. Basic research establishes a reservoir of data, theoretical explanations, and concepts that can be tapped by the applied researcher. Without this source, applied research would soon dry up and sputter to a halt, unless applied researchers became of necessity basic researchers. It takes quite a while for a concept developed by basic research to find some useful application in society. Adams (1972) traced five socially important products to discover the impact, if any, of basic research. Although basic research accounted for 70 percent of the significant events, these events occurred twenty to thirty years before the ultimate use of the product. This long time lag obscures the crucial role of basic research so that many persons incorrectly believe that basic research is not very useful to society. It is quite difficult to tell what basic research being done today will have an impact thirty years from now. But this inability to predict hardly means that we should stop doing basic research.

Although the scientific quest for knowledge may be for one purpose only, usually basic and applied interests eventually intermingle in interesting ways, as demonstrated by the various kinds of research done on social loafing. Ringelmann's early observations of social loafing in the laboratory were also documented in the workplace (Marriott, 1949). A potentially useful way to improve group productivity then arose from the laboratory work of Latané and his colleagues, who found that individual performance assessment can reduce social loafing.

Although the division of research into basic and applied categories is common, a far more important distinction is between good and bad research. The principles and practices covered in this text apply with equal force to basic and applied research. You can and should use them to evaluate all the psychological research you encounter, whether as a student, a professional psychologist, or an educated person reading the daily newspaper.

Are Experiments Too Far from Real Life? Students of psychology typically demand a higher level of relevance in their psychology courses than they expect from other sciences. Students who are not at all dismayed that their course in introductory physics did not enable them to repair their automobile are often disturbed that their course in introductory psychology did not give them a better insight into their own motivations, did not cure their neuroses, and failed to show them how to gain eternal happiness. If you did not find such information in introductory psychology, we doubt that you will find it in this text either. If this seems unfair, read on.

The data that psychologists gather may at first seem unimportant, because an immediate relationship between basic psychological research and pressing social or personal problems may be difficult to establish. It is natural then to doubt the importance of this research and to wonder why the federal government, through various agencies, is funding researchers to watch rats press bars or run through mazes.

The difficulty, however, is not with the research but with the expectations as to how "useful" research should be conducted. As noted by Sidman (1960), people expect progress to occur by the establishment of laboratory situations that are analogous to real-life situations: "In order to study psychosis in animals we must learn how to make animals psychotic." This is off the mark. The psychologist tries to understand the underlying *processes* rather than the physical situations that produce these processes. The physical situations in the real world and the laboratory need not be at all similar, provided that the same processes are occurring.

Suppose we would like to know why airplane accidents occur, or more specifically, what the relationship is between airplane accidents and failure of attention on the part of the pilot and/or the air traffic controller. A basic researcher might approach this problem by having college sophomores sit in front of several lights that turn on in rapid succession. The sophomore has to press a key as each light is illuminated. This probably seems somewhat removed from mid-air collisions of aircraft. Yet although the physical situations are quite different, the processes are similar. Pressing a key is an index of attention (see chapter 8). Psychologists can overload the human operator by presenting lights faster than he or she can respond. Thus, this simple physical situation in a laboratory allows the psychologist to study failure of attention in a carefully controlled environment. In addition to the obvious safety benefits of studying attention without having to crash airplanes, there are many scientific advantages to the laboratory environment (see chapter 3). Because failures of attention are responsible for many kinds of industrial accidents (DeGreene, 1970, chapters 7 and 16), studies of attention by use of lights and buttons can lead to improvements outside the laboratory.

By the same token, establishing similar physical situations does not guarantee similarity of processes. One can easily train a rat to pick up coins in its mouth and bury them in its cage. But this does not necessarily mean that the "miserly" rat and the miserly human who keeps coins under his mattress do so because the same psychological processes are controlling their behaviors.

We should not only be concerned with the psychological processes that may generalize from the laboratory to an application, but also be aware of two important reasons for doing research, the purpose of which (at least initially) may not be directly related to practical affairs (Mook, 1983). One reason that basic research aids understanding is that it often demonstrates what *can* happen. Thus under controlled conditions, it can be determined whether social loafing does occur. Furthermore, the laboratory affords an opportunity to determine the characteristics of social loafing more clearly than does the workplace, where a number of uncontrolled factors, such as salary and job security, could mask or alter the effects of social loafing (see chapter 3).

A second reason for the value of basic research is that the findings from a controlled, laboratory setting may have more force than similar findings obtained in a real-life setting. Showing that the human operator can be overloaded in a relatively nonstressful laboratory task suggests that attentional factors are crucial for performance; individuals could be even more likely to be overloaded under the stressful conditions of piloting large passenger planes in crowded airspaces.

Of course, if a researcher wants to test a theoretical prediction or apply a laboratory result in an applied setting, then "real-life" tests will be necessary. Installing a way of assessing individual performance to reduce social loafing in a group manufacturing situation without first testing its applicability in that setting would be foolhardy. The moral, then, is that the researcher needs to be concerned with the goal of the experiments. The researcher or the evaluator of a piece of research should consider well that goal.

Neither the practice nor the use of science is easy. The benefits that can be derived from scientific knowledge and understanding depend on critical and well-informed citizens and scientists. Your involvement with a career, a family, and social affairs will partially be determined by scientific findings. You must be in a position to evaluate those findings accurately and accept those that seem most reliable and valid. Unless you plan to hibernate or drop out of society in some other way, you are going to be affected by psychological research. As a citizen you will be a consumer of the results of psychological research, and we hope that the material discussed in this book will help to make you an intelligent consumer.

Some of you, we hope, will become scientists. We also hope that some of you budding scientists will focus on why people think and act as they do. We wish you future scientists good fortune. Your scientific career will be exciting, and we hope that your endeavors will be positively influenced by the principles of psychological research presented herein.

About a hundred years ago, T. H. Huxley, a British scientist, said: "The chessboard is the world, the pieces are the phenomena of the universe, the rules of the game are what we call the laws of Nature. The player on the other side is hidden from us. We know that his play is always fair, just, and patient. But we also know, to our cost, that he never overlooks a mistake, or makes the smallest allowance for ignorance."

SUMMARY

1. Scientific psychology is concerned with the methods and techniques used to understand why people think and act as they do. This curiosity may be satisfied by basic or applied research, which usually go hand in hand to provide understanding.

2. Our beliefs are often established by the method of authority, the method of tenacity, or the a priori method. The scientific method offers advantages over these other methods because it relies on systematic observation and is self-correcting.

3. Scientific procedures include naturalistic observation, correlation, true experiments, and quasi-experiments.

4. Scientists use both inductive and deductive reasoning to arrive at explanations of thought and action.

5. A theory organizes sets of data and generates predictions for new situations in which data have not been obtained. A good theory is parsimonious, precise, and testable.

6. Laboratory research is concerned with the processes that govern behavior and with showing the conditions under which certain psychological processes can be observed.

KEY TERMS

a priori method	method of authority
applied research	method of tenacity
basic research	observation
correlation	organization
data	parsimony
deduction	precision
description	prediction
diffusion of responsibility	quasi-experiment
empirical	scientific method
experimentation	self-correcting
explanation	social loafing
falsifiability view	strong inference
induction	testability
intervening variables	theory

DISCUSSION QUESTIONS

1. Make a list of five statements that might be considered true. Include some controversial statements (for example, men have lower IQs than women), as well as some you are sure are correct. Survey some of your friends by asking if they agree with these statements. Then, ask their justifications for their opinions. Classify their justifications into one of the methods of fixing beliefs discussed in this chapter.

2. Compare and contrast inductive and deductive approaches to science. Clarify your answers by referring to at least one branch of science outside of experimental psychology.

3. Discuss social loafing research from the standpoint of strong inference.

4. Is it necessary (or even desirable) for experimental psychologists to justify their research in terms of applied benefits to society?

5. Read this article: Skinner, B. F. (1956). A case history in scientific method. *American Psychologist, 11*, 221–233. Analyze Skinner's views from the standpoint of the issues discussed in this chapter.

2

Research Techniques: Observation and Correlation

Scientific observation does not differ from everyday observation by being infallible although it is quantitatively less fallible than ordinary observation. Rather, it differs from everyday observation in that the scientist gradually uncovers his previous errors and corrects them. . . . Indeed, the history of psychology as a science has been the development of procedural and instrumental aids that gradually eliminate or correct for biases and distortions in making observations.

—RAY HYMAN

SCIENCE IS PERHAPS THE ONLY intellectual enterprise that builds cumulatively. From a scientific perspective, we know more about the world today than people have known at any other time in history. On the other hand, literature, art, and philosophy may be different today than they were in ancient Greece, but we probably cannot say that these disciplines are in a better state or more accurately represent the world.

One primary reason that science cumulates is that scientists strive for the most accurate observation possible of the world. Science is self-correcting in that theories and hypotheses are put forward that allow prediction about what should happen under specified conditions, and then these ideas are tested by comparing the predictions to carefully collected observations. When the facts differ consistently and drastically from the predictions, it is necessary to modify or abandon our theoretical conceptions. Much of the scientific enterprise is concerned with observation: the collection of data on some particular aspect of the world.

In this chapter we will discuss several nonexperimental methods of gathering psychological data. One such method is *naturalistic observation*, which is the most obvious and, perhaps, the most venerable way of gathering data. Many people, such as bird watchers, are amateur naturalists, but scientific naturalists, as we will see, are more systematic in their observations. For example, recent work has shown that when the risk of attack by predator hawks is imminent, chickadees give a much higher alarm call than when the risk posed by the predator is not so serious (Ficken, 1990).

An additional classic way of obtaining information is the *case study*, in which detailed information is gathered about a single individual. A recent case study revealed that when Ruth L., age 30, came to therapy, she was showering six or more times daily, washing her hands three times an hour, and completely cleaning her apartment twice daily (Leon, 1990).

Similar to the case study is the *survey*, in which detailed information is gathered from a number of individuals. Colasanto (1989) interviewed people in the San Francisco Bay Area the day following the earthquake that occurred on October 17, 1989. Thirty-seven percent of those people claimed to have been very frightened by the earthquake, and 15 percent of the Bay Area people were not frightened at all.

Another recent survey attempted to determine the sorts of memory problems suffered by elderly Americans (Lovelace and Twohig, 1990). Healthy, older adults with an average age of 68 claim that the most vexing memory problem they have is an inability to remember someone's name. However, most of these respondents report that memory difficulties have little effect on their daily functioning.

The descriptive information gathered by the procedures just outlined are often combined in various ways so that predictions about a person's activities can be made. This attempt at prediction is a *correlational technique*. A recent example of that procedure reveals that a person's confidence in his or her ability to identify a criminal correctly does not predict how well she or he can pick the criminal out of a police lineup (Cutler and Penrod, 1989).

As the results above indicate, the observational and correlational methods can yield interesting data. We will examine these methods in some detail, showing both their strengths and weaknesses as ways of determining why people and animals think and act as they do.

Naturalistic Observation

As we all know, observers are fallible. Seeing should not be believing—at least not always. Often our perceptions fool us, as we can see by the way we perceive the optical illusions in figure 2–1. We have all seen magicians perform seemingly impossible feats before our eyes, when we knew that we were being tricked by natural means. Such tricks demonstrate that direct perceptions can be inaccurate if we are not careful, and sometimes even if we are.

Scientists, being human, are also subject to errors of observation. Essentially the research techniques employed by scientists—including logic, use of complicated apparatus, controlled conditions, and so on—are there to guard against errors of perception and to ensure that observations reflect the state of nature as accurately as possible. Even with our best methods and most

FIGURE 2–1.   (a)

(b)

(c)

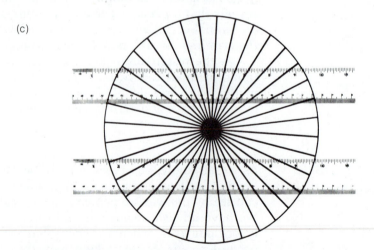

Visual illusions. (a) The Müller-Lyer illusion. The vertical lines are the same length, but appear unequal due to the different directions of the fins in the two cases. (b) The illusion apparently distorts even an objective measuring device, the ruler. But close examination indicates that the ruler is not really distorted and that the lines are of equal length. (c) The rulers now appear bent, due to the influence of the circle. These illusions are mantained even though we "know," as in (b), they cannot be so. Our observations can suffer distortions no matter how careful we are (examples taken from R. L. Gregory, 1970, pp. 80–81).

careful techniques of observation, however, we can only approximate this ideal.

Miller (1977) enumerated several important roles that naturalistic observation can play in psychology. One way to summarize Miller's thinking is to say that observation provides a major part of the data base that can lead to subsequent, more highly controlled research. Naturalistic observation describes the thoughts and behaviors of organisms, which is a necessary first step in understanding. A familiar example is Harlow's (1958) work on mother love in infants. Prior to his experiments, Harlow needed to know what behaviors infant monkeys exhibited; he also needed to know some of the things infant monkeys seemed to like (their soft blankets) and dislike (the wire floor of the cage). With this background information, Harlow could attempt to explain the behavior via experimentation. Thus, we should not view observation as somehow secondary or subordinate to experimentation because it lacks control. In the sense just mentioned, observation is prior and superior to experimentation.

In making scientific observations, we confront two basic problems that threaten the validity or soundness of the observations. (The following two problems can plague experimentation as well, which we will examine later.) One problem has to do with *delimiting* the choice of behaviors to observe. Human observers have a finite capacity to perceive and think about events. Although most of us may be able to walk and chew gum at the same time, most of us cannot attend to and remember twenty different behaviors occurring over short periods of time. Thus, there has to be some boundary on the range of behaviors that we plan to observe. The second problem concerns the participant's reaction to being observed. This problem, called *reactivity*, presents problems in conducting any sort of psychological research.

What Do We Observe?

How do we delimit the range of behaviors to be studied? Part of this answer seems straightforward. If we are interested in human nonverbal communication, we observe human nonverbal communication. However, this is not necessarily easy to do. In the first place, nonverbal communication is highly complex, which means that we observers are faced with the same problem we started out trying to avoid. In the second place, examining nonverbal behaviors presupposes that we already know some of the behaviors to observe. Obviously, we do not enter a research project devoid of all knowledge, but neither do we start out with all the answers. What usually happens is that we begin a series of observational studies, in which successive projects rely on previous data to refine and delimit the field of inquiry. Let us consider some examples to illustrate the refinement procedure.

An ethogram. Naturalistic research of interest to psychologists is perhaps most prevalent in the area of *ethology*, the study of naturally occurring behavior (often in the wild). Simply observing the behavior of animals or humans allows one to gain a global impression of the characteristics and range of behavior. However, one may soon desire more systematic observation. One way ethologists make more systematic observations is by identifying different categories of experience for the organism under study and then recording the number of times the organism engages in each behavior. These behaviors can be divided into large units such as mating, grooming, sleeping, fighting, eating, and so on, or into much smaller units. For example, an *ethogram* of the various behaviors involved in the courtship pattern of a fish, the orange chromide, is shown in figure 2–2. (An ethogram is a relatively complete inventory of the specific behaviors performed by one species of animal.) By counting the number of times that any specific behavior occurs, ethologists can begin to get some idea of the significance of the behavior.

FIGURE 2–2.

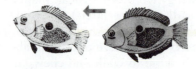

a. *Charging:* An accelerated swim of one fish toward another.

b. *Tail Beating:* An emphatic beating of the tail toward another fish.

c. *Quivering:* A rapid, lateral, shivering movement that starts at the head and dies out as it passes posteriorly through the body.

d. *Nipping:* An O-shaped mouth action that cleans out the (presumptive) spawning site.

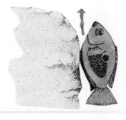

e. *Skimming:* The actual spawning movement whereby the fish places its ventral surface against the spawning site and meanders along it for a few seconds.

Ethogram showing courtship pattern in orange chromide. An ethogram can be compiled for all behaviors of a species, or for only selected aspects of behavior. (From Drickamer, L. C., and Vesey, S. H. *Animal Behavior: Concepts, Processes, and Methods.* Boston: Willard Grant Press, 1982, p. 28).

This was the way in which Ficken (1990) was able to isolate the types of alarm calls made by chickadees. Obviously, however, Ficken had to be able to record and analyze the chickadees' vocal output. Often it is difficult to obtain accurate records of an animal's behavior in the wild. It may be hard to observe an animal continuously in its natural habitat. Researchers cannot remain forever vigilant. The presence of human observers may make the measures reactive. These are only some of the greatest problems. Applying similar techniques to human behavior is even more difficult, for people do not usually appreciate having their every action noted by curious scientists.

Barker and his associates (for example, Barker and Wright, 1951; Barker, 1968) were pioneers in applying methods of naturalistic observation to humans in a number of settings. Let us examine some recent naturalistic observations of humans.

Flashing eyebrows. The famous ethologist of human behavior Eibl-Eibesfeldt (for example, 1970, 1972) has done a substantial amount of field research on human facial expressions. He and his colleagues traveled around the world taking pictures of facial expressions in a variety of contexts. Careful examination of the expressions indicated that many are similar across cultures, and some are not. In the process of examining facial expressions associated with people greeting each other, Eibl-Eibesfeldt discovered that most humans give a brief eyebrow flash. He went on to examine this phenomenon in detail.

Generally, the eyebrow flash is a brief (one-sixth of a second) raising of the eyebrows, accompanied by a slight smile and a quick nod of the head. The eyebrow flash has been observed in people of many cultures, including Bushmen, Balinese, and Europeans. However, some cultures seem to differ in their uses of the eyebrow flash. The Japanese do not use the flash, because in Japan it is considered suggestive or indecent. Furthermore, Eibl-Eibesfeldt found that the flash occurred in other circumstances, such as in flirting and acknowledging a gift or service (that is, as a kind of thank you), in addition to greeting.

We can see from his work that previous observations suggested additional ones for Eibl-Eibesfeldt, and by delimiting his range of inquiry he was able to garner substantial information about a common human behavior.

Testing neonates. Our second example of refinement comes from studies of newborn humans (neonates). What do neonates do and what can we look for in their behavior? Most people think of neonates as being limited in their behavior. However, neonates can do more than eat, sleep, eliminate, and cry. All their senses are operative, and they possess a number of complex reflexes. Brazelton and his associates (for example, Lester and Brazelton, 1982) have spent many years refining a scale to assess the optimal performance of neonates in a variety of behaviors. Initially, the scale assessed reflexes (squeezing, blinking) and a few behaviors. Repeated observations of neonates from a variety of cultures and in a variety of situations led to changes, which, in turn, caused more changes. The resulting Brazelton Neonatal Behavioral Assessment Scale contains measurements of sixteen reflexes and twenty-six behaviors. The reflexes are rated on a three-point scale (low, medium, and high), and the behavioral items, such as responses to a pinprick and hand-to-mouth activity, are rated on nine-point scales.

Earlier observations had suggested that the level of arousal was very important in respect to the appearance and magnitude of certain behaviors, so the current scale indicates when the neonate should be assessed on the various behaviors. For example, responses to a pinprick are assessed when the neonate is asleep or quiet, but not when the neonate is alert or crying. Hand-to-mouth behaviors can be assessed during any state.

Brazelton and his coworkers have been particularly concerned with individual and cultural differences in development, and they have conducted numerous quasi-experiments to examine these differences. The quasi-experiments would not have been possible had they not made the exhaustive series of observations that led to the development of the assessment scale.

Reactivity

There are two general ways to guard against the participants' reactions ruining observations: (1) we can make *unobtrusive observations*, or (2) we can take *unobtrusive measures* (Webb and others, 1966). We will consider these in turn.

Unobtrusive observations. Imagine that you are walking down a street in your hometown. Occasionally you greet a friend (perhaps with a handshake, perhaps with an eyebrow flash). As your walk continues, a man with a large camera approaches and proceeds to take a moving picture of you every time you greet one of your friends. How are you likely to react to this attention? Quite likely, your mode of greeting people will change dramatically. (Have you ever noticed how spectators behave at sporting events when they know the television camera is on them?) Eibl-Eibesfeldt guarded against participant reactivity in his research by using a camera with a special sideways lens. This lens permitted him to aim the camera away from the subject 90 degrees; presumably, the subject would think that Eibl-Eibesfeldt was photographing something else. Thus, the subject would not react abnormally to the presence of the observer and his camera; instead, the subject would act naturally, which is what Eibl-Eibesfeldt intended. The special camera lens allowed the researcher to observe without intruding on the subject. We say that Eibl-Eibesfeldt used an unobtrusive observation technique.

In general, unobtrusive observations of subjects are likely to reveal more natural behavior than those in which the subjects are aware of being observed. In studying animals, researchers use unobtrusive observations whenever possible.

Sometimes, however, either the subjects themselves, the terrain, or some other aspect of the project demands close contact. In these situations, *participant observation* often provides a solution. As the phrase suggests, the observer becomes an active (and intrusive) participant in the lives of the subjects being observed. For example, Fossey (1972) spent a great amount of time observing the mountain gorilla. The mountain gorilla lives in central Africa, and its habitat is threatened by human beings who are moving into that area. The mountain gorilla's natural habitat is the mountainous rain forest; this makes long-range, unobtrusive spying out of the question. Fossey was particularly concerned with the free-ranging behavior of the gorillas, so she decided to become a participant observer. This was difficult, because the gorillas are not tame. She had to act like a gorilla in front of the gorillas so that they would become accustomed to her presence. She mimicked aspects of the animal's behavior, such as eating, grooming, and making weird gorilla-like vocalizations. As she said, "one feels like a fool thumping one's chest rhythmically or sitting about pretending to munch on a stalk of wild celery as though it were the most delectable morsel in the world. But the gorillas have responded favorably" (p. 211). It took several months for Fossey to gain the confidence of the gorillas, and she continued to live with and study the gorillas until her death in 1986. How would you like to act like a gorilla for ten or fifteen years?

Unobtrusive measures. Unobtrusive measures, in contrast to unobtrusive observations, are usually indirect observations of behavior. Unobtrusive measures are indirect because it is the result of behavior, not the behavior itself, that is being studied. Thus, instead of measuring behavior directly, we examine it after the fact by looking at what the behavior has accomplished. Instead of observing a student's studying activities, we examine his or her transcript. Instead of living with the gorillas, we look at their effect on the environment.

Obviously, unobtrusive measures are not suitable for all questions being investigated (an unobtrusive measure of an eyebrow flash might be difficult), but for some research problems these measures are not merely good: they are the only ones that are feasible. Consider the question of graffiti in public restrooms. Who does it? What does it usually concern? A number of serious ethical questions (ethics are discussed in chapter 4) would be raised if a researcher stood around in restrooms observing the patrons. However, the graffiti itself can be examined and can provide substantial information. Kinsey, Pomeroy, and Martin (1953) discovered that graffiti in men's restrooms was more erotic than graffiti in women's restrooms. Furthermore, they found more graffiti in men's rooms than in women's rooms.

Using unobtrusive measures is akin to a hunter following animal tracks or a police officer examining such clues as fingerprints. Tracks and clues are left behind that often allow us to infer things about the behavior that caused them. Recently, a popular psychological and anthropological unobtrusive measure has been to examine the garbage and other refuse that people discard. From the characteristics of the discarded objects, the observer attempts to understand some aspect of the behavior behind that refuse (for example, a discarded liquor bottle or a love letter that has been thrown away could reveal information about behavior).

Naturalistic observation is often difficult to undertake because of reactivity and an inability to delimit the observations. Variants of the naturalistic approach have been used to study human behavior; two of them are briefly described here.

The Case Study

One of the most venerable forms of inquiry in psychology is the *case study*. Freud's psychoanalytic theory arose from his observations and reflections on individual cases. In general, a case study is the intensive investigation of a single case of some sort, whether of a neurotic patient, a spiritual medium, or a group awaiting the end of the world. An interesting case study of this last instance was provided by Festinger, Riecken, and Schachter (1956), who infiltrated a small group of persons who were indeed awaiting the end of the world. The members thought themselves to be in contact with beings from another planet, who had communicated to one member that the destruction of the earth was near. The group was expecting to be rescued by spacecraft before the catastrophe. Festinger and his colleagues were especially interested in the reactions of the group when (if?) the calamity did not occur. They observed that for many of the members of the group, belief in its delusional system actually increased rather than decreased after the predicted date of catastrophe had passed.

The case study is a type of naturalistic observation and is subject to all the disadvantages and the few advantages (to be discussed shortly) of that method. One chief disadvantage is that case studies usually do not allow firm inferences to be made about what causes what. Typically, all one can do is describe the course of events. Often, however, case studies provide implicit comparisons that allow the researcher to make some reasonable guesses as to what causes what. The case study of Ruth L., the compulsive cleaner mentioned at the beginning of the chapter, revealed a very stern upbringing that involved an excessive emphasis on cleanliness and neatness. Because the severity of this emphasis on cleanliness was greater than that experienced by most people, the therapist concluded that it was a causal factor in her current compulsion to be neat and clean. This sort of conclusion needs to be tentative, however, because we do not know what kind of adult Ruth L. would have become had she had a more ordinary childhood.

A type of case study that best attempts to minimize the difficulties of making inferences is the *deviant-case analysis*. Here the researcher considers two cases that bear a number of similarities and yet differ in outcome. For example, one twin brother might become schizophrenic and the other not. The researcher attempts to pinpoint, through a careful comparison of the two cases, the factors that are responsible for the difference in outcome. Such comparisons usually cannot be made, because comparable cases that differ in only one factor are rare. Furthermore, any conclusions even from this method cannot really be considered firm or well established, because the researcher can never be certain that he or she has identified the critical causes in the differing outcomes.

These cautions notwithstanding, let us consider a case study recently reported by Butters and Cermak (1986) that illustrates how judicious use of the procedure can provide valuable information. The study is about P.Z., a world-famous scientist who suffered from severe memory loss (amnesia) in 1981 after long-term alcohol abuse. He had extreme difficulty both in remembering new information and in recollecting past events and people. The latter memory deficit was easy to determine, because two years prior to the onset of amnesia, P.Z. had written his autobiography. When he was queried about the names and events mentioned in his autobiography, he showed a drastic memory deficit. P.Z.'s memory for these events was compared with the retention of a similar-aged colleague (the comparison person for deviant-case analysis) who did not have a history of alcohol abuse. Since the comparison case did not show a memory deficit as serious as P.Z.'s, Butters and Cermak reasoned that the long-term alcohol abuse was an important causal factor in P.Z.'s amnesia. Furthermore, P.Z.'s memory deficit for new information was very similar to that shown by other people with a history of alcohol abuse. This latter technique of comparing the case's behavior with that of others is essentially an experimental one, and it will be illustrated again in chapter 6.

Survey Research

Case studies usually involve only a few subjects, and often these individuals are not at all representative of the population at large. P.Z., for example, was both a brilliant scientist and an amnesiac. Often researchers want to obtain information on a large random sample of people in a large geographic area (such as the Bay Area survey mentioned at the beginning of the chapter), even though the amount of information obtained from any one person is necessarily limited. This technique is little used in most areas of psychology, though it is familiar to most of you through its use in predicting elections and the like. With the precise sampling procedures now available, relatively few people can be queried, and the results will nonetheless generalize well to the population at large.

Because the survey leads to results that are generally descriptive in nature, this method is not particularly popular with psychologists. Nevertheless, clever use of the method may allow contributions to some areas of psychology. The work by Lovelace and Twohig (1990) that was summarized briefly at the outset of the chapter is a good example. The elderly subjects whom they surveyed reported that they relied very strongly on notes, lists, and other external memory aids to help them remember to do things. Further, the elderly respondents claimed not to rely on various memory "tricks" such as mnemonic devices. The results reported by Lovelace and Twohig agree with other survey data (Moscovitch, 1982), which show that compared with younger people, the elderly are much more likely to make lists and use date books and are less likely to resort to internal memory procedures, such as mnemonic devices. These results are provocative, because they suggest that the elderly are somehow aware that they may have some memory limitations, which they try to minimize by relying on external memory aids. However, more controlled research is necessary before that conclusion can be confirmed.

Advantages and Disadvantages of Naturalistic Observations

As noted earlier, naturalistic observation is extremely useful in the early stages of research, when one desires simply to gain some idea as to the breadth and range of the problem of interest (Miller, 1977). It is primarily descriptive, however, and does not allow one to infer how factors may be related. In some cases, there is no way to employ more controlled methods of observation; therefore, only naturalistic ones are available. If you want to know how penguins behave in their natural habitat, you simply have to observe them there. Still, for most psychological problems, naturalistic observation is useful primarily in defining the problem area and raising interesting questions for more controlled study by other means, especially experimental ones. For example, the case study by Festinger and his colleagues of the group predicting the end of the earth helped lead to Festinger's (1957) cognitive dissonance theory of attitude change, which has been quite important in guiding social psychological research.

The primary problem unique to naturalistic observation is that it is simply descriptive in nature and does not allow us to assess relationships among events. An investigator might note that grooming behavior in free-ranging monkeys occurs at certain times, following five different prior conditions (such as eating). If one is interested in finding out which antecedent conditions are necessary to produce grooming, naturalistic observation cannot provide an answer, since it is not possible to manipulate these antecedent conditions. For this, one needs an experiment.

Naturalistic observation typically produces data that are deficient in other ways, too. Scientific data should be easy to reproduce by other people using standardized procedures, if these people doubt the observations or are interested in repeating them. Many naturalistic methods, such as the case study, do not allow reproducibility; they are thus open to question by other investigators.

Another problem in naturalistic approaches is maintaining as strictly as possible a descriptive rather than an interpretive level of observation. In the study of animals, the problem is often one of *anthropomorphizing,* or attributing human characteristics to animals. When you come home and your dog wags its tail and moves about excitedly, it seems perfectly natural to say that it is happy to see you. But this is anthropomorphizing, and if one were engaged in naturalistic observation of the scene, it would be inappropriate. Instead, one should record the overt behaviors of the dog with the least possible attribution of underlying motives, such as happiness, sadness, or hunger.

Of course, the case studies of Freud are based entirely on just such interpretations of the facts. Besides being nonreproducible, such cases suffer from the possibility that if we are allowed to (a) select our data from case studies and answers people give to the questions we ask, and then (b) weave these "facts" into a previous conceptual system of our own devising, case studies could probably be used to "prove" any theory. (This is not to detract from the creative flair and genius that are evident in Freud's system; he is, however, certainly open to criticism in terms of the evidence on which it is based.)

Another instance of this interpretive problem that is closer to scientific psychology is reported by Pavlov in his early research on the conditioned reflex (see chapter 9). When they began to study the dog's psychological processes, he and his coworkers discovered they had a problem that had not been apparent when they had previously been concerned only with the digestive system. The problem was severe, for they could not agree on the anthropomorphic observations they were making. Pavlov describes the problem of studying conditioned reflexes:

> But how is this to be studied? Taking the dog when he eats rapidly snatches something in his mouth, chews for a long time, it seems clear that at such a time the animal strongly desires to eat, and so rushes to the food, seizes it, and falls to eating. He longs to eat ... When he eats, you see the work of the muscles alone, striving in every way to seize the food in the mouth, to chew and to swallow it. From all this we can say that he derives pleasure from it. ... Now when we proceeded to explain and analyze this, we readily adopted this trite point of view. We had to deal with the feelings, wishes, conceptions, etc., of our animal. The results were astounding, extraordinary; I and one of my colleagues came to irreconcilable opinions. We could not agree, could not prove to one another which was right. ... After this we had to deliberate carefully. It seemed probable we were not on the right track. The more we thought about the matter, the greater grew our conviction that it was

necessary to choose another exit. The first steps were very difficult, but along the way of persistent, intense, concentrated thinking I finally reached the firm ground of pure objectivity. We absolutely prohibited ourselves (in the laboratory there was an actual fine imposed) the use of such psychological expressions as the dog guessed, wanted, wished, etc. (Pavlov, reprinted 1963, pp. 263–264)

One further problem will be discussed here, though it is relevant to all types of observation in all types of research. This is the issue of how much our conceptual schemes determine and bias what we "see" as the facts. Pavlov's statement is eloquent testimony of how difficult it is to establish objective methods so that we can all see the facts in the same way. He had found it initially "astounding" and "extraordinary" that this was so and was surprised at the elaborate precautions needed to insure objectivity. Philosophers of science have pointed out that our observations are always influenced by our conceptions of the world—if in no other way, at least by the particular observations we make (see, for example, Hanson, 1958, chapter 2). "Pure objectivity," to use Pavlov's phrase, is quite elusive, if not impossible. One illustration Hanson uses is that of two trained microbiologists viewing a stained and prepared slide through a microscope and "seeing" different things. (As is well known, the primary thing a novice typically reports seeing in a microscope is his or her own eyeball.) Objective and repeatable observation in science is an ideal to be approximated, but we may never be completely confident that we have achieved it. Certainly, however, we must make every possible step toward this ideal, which is what much of the technical paraphernalia of science is concerned with.

The problem of observations being unduly influenced by expectations is not automatically overcome by the use of the technical equipment of hard science, however, as is evident in an illustration cited by Hyman (1964, p. 38). In 1902, shortly after X rays were discovered, the eminent French physicist Blondlot reported the discovery of "N rays." Other French scientists quickly repeated and confirmed Blondlot's discovery; in 1904, no fewer than 77 publications appeared on the topic. However, the discovery became controversial when American, German, and Italian scientists failed to replicate Blondlot's findings.

The American physicist R. W. Wood, failing to find N rays in his own lab at Johns Hopkins University, visited Blondlot. Blondlot displayed a card to Wood with luminous circles painted on it. Then he turned down the room light, fixed N rays on the card, and pointed out to Wood that the circles increased in luminosity. When Wood said he could see no change, Blondlot argued that this must be because Wood's eyes were too insensitive. Next, Wood asked if he could perform some simple tests, to which Blondlot consented. In one case, Wood moved a lead screen repeatedly between the N rays and the cards, while Blondlot reported the corresponding changes in luminosity of the circles on the card. (The lead shield was to prevent passage of the N rays.) Blondlot was consistently in error, and often reported a change in luminosity when the screen had not been moved! This and other tests clearly indicated that there was no evidence for the existence of N rays, despite their "confirmation" by other French scientists.

After 1909, there were no further publications on N rays. The mistake was too much for Blondlot. He never recovered, and died in disgrace some years later. We can see from this dramatic example that even with the sophisticated apparatus of physicists, errors of observation are possible and must be guarded against.

The Correlational Approach

Scientists are not long contented with the type of descriptive information that is derived from observational studies. Of much greater interest is how two *variables* are related to one another. (A variable is something that can be measured or manipulated. More on this in the next chapter.) The use of correlational techniques permits us to assess and specify the degree of relationship between two variables of interest, generally with the hope that given one variable, we can predict the other. The assessment is usually made *ex post facto*, or after the fact. All this means is that the observations of interest are collected and then a *correlation coefficient*, which indicates the degree of relation between the two variables or measures, is computed.

One typical example of the correlational approach is the exploration of the relationship between cigarette smoking and lung cancer. Studies in the 1950s and early 1960s consistently found a moderately high positive correlation between cigarette smoking and lung cancer: the greater the number of cigarettes a person smoked, the more likely that person was to have lung cancer. Knowledge of this relationship allows predictions to be made. From the knowledge of how much someone smokes, we can predict (though not perfectly) how likely that person is to contract cancer, and vice versa. The Surgeon General's report in 1964, which concluded that smoking was dangerous to health, was based almost entirely on correlational evidence. We shall consider some problems in interpreting correlational evidence; but first, let us consider the properties of the correlation coefficient itself.

The Correlation Coefficient

There are several different types of correlation coefficients, but almost all have in common the property that they can vary from -1.00 through 0.00 to $+1.00$. Commonly, they will not be one of these three figures, but something in between, such as $+.72$ or $-.39$. The **magnitude** of the correlation coefficient indicates the degree of relationship (larger numbers reflecting greater relationships), and the **sign** indicates the direction of relationship, positive or negative. It is important to put the appropriate sign in front of the correlation coefficient, since otherwise one cannot know which way the two variables are related, positively or negatively. It is common practice, though, to omit the plus sign before positive correlations, so that a correlation of .55 would be interpreted as +.55. It is a better practice always to include the sign. An example of a *positive* correlation is the relationship between lung cancer and smoking. As one variable increases, so does the other (though not perfectly, that is, the correlation coefficient is less than +1.00). There is also a documented *negative* correlation between smoking and another variable, namely, grades in college. People who smoke a lot have tended to have lower grades than those who smoke less (Huff, 1954, p. 87).

As mentioned, there are actually several different types of correlation coefficients, and which is used depends on the characteristics of the variables being correlated. We shall consider one commonly used by psychologists; *Pearson's product-moment correlation coefficient,* or *Pearson r.* You should remember that this is only one of several; if you actually need to compute a correlation on some data, you should consult a statistics text (such as Kerlinger, 1973) to determine which is appropriate for your particular case.

Let us imagine that we are one of the bevy of psychologists who devote their careers to the study of human memory. One of these psychologists hits upon a simple, intuitive idea concerning head size and memory, which goes like this. Information from the outside world enters the head through the senses and is stored there. An analogy can be made between the head (where information is stored) and other physical vessels, such as boxes, where all kinds of things can be stored. On the basis of such analogical reasoning, which is common in science, the psychologist makes the following prediction from his or her knowledge of the properties of physical containers: as head size of a person increases, so should the person's memory. More things can be stored in bigger boxes than in smaller, and similarly more information should be stored in larger heads than in smaller ones.

This "theory" proposes a simple relationship: that as head size increases, so should memory. A positive correlation between these two variables is predicted. A random sample of the local population could be taken. The persons chosen could be measured on two dimensions: head size and the number of words they can recall from a list of thirty, presented to them once, at the rate of one word every three seconds. Three hypothetical sets of results from ten subjects are presented in table 2–1. For each individual there are two measures, one of head size and the other of number of words recalled. Also, the two types of measures need not be similar in any way to be correlated. They do not have to be on the same scale. Just as one can correlate head size with number of words recalled, one could also correlate I.Q. with street-address number, or any two sets of numbers at all. The way to calculate a Pearson *r* is illustrated in the statistical appendix.

To give you a better idea of the graphical representation of correlations, the data in the three panels of table 2–1 are presented

TABLE 2–1.   Three hypothetical examples of data taken on head size and recall, representing (a) a positive correlation, (b) a low (near-zero) correlation, and (c) a negative correlation.

Sub-ject	(a) Head size (cm.)	Recall (words)	Sub-ject	(b) Head size (cm.)	Recall (words)	Sub-ject	(c) Head size (cm.)	Recall (words)
1	50.8	17	1	50.8	23	1	50.8	12
2	63.5	21	2	63.5	12	2	63.5	9
3	45.7	16	3	45.7	13	3	45.7	13
4	25.4	11	4	25.4	21	4	25.4	23
5	29.2	9	5	29.2	9	5	29.2	21
6	49.5	15	6	49.5	14	6	49.5	16
7	38.1	13	7	38.1	16	7	38.1	14
8	30.5	12	8	30.5	15	8	30.5	17
9	35.6	14	9	35.6	11	9	35.6	15
10	58.4	23	10	58.4	16	10	58.4	11
	$r = +.93$			$r = -.07$			$r = -.89$	

in the three panels of figure 2–3; head size is plotted along the horizontal X-axis (the abscissa), and number of words recalled is plotted along the vertical Y-axis (the ordinate). The high positive correlation between head size and number of words recalled in the (a) panel in table 2–1 is translated into a visual representation that tilts upward to the right, whereas the negative correlation in panel (c) is depicted as sloping downward to the right. Thus you can see how knowing a person's score on one variable helps predict (though not perfectly in these cases) the level of performance on the other. So knowing a person's head size in the hypothetical data in the (a) and (c) panels helps predict recall, and vice versa. This is the primary reason correlations are useful: they specify the amount of relationship and allow predictions to be made. This last statement cannot be made about the data in panel (b), where there is essentially a zero correlation. The points are just scattered about, and

FIGURE 2–3.

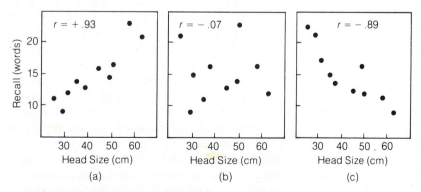

(a)   (b)   (c)

Graphical representation of the data in Table 2–1, showing the characteristic pattern of (a) a high positive correlation, (b) an essentially zero correlation, and (c) a strong negative correlation.

there is no consistent relationship, which is just what a low Pearson *r* reflects. Even in the cases where the size of the correlation is rather large, it will not be possible to predict perfectly an individual's score on one variable given his or her position on the other. Even with $r = +.75$ between head size and number of words recalled, it is still quite possible for a person with a large head size to recall few words, and vice versa. Unless the correlation is perfect ($+1.00$ or -1.00), prediction of one score when given the other will not be perfect, either.

What do you think the real correlation would be between head size and recall for a random sample of the population at large? Although we have not actually done such a study, we think it quite likely that it would be rather large and positive (perhaps $+.60$ to $+.70$), in support of the theory of memory storage based on head size. What can we conclude from this? How can correlation coefficients be interpreted? We turn to this issue next.

Interpreting correlation coefficients. An important warning is always given in any discussion of correlation: The existence of even a sizable correlation implies nothing about the existence of a causal relationship between the two variables under consideration. On the basis of a correlation alone, one cannot say whether factor *X* causes factor *Y*, factor *Y* causes factor *X*, or some underlying third factor causes both. Let us consider some examples. Suppose we have found a correlation of $+.70$ between head size and recall of words. This is in general agreement with our theory that larger heads hold more information, but certainly there are other interpretations of this relationship. It could be argued that the high positive correlation between head size and recall is *mediated* or produced by some third factor underlying both, such as age. We know that people's heads grow as they age, and that recall also improves with age. Therefore, age (or one of its correlates) might actually be responsible for the large positive correlation we have found between head size and number of words recalled.

In correlational studies, we cannot conclude that any one factor produces or causes another, since there are likely to be a number of factors that vary simultaneously with those of interest. In an experiment, we attempt to avoid this problem by directly manipulating one factor while holding all the others constant. If we are successful in holding other factors constant, which is very difficult to do, then the influence of the manipulated factor on whatever we are measuring can be directly attributed to the factor of interest. When two factors (or more) are varied at the same time, so that we cannot know whether one factor, the other factor, or both operating together produce some effect, we say that the factors are *confounded*. Confounding is inherent in correlational research and leads to the interpretational difficulties with such research. In the example of the correlation between head size and recall, we cannot say that variations in head size produced or caused differences in recall, since head size was confounded with at least one other factor: age.

In other cases, the relationship between two factors may seem to allow a causal interpretation, but again this is not strictly permitted. Some studies have shown a positive correlation between the number of handguns in a geographic area and the number of murders in that area. Proponents of gun control might use this evidence to support the contention that an increased number of guns leads to (causes, produces) more murders, but again this is not the only plausible interpretation. It may be that people in high-crime neighborhoods buy handguns to protect themselves, or that some third factor, such as socioeconomic class, actually mediates both. We can see, therefore, that no conclusion is justified simply on the basis of a moderate or even a high correlation.

Because correlations can be calculated between any two sets of scores, often even very high correlations are accidental and not linked to one another at all. There may be a very high correlation between the number of preachers and the number of pornographic movies produced each year since 1950, with both being on the increase. But it would take an unusual theory to relate these two in a causal manner.

A high degree of correlation is given greater weight in cases in which obvious competing explanations (from confounding factors) seem less plausible. We have already mentioned that most of the early evidence linking cigarette smoking to lung cancer was correlational; yet the conclusion was drawn (over the protests of the cigarette manufacturers) in the 1964 Surgeon General's report that cigarettes were likely to lead to or cause cancer. This eventually led to warnings on cigarette packages and a ban on advertising cigarettes on television, among other things. The correlation was taken as indicative of a causative relationship, probably because competing hypotheses seemed implausible. It seems unlikely, for example, that having lung cancer causes one to smoke more cigarettes (to soothe the lungs?).

More plausible, perhaps, is the possibility that some underlying third factor (such as anxiety) produces the relationship. In fact, Eysenck and Eaves (1981) have recently argued that the correlation between lung cancer and smoking in humans is produced by personality differences. Certain personality types, according to Eysenck and Eaves, are more likely to smoke and also to get lung cancer. Thus they argue that the smoking-cancer correlation does not imply causation. We should mention, though, that the link between cigarette smoking and lung cancer has now been established by experimental studies with nonhuman animals, typically beagles. Most authorities disagree with the view of Eysenck and Eaves.

As a final example of the pitfalls of the correlational approach, consider the negative relationship mentioned previously between cigarette smoking and grades. More smoking has been related to poorer grades. But does smoking cause poorer grades? This seems unlikely, and certainly there are ready alternative interpretations.

Students with poor grades may be more anxious and thus smoke more, or more sociable students may smoke more and study less, and so on. No firm conclusions on the causal direction of a relationship between two variables can be established simply because the variables are correlated, even if the correlation is perfect. As is true for the observational method, the correlational method is very useful for suggesting possible relationships and directing further inquiry, but it is not useful for establishing direct causal relationships. The correlational method is superior to the observational method, because the degree of relation between two variables can be precisely stated and thus predictions can be made about the (approximate) value of one variable if the value of the other is known. Remember, the greater the correlation (nearer +1.00 or −1.00), the better the prediction.

Low correlations: A caution. If high correlations cannot be interpreted as evidence for some sort of causal relationship, one might think it should at least be possible to rule out a causative relationship between two variables if their correlation is very low, approaching zero. If the correlation between head size and recall had been −.02, would this have ruled out our theory that greater head size leads to better recall? Or if the correlation between smoking and lung cancer had been +.08, should we have abandoned the idea that they are causally related? The answer: sometimes, under certain conditions. But other factors can cause low or zero correlations and may mask an actual relationship.

One common problem is that of *truncated range*. For a meaningful correlation coefficient to be calculated, there must be rather great differences among the scores in each of the variables of interest; there must be a certain amount of spread or variability in the numbers. If all the head sizes were the same in the panels of table 2–1 and the recall scores varied, the correlation between the two would be zero. (You can work it out yourself using equation B–5 in appendix B.) If we looked only at the correlation between head size and recall in college students, it might be quite low, because the differences in head size and recall among college students might not be very great, compared with the population at large. This could happen even though there might be a positive (or negative) correlation between the two variables if head size were sampled over a wider range. The problem of restricted range can produce a low correlation, even when there is an actual correlation present between two variables.

You might think that everyone would recognize the problem of truncated range and avoid it, but it is often subtle. Consider the problem of trying to predict success in college from Scholastic Aptitude Test (SAT) scores at a college with very high admission standards. The scores on the verbal and quantitative subtests can range from 200 to 800, with average (mean) performance of just below 500. Imagine that mean scores at our hypothetical college are 700 on each subtest. The admissions officer at this college computes a correlation between combined SAT scores and freshman grades and finds it to be +.10, very small indeed. Her conclusion: SAT scores cannot be used to predict grades in college. The problem, however, is that the only scores considered are ones from a very restricted range, specifically very high ones. People with low scores are not admitted to the college. Obviously, the truncated-range problem is very likely to be a factor here, or in any research situation involving a limited sample of subjects with homogeneous characteristics. If the college had randomly admitted people, and if the correlation had then been determined between SAT scores and grades, it would probably have been much higher. Since psychologists often use homogeneous populations such as college students, the restricted-range problem must be carefully considered in interpreting correlations.

A final problem in interpreting low correlations is that one must be certain that the assumptions underlying the use of a particular correlation coefficient have been met. Otherwise, its use may well be inappropriate and lead to spuriously low estimates of relationship. These have not been discussed here, but it is imperative to check on these assumptions in a statistics book before employing Pearson r or any other correlation coefficient. For example, one assumption underlying Pearson r is that the relationship between the two variables is linear (can be described by a straight line) rather than curvilinear, as in the hypothetical (but plausible) relationship in figure 2–4 between age and long-term memory. At very young ages, the line is flat; then it increases be-

FIGURE 2–4.

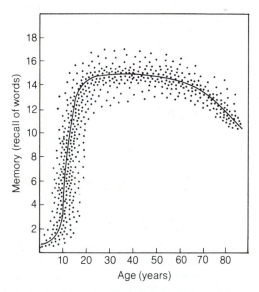

A hypothetical figure depicting a curvilinear relationship between long-term memory and age. Although memory is related to age in a systematic fashion and one could predict recall by knowing age, Pearson r would be quite low, since the relationship is not linear.

tween ages three and sixteen, where it again levels off until late middle age, where it drops slightly, until very old age, where it decreases at a greater rate (Craik, 1977). Thus one can predict recall of words from age fairly well, but Pearson *r* will be rather low, since the relationship between the two variables is not linear. This could, of course, always be checked by plotting a scatter diagram, as in figure 2–4. Low correlations, then, may not reflect that a relationship is absent, but only that the assumptions of the particular coefficient employed have not been met.

Complex Correlational Procedures

Does watching violent TV programs cause aggressive behavior? Eron, Huesmann, Lefkowitz, and Walder (1972) measured children's preferences for violent programs and the children's aggressiveness as rated by their peers. For these third-graders, Eron and coworkers found a moderate positive correlation, *r* = +.21, indicating that children who were more aggressive tended to watch more violent TV (and less aggressive children tended to watch less violent programs). How are we to interpret this positive correlation? Can we say that watching violent programs causes aggressiveness? The answer is no. To see why this is the case, all we have to do is to turn our causal statement around and assert that being aggressive causes a preference for violent TV. We have no reasonable way to decide on the direction of causality, based on this one correlation coefficient. As we noted earlier, a valid causal statement cannot be made on the basis of a single correlation.

When we do not know the direction of causality (violent TV causes aggression versus aggressive traits cause a preference for violent programs), there is a strong possibility that some third, confounded variable is the cause of the obtained relation. Since the researchers have not controlled either the programs watched or the initial aggressiveness, they cannot rule out other variables, such as genetic differences in aggressiveness or differences in home life. Causal statements are difficult, if not impossible, to make on the basis of a single correlation coefficient.

The explanatory power of correlational research may be enhanced by examining patterns of correlations. One technique is called the *cross-lagged-panel correlation procedure,* and Eron and coworkers used it in a ten-year follow-up study of the same children in the "thirteenth" grade. The results are summarized in figure 2–5. The correlation between a preference for violent TV and aggression was essentially zero (*r* = −.05) in the thirteenth grade. Similarly, they found a negligible relation between preference for violent TV in the third and the thirteenth grade (*r* = +.05). They did obtain a moderate relation between aggressiveness in the two grades (*r* = +.38), indicating that it is a somewhat stable trait. Of more interest are the cross-lagged correlations (the ones along the diagonals of the figure) in assessing the direction

FIGURE 2–5.

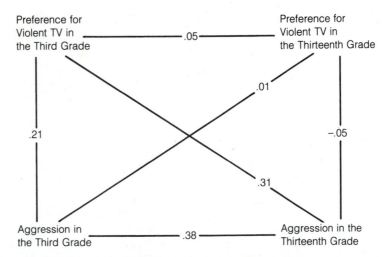

Correlations between a preference for violent television programs and aggression, as rated by peers for 211 males over a ten-year period. The important cross-lagged correlations are on the diagonals. (After Eron, Huesmann, Lefkowitz, and Walder, 1972. Copyright (1972) by the American Psychological Association. Reprinted by permission of the author.)

of the relationship. Do aggressive people watch violent TV, or does watching violent TV produce aggressiveness? We can determine which of these two possibilities holds true by examining the diagonal correlations. Essentially no relationship exists between aggressiveness in the third grade and watching violent TV in the thirteenth ($r = +.01$). However, a fairly substantial correlation exists between a preference for watching violent TV in the third grade and exhibiting aggressiveness in the thirteenth ($r = +.31$). In fact, the relationship is even greater than the relationship between these two variables in the earlier study, when the subjects were third-graders. Thus the direction of relationship seems to be that watching violent TV programs in the third grade may produce aggressiveness later. The underlying assumption is that if one variable causes the other, the first (watching violent TV programs) should be more strongly related to the second (aggressiveness) later in time than when the second (effect) variable is measured at the same time as the first cause). In other words, causes should take some time to produce their effects (see figure 2–5).

Using these cross-lagged-panel correlations and other complex analyses, Eron and colleagues concluded that watching violent TV programs early in life probably causes, in part, aggressive behavior later in life. Recent research by Eron (1982) supports this conclusion (also see Huesmann and others, 1973). Of course, many other factors contribute to aggressiveness; this is just one example of how cross-lagged-panel correlations can aid in arriving at an explanation from correlational research. However, causal statements cannot be as strong as those that come from experiments, because the variables have not been manipulated by the researcher.

The general strategy of the cross-lagged procedure, then, is to obtain several correlations over time, and then, on the basis of the size and direction of the rs, determine what leads to what. The cross-lagged technique is fairly new to psychological research and has the obvious drawback that the research project may be very time consuming. Nevertheless, this method for determining causation from correlational research has been used in several problem areas, for example, to show that a large vocabulary enhances the ability to spell, rather than the other way around, and that air pollution is an important cause of death in large cities, rather than death being a cause of pollution (Cook and Campbell, 1979, chapter 7).

In addition to cross-lagged-panel correlations, there are several other statistical procedures used to try to gain a better understanding of causation in correlational research. Some of these include partial correlation, multiple-regression analysis, and path analysis. As is true of the cross-lagged procedure, these other techniques involve an examination of several relationships, not just a single correlation. These statistical techniques are described in numerous texts (see especially Cook and Campbell, 1979), and since this book is not concerned primarily with statistical techniques, we shall only note their existence here as an aid to interpreting correlational research.

As a general rule, remember that causal statements are always suspect in correlational research, because of possible third-variable confounding. Cook and Campbell, as well as others (for example, Rogosa, 1980), have noted that many of the assumptions underlying complex correlational research are questionable. Thus, we have additional reasons to suspect causal statements made on the basis of correlational evidence.

Cause: A Note

We have repeatedly cautioned you about incorrectly concluding that a correlation means causation. Causation is a controversial subject in science and philosophy, and we will now consider some of the issues. Owing to the influence of some philosophers of science, it has become unpopular among contemporary scientists to use the term *cause*, because the philosophical implications become frightfully complicated. Thinking too long about the cause of even a very simple event leads to an infinite regress of causes for that event. For this and other reasons, the term *cause* has dropped out of use in some circles (see Kerlinger, 1973, pp. 392–393). In this book we muddle through, using the term *cause*, since its meaning is always limited; experiments lead to causal inferences because one factor is varied while all others are, in the ideal case, held constant. Thus we can say that whatever effect occurs in such cases has been caused by the factor that varied. We limit ourselves to this usage, but others prefer various circumlocutions. Instead of saying that there is evidence that cigarette smoking causes cancer, we can say that it leads to, produces, is an antecedent condition of, determines, or directly affects cancer. We use these terms interchangeably with *causes.*

A more interesting point is that many factors that are experimentally varied are themselves quite complicated sets of independent events, any one of which could be the cause of an experimental effect. Time is a good example of such a variable. If we are interested in the effects of the length of time one studies a persuasive communication on the amount a person's attitude changes toward the communication, we vary the amount of time people spend studying the message. Suppose we find an increase in attitude change with increases in study time, when other factors are held constant. Can we say that time has caused an increase in attitude change? In a sense this is true, but in a more fundamental sense it is not. Presumably, it is some psychological process, acting over time, that causes the attitude change. It is something correlated with time, but not time itself, since time is not a causative agent. If we leave a bicycle outdoors in the rain and it rusts, we do not say that time caused the rust; chemical processes acting over time caused it.

Usually, a manipulated variable is actually composed of a number of complex and interacting parts, any one or set of which may actually cause some effect. For this reason, it is sometimes said that experiments are only controlled correlations, since the variable manipulated is actually composed of a number of confounded parts. This is certainly an accurate characterization in at least some cases; even so we are far ahead of having a simple correlation, because we know the direction of effect. Take the example of how amount of time spent studying a persuasive communication affects attitude change. We could simply give the message to a number of people and let them read it for as long as they desired. We could time this for each person, and then see how much the person's attitude changed. If we found a positive correlation, we would not know whether the time people spent studying the passage caused more attitude change, or whether the more people decided to change their attitudes, the more they studied the passage to make sure they knew the facts. There are other possible reasons for the relationship, too. But in the experiment in which time is varied while other factors are held constant, we can say that more study time leads to (determines, produces, causes) more attitude change.

Experiments allow us to know the direction of the relation. This is their overwhelming advantage to correlations. They also inform us (which a correlation does not) that the causal factor is at least embedded in the independent variable, and not some third outside factor. It is in this sense that they tell us about causes. We turn to this important scientific tool—the experiment—in the next chapter.

SUMMARY

1. Much of science is concerned with the careful observation and study of the natural world. Two basic techniques discussed in this chapter are naturalistic observation and the correlational

approach. Both of these are fairly weak scientific methods relative to the experiment, since they do not allow us to make statements about what factors cause what effects. But they are very useful in early stages of exploration of a topic and in studying topics that cannot practically or ethically be studied by experimental means.

2. After delimiting the range of events to be studied, naturalistic observation typically involves the unobtrusive (nonreactive) observation or unobtrusive measurement of events naturally occurring in the environment. Of more use to psychologists are two reactive variants of naturalistic observation: case studies and surveys. However, all these methods of simple observation have the disadvantage of being descriptive and not allowing statements about how factors are related to one another.

3. The correlational approach allows statements of relationship, of what goes with what. Correlations can vary from -1.00 to $+1.00$, with the magnitude of the number reflecting the strength of the relationship and the sign indicating the direction. For example, height is positively correlated with weight, and mean yearly temperature is negatively correlated with distance of location from the equator. There are several measures of correlation, but the one most commonly used by psychologists is the Pearson product-moment correlation coefficient, or Pearson r.

4. The correlational approach allows one to establish the amount of relationship between two variables, which is useful for prediction. However, its primary drawback is that it cannot establish the direction of relationship. Even if two variables, X and Y, are strongly related, we cannot say whether the relationship is accidental, or X caused Y, or Y caused X, or some third factor caused both.

5. In correlational studies a number of factors usually vary together, so that the results are confounded. But correlational research is quite appropriate in situations where it is impossible to perform experiments, for example, in studying conditions related to race riots.

6. When researchers discover that the correlation between two measures is near zero, they will often conclude that there is no relation between the measures. Before drawing such a conclusion, even though it often is correct, researchers must determine if assumptions underlying the use of the correlational measure have been met. One common problem is that of truncated range, or a lack of variation in the distribution of one set of scores. If all the measures on one variable are about the same, the correlation coefficient will approach zero, even if there is a true relation between the measures when a wider sampling of scores is taken.

7. Much research attempts to introduce a measure of control into correlational studies to better determine cause-and-effect relations. In some cases, statistical techniques, such as the cross-lagged correlational procedure, can be used to try to determine causes in correlational studies.

KEY TERMS

anthropomorphize
case study
cause
confounding
correlation
correlation coefficient
correlational technique
cross-lagged-panel correlation
   procedure
delimiting observations
deviant-case analysis
ethogram

ethology
ex post facto research
naturalistic observation
participant observation
Pearson r
reactivity
survey
truncated range
unobtrusive measures
unobtrusive observations
variable

DISCUSSION QUESTIONS

1. Imagine that you are a researcher just beginning a study of how mothers interact with their babies. You want to gain some idea as to the frequency (1) of the mother's performance of some act regarding the baby that is relatively independent of the baby's immediate needs, (2) of the baby's acting in various ways when the mother is not attending to it, and (3) of the mother's and child's actions when they are interacting. Make a list of all the behaviors that you think might occur with relatively great frequency in the three categories. This would be a type of ethogram, as discussed in this chapter. If you observed mothers and babies for five hours a day over a period of weeks, what kinds of conclusions could you draw? What kinds of information would you want to know, but not be able to obtain, from this sort of naturalistic observation?

2. One of the first pieces of evidence that linked lung cancer with cigarette smoking was published by Doll (1955). He tabulated the average number of cigarettes consumed by the people of eleven countries in 1930 and the number of deaths from lung cancer among men in 1950. The measure of deaths was taken twenty years after the measure of cigarette consumption, since it seems natural that it would take years for a cause-and-effect relation to be seen, if one were there. Since very few women smoked in 1930, it also seemed best to relate the smoking rates to male deaths. The following table is an adaptation of Doll's important results.

Country	1930 Cigarette consumption	1950 Deaths per million
Australia	480	180
Canada	500	150
Denmark	380	170
Finland	1,100	350
Great Britain	1,100	460
Holland	490	240
Iceland	230	60
Norway	250	90
Sweden	300	110
Switzerland	510	250
United States of America	1,300	200

(a) Examine the results. What do the two columns of numbers seem to show?

(b) Plot a graph relating the two measures, such as the one in figure 2–3. What does it show?

(c) Now calculate the exact relation between the two variables by using the formula for Pearson r given in the statistical appendix. What is the exact magnitude and sign of the correlation coefficient you have obtained?

3. Do the analyses you performed in 2(c) permit the conclusion that smoking causes lung cancer? If the correlation coefficient were higher, say +.95, would you be more certain of the cause-and-effect relation? If you think these data do not argue that smoking causes lung cancer, how else might you explain the results?

4. Make a list of pairs of variables that you believe are highly correlated (either positively or negatively), but between which you think there is little chance of a causal connection. How could you determine whether the correlation does indicate a cause-and-effect relation?

3

Research Techniques: Experiments

No one believes an hypothesis except its originator, but everyone believes an experiment except the experimenter.

—W. I. B. BEVERIDGE

IMAGINE YOU ARE A STUDENT in a class in environmental psychology and have received the following assignment: Go to the library and "defend" a table by preventing anyone else from sitting down for as long as you can. You must use only nonverbal and nonviolent means to accomplish this. To carry out this task, you might wait in the crowded library until a table was vacant, quickly sit down, and proceed to strew your books, clothing, and other belongings all over the table in hopes that this disarray might keep others away. After some time, say fifteen minutes or so, someone finally does sit down at your table, ending your assignment. Have you performed an experiment?

Before answering this question, let us sketch out the major criteria for an experiment, which have been briefly discussed in the preceding chapters. An experiment occurs when the environment is systematically manipulated so that the causal effect of this manipulation on some behavior can be observed. Aspects of the environment that are not of interest, and hence not manipulated, are held constant, so as not to influence the outcome of the experiment. We can then explain that the behavior resulted from the manipulation. We must explain two special terms briefly introduced in chapter 1—*independent* and *dependent variables*—to describe how the environment is manipulated and how behavior is observed.

What Is an Experiment?

Many students are surprised to discover that the actions described in our library table exercise do not constitute an experiment. All experiments require at least two special features, called independent and dependent variables. The *dependent variable* is the behavior recorded by the experimenter: in this case, the time that elapsed until someone else sits down at the table. The *independent variable* is a manipulation of the environment controlled by the experimenter: in this case, the strewing of articles on the table. (An exception is the quasi-experiment, which is discussed later in this chapter.)

But an experiment must have at least two values, or *levels,* of the environment. There must be two conditions that are compared with each other to determine if one of the conditions makes a difference in a behavior or outcome. Sometimes, these two levels might be just the presence or absence of manipulation. The library example fails to meet this criterion, since it involves only one level of the independent variable.

How might we change the procedure to obtain an experiment? The simplest way would be to sit down again, this time without scattering anything. Then our independent variable would have the necessary two levels: the table with items strewn about, and the bare table with no items strewn about. Now we have something to compare with the first condition.

The possible outcomes of this experiment are three: (1) strewing articles on the table results in a longer time before the table is invaded by another person; (2) the time until invasion is the same, whether or not articles are strewn about; (3) scattering articles results in a shorter time until invasion. Without the second level of the independent variable (the table with no articles strewn about), these three outcomes cannot be formulated. Indeed, it is impossible to say anything about how effective articles are in defending library tables until there are two levels of the independent variable.

When this library experiment is performed properly, the first possible outcome is obtained. A table can be better protected by a person plus assorted articles than by a person alone.

We can see, then, that experiments must have at least independent and dependent variables. The research techniques discussed in the preceding chapter do not allow or require manipulation of the environment; but before an *experiment* can be established, independent variables with at least two levels are necessary.

Advantages of Experiments

The main advantage of experiments over the techniques discussed in chapter 2 is better control of extraneous variation. In the ideal experiment, no factors (variables) except the one being studied are permitted to influence the outcome; in the jargon of experimental psychology, we say that these other factors are *controlled*. If, as in the ideal experiment, all factors but one (that under investigation) are held constant, we can logically conclude that any differences in outcome must be caused by manipulation of that one independent variable. As the levels of the independent variable are changed, the resulting differences in the dependent variable can occur only because the independent variable has changed. In other words, changes in the independent variable *cause* the observed changes in the dependent variable. Whereas nonexperimental research techniques are limited to statements about description and correlation, experiments permit statements about causation—that is, independent variable *A* causes dependent variable *B* to change.

Thus, in principle, experiments lead to statements about causation. In practice, these statements are not always true. No experiment is 100 percent successful in eliminating or holding constant all other sources of variation but the one being studied. However, experiments eliminate more extraneous variation than do other research techniques. Later in this chapter, we will discuss specific ways in which experiments limit extraneous variation.

Another advantage of experiments is economy. Using the technique of naturalistic observation requires that the scientist wait patiently until the conditions of interest occur. If you lived in Trondheim, Norway—near the Arctic Circle—and wanted to study how heat affects aggression, relying on the sun to produce high temperatures would require great patience and lots of time. The experimenter controls the situation by creating the conditions of interest (various levels of heat in a laboratory setting), thus obtaining data quickly and efficiently.

Why Experiments Are Conducted

The same general reasons that apply to the conduct of any research also explain why psychologists perform experiments. In basic research, experiments are performed to test theories and to provide the data base for explanations of behavior. These kinds of experiments are typically well planned, with the investigator having a clear idea of the anticipated outcome. As an example of strong inference (see chapter 1), so-called *critical experiments* try to pit against each other two theories that make different predictions. One outcome favors Theory A; the other, Theory B. Thus, in principle, the experiment will determine which theory to reject and which to keep. In practice, these critical experiments do not work out so well, since supporters of the rejected theory are ingenious in thinking up explanations to discredit the unfavorable interpretation of the experiment. One example of such an explanation is found in a study of how people forget. Two major explanations of forgetting are that (1) items decay or fade out over time, just the way an incandescent light bulb fades when the electricity is turned off (this explanation is called "trace decay"), or (2) items never fade, but because of this they interfere with each other, causing confusion. A simple "critical" experiment would vary the time between introduction into the memory of successive items, holding the number of items constant (Waugh and Norman, 1965). Memory should be worse with longer times, according to trace-decay theorists, since there is more time for items to fade out. But since the number of items remains the same regardless of the time they are introduced, interference theory predicts no differences in forgetting. When this experiment is performed, there is no difference in memory; this would seem to nullify the trace-decay explanation. The rejoinder by trace-decay theorists, however, is that the extra time given between items allows people to rehearse—that is, repeat the item to themselves—which prevents forgetting.

Less often, researchers perform an experiment just to see what happens; we can call this a *what-if experiment*. Students often come up with what-if experiments, since these experiments require no knowledge of theory or the existing data base and can be formulated on the basis of personal experience and observations. Some scientists frown on what-if experiments; the main objection to them is their inefficiency. If, as is often the case, nothing much happens in a what-if experiment—say, the independent variable has no effect—nothing is gained from the experiment. By contrast, if nothing much happens in a careful experiment for which a theory predicts something will happen, the null result can be useful. We must admit to having tried what-if experiments. Most of them did not work, but they were fun. Our advice is to check with your instructor before trying a what-if experiment. He or she probably can give you an estimate of the odds of your coming up with anything, or may even know the results of a similar experiment that has already been performed.

This brings us to the last major reason for doing experiments in basic research. This is to repeat or replicate a previous finding. A single experiment by itself is far less convincing than a series of related experiments. The simplest replication is the direct repetition of an existing experiment, with no change in procedures. Although this is a useful exercise for the student, the scientist finds this boring and inefficient, unless the original experiment was quite novel. Instead, a better way to replicate is to *extend* the previous procedure by adding something new while retaining something old. Thus, part of the replication is a literal repetition, but the additional part adds to scientific knowledge. This kind of repetition demonstrates the generality of a result by showing how it is (or is not) maintained over different independent variables.

Variables

Variables are the gears and cogs that make experiments run. Effective selection and manipulation of variables makes the difference between a good experiment and a poor one. This section covers the three kinds of variables that must be carefully considered before starting an experiment: *independent, dependent,* and *control* variables. We conclude by discussing experiments that have more than one independent or dependent variable.

Independent Variables

In true experiments, *independent variables* are those *manipulated* by the experimenter. The brightness of a lamp, the loudness of a tone, the number of food pellets given to a rat—all are independent variables, since the experimenter determines their quality and quantity. Independent variables are selected because an experimenter thinks they will cause changes in behavior. Increasing the intensity of a tone should increase the speed with which people respond to the tone. Increasing the number of pellets given to a rat for pressing a bar should increase the number of times the bar is pressed. When a change in the level (amount) of an independent variable causes a change in behavior, we say that the behavior is under control of the independent variable.

Failure of an independent variable to control behavior, often called *null results*, can have more than one interpretation. First, the experimenter may have guessed incorrectly that the independent variable was important: the null results may be correct. Most scientists will accept this interpretation only reluctantly, and so the following alternate explanations of null results are common. The experimenter may not have created a valid manipulation of the independent variable. Let us say you are conducting an experiment on second-grade children, and your independent variable is the number of small candies (M&Ms, jelly beans, et cetera) they get after each correct response. Some children get only one whereas others get two. You find no difference in behavior. Perhaps if your independent variable had involved a greater range—that is, from one piece of candy to ten pieces of candy—you would have obtained a difference. Your manipulation might not have been sufficient to reveal an effect of the independent variable. Or perhaps, unknown to you, the class had a birthday party just before the experiment started and their little tummies were filled with ice cream and birthday cake. In this case, maybe even ten pieces of candy would not show any effect. This is why, in studies of animal learning with food as a reward, the animals are deprived of food before the experiment starts.

We can see that experimenters must be careful to produce a strong manipulation of the independent variable. Failure to do so is a common cause of null results. Other common causes of null results are related to dependent and control variables, to which we now turn.

Dependent Variables

The *dependent variable* is that *observed* and *recorded* by the experimenter. It *depends* on the behavior of the subject. That behavior is dependent on the independent variable. The time taken to press a switch, the speed of a worm crawling through a maze, the number of times a rat presses a bar—all are dependent variables, because they are observed and recorded by the experimenter.

One criterion for a good dependent variable is stability. When an experiment is repeated exactly—same subject, same levels of independent variable, and so on—the dependent variable should yield the same score as it did previously. Instability can occur because of some deficit in the way we measure some dependent variable. Assume that we wish to measure the weight in grams of an object, say, a candle, before and after it is lit for fifteen minutes. We use a scale that works by having a spring move a pointer. The spring contracts when it is cold and expands when it is hot. As long as our weight measurements are taken at constant temperatures, they will be reliable. But if temperature varies while objects are being weighed, the same object will yield different readings. Our dependent variable is then unreliable.

Null results can often be caused by deficits in the dependent variable, even if it is stable. The most common cause is a restricted or limited range of the dependent variable, so that it gets "stuck" at the top or bottom of its scale. Imagine that you are teaching a rather uncoordinated friend how to bowl for the first time. Since you know from introductory psychology that reward improves performance, you offer to buy your friend a beer every time he or she gets a strike. Your friend gets all gutter balls, so you drink the beer yourself. Thus you can no longer offer a reward; you therefore expect a decrement in performance. But since it is impossible to do any worse than all gutter balls, you cannot observe any decrement. Your friend is already at the bottom of the scale. This is called a *floor effect*. The opposite problem, getting 100 percent correct, is called a *ceiling effect*. Ceiling and floor effects (see chapter 10) prevent the influence of an independent variable from being accurately reflected in a dependent variable.

Control Variables

A *control variable* is a potential independent variable that is held constant during an experiment. It is a variable that does not vary, because it is *controlled* by the experimenter. For any one experiment, the list of desirable control variables is quite large, far larger than can ever be accomplished in practice. In even a relatively simple experiment, for example, requiring people to memorize three-letter syllables, many variables should be controlled. Time of day (diurnal cycle) changes your efficiency; ideally, this should be controlled. Temperature could be important, since you might fall asleep if the testing room were too warm. Time since your last meal might also affect memory performance. Intelligence is also related. The list could be extended. In practice, an experimenter tries to control as many salient variables as possible, hoping that the effect of uncontrolled factors will be small relative to the effect of the independent variable. The smaller the size of the effect produced by the independent variable, the more important it is to carefully control other extraneous factors. Holding a variable constant is not the only way to remove extraneous variation. Statistical techniques (discussed later in the chapter) also control extraneous variables. However, holding a variable constant is the most direct experimental technique for controlling extraneous factors, and so we shall limit our definition of control variables to only this technique. Null results often occur in an experiment because there is insufficient control of these other factors—that is, they have been left to vary unsystematically. This is especially true in studies outside of laboratories, where the ability to hold control variables constant is greatly decreased.

INDEPENDENT variable is **MANIPULATED**
DEPENDENT variable is **OBSERVED**
CONTROL variable is held **CONSTANT**

Name the Variables

Because understanding *independent*, *dependent*, and *control* variables is so important, we have included some examples for you to check your own understanding. For each situation, name the three kinds of variables. Answers are provided at the end of this section. No peeking!

1. An automobile manufacturer wants to know how bright brake lights should be in order to minimize the time required for the driver of a following car to realize that the car in front is stopping. An experiment is conducted to answer this. Name the variables.

2. A pigeon is trained to peck a key if a green light is illuminated, but not if a red light is on. Correct pecks are rewarded by access to grain. Name the variables.

3. A therapist tries to improve a patient's image of himself. Every time the patient says something positive about himself, the therapist rewards this by nodding, smiling, and being extra-attentive. Name the variables.

4. A social psychologist does an experiment to discover whether men or women give lower ratings of discomfort when six people are crowded into a telephone booth. Name the variables.

Answers

1. *Independent (manipulated) variable:*

    Intensity (brightness) of brake lights.

    Dependent (observed) variable:

    Time from onset of brake lights until depression of brake pedal by following driver.

    Control (constant) variables:

    Color of brake lights, shape of brake pedal, force needed to depress brake pedal, external illumination, etc.

2. *Independent variable:*

    Color of light (red or green)

    Dependent variable:

    Number of key pecks

    Control variables:

    Hours of food deprivation, size of key, intensity of red and green lights, etc.

3. *Independent variable:*

    Actually, this is not an experiment, because there is only one level of the independent variable. To make this an experiment, we need another level—say, rewarding positive statements about the patient's mother-in-law and ignoring negative ones. Then the independent variable would be: Kind of statement rewarded.

    Dependent variable:

    Number (or frequency) of statements

    Control variables:

    Office setting, therapist

4. *Independent variable:*

    Sex of participant[1]

    Dependent variable:

    Rating of discomfort

    Control variables:

    Size of telephone booth, number of persons (6) crowded into booth, etc.

---

[1]Sex is a special type of independent variable called a subject variable, discussed later in this chapter.

More Than One Independent Variable

It is unusual to find an experiment reported in a psychological journal in which only one independent (manipulated) variable is used. The typical experiment manipulates from two to four independent variables simultaneously. There are several advantages to this procedure. First, it is often more efficient to conduct one experiment with, say, three independent variables, than to conduct three separate experiments. Second, experimental control is often better, since with a single experiment some control variables—time of day, temperature, humidity, and so on—are more likely to be held constant than with three separate experiments. Third, and most important, results generalized—that is, shown to be valid in several situations—across several independent variables are more valuable than data that have yet to be generalized. Just as it is important to establish generality of results across different types of experimental subjects (see chapter 12), experimenters also need to discover if some result is valid across levels of independent variables. Fourth, this allows us to study interactions, the relationships among independent variables.

Let us say we wish to find out which of two kinds of rewards facilitate learning geometry by high-school students. The first reward is an outright cash payment for problems correctly solved; the second reward is early dismissal from class—that is, each correct solution entitles the student to leave class five minutes early. Assume that the results of this (hypothetical) experiment show early dismissal to be better. Before we make early dismissal a universal rule in high school, we should first establish its generality by comparing the two kinds of reward in other classes, such as history, biology, etc. Here, subject matter of the class would be a second independent variable. It would be better to put these two variables into a single experiment than to conduct two successive experiments. This would avoid problems of control, such as one class being tested the week of the big football game (when no reward would improve learning), and the other class being tested the week after the game is won (when students felt better about learning).

When the effects produced by one independent variable are not the same at each level of a second independent variable, we have an *interaction*. The search for interactions is a major reason for using more than one independent variable per experiment. This can best be demonstrated by example.

Piliavin, Piliavin, and Rodin (1975) were interested in discovering under what conditions an innocent bystander would help someone in an emergency. The emergency was faked on a New York City subway car (the F train, appropriately enough). A white male carrying a cane stumbled and fell to the floor. Would other passengers aid this "victim"?

There were two independent variables. For half of the trials, victims had an ugly red birthmark placed on their face with theatrical makeup. The presence or absence of this birthmark was the first independent variable. For half of the trials, an observer wearing a white medical jacket (identifying him as a medical intern) was present. The same observer was present without the white jacket for the remaining half of the trials. So the presence or absence of a medical intern was the second independent variable. The dependent variable was the percentage of trials in which passengers came to the aid of the victim by either touching the victim or asking him if he needed help.

Results of this experiment are shown in figure 3–1, with each independent variable plotted alone. People were more willing to help victims who lacked an ugly birthmark. They were also more willing to help when no intern was present.

Figure 3–2 shows, however, that this interpretation of the results can be misleading. If, as figure 3–1 implies, both independent variables have their own effect, the results should look like the two parallel lines plotted in figure 3–3. Instead, the lines in figure 3–2 are not parallel. This indicates the possibility of an interaction between the two independent variables. The percentage of trials in which help was given depends on the levels of both independent variables. If the victim had no birthmark, then the presence or absence of an intern had little effect on helping. But when the

FIGURE 3–1.

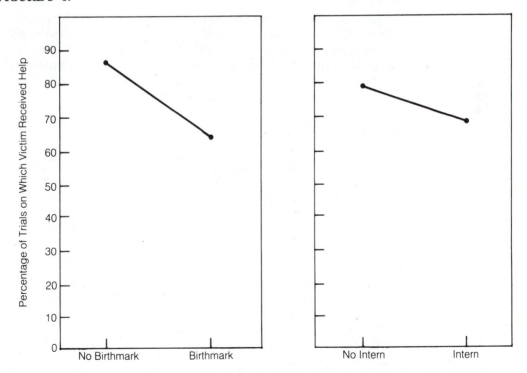

Effects of two independent variables on helping behavior. Each variable is plotted separately. (Data from Piliavin et al., 1975).

FIGURE 3–2.

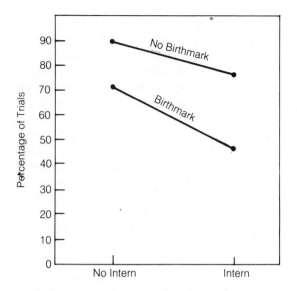

Effect of two independent variables on helping behavior. (Data from Piliavin et al., 1975).

victim had a birthmark, passengers were far less willing to help when an intern was present.

Now let us imagine that this experiment was performed in two separate parts. In the first part, only the birthmark was manipulated. The experimenter would not have known that the presence of an intern would have reduced helping. In the second part, only the presence of the intern would vary. Results would have been quite different, depending on whether the victim had a birthmark.

FIGURE 3–3.

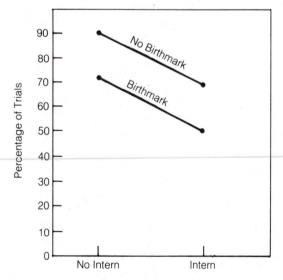

Fictitious data showing no interaction between the two independent variables.

You can see that by doing the experiment in two parts, we would have lost a great deal of information.

Figure 3–2, which contains the actual results, shows an interaction. The effects of one independent variable depend on the level of the other independent variable. The least amount of help was given when the victim had a birthmark and an intern was present.

Many experiments include two or more independent variables; this means that the results may contain an interaction. Because of the frequency with which you are likely to encounter interactions, we will present another example of a two-variable experiment to help you practice interpreting the results of complex experiments.

In this experiment on social loafing (see chapter 1) by Brickner, Harkins, and Ostrom (1986), the authors wanted to determine the effect of personal involvement in a task on the amount of social loafing shown on that task. Brickner and her associates noted that low-involvement tasks, such as clapping and generating uses for a knife, had been used in earlier research on social loafing. The authors reasoned that the effort devoted to a task should be related to the intrinsic importance or personal significance that the task has for the individual. High personal involvement in a task should reduce social loafing, because individuals should put forth a substantial amount of effort on such tasks, regardless of whether their individual performance is monitored. So, the researchers varied the involvement in the task and also varied the amount that individual effort could be assessed. If their reasoning was correct, there should be an interaction: low involvement should lead to social loafing (reduced effort when the individual's effort can be assessed), but high involvement should lead to about the same amount of effort, whether or not individual effort could be identified.

Brickner and associates had college underclass students generate as many thoughts as they could in a twelve-minute period about a proposal to implement senior comprehensive exams, which a student would have to pass in order to graduate. In the high-involvement condition, the students were led to believe that the proposal would be instituted at their college prior to their graduation. Thus, the addition of comprehensive exams as one prerequisite to graduation should have high personal relevance. In the low-personal-involvement condition, the students were led to believe that the exams would be instituted later, at another college. The possible identifiability of individual effort was also manipulated by instructions. Subjects wrote each of their thoughts about comprehensives on an individual slip of paper. In the low-identifiability condition, the subjects were told that their thoughts would be collected together with those of other subjects, because the committee evaluating the thoughts wanted to assess the range of opinions for the group as a whole. In the high-identifiability condition, the subjects were told that their opinions would be considered separately from those of others, because the committee in charge wanted to assess individual responses.

To summarize, the dependent variable was the number of thoughts generated in the four conditions: low identifiability and low involvement; low identifiability and high involvement; high identifiability and low involvement; and high identifiability and high involvement.

The results are shown in figure 3–4, which plots the number of thoughts generated against identifiability for the two involvement conditions. Earlier social loafing research is replicated in the low-involvement condition: fewer thoughts were generated when the subjects believed that their individual performance was not being assessed. Now examine the results when there was high involvement: the number of thoughts was about the same, regardless of identifiability. Thus, the variables interact: the effects of identifiability depend on the level of task involvement. Put another way, social loafing, and therefore diffusion of responsibility, is less likely to occur when a person is confronted with a personally involving task than when the task does not have much intrinsic interest.

In summary, an interaction occurs when the levels of one independent variable are differentially affected by the levels of other independent variables. When interactions are present, it does not make sense to discuss the effects of each independent variable separately. Because the effects of one variable also depend on the levels of the other variables, we are forced to discuss interacting variables together.

FIGURE 3–4.

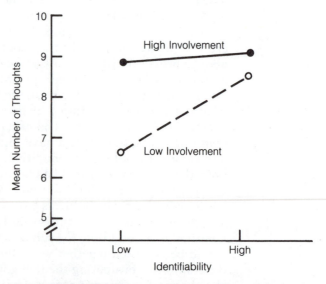

Results of the experiment by Brickner, Harkins, and Ostrom (1986), showing an interaction. Social loafing (low numbers of thoughts generated with low as opposed to high identifiability) occurs with a low-involvement task, but not with a high-involvement one.

More Than One Dependent Variable

The dependent (observed) variable is used as an index of behavior. It indicates how well or poorly the subject is performing. It permits the experimenter to score behavior. The experimenter must decide which aspects of behavior are relevant to the experiment at hand. Although some variables are traditional, this does not mean that they are the only, or even the best, indexes of behavior. Take, for example, the behavior of a rat pressing a bar or a pigeon pecking a key. The most common dependent variable is the number of presses or pecks observed. But the force with which a key is pecked can also lead to interesting findings (see Notterman and Mintz, 1965), as can the latency (time taken to respond). Researchers can usually come up with several dependent variables that may be appropriate. Let us say we wish to study the legibility of the typeface that you are now reading. We cannot observe "legibility," of course. What dependent variables might we observe? Here are some that have been used in the past: retention of meaningful information after reading text, time needed to read a fixed number of words, number of errors in recognizing single letters, speed in transcribing or retyping text, heart rate during reading, and muscular tension during reading. And this list is far from exhaustive.

Reasons of economy argue for obtaining as many dependent measures at the same time as is feasible. Despite this, the typical experiment uses only one, or at the most, two dependent variables simultaneously. This is unfortunate: just as the generality of an experiment is expanded by having more than one independent variable, it is also expanded with several dependent variables. The reason that more dependent variables are not used is probably that it is statistically difficult to analyze several dependent variables at once. Although modern computer techniques make the calculations quite feasible, many experimental psychologists have not been well trained in these multivariate statistical procedures, and thus hesitate to use them. Separate analysis could be conducted for each dependent variable by itself, but this loses information in much the same way that separate analysis of independent variables ignores interactions. Multivariate analysis is complex; nevertheless, you should be aware that it is often advantageous to use more than one dependent variable in an experiment.

Experimental Design

The purpose of experimental design is to minimize extraneous or uncontrolled variation, thereby increasing the likelihood that an experiment will produce sound, stable results. Entire books have been written about experimental design. Here we will cover a sample of some common techniques used to improve the design of experiments.

Within- and Between-Subjects Designs

One of the first design decisions an experimenter must make is how to assign subjects to the various levels of independent variables. The two main possibilities are to assign only some subjects to each level, or to assign each subject to every level. The first possibility is called a *between-subjects design* and the second a *within-subjects design*. The difference can be shown with a simple example. Thirty students in introductory psychology have signed up for an experiment that you are conducting to test ability to remember nonsense words. Your independent variable is the number of times you will say each item: one time or five times. You expect that an item presented five times will be learned better than an item presented only once. The between-subjects design calls for you to divide your subjects in half—that is, into two groups of fifteen students each—with one group receiving five repetitions, and the other, one repetition. (How to select which subjects to put in each group will be discussed shortly.) The within-subjects design has all thirty subjects learning with both levels of the independent variable—that is, each is tested with one repetition and again with five repetitions. (How to determine the order in which each subject gets these two treatments will also be discussed later.) Which design should you use?

The between-subjects (two groups) design is conservative. There is no chance that one treatment will contaminate the other, because the same person never receives both treatments. Nevertheless, most experimental psychologists would prefer the within-subjects (one group) design. It is more efficient, since each subject is compared with herself or himself. Any differences resulting from one versus five repetitions cannot be the result of differences between the people in the two groups, as might be the case for the between-subjects design. The between-subjects design must deal with differences among people; and this decreases its efficiency—that is, its ability to detect real differences between one and five repetitions of the memory items.

There is a risk, however, in the more efficient within-subjects design. Imagine that all thirty subjects first learn items with five repetitions and then learn with one repetition. As a result of their earlier experience with five repetitions, they might decide to repeat to themselves four more times the item that was only presented once. This would destroy any differences between the two levels of the independent variable. The danger is that an early part of the experiment might change behavior in a later part of the experiment. This, of course, ruins the experiment. We can minimize this danger by *counterbalancing* (discussed shortly), but cannot eliminate it entirely. If an experimenter suspects that the effects of one treatment may linger on to alter a later treatment, the between-subjects design should be used. Because it is less efficient, it will require that a much greater number of subjects be tested, but this is preferable to a within-subjects design in which effects have been carried over or transferred from one part of the experiment to another.

Randomization and matching. In any between-subjects design, the experimenter must try to minimize differences among the subjects in the two or more treatment groups. Clearly, if we took the five best memorizers and deliberately placed them in the one-repetition group, and put the five worst in the five-repetition group, we might wind up with no difference in results—even, perhaps, with the one-repetition group doing better. To prevent this outcome, the experimenter must ensure that both groups are equivalent at the start of the experiment. One way to do this would be to administer a memory test to all thirty subjects before the regular experiment started. Then, pairs of subjects could be formed from those subjects who had equal or very similar scores. One member of each pair would be randomly assigned to one group, and the other member to the second group. This technique is called *matching.* One difficulty with matching is that an experimenter cannot match for everything. Thus, there is always the possibility that the groups, even though matched on some characteristic(s), differ on some other characteristic that may be relevant (matching is treated further later in this chapter).

A more common technique to ensure that equivalent groups are formed is *randomization.* Randomization means that each person participating in an experiment has an equal chance to be assigned to any particular group. In our repetition experiment, one way to form two groups by randomization would be to draw names out of a hat. Or, we could ask each person to step forward, and then throw a die. Even throws would be assigned to one group and odd throws to the other. If we did not have any dice, a table of random numbers could be used to generate even and odd digits. This method of assigning subjects to experimental conditions has no bias, since it ignores all characteristics of the subjects; we expect that groups so created would be equivalent on any and all relevant dimensions. However, randomization does not guarantee that the groups will always be equal. By chance, a greater number of better memorizers might be assigned to one of the groups. The odds of this rare occurrence can be calculated by the methods of probability theory as applied to statistics. This is one reason that experimental design and statistics are often treated as the same topic. However, design is concerned with the logic of arranging experiments, whereas statistics deals with calculating odds, probabilities, and other mathematical quantities.

If we are sure that all relevant dimensions have been dealt with, matching is preferable to randomization. Since we seldom are sure, randomization is used more often.

Counterbalancing. Although the within-subjects (one-group) design avoids problems of forming equivalent groups (since there is only one group), it has the analogous difficulty of determining the order in which treatments should be given to subjects. Again, one solution is to use randomization by drawing the treatment titles out of a hat, using a random-number table, or using a computer. The logic behind this is discussed above. However, although randomization of treatments produces equivalent orders in the long run, it is less likely to be suitable when there are only a small number of treatments. In most experiments, the number of subjects exceeds the number of treatments, so randomization is a good technique for assigning subjects to treatments.

Complete counterbalancing makes sure that all possible treatment orders are used. In the repetition experiment, this is easy, since there are only two orders: one and five repetitions, five and one repetition. Half the subjects would receive one repetition followed by five repetitions, and the other half would get the opposite order. As the number of treatments increases, the number of orders becomes large indeed. Three treatments have six different orders; four treatments have twenty-four different orders; five treatments have 120 different orders; and so on. As the levels of an independent variable increase, complete counterbalancing soon becomes impractical.

Counterbalancing does not eliminate the effects of order. It does allow experimenters to evaluate possible order effects. If such effects are present, and especially if they form interactions with other more important independent variables, steps need to be taken to correct the design. The experimenter might decide to repeat the experiment, using a between-subjects design to avoid order effects. Alternatively, the original experiment could be reanalyzed as a between-subjects one, by examining behavior in just the initial condition experienced by each subject.

Mixed designs. Experiments need not be exclusively of within-subjects or between-subjects design. It is often convenient and prudent to have some independent variables treated as between-subjects and others as within-subjects in the same experiment (assuming the experiment has more than one independent variable, of course). If one variable—for example, the administration of a drug—seems likely to affect others, it can be made a between-subjects variable, while the rest of the variables are within-subjects. When trials or repeated practice on a task are of interest, it is of necessity a within-subjects variable. Frequently a mixed design is used, in which some variable is imposed between subjects to see its effect across practice trials (within subjects). This compromise design (*mixed design*) is not as efficient as a pure within-subjects design, but it often is safer.

Control Conditions

Independent variables must be varied (or manipulated) by the experimenter. This implies that each and every independent variable must have at least two settings or values within the experiment. For example, if intensity of an electric shock given to a rat is an independent variable, the settings chosen by the experimenter might be 1 and 4 milliamperes of electric current. The technical term for the setting of an independent variable is *level*. We would state that the levels of the independent variable are 1 and 4 milliamperes.

Most experiments contain, in addition to independent variables, some *control group* (between-subjects design) or *control condition* (within-subjects design). In its simplest form, the control group does not receive the levels of interest of the independent variable. In the electric-shock example just described, a control group of rats would receive no shock. Or an experimenter might be interested in the effect of noise on studying. Using a between-subjects design, the experimenter would expose one group of subjects to loud noise for half an hour while they were studying; this is the level of interest of the independent variable. A control group would study the same material for half an hour in a quiet setting (a very low level of noise). Then both groups would be tested on the material. Any obtained difference on the test between the two groups would be attributed to the effect of noise.

The control group sometimes does receive treatment. In the helping experiment discussed previously (figure 3–2), the observer was either dressed as a medical intern or dressed normally. The normal dress could be considered a control condition. It allows us to determine how much less help is given when an intern is present. The important characteristic of a control condition is that it provides a *baseline* against which some variable of interest can be compared.

Sometimes the best baseline is no treatment, but often the best baseline requires some activity. A frequent example occurs in memory research, where a group of subjects is required to learn two different lists of words; the experimenter is interested in how learning one list interferes with learning the other. The experimental group (receiving the level of interest of the independent variable) first learns list A, then learns list B, and then is tested again on list A. The experimenter would like to show that learning list B interferes with learning list A. But before any conclusion of this sort can be reached, a comparison control condition is required. Merely comparing the final test of list A with the first test is insufficient: since subjects might do worse on the last list-A test simply because they are tired, or do better because they have had extra practice. A control condition with no treatment would have a control group learn list A, then sit around for the time it took the experimental group to learn list B, and then be tested again on list A. But this would be a poor control condition, because subjects might practice or rehearse list A while they were sitting around. This would improve their final performance on the last list-A test and incorrectly make it appear that in the experimental group, list B interfered more than it really did with list A. A proper baseline condition would occupy the control group during the time the experimental group was learning list B; perhaps the experimenter would have them do arithmetic or some other "busy work" that would prevent rehearsal (see figure 3–5).

Sometimes the control condition is contained implicitly within the experiment. Recall the memory experiment discussed earlier, in which the independent variable was the number of repetitions of an item: one or five. No experimenter would bother to include a control group or condition with zero repetitions, since no learning could occur under this odd circumstance. The control condition is implicit, in that five repetitions can be compared with one, and vice versa. Since the experimenter might well be as interested in effects of a single repetition as in five repetitions, we probably would not explicitly call the one-repetition level a control condition. But it does provide a baseline for comparison—and so, for that matter, does the five-repetition condition, since the one-repetition results can be compared with it.

Many types of experiments require more than one baseline. In physiological and drug research, for example, a control for surgical or injection trauma is needed. So, a subject might receive a sham operation or the injection of an inert substance (a placebo) in the control condition; those would also be compared with other controls that received no operation or no injection.

Pitfalls

It is quite easy to formulate an inadequate experimental design; most experimental psychologists have hidden away, either in a dusty file cabinet or in a journal article, mistakes of this kind. In this section we discuss only a small sample of errors in design, ones that are so common you should be aware of them. You should not let this discussion of error fool you into believing that any experiment that is free from error is guaranteed to produce results that merit publication.

Demand characteristics. Laboratory experiments attempt to capture behavior as it really is influenced by the independent variable. Sometimes the laboratory setting itself, or the knowledge that an experiment is under way, may alter patterns of behavior. Try this simple demonstration to convince yourself that such effects occur. Tell five of your friends that you are conducting an experiment for your psychology class and would like their cooperation as subjects.

FIGURE 3–5.   Examples of experimental and control groups for list learning.

Experimental Group	Learn List A	Learn List B	Test List A
Control Group	Learn List A	Do Arithmetic	Test List A

If they agree, ask them to hold three ice cubes in their bare hands. Note how many hold the cubes until they melt. Now ask five other friends to hold the ice cubes, without mentioning anything about an experiment. Instead of holding the ice cubes until they melt, they probably will consider your request somewhat strange, and soon so inform you. There is something unusual about the ready compliance of those friends who knew they were participating in an experiment: more of them were willing to hold the ice cubes for a longer period of time. Psychologists call the cues available to subjects that may enable them to determine the purpose of the experiment, or what is expected by the experimenter, *demand characteristics*. To the extent that the behavior of research participants is controlled by demand characteristics instead of by independent variables, experiments are invalid and cannot be generalized beyond the test situation.

A well-known example of a demand characteristic is the *Hawthorne effect*, named after the Western Electric Company plant where it was first observed. The company was interested in improving worker morale and productivity and conducted several experiments (such as improving lighting) to better the workers' environment. No matter what experimental manipulation was tried, worker productivity improved. The workers knew they were in a "special" group, and therefore tried to do their best at all times. (See Parsons, 1974, and Bramel and Friend, 1981, for alternate interpretations of these results.) The demand characteristics were more important in determining the workers' productivity than were the experimental manipulations.

Experimenter effects. A pitfall closely related to demand characteristics is the *experimenter effect*, which influences the outcome accidentally by providing participants with slight clues as to his or her expectations. For example, an experimenter might not be aware that he or she nods approvingly when a correct response is given and frowns after errors.

These effects are not limited to experiments with humans. The experimenter effect can also occur in seemingly objective experiments with animal subjects. Rosenthal and Fode (1963) told student experimenters that the rats they were to test in a maze were from special strains: either maze-bright or maze-dull. Actually, the rats came from the same population. Nevertheless, the rats that were labeled maze-bright had fewer errors than those labeled maze-dull, and this difference was statistically reliable. The student experimenters were observed while they tested the rats: they did not cheat or do anything overt to bias the results. It seems reasonable that the lucky students who got supposedly bright rats were more motivated to perform the experiment than those unfortunates who had to teach stupid rats to go through the maze. Somehow, this affected the results of the experiment—perhaps because experimenters handled the two groups of rats differently.

The best way to eliminate this kind of experimenter effect is to hide the experimental condition from the experimenter on the premise that experimenters cannot communicate what they do not know. Such a procedure was, for instance, used in a study of the behavioral effects of air pollution. Subjects breathed either pure air or air taken from a busy roadway. The air was contained in tanks; the experimenter did not know which tank held pure air and which tank held polluted air. The subjects' poorer performance in polluted air cannot, then, be attributed to the experimenter's giving away the independent variable.

Experimenter effects are not always this subtle. One of the authors was once involved in an experiment concerning the human eye-blink response. Several experimenters helped conduct the same experiment, and it was soon noticed that one of them obtained results that were quite different from those of the rest of us. His subjects started out experimental sessions with massive flurries of frenzied blinking. The cause of this odd behavior was easily discovered. To record eye blinks, the experimenter must attach a tiny metal rod to the subject's eyelid with special tape—ordinarily a painless procedure. However, the experimenter in question had a very heavy thumb and was unable to attach the rod without irritating the eye, causing the strange flurries of blinking.

Automation of experiments. Experimenter effects can be eliminated or greatly reduced by having computers or other equipment conduct the experiment, so that the subject is untouched by human hands. In many laboratories, a subject enters a testing booth and sees a message on a screen that tells her or him to push a button to begin. Pushing the button causes instructions for the experiment to appear on the screen. The entire experiment is then conducted by a computer. The experimenter appears at the end of the data collection to debrief the participant, giving the aims of the study and explaining how the subject has helped advance science. Until then, the experimenter simply monitors the equipment and the subject to ensure that the subject is following instructions and that nothing untoward happens. Since you probably will not have such sophisticated experimental equipment, it is especially important for you to watch out for experimenter effects in your own research efforts.

Quasi-Experiments

For one reason or another, there are many variables that cannot be manipulated directly. One deterrent to manipulation of variables in experiments is the ethical considerations all scientists must have (see chapter 4). It is ethical to survey or otherwise observe the use of drugs by college students as long as permission is obtained. By no stretch of the imagination, however, would it be ethical to create a group of drug abusers and compare their activities with a nonabusing group that we created. A second barrier to manipulation is mother nature. Some variables, such as the sex of our subjects, cannot be varied by the experimenter (except in very rare and controversial circumstances); there are other variables, such as natural disasters (such as tornadoes) or unnatural disasters (such as wars and airplane crashes) that are both physically and morally difficult to implement. Can we do experiments that concern these phenomena? After all, such variables and others like them are fascinating and may play an important part in human experience.

The answer to the question (assuming you are an ethical scientist) is this: you can and you cannot. We are not being silly here; rather, we are emphasizing the fact that you cannot do real experiments on phenomena such as the ones just listed. You can, however, conduct *quasi-experiments*. The technique here is similar to the ex post facto examination in correlational research, except that two or more levels of the variable of interest are examined rather than correlated. We wait for mother nature to do her work, and then we compare the effects of that "independent variable" with the effects that occur when that variable is not present or differs in some way. If we compare the reading ability of men with that of women or that of speed readers with that of average adults, we have conducted a quasi-experiment.

The advantages of quasi-experiments are obvious: they use naturally occurring independent variables, most of which have a high degree of intrinsic interest and important practical implications. In a quasi-experiment, we take advantage of observational and correlational procedures and combine them with the power of experimentation. The typical quasi-experiment has a *subject variable* as an independent variable. If we want to find out about almost any inherent subject variable (age, sex, race, ethnic group), socially caused subject attribute (social class, region of residence), disease- and illness-related subject attribute (limb loss, mental illness, dietary phenomena, effects of disasters), we are going to have to select rather than vary our independent variables, unless it is possible to do the experiment directly on infrahuman organisms. Although quasi-experiments are interesting and can contribute very important research, we should caution you here that the advantages of quasi-experiments are gained at the expense of control. When the researcher has to take what is given, what is given may include several important confounding variables.

Because much research in psychology is concerned with subject variables, and because quasi-experiments using subject variables are likely to be confounded, we will examine the problems and possible solutions.

An experimenter cannot manipulate a subject variable while holding other factors constant; she or he can only select subjects who already have the characteristic in some varying degree, and then compare them on the behavior of interest. If the subjects in the different groups (say, high, medium, and low I.Q.) differ on the behavior, we cannot conclude that the subject-variable difference has produced, or is responsible for, the difference in behavior. The reason is that other factors may covary with the subject variable and be confounded with it. If high-I.Q. subjects perform some task better than low-I.Q. subjects, we cannot say that I.Q. produced or caused the difference, because the different groups of subjects are likely to vary on other relevant dimensions such as motivation, education, and the like. When subject variables are investigated, we cannot safely attribute differences in behavior to this variable, as we can with true experimental variables. Such designs, then, essentially produce correlations between variables. We can say that the variables are related, but we cannot say that one variable produces or causes the effect in the other variable.

This is a very important point; let us consider an example. Suppose an investigator is interested in the intellectual functioning (or lack thereof) of people suffering from schizophrenia. People diagnosed as belonging to this group are given numerous tests that are meant to measure various mental abilities. The researcher also gives these tests to another group of people, so-called normals. He or she discovers that schizophrenics do especially poorly relative to normals in tests involving semantic aspects of language, such as those that involve understanding the meanings of words or comprehending prose passages. The investigator concludes that the schizophrenics perform these tests more poorly *because* they are schizophrenics and that their inability to use language well in communication is a likely contributing cause of schizophrenia.

Studies such as this are common in some areas of psychology. Despite the fact that conclusions similar to this are often drawn from such studies, they are completely unwarranted. Both conclusions are based on correlations, and other factors could well be the critical ones. Schizophrenics may do more poorly than normals for any number of reasons. They may not be as intelligent, as motivated, as educated, or as wise at taking tests. It may simply be that they have been institutionalized for a long time, with a resulting poverty of social and intellectual intercourse. So we cannot conclude that the reason that the two groups differ on verbal tests is schizophrenia or its absence in the two groups. Even if we could conclude this, it would certainly not imply the other conclusion, that language problems are involved in causing schizophrenia. Again, all we would have is a correlation between these two variables, with no idea of whether or how the two are causally related.

Use of subject variables is very common in all psychological research, but it is absolutely crucial in such areas as clinical and developmental psychology. Therefore, the problems with making inferences from such research should be carefully considered. A primary variable in developmental psychology is age, a subject variable; this means that much research in this field is correlational in nature. In general, the problem of individual differences among subjects in psychology is one that is often ignored, though there are often appeals to consider this problem as crucial (see Underwood, 1975). We devote a chapter later in the book to individual differences (chapter 12). Let us consider here one way of attempting more sound inferences from experiments employing subject variables.

Matching again. The basic problem in the investigation of subject variables, and in other ex post facto research, is that whatever differences are observed in behavior may be caused by their confounded variables. One way to try to avoid this problem is by *matching* subjects on the other relevant variables. In the comparison of schizophrenics and normals, we noted that the two groups were also likely to differ on other characteristics, such as I.Q., education, motivation, institutionalization, and perhaps even age. Rather than simply comparing the schizophrenics with normals, we might try to compare them with another group more closely matched on these other dimensions, so that, we hope, the main difference between the groups would be the presence or absence of schizophrenia. For example, we might use a group of patients who, on the average, are similar to the schizophrenics in terms of age, I.Q., length of time institutionalized, sex, and some measure of motivation. When the two groups have been matched on all these characteristics, then we can more confidently attribute any difference in performance between them to the factor of interest, namely, schizophrenia. By matching, investigators attempt to introduce the crucial characteristic of experimentation—being able to hold constant extraneous factors to avoid confoundings—into what is essentially a correlational observation. The desire is to allow one to infer that the variable of interest (schizophrenia) produces the observed effect.

There are several rather severe problems associated with matching. For one thing, it often requires a great deal of effort, because some of the relevant variables may be quite difficult to measure. Even when one goes to the trouble of taking the needed additional measures, it may still be impossible to match the groups, especially if few subjects are involved before matching is attempted. Even when matching is successful, it often greatly reduces the size of the sample on which the observations are made. We then have less confidence in our observations, because they may not be stable and repeatable.

Matching is often difficult, because crucial differences among subjects may have subtle effects. In addition, the effects of one difference may interact with another. Thus, *subtle interactions* among matched variables may confound the results. To illustrate these difficulties, let us reconsider some of the work done by Brazelton and associates on neonatal behavior, mentioned in the previous chapter (Lester and Brazelton, 1982).

Brazelton's primary interest is in cultural differences in neonatal behavior, as measured by the Brazelton Neonatal Behavioral Assessment Scale. The general strategy is to compare neonates from various cultures and ethnic groups with neonates from the United States. In these quasi-experiments, culture or ethnic group, which is a subject variable, is the quasi-independent variable. Attempts are usually made to match the neonates from different cultures along various dimensions, such as birth weight, birth length, and obstetrical risk (including whether the mother received medication during birth, whether the baby was premature, and so on). Lester and Brazelton show that there is a synergistic relationship among these factors. *Synergism* in a medical context means that the combined effects of two or more variables are not additive: the combined effect is greater than the sum of the individual components. This means that the variables interact.

The way in which neonatal characteristics and obstetrical risk interact is as follows. Studies have shown that the behavior (as measured by the Brazelton scale) of slightly underweight infants is more strongly influenced (negatively) by small amounts of medication taken by the mother than is the behavior of neonates who are closer to the average in weight. Even though the neonates are carefully selected, subtle and interactive effects of the matched variables can influence the results. This is an especially difficult problem in Brazelton's work, because much of his research has examined neonates from impoverished cultures, where birth weight is low and obstetrical risk is very high. Generally, you should remember that matched variables are rarely under direct control, which means that the possibility of confounding is always present.

Another problem with matching involves the introduction of the dreaded *regression artifact*. This is discussed in chapter 12, but we will explain it briefly here. Under certain conditions, in many types of measurements a statistical phenomenon occurs known as *regression to the mean*. The mean of a group of scores is what most people think of as the average: the total of all observations divided by the number of observations. For example, mean height in a sample of sixty people is the sum of all their heights divided by sixty. Typically, if people who received extreme scores (that is, very high or very low) on some characteristic are retested, their second scores will be closer to the mean of the entire group than were their original scores. Consider an example. We give two hundred people a standard test of mathematical reasoning for which there are two equivalent forms, or two versions of the test that we know to be equivalent. The average (mean) score on the test is 60 of 100 possible points. We take the fifteen people who score highest and the fifteen who score lowest. The mean of these groups is, say, 95 and 30, respectively. Then we test them again on the other version of the test. Now we might find that the means of the two groups are 87 and 35. On the second test, the scores of these two extreme groups regress toward the mean; the high-scoring group scores more poorly, and the low-scoring group does somewhat better. Basically, this happens for the high-scoring group because some people whose "true scores" are somewhat lower than actually tested lucked out and scored higher than they should have on the test.

When retested, people with extremely high scores tend to score lower, nearer their true score. The situation is reversed for the low-scoring group. That is, some of them scored below their "true scores" on the first test; retesting leads to their scoring higher or nearer the true score.

This regression toward the mean is always observed under conditions when there is a less-than-perfect correlation between the two measures. The more extreme the selection of scores, the greater the regression toward the mean. It also occurs in all types of measurement situations. If abnormally tall or short parents have a child, it will likely be closer to the population mean than the height of the parents. As with most statistical phenomena, regression to the mean is true of groups of observations and is probabilistic (that is, it may not occur every time). For example, a few individual subjects may move away from the mean in the second test of mathematical reasoning, but the group tendency will be toward the mean.

How does regression toward the mean affect quasi-experiments, in which subjects have been matched on some variable? Again, consider an example. This one, like much ex post facto research done on applied societal problems, has important implications. Let us assume that we have an educational program that we believe will be especially advantageous for increasing the reading scores of black children. This is especially important because black children's scores are typically lower than those of whites, presumably because of different cultural environments. We take two groups of children, one black and one white, and match them on several criteria, including age, sex, and most important, initial reading performance. We give both groups of children the reading improvement program and then test their reading scores after the program. We find, much to our surprise, that the black children actually perform *worse* after the reading program than before it, and the white children improve. We conclude, of course, that the program helped white children but actually hurt black children, despite the fact that it was especially designed for the latter.

This conclusion, even though it may seem reasonable to you, is almost surely erroneous in this case, because of regression artifacts. Consider what happened when the black and white children were matched on initial reading scores. Since the populations differed initially, with blacks scoring lower than whites, in order to match two samples it was necessary to select the black students having higher scores than the mean for their group and the white students having lower scores than their group mean. Having picked these extreme groups, we could predict (because of regression to the mean) that when retested, the black children would have poorer scores and the white children would have better ones, on the average, even if the reading improvement program had no effect at all! The exceptionally-high-scoring black children would tend to regress toward the mean of their group, and the low-scoring whites would regress toward the mean for their group. The same thing would have happened even if there had been no program and the children had been simply retested.

The same outcome would likely have been obtained if children had been matched on I.Q.s instead of reading scores, since the two are probably positively correlated. So simply finding another matching variable may not be a solution. One solution would be to match very large samples of black and white children and then split each group, giving the reading program to one subgroup but not the other. All would be retested at the end of the one subgroup's participation in the program. (Assignment of subjects to the subgroups of black and white children should, of course, be random.) Regression to the mean would be expected in both subgroups, but the effect of the reading program could be evaluated against the group that had no program. Perhaps black children with the reading program would show much less drop (regression to the mean) than those without, indicating that the program really did have a positive effect.

Because quasi-experimental research with subject variables is conducted quite often to evaluate educational programs, its practitioners need to be aware of the many thorny problems associated with its use. One may not be able to say much with regard to the results, or draw important conclusions, because of confoundings. Matching helps alleviate this problem in some cases where its use is possible, but then one introduces the possibility of regression artifacts. And many researchers seem unaware of this problem. One famous blooper in such evaluational research, very similar to the hypothetical study outlined here, is discussed in chapter 12.

When matching is a practical possibility, and when regression artifacts are evaluated, we can feel somewhat more confident of conclusions from our results. But we should remember that what we have is still only a correlation, albeit a very carefully controlled one. Matching is sometimes useful, but it is not a cure-all. In our earlier example comparing schizophrenics with others on mental test performance, if the schizophrenics still performed worse than the new matched control group, could we then conclude that schizophrenia *produced* inferiority in language usage? No, we could not. It could still be something else, some other difference between the two groups. We can never be absolutely sure we have matched on the relevant variables.

From Problem to Experiment: The Nuts and Bolts

Problem: Conducting an Experiment

Many of the decisions that go into creating an experiment are not clearly explained in journal reports of research. Although some of this brevity can be attributed to the economy imposed by journal editors who like short articles, a larger part is based on the assumption that experimental psychologists, or indeed psychologists researching any specialty, share a common background knowledge. This is true in all branches of science. For example, a physicist writing in a journal assumes that the readers already know that a dyne is a unit of force and will not bother to explain that term. Similarly, psychologists usually assume the reader knows what the terms *stimulus* and *response* mean, although these may be defined anyway. One purpose of this text is to give you some of the vocabulary necessary if you wish to read (or write) about psychological research.

Another problem for the new researcher is related to the "lore of the laboratory." "Everybody" knows there are certain "obvious" ways to perform certain kinds of research. These ways differ from area to area, but are well known within each category. They are so well known that researchers seldom bother to explain them and indeed are quite surprised when new researchers are ignorant of these "obvious" tricks and techniques. Animal researchers often deprive animals of food for many hours before the experiment, or keep their pigeons at a certain percentage of the weight the pigeons would attain if they had food continuously available. Although the reasons for this are obvious to the researcher, they may not be obvious to you. How does an experimenter know how many items to use in a memory experiment? How long should an experiment take? Why is one dependent variable selected from a set of what appear to be equally valid dependent variables? How many subjects should be used in an experiment? This section in the chapters of Part Two will answer such "obvious" questions as these.

From Problem to Experiment

All research aims at solving a problem. This problem can be abstract and theoretical, or concrete and applied. The problem may arise from an observation made more or less casually, such as that people seem to be more aggressive during the summer. Here the problem can be stated as "Why does summer heat cause aggression?" or even more skeptically as "Does high temperature cause aggression?" A problem may arise from an accidental discovery in a laboratory, such as the finding of mold on a piece of bread. Solving this problem—why is the mold growing here?—led to the discovery of penicillin. Finally, a problem may arise directly from a theoretical model, as when we ask, "Why does reinforcement increase the probability of the occurrence of the behavior that preceded it?"

The first step the experimenter must take is to translate the problem into a testable hypothesis. Then the hypothesis must be transformed into an experiment with independent, dependent, and control variables.

From problem to hypothesis. A problem is, more or less, a vague statement that must be verified or a question that must be answered. Unless either is made specific and precise, it cannot be experimentally tested. Any hypothesis is a particular prediction, derived from a problem, often stated in this form: if A, then B. The crucial distinction between a problem and a hypothesis is that a hypothesis is directly testable, whereas a problem is not. An experimental test must be capable of disproving an hypothesis.

Data

The purpose of any experiment is to obtain data. Once obtained, these data must be analyzed. Once analyzed, data must be reported. We briefly discuss these aspects in turn.

Obtaining Data

Fixing an experimental design does not establish all the conditions needed for data acquisition. Although the design tells you how to assign subjects to experiments, it does not tell you how to get the subjects. Without subjects, there are no data.

Psychologists who investigate animal behavior have much more control over subject selection than those who study humans. Although animal psychologists must bear the additional expense of obtaining, housing, and feeding their subjects, they can select the strain they wish to purchase and always have subjects available, barring some catastrophe.

Research with humans most often uses as subjects college students enrolled in introductory psychology. Provided that this participation is used as a learning experience for the student, it is considered ethical and proper (APA, 1973). If the experiment is not used as a learning experience, the experimenter should pay subjects. Since college students are a select population, experimenters need to be careful about generalizing results to other subject populations. For example, techniques from a programmed learning system designed to teach inorganic chemistry might not prove successful in the teaching of plumbing.

The technique of selecting subjects from some population is called *sampling*. Sampling is necessary because it is usually impossible to test the entire population, say, all college sophomores in the United States. *Random sampling* means that any member of a population has an equal chance of being selected as a subject. Furthermore, each selection is independent of other selections, so that choosing one person does not affect the chances of selecting anyone else. Since the typical researcher does not have access to all college students, what this means in actual practice is that the experimenter tries to randomly select from the population that is available to him or her. Statistical implications of sampling are discussed in appendix B.

After your sample has been selected and your design is fixed, one major decision remains. Should you test your subjects one at a time or in a group? Both procedures have advantages and disadvantages. The biggest advantage of group testing is economy. It takes only one hour to test thirty subjects for an hour as a group, whereas it takes thirty hours to test them singly. So, all other things being equal, it is faster, and therefore better, to test subjects in groups. But there are many instances where all other things are far from equal. For example, take a listening experiment in which separate words are presented to left and right ears. One hurried doctoral student decided to save time and test her subjects in a group. She forgot that, unless subjects were positioned exactly between the two loudspeakers, one message would reach one ear before the other message reached the other ear. This invalidated the independent variable. Of course, it would have been fine to test subjects in a group if each subject wore earphones, thus avoiding this difficulty. The other problem in group testing is the possibility that subjects will influence one another, thus influencing the data. Perhaps a subject may cheat and copy answers from another, or the sexual composition of the group may alter motivation. Sometimes these problems can be prevented by placing subjects in individual booths that prohibit social interaction.

Analyzing Data

The immediate result of an experiment is a large series of numbers that represent behavior under different conditions. As Sidman (1960) humorously describes it, scientists believe that all data are tainted at birth. Data belong to Chance or to Science—but never to both. Before the psychologist can be sure that data belong to Science, the demon Chance must be exorcised. This is done by a ritual called inferential statistical analysis.

Once statistical analysis tells you which data are reliable, you still have to decide which data are important. No mathematical calculation can guess what hypotheses are being tested, what is predicted by the theories, and so on. Statistics are never a substitute for thought. Statistical analysis is a theoretically neutral procedure that serves theory and hypothesis testing. Except in the case of a what-if experiment, the theories and hypotheses precede the statistics.

Since it is virtually impossible to grasp the meaning of the large set of numbers an experiment produces, data are usually condensed by descriptive statistics. The most common are the mean and the standard deviation. As part of the data analysis, means are calculated for each level of each independent variable, as well as for combinations of independent variables to show interactions.

Reporting Data

Data are presented in tables or figures. Usually, figures are easier to understand. Figure 3–3 is a typical example of how results of an experiment are reported. The dependent variable is plotted on the *ordinate*—the vertical scale. The independent variable is graphed on the *abscissa*—the horizontal scale. More than one independent variable can be shown in the same graph by using solid and dotted lines and/or differently shaped symbols for each independent variable.

Raw (unanalyzed) data are hardly ever reported. Instead, some descriptive statistic, like the mean, is used to summarize data. Other statistics often accompany data to tell the reader about the reliability of these data.

Many different styles and formats can be used to report data. We recommend the format given in the *Publication Manual* of the American Psychological Association. This book will tell you more than you would like to know about every aspect of preparing the report of an experiment. If it is not in the library or bookstore, you can purchase it by sending to Order Department, American Psychological Association, P.O. Box 2710, Hyattsville, MD 20784.

SUMMARY

1. An experiment is a controlled procedure for investigating the effects of one or more independent variables on one or more dependent variables. The *independent variable* is manipulated by the experimenter, whereas the *dependent variable* is observed and recorded. Experiments offer the investigator the best chance of eliminating or minimizing extraneous variation. Experiments are performed to test theories, to show that a published experiment is in some way deficient, and to replicate and expand previous findings. Only rarely are experiments performed just to see what might happen.

2. Independent variables are chosen because an experimenter thinks they will control behavior. If they do not, this may mean that the manipulation was inadequate or that the experimenter was wrong. Dependent variables must be *stable*—that is, they must consistently produce the same results under the same conditions. *Ceiling* and *floor effects* result from inadequate range of the dependent variable. *Control variables* are potential independent variables that are not manipulated during an experiment.

3. Most experiments test more than one independent variable at a time. In addition to providing economy, this allows the experimenter to gain important information about interactions. *Interactions* occur when the effects of one independent variable are not the same for different levels of another independent variable. Occasionally, experiments use more than one dependent variable.

4. Experimental design assigns subjects to different conditions in ways that are expected to minimize extraneous variation. In a *between-subjects design*, different groups of subjects experience different treatments. In a *within-subjects design*, the same subjects go through all treatments. The between-subjects design is

safer, but the within-subjects design is more efficient. *Mixed designs* have some independent variables that are between-subjects and others that are within-subjects. In between-subjects designs, equivalent groups are formed by *matching* and by *randomization*. Order effects in within-subjects designs are evaluated, but not eliminated, by *counterbalancing*. Control conditions provide a clear baseline against which the condition(s) of interest can be compared.

5. There are many pitfalls in experimental design. *Demand characteristics* result from the subject's knowledge that he or she is participating in an experiment. *Experimenter effects* are artifacts introduced accidentally, when the experimenter provides clues to the subject or influences the subject unsystematically. The latter can be minimized by the use of machinery to conduct the experiment.

6. Selecting subjects from some population is called *sampling*. *Random sampling* means that each member of the population has an equal chance of being selected. It is more efficient to test subjects in groups, but care must be taken to avoid contaminating the experiment.

7. Quasi-experiments in psychology often employ subject variables. These variables are measures such as age, I.Q., mental health, height, hair color, and sex, as well as the myriad other characteristics that differ from one person to the next. Such variables are determined after the fact, since they are often inherited dispositions (or at least, people come to the psychological study with the variable already determined). Because it is not possible to randomly assign people to the conditions of interest, studies that use subject variables are inherently correlational in nature.

8. To attempt cause-and-effect statements from manipulation of subject variables, researchers often match subjects on other variables. Thus, if a researcher were interested in the effects of hair color on peformance in some task or on the reaction from others in some situation, he or she would attempt to control as many other variables as possible to ensure that hair color was the only aspect on which people in the various conditions differed. Matching is often a useful tool for these purposes, but one must be certain that the possibility of regression artifacts does not cloud the conclusions.

9. *Regression to the mean* refers to the fact that when a subgroup with extreme scores is taken from a larger group and retested, members will tend to score nearer the mean of the whole group on the second test. If, in matching two groups on the basis of a first test, the researcher is taking high scorers from a group that generally does poorly and low scorers from a group that generally does well, then even if the groups are not treated differ-

ently in an experiment, the researcher can expect them to score differently on a second test—simply because of regression to the mean. This problem is referred to as a *regression artifact*.

KEY TERMS

abscissa
baseline
between-subjects design
ceiling effect
control conditions
control group
control variable
counterbalancing
critical experiment
data
demand characteristics
dependent variable
experiment
experimenter effects
floor effect
Hawthorne effect
independent variable

interaction
level
matching
mixed designs
null results
ordinate
quasi-experiments
randomization
random sampling
regression artifact
regression to the mean
sampling
subject variables
synergism
what-if experiment
within-subjects design

DISCUSSION QUESTIONS

1. Design an experiment to discover why plumbers get paid more than college professors. Take a random sample of plumbers and professors. Have half of each group perform the job of the other occupation, while the other occupation either (a) observes quietly or (b) offers advice. Name the dependent, independent, and control variables you would select for this experiment. What are some of the design problems associated with such an experiment?

2. Transform each of the following problems or statements into at least two testable hypotheses:

   (a) You can't teach an old dog new tricks.

   (b) Eating junk food lowers your grade point average.

   (c) A penny saved is a penny earned.

   (d) The best way to study is cramming the night before an exam.

3. Create a fictitious experiment with two independent variables. Draw hypothetical results that illustrate interaction and lack of interaction. Label your graphs carefully.

4. Explain the quotation by Beveridge at the head of this chapter.

5. Suppose you wanted to determine whether people with long noses have a better sense of humor than people with shorter

noses. Nose length is, of course, a subject variable. You decide to give two groups of people with different-sized noses a series of twenty jokes (which experts have rated as excellent) to see if the people with long noses like them better than those with short noses. What steps would you take to ensure that some other variable was not confounded with nose length in your two groups of people? How would you go about selecting people for the study, assuming that you had two hundred people for whom you had measures of nose length and many other characteristics?

CHAPTER

4

Ethics in Psychological Research

The scientific enterprise creates ethical dilemmas. Scientific knowledge and techniques that can be used for human betterment can be turned to manipulative and exploitative purposes as well. Just as results of research in atomic physics can be used for the treatment of cancer as well as for destructive weapons, so methods discovered to reduce prejudice toward minority groups, to eliminate troublesome behavior problems, or to facilitate learning in school may also be used to manipulate political allegiance, to create artificial wants, or to reconcile the victims of social injustice to their fate. The double-edged potentiality of scientific knowledge poses ethical problems for all scientists.

—AMERICAN PSYCHOLOGICAL ASSOCIATION, 1982, P. 16

Research with Human Participants

THE QUOTATION INTRODUCING THIS CHAPTER is from a publication of the American Psychological Association. The quote comes from a preamble to a lengthy discussion of ethical principles covering all aspects of psychology and is presented in abbreviated form here to emphasize the ethical obligations of researchers in all areas of science. These obligations are straightforward in principle but difficult to implement. We will examine both the ethical principles and the problems associated with putting them into practice in psychology. Psychologists are concerned with the ethics of research involving both human participants and animals. Although some of this concern is selfish, owing to fear of restriction of research funds and loss of access to subject populations, most psychologists are ethical persons who have no desire to inflict harm on anyone. The mad researcher, who will do anything to obtain data, is largely fictional.

Since it is difficult for an experimenter to be completely impartial and objective in judging the ethical issues concerning his or her own research, most universities and research institutions have peer committees that judge the ethicality of proposed research. Indeed, any federally funded research must be approved by such a committee before any funding is granted.

Let us consider a specific experimental situation to illustrate the implementation of ethical principles. Imagine that you are a psychologist interested in determining to what extent depressive feelings influence how well people remember information. One of the major reasons you want to study this topic is that depression is a fairly common emotional problem among college students, and you would like to have some idea how this problem could affect academic performance. You decide to do a tightly controlled laboratory experiment to determine the effects of depression on memory. Your general strategy is to induce depression in some of your subjects and then compare their memory to that of other subjects who were not induced to be depressed. The manner in which you induce depression in your subjects follows a procedure devised by Velten (1968). To induce a mood by this procedure, the investigator has the subject read aloud sixty self-referent statements that are associated with the mood in question. In this case, the participant reads statements that are supposed to induce depression, beginning with relatively mild statements such as "Today is neither better nor worse than any other day," and progressing to "I feel so bad that I would like to go to sleep and never wake up." This procedure has been shown to induce a mild, temporary depression; participants report feeling depressed, and their behavior suffers on a variety of tasks.

Even though many details of this experiment have not been specified, it should be obvious that the welfare of the research participants in this study could be jeopardized (for complete details of this experiment, see Elmes, Chapman, and Selig, 1984). Inducing a negative mood (such as depression) in college students could have disastrous effects on their social and intellectual functioning. How can you as an ethical researcher try to preserve and protect the fundamental human rights of your participants? What would you do to protect their welfare and at the same time conduct an internally valid experiment?

In a recent review of research on mood and memory, Blaney (1986) listed a number of studies in which depression was induced in college students. In some experiments, a happy mood was induced in subjects. Do the ethical considerations depend on the kind of mood—happy or sad—that is induced in a subject? Also, researchers have used several different mood-induction procedures in their experiments. Besides the Velten (1968) procedure described above, hypnosis and music have been used to induce a depressed or happy mood. Do ethical considerations depend on the mood-induction technique? These questions concerning mood-induction research illustrate how ethical issues associated with psychological research may vary according to the specific circumstances in the experiment.

The American Psychological Association (1981a, 1987) has provided ethical guidelines for researchers. The association outlined ten general principles governing the conduct of research with human participants. To consider how the welfare of the students was protected in those studies, we will examine the principles that guide research involving human participants. *You should read and understand these ethical principles before you conduct a research project with human participants.*

The decision to undertake research rests on a considered judgment by the individual psychologist about how best to contribute to psychological science and human welfare. Having made the decision to conduct research, the psychologist considers alternative directions in which research energies and resources might be invested. On the basis of this consideration, the psychologist carries out the investigation with respect and concern for the dignity and welfare of the people who participate and with cognizance of federal and state regulations and professional standards governing the conduct of research with human participants.

1. In planning a study, the investigator has the responsibility to make a careful evaluation of its ethical acceptability. To the extent that the weighing of scientific and human values suggests a compromise of any principle, the investigator incurs a correspondingly serious obligation to seek ethical advice and to observe stringent safeguards to protect the rights of human participants.

2. Considering whether a participant in a planned study will be a "subject at risk" or a "subject at minimal risk," according to recognized standards, is of primary ethical concern to the investigator.

3. The investigator always retains the responsibility for insuring ethical practice in research. The investigator is also responsible for the ethical treatment of research participants by collaborators, assistants, students, and employees, all of whom, however, incur similar obligations.

4. Except in minimal-risk research, the investigator establishes a clear and fair agreement with research participants, prior to their participation, that clarifies the obligations and responsibilities of each. The investigator has the obligation to honor all promises and commitments included in that agreement. The investigator informs the participants of all aspects of the research that might reasonably be expected to influence willingness to participate and explains all other aspects of the research about which the participants inquire. Failure to make full disclosure prior to obtaining informed consent requires additional safeguards to protect the welfare and dignity of the research participants. Research with children or with participants who have impairments that would limit understanding and/or communication requires special safeguarding procedures.

5. Methodological requirements of a study may make the use of concealment or deception necessary. Before conducting such a study, the investigator has a special responsibility to (i) determine whether the use of such techniques is justified by the

study's prospective scientific, educational, or applied value; (ii) determine whether alternative procedures are available that do not use concealment or deception; and (iii) ensure that the participants are provided with sufficient explanation as soon as possible.

6. The investigator respects the individual's freedom to decline to participate in or to withdraw from the research at any time. The obligation to protect this freedom requires careful thought and consideration when the investigator is in a position of authority or influence over the participant. Such positions of authority include, but are not limited to, situations in which research participation is required as part of employment or in which the participant is a student, client, or employee of the investigator.

7. The investigator protects the participant from physical and mental discomfort, harm, and danger that may arise from research procedures. If risks of such consequences exist, the investigator informs the participant of that fact. Research procedures likely to cause serious or lasting harm to a participant are not used unless the failure to use these procedures might expose the participant to risk of greater harm, or unless the research has great potential benefit and fully informed and voluntary consent is obtained from each participant. The participant should be informed of procedures for contacting the investigator within a reasonable time period following participation should stress, potential harm, or related questions or concerns arise.

8. After the data are collected, the investigator provides the participant with information about the nature of the study and attempts to remove any misconceptions that may have arisen. Where scientific or humane values justify delaying or withholding this information, the investigator incurs a special responsibility to monitor the research and to ensure that there are no damaging consequences for the participant.

9. Where research procedures result in undesirable consequences for the individual participant, the investigator has the responsibility to detect and remove or correct these consequences, including long-term effects.

10. Information obtained about a research participant during the course of an investigation is confidential unless otherwise agreed upon in advance. When the possibility exists that others may obtain access to such information, this possibility, together with the plans for protecting confidentiality, is explained to the participant as part of the procedure for obtaining informed consent.

Principles 9 and 10 are the ones most relevant to protecting welfare, and they can be summarized by noting that the experimenter has an obligation to minimize harm to the participant. The subject should be warned ahead of time if there is potential harm, the subject should be able to withdraw if he or she chooses, and deception should be used carefully. The experimenter is obligated to undo any harm, and the results should remain confidential with regard to a particular participant unless agreed otherwise. These principles need to be reckoned with in any research project.

Informed Consent and Deception

The ethical researcher tells the subjects, prior to participation, of "all aspects of the research that might reasonably be expected to influence willingness to participate and explains all other aspects of the research about which participants inquire." This means that the participants must be forewarned about those aspects of the research that may have detrimental effects.

In a simple memory study, in which mode of presentation is the independent variable, probably little more than a general description of the task is required. However, the researchers sometimes must go into more detail when a chance exists that the participant might misinterpret the purpose of the experiment. Often in studies requiring memory or other cognitive abilities, the researcher assures the subjects that the task is not a personality or intelligence test. This is done to reassure the participant and to reduce evaluation apprehension.

In riskier research, such as the depression experiment just outlined, even greater caution is necessary. At the very least, the experimenter should tell the participants that they will be doing something that may make them feel unhappy. This warning allows the potential subject to decide whether to participate in the research. Enough information should be provided so that the person can either withdraw or give informed consent for participation.

There are at least two difficulties in implementing this safeguard. First, many people may not understand the prior information given them (such as children or people with learning disabilities), which puts a special burden on the experimenter to find someone capable of giving informed consent. Second, having to divulge too many details of an experiment could result in an internally invalid research project. Here, there are no easy solutions. If a researcher divulges everything about the study, the possibility of subject reactivity is very strong. For example, Brownell and Stunkard (1982) report that informed consent in medical research can severely hamper the use of a double-blind design. They conducted a study on the effectiveness of an appetite suppressant on overeating. The drug was compared with a placebo in a double-blind design in which neither the attending physician nor the subjects knew who was receiving the drug and who was getting the placebo. So, they attempted to deceive both the participants and the experimenter. The drug, fenfluramine hydrochloride, has many side effects, including drowsiness, diarrhea, dry mouth, and dizziness, which have different degrees of severity for different people. Consequently, prior to the experiment, all subjects were informed of the side effects that could occur if they were given the drug. Brownell and Stunkard found that both the patients and the attending physicians could correctly identify the assignment of medication in 70 percent of the cases. The information given prior to the experiment was enough to sabotage the double-blind design, and the deception did not work. More important, this breakdown in design resulted in unwanted changes in behavior, because correct identification of the medicated group was highly correlated with a favorable outcome of the treatment.

By providing enough information for informed consent, the researcher may undermine the validity of the experimental design. Thus, the ethical researcher is in a dilemma as to how much information should be provided. Obviously, participants should be forewarned of a life-threatening manipulation, and deception about such a variable would be unethical. But the costs and benefits associated with complete disclosure of a less detrimental manipulation are more difficult to assess. In the depression and memory experiment, the people who signed up to participate were told that some of the things they were going to do in the experiment might make them feel unhappy, and they were given the opportunity to refuse to participate. However, the specific nature of the manipulation, such as the Velten technique and who was going to serve in the experimental group, was not disclosed ahead of time. Complete disclosure might have resulted in reactivity. Since the effects of the manipulation involving depression are temporary, the researchers believed that partial information was enough to permit informed consent.

Since the solution to the informed-consent dilemma is not always apparent, the prudent researcher should seek the advice of others who can be objective about the situation. In the depression and memory study, the following people were consulted prior to the experiment: another experimental psychologist, a dean of student affairs and his assistant, an expert in biomedical ethics, and a counseling psychologist. They commented on deception and the informed-consent issue as well as on other ethical problems, which will be considered next.

Freedom to Withdraw

Participants should be allowed to decline to participate or to withdraw at any time. Everyone would agree that the mad scientist who straps participants to the chair is unethical. Most also would agree that people who are unhappy about participating should have the right to withdraw. So, what is the ethical dilemma? The major problem revolves around the definition of a willing volunteer participant. Consider the subject pool for the depression and memory experiment: undergraduate students (mostly freshmen and sophomores) taking introductory psychology. They sign up to participate in experiments, and they usually receive some sort of course credit for their service. Are they volunteering when they sign up, or are they under some sort of coercion that they have inferred from the situation? If the students actually receive extra credit, they are likely to be acting on their own volition. If they must participate as part of a course requirement, then the freedom to participate or not is less obvious. When students are required to participate, they should have some optional way of fulfilling the requirement, such as writing a paper or attending a special lecture. The point, then, is to provide freedom to the potential subjects, so that they can participate or not as they choose.

Generally, when the pool of potential participants is a captive audience, such as students, prisoners, military recruits, and employees of the experimenter, then the researcher needs to consider the individual's freedom to withdraw or to participate. In the depression and memory experiment, volunteer students were recruited with the lure of extra credit (participation was not mandatory). When they signed up, they were forewarned about the possibility of unhappiness (they could agree to participate or not). In the instructions at the beginning of the experiment, the students were advised that they had the option of quitting any time they wanted and they would still receive the full extra credit that had been promised (they were free to withdraw).

Protection from Harm

One additional safeguard to protect research participants from harm is suggested by the American Psychological Association: a way for the subjects to contact the investigator following their participation in the research. Even the most scrupulously ethical project of the minimal-risk sort may have unintended aftereffects. Thus, the participant should be able to receive help or advice from the researcher if problems should arise. We have had participants cry (out of frustration and embarrassment) during what was supposed to be a standard, innocuous memory experiment. Those subjects may have carried away from the experiment a negative self-image or strong feelings of resentment toward the experimenter in particular or research in general.

Because of such unintended effects, the prudent researcher provides for subsequent consultation, or what is called *debriefing*. Debriefing means that the investigator explains the general purposes of the research and the nature of the manipulations so that any questions or misunderstandings the subjects may have are removed.

Let us apply the principles of debriefing and protection from harm to the depression and memory experiment. At the end of that project, the participants were given a list of phone numbers of people who could be contacted in the unlikely event that the subjects felt depressed following the experiment. The list of contacts included the principal investigator, a counselor, and the dean of student affairs and his assistant. Also, the day after participation, each subject who had read the depression-inducing statements was phoned by one of the experimenters, who tried to determine whether the participant was having any negative aftereffects.

The participants were also thoroughly debriefed. They were told about the mood-induction procedure and how its effects were temporary. In addition, other details of the experimental design and rationale were outlined, and any questions the participants had were answered.

Removing Harmful Consequences

Debriefing subjects and giving them phone numbers may not be sufficient in a risky project. If a participant could indeed suffer long-term consequences as a result of serving in a research project, the investigator has the responsibility to remove those consequences. It may be difficult to reverse the feelings of resentful subjects, because the resentment may be unintended and undetected. However, where the risks are known, the ethical investigator must take steps to minimize them.

Prior to the debriefing in the depression and memory experiment, the participants read a series of self-referent statements designed to induce elation. This exercise was supposed to counteract the effects of the negative mood induced earlier. Then the participants were questioned about their current feelings, and they were also asked to sign a statement which said they left the experiment feeling no worse than when they began it. All participants signed the statement, but had they not, a contingent plan was to keep them in the laboratory under the supervision of one of the experimenters until they felt better.

Confidentiality

What a subject does in an experiment should be confidential unless otherwise agreed. An ethical researcher does not run around saying such things as: "Bobby Freshman is stupid; he did more poorly than anyone else in my experiment." Also, personal information about particular participants, such as their attitudes toward premarital sex or their family income, should not be revealed without the subjects' permission. The principle of confidentiality seems straightforward, but a researcher can be faced with an ethical dilemma when trying to uphold confidentiality.

This dilemma arose in the depression and memory experiment. The experimenter was confronted with an ethical problem, because he believed it was necessary to violate the principle of confidentiality in order to uphold the principle of protection from harm. Let us see how this problem developed. One of the first tasks of the participants was to answer some questions concerning their mental health. They were to indicate whether they were currently seeking professional help for a personal problem and to give some details about the problem and the therapeutic procedure. The participants were assured that their answers were confidential. Then the subjects completed a clinical test that assessed their current level of depression. If a participant indicated that he or she was being treated for depression and scored high on the test, the experiment was discontinued at that point. Confidentiality was promised so that honest responses could be obtained, and the test was administered to prevent a depressed person from becoming even more depressed by the mood-induction procedure. Thus, the intent was to minimize harm. In the course of the experiment, two students scored very high on the depression test, and one of them was not undergoing therapy. Since the test was known to be a reliable and valid predictor of clinically serious depression, the principal investigator believed that it was necessary to warn one of the college's counselors about the two students who appeared to have very high levels of depression. Then, under the guise of a routine interview, the counselor talked to these students.

This type of dilemma occurs frequently in research. The researcher may find it necessary to violate one ethical principle in order to adhere to another. There are no easy choices when this happens. If the highly depressed students had suspected that the investigator had betrayed their confidence, permanent resentment and mistrust could have resulted. On the other hand, had the one student who was not undergoing therapy committed suicide, the investigator would have felt responsible for an awful tragedy. At that time, preventing such a tragedy seemed much more important than upholding the participants' right to confidentiality.

Thus, ethical decisions rarely are made on the basis of empirical facts. Rather, the decisions usually are based on the pragmatic criterion. This criterion focuses on how to best protect the participants and at the same time conduct a meaningful, valid project.

Ethics in Research with Animals

Animals are used extensively in psychological research to answer questions that would be impossible or impractical to answer by using human beings. However, some people believe that animals should not be used in various kinds of research, on ethical grounds (Bowd, 1980). For example, Rollin (1985) has argued that if the concept of legal and moral rights can be applied to human research, it can also be applied in the same way to animal research. He suggested that the status of research animals needs to be elevated to that of human subjects, with many of the same rules that currently govern human research applied to animals. Recently, many sensational reports in the media have discussed the purported mistreatment of laboratory animals and the attempts of animal-rights advocates to limit the use of animals in research. Therefore, a consideration of why animals are used in research is important, and an understanding of the ethical safeguards for animals is necessary.

Animals are often the subjects of research because they are interesting and because they form an important part of the natural world. The number of bird-watchers and other amateur naturalists, as well as the numerous comparative psychologists and ethologists, readily attest to the interest. More important in terms of ethical concerns, however, is that animals serve as convenient, highly controlled models for humans *and* other animals.

Ethics prohibit experimentally induced brain damage in human beings, preclude deliberate separation of a human infant from its parents, forbid testing of unknown drugs on human beings, and generally exclude dangerous, irreversible, and immoral manipulations of human beings. Animal-rights advocates believe that research on animals should have the same prohibitions. According to the animal-rights advocates, researchers need to uphold the rights of both human beings and animals, because, for example, they believe that experimental destruction of a monkey's brain is as ethically reprehensible as the destruction of the brain of a human being. Three points summarize the animal advocates' position: (1) animals feel pain and their lives can be destroyed, as is true of humans (Roberts, 1971); (2) destroying or harming any living thing is dehumanizing to the human scientist (Roberts, 1971); and (3) claims about scientific progress being helped by animal research are a form of racism, called *speciesism* by Singer (1978), and, like interracial bigotry, are completely unwarranted and unethical. Most experimental psychologists, especially psychobiologists, have strong reservations about the validity of these points. Let us consider each in turn.

Surely animals feel pain and suffering. However, ethical standards exist in all scientific fields that use animals as research subjects. A major portion of these principles concerns the proscription of undue pain and inhumane treatment. No ethical psychologist would deliberately mistreat research animals, nor would an ethical psychologist deliberately inflict undue harm on an animal. Again, the vision of the mad scientist is merely that—a vision, and not a reality. A second reservation about pain and suffering as a deterrent to using animals should be mentioned. Many scientists believe that the disruptive effects of harm deliberately produced during a scientific investigation are much less tragic for animals than for human beings. Hoff (1980) argues that an animal stricken by blindness suffers less than a person stricken by blindness. Hoff does not advocate cruelty. Rather, her point is that harmful outcomes of research, though unpleasant and, perhaps, morally wrong, affect animals less than they do human beings.

Of course, Hoff's position is arguable. Roberts (1971) would consider Hoff's position as supporting her argument that many forms of animal research dehumanize the human investigator. Only a bloodless and unethical monster would remove the brain from a monkey and then keep the brain alive through a variety of ghastly means. To us, this argument seems specious for two reasons. In the first place, most animal-rights advocates exploit living things in one way or another. Even if they do not eat the flesh of animals (and most do), they do eat other living things, such as vegetables and fruits. Is it dehumanizing to kill a radish? If animal life is different from plant life, then it may be reasonable to argue that human life is different from animal life, as Hoff believes. In the second place, a substantial amount of animal research is undertaken to understand and help animals. Consider your favorite dog or other domestic pet. You may feel uneasy about the fact that many psychologists, physiologists, and veterinarians conduct experiments on dogs—experiments that we all agree would be unethical to conduct on human beings. However, there is a serious pragmatic and ethical dilemma here. If we love dogs and if we want them to be as happy and as healthy as possible, some kinds of dangerous research must be done on these animals so that humane care can be given to them. It seems ironic to us that those who appear to love animals the most would advocate measures that could be disastrous for those animals.

As a model for human behavior, animal research is essential for scientific progress. This may be a form of speciesism, but given the validity of our previous arguments, speciesism may not be so bad. Consider these two quotes from Robert J. White, an eminent neuroscientist and neurosurgeon, who conducted the brain-removal studies alluded to earlier: "As I write this article, I relive my vivid experiences yesterday when I removed at operation a large tumor from the cerebellum and brain stem of a small child. This was a surgical undertaking that would have been impossible a few decades ago, highly dangerous a few years ago, but is today thanks to extensive experimentation on the brains of lower animals, routinely accomplished with a high degree of safety" (1971, p. 504). "I consider the employment of animals in biological and medical research so critical to continued human existence and survival as to be beyond logical challenge" (p. 512).

Gallup and Suarez (1985) reviewed the rationale, extent, and use of animals in psychological research. They considered the possible alternatives and concluded that in many cases there is no viable alternative to the use of animals in psychological research.

The American Psychological Association (1981a) has provided guidelines governing animal research. As a general principle,

> An investigator of animal behavior strives to advance understanding of basic behavioral principles and/or to contribute to the improvement of human health and welfare. In seeking these ends, the investigator ensures the welfare of animals and treats them humanely. Laws and regulations notwithstanding, an animal's immediate protection depends upon the scientist's own conscience.

The five primary considerations for researchers using animal subjects are listed below.

1. The acquisition, care, use, and disposal of all animals are in compliance with current federal, state or provincial, and local laws and regulations.

2. A psychologist trained in research methods and experienced in the care of laboratory animals closely supervises all procedures involving animals and is responsible for insuring appropriate consideration of their comfort, health, and humane treatment.

3. Psychologists ensure that all individuals using animals under their supervision have received explicit instruction in experimental methods and in the care, maintenance, and handling of the species being used. Responsibilities and activities of individuals participating in a research project are consistent with their respective competencies.

4. Psychologists make every effort to minimize discomfort, illness, and pain of animals. A procedure subjecting animals to pain, stress, or privation is used only when an alternative procedure is unavailable and the goal is justified by its prospective scientific, educational, or applied value. Surgical procedures are performed under appropriate anesthesia; techniques to avoid infection and minimize pain are followed during and after surgery.

5. When it is appropriate that the animal's life be terminated, it is done rapidly and painlessly.

The above guidelines were designed for experienced researchers. The APA (1981b) has also provided guidelines for the student researcher, which are reproduced below.

Both sets of guidelines emphasize decent care and treatment. Both also mention additional regulations. Before using animal subjects, you should understand the contents of both sets of guidelines, and you should become familiar with relevant state and local humane regulations. *An ethical psychologist does not mistreat animal subjects, nor does an ethical psychologist submit animal subjects to undue pain or harm.*

Guidelines for the Use of Animals in School Science Behavior Projects

1. In the selection of science behavior projects, students should be urged to select animals that are small and easy to maintain as subjects for research.

2. All projects *must* be preplanned and conducted with humane considerations and respect for animal life. Projects intended for science fair exhibition must comply with these guidelines as well as with additional requirements of the sponsor.

3. Each student undertaking a school science project using animals *must have a qualified supervisor*. Such a supervisor shall be a person who has had training and experience in the proper care of the species and the research techniques to be used in the project. The supervisor *must* assume the primary responsibility for all conditions of the project and must ensure that the student is trained in the care and handling of the animals as well as in the methods to be used.

4. The student shall do relevant reading about previous work in the area. The student's specific purpose, plan of action, justification of the methodology, and anticipated outcome for the science project shall be submitted to and approved by a qualified person. Teachers shall maintain these on file for future reference.

5. No student shall inflict pain, severe deprivation, or high stress levels or use invasive procedures such as surgery, the administration of drugs, ionizing radiation, or toxic agents *unless* facilities are suitable both for the study and for the care and housing of the animals and *unless* the research is carried out under the extremely close and rigorous supervision of a person with training in the specific area of study. These projects must be conducted in accordance with the APA *Principles for the Care and Use of Animals*.

6. Students, teachers, and supervisors *must* be cognizant of current federal and state legislation and guidelines for specific care and handling of their animals (e.g., the Animal Welfare Act). Copies of humane laws are available from local or national humane organizations. A recommended reference is the *Guide for the Care and Use of Laboratory Animals*, available from the Superintendent of Documents, U.S. Government Printing Office, Washington, D.C. 20402, Stock Number 017-040-00427-3.

7. The basic daily needs of each animal shall be of prime concern. Students *must* ensure the proper housing, food, water, exercise, cleanliness, and gentle handling of their animals. Special arrangement *must* be made for care during weekends, holidays, and vacations. Students must protect their animals from sources of disturbance or harm, including teasing by other students.

8. When the research project has been completed, the supervisor is responsible for proper disposition of the animals. If it is appropriate that the animal's life be terminated, it shall be rapid and painless. *Under no circumstances should students be allowed to experiment with such procedures.*

9. Teachers and students are encouraged to consult with the Committee on Animal Research and Experimentation of the American Psychological Association for advice on adherence to the guidelines. In cases where facilities for advanced research by quaified students are not available, the Committee on Animal Research and Experimentation will try to make suitable arrangements for the students.

10. A copy of these guidelines shall be posed conspicuously wherever animals are kept and projects carried out, including displays at science fairs.

From *American Psychologist*, Vol. 36, 1981. Copyright 1981 by the American Psychological Association. Reprinted by permission of the publisher.

Ethics in Drug Research

The APA guidelines for the use of drugs in research involving both humans and animals are printed below. The primary purpose for reprinting these guidelines is to discourage most undergraduate research on drugs, especially projects using human beings. Special government permits are required for research with controlled substances (including marijuana), and most student projects neglect to include appropriate *aftercare* for their human participants. You are responsible for accidents, antisocial behavior, and worse yet, addiction that could result from an experimentally induced high. If you are compelled to engage in drug research, use animals as your subjects and use legal substances. If you do, be sure you understand the following rules as well as the other legal documents that are mentioned therein.

APA Guidelines for Psychologists on the Use of Drugs in Research

General Principle: A psychologist or psychology student who performs research involving the use of drugs shall have adequate knowledge and experience of each drug's action or shall work in collaboration with or under the supervision of a qualified researcher. Any psychologist or psychology student doing research with drugs must comply with the procedural guidelines below. Any supervisor or collaborator has the responsibility to see that the individual he supervises or collaborates with complies with the procedural guidelines.

Definition of a qualified researcher

1. A qualified researcher possesses a Ph.D. degree based in part upon a dissertation that is experimental in nature and in part upon training in psychology, pharmacology, physiology, and related areas, and that is conferred by a graduate school of recognized standing (listed by the United States Office of Education as having been accredited by a recognized regional or national accrediting organization).

2. A qualified researcher has demonstrated competence as defined by research involving the use of drugs which has been published in scientific journals; or continuing education; or equivalent experience ensuring that the researcher has adequate knowledge of the drugs, their actions, and of experimental design.

Definition of a drug
In these Guidelines, the term drug includes (a) all substances as defined by the term drug in the "Federal Food, Drug, and Cosmetic Act" (21 USC 321) and (b) all substances, Schedules 1–V, as listed in the "Comprehensive Druge Abuse Prevention and Control Act of 1970" (21 USC 812; PL 91-513, Sec. 202) in its present form or as amended (Federal Food, Drug and Cos-

metic Act, 21 USC, Sec. 201 (g), Appendix A). Copies of these acts are available from the Superintendent of Documents, United States Government Printing Office, Washington, DC 20402.

Procedural guidelines

1. All drugs must be legally obtained and used under conditions specified by state and federal laws. Information concerning these laws should be obtained from federal or state authorities.

2. Proper precautions must be taken so that drugs and drug paraphernalia that are potentially harmful are available only to authorized personnel. All such drugs used in experiments should be kept in locked cabinets and under any additional security prescribed by law.

3. All individuals using or supervising the use of drugs in research must be familiar with PL 91-513, the "Comprehensive Drug Abuse Prevention and Control Act of 1970," and its implementing regulations as well as all amendments to the act and other drug laws relevant to their research.

4. The use of drugs must be justified scientifically.

5. All individuals using or supervising the use of drugs in research must familiarize themselves with available information concerning the mode of action, toxicity, and methods of administration of the drugs they are using.

6. In any experiment involving animals, the welfare of the animal should be considered as specified in APA's "Precautions and Standards for the Care and Use of Animals."

7. Research involving human subjects is governed by additional guidelines as set forth in APA's "Ethical Standards for Psychological Research."

8. The present Guidelines should be brought to the attention of all individuals conducting research with drugs.

9. The present Guidelines should be posted conspicuously in every laboratory in which psychologists use drugs.

Source: American Psychological Association Ad Hoc Committee on Guidelines for the Use of Drugs and Other Chemical Agents in Research. From *American Psychologist*, Vol. 27, 1972. Copyright 1972 by the American Psychological Association. Reprinted by permission of the publisher.

Monitoring Ethical Practices

The American Psychological Association provides ethical guidelines for psychological research. Acceptance of membership in the association commits the member to adherence to these principles. The principles are also intended for nonmembers, including students of psychology and others who work on psychological research under the supervision of a psychologist.

The American Psychological Association established an Ethics Committee that fulfills a number of purposes. Through publications, educational meetings, and convention activities, the Ethics Committee educates psychologists and the public about ethical issues related to psychological research. The committee also investigates and adjudicates complaints concerning unethical research practices. Examples of these cases can be found in an APA (1987) publication titled, *Casebook on ethical issues*. The Ethics Committee also publishes an annual report in *American Psychologist*.

Most institutions involved in psychological research have guidelines regarding research with animals and humans in addition to the APA ethical guidelines. Many universities have a special committee that monitors the use of human and animal subjects. Researchers must submit a detailed outline of the planned research to the committee. The committee evaluates the types and levels of risk involved in the research and considers the potential value of the research. It often proposes additional or alternative procedures that will reduce the level of risk to the subject.

In addition to the above guidelines, there are federal government regulations concerned with the protection of human and animal subjects. These regulations require that any individual or institution that applies for federal grants must follow certain research practices designed to minimize the level of risk to the subject. These regulations also require that institutions monitor research to protect the rights of the subjects of such research.

SUMMARY

1. An ethical investigator protects the welfare of research participants by following the ethical standards of the American Psychological Association.

2. Minimal use of deception on the part of the investigator as well as informed consent permit the participant to make a reasoned judgment about whether to participate.

3. The ethical investigator respects the participant's right to decline to serve in the research or to withdraw at any time.

4. In an ethical investigation, the participant is protected from physical and mental harm.

5. After the data have been collected, participants should be debriefed to remove any misconceptions that may have arisen.

6. An ethical investigator will attempt to remove any harmful consequences that resulted from the research.

7. Unless otherwise agreed, information about a research participant is confidential.

8. Attempts to uphold these ethical principles sometimes lead to a dilemma in that adherence to one principle may violate another.

9. An ethical investigator treats animal subjects in a humane fashion.

10. Research with drugs poses special welfare problems, especially those concerned with the aftercare of the participants.

KEY TERMS

aftercare
confidentiality
debriefing
deception
ethical principles of the
   American Psychological
   Association

freedom to withdraw
informed consent
protection from harm
removing harmful
   consequences
speciesism

DISCUSSION QUESTIONS

Reconsider the ethical principles presented in this chapter and read the list of ethical principles published by American Psychologist Association (1981, 1987).

1. Read selections from the *Casebook on Ethical Issues* published by the American Psychological Association (1987), which is probably available in your library. This book describes the background of different ethical complaints, how the complaints came to be sent to the Ethics Committee, and how the cases were adjudicated. Select two cases and consider the ethical principles involved in the case. Describe why you agree or disagree with the adjudication of the Ethics Committee.

2. Read two of the articles listed below. These articles describe the ethical issues associated with different types of psychological research. Consider the general ethical principles that apply in both cases. Describe how the ethical issues differ between the two types of research discussed in the articles.

SUGGESTED READINGS

Bowd, A. D. (1980). Ethical reservations about psychological research with animals. *Psychological Record, 30*, 201–210.

Imber, S. D., Glanz, L. M., Elkin, I., Sotsky, S. M., Boyer, J. L., & Leber, W. R. (1986). Ethical issues in psychotherapy research: Problems in a collaborative clinical study. *American Psychologist, 41*, 137–146.

Melton, G., & Gray, J. (1988). Ethical dilemmas in AIDS research: Individual privacy and public health. *American Psychologist, 43*, 60–64.

Milgram, S. (1977). Ethical issues in the study of obedience. In S. Milgram (Ed.), *The individual in a social world* (pp. 188–199). Reading, MA: Addison-Wesley.

Scarr, S. (1988). Race and gender as psychological variables: Social and ethical issues. *American Psychologist, 43*, 56–59.

Sieber, J. E., & Stanley, B. (1988). Ethical and professional dimensions of socially sensitive research. *American Psychologist, 43*, 49–55.

Smith, C. P. (1983). Ethical issues: Research on deception, informed consent, and debriefing. In L. Wheeler & P. Shaver (Eds.), *Review of personality and social psychology* (Vol. 4, pp. 297–328). Beverly Hills, CA: Sage.

How to Read and Write Research Reports

"I couldn't afford to learn it," said the Mock Turtle with a sigh. "I only took the regular course." "What was that?" inquired Alice. "Reeling and Writhing, of course. . . ."

—LEWIS CARROLL

TRYING TO READ A PSYCHOLOGY journal article for the first time can be a challenging experience. Researchers write articles for other researchers, and so use jargon and a terse writing style. These features aid communication among scholars in a particular field, because they can read short reports and understand them. But such writing can be difficult to comprehend for students beginning their study of a field. This chapter is designed to prepare you for your first encounter with the literature of experimental psychology in two ways. First, the format and style most often used in journal articles will be explained, so that you will know what to expect in each section of an article. Second, hints will be provided to help you become a critical reader, skilled at objectively evaluating an article. With some practice, you will far surpass the Mock Turtle and not have to "reel and writhe" your way through every psychology article you read. The chapter ends with some recommendations for writing a research report.

The Parts of an Article

The basic psychology article consists of seven parts: title and author(s), abstract, introduction, method, results, discussion, and references. Each part has an important function and is a necessary component of the article.

Title and Author(s)

The *title* gives you an idea of the contents of an article. Since titles must be short, the most common type of title states only the dependent and independent variables—for example, "Rate of bar pressing as a function of quality and quantity of food reward." Although this title is not particularly appealing, it conveys important information. The title and authors of each article in a given issue usually appear on the inside front cover.

As you continue to gain knowledge in a particular content area, you will become familiar with many researchers. You may start to pay attention to the authors first, and then look at the titles. After you have read several articles published by the same *author*, you will grow in understanding of that writer's viewpoints and how they differ from those of other researchers.

So many psychology articles are published each month that no one has the time to read all of them. The table of contents is a first step to selecting those articles relevant to your own interests. But an even better decision can be made by consulting the abstract and the references of an article.

Abstract

The *abstract* is a short paragraph (100 to 150 words) that summarizes the key points of an article. According to the *Publication Manual* of the American Psychological Association (1983), it should be "accurate, succinct, quickly comprehensible, and informative" (p. 24). The abstract is the best way to discover quickly what an article is about. If you are new to an area, you can use the abstract to decide if a particular article warrants further reading. As you gain experience and become familiar with authors in the field, you will want to consult the references as well before making this decision.

References

References are found at the end of the article. In contrast to journals in other disciplines, psychology journals list full titles of referenced articles. This practice helps to inform the reader as to what the article is about. Furthermore, the references are valuable as a guide for related information. They can also be used as an index of the merit of the article. Articles should refer to the most recently published works in the area, as well as to the most important previous publications. The *Social Sciences Citation Index* (available in most university libraries) is a useful source of additional references.

Introduction

The *introduction* specifies the problem to be studied and tells why it is important. The author also reviews the relevant research literature on the topic. A good introduction also specifies the hypotheses to be tested and gives the rationale behind the predictions.

Science does not always take giant steps forward. Knowledge may be acquired in small steps, with several readjustments. Since it is impossible to predict experimental outcomes accurately all the time, many an experiment starts out as an educated hunch, based on the author's prior work and theoretical orientation. Therefore, the sample of published articles does not represent the population of experiments that have been performed. Several studies may have been done prior to those appearing in the article under consideration. Although the results of these preliminary studies may never be published directly, information gained will help the author formulate and refine a set of hypotheses and obtain results that are publishable. What finally appears in print can represent the culmination of a great deal of time, energy, hope, surprise, and disappointment. Beveridge (1957) emphasizes this:

> Unfortunately research has more frustrations than successes and the scientist is more often up against what appears to be an impenetrable barrier than making progress. Only those who have sought know how rare and hard to find are those little diamonds of truth which, when mined and polished, will endure hard and bright. Lord Kelvin wrote: "One word characterises the most strenuous of the efforts for the advancement of science that I have made perserveringly during fifty-five years; that word is failure."

These words from a famous scientist are comforting when our own efforts at research lead to disappointment.

Method

The *method* section describes in detail the operations performed by the experimenter. It is usually printed in smaller type to conserve space, but this does not mean it is an unimportant part of the article to be quickly skimmed over. The method section should contain enough information that another experimenter could replicate the study.

It is customary to divide the method section into subsections that cover subjects, apparatus, and procedure. The *subject* section tells how many subjects there were, how they were selected (randomly, haphazardly, only the investigator's relatives, etc.) and who they were (college undergraduates taking introductory psychology, paid volunteers obtained by an ad in a newspaper, a particular strain of rats purchased from a supply house). The *apparatus* section describes any equipment used to test the subjects. This section might include details such as the model number of a computer or the size of a conditioning chamber. The *procedure* explains what happened to the subjects and includes instructions (for human subjects), statistical design features, and so forth. If an uncommon statistical technique was used—that is, one that cannot be looked up directly in an advanced statistics text and cited—an extra design subsection is often included. Sometimes even a standard statistical technique is described in a design subsection.

Results

The *results* section tells what happened in the experiment. It is unusual to find raw data or individual scores reported in a journal article; instead, descriptive statistics are presented that summarize the data. Inferential statistics present the probability of whether the observed differences between the various experimental conditions have been produced by random, or chance, factors. This information helps the reader to decide whether to believe the data. (See Appendix B: Statistical Reasoning, for further explanation and review.) Both kinds of statistics are important and help psychologists understand the outcome of an experiment.

Either tables or graphs may be used to describe and summarize data. It is often helpful to draw a graph for yourself from the tabular data. If an article contains several figures, check that the scales are comparable, so that effects can be easily compared across different figures. The way a graph is drawn can be misleading, as the following example illustrates.

Imagine that a psychologist is interested in how people perceive written English words. Either a word or a nonword—letters that follow the pattern of written English but do not spell a real word, e.g., nale—is presented visually. The participants must press one button if it is a word or press a different button if it is a nonword. This is called a *lexical decision*. In another condition, the participant must pronounce the word or nonword when it is presented. This is called *naming.* An experiment to compare naming and lexical decisions was performed by Frost, Katz, and Bentin (1987). Their results showed how long it took people to respond to high-frequency English words and nonwords.

We have replotted their data in figure 5–1. At first glance, the two panels look quite different. Examining panel (a), we might conclude that naming and lexical decisions are quite similar. But from panel (b), we might conclude not only that naming is faster, but also that the difference between words and nonwords is greater for lexical decisions than for naming. Actually, the same data are presented in both panels. The trick is that the vertical scales are plotted differently. One panel has reaction time (the time between the visual presentation and responding) measured in seconds, whereas the other plots reaction time in milliseconds. Since a millisecond is one one-thousandth of a second, the two graphs appear to be different. Also, the scale is "broken" in panel (b), so that measures begin at 520 milliseconds, which further dramatizes the difference. Clearly, the way a graph is drawn can emphasize or conceal results. (See appendix B for a further example of this point.)

But which way of graphing the results is right? In a sense, both are, because both can be argued to portray matters accurately.

FIGURE 5–1(a).

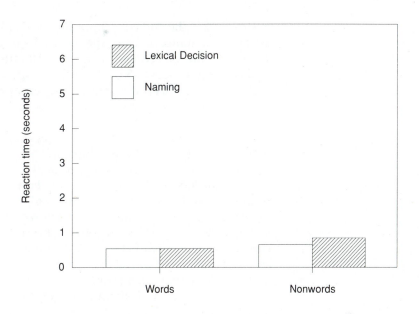

5–1(b).

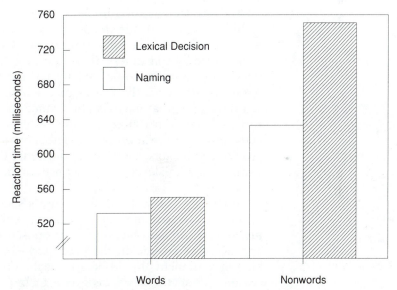

Exaggerated scales. Exactly the same data are presented in the two panels of figure 5–1, but the scale in panel (a) is in seconds and that in panel (b) is in milliseconds (with a scale break indicated, too). Thus the differences appear very small in (a) and very large in (b).

However, if statistical tests have shown a difference to exist between the two measures, then the graph in panel (b) more accurately captures the relation between measures. This was the scale used by Frost, Katz, and Bentin (1987) to portray their results.

Inferential statistics permit the assessment of whether differences that appear in the results, as in panel (b), can be trusted as real and not due to chance factors. Inferential statistics about the data appear in statements such as "$F(4,60) = 2.03, p < .05$." All this means is that the odds for obtaining an *F*-statistic at least as large as 2.03 by chance if the experiment were repeated would be 5 percent; if the experiment were done 100 times, the results would be similar in at least 95 of the 100 repetitions.

There is no fixed rule for setting an appropriate level of significance. It is up to the researcher to decide if the odds are just right, too high, or too low. Depending on the import of your conclusions, you may require more or less certainty that what happened has not happened by chance.

Imagine the problem of a graduate-student admissions officer who has been told that resources at the university are extremely limited. It has been suggested that she discriminate against women in accepting students into the program, since they are less likely to finish. She would like to put such unsubstantiated notions to rest and so commissions a statistical analysis to test this hypothesis. Here, odds of 5 in 100 to reject the null hypothesis that women are less likely than men to finish are too high, because the import is so great. A level of significance of 1 in 1,000 would be more appropriate.

Or take the case of a breakfast-cereal company that wishes to include a "prize" inside the box. It performs a statistical analysis to decide which of five potential prizes, all of which cost the same, is preferred by consumers. If there is any difference among prizes, the company wants to be sure to find the best one. If the firm is wrong and incorrectly selects one, when in fact all are equally attractive, no great harm is done, since each prize costs the same. Here, odds of 5 in 100 are too low. A level of significance of 50 in 100 might be more appropriate. The situation determines what the level of significance should be. Additional discussion of inferential statistics and the level of significance can be found in the statistical appendix.

In the results section, the author's specific choice of words is important. Beware of such statements as this: "Although the data just barely missed reaching the proposed level of significance, it appears that a trend in the predicted direction did occur." This kind of statement should be approached with caution for several reasons. First, the word *trend* is a technical term: existence of a trend can be determined only by an appropriate statistical test. Second, it implies that results that are significant go beyond a trend—that is, they are true and utterly reliable—and that failure to reach a prescribed level only means that "truth" is latent rather than explicit. This implication is false: even significant results are reliable only in a probabilistic sense—for example, ninety-five times in a hundred.

Discussion

The *discussion* is the most creative part of an article. Here, an author is permitted to restate what the data show (if he or she so desires) and to draw theoretical conclusions. Most editors have firm standards for both method and results sections, but the author is given greater latitude in the discussion. Hence, although skepticism is healthy when approaching any article, an extra degree of caution is required when reading the discussion. In the words of the APA *Publication Manual* (1983): "In the Discussion section, you are free to examine, interpret, and qualify the results, as well as to draw inferences from them" (p. 27). Keep in mind that research results are not incontestable truths and that experimental findings are relative to the context in which they are found. Freedom for the author requires caution from the readers.

Checklist for the Critical Reader

In this section we offer some hints that have helped us to become better consumers of the information presented in psychological journals. Our major suggestion is to avoid rushing through an article. Instead, you might deliberately stop after each section and write down the answers to the questions we shall list here. This can be difficult at first, but with practice this process becomes automatic and requires little extra time.

Introduction

1. *What is the author's goal?* The introduction explains the reasons behind the experiment. If one or more theories are related to the research, the introduction gives the predictions the theories make. As with scientists in other areas, psychologists do not necessarily agree as to the underlying mechanisms and theoretical interpretations of behavior. The author may present a particular theory that he or she thinks provides a useful explanation of behavior. Although the author may present more than one theory in the introduction, he or she will proceed later on to demonstrate that they do not all help equally to predict and explain the obtained results. Try to figure out which of the several theories the author believes and which are slated for subsequent rejection.

2. *What hypotheses will be tested in the experiment?* The answer to this should be obvious and stated directly within the introduction section.

3. *If I had to design an experiment to test this hypothesis, what would I do?* This is the key question for the introduction. You must try to answer this *before* continuing on to the method section of the article. Remember that the writer is frequently biased. Many experiments are done within the context of a systematic investigation of behavior to test and support a particular theoretical framework developed by the author. If the author has any skill as a wordsmith, once you have finished the next section, you are likely to agree with the method that the author has advocated in the article. A clever author will plant the seeds to

this answer in the introduction itself; this practice makes it harder for you to state a method independently. Write down the major ideas for your method of testing the hypothesis.

Method

Compare your answer to question 3 with that of the author of the article. They probably will differ, if you have not peeked. Now answer questions 4a–c.

4a. *Is my proposed method better than the author's?* Regardless of who has the better method, you or the author, this forced comparison will make you think about the method section critically, instead of passively accepting it.

4b. *Does the method actually test the hypothesis?* The hypothesis is sometimes the first casualty, disappearing between the introduction and method sections. Always check that the method used is adequate and relevant to the hypothesis at hand.

4c. *What are the independent, dependent, and control variables?* This is an obvious question and can be answered quickly. Listing the variables helps you avoid passive reading of the method section. After you have resolved differences between your proposed method and the author's, answer the next question.

5. *Using the subjects, apparatus, and procedures described by the author, what results would I predict for this experiment?* You must answer this on your own before reading the results section. To help yourself, review the hypotheses and the independent and dependent variables. You may find it impossible to predict a single outcome. This is not really a problem, since the author probably also had more than one prediction originally. He or she may have done some preliminary investigations to narrow down possible outcomes; alternatively, he or she may have been surprised by the results and had to rethink the introduction once the results were in. Draw a rough sketch illustrating the most likely outcomes you have predicted.

Results

Compare the results with your predictions. If they are the same, go on to question 7. If not, answer question 6.

6. *Did the author get the "wrong" results?* After some thought, you will reach one of two conclusions: either your prediction was wrong, or the results are hard to believe. Perhaps the method the author selected was inappropriate and did not adequately test the stated hypotheses or introduced sources of uncontrolled variance. Or perhaps these results would not be obtained again if the experiment were repeated. You might even try your own experiment. See if you can replicate the reported results.

7. *How would I interpret these results?* Try to answer this on your own, before reading the discussion.

Discussion

Compare your interpretation with the author's. Answer question 8a or 8b, whichever is appropriate.

8a. *Why didn't I think of that?*

8b. *Why didn't the author think of that?* The discussion section is the most difficult to evaluate. Often, only future research can decide if it is correct. Conducting experiments and collecting data are ongoing processes. Often, authors have already done some of this future research, but have not gotten around to reporting it yet. There is a lag between the date an experiment is completed and the date it is written up for publication. Therefore, in writing up the current work, a scientist may already have gained a preview of the results of his next investigation and anticipate this in his current discussion section.

Checklist Summary

As you are reading your first article carefully, try to write down the answers to all eight questions. It is hard work the first several times, so do not be discouraged. The following is a typical psychological article. It has been analyzed according to the checklist summarized in table 5–1.

TABLE 5–1. | **Questions for Critical Readers**

Introduction
   1. What is the author's goal?
   2. What hypothesis will be tested in the experiment?
   3. If I had to design an experiment to test this hypothesis, what would I do?

Method
   4a. Is my proposed method better than the author's?
   4b. Does the method actually test the hypothesis?
   4c. What are the independent, dependent, and control variables?
   5. Using the subjects, apparatus, and procedures described by the author, what results would I predict for this experiment?

Results
   6. Did the author get the "wrong" results?
   7. How would I interpret these results?

Discussion
   8. Is my interpretation better than the author's?

A Sample Journal Article

In this section, we have reprinted a short article from the *Bulletin of the Psychonomic Society*. The answers to the checklist questions were distilled from answers given in one of the author's classes. Most of those students were college sophomores who had taken two courses in psychology. The article is about experiments that have been interpreted as showing that a particular type of brain wave (alpha waves) can be conditioned in human subjects.

Most articles are written for experts in a particular area, so the authors of a report assume that their readers have some knowledge of the topic under investigation. In addition, most journals set page limitations on articles, which means that some information may be missing or presented very tersely. The assumptions made by the authors and the brevity of many articles pose a problem for the novice reader. The novice may have to read other articles or textbooks in order to understand a particular report. To help you understand the following report, we present some background information.

The article by Lindholm and Lowry (1978) is about learning to control a particular brain wave—the alpha wave. Alpha waves are prominent during meditation and relaxed wakefulness, and these waves are often associated with a pleasant emotional state that is called the alpha experience.

In a typical study about learning to control brain waves, the subject is connected to an electroencephalograph (EEG), a device that measures brain waves. The EEG is constructed so that it can provide a feedback signal to the subject when a particular brain wave, such as the alpha wave, is present. The feedback, usually a tone, is supposed to work as a reinforcer does in operant conditioning; that is, the feedback tells the subject when alpha is occurring. So, when the feedback is contingent on the appearance of alpha waves (feedback occurs only when alpha occurs), the alpha waves should occur more often than when feedback is noncontingent (the occurrence of feedback is unrelated to the occurrence of alpha). The logic here is precisely the same as that of reinforcing a hungry rat with food when the rat makes a particular response. If food is contingent on a particular response, then that response will increase in likelihood. If food is presented noncontingently with respect to that response, then it will not increase in likelihood.

Some earlier alpha-wave studies seemed to show that alpha would increase even when the feedback was noncontingent. Thus, Lindholm and Lowry wanted to examine the effects of false (noncontingent) feedback on alpha-wave production. If alpha waves increase when feedback is noncontingent, then we can conclude that something other than operant conditioning increases the frequency of alpha production.

Lindholm and Lowry also studied the effects of relaxation on the production of alpha. They do not detail the method of inducing relaxation, but we will. The procedure used was Jacobson's (1978) method of progressive relaxation. This technique involves training people to alternately tense and relax small groups of muscles until the entire body is in a state of relaxation. This progressive relaxation usually starts with the toes, works up through the legs, the torso, arms, neck, and finally the face.

The following report is brief. One question you might try to answer is: "Could I replicate this study on the basis of the information presented?"

Alpha Production in Humans Under Conditions of False Feedback*

Ernest Lindholm and Steven Lowry
ARIZONA STATE UNIVERSITY
TEMPE, ARIZONA 85281

Subjects were pretrained in either Jacobson's relaxation or a control relaxation technique, then served in four daily sessions of biofeedback training. On some days, the feedback was veridical with respect to alpha production, while on other days, the feedback falsely indicated either success or failure at the control task. The results showed that alpha increased over trials, but this increase was independent of feedback contingency. Subjective reports of mood were not influenced by feedback falsely indicating success or failure at the control task, and there were no reliable relationships between mood and amount of alpha actually produced. Prior training on Jacobson's relaxation did not enhance alpha production. It is concluded that alpha production and positive mood states are not systematically related and that neither of these variables is operantly conditioned through biofeedback.

Brown (1970, 1971, 1974), Kamiya (1968, 1969) and others have reported that humans can learn to control their alpha production and that successful learning is accompanied by a variety of positive mood states (e.g., euphoria, well-being) collectively referred to as the "alpha experience." Others (e.g., Lynch, Paskewitz, & Orne, 1974) have argued that alpha production is not learned, that rather, subjects habituate to the strangeness of the experimental environment and over time, engage in fewer activities that tend to block alpha, such as visual fixation on objects in the room. Regarding mood states, Plotkin, Mazer, and Lowery (1976) found no relationship between mood and the amount of alpha produced, although they suggested the possibility that the subjects' perceived success or failure might influence subjective reports of mood; that is, subjects who thought they were successful might report more positive mood states than subjects who thought they were not successful at the control task.

---

*Copyright 1978 by The Psychonomic Society, Inc. Reprinted by permission of the author and publisher. Lindholm and Lowry. *Bulletin of the Psychonomic Society*, vol. 11, 1978.

The Lynch et al. (1974) position that alpha enhancement is not learned is questioned by the results of Brolund and Schallow (1976), who showed that combining feedback and reward led to greater alpha enhancement than feedback alone, suggesting that experimental contingencies were controlling the behavior (alpha production) to some reliable degree. Further, Lynch et al. (1974) employed a noncontingent feedback control in which the noncontingent feedback of one subject is a replay of the contingent feedback received by another. This may well be inappropriate for alpha learning experiments, since subjects do (by whatever means) increase alpha over trials, thus the replay of increasing density of feedback over trials might serve to fortuitously reinforce almost anything the control subject does which works in the direction of increasing alpha. This could introduce a bias in the direction of reducing group differences between contingent and noncontingent groups and obscure real differences between groups.

The other type of control group used in alpha experiments is the no-feedback control, which simply requires subjects to sit in a comfortable chair in a quiet room for the duration of the experiment (Brolund & Schallow, 1976). The problem here is that these subjects receive less stimulation than subjects receiving feedback (contingent or otherwise) and thus might display enhanced alpha due to a movement toward a sleep or semisleep state. It appears, therefore, that while some argue that alpha enhancement is not a learned phenomenon, the lack of appropriate control groups detracts from the force of these arguments.

There appear to be four important questions that require evaluation before the worth of alpha conditioning experiments can be adequately evaluated: (1) Are alpha increases learned as a result of experimental contingencies? (2) Is the "alpha experience" closely related to the amount of alpha actually produced? (3) Is the intensity of the "alpha experience" influenced by the subject's perceived success or failure? (4) Is the amount of alpha produced and the intensity of the "alpha experience" influenced by the subject's ability to relax? There is an implicit assumption that alpha density and relaxation are closely related, yet this assumption has never been directly tested by manipulating relaxation as an independent variable.

Question 1. What is the author proposing? The authors propose that the results of research concerned with learning to control alpha waves are equivocal. They seem to favor the idea that you cannot learn to control alpha.

Question 2. What hypotheses will be tested? The hypotheses are listed as questions to be answered before one can accept alpha conditioning: (1) Does alpha increase because of the feedback provided? (2) What is the relation between the amount of alpha produced and the alpha experience? (3) What is the relation between the alpha experience and the subject's perceived failure or success? (4) What is the relation between the subject's ability to relax and the production of alpha (and the alpha experience)?

Question 3. How would I test these hypotheses? With respect to the first one, you could try to fool the subject in some way so that the feedback provided on the production of alpha is not correct. You could, for example, randomly present feedback to the subject—sometimes when alpha is being produced, and sometimes when it is not being produced. If alpha increases under random feedback, then it is not learned. With regard to the second hypothesis, you could correlate some measure of the subject's mood (the alpha experience) and the amount of alpha that is produced. For the third hypothesis, you could tell some subjects that they are doing well and compare their alpha production with that of subjects who are told that they are not doing well. One way to examine the final hypothesis would be to provide a relaxing atmosphere for some subjects and compare their alpha with the alpha of subjects who are trained in a more tense environment.

Method

Subjects

Ten male and 10 female subjects were solicited by advertisement to participate in an experiment in which they could learn self-relaxation techniques and control of brainwaves. All were members of psychology classes regularly offered at Arizona State University.

Apparatus

Brain activity was recorded from occipital-occipital placements referenced to left mastoid using Grass silver disk electrodes and Grass electrode paste. Signals were amplified by a Beckman Type 411 dynograph, the high-level output of which was fed to the input of a DEC-LAB-8 computer that was programmed to detect alpha activity according to the following criteria: (1) There must be 1½ cycles of activity falling within the 8- to 12-Hz frequency band, and (2) the amplitude of the activity must exceed the Schmitt trigger threshold set for each subject during the baseline sessions. When both criteria were met, the computer software turned on the biofeedback display which consisted of a 61 × 61 cm sheet of milk-white Plexiglas located 61 cm from the subject's face and back-lighted by a 15-W ac bulb. The Plexiglas formed the face of a plywood box, thus providing a diffuse low-intensity glow that covered a large portion of the visual field and minimized focusing.

Procedure

Relaxation training. The 20 subjects were divided into two groups of 5 males and 5 females each. The subjects in the Jacobson's group received 3 h of relaxation training, as did the subject in the control relaxation group; the latter were told only to listen to white noise played at a low intensity and to relax as best they could.

Biofeedback training. Four 54-min sessions of biofeedback training were employed. Subjects were told that each session investigated a different brainwave, and that recent research indicated that relaxation enhanced control of all brain-waves, thus they should use their prior relaxation training to keep the feedback light on as much as possible. This was deception. In fact, the four sessions operated as follows: Contingent Day 1 (CD1) was the first day of feedback for all subjects. Feedback was contingent on alpha production and this was true also for the fourth day (Contingent Day 4, abbreviated (CD4). Days 2 and 3 were either false increasing (FI) or false decreasing (FD) feedback, counterbalanced across subjects. Under FI, the feedback density started at low level and increased over trials while the reverse was true for the FD condition. To make the illusion of "real" feedback convincing, the amounts delivered on Days 2 and 3 were based on individual subject's Day 1 performance, and were programmed for delivery according to an unpredictable computerized schedule, the only constraint being that feedback increased and decreased over trials for the FI and FD groups, respectively. Thus, the amount of feedback presented to each individual subject was both a familiar and credible amount, referenced to his or her Day 1 performance. The rationale for this particular design was as follows: The first day must be contingent to establish baseline performance, and the last day should also be contingent to assess time-dependent changes in alpha production. The middle 2 days were FI and FD to assess perceived success on mood and also to determine whether feedback contingency was systematically related to alpha production.

Question 4a. Is my method better than the authors'? Their methods are at least as good as ours, if not better.

Question 4b. Does the method actually test the hypotheses? Yes, the methods should test the four hypotheses. One problem that does exist is that all subjects receive contingent feedback on the first day. Although that procedure seems necessary to provide a baseline of alpha production, its effects could carry over throughout the next three days and mask the other manipulations. However, the effects of false feedback on the second two days probably will not carry over because the order of presenting the two conditions was counterbalanced across subjects. Counterbalancing means that some subjects received false increasing feedback about their brain waves on the second day and decreasing feedback on the third day. The rest of the subjects received those conditions in the reverse order.

Question 4c. What are the variables (independent, dependent, subject, control)? Independent variables: type of feedback, type of relaxation training, trials, and days. Dependent variables: amount of alpha, mood. It is not clear how or when mood will be assessed. Subject variables: sex. Control variables: amount of feedback on the false feedback days determined by the subject's alpha level on the first day. Session length was controlled, as were the number of training days.

Question 5. What do I predict? Since previous studies have reported reliable alpha conditioning, we predict that increases in alpha will be observed only on the first and last days (that is, only when the feedback is contingent on alpha production). Furthermore, we expect that alpha will increase with increases in the alpha experience and with perceived success. We expect that the ability to relax will enhance alpha.

Results and Discussion

The .95 confidence level was adopted throughout as indicating the presence of a reliable difference.

The percent alpha produced during all phases of the experiment are displayed in Figure 1. All functions superficially resemble "learning curves," since performance during Trial 4 was generally superior to performance during Trial 1. An ANOVA revealed main effects for trials and rest vs. feedback. The main effect for sessions approached the .05 level and was therefore further analyzed by comparing CD1 alone with CD2, as a test for extreme differences. This analysis also failed to detect reliable sessions differences. No other main effect or interaction approached significance in either ANOVA.

The interpretation of these results is straightforward: The Jacobson's relaxation and control relaxation groups behaved similarly throughout the experiment. Both displayed more alpha as a function of trials and both displayed more alpha during feedback than during

FIGURE 1.

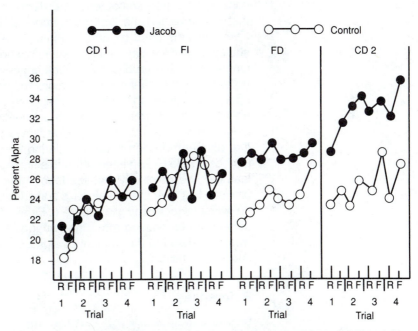

Percent alpha produced by the Jacobson's relaxation group (solid circles) and the control relaxation group (open circles) as a function of sessions and trials. Abbreviations: CD1 and CD2, Contingent Days 1 and 2, respectively; FI and FD, false increasing and false decreasing biofeedback, respectively. R and F, rest and feedback, respectively. The first R period in each session is the mean of the baseline recording period.

rest periods. However, the amount of alpha produced was not affected by whether the feedback was veridical or false, demonstrating that alpha production was not under the control of the experimental contingencies. We also analyzed the data from the viewpoint of net alpha change, for example, alpha produced during each feedback period minus alpha produced during the preceding rest period. This "change score" produced functions (not shown) that varied in a nonsystematic manner and remained close to 0% change. An ANOVA in this case produced no main effects or interactions that approached reliability.

The mood scores (responses on the Mood Adjective Check List, MACL, Nowlis, 1965) were analyzed by ANOVA, Mann-Whitney U, and parametric and nonparametric correlational methods. None of these analyses even hinted at a reliable relationship among the variables of amount of alpha actually produced, subjective report of mood, prior exposure to relaxation training, or perceived success or failure on the control task. Differences attributable to sex of subject were sought in all of the above analyses, but none were found.

We purposely used visual feedback since the early positive reports of alpha conditioning used visual feedback while more recent, negative findings employed nonvisual feedback designs. Also, we designed control groups that we feel eliminated or circumvented the problems inherent in the control groups used by others. Additionally, we used a computerized system for detecting alpha activity that circumvented the "roll off" problems inherent in the "active filter" systems used by others. Finally, we gathered data on our subjects over a 4-day period (plus relaxation pretraining) which is longer than other published experiments. Nonetheless, there was no evidence that changes in alpha production were learned through operant conditioning, since the response (alpha production) was not under the control of reinforcement contingencies (biofeedback being veridical or false). We did replicate Brown's (1971) finding that alpha production is greater during feedback than during rest periods. While Brown interpreted this finding as evidence for alpha learning, we point out that feedback need not be contingent to produce this effect, and if alpha is considered to be change scores, no evidence for learning is apparent. Finally, the "alpha experience" appears to be nothing more than suggestibility; empirically, mood was not related to the amount of alpha produced nor to perceived success or failure.

References

Brolund, J. W., & Schallow, J. R. (1976). The effects of reward on occipital alpha facilitation by biofeedback. *Psychophysiology, 13* 236–241.

Brown, B. B. (1970). Recognition of aspects of consciousness through association with EEG activity represented by a light signal. *Psychophysiology, 6,* 442–452.

Brown, B. B. (1971). Awareness of EEG subjective activity relationships within a closed feedback system. *Psychophysiology, 7,* 451–464.

Brown, B. B. (1974). *New mind, new body.* New York: Harper & Row.

Kamiya, J. (1968). Conscious control of brainwaves. *Psychology today,* **1,** 57–60.

Kamiya, J. (1969). Operant control of the EEG alpha rhythm and some of its reported effects on consciousness. In C. Tart (Ed.), *Altered states of consciousness: A book of readings.* New York: Wiley.

Lynch, J. J., Paskewitz, D. A., & Orne, M. T. (1974). Some factors in the feedback control of human alpha rhythm. *Psychosomatic Medicine,* **36,** 399–410.

Nowlis, V. (1965). Research with the mood adjective check list. In S. S. Tomkins & C. E. Izard (Eds.), *Affect. cognition, and personality.* New York: Springer.

Plotkin, W. B., Mazer, C., & Lowey, D. (1976). Alpha enhancement and the likelihood of an alpha experience. *Psychophysiology,* **13,** 466–471.

(Received for publication November 9, 1977.)

Question 6. Did the author get unexpected results? The only prediction of ours that was correct concerned the positive effect of false increasing feedback on the amount of alpha. However, this is a small victory, since alpha also increased under false decreasing feedback. It looks as if the subjects who received real relaxation training did better on the last day or two than did the control subjects. However, the authors report that there were no interactions between relaxation and sessions. This means that the effects of relaxation training did not differ reliably across sessions. "ANOVA" refers to "analysis of variance," a type of statistical test discussed in appendix B.

Question 7. How would I interpret the results? Subjects might have increased alpha because they wanted to. In other words, the important variable in an alpha conditioning study is not the relation between feedback and alpha production. Rather, subjects may perceive alpha waves as being desirable, and thus may try to have an alpha experience. Since most college students have heard about meditation and brain waves, these subjects may well have tried to relax in order to increase alpha. Furthermore, since these subjects were introductory psychology students, it is likely that they knew quite a bit about alpha waves and the alpha experience.

Question 8. Is my interpretation better than the authors? The authors simply point out that the results are not owing to conditioning (alternative explanations are mentioned in the introduction). They do argue that the alpha experience is caused by suggestibility, which is somewhat similar to our interpretation of the conditioning results.

If you are interested in alpha experiences and alpha conditioning, you will find a review by Plotkin (1979) to be thought provoking. Plotkin suggests that there are no unequivocal demonstrations of alpha conditioning, and he offers eight hypotheses for the development of the alpha experience during laboratory studies of alpha.

Writing a Research Report

You have gotten an idea, reviewed the pertinent literature, designed a procedure, collected your data, and analyzed the results. Your course may require a written record of your research. Even if it does not, you are obligated to publicize the results of a carefully done project. We believe that to maintain the self-correcting nature of science, it is important to publish good data. However, this does not mean that journals should be cluttered with information derived from every undergraduate project. If your research is promising, you will receive encouragement from your instructor.

In this section, we will review the format of a typical report and discuss some of the stylistic considerations that make up a comprehensible paper. If you follow our suggestions for reading articles, you will have a pretty good idea about the format of a research report, and you will probably have a good feel for technical writing style. Some aspects of technical writing are not too obvious, so we will discuss them here. What we present are general guidelines. If you need additional information, examine R. J. Sternberg's book, *The Psychologist's Companion,* and D. J. Bem's (1987) chapter, "Writing the Empirical Journal Article." The 1983 revision of the *Publication Manual of the American Psychological Association* (third edition) will also help, because it is the official arbiter of style for almost all of the journals in psychology and education.

Format

The outline of a typical report in figure 5–2 emphasizes the sequence of pages you will have to put together in your APA-style manuscript. This version of the article is known as the *copy* manuscript and is assembled in a particular manner to facilitate the editorial and publication processes. A run through that sequence will give you an idea of what you are supposed to include. Your cover page contains the title of your project, your name, and your affiliation (your institution or place of business). The short title that appears at the top of each page of the copy manuscript consists of the first few words of the title and is used to identify the manuscript during the editorial process only. The heading that will appear at the top of each page of the *published* article is called the *running head,* and this is typed in capital letters near the bottom of the cover page of the copy manuscript. The short title and running head should not be confused. The next page, page 2, contains the heading "Abstract" and the abstract itself. On this page and on all subsequent ones (except the figures), you should have an abbreviated title and the page number in the top right-hand corner of the page. Page 3 repeats the whole title and includes your introductory material. Ordinarily, you do not have a heading for the introduction. After your introduction is finished, the method section begins. Note the format shown for the headings on page 4 in figure 5–2. The side headings, such as "Subjects" and "Apparatus," help guide the reader to pertinent information. The results section immediately follows the method. Do not include *figures* and *tables*

FIGURE 5–2.

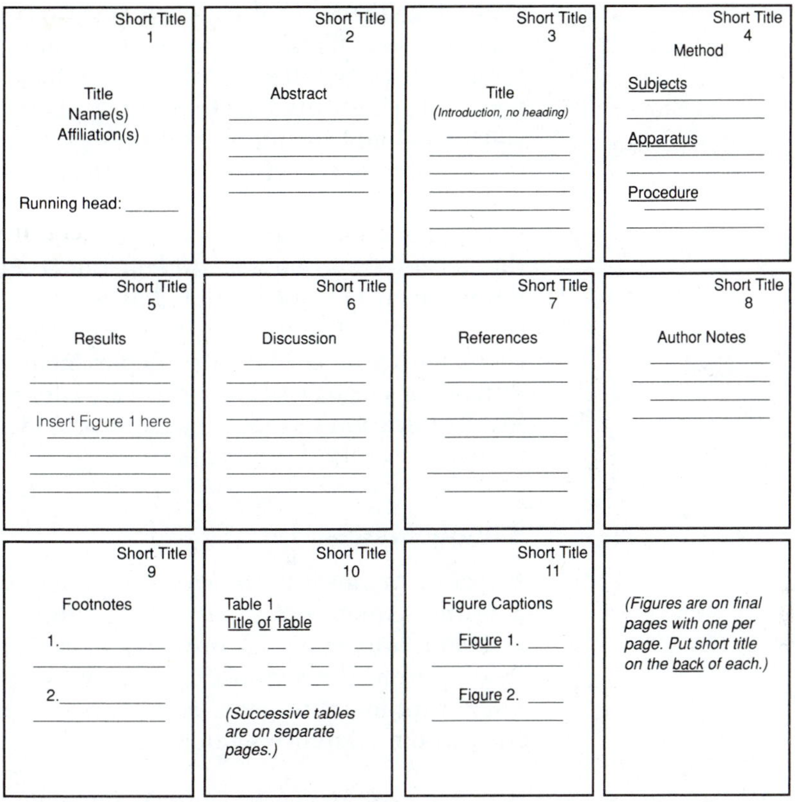

Short Title 1 Title Name(s) Affiliation(s) Running head: _____	Short Title 2 Abstract _____ _____ _____ _____	Short Title 3 Title *(Introduction, no heading)* _____ _____ _____	Short Title 4 Method Subjects _____ Apparatus _____ Procedure
Short Title 5 Results _____ _____ Insert Figure 1 here _____ _____	Short Title 6 Discussion _____ _____ _____ _____ _____	Short Title 7 References _____ _____ _____	Short Title 8 Author Notes _____ _____
Short Title 9 Footnotes 1._____ _____ 2._____ _____	Short Title 10 Table 1 Title of Table __ __ __ __ __ __ __ __ __ __ __ __ *(Successive tables are on separate pages.)*	Short Title 11 Figure Captions Figure 1. ____ _____ Figure 2. ____ _____	*(Figures are on final pages with one per page. Put short title on the back of each.)*

Page sequence for a report in APA format.

in the body of this section (they come at the end of the report). Instead, indicate their approximate location as shown on page 5 of figure 5–2. Next comes the discussion, which ends the major textual portion of your report.

The references begin on a separate page. The format for presenting references is complex, and you should use care in preparing them. The article reprinted in this chapter contains most of the different styles of references that you will have to document. Look them over carefully, and, if you have any questions, ask your instructor. You might also study the APA manual and recent journal articles. Any author notes and footnotes appear on separate pages after the references. For most college laboratory reports, footnotes are not necessary. When you prepare something for publication, you may acknowledge financial and intellectual support, which should appear on the author-note page. General acknowledgments are not numbered. Other, perhaps peripheral, information should appear as numbered footnotes on a separate footnote page, but such footnotes are generally discouraged.

Following the footnotes are your data tables mentioned in the results section. Each table should be on a separate page and numbered consecutively, according to its appearance in the results section. Make the titles of your tables short but communicative. Captions for your figures are numbered consecutively and appear on a separate page following the data tables. Finally, you have your figures, each on a separate piece of paper. Put your name (or the short title) and the number of the figure on the back.

As mentioned before, copy manuscripts are organized in this fashion to accommodate the publisher. However, you should note that there is a special section in the *APA Publication Manual* about the accepted format for student papers submitted for a course requirement but not for publication. For example, in student papers, tables and figures may be interspersed in the text. You should check with your professor or department regarding the preferred format for class projects. However, we recommend learning that APA publication format because it provides good practice for preparing your future publications.

Sample Manuscript

A sample manuscript appears on the following pages. You should note the sequence of pages, where typing begins on a new page, and what information is provided in each section. The only aspect missing from this manuscript that may appear in one of yours is a separate footnote page. Note carefully how the references are cited in the reference section.

The following paper is copyright 1987 by the American Psychological Association. Reprinted by permission of the author and publisher. Comish, S. E. (1987). Recognition of facial stimuli following an intervening task involving the Identi-kit. *Journal of Applied Psychology, 72,* 488–491.

Recognition of Facial Stimuli

1

Recognition of Facial Stimuli Following an Intervening

Task Involving the Identi-kit

Sara Elizabeth Comish

University of Alberta

Running head: RECOGNITION OF FACIAL STIMULI

Abstract

The Identi-kit is a tool for constructing a facial composite. The types of errors made on a recognition task, following an intervening task involving the Identi-kit, were examined in this study. One hundred and eight introductory psychology students viewed a target composite-face and made an Identi-kit reconstruction. Subsequently, they were required to identify the original composite-face from a lineup of six composite-faces. Subjects who made an Identi-kit reconstruction were prone to make more errors on the recognition task than participants in a control condition, p < .01. False alarms were promoted when the subjects saw a lineup containing foils modified to resemble the subjects' own reconstruction errors, p < .05. This finding suggests that memory for facial stimuli can be influenced by viewing misleading information.

Recognition of Facial Stimuli

3

Recognition of Facial Stimuli Following an Intervening Task Involving the Identi-kit

There is a commonly held belief that memory for faces is immune to interference; this belief is expressed by the oft heard statement, "I never forget a face." Support for the role of interference in facial memory, however, can be found in experimental studies. Deffenbacher, Carr, and Leu (1981) found that individual's memory for photographs of faces was highly susceptible to retroactive interference, unlike their memory for nouns and objects, which was relatively immune to the interference. Loftus and Greene (1980) examined the extent to which facial memory was influenced by reading misleading descriptions of a previously shown target face. In a later recognition task with the target face absent, the majority of subjects who had read the misleading information picked a face with the misleading information. This finding raises the issue of whether facial memory can be altered by viewing misleading information.

A useful tool for studying this issue is the Identi-kit, a technique that consists of transparencies of line drawings of different facial features that can be superimposed on each other to make a composite-face. A similar system is the Photofit, which consists of actual photographs of features instead of line drawings. Studies that have used composite techniques to examine interference in memory for faces have yielded conflicting results. Mauldin and Laughery (1981) found that use of the Identi-kit to construct a target face improved recognition of the same target face in a later recognition task. On the other hand, Davies, Ellis, and Shepherd (1978) found different results. They found a trend in the opposite direction, which indicated that making a Photofit reconstruction could interfere with later recognition of a target face (although this difference failed to attain statistical significance). In both of these studies, subjects viewed a target face and then made a composite reconstruction. The recognition tasks that were used to assess memory involved photograph lineups that were not altered to resemble subjects' composite reconstructions.

It is reasonable to assume, however, that the source of any interference from Identi-kit reconstruction may result from viewing one's own errors in Identi-kit reconstruction as a holistic face and that maximum interference can be expected when the distractors used during the recognition task are similar to the individual's errors in Identi-kit reconstruction. The purpose of this study was to determine the effect of an intervening task involving misleading information on later recognition. In order to test this, subjects in two conditions made Identi-kit reconstructions of a target composite-face. The third condition was a control condition in which subjects did not make an Identi-

kit reconstruction. For the subsequent recognition task, subjects
saw a lineup consisting of the original target composite-face and
five foils. The subjects were yoked on the recognition task to
allow for the determination of whether interference was a result
of making Identi-kit reconstructions per se or if it occurred only
when the distractor foils resembled the participants' own Identi-
kit reconstruction errors.

Method

<u>Subjects</u>

One hundred and eight introductory psychology students
participated in partial fulfillment of a course requirement.
Thirty-six subjects were randomly assigned to each of the three
conditions.

<u>Materials</u>

The Identi-kit, available from Smith and Wesson, Inc., is a
box containing transparencies of facial features. It is
accompanied by the Identi-kit Handbook, which is a pictorial index
of the features available in the kit.

<u>Design</u> <u>and</u> <u>Procedure</u>

A three-group design was employed. In the Identi-kit/own-
errors condition, subjects made an Identi-kit reconstruction of a
target composite-face and, in a later recognition task,
encountered foils modified to resemble the subjects' own Identi-

kit reconstruction errors. Subjects in the Identi-kit/other-errors conditions also made an Identi-kit reconstruction but were yoked to a subject in the Identi-kit/own-errors condition so that the foils in the recognition task were those of a subject in the Identi-kit/own-errors condition. In the control/other-errors condition, subjects saw the target composite-face but did not make an Identi-kit reconstruction. They were also yoked so that the foils in the recognition task were those of a subject in the Identi-kit/own-errors condition.

Initially, all subjects viewed one of two target composite-faces -- photocopies of an Identi-kit reconstruction of either a man or a woman -- for 10 s until it was removed. Subjects in the Identi-kit/own-errors condition and the Identi-kit/other-errors condition then made an Identi-kit reconstruction that involved an initial choice of facial features from the Identi-kit Handbook. A composite face was made using these features and shown to the subjects, who were allowed to change any of the features. On average, the reconstruction process took 13 min. Following this, subjects performed a filler task in which they were given 7 min to rate two photograph faces on trait dimensions. In order to ensure that the time that elapsed between the initial exposure to the target composition-face and the recognition task was the same for subjects in all conditions, the subjects in the control/other-errors condition spent 20 min rating the two photograph faces.

Finally, the subjects performed the recognition task, in which they were asked to select the original composite-face from a lineup consisting of the original target composite-face and five distractors. This task was not a forced choice and subjects were allowed to indicate that the target composite-face was not present in the lineup. In the Identi-kit/own-errors condition, each distractor foil was the same as the original target composite-face except that one error from the individual's Identi-kit reconstruction was substituted for one feature of each distractor. Thus, the first distractor was the same as the target except for the hair, the second distractor was the same as the target except for the nose, the third differed on the lips, the fourth differed on the eyes, and the fifth differed on the eyebrows (see Figure 1 for an example of a typical lineup). These distractor foils were photocopied and placed in a lineup, counterbalanced to vary the order of the target and the foils. Using this technique the target appeared in each position six times in each condition, with the positions of the foils randomly determined. Subjects in the Identi-kit/other-errors condition and control/other-errors condition saw the same lineup in the recognition task as the subject in the Identi-kit/own errors condition to whom they were yoked.

\-

Insert Figure 1 about here

\-

The data from an additional four participants in the Identi-kit/own-errors condition and from an additional three subjects in the Identi-kit yoked condition were not included in the analyses because one or more features in the Identi-kit reconstruction was identical to the original target composite-face. When the correct feature was selected for the Identi-kit reconstruction, it was not possible to modify the lineup distractor foils in the manner described previously. These subjects were replaced.

The dependent variable was scored as a <u>hit</u>, a <u>miss</u>, or a <u>false alarm</u>. A hit was a correct recognition of the original target composite-face; a miss was an incorrect "not present" decision; and a false alarm was an incorrect selection of a distractor foil. In addition, subjects' satisfaction with their reconstruction and the subjects' certainty with regard to their recognition were obtained on scales from <u>not at all satisfied</u> (1) to <u>totally satisfied</u> (7) and from <u>not at all certain</u> (1) to <u>totally certain</u> (7), respectively.

Results

All data were collapsed over the two target composite-faces and converted to percentages, which are presented by condition in Table 1. A one-way analysis of variance (ANOVA) across the three

Recognition of Facial Stimuli

9

conditions was performed on the number of overall errors. A significant difference was found for the overall number of recognition errors, $F(2, 105) = 4.86$, $p < .01$. A Newman-Keuls comparison revealed that the control/other-errors condition produced significantly fewer errors than either of the Identi-kit reconstruction conditions. The estimated ω^2 was .065.

Insert Table 1 about here

A further one-way ANOVA was performed on the number of false alarms. A significant difference was found among the conditions, $F(2, 105) = 4.46$, $p < .05$. A Newman-Keuls comparison revealed that the Identi-kit/own-errors condition differed significantly from the other two conditions, demonstrating that when the foils resembled subjects' Identi-kit errors, subjects were more prone to incorrectly identify the modified foils. In this case, the estimated ω^2 was .059.

Although an ANOVA on the number of overall errors and on both of the types of errors is redundant -- because the two types of errors sum to give the number of overall errors -- the effect of Identi-kit use on the different types of errors is of particular interest in this study. Therefore, an additional ANOVA was performed on the number of "not present" responses (misses). There was a significant different among the conditions, $F(2, 105)$

= 3.75, $\underline{p}$ < .05, and the Newman-Keuls comparison revealed that the subjects in the Identi-kit/other errors condition made significantly more "not present" responses than subjects in either the Identi-kit/own-errors condition or the control/other-errors condition. The estimated ω^2 was .047.

An ANOVA was performed on subjects' confidence ratings, and there were no significant differences among the conditions, $\underline{F}$(2, 105) = 1.46, ns. Wells and Lindsay (1985) have suggested that confidence ratings of "choosers only" (i.e., those subjects that make a recognition choice rather than those that indicate that the target composite-face was not present) should be analyzed separately to determine whether confidence ratings have predictive use. No significant differences were found among the conditions when a one-way ANOVA was performed on the confidence ratings of "choosers only," $\underline{F}$(2, 89) = 0.422, ns. The low accuracy-confidence correlation, however, is consistent with previous eyewitness studies (see Wells & Murray, 1984).

A point-biserial correlation between confidence and accuracy was performed for "choosers only" by condition and was not significant, highest $\underline{r}$ = -.221. Further, it was not significant when performed on the data of all subjects, highest $\underline{r}$ = -.24. A point-biserial correlation between subjects' satisfaction with their Identi-kit reconstruction and accuracy of recognition was also not significant for all subjects ratings nor was it

Recognition of Facial Stimuli

11

significant when the analysis was performed on "choosers only,"
highest r = -.27.

Discussion

The use of the Identi-kit itself promotes overall errors on
the recognition task. The lineup foils in this study were
modified by only one feature to resemble the Identi-kit
reconstructions. This was sufficient, however, to bias people in
favor of foils that resembled their own Identi-kit
reconstructions. When the lineup foils resemble people's own
Identi-kit reconstructions, the errors that are promoted are false
alarms to composite-faces that resemble their Identi-kit
reconstructions. Errors are promoted even when the composite-
faces in the lineup are not similar to the subject's original
Identi-kit reconstruction. In these cases, the predominant errors
are misses, that is, failures to correctly identify the original
target composite-face by saying that it is not present.
Therefore, it appears that people who make an Identi-kit
reconstruction are biased away from the original target composite-
face.

The findings in this study appear to conflict with the
results obtained by Davies et al. (1978) and Maudlin and Laughery
(1981). The differences between the present study and the
experiments of Davies et al. and Mauldin and Laughery are,

however, numerous. Their null results, for example, may be due to

a failure to allow the subject to make a "not present" response.

Alternatively, the high similarity between distractors and target

achieved in the present study, compared with the others, might

account for the different results. Most important, no study prior

to this has used Identi-kit reconstruction errors to build

distractor composite-faces in which the target is embedded. This

contingency between Identi-kit reconstructions and the recognition

task in the Identi-kit/own-errors condition allowed for an optimal

test of the potential interference effects of the Identi-kit task

on subsequent recognition.

What is the source of the recognition errors? It is possible

that the Identi-kit task creates interference because it involves

viewing the misleading errors incorporated into a complete face.

A person making a recognition decision may be easily confused

between the original memory and the memory of the Identi-kit

reconstruction. This is particularly likely to occur when a

composite-face similar to a person's own Identi-kit reconstruction

is present in the lineup.

The distribution of facial features in the foils that

subjects had falsely identified was also examined. In general,

people seem to make more recognition errors when features of less

importance, such as eyebrows and lips, were altered. This is

consistent with previous studies (see Ellis, 1984, for a review).

Recognition of Facial Stimuli

13

Recognition errors involving the more important features, hair and eyes, were primarily made only when the altered features resembled the Identi-kit reconstruction. This suggests that more confusions occur for less important features and for important features that resemble Identi-kit reconstructions.

Although the Identi-kit task was shown to interfere with recognition in this study, there are a number of caveats to consider in generalizing these findings to police lineups. First, it is not known how representative Identi-kit composite-faces are of photographs of real individuals, let alone the extent to which Identi-kit encoding operations compare with the encoding of live faces. Thus, performance on an Identi-kit lineup task may not be indicative of performance on a real lineup task. Second, the lineups used in this experiment consisted of highly similar composite-faces, faces much more similar than a typical police lineup. In the first condition, the foils were altered so that one feature was precisely the same as the subjects' Identi-kit reconstruction--an occurrence that is highly unlikely in a typical police lineup. Third, the target stimuli in this study were limited to only two Identi-kit composites that may not be representative of other faces. Fourth, the reconstructions from which the lineups were created shared no features with the target composite. Finally, the subjects in this study may have had poorer memories for the target than aroused witnesses to a crime

and thus made poorer reconstructions. For these reasons, it is
necessary to be cautious in extrapolating from these results to
police lineups.

Recognition of Facial Stimuli

15

References

Davies, G. M., Ellis, H. D., & Shepherd, J. W. (1978). Face

identification: The influence of delay upon accuracy of

Photofit construction. Journal of Police Science and

Administration, 6, 35-42.

Deffenbacher, K. A., Carr, T. H., & Leu, J. R. (1981). Memory for

words, pictures and faces: Retroactive interference,

forgetting and reminiscence. Journal of Experimental

Psychology: Human Learning and Memory, 7, 299-305.

Ellis, H. D. (1984). Practical aspects of face memory. In G. L.

Wells & E. F. Loftus (Eds.), Eyewitness testimony:

Psychological perspectives (pp. 12-37). New York: Cambridge

University Press.

Loftus, E., & Greene, E. (1980). Warning: Even memory for faces

may be contagious. Law and Human Behavior, 4, 323-334.

Mauldin, M., & Laughery, K. (1981). Composite production effects

on subsequent facial identification. Journal of Applied

Psychology, 66, 351-357.

Wells, G. L., & Lindsay, R. C. L. (1985). Methodological notes on

the accuracy-confidence relation in eyewitness identifications.

Journal of Applied Psychology, 70, 413-419.

Recognition of Facial Stimuli

16

Wells, G. L., & Murray, D. M. (1984). Eyewitness confidence. In

G. L. Wells & E. F. Loftus (Eds.), <u>Eyewitness testimony:</u>

<u>Psychological perspectives</u> (pp. 155-170). New York: Cambridge

University Press.

Recognition of Facial Stimuli

17

Author Notes

Portions of this article were presented at the meeting of the Canadian Psychological Association held in Toronto, Canada, June 1986.

I am indebted to Gary Wells for the thoughtful help and guidance he provided during the course of this research. In addition, I am grateful to John Pullyblank, John Turtle, and Brendan Rule for their comments on an earlier version of this article; to Constable Bates of the Royal Canadian Mounted Police for his time and comments; and to two anonymous reviewers for their extremely helpful and meticulous comments.

Correspondence concerning this article should be addressed to Sara Elizabeth Comish, who is now at the Department of Psychology, University of Victoria, P. O. Box 1700, Victoria, British Columbia, Canada, V8W 2Y2.

Table 1

Performance on the Recognition Task: Data Converted Into

Percentages by Condition

| | Condition | | |
Performance	Identi-kit (own errors)	Identi-kit (yoked)	Control (yoked)
Total errors	86.11_a	77.78_a	56.56_b
Misses	8.33_a	27.78_b	8.33_a
False alarms	77.78_a	50.00_b	47.22_b
Correct (hits)	13.89	22.22	44.44

Note. Percentages that do not share a common subscript differ at $p < .05$.

Recognition of Facial Stimuli

19

Figure Caption

<u>Figure</u> 1.   The original target face, a typical Identi-kit

reconstruction, and the subsequent lineup.   (Foils are identical

to the original target face, except for the indicated facial

feature obtained from the reconstruction.)

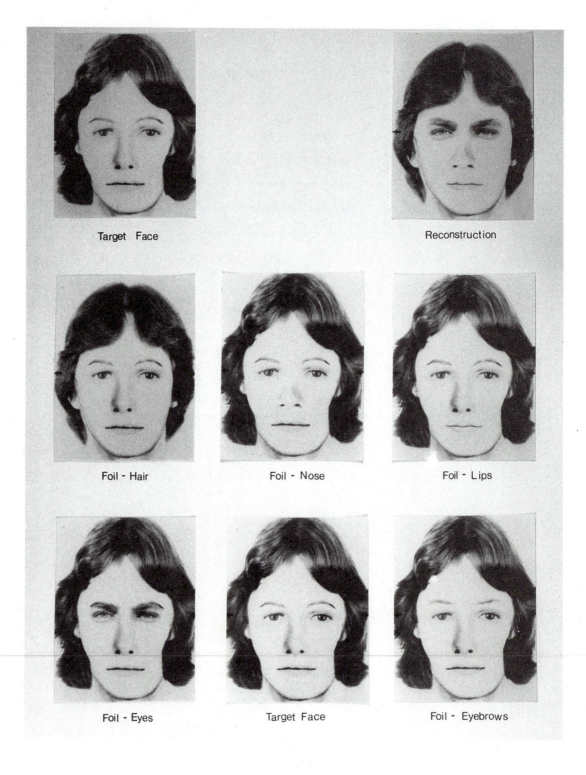

Target Face

Reconstruction

Foil - Hair

Foil - Nose

Foil - Lips

Foil - Eyes

Target Face

Foil - Eyebrows

Style

Now that you have some idea of format, let us consider style. After you have suffered through some obscurely written article, you will no doubt recognize the advantage of clear, unambiguous writing. The *APA format* helps standardize the order and general content. However, making sure that the reader understands what you are saying is up to you. We have read many research reports prepared for our classes—some good, some awful, most of them in between—and we have found that the biggest problem is transition, or flow, from one section to the next. Deliberately or not, many students write as if they were composing a surprise-ending short story, even though their report should be as straightforward as possible.

Your abstract should include your variables (independent, dependent, and important control variables), number and type of subjects, major results, and important conclusions. The body of your report should expand on the abstract. (This is why most abstracts are written last, even though the report might be clearer if it were written first, as an outline for the main part of the work.) You should remember the following: In the introduction, state why you are interested in particular variables and what other investigators have found; in the method section, state how you examined those variables; in the results section, state what happened when you examined the variables; and in your discussion, state what the effects of the variables mean. Thus, the body of your report should represent a tight package, not a disjointed essay containing sections that seem independent of each other. You have to tell your readers what you were trying to do, over and over again. Do not be afraid to be somewhat redundant by having each section build on the previous one. If you repeat the purpose of the your research often enough, even the dullest reader will have gotten something from your report by the time he or she gets to the reference list. Table 5–2 summarizes the information that should be included in each section of your report.

The APA publication manual outlines style considerations as follows: Use the precise word, avoid ambiguity, order presentation of ideas, and consider the reader. These guidelines warrant some discussion.

Scientific writing demands clarity, so each word has to be chosen carefully. Consider these sentences that regularly appear in undergraduate research reports: "I ran the subjects individually." "The white albino rat was introduced to the Skinner box." Actually, none of the subjects in the study from which the first sentence was pulled did any running during the course of the project. What the author meant to say was, "I tested the subjects individually." From reading about rats introduced to Skinner boxes, you might conclude that the researcher had very clever rats. The rat did not shake hands with a box; all that happened was that the rat was put into the operant-conditioning chambers. Furthermore, "white albino" is redundant. All albino rats are white. The lesson here is that in

TABLE 5–2.   A summary of the information in each section of a research report.

Section	Information
Title	Experiments: State independent and dependent variables— "The effects of X on Y." Other studies: State the relationships examined— "The relation between X and Y."
Abstract	In less than 150 words, state what was done to whom and summarize the most important results.
Introduction	State what you plan to do and why (you may have to review results from related research). Predicted results may be appropriate.
Method	Present enough information to allow someone else to repeat your study exactly the way you did it. For clarity use subheadings (*Subjects, Apparatus*, etc.), and make sure that dependent, independent, subject, and control variables are specified.
Results	Summarize important results in tables or figures. Direct the reader to data that seem most relevant to the purpose of the research.
Discussion	State how the results relate to the hypotheses or predictions stated in the introduction. Inferences and theoretical statements are appropriate.
References	In APA format, list only those references that were cited in your report.

scientific writing you must be careful to choose the correct word or phrase and avoid ambiguity. Also, be cautious when using pronouns such as *which, this, that, these,* and *those.* Many students find it irresistible to begin a paragraph with one of these pronouns, and more often than not the referent for the pronoun is not very easy to determine. You can usually avoid any ambiguity by including the referent of the pronoun each time it is used.

After you have decided on your words and phrases, put them together carefully. A common problem among some writers is to shift verb tenses abruptly. In general, use the past tense in the review of other studies in your introduction (Smith *found*) and in your method (the subjects *were*). When you are describing and discussing your data, the present tense is usually appropriate (The data *show* that . . ., which *means* that).

Make sure that collective and plural nouns agree with their verbs and pronouns. Plural words that end in *a* are troublesome, such as *data, criteria,* and *phenomena.* Each of these nouns is plural, so they require plural verbs and pronouns. "These data *are*" is correct, but "this phenomena *is*" is not correct. The singular forms for these nouns are: *datum, criterion,* and *phenomenon* (this phenomenon *is*).

Many scientific writers overuse the passive voice in their reports. Consider this statement: "It is thought that forgetting is caused by interference." Although this sentence is fairly concise (and it is precise), it is also stuffy and less direct than "We think that interference causes forgetting," which is really what was meant. Be careful about using either the active or passive voice too much.

If you overuse the passive voice, your report sounds stuffy. If you overuse the active voice, you may take interest away from what you did and place too much emphasis on yourself (I think, I did, and so on). If you want to emphasize what was done and not who did it and why, use the passive construction. On the other hand, if you think that the agent of the activity is also important, or if the reason for the action is important, use the active voice.

The careful writer tries to avoid language that is sexist. The APA recommends that the use of *he* (and *his* and *him*) as a generic pronoun be avoided by changing to a plural construction or by using *he and she*. Generally, the writer should strive for accurate, unbiased communication.

Writing a cogent, well-organized research article is a skill that requires considerable effort and practice. More is involved than simply allocating information to the correct sections. There are many fine points of style, usage, and exposition that distinguish lucid, well-written articles from obscure and tortuous ones. While writing your report, you should make frequent use of standard references for points of style and grammar. In addition, consult the *APA Publication Manual* regarding aspects of technical writing that are particularly relevant to psychology journal articles, including the organization and content of each section, economy and precision in the expression of ideas, the presentation of data and statistics, and so forth. Finally, we highly recommend the aforementioned book by Sternberg (1987) and the chapter by Bem (1987) for excellent advice and specific examples of good and poor style, phrasing, and organization in psychology articles.

Publishing an Article

Assume that your article has been written, proofread, corrected, and the last page has just emerged from a steaming typewriter. Now what? Although it is unlikely that your first student effort will produce an article of professional quality, you may nevertheless find it interesting to discover what happens when an article is submitted to a journal by a professional psychologist.

The first step is to send copies of the manuscript (the technical term for an unpublished work) to a small number of trusted associates who can check it over to make sure that it has no obvious or elementary flaws and that it is written clearly. Once the comments come back, the indicated corrections are made and, with some trepidation, the author commits the manuscript to the mail, addressed to the editor of the most appropriate journal. After this, it is necessary to forget about it entirely for the next few months or otherwise exhibit great patience. The review process is slow. (The editor who receives the manuscript is a harried, overworked, tired individual who often regrets accepting the editorship. Editors of journals, like elected politicians, serve a fixed term of office, usually four to six years.) About two or three weeks after submitting the article, the author receives a form letter that thanks him or her for interest in the journal and acknowledges receipt of the manuscript. The manuscript gets a number (such as 91–145) and if an associate editor has been assigned to handle it, the author is instructed to direct all future correspondence to that editor.

The editor then sends copies of the manuscript to two or three reviewers. Some journals allow the author to have anonymous (or blind) reviewing, where the author conceals his or her identity. Anonymous reviewing is for those who do not believe in the impartiality of reviewers. The reviewer, who may also review for several other journals, puts the manuscript in the pile on his or her desk. A conscientious reviewer may take up to a day or two to carefully read and evaluate a manuscript. When each reviewer gets around to it, a summary statement is sent to the editor. When the reviewers are in agreement, the editor's decision is easy. Should the reviewers disagree, the editor must carefully read the manuscript and sometimes may request a third opinion. Finally, an editorial decision is reached and the author receives a letter stating either (1) why the manuscript cannot be published, (2) what kind of revisions are needed to make the manuscript acceptable, or (3) that the journal will publish the article. Since rejection rates for manuscripts are quite high in most journals (above 70 percent), editors spend a great deal of time devising tactful letters of rejection.

Whether or not the article was accepted, the comments of the reviewers are most valuable. The best psychologists in the area have provided, free of charge, their careful opinions about the research. Of course, reviewers can also make mistakes. Any author who disagrees with a review has the privilege, even the responsibility, of writing to the editor. Although this action will usually not result in the article being accepted, it is important that rejected authors have the right to appeal or protest. Anyway, there are always other journals.

If the article was accepted for publication, the author is still not yet finished. Some revision of the manuscript may be required. The copyright for the article is signed over to the publisher. Some months later, the author receives galley or page proofs from the publisher. These must be carefully checked to ensure that the words and tables set in type by the printer match those in the original manuscript. After making corrections (and the author is charged for excessive changes that do not result from the printer's errors), the author returns the article to the publisher. Several months later, the article finally appears in the journal. The entire process, from submission of the manuscript until final publication, takes a year or more. Authors do not get paid for articles in journals, but on the other hand, neither do they get charged for the privilege of appearing in print.

As you might expect, it is a great thrill to see your name in print, especially the first time. An even greater thrill, however, is the knowledge that you may have added some small amount to our understanding of why people and animals think and act as they do.

SUMMARY

When you read a research report, you should read actively and critically, so that you can derive maximum benefit from other people's research. The checklist for critical readers is designed to get you into the habit of actively asking questions about the reports you read: What hypotheses are being tested? How are they being tested? Does the method test the hypotheses? Do the results apply to the hypotheses? How does the author relate the results to the purposes of the research? What interpretations and inferences are made by the author? You should also consider these questions when you write your own report. The APA format provides a framework for your report, but it is up to you to write clearly. Several suggestions that help produce a clear unambiguous style of report writing are provided. The chapter concludes with a brief description of the publication process. For psychological science to progress, reports must be published, and knowledgeable consumers must read them critically.

KEY TERMS

abstract
APA format
apparatus
author
checklist for critical readers
discussion
figures
introduction

method
procedure
references
results
running head
subjects
tables
title

PART TWO

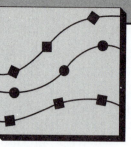

Principles and Practices of Experimental Psychology

*I*N EACH CHAPTER OF PART two, we will discuss two or three topics that are important in psychological research. The discussion does not pretend to supply a comprehensive survey of each research area, but is intended to illustrate the topics in a concrete way. Of course, the various topics have application beyond the particular content areas chosen to illustrate them. We will bring methodology—the special techniques employed to make data useful and appropriate—into play only to solve problems related to specific content areas. Both the principles and the topics, as well as the specific content areas used to illustrate them, will be listed at the head of each chapter. You can also locate specific topics by looking them up in the table of contents, which shows which chapters discuss each topic. Very important topics are covered in more than one chapter.

The introduction to each chapter will tell you what these topics are and why they are important in the context of the particular subject discussed in the chapter. You can tell that the introduction has ended when you encounter the first heading. It looks like this:

This Is the First Heading

Headings in this kind of type mark off major sections. This first section is designed to orient you to the chapter contents. In it, we will discuss some general problems that psychologists are trying to understand in this area. In this section, we may talk about some of the people who were important in establishing the area of inquiry. Or, we may use the section to explain how a general issue in science applies to some specific psychological problem area.

Smaller headings are often used within each major section to help you organize the chapter. The next kind of heading you will encounter looks like this:

This Is a Secondary Heading

This kind of heading refers to a more specific topic within the general issue indicated by its preceding major heading. Sometimes this is further divided with a minor heading.

This is a minor heading. It is run into the text, like this. If you find yourself getting lost in the details of a chapter, look back at the preceding headings. Find the minor heading, and then see how it relates to the headings above it. If you are not sure about this relation, back up to the next highest heading and reread from there. No good explorer continues into the unknown without a landmark, and you should not either. The three different kinds of headings have been carefully constructed to guide you through the chapter. Use them to keep on the right path.

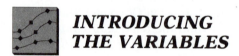

INTRODUCING THE VARIABLES

Next you will find a section set in a box like this. This section introduces you to some of the independent, dependent, and control variables you will find in the chapter. It is not an exhaustive list of all the variables you would read about if you ventured into the depths of psychology journals. Instead, it illustrates a few key variables that are important in the context of the chapter.

Independent, dependent, and control variables are the most important components of psychological research. Without them, there would be no research. The independent variable is the variable manipulated by the experimenter. The dependent variable is the variable observed or recorded by the experimenter. The control variable is a potential independent variable that is not varied in some particular experiment. Instead, it is held at a constant value or level. If these crucial concepts are not entirely clear to you, go back to chapter 3, where several examples can be found.

Later on in the chapters, you will discover summaries of actual experiments. Make sure you know the independent, dependent, and control variables used in these studies.

0.0 Experimental Topics and Research Illustrations

Topic:
Illustration:

This section is the meat of the chapter. Principles that guide psychological research will first be defined and discussed. Then, specific studies will be used to illustrate how these principles have been used (or not used, as the case may be) to insure sound research.

The first experimental topic discussed in each chapter will be illustrated by two or more studies. You should try to compare these studies to see not only how they differ but also what they have in common that relates them to the same principle. Then, check your comparison against that given in the chapter. The second topic (and third topic, if included) will most often be illustrated by a single study.

When you design your own research project, take these topics and principles into account. They will help you avoid the most common types of errors in psychological research. The table of contents will help you locate these principles when you need them.

From Problem to Experiment: The Nuts and Bolts

Problem:

This section takes you behind the scenes in research and answers hidden questions. You may be surprised to discover that many answers are quite arbitrary. An experiment with human subjects may be designed to last one hour because it is more convenient for the students who will serve as participants. The number of studied items in a memory experiment might be determined by how many slides fit in a slide-projector tray. Although not every detail will be covered in each experimental design, after reading several "Nuts and Bolts" sections, you should have a good understanding of some hidden factors that are not made explicit in journal reports.

The general format of each "Nuts and Bolts" section is simple. We look at a psychological problem and work out the nuts-and-bolts details to come up with an answer. First, we formulate a hypothesis; then, we design an experiment to test that hypothesis.

Chapter Aids: Summary, Key Terms, and Discussion Questions

The summary, list of key terms, and discussion questions allow you to check your understanding of each chapter in part two. The summary is a brief reminder of the highlights of a chapter. It is not a substitute for reading the chapter. The numbered statements are short reviews of important chapter sections. If you do not understand one of them, go back and reread that part of the chapter. You can also review the chapter by looking over the headings listed at the beginning of each chapter.

The list of key terms is another form of review. You probably will not be able to define all the key terms after just one reading of the chapter. Go back and find the key terms you have missed. An even better way to review is to write down your own definition for each key term. Then, go back and check your definition against the text.

The discussion questions give you one more way to check your understanding. Questions range from very specific mathematical calculations with only one correct answer to broad (and even far-out) topics relating philosophy to experimental design. There is no unique correct answer to these broad questions; they are included to promote discussion and thought (not in that order, we hope). Even if your instructor does not go over these in class, you should spend some time thinking about possible answers. The wide range of questions is intended to demonstrate that experimental psychologists encourage (or at least tolerate) many different viewpoints. There is no single approach to experimental psychology that has a monopoly on truth.

CHAPTER

6

Psychophysics

Observation is a passive science, experimentation an active science.
—CLAUDE BERNARD

S UPPOSE YOU WANTED TO DETERMINE whether aspirin alleviated pain. How would you try to do it? You would need to do an experiment; in this experiment, you would measure pain reactions with and without the ingestion of aspirin. This general outline seems straightforward and is the standard way that the effects of analgesics (substances that may reduce pain, such as aspirin) have been tested.

In a large number of experiments, Hardy, Wolff, and Goodell (1952) examined people's reactions to radiant heat presented to their forearms by a piece of equipment similar to a hair dryer, called a *dolorimeter*. A small spot of stimulation was presented at various intensities (usually defined in terms of calories per unit area stimulated, rather than in terms of a temperature scale). The researchers' approach was to determine the intensity of heat necessary for a person to report pain—first without an analgesic such as aspirin, and then when aspirin had been taken prior to the presentation of heat. An increase in the intensity needed to elicit pain after the subjects had taken aspirin would indicate that aspirin had analgesic properties. Indeed, this is what Hardy and associates found. Or, at least, that is what they observed when they used highly experienced subjects (themselves) in the experiment. Much to their surprise, when they tested naive subjects (80 military recruits, in this case), they found that for more than half of their subjects, the heat intensity required to evoke pain actually went *down* following the ingestion of aspirin.

Measuring Sensations

This unexpected result is owing to several factors, some of which will be addressed in this chapter. We will examine these issues in the context of a venerable area of investigation in scientific psychology called *psychophysics*. Psychophysics involves the determination of the psychological reaction to events that lie along a physical dimension. Edwin G. Boring (1950), the eminent historian of experimental psychology, claims that the introduction of techniques to measure the relation between internal impressions (the "psycho" of psychophysics) and the external world (the "physics") marked the onset of scientific psychology.

Boring marked psychophysics as the beginning of scientific psychology primarily because the scientists using psychophysical techniques were able to formulate the first mathematical laws of psychological phenomena. Although the characteristics of these laws are of interest in and of themselves, their development has other important implications. First, measuring sensations is very difficult, because they are not open to public measurement as is light intensity or the weight of a stone. Second, the internal judgments are not identical to the amount of physical energy influencing the sensory apparatus. We will examine each of these legacies of psychophysics now and expand on them throughout this chapter.

Gustav Fechner, shown in figure 6–1, formalized the *psychophysical methods*, which measure attributes of the world in terms of their psychological values (1860, republished, 1966). His methods, which are detailed later in the chapter, showed that psychological judgments varied in particular ways according to the intensity of the stimulus and according to the particular sensory modality of the stimulus (that is, judgments of visual stimuli differed from judgments of auditory stimuli, which differed from

FIGURE 6–1.

Gustav Fechner (1801–1887), the father of psychophysics.

judgments of taste stimuli, and so on). Since these relations held, at least approximately, for many different people, Fechner and other researchers concluded that private, internal judgments had been measured accurately. Just as physicists could measure light intensity, auditory intensity, and weight, so too could psychophysicists measure the corresponding psychological attributes of brightness, loudness, and heaviness.

In the 1800s, the psychophysical methods were used to measure seemingly simple sensations such as brightness, pitch, and so on. At first, this might seem to be an unnecessary enterprise. You may think it is easy to decide how loud a sound is or how painful a stimulus feels. However, it turns out that there is rarely a direct one-to-one relation between physical values and psychological values. If a rock band turned up its amplifiers to produce twice as much energy as it had produced before (a doubling of the physical units), this twofold increase of energy would not result in listeners experiencing a sound twice as loud as before. For a listener to judge the sound to be twice as loud, the energy level would have to be increased roughly ten times. Such discoveries derived from the psychophysical methods have important practical applications. For example, the amplifier or radio dial that you turn to increase volume (that is, the perceived loudness) cannot bear a one-to-one relation between movements of the dial and increases in energy. Rather, the dial has to be calibrated so that its movements increase intensity proportional to increments in loudness. Thus, doubling the volume level on the dial has to increase physical energy about ten times to produce a twofold increase in loudness. Telephones are also designed so that their microphones and amplifiers work in accord with this psychophysical relation between auditory intensity and perceived loudness.

The psychophysical relation between stimulus and judgment depends on the particular sensory modality that is stimulated. Pain judgments in response to increases in electrical intensity of shocks applied to the skin grow much more rapidly than do loudness judgments in response to increases in sound energy. For one shock to be judged twice as painful as another, the intensity of the shock needs to have been increased by about one-third. We can see, then, that merely measuring changes in physical units does not always help us accurately determine changes in psychological units.

In this chapter, psychophysical methods are used to illustrate three scientific topics. *Operational definitions* describe the procedures used to produce a concept and allow us to communicate successfully about the concepts we are studying. What does it mean when a subject reports that he or she detects a painful stimulus? An operational definition of detection and one of pain will help to ensure that scientists use technical terms in similar ways.

A related issue has to do with *measurement scales:* the assignment of numbers or names to objects and their attributes. How do we determine whether one light intensity appears twice as bright as another? Not all psychophysical techniques permit accurate statements about the ratio of one sensation to another.

Finally, we shall discuss *small-n designs,* or those based on small numbers of subjects. In this context, we explain why it is often appropriate to formulate psychophysical laws that are based on large numbers of observations, but that are taken from a small number of observers (the small *n*). This technique differs from that often used in psychology experiments, in which large numbers of subjects are used, but few observations are taken on each person.

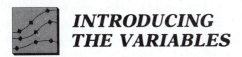

INTRODUCING THE VARIABLES

Dependent Variables

Observers in psychophysical studies are asked to make one of two kinds of judgment about stimuli that have been presented. If only one stimulus has been presented on a particular trial, an absolute judgment is required. Absolute judgments can be simple statements about the presence or absence of a signal (Yes, I saw it, or No, I did not) or direct estimates about some property of the stimulus (How many grams does this weigh?). If two stimuli must be compared on a particular trial, a relative judgment is required. Again, simple statements, such as "Stimulus *A* is a larger than (or smaller than) stimulus *B*," can be made; or direct estimates, such as "Stimulus *A* is twice as large as stimulus *B*," can be given.

Independent Variables

The major independent variables manipulated in psychophysical studies are the magnitude and the quality of stimuli. Changing the intensity—the physical correlate of loudness—of a tone would be a manipulation of stimulus magnitude, as would be changing the weight of an object or the concentration of an odor. The frequency—the physical correlate of pitch—of a tone would be manipulated to produce a qualitative change in the stimulus. Other qualitative judgments could require that observers compare various foods (spinach versus turnips) or the styles of different singers (Madonna versus Tammy Wynette).

Control Variables

The main thing to be controlled in a psychophysical experiment is the observer's willingness to make a particular response. This attitude must remain constant from trial to trial. An observer who is very willing to make a positive judgment (Yes, I saw it) should maintain this same willingness over the course of an experiment. If the criteria for making a response vary, then an inaccurate picture of sensitivities is obtained. Classical or traditional psychophysics assumed that observers could accomplish this constancy without too much difficulty. Once an observer was trained, attitude was supposedly controlled. Modern psychophysical theories, such as the theory of signal detection (to be discussed later), do not accept this assumption. They assume that the observer makes a response based on a decision that depends both on the stimulus and on the psychological factors involved, such as the relative costs and benefits of the decision. So, as will be detailed later, modern psychophysical methods incorporate special techniques to guarantee (or at least to test) the assumption that the observer maintains a constant strategy.

6.1 Experimental Topics and Research Illustrations

Topic: Operational Definition
Illustration: Thresholds

No serious discussion, scientific or otherwise, can progress very far unless the participants agree to define the terms they are using. Imagine that you and your date are having a friendly argument about who is the best athlete of the year. How do you define "athlete"? You both might agree about such common sports as tennis, swimming, and gymnastics. But what about more esoteric sports, such as frisbee throwing, hang gliding, and hopping cross-country on a pogo stick? Should practitioners of these activities be considered for your athlete-of-the-year award? Until this question of definition is answered, your discussion may just go around in circles.

Similar problems can arise in scientific discussions. One way to describe the unusual analgesia results reported by Hardy and associates is that untrained observers become more sensitive to pain after taking aspirin. For ordinary conversation, this might be a perfectly adequate way to make sense of the situation. However, *common* usage and *technical* usage have different requirements: in technical discourse, precision is necessary, so that needless arguments over the meaning of scientific results do not occur. Technically, a change in sensitivity would imply that the body's pain receptors became more acute after taking aspirin. This unlikely possibility would have important implications for drug companies, doctors, and headache sufferers.

What the scientist needs to know are the operations used to produce the outcome. Then, the scientist can decide whether the concept so defined is a sensible way to think about the outcome. In this instance, the procedure used by Hardy (described in detail in the next section) was supposed to measure sensitivity; however, his technique did not permit the assessment of an alternative interpretation—namely, that aspirin altered the willingness of the observers to say that a stimulus was painful. We can see that it is crucial to know the procedures and operations scientists use to study the processes they say they are studying. Words and phrases such as "pain," "sensitivity," and "willingness to respond" have broad everyday meanings that must be precisely limited when they are used in a technical, scientific context.

The most common way of providing technical meaning is by way of an *operational definition*. An operational definition is a formula for building a construct in a way that other scientists can duplicate, by specifying the operations used to produce and measure it. "Take the eye of a newt, the leg of a frog, three oyster shells and shake twice" is an operational definition, although it is not entirely clear what is being defined. However, this recipe can be duplicated and so meets the major criterion for an operational definition. You can tell from this example that an operational definition does not have to be entirely sensible, as long as it is clear and can be copied. For instance, we might operationally define a construct called *centigrams* as the product of your height in centimeters and your weight in grams. Since any scientist can easily determine the centigram score, this is a valid operational definition. Of couse, it probably could not be used for any important scientific purpose, but the potential utility of an operational definition is an issue separate from its validity. Typically, however, operationally defined constructs are tied to a theory or body of research literature, so they do make sense and do have some validity.

In the following sections we will discuss the operational definition of a theoretical construct called a *threshold*. First, we will give the common-language meaning of this term; then, we will see how attempts at increasing the precision of definition have led to rather sophisticated methodological techniques to improve the operational definitions of a threshold.

Thresholds: Classical psychophysics. In common language, a threshold is the part of a doorway you step through or over to enter a room. Classical psychophysicists believed that stimuli had to cross such a (hypothetical) barrier to enter the brain or the mind. If a stimulus were strong, it could easily jump over the threshold. A crude analogy that may be helpful is to think of the stimulus as a pole vaulter. The bar corresponds to the threshold. A good jump will put you over the bar (across the threshold), whereas a feeble jump will not. The obvious question, then, is how strong a stimulus is necessary for a signal to cross the threshold. Answering this question was of major concern to classical psychophysicists.

At first, the answer may seem obvious. All we have to do is slowly increase the intensity of a stimulus, such as a tone or a dim light, until the observer responds, "Yes, there it is." Unfortunately, when we try to repeat this process, the point at which an observer suddenly detects the stimulus changes from trial to trial. To deal with this variability, classical psychophysicists developed statistical methods to estimate the best value for the threshold. We will discuss only one of the methods, developed by Fechner, and known as the *method of limits*.

If we performed an experiment using the method of limits to determine the threshold for a tone, results would look like those shown in table 6–1. Each column represents data from one block of trials. The first block starts with a clearly audible tone, to which the observer responds "Yes." The tone intensity is lowered in successive steps until the observer reports "No," thus ending that trial block. The next block of trials starts with an intensity so low that the observer cannot hear the tone and responds "No." On successive trials, the intensity is gradually increased, until the observer reports hearing the tone. This process of alternating trial blocks continues until table 6–1 is complete. Each block is started at a different intensity, to avoid extra cues that might mislead the observer.

TABLE 6-1.   **Using the Method of Limits to Determine an Absolute Threshold**

Stimulus Intensity	Response				
	↓		↓		
200			Yes		
180	Yes		Yes		
160	Yes		Yes		
140	Yes	Yes	Yes		
120	Yes	No	No	Yes	
100	Yes	No		No	
80	No	No		No	
60		No		No	
40		No		↑	
20		No			
		↑			Mean
Threshold	90	130	130	110	115

Note: In the first series of trials, the experimenter starts with a strong stimulus and decreases its intensity until the observer can no longer detect it. The threshold is the mean of the stimulus intensities that yield the first "No" response and the last "Yes" response. In the next series of trials, a weak stimulus is increased in intensity until it is detected. It is customary to start each series at a different stimulus intensity, to make it less likely that the observer's responses will be influenced by the length of a series. Stimuli are in arbitrary units—that is, the intensities ranging from 20 to 200 could represent weight, or anything else that might vary in intensity.

If the observer were a perfect stimulus detector, the point at which responses switched from "Yes" to "No" (or vice versa) would always be the same. This ideal point would be the threshold. Stimuli less intense than this value would never be detected, and stimuli greater than or equal to this ideal threshold would always be detected. Unfortunately, real data from real people do not have this ideal characteristic; instead, they look like the data in table 6-1.

Observers are influenced by their expectations as to when it is time to change their response from "Yes" to "No," or vice versa. For example, if a series requires several "Yes" responses before the threshold is reached, some observers may decide that they are giving too many "Yes" responses and prematurely respond "No." Other observers may be very cautious about changing their responses and so may delay too long. Indeed, the same observer at different times may commit both of these kinds of errors. So the threshold is operationally defined as the mean (average) of the points in each trial block at which the observer switches from "Yes" to "No" (or "No" to "Yes"). This is a statistical definition. A threshold defined this way, based on an observer's ability to detect a signal, is called an *absolute threshold*, since the "Yes"-"No" judgments are not based on a comparison of two stimuli, but are absolute judgments about a single stimulus. Hardy and his colleagues used the method of limits to obtain the absolute threshold for pain, using different intensities of heat as the stimuli, rather than tones.

Since the absolute threshold is a statistical concept, much like the "average taxpayer," it has other statistical properties in addition to the mean. These will now be illustrated by computing a *difference threshold* in table 6–2. Difference thresholds are based on relative judgments, in which a constant unchanging comparison stimulus is judged relative to a series of changing stimuli. The question being asked by the experimenter is this: "How different must two stimuli be before they can reliably be distinguished?"

The traditional example of a difference threshold requires the observer to lift pairs of weights—one weight always remaining the same—and to judge if the new weight is heavier, lighter, or equal to the standard weight. Several series of ascending and descending trials are given. The upper threshold is the average point at which the observer changes from "Heavier" responses to "Equal" responses. The lower threshold is the point at which "Equal" responses give way to "Lighter" responses. The difference between these two values is called the *interval of uncertainty*. The difference threshold is operationally defined as half the interval of uncertainty. In table 6–2, this equals 10 grams. The mean of upper and lower thresholds is called the *point of subjective equality* (300 grams in table 6–2).

TABLE 6–2. **Using the Method of Limits to Determine a Difference Threshold**

Comparison Stimulus (grams)	Response				Mean
	↓		↓		
350			Heavier		
340	Heavier		Heavier		
330	Heavier		Heavier		
320	Heavier	Heavier	Heavier	Heavier	
310	Equal	Equal	Heavier	Equal	
300 (Standard stimulus)	Equal	Equal	Heavier	Lighter	
290	Equal	Lighter	Equal	Lighter	
280	Lighter	Lighter	Equal	Lighter	
270		Lighter		Lighter	
260		Lighter			
	↑		↑		Mean
Upper Threshold	315	315	295	315	310
Lower Threshold	285	295	275	305	290
Interval of Uncertainty = 310 − 290 = 20 grams					

Note: For descending series, the upper threshold is the mean of the stimuli leading to the last "Heavier" response and the first "Equal" response. The lower threshold is the mean of the stimuli producing the last "Equal" response and the first "Lighter" response. The standard stimulus is always 300 grams. The difference threshold is one-half of the interval of uncertainty (10 grams, in this example).

Weber, whose pioneering work in psychophysics preceded Fechner's by about twenty years, discovered some important properties of the difference threshold. One property that Weber determined was that the magnitude of the difference threshold increases with increases in the magnitude of the standard stimulus. This means that if 10 grams is the difference threshold when 300 grams is the standard, the corresponding value for a 600-gram standard stimulus would be a difference threshold of 20 grams. A familiar example will illustrate this psychophysical finding. In a room lit by a single candle, the addition of another lit candle will make the room noticeably brighter. However, in a room illuminated by several intense lamps, adding a single lit candle will not noticeably increase the brightness of the room.

Weber is famous for determining a second property of the difference threshold: *For a particular sensory modality, the size of the difference threshold relative to the standard stimulus is constant.* To return to our earlier example, the ratio of 10 grams to 300 grams is the same as the ratio of 20 grams to 600 grams, 1/30 in this case (the ratio that Weber actually obtained in his experiments). According to Weber's discovery, this means that the difference threshold for a 900-gram standard stimulus should be 30 grams, and it should be 40 grams for a 1,200-gram standard. What should the difference threshold be for a standard stimulus of 50 grams?

Fechner called relative constancy of the difference threshold *Weber's law*. This law is usually written as $\Delta I/I = K$, where I refers to the magnitude of the standard stimulus, ΔI is the difference threshold, and K is the symbol for constancy.

Weber's law, or the Weber fraction, as it is sometimes called, varies in size for different senses. For example, it is somewhat larger for brightness than it is for heaviness. A substantial amount of research has shown that Weber's law holds true for greater than 90 percent of the range of standard stimuli tested in a particular sensory modality. It fails to hold for very weak stimuli, such that the Weber fraction for very light standard stimuli is much larger than 1/30, which is what is found in the middle range.

You may think that the method of limits is quite inefficient, since each column contains many successive responses (in table 6–1, either "Yes" or "No") that do not change. A newer version of the method of limits, called the *staircase method* (Cornsweet, 1962), concentrates responses around the threshold. For the first trial, it is similar to the method of limits. However, once an estimate of the threshold is obtained, the staircase method never presents stimuli that are far from this estimate. This is shown in table 6–3. As soon as the threshold estimate is crossed, the direction of stimulus intensity reverses. This improves the efficiency of the method by keeping the stimuli much closer to the threshold than is the case for the method of limits. The threshold is calculated as the mean value of all stimuli presented, starting with the second trial (column 2 in table 6–3).

TABLE 6–3.

Using the Staircase Method to Determine an Absolute Threshold

Stimulus Intensity	Response			
	↓			
180	Yes			
160	Yes			
140	Yes	Yes	↓	Yes
120	Yes	No	No	↑
100	Yes	No		
80	No	↑		

Threshold = 124

From the time of Fechner until about twenty-five years ago, the method of limits was a major psychophysical technique. But a new development, called the *theory of signal detection,* has now become the dominant psychophysical method. In an exciting modification of earlier work, signal-detection theory alters the concept of a threshold dramatically.

No thresholds: The theory of signal detection. According to signal-detection theory, perception in general is controlled by two basic internal processes. Arrival of a signal or stimulus at a receptor creates a (hypothetical) sensory impression that on the average is dependent on the intensity of the signal. But this impression is not sufficient to cause a "Yes" response—even for strong signals. Instead, the magnitude of this sensory impression is evaluated by a subsequent decision process. For an observer to report sensing a signal, both sensory and decision processes must be involved. We will first discuss the decision process, since it is easier to understand.

Any decision you make is dependent on the costs and benefits associated with it. Imagine that a friend has set up a blind date for you. The costs (a wasted evening) are probably less than the possible benefits (an exciting evening now and more exciting evenings in the future); many of us would accept a blind date, even though we knew nothing about the person we would be dating. So you might be likely to respond "Yes." This decision would be based mostly on costs and benefits, since you would lack information about the stimulus (the person who is your date).

Now let us imagine a situation in which costs are high: accepting or offering a proposal of marriage. Even those of us who are eager to accept a blind date would not get married if we were offered only the information that was needed to help us decide whether to go on a blind date. The costs of an unsatisfactory marriage are much greater than those of a blind date that does not pan out. In terms of decision theory, most of us are conservative decision makers when considering marriage, but liberal decision makers when considering a blind date. This decision bias does not depend on the stimulus—indeed, the same person could be involved in both instances—but only on the costs and benefits of the decision.

Now, we can return to the sensory end (beginning) of signal detection. The sensory process transmits a value to the decision process. If this value is high, the decision process is more likely to yield a "Yes" response once costs and benefits have been considered. If this value is low, the decision process is more likely to yield a "No" response, even if costs and benefits favor a "Yes" decision. How does the sensory process find a value to send?

Signal-detection theory assumes that *noise,* a disturbance that can be confused with signals, is always present when a human attempts to detect signals. This background disturbance is owing to such things as environmental changes, equipment changes, spontaneous neural activity, and direct experimental manipulations. Just to make sure that the assumption that noise is present during attempts at detection, a typical signal-detection experiment will present white noise—a hissing sound you can hear turning your television to an unoccupied channel—along with the signal. Noise can be auditory or visual (see figure 6–2), or indeed can occur in any modality; we will consider only the auditory system for now. Imagine that you are sitting in a soundproof booth, wearing headphones. On each trial you must decide whether you hear a faint tone combined with white noise or only the white noise by itself. Signal-detection theory assumes that any stimulus, even noise, produces a distribution of sensory impressions. The sensory impression on each trial is only one point, and the distributions are built up from many sensory impressions, each occurring at a different point in time (see discussion of distributions in appendix B). Since sensory impressions cannot be directly observed, the distributions for stimulus trials and for noise trials are hypothetical. The sensory impression arising from a trial for which only noise occurred will tend to be small, so that over many trials a (hypothetical) distribution with a small mean will be established. When

FIGURE 6–2.

Noise can make it difficult to detect a signal.

By permission of Johnny Hart and NAS, Inc.

FIGURE 6–3.

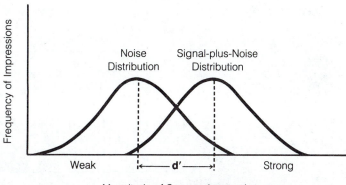

Hypothetical distributions of the sensory impressions resulting from noise and signal plus noise. The frequency of the impressions is the *y*-axis, and the magnitude is the *x*-axis. The strength of the signal and the sensory acuity of the observer determine the amount of overlap of the two distributions. A stronger signal or a more sensitive observer would move the signal-plus-noise distribution to the right (toward the strong end of the *x*-axis). The dashed vertical lines are the mean (average) of each distribution, and the distance between the two means is called **d'**.

a signal plus noise is presented, the sensory impression will be larger, so that a distribution with a greater mean will be formed over many trials.

Repeated trials generate two distributions—one for noise only, and one for the signal plus noise—as shown in figure 6–3. Since the two distributions overlap in the middle, some values of sensory impression are ambiguous, because they could have occurred as a result of either noise or the signal. Of course, if the two distributions were far enough apart, this problem would be minimized—but even in the laboratory, life is usually not that simple.

A criterion, shown as a vertical line in figure 6–4, must be set to determine whether a response will be "Yes" or "No." The position of this *criterion* is set by the decision process. If costs and benefits favor a liberal decision policy, the criterion will be set far to the left, so that most responses will be "Yes." If a conservative policy is used, the criterion moves to the right, so that most responses will be "No." In either case, some errors will be made. As shown in figure 6–4, correctly detecting a signal when it is presented is called a *hit*. Incorrectly responding "Yes" when only noise is presented is called a *false alarm*. With a liberal decision strategy—criterion set to the left—the number of hits will be high; but since there are numerous "Yes" responses, the number of false alarms will also be high. (If someone said "Yes" on every trial, both the hit rate and the false alarm rate would be 100 percent.) With a conservative decision strategy, false alarms will be low—but so will hits. (If someone said "No" on every trial, the false alarm rate would be 0 percent, as would the hit rate.) If we plot hits as a function of false alarms, as the criterion moves from

FIGURE 6–4.

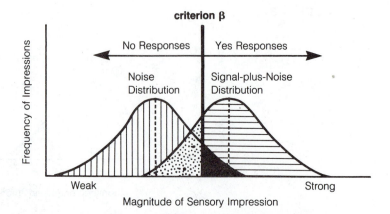

Hypothetical distributions of "Yes" and "No" responses as a function of the criterion and the magnitude of the sensory impression. Once a particular sensory impression occurs, the decision *criterion* (β) determines whether a "Yes" or "No" response will be made. Strong impressions to the right of the criterion will lead to "Yes" responses, and weak impressions to the left will lead to "No" responses. Correct detection of the signal ("Yes" responses in the horizontally striped area) are called *hits.* Correct "No" responses when noise occurs (the vertically striped portion) are called *correct rejections. Misses* occur when a "No" response occurs to weak signals to the left of the criterion (the dotted portion of the signal-plus-noise distribution). *False alarms* are incorrect "Yes" responses to noise that is to the right of the criterion (the black portion of the noise distribution).

conservative to liberal we get the representation depicted in figure 6–5.

This figure is called a *receiver-operating characteristic* (or ROC) function. Both hits and false alarms are infrequent (conservative criterion) at the lower left of the curve. As the criterion becomes more liberal, both hits and false alarms become more likely, and the ROC curve moves upward to the right. The slope of the ROC function tells us the criterion. Flat slopes reveal a liberal decision criterion (generally, the upper right of the curve) and steep slopes a conservative criterion (usually, the lower left of the curve).

The slope of curves such as the ROC function is determined by the slope of a line that is drawn tangent to a particular point on the function and intersects one of the axes of the graph. There are tables such as 6–4 that contain values of the criterion. The distance from the diagonal to the ROC curve tells us how far apart the noise and signal-plus-noise distributions of figure 6–3 lie. When the two distributions are far apart, indicating either a more discernible signal or a more acute observer, the ROC curve moves upward to the left, away from the diagonal, as shown by the heavy ROC function in figure 6–5. When the signal is less detectable or when the observer is less acute and the two distributions are close together, the ROC curve moves closer to the diagonal. Thus, the ROC function tells us about both the sensory process (d', distance between signal-plus-noise and noise-only distributions) and the decision process (β, the slope). Since a single experimental condition

FIGURE 6–5.

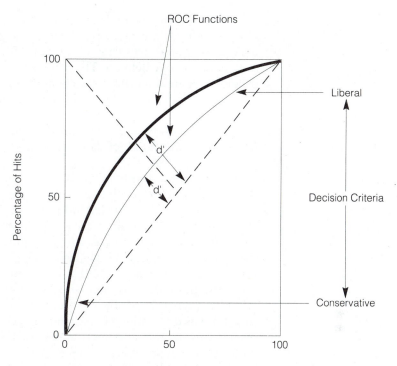

Receiver-operating characteristic (ROC functions). The distance from the diagonal to the center of the curve is proportional to d′. The diagonal represents chance performance, with the observer guessing about the presence or absence of a signal. Thus, the percentage of hits equals the percentage of false alarms along this "guessing" diagonal. The heavy ROC function is farther away from the diagonal than is the lighter ROC function, which means that d′ is greater for the heavy curve than for the light one. A larger d′ can result from a stronger signal or a more acute observer.

generates only a single point on the ROC curve, many conditions are needed to alter the hit and false-alarm rates. Usually, hit and false-alarm rates are manipulated by altering the payoff associated with them (see figure 6–10). (If a hit were worth two dollars and a false alarm penalized you fifty cents, would you be more liberal or more conservative than if a hit were valued at fifty cents and a false alarm penalized you two dollars?) Another way of manipulating the rate of hits and false alarms is to vary how often the signal occurs (see figure 6–9). If, over a series of trials, a signal had occurred 90 percent of the time, you would be more likely to say "Yes" on any trial than when the signal had occurred very infrequently on the previous trials.

By now, you may be wondering what all this has to do with thresholds. Nowhere does the ROC curve have a label that reads "threshold." Whether an observer will respond "Yes" or "No" depends on the sensory impression and the decision criterion. Signal intensity may be held constant, but since there are varying payoffs for hits and false alarms, you can generate an ROC curve showing *d'* (sensitivity) and the slope of the curve at various points. There is no operational definition of a threshold. Instead, two quantities are operationally defined. The sensitivity of the observer is called *d'* and is defined as the distance between signal and noise distributions in figure 6–3, or as the maximum distance between the ROC curve and the diagonal in figure 6–5. The criterion of the decision processes is called *beta* (β) and is the slope of the ROC function at the point of interest—for example, a hit rate of 55 percent.

So, what is a threshold? As shown in figure 6–3, signal-detection theory supposes that the sensory impression of a stimulus is a continuous distribution that takes on a zero value only when the stimulus intensity itself is zero. We do not have a threshold that splits the stimulus dimension into detectable and undetectable components, as classical psychophysics would lead us to believe. Rather, a stimulus must yield a sensation that exceeds the decision criterion (β) in order for a person to report having detected a weak stimulus (figure 6–4). In a sense, then, the notion of an absolute threshold as determined by a stimulus of a particular intensity has been denied by signal-detection theory. What we have left, as D'Amato (1970) suggests, is a response or *decision threshold*. Only when a stimulus yields a sensation that exceeds the decision threshold, what we have been calling β or the criterion, do we have correct detection of the signal. Of course, *d'* determines the detectability of the signal, but not necessarily what the subject reports. This means that *detecting and reporting* the presence of a signal is determined by *d'* and β; together, these two quantities determine what a classical psychophysicist would call a threshold.

Calculating d'. Given a set of data, we can easily calculate *d'* by using tables based on the area under the normal curve. Suppose you know that the hit rate is .875 and the false-alarm rate is .21. What is *d'*? First, draw the noise distribution, as in figure 6–6. Since the false-alarm rate represents the area under the curve from the criterion to plus infinity on the right, it equals .21. Since the normal curve is symmetrical, half of its area (.5) lies between zero and plus infinity. Therefore, the area between zero and the criterion must be .5 − .21, which equals .29. Now look up .29 in the normal table (table 6–4). You will find that *t* = .8. This is the normalized distance of the criterion from zero.

Second, repeat this process for the signal distribution shown at the bottom of figure 6–6. Since the hit rate is .875, this is the area under the curve from the criterion to plus infinity. Again, because of symmetry, half the area under the curve (.5) is between *d'* and plus infinity. Therefore, the area between the criterion and *d'* is .875 − .5, which equals .375. Consulting table 6–4, we find that an area of .375 corresponds to a *t* of about 1.15.

We can now put these two *t* values together to find *d'* (see figure 6–7). Since the mean of the noise distribution is given the value

FIGURE 6–6.

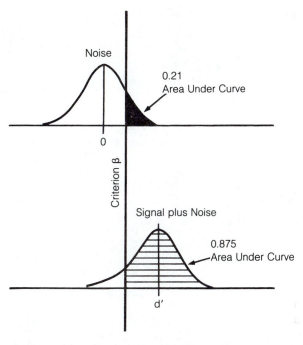

Calculating d' on the basis of false alarms (black area under the noise-distribution curve) and hits (horizontally striped area under signal-plus-noise distribution curve).

of zero, d' is the sum of the two *t* values: $0.8 + 1.15 = 1.95$. Our calculation of d' is now complete. Obviously, then, the larger the d', the greater the distance between the means of the two distributions. Therefore, a large d' indicates either a strong signal or an acute observer.

Advantage of signal-detection methods. A major advantage of signal-detection methods over a classical psychophysical procedure, such as the method of limits, is the ability to measure both sensitivity and response bias. In many areas of applied psychology, the ability to distinguish between these two processes is very important. Let us return to the problem that opened this chapter: the problem of measuring the effectiveness of analgesics.

Hardy and associates (1952) used the method of limits to determine the absolute threshold of pain and changes in such thresholds resulting from a supposed analgesic, such as aspirin. Among other things, they found that aspirin elevated pain thresholds more consistently in trained observers than in naive ones, and they also noted that various kinds of suggestion would alter pain thresholds. For example, thresholds were raised more when people believed they had taken an analgesic than when they did not believe so. Furthermore, Hardy and his associates showed that this suggestion elevated thresholds both when people took a real analgesic (say, aspirin) and when they took a *placebo* (inert) pill. Is this result owing to a change in sensitivity (d'), or is there a change in the decision criterion (β)?

TABLE 6–4.

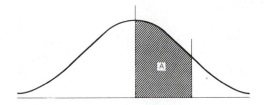

Tabled Values of the Normal Curve	
t	Area (from 0 to t)
0	0
0.1	.039
0.2	.079
0.3	.118
0.4	.155
0.5	.192
0.6	.226
0.7	.258
0.8	.288
0.9	.316
1.0	.341
1.1	.364
1.2	.385
1.3	.403
1.4	.419
1.5	.433
1.6	.445
1.7	.455
1.8	.464
1.9	.471
2.0	.477
2.1	.482
2.2	.486
2.3	.489
2.4	.492
2.5	.494

(From Kantowitz and Sorkin, 1983)

To determine how analgesics worked, Clark and his co-workers (Clark, 1969; Clark and Yang, 1974) conducted a number of experiments on pain analgesia. Rather than using the method of limits, Clark used a signal-detection procedure, so that both changes in sensitivity and decision processes could be assessed. In these experiments, a dolorimeter was used to evoke pain by means of thermal stimulation. Initially, Clark found that analgesics such as aspirin reduced d′, which means that the drug lowered the acuity of the sensory system with the outcome being that the aspirin reduced the ability of people to distinguish between painful and nonpainful stimuli. Clark then investigated whether placebos and acupuncture (a Chinese medical procedure of inserting needles into the skin, which is sometimes used to reduce surgically-induced

FIGURE 6 – 7.

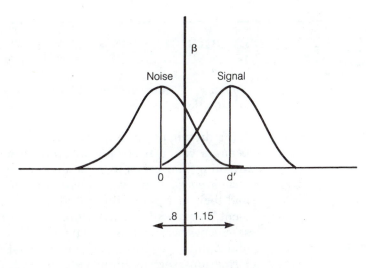

Calculating d′: the sum of the two *t* values yields d′. d′ = .8 + 1.15; d′ = 1.95.

pain and has other medical uses) altered d′ (reduced sensitivity), or whether placebos and acupuncture changed the willingness of the subjects to report pain. In both experiments, Clark found that placebos and acupuncture reduced the reports of pain and the number of times that the subjects attempted to withdraw from the painful stimuli. Did these procedures induce analgesia for pain? No: in both experiments, d′ was unaffected by the manipulation. What happened was that acupuncture and placebos elevated the subjects' decision criterion, so that stronger stimuli than before were required to elicit a detection response. This does not mean that placebos and acupuncture do not work; following an acupuncture treatment or the ingestion of a placebo, people report less pain. What Clark's results do show is the way in which these procedures work to alleviate pain. They do not deaden the sensory systems; rather, they change the decision threshold for reporting that pain has been experienced.

Let us return briefly to the work by Hardy and associates (1952). Using the method of limits, they found that suggestion altered the absolute threshold. Given the signal-detection results found by Clark, it is reasonable to suppose that suggestion changed the absolute threshold determined by the method of limits, by altering the decision criterion of the subjects. How are we to account for the fact that trained observers—but not naive ones—have higher pain thresholds following the ingestion of aspirin? Why do most naive observers have a lower pain threshold? We could guess that this too is a criterion shift, owing to the fact that the trained observers know all about the experiment and the supposed effects of aspirin, whereas the naive subjects are nervous after taking a drug and more likely to report pain. In the absence of doing a signal-detection analysis, however, we can only speculate about the data. An enigma in the literature on pain relief could be cleared up with an appropriately conducted signal-detection experiment.

6.2 Experimental Topics and Research Illustrations

Topic: Measurement Scales
Illustration: Fechner's Law and Stevens' Law

It is a dictum in psychophysics that anything that exists, be it jelly beans or your attitude toward spinach, exists in some amount. And anything that exists in some amount can be measured. *Measurement* is a systematic way of assigning numbers or names to objects and their attributes. But not all measurement systems are equivalent. In particular, different scale types result from different measurement operations. A scale type is mathematically defined (Suppes and Zinnes, 1963) by its uniqueness—that is, the kinds of transformations, such as adding a constant or multiplying by a constant and so forth, that can be performed without altering the unique mathematical properties of the scale. Psychologists are most concerned with four types of scales, called *nominal, ordinal, interval,* and *ratio,* although other types also exist. These four scale types have been listed according to increasing power of measurement, with each successive scale type having the properties of the preceding types, plus other new ones. This means, for example, that data obtained using a ratio scale of measurement could be analyzed by methods appropriate to any of the three lesser scales. However, methods of analysis appropriate only for a ratio scale would not fit the other scales.

It is interesting that the simplest measurement operation (counting) produces the highest scale type (ratio). A *ratio scale* remains unique if all the scale numbers are multiplied by a constant. Any other arithmetic operation destroys the ratio properties of the scale. The easiest way for you to tell whether a scale has ratio properties is to look for two characteristics. First, the scale has a real zero, corresponding to no objects, or none of the scale property. A physical scale that satisfies this condition is weight in grams. Zero grams truly means no weight. The second characteristic of the ratio scale, from which its name derives, is that ratios of scale values make sense. Thus, a 10-gram weight has the same relationship to a 5-gram weight as a 24-gram weight has to a 12-gram weight, since the ratio of two weights is 2.0 in both cases.

An *interval scale* is unchanged if a constant is added, or if scale values are multiplied by a constant. In an interval scale, there is an arbitrarily chosen zero point, and although distances between adjacent scale numbers are equal, the actual size of the interval is not very important. Ratios of pairs of scale values are not meaningful. Fahrenheit and Centigrade are interval scales. Although the zero value will change depending on whether Fahrenheit or Centrigrade scale units are chosen, the distance between adjacent units is equal. A temperature increase from 34 to 35 produces the same change as an increase from 35 to 36 (on either scale). Most course grades are assumed to be on an interval scale. The intervals between As and Bs are about the same as the intervals between Bs and Cs, and so on. However, the typical letter grade scale does not permit one to assume that a person who receives an A does twice as well as someone who does C work, or that the A student is half again better than the B student.

In fact, most grading schemes and many measures of sensation are best viewed as examples of ordinal scales. An *ordinal scale* is unchanged by any monotonic (steadily increasing or decreasing) operation, such as taking the square root, adding or multiplying by a constant, or taking a logarithm. It lacks an absolute zero, and the distances between adjacent scale values are unequal. This scale type is achieved most often by asking people to rank order a set of objects—for example, to list all their friends of the opposite sex according to attractiveness. If Person A is the most attractive, Person B the next most, and so on, the difference in attractiveness between adjacent persons changes as we go down the list. When someone reports that light X is brighter than light Y, we will soon see that it is very difficult to determine whether this judgment is on a scale higher than an ordinal one.

A *nominal scale* is the weakest type of measurement, since it merely sorts objects into different categories. Just about any arithmetic transformation can be used without the scale properties changing, as long as objects are not pulled out of one bin and pushed into another. Numbers on an athlete's jersey represent nominal measurement: all they do is identify particular individuals, without telling you anything about them (for that you need a scorecard). It would be silly to add the numbers that two athletes are wearing and expect the result to be meaningful. Sex is also a nominal measurement, since all individuals can be classified into one of two categories: male and female.

Importance of measurement scales. Some of the discussion of scales may seem to you too abstract to be pertinent to an understanding of psychophysics or the measurement of any psychological characteristic. The examples we have included should indicate that the different scales provide different kinds of information. Since a ratio scale represents the most powerful form of measurement, psychologists should always strive for ratio measurement of their dependent variables. Unfortunately, this is easier said than done. It turns out that the majority of psychological measurement is at the ordinal and interval level.

What does this mean to you? For one thing, when you evaluate the assertions of a researcher, you should be able to identify the measurement scale underlying the assertions. You should recognize that it is invalid to say that "this temperature is twice as hot as that one," unless your measurement of temperature sensation is at the level of a ratio scale. Scale type will also play an important part in your own research. If you know that one object feels heavier than another but you do not know how much more (an ordinal scale), then you are constrained as to what you can say about those sensations. You are even further limited if all you know is that one object feels heavy and the other does not (a nominal scale).

We will now examine two approaches toward the measurement of sensation. Both approaches have the goal of devising a ratio scale of an internal psychological dimension. The first approach was undertaken by Fechner; he relied on the results of classical psychophysical methods to provide the data for his psychological scale. The second approach we examine is a more modern one, devised by S. S. Stevens.

Fechner's law. According to Weber's law, the difference threshold bears a constant relation to the standard stimulus: $\Delta I/I = K$. Fechner assumed that Weber's law was correct, and with two additional assumptions developed his own law of sensation measurement. Fechner first assumed that the absolute threshold indicates the point of zero sensation. Then, he assumed that the *just-noticeable difference* (JND), which is the internal sensation evoked by two stimuli that differ by one difference threshold, is the unit defining the intervals of an internal psychological scale. Because Weber's law was assumed to be accurate, Fechner believed that all JNDs produce equal increments in sensation, as shown in figure 6–8. Each JND step on the psychological scale corresponds to the physical stimulus that is one difference threshold greater than the preceding stimulus. The first unit beyond the zero point corresponds to the physical stimulus that is one JND above the absolute thresh-

FIGURE 6–8.

Presumed Internal Psychological Scale (ψ)

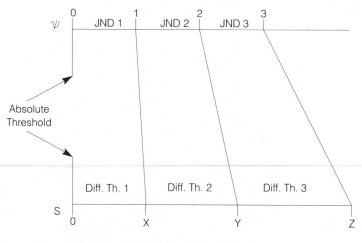

Values of the Physical Stimulus (S)

Fechner's law. Equal units on an internal psychological scale correspond to progressively greater units on an external physical scale (the difference thresholds): $\psi = K \log (S)$.

old. The next point will be one JND above that, or two JNDs above the absolute threshold.

This process can be continued to build a psychological scale. Once this is done, there is a fixed mathematical relationship between the value of the physical scale corresponding to some point on the psychological scale and the physical value corresponding to the preceding point on the internal psychological scale. To find the physical-scale value that corresponds to a particular psychological value, we first take the physical value of the previous step on the external scale (for example, X in figure 6–8) and multiply it by the Weber fraction. Then we add this product to our original value, so that $Y = X + X$ times the Weber fraction in figure 6–8 (likewise, $Z = Y + Y$ times the Weber fraction). Summing in this fashion yields successive physical values that correspond to successive just-noticeable differences on the internal psychological scale. When this relationship is expanded and solved mathematically, we find that the psychological-scale value (ψ) is proportional to the logarithm of the physical-stimulus value. This equation ($\psi = K$ log stimulus) is called *Fechner's law.*

According to Fechner's law, all JNDs produce equivalent increments in sensation; therefore, it appears that we have a ratio scale (D'Amato, 1970). The sensation corresponding to six JNDs should be twice the sensation of three JNDs. Two factors we have already discussed should lead you to question whether Fechner has actually devised a ratio scale of sensation. First, Fechner's zero point is arbitrary rather than absolute. The absolute threshold is defined statistically and includes many sensations that do not exceed the decision criterion (see the discussion on thresholds and signal detection). Second, we know that Weber's law is only approximately true; this could result in psychological and physical units of varying sizes. There is an additional difficulty with Fechner's formulation. Fechner assumed that each JND was psychologically equal, but if you ask people about the magnitude of the sensory effects produced by stimuli of varying JNDs above threshold, there is poor correspondence between the two (D'Amato, 1970). Thus, Fechner's work is neither a ratio scale nor an interval scale. At best, it is an ordinal scale indicating that sensations are ordered in a particular way with regard to the physical stimuli that produce them.

Stevens' power law. S. S. Stevens (1961) attempted to develop an internal scale of sensation more directly than did Fechner. Fechner used an *indirect scaling* method, in which the psychological scale was built up by putting successive JNDs in a row. The observers did not judge the magnitudes of the JNDs directly, so the psychological-scale values are derived from measures of discrimination; therefore, they are indirect. Stevens used several *direct scaling* techniques, in which the observer responded in psychological-scale units in the first place.

The primary direct scaling procedure used by Stevens was the method of *magnitude estimation*, which requires the observer to state a number that represents his or her sensation of the stimulus intensity. The first stimulus that the experimenter presents is arbitrarily assigned some convenient number, say, 100. Then other stimuli are assigned numbers, depending on how close the perceived intensity is to the first stimulus. For example, the experimenter could present a tone of moderate intensity and tell you it has a value of 100. Then a weaker tone might be presented. So you would give it a lower number, say, 87. These numbers reported by the observer represent perceived psychological values directly. When data are gathered in this way, the equation relating psychological value to physical value differs from the logarithmic relationship of Fechner's law. Instead, the equation obtained by Stevens (1961) is $\psi = K (\text{Stimulus})^n$, where n is an exponent. This equation is called *Stevens' law*.

The method of magnitude estimation is not limited to psychological scales that have a physical correlate. Essay exams are often graded by this method. Similarly, legal penalties, severity of crimes, works of art, and so forth, can be scaled by magnitude estimation.

If we assume that a stimulus of zero intensity always produces zero sensation (that is, there are no false alarms), then we can accept Stevens' law as a ratio psychological scale. With a true zero, and with equal stimulus ratios producing equal sensation ratios (a power relation), we have satisfied the criteria for a ratio scale. If this is the case, then it seems reasonable to accept $\psi = K S^n$ as the way in which our internal sensations are related to the external world.

However, Stevens' work and conclusions have not gone without criticism. There is some debate as to what the observer is really reporting in the method of magnitude estimation. One controversy centers on whether observers report the intensity of sensation, as claimed by Stevens, or whether they instead report a learned association based on a correlation with a physical attribute linked to the stimulus—such that, for example, judgments of loudness reflect the experience that softer sounds are farther away from the subject (Warren, 1963).

A related problem has to do with the fact that different people use numbers differently. Some people, for example, always produce very large exponents in the equation of Stevens' law, and it has been found that Stevens' law varies with the range of numbers used by the subjects (Marks, 1974).

A final problem with the magnitude estimation approach is related to operational definitions (discussed earlier in this chapter). A substantial amount of research has shown that a particular sensory scale, such as brightness or pain, does not have just one psychophysical function that characterizes it. As Marks (1974) notes, you can accurately describe a power function for brightness only if you specify all of the other variables relevant to the perception of brightness—the color and duration of the light, the sensory adaptation of the observer, and so on. Varying these latter factors changes the value of the exponent in Stevens' law. Thus, we must operationally define the psychophysical function we obtain; otherwise, we would present a misleading view of the power function relating sensation to stimulus.

6.3 Experimental Topics and Research Illustrations

Topic: Small-*n* Design
Illustration: Psychophysical Methods

Unlike most other areas of psychology, psychophysical research uses only small numbers of observers (subjects). Experimental control replaces statistical control as a method for reducing error variance and for increasing the reliability of data. When an experiment is complicated with many uncontrolled sources of variance, as in, say, a field experiment in social or environmental psychology (see chapters 13 and 14), it is unlikely that the same results will be obtained when the experiment is repeated, even with the same subject. But psychophysical techniques are characterized by extremely fine control of the experimental situation. The same results can be obtained again and again. For example, if an observer returns to the laboratory and the experimenter uses the same conditions in a repeat experiment, the same ROC function should be obtained. Because the ROC function is so precisely replicated, there is little need for the more complex statistical operations, such as analysis of variance. It is simpler and more elegant to manipulate independent variables directly and to replicate previous data precisely.

An example of the precise control possible in psychophysical experiments is shown in figures 6–9 and 6–10. The same observer has generated both ROC functions. In figure 6–9, the probability that a stimulus, rather than noise only, would be presented is varied from low to high. When signal probability is low, the observer acts like a conservative decision maker, since it is not likely that on any given trial a signal has been presented. As signal probability increases, the observer becomes more liberal, since the odds in favor of a signal trial are better. This change in the decision criterion—from conservative to liberal—sweeps out the ROC function in figure 6–9, starting from the lower left and moving along the curve to the upper right.

To generate the ROC function of figure 6–10, the experimenter keeps the signal probability constant and varies the payoff. This manipulation also affects the decision process. When the cost of false alarms is high relative to the cost of hits, the observer is conservative. As the relative cost of false alarms decreases, the

FIGURE 6–9.

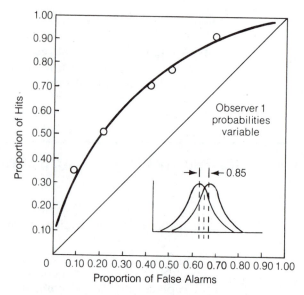

ROC graph obtained by varying signal probability. The insert shows hypothetical noise and signal-plus-noise distributions (data from Green & Swets, 1966).

observer becomes more willing to respond "signal" and adopts a liberal decision criterion.

The insert in both figures shows the hypothetical noise and signal-plus-noise distributions. Both curves are well fitted by a d' equal to .85—that is, the solid curve passes close to the actual data points. This exact fit is even more impressive when we stop to realize that the two ROC functions are generated in slightly different ways: two different operations are used to vary the decision criterion. The extreme similarity of the two ROC functions shows a high degree of experimental control.

Psychophysical experiments usually require thousands of trials, even though a small number of observers is used. The total effort—number of trials times number of observers—in psychophysical experiments often exceeds that of less controlled experiments, so that using a small number (n) of subjects is not an economy to lessen overall experimental effort, or a cheap way to avoid the terrors of statistics. Indeed, the psychophysicist does use very refined statistical techniques based on fitting psychophysical models rather than analysis of variance.

By now you may be wondering whether it is better to use large numbers of subjects and analysis of variance or small numbers with lots of trials. There is no absolute answer to this question. But most psychologists prefer experimental control to after-the-fact statistical control. The greater the degree of experimental control, the less the need for analysis of variance.

FIGURE 6–10.

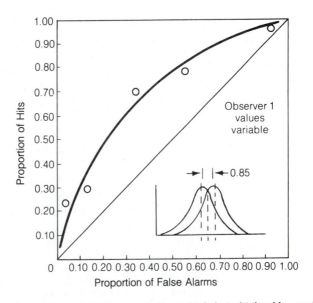

ROC graph from the same observer as in figure 6–9, but obtained by varying the values of the decision outcomes and holding signal probability constant at 0.5. Notice how closely the two functions agree (data from Green & Swets, 1966).

From Problem to Experiment: The Nuts and Bolts

Problem: Do pigeons have visual thresholds?

Problem: *How can we measure a pigeon's visual threshold?*

Since this problem is based more on methodology than on content, we do not require much in the way of a formal hypothesis. Content issues would arise when the feasibility of measuring a pigeon's visual threshold was first established. Primarily for the sake of completeness, we offer the following hypothesis.

Hypothesis: *Pigeons are sensitive to different intensities of light, and their absolute thresholds will be influenced by variables that influence human thresholds, such as the wavelength (color) of the light and certain drugs.*

The first problem we must overcome is obvious: pigeons cannot talk. Therefore, we will put them into a conditioning chamber with two response keys to peck: one for "Yes, I see the light" and the other for "No, I don't see it." Our dependent variable is the absolute threshold (see below). Our independent variables are light intensity, light color, and the presence or absence of a drug. Control variables will include the conditioning chamber and the reward schedules used to maintain pecking. We want the pigeon to peck the Yes key when the light is visible and the No key when it is not, but we have no way of determining just from looking at the light whether it is visible to the pigeon.

Blough (1958, 1961) has developed a way to get the pigeon to indicate the visibility of the light. He uses a variant of the staircase method to determine the absolute threshold. Pecks on the Yes key gradually reduce the intensity of the light, and pecks on the No key gradually increase it. Occasionally, pecks on the Yes key completely cut out the light, and subsequent pecks on the No key are rewarded with food. As Blough notes, this procedure can be described anthropomorphically as having the pigeon peck the Yes key to turn out the light and peck the No key to get the food reward. (You should note that these lights were never intense enough to be aversive to the pigeon.) What happens is that when the light is too dim for the pigeon to see, it switches from the Yes key to the No key in order to receive the reward. When the light is visible, it switches from the No key to the Yes key in order to dim the light.

Since the bird is shifting back and forth between keys in response to changes in intensity, we can determine the absolute threshold by taking the average of the intensities just prior to the switch from one key to the other. This is what is done to determine a human's absolute threshold with the staircase method. Blough reports that when the color of the light is varied, the pigeon's absolute threshold changes, just as the human absolute threshold changes. Furthermore, minute doses of LSD raise the absolute threshold of light—for both pigeons and humans.

SUMMARY

1. Operational definitions are required in science, both to make experiments more public and to increase the precision of technical terms beyond their use in ordinary conversation. The method of limits gives an operational definition for the concept of threshold. Classical psychophysics was largely aimed at evaluating thresholds. The more modern theory of signal detection replaces the threshold concept with two other operationally defined constructs; d' and beta. Sensory processes are measured by d', and beta is a measure of the decision-making process. Both d' and beta can be computed from ROC (receiver-operating characteristics) functions that plot hits against false alarms. Signal-detection methods have many applied uses.

2. Measurement scales result when numbers are assigned systematically to objects. Psychologists deal most often with nominal, ordinal, interval, and ratio scale types. Only certain kinds of data analysis and scale transformations are appropriate for each scale type. Fechner's law probably yields an ordinal scaling of an internal psychological continuum. Stevens' law yields a ratio scale.

3. Psychophysical experiments often use only small numbers of observers, in contrast to most areas of psychology, in which large numbers are typical. This procedure is highly acceptable, or even preferred, because of the high degree of experimental control in psychophysical experiments, which greatly reduces error variance. Even with a single subject, the psychophysicist can manipulate an independent variable to replicate earlier results quite precisely.

KEY TERMS

absolute threshold
beta (β)
criterion
d′
decision threshold
difference threshold
direct scaling
dolorimeter
false alarm
Fechner's law (ψ = K log(s))
hit
indirect scaling
interval of uncertainty
interval scale
just-noticeable difference (JND)
magnitude estimation
measurement
measurement scales

method of limits
noise
nominal scale
operational definition
ordinal scale
placebo
point of subjective equality
psychophysical methods
psychophysics
ratio scale
receiver-operating characteristic (ROC)
theory of signal detection
small-n designs
staircase method
Stevens' law (ψ = KS^n)
threshold
Weber's law (ΔI/I = K)

DISCUSSION QUESTIONS

1. Although the method of limits may not yield the best definition of sensory thresholds, it has many practical uses—especially for the determination of difference thresholds. The sensory effects of food flavorings are often determined this way. See if you can think of additional practical uses of the method of limits. A brief literature search in a journal such as *Ergonomics* may be of use.

2. Does either the method of limits or the staircase method offer a better operational definition of the concept of a threshold—or are the two methods equivalent insofar as operational definition is concerned?

3. Calculate d′ for the following pairs of hit and false-alarm rates: (.90, .10), (.90, .25), (.90, .50), (.90, .90).

4. What is the difference between an absolute threshold and a decision threshold?

5. Give two examples of each kind of measurement scale.

6. Contrast the following experimental-design approaches: (1) use of large numbers of subjects and analysis of variance, (2) use of small numbers of subjects with large numbers of trials.

Weber's Law

FOR THIS DEMONSTRATION YOU will need several empty cardboard milk containers; a supply of sand, gravel, lead shot, or similar material to partially fill them; and a scale. Fill one of the containers about one-eighth full and add slightly more to another container. Ask a friend to lift them and tell you which weighs more. At first your subject will tell you they are equal in weight. Keep adding material to the heavier container until your subject can tell which is heavier. Do not let your subject see you filling the heavier container, which should not always be lifted with the same hand.

Once the heavier container is determined, it becomes the new standard stimulus. Add material to a new container until it is just noticeably heavier than the standard container. Keep on repeating this procedure until the last container is almost completely filled. Now weigh each of the containers, making careful notes of the differences in weight between adjacent containers.

See if you replicate Weber's results described in the chapter. You should find that adding a constant amount of material is not enough to produce a noticeable difference. Imagine that you are holding a three-pound package. You certainly would notice if someone quietly tiptoed up and added another pound. But if you were carrying a hundred-pound load, the addition of another pound would go unobserved. Although x amount is sufficient to distinguish the first two containers, amounts greater than x are required to tell containers apart later in the series. If you have done your experiment carefully, you should find that a constant percentage of the weight of a container is required before the next container seems heavier. This percentage is called the Weber fraction. Weber's law can be stated as follows: the difference threshold divided by the stimulus magnitude equals a constant (Weber's law, $\Delta I/I = K$). Weber's law does not hold for extreme values of stimulus magnitude. Thus, if you repeated your experiment with barbells or paper clips instead of milk containers, you would not get this result. The Weber fraction also differs for different individuals and for different tasks, such as judging line length instead of weight. You might try to verify these characteristics of Weber's law.

CHAPTER 7

Perception

Discovery consists of seeing what everybody has seen and thinking what nobody has thought.

—ALBERT SZENT-GYÖRGYI

IMAGINE THAT YOU ARE ACTUALLY viewing the town of Ålesund, Norway, from the camera angle that yielded figure 7–1. A standard way of conceptualizing the visual receptive process of such a scene is that you first detect the presence of objects; then, this *sensation* provides you with the elements necessary for your *perception* of the town. According to this approach, perception is the interpretation and recognition of the objects and events that we sense. This simple and intuitively appealing theory of perception provides the background for most of the theoretical and methodological issues that confront psychologists interested in studying perception (for additional details of the issues, see Frisby, 1979; Kaufman, 1979).

Issues in Perception

One set of issues has to do with how the observer uses sensory information to make perceptual interpretations. Look again at figure 7–1. If you were actually viewing Ålesund, you would perceive the mountains as farther away than the buildings in the foreground. This natural and unambiguous perception is the result of several cues that provide information about the distance and depth of objects in the scene. In a moment we will consider what these cues are. Now let us focus on how they enter into perception.

Direct and Indirect Perception

Gibson (1979) argues that the usually reliable cues in the optic array of a scene *directly* provide information about depth and distance. The direct view assumes that the perceiver picks up the information afforded by the environment naturally and essentially, without reflecting upon them. In contrast, the *indirect approach* argues that our judgments of depth are made on the basis of our past experience with the depth cues (Gregory, 1970). According to the indirect approach, we interpret the scene to produce a perception of depth and distance.

In contemporary cognitive psychology, the direct/indirect controversy is often described as a contrast between *bottom-up* and *top-down* perceptual processing. The bottom-up view emphasizes the role of sensory data in determining what is perceived, and the top-down approach stresses the role of previously established concepts in determining perceptions. Because of these contrasts, you will also see the two aspects of perception labeled as a distinction between *data-driven processing* (the bottom-up emphasis) and *conceptually driven processing* (the top-down emphasis). With regard to the Ålesund photograph (figure 7–1), the bottom-up analysis would focus on the gradient of texture that appears to recede into the distance toward the mountains in the background. Because this receding texture is a component of depth and distance in our three-dimensional world, we directly see the picture as containing depth.

The indirect or top-down approach has an alternative interpretation of your perception of Ålesund. The interpretation from the top-down position focuses on the fact that your perception of depth and distance in a *photograph* is an *illusion*.

An illusion is a mistaken or distorted perception. Why is your perception of these qualities in the Ålesund photograph an illusion? The small buildings near the top of the photograph could be min-

FIGURE 7–1.

A view of the town of Ålesund, Norway.

iature buildings, or they could be farther away than the large buildings at the bottom. However in the photograph, both sets of buildings are equally distant from you (assuming that your eyes and the plane of the picture are parallel). On the basis of your past experience with small buildings being distant from you, you confer illusory depth cues to the two-dimensional photographic representation of Ålesund. This interpretation of depth leads to a three-dimensional percept. Since there is not real depth in the two-dimensional photograph, the depth and distance that we do perceive can be attributed to an indirect process resulting from our interpretation of the (illusory) cues in the scene.

Attempts to understand how the world is perceived often involve illusory or ambiguous stimuli. Such figures are used so that the importance of various cues for ordinary perceptions can be determined. When the observer is tricked by conflicting cues for depth perception, for example, it may be possible to determine which of the cues is more important for interpreting the perception of depth in the scene. In the following two sections, we will examine how this strategy has been used.

Impossible figures. Look at the waterfall in figure 7–2. At first, it seems to be quite ordinary. Each component of the picture is perfectly all right by itself. But as you stare at it, you soon notice that something is amiss. The parts of the figure do not go together properly. Although the presumed source of the waterfall is at the top of the painting to make it appear far from the water at the bottom, there is no start or finish to this waterfall. This illusion succeeds—that is, it causes an inaccurate perception—because of ambiguous and inconsistent cues about depth. There are many cues to depth that we have learned from experience. Relative size is one of them. All other things being equal, smaller objects are perceived as farther away than larger objects. Haze is another cue to depth. Loss of detail occurs under natural conditions when objects are far away. Photographs taken with telephoto lenses restore this missing detail and thus appear more novel than pictures taken with standard lenses (see figure 7–3).

Size constancy occurs when we use depth cues to allow us to take into account the distance between us and an object being perceived. An automobile you are standing next to appears to be about the same size as one parked down the block. If you reported your perception that both cars looked about the same size, you would be displaying size constancy. This phenomenon creates serious problems for psychologists studying perception. The image formed on the retina of your eye is far smaller for the distant car than for the nearby car. Nevertheless, your perceptual report that they look the same implies that the image on the retina should be the same for both cars. Your knowledge of the world has acted on your perception. Psychologists would prefer people to report what they see, but often people instead report what they know. We shall

FIGURE 7–2.

A perpetual-motion waterfall. M. C. Escher's *Waterfall,* © 1990 M. C. Escher Heirs/
Cordon Art—Baarn—Holland.

return to this important distinction often in this chapter, but for
now we shall continue to show you that perception can be fooled.

Our last set of *impossible figures,* which yield apparently accurate perceptions from drawings of objects that cannot occur,
includes the Freemish crate for shipping optical illusions and the
endless staircase (see figure 7–4). As you study these ambiguous
figures, the contradictions that result from conflicting depth cues
become obvious.

Although there may seem to be something artificial about the
figures shown so far, situations in which cues are ambiguous usually will produce errors of perception. For example, illusions have
been responsible for airplane crashes (Kantowitz and Sorkin, 1983,
p. 132). Examine figure 7–5. Most people lack the experience to
interpret this scene quickly. It is not an illusion, but an accurate
representation of a real-world scene, with no trick photography.
But this scene happens to be fifty feet underwater, off the island
of Bonnaire. It is a closeup photo of a Christmas-tree worm embedded in a coral reef. Although the figures that psychologists study
in the laboratory are specially created to highlight perceptual unreliability, these ambiguous figures merely abstract essential com-

FIGURE 7–3.

(a) A view of the town of Ålesund, Norway, taken with a wide-angle lens. This illustrates several depth cues. Haze and lack of detail become more pronounced as your gaze shifts from the foreground to the background. Perspective gives the appearance of two converging lines that come together at the two low peaks in the background. (b) The same view taken with a telephoto lens. Depth cues are minimized relative to the wide-angle photo. There is more detail and less perspective. The telephoto lens also compresses the picture, as you can see by estimating the distance from the warehouses in the foreground to the hills in the background. This distance seems greater in panel (a). (© B. Kantowitz, Text-Eye)

ponents of everyday perception to help us understand how perception works outside the laboratory.

Illusions of perspective. Another important depth cue is *perspective*. A railroad track that disappears into the distance gives the impression that the two rails converge. Of course, we know that the rails remain the same distance apart—it would make it rather difficult for trains if rails did converge—but even so, the appearance of convergence remains. Artists use this depth cue of perspective to create the illusion of distance in their paintings, photographs, and other visual arts.

Psychologists have manipulated perspective to yield misleading illusions, as shown in figure 7–6. There are two possible interpretations of this figure. The face at the left is smaller, and ordinarily you would conclude that this person is farther away from you than is the larger person. But this first interpretation does not seem to hold because of constraints imposed by the wall of the room. You know that rooms are rectangular, and so the two windows must be equally distant from you. Hence, the second interpretation—that the person on the left must be a midget, and the one on the right a giant. This is an implausible interpretation and may seem odd to you—but how else can figure 7–6 be explained?

FIGURE 7–4.

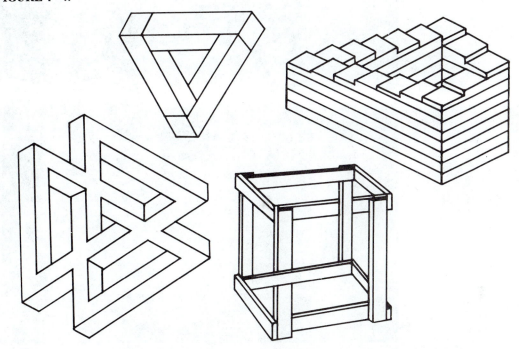

Impossible figures. The lower right-hand figure is the Freemish crate, designed by Cochran. The other figures were constructed by Penrose and Penrose. The upper right-hand figure has proved so popular that it has a well-known name in psychology: it is called the endless staircase. (From Baron, Byrne, and Kantowitz, 1977).

The conflict between these two explanations can be resolved by looking at figure 7–7. The room is trapezoidal, not rectangular. Thus, the person on the left really is farther away, and the first interpretation is correct. Since midgets, giants, and trapezoidal rooms all are rare, figure 7–6 was difficult to interpret. But since you probably have seen more midgets and giants than trapezoidal rooms, you naturally misinterpret the figure by letting your knowledge govern your perception. Now that you know the room is not rectangular, look again at figure 7–6. This time, imagine the wall tilting away from you, as shown in figure 7–7, with the left side much farther back than the right side. The illusion should be weaker—because your new knowledge allows a correct, although unusual, perception of the scene.

However, if we now had a young girl walk from point A to point B in the room, she would appear to increase in size—a very rare perception. Knowledge of the conflicting depth cues does not diminish our unusual perceptions very much, so the figure remains ambiguous and difficult to interpret.

Similar principles explain the card illusion of figure 7–8. It seems obvious that in each row, the cards on the left are closest to you, and the cards on the right farthest away. Even though the card on the right is largest in each row, the depth cue of overlap

FIGURE 7–5.

Underwater photo of a Christmas-tree worm. The body of the worm is hidden in a tube bored in to the coral. The plumes of the worm gather food and oxygen. The cratered surface is a piece of coral. (© B. Kantowitz, Text-Eye)

FIGURE 7–6.

The two men appear to be of quite different size, even though the same distance from the viewer. (From Ittelson and Kilpatrick, 1952)

FIGURE 7–7.

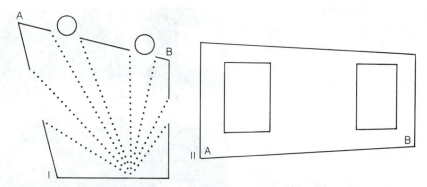

Top (I) and frontal (II) views of the distorted room shown in the preceding figure. The man on the left is really further away from the viewer and hence appears smaller. (From *Principles of Perception,* by S. Howard Bartley, Ph.D. Pub. 1958 by Harper and Brothers, N.Y.)

is more important than that of relative size. We know from experience that something that blocks another object must be in front of that object. Now look at figure 7–9. The cards on the right are really the closest. Once again, you have been tricked, because you have relied on your knowledge of the world to interpret a set of stimuli. It may still look as if the card on the right is farthest away from you. It is difficult to undo your habits of perception, even when you know for sure that you are seeing an illusion.

There are three reasons for presenting these illusions and ambiguous figures. First, you should now be convinced that seeing and believing do not necessarily coincide. Perception can be inaccurate, and you may be tricked into making several different perceptions of the same figure. Second, knowledge of the true state of the external world does not always improve perception, as is the case when you reexamine figure 7–8; this may cause misperceptions in unusual circumstances. If you yourself have difficulty deciding what you are perceiving, imagine how much trouble a psychologist might have in trying to decide how to interpret your

FIGURE 7–8.

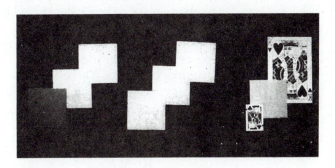

Which of the three cards in each set appears closest? (From Ittelson and Kilpatrick, 1952)

FIGURE 7–9.

The cards on the right are closest. Misleading cues for depth (size and overlap) have fooled you in the preceding figure. (From Ittelson and Kilpatrick, 1952)

perceptual report. Are you reporting what you know should be there, what is there even if it contradicts your preconceptions about the world (for example, rooms are rectangular), or something in between?

Third, you should also be convinced that most perceptions involve a complex interplay between direct and indirect factors (or bottom-up and top-down processes). Contemporary theories emphasize the interplay of the two. Examine figure 7–10. Most people readily read *THE CAT*, even though there is neither an *H* nor an *A* in those wordlike configurations. Perception of the middle letter in each of the "words" apparently is determined both by the surrounding letters (particular bottom-up sensory data) and by what we know about words in English (top-down conceptual processing). A theory of how both top-down and bottom-up processes work together to determine a percept is illustrated in figure 7–11, which is a schematic of a theory developed by McClelland and Rumelhart (1981).

McClelland and Rumelhart assume that there are three levels of perceptual recognition, each of which comprises hypothetical neuronlike elements. The initial level is the *feature level*, in which the aspects of a letter such as a straight line are recognized. The

FIGURE 7–10.

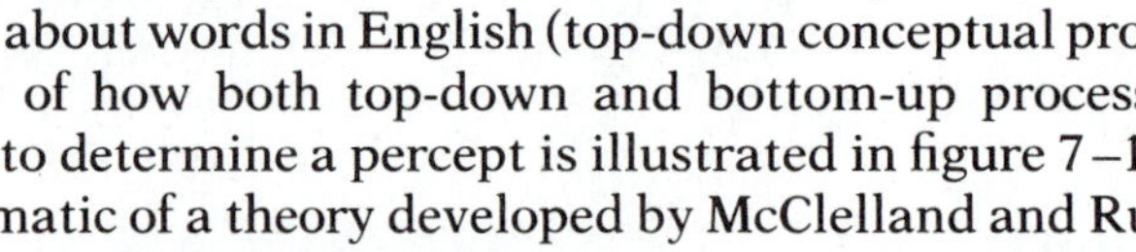

THE CAT

Most people easily perceive this as *THE CAT*, even though the middle letters of the two "words" are neither an *H* nor an *A*.

second level is the *letter level*, in which letter recognition units are activated by the feature data. The third level in the perceptual process is the *word level*, in which elements are activated by the letter units. The theory adds the interesting twist that as soon as a word unit is activated by letters, then it, in turn, reactivates the letters. This top-down feedback is circular, so that, as shown in the example, as word elements beginning with *th* become active, those words heighten the activation of the letter units *t* and *h*, which, in turn, heighten the activation of the word unit *THE*. This means that we perceive the information in figure 7–10 as *'THE CAT'*, even though neither *'THE'* nor *'CAT'* is there.

FIGURE 7–11.

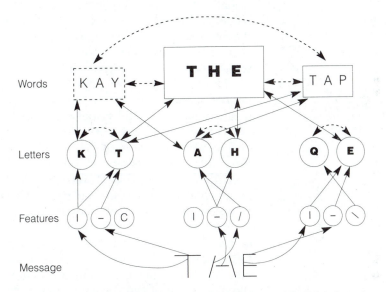

A schematic of the McClelland and Rumelhart computer model of visual word recognition that illustrates how a distorted word could activate *THE*. The arrows with solid lines indicate that one element excites or activates another, and the arrows with the broken lines indicate an inhibitory relationship between elements. Not all of the connections have been included. Letters are activated position by position simultaneously (at least in short words). *Feature level.* Initially, the visual message activates feature detectors (all features have not been shown). *Letter level.* In turn, the feature detectors activate letter detectors that contain their feature. Activation of letters is specific to the position of the letter in the message. Letter detectors mutually inhibit each other position by position (there can be only one first letter in a word). Letter detectors also receive top-down excitation from the words that they activate. *Word level.* The letter detectors excite word recognition units that contain their letter. The word units mutually inhibit each other. As shown by the double-headed excitatory arrows, when word units become active, they feed back excitation to the letter level. The word perceived is the one whose unit has a higher level of excitation than other word units. So, in this example the word *THE* has more excitation than does *TAP* because *T* is excited, *H* is partially excited, and *E* is excited. The total excitation for the letters in *TAP* is less. Furthermore, the feedback between *THE* and its letters increases the likelihood of seeing *THE*. The top-down activation of *H* by the word-unit *THE* means that we actually see the *H* even though it is not there.

Nature and Nurture in Perception

A second issue in research on perception, which is closely related to the direct/indirect controversy, concerns the relative importance of past experience and innate factors. This is a venerable controversy in perception, and in psychology as a whole (see chapter 12). The debate about the roles of nurture (experience) and nature (native or innate properties) in perception was clearly outlined by the eminent scientist Helmholtz (see appendix A) in the middle of the nineteenth century (for a modern translation of his work, see Helmholtz, 1962).

Helmholtz believed in a version of the indirect view we have just outlined. He thought that all our knowledge of depth (and the rest of visual perception, for that matter) resulted from our past visual experiences. When we are confronted with a new visual scene, such as that in figure 7–1, we interpret it by inferring that the perspective cues we sense mean depth. These *unconscious inferences*, as Helmholtz called them, occur rapidly and without conscious thought—the inferences are a visual habit.

The *empirical theory* of perception espoused by Helmholtz can be contrasted to a *nativistic theory*. According to the nativistic view, it is the nature of the visual system (the eye and the brain) that determines visual perception (for one example of a nativistic theory, see the discussion of the Gestalt psychologists in appendix A). Since infant organisms with minimal visual experience often show good depth perception (Kaufman, 1979), it is likely that native factors play an important role in many aspects of visual perception. Nevertheless, there is no denying that experience is an important determiner of perception as well: your perception of the word *perception* both as a word and as a word with a particular interpretation cannot be the result of just built-in processes in your nervous system. Experience must play a role in meaningful perceptions, as the discussion of the theory proposed by McClelland and Rumelhart indicates.

Most acts of perception are a complex interaction of native and empirical components. If perception results from the interplay of these two components, then the traditional idea that sensation provides the elements of perception will have to be modified. Consider an extreme possibility. If the characteristics of the eye and the built-in wiring of the nervous system completely determined depth perception—that is, experience is almost entirely irrelevant—then what is the interpretive component? Put more bluntly, what is the difference between sensation and perception? The possibility that sensation and perception are one and the same has been pursued by some (for example, Gibson, 1979), but most psychologists believe that at least some aspects of perception involve interpretations of sensory data.

Awareness and Perception

If the perceiver adds meaning and interpretation to sensations, the question arises as to whether these additions are the result of conscious deliberation. The controversial topic in perception on which we will focus for the remainder of this chapter concerns the role of conscious *awareness* in perception. The gist of the awareness issue is this question: Can meanings and interpretations be applied to sense data automatically, without our being verbally aware of them, or is verbal awareness a necessary part of perception? Helmholtz, you will remember, argued that our inferences and conclusions are unconscious. However, perception has to do with one's experience of an event, and much research on perception has attempted to understand the nature of this phenomenal experience (Kaufman, 1974). After all, the argument goes, if perception includes an experience or a feeling of "something," then we must be consciously aware of that "something."

Currently, a substantial amount of research is being undertaken to determine the relation between conscious awareness and perception. As you might expect, studying a private process such as consciousness (see appendix A) is fraught with numerous methodological problems. We will examine some of these in this chapter. To set the stage for our examination, we will first consider a remarkable neuropsychological case study, the patient D.B.

Blindsight: Detection without awareness. D.B. is an Englishman in his late forties. Except for the particular neuropsychological problem that he has, D.B.'s life (medically, socially, and psychologically) can be described as ordinary or typical. What follows is a précis of a detailed case study resulting from an intensive examination of D.B. over a thirteen-year period (Weiskrantz, 1986).

When D.B. was about fourteen, he began to experience violent headaches every six weeks or so, accompanied by a temporary oval of blindness in the left portion of his visual field. In his early twenties, the attacks increased in frequency, and a partial blindness remained permanently after one of the headache attacks. An angiogram, which is an X-ray picture of the head taken after an opaque substance has been injected into the bloodstream, revealed a mass of enlarged blood vessels at the tip of the visual cortex on the right side of the brain. This visual part of the brain and the distorted blood vessels were removed surgically. Immediately, his headache attacks stopped, and D.B. was able to lead a reasonably normal, productive life. However, after the operation, D.B. was blind in the left half of his visual field.

The reason that D.B. was blind in the left half of his visual field can be determined from figure 7–12. The right visual cortex contains the information in the left visual field, and the left visual cortex contains the information in the right visual field. Since D.B. had a large portion of his right visual cortex surgically removed to eliminate the headaches, the left visual field did not have the same representation in the brain as did the right visual field.

D.B.'s blindness was determined by a procedure called *dynamic perimetry*, which is the standard way of assessing visual field defects following accident or surgery. The procedure is a variant of ascending method of limits trials (see chapter 6). With the patient's

FIGURE 7–12.

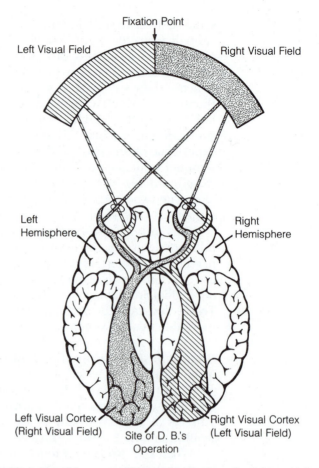

A simplified top view of the eyes and brain showing how the right and left visual fields are represented in the visual cortex at the back of the brain. The left visual field is represented in the right visual cortex, and the right visual field is represented in the left visual cortex. Because the site of D.B.'s operation was in the right visual cortex, he was blind in the left visual field.

head kept still, a spot of light is slowly moved across the visual field of one eye, starting at the perimeter. When the light is seen by the patient, it is returned to the perimeter and brought across the field again from a different angle. This procedure is repeated several times and results in a map of sensitive and blind areas in the visual field. Then the perimetry is repeated on the other eye. The blind part of the visual field is called a *scotoma;* D.B. had a scotoma in the left half of the visual field of each eye.

So far this blindness, though unfortunate, was as expected, given that brain tissue from the right visual cortex had been removed. However, some informal observations seemed to show that D.B. could locate objects in his blind field. For example, he could reach for a person's outstretched hand accurately, even though he could not see it. Furthermore, he could correctly guess the orientation (horizontal or vertical) of a stick that he claimed he could not see. In fact, D.B. vehemently denied that he saw anything in a portion of his left visual field, and he attributed his success on these informal tasks to lucky guesses.

Suppose you were Weiskrantz, the psychologist who observed this odd behavior. What would you conclude? On the one hand, D.B. was blind. He did not report seeing stimuli in his left visual field. On the other hand, D.B.'s behavior indicated that he could detect and locate stimuli in the same area. Weiskrantz and his associates believed D.B.'s verbal report that he could not see objects in his left visual field, so they undertook a series of controlled experiments to determine the visual capacity of D.B.'s scotoma.

Since D.B. could not see objects in the blind field, he was asked to make forced-choice guesses about the location and the presence or absence of small patches of light. Other tests required him to guess the orientation of very small lines. All the tests were done under controlled lighting conditions, and D.B.'s head and direction of gaze were kept fixed. Sometimes, the visual stimuli were presented so briefly in the blind area that D.B. could not move his eyes quickly enough to change his focus to the good visual field. The line and dot stimuli were small in size and not very intense, but their size and intensity may have influenced both good and bad visual fields simultaneously. Therefore, detection of these targets in the blind visual field was compared with detection in the good field and in the blind spot. Everyone has a blind spot in each eye. It is the part of the retina where the nerves exit the eyeball and thus is insensitive to light. If D.B. were able to detect a target in his blind spot, it would mean that the target was so intense or so big that it "leaked" out to sensitive areas of the eye. Since the blind spot was much smaller than D.B.'s field of blindness, and since he could not detect targets in his blind spot, Weiskrantz had chosen target stimuli with appropriate characteristics to test in the blind field.

Weiskrantz then presented D.B. with dots and lines of either horizontal or vertical orientation. The results of the controlled tests were very interesting. Localization, detection, and guessing of orientation of targets presented to the blind field were much better than could be expected by chance. In many cases, the visual performance from the blind field was nearly as good as that from the good visual field. D.B. could not identify objects presented to his blind field, and throughout the testing he claimed not to see the targets for which he was required to make forced-choice judgments. D.B.'s reaction to his success on the forced-choice trials was one of incredulity. He attributed his success to lucky guesses, because he simply could not see the target stimuli.

Blindsight is the name that Weiskrantz used to describe visual capacity in a scotoma (the blind field) when there is no acknowledged awareness of perception. Other cases of blindsight have been reported, and there is currently a substantial amount of theorizing and debate about the syndrome (Campion, Latto, and Smith, 1983). However, the generality of a dissociation between verbal awareness and perceptual capacity is not the issue, because other neuro-psychological studies have shown that different types of brain damage can result in disorders similar to blindsight. For example, Paillard and associates (1983) report the case of a brain-injured woman who was insensitive to touch on the right side of her body; yet, when she was asked to locate where she was touched on her unfeeling side, she could do so with considerable accuracy. She could also correctly guess the direction of movement on her skin, even though she could not feel the moving stimulus. Furthermore, as we will soon see, non-brain-damaged people can be induced to show a similar dissociation between awareness and perceptual behavior under controlled laboratory conditions. The issue, then, is to try to understand the relation between verbal reports of awareness and perception.

Before introducing the variables in perception research, we should note that blindsight and related phenomena pose serious problems for the view that perception is the interpretation of sensation. D.B. was making complicated sensory judgments in the absence of awareness. D.B. was sensing without perceiving. Examples later in this chapter will show that very complicated sensations involving meaning can occur without conscious interpretation. Does this mean that there is no difference between sensation and perception? Or does it mean that a new boundary line between sensation and perception needs to be determined? In either case, further research and theorizing are needed to clarify an extremely puzzling problem. Current research on vision suggests that there are two types of visual systems in the brain: one is important for identifying objects, and the other system has to do with detection and movement. Apparently, the problem suffered by D.B. was that the system concerned with identification was destroyed during the operation done to cure his headaches.

INTRODUCING THE VARIABLES

Dependent Variables

The simplest dependent variable is the verbal description given by an observer. Although this is the easiest measure to obtain, it often has several disadvantages. An untrained observer seldom is able to give a precise report. Although this can be corrected by proper training, there is always the possibility that the training, rather than the stimulus, is controlling the observer's report. We shall return to properties of subjective reports in a later section.

More objective measures of perception include reaction time and reports that can be verified directly by the experimenter. For example, if a string of six letters is presented in a *tachistoscope* (a device for controlling illumination and duration of stimuli) for 50 milliseconds and the observer is asked to report the letters, the experimenter can easily determine whether this report is correct. Observers are often asked to rate their confidence that their report is correct. Such rating measures, although not objective, can provide converging operations when used with other objective measures, such as reaction time.

As you can see, the major dimension for classifying dependent variables in perception is verifiability. Of course, all dependent variables must be verifiable and consistent. But some dependent variables can be verified directly, whereas others require subtle statistical methods, such as scaling, before verification can be achieved. So we will divide dependent variables into those that can be *immediately* verified (judged as correct or incorrect) by the experimenter, and those that cannot.

Independent Variables

As you might expect, the independent variables that are most common in studies of perception are those that alter the physical characteristics of stimuli. Psychologists change the size, shape, backgrounds, perspective, and angle of view of visual stimuli. Auditory stimuli can be varied according to frequency (pitch), intensity (loudness), waveform (timbre), and complexity (number of separate waveforms and their relationship to one another). The time course of perception is studied by presenting parts of a stimulus separated by short time intervals, or by limiting the presentation time of the entire stimulus to tens or hundreds of milliseconds.

Another class of perceptual independent variables is more qualitative than quantitative. Animals and people have been placed in abnormal circumstances where the usual perceptual inputs are either absent or grossly distorted. Some examples of this type of manipulation would be raising animals in the dark,

having people wear special goggles that distort their vision, allowing normal perception but preventing motor movements, and having a uniform visual field with no patterns or lines. Many such studies try to determine whether perception is learned like other behavior, or is innate. At one time, the distinction between innate and learned perception was a major controversy in psychology. Now, as noted earlier, most psychologists admit there are both innate and learned components in perception.

Control Variables

This chapter is concerned with what might be termed the intellectual aspects of perception; however, it cannot be denied that perception has emotional and motivational aspects as well. Thus when people are asked to report "taboo" four-letter words, these words require a greater display duration than do innocent control words. Similarly when hungry people observe an out-of-focus image, they report seeing food-related objects more often than people who have eaten recently. Although these phenomena are interesting in their own right, when we focus on the stimulus as the most important determinant of perception, these other effects become artifacts and must be controlled. In terms of signal-detection theory (see chapter 6), the decision aspects of perception must be held constant. Reporting a taboo word requires a greater display duration not because the word is harder to perceive, but because, as we will discuss later, observers are more reluctant to say a taboo word to the experimenter and hence alter their decision criterion.

Physical aspects of the stimulus that are not being investigated must also be controlled. Stimulus duration, intensity, illumination, contrast, and so on need to be held constant when they are not manipulated as independent variables.

7.1 Experimental Topics and Research Illustrations

Topic: Verbal Report
Illustration: Perception Without Awareness

A compelling aspect of research on perception is that the dependent variables seem to provide insight into the observer's *phenomenological experience,* which is the internal awareness of the external world. This insight seems especially strong when a *verbal report* is elicited from an observer. It seems apparent that the verbal report, or what the observer says is perceived, must be correlated with his or her awareness of the experience. However, when a verbal report is elicited, the psychologist must determine whether the verbal report is a useful dependent variable that provides a reliable and valid indicator of the observer's experience.

Reconsider the discussion of psychophysics in the previous chapter. One way to view the difficulty in establishing a true threshold by the method of limits is that what the subject reports is not solely a function of what is perceived. Sensitivity to the signal and the subject's willingness to respond combine to determine the decision threshold; this is the reason signal-detection methods were developed.

Psychologists are likely to accept most reports from psychophysical research as valid indicators of phenomenological experience for two reasons. In the first place, d′ and β can be determined under appropriate conditions. In the second place, most people report approximately the same fluctuations in experience when external stimuli are varied. The generality and regularity of the results increase our confidence in the utility of the verbal reports that are given in such experiments.

It is for this latter reason that the verbal reports occurring during magnitude estimation (see chapter 6) are accepted. If a rock band increases its amplification by a factor of ten and you report that it then sounds twice as loud, the psychologist has no direct check on your phenomenological experience. However, the fact that most observers respond in roughly similar ways to changes in stimulus energy suggests that the verbal report has some generality and thus is a valid way of assessing the observer's perceptual experience.

Deciding on the usefulness of a verbal report is sometimes very difficult. Imagine that you are confronted by a woman who claims to see little green people from Mars. Does she really *see* little green people? Since you and several others do not see these people, and since it is highly improbable that there is humanlike life (of any color) on Mars, you are likely to assume that the woman is demented—she is hallucinating. A *hallucination* is the report of an experience in the absence of any apparent corresponding stimulation.

Assuming that the woman is not lying, what are we to make of her verbal report that she sees little green people from Mars? Unlike the situation in a psychological experiment, in this instance there is a dramatic discrepancy between the stimulus (none or an irrelevant one) and the verbal report of the experience (green people). A psychologist interested in perception might not believe that the verbal report is an adequate indicator of perceptual experience. This is not to deny that the woman is actually experiencing the little green people. But her experience is unlikely to be a product of perception; rather, it probably is the result of mental pathology or the influence of drugs.

Now, reconsider the case of D.B. What are we to conclude from his verbal report, "I can't see the objects"? His verbal report did not coincide with his behavior in the presence of some kinds of stimuli. Was D.B. having a sort of negative hallucination (not seeing something that was actually there and otherwise detectable), or was his verbal report an accurate reflection of his perceptual experience? How do we decide on the utility of a report? D.B.'s verbal report was troublesome for an understanding of his perceptions, because from the standpoint of the experimenter there was an obvious discrepancy between the presence or absence of a stimulus and D.B.'s report of his perceptual experience (Weiskrantz, 1986). This discrepancy seems to be different from the lack of direct check seen in scaling experiments, because failing to identify an object while accurately localizing it represents a paradox.

How does the psychologist know when the response of the observer qualifies as a useful dependent variable? The answer is deceptively simple: It qualifies only when a verifiable relationship between the response and a previous perceptual event can be directly inferred. Natsoulas (1967) defined a report as

> a presumed or confirmed relationship between some preceding or synchronous event (e_i) and the response. This relationship must be such as to make possible direct inferences from knowledge of the response to e_i (p. 250).

This definition is purposely abstract and will make more sense once we have examined another concrete example.

In the preceding chapter, we discussed how a pigeon could be trained to tell us its absolute visual threshold (Blough, 1958). You will recall that the pigeon pecked one key when it saw the stimulus and a different key when it did not. Appropriate reinforcement contingencies were used to ensure that the pigeon's behavior was controlled by the stimulus. According to the definition just given, do the pigeon's pecking responses qualify as reports?

In this instance, the preceding event (e_i) is the stimulus with particular reference to its intensity. A peck on one key indicates that the stimulus is below the threshold, whereas a peck on the other shows that the pigeon can see the stimulus. This relationship is the direct inference called for in the definition. Knowing the response—that is, which key is pecked—allows a direct inference as to whether the pigeon is able to see the stimulus. We must conclude, therefore, that the pecking responses do indeed qualify as reports.

The essential characteristic of an adequate report of a perception is the relation between it and the preceding perceptual event. To the extent that alternate relations or inferences can be proposed, the report is weakened. For example, had Blough not been careful to eliminate the possibility that the pigeon learned to switch between keys only after a long string of pecks on a single key, this alternate relation could have also explained the pecking behavior. In that case, the pecking could not have been correctly interpreted as a perceptual report.

The pecking example also illustrates that the qualitative nature of the report is relatively unimportant. A key press is every bit as good as a verbal statement that the stimulus is or is not seen. Verbal statements can be responses to stimuli, rather than unverifiable reports. It is only the relation between the preceding event and the report that needs to be considered in order to establish whether a response is an adequate dependent variable. And just because a statement is verbal does not guarantee that it is also a report.

Now we can consider D.B.'s case in a slightly different way. His two classes of perceptual reports—the verbal one and the detection/localization one—are in conflict. The difficulty in understanding this conflict arises for two reasons. First, humans tend to place a great deal of emphasis on verbal reports as indicators of phenomenological experience. Thus, the verbal report must be the "correct" one, the cases of the demented woman and Blough's pigeons notwithstanding. Second, people make the incorrect assumption that all perceptual reports will have the same preceding synchronous event. It is logically possible (and empirically likely, as we shall soon discover) that the e_i for a verbal report is different from the e_i associated with other indicators of perceptual experience. Thus, it may be entirely possible for one report to indicate a perceptual experience and another to fail to do so. Let us see how one could study perception without verbal awareness. What are the indicators of perceptual experience in the absence of verbal reports of that experience?

Lack of verbal awareness. The topic of perception without awareness has had a long and controversial history (Eriksen, 1960). Recently, Marcel (1983) revived the controversy when he reported the results of a series of experiments that seemed to show the perception of meaning in the absence of verbal awareness. The normal college students who participated in Marcel's research behaved much like D.B.: they claimed that they could not perceive a word, yet their behavior indicated that they were sensitive to the meaning of the unperceived word.

In one of his experiments, Marcel combined several different research techniques. His basic task was a variant of the *Stroop effect*—named after Stroop (1935), who first reported on the phenomenon. A standard Stroop task is illustrated in figure 7–13. The subject sees a list of words and is supposed to rapidly name the ink color of each word. Compared with naming the ink color of a neutral noncolor word (such as *house* in red ink), color naming is slower when the word and ink color conflict (*red* printed in blue ink) and faster when the word and the ink color are congruent (*green* in green ink). The slower or faster color naming under conditions of word/color conflict or congruency define the Stroop effect.

Marcel modified the Stroop procedure by using a form of *priming*. Priming occurs when a word or other perceptual event biases the observer to perceive a subsequent event in a particular way. Seeing the word *red* printed in black ink could prime you to think of the color red, much like the old joke, "Don't think of an elephant" makes you think of an elephant. So if you had been primed by the word *red* to think of the color red, a subsequent color, such as green, might be unexpected, and a Stroop-like conflict would be produced. In Marcel's experiment, a priming word (for example, *red*) was presented just prior to a patch of color (for example, green), and the subject was to indicate quickly the color of the color patch (the observer was to say "green"). If priming works to produce a Stroop effect, then compared with a neutral word prime such as *house*, a congruent word prime (*green*) should speed up color naming of a green-colored patch, and an incongruent color-word prime (*red*) should slow down color naming of green. That is what Marcel found.

In the priming Stroop test, Marcel employed a clever technique to manipulate the observers' awareness of the priming word. The

FIGURE 7–13.

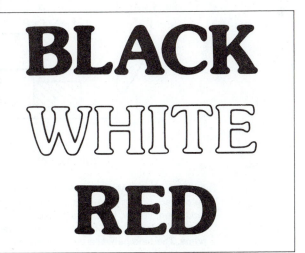

Stimuli used in Stroop test. The correct responses from top to bottom would be "black," "white," "black," because the subject names the ink color and ignores the color words.

perception of the priming word was prevented on some trials by a procedure called *masking*. Masking, in this context, involves presenting a jumbled pattern of letters immediately after the onset of a priming word. The mask will prevent the detection and identification of the word when it follows the word immediately; as the interval between the word and the mask increases, detection and accurate identification of the word also increase. An effectively masked prime should not be reportable by the observer, because he or she cannot detect or identify the prime. Marcel reasoned that if perception can occur without awareness, then an effective mask should not eliminate the Stroop effect induced by the prime. Regardless of whether the subjects are aware of the prime, their color naming should be sensitive to it, if the perception of meaning does not depend on verbal awareness. Alternatively, if awareness is necessary for the perception of meaning, then masking the prime should eliminate the Stroop effect.

Marcel's procedure for part of one of his experiments is outlined in figure 7–14. To present the stimuli, he used a tachistoscope, which is a device that allows very brief presentations. The time between prime and the patch of color was 400 milliseconds (ms), which is four-tenths of a second. Awareness of the prime was de-

FIGURE 7–14.

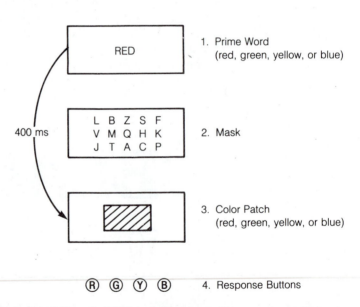

An illustration of Marcel's (1983) procedure (part of his experiment 3). A color patch (red, green, yellow, or blue) appeared 400 ms after a prime word (no word, red, green, yellow, blue, or a noncolor word). The mask on aware trials occurred with the color patch. On unaware trials, the mask was presented just after the prime. The time between prime onset and mask onset on unaware trials was determined separately for each subject, such that they could determine the presence of the prime no more than 60 percent of the time (chance detection would have been 50 percent). When the color patch appeared, the subject indicated the color by pressing a button corresponding to red, green, yellow, or blue.

termined by how much later the mask followed the prime. On aware trials, the mask was presented at the same time as the color patch (400 ms after the prime). This interval is long enough for the prime to be detected and identified.

On unaware trials, the interval between the onset of the mask and the onset of the prime was very short. Prior to the start of the Stroop test, the exact interval between prime and mask was determined individually for each subject. The color words were followed by a mask, and the observer was to detect the presence of the prime. The detection threshold was determined by the method of limits and was defined as the prime-mask interval that yielded detection less than 60 percent of the time, with 50 percent being chance performance. During the Stroop test, an interval 5 ms shorter than the detection interval was used on unaware trials.

On some Stroop trials, a prime was not presented. The remaining trials were defined by the relation between the prime and the color patch: neutral, congruent, or incongruent. The materials included four colors (red, green, yellow, and blue), four color words (red, green, yellow, and blue), and three neutral words (cough, kind, and water). After the color patch appeared, the observers pressed one of four buttons to indicate the color of the color patch. The reaction time to press the correct button was the primary dependent variable.

The results were straightforward. On both aware and unaware trials, a typical Stroop effect was obtained. Compared with neutral primes and no prime at all, color identification (for example, yellow) was slower following incongruent primes (for example, the word *blue*) and faster following congruent primes *(yellow)*—regardless of whether the subjects were aware of the primes. On the basis of these results and the results of other experiments that he did, Marcel concluded that meaning can be perceived without awareness.

In Marcel's experiment, the observers' behavior on the Stroop test showed that meaning had been registered, even though their verbal reports indicated that the primes had not been perceived. Cheesman and Merikle (1984) questioned the awareness interpretation of the results. They noted that Marcel's detection threshold of 60 percent allowed for the possibility of true detection on some trials (see chapter 6 on the distribution of responding in signal detection). Furthermore, Cheesman and Merikle reasoned that verbal reports of awareness may have a higher threshold than does differential responding to the meaning of words. If this is the case, then it is possible that Marcel may have inadvertently determined the wrong threshold when he adjusted the prime-mask interval to obtain less than 60 percent detection. Marcel's procedure may have resulted in a threshold that was below the observers' threshold for making a verbal report, but above their detection threshold.

Cheesman and Merikle tested the idea that the inappropriate threshold had been determined by replicating Marcel's Stroop experiment with a few important changes. First, they altered the way in which the detection threshold for the prime was determined. Instead of having the observer make judgments of the presence or absence of the prime, as in Marcel's work, Cheesman and Merikle forced the subjects to report which color word had been presented. This was done to minimize response bias in reporting the presence of a prime. In the forced-choice procedure, each prime is presented equally often, followed by a mask. Over an extensive series of trials, the observers responded equally often with each of the choices available (the same four color words Marcel used—red, green, yellow, and blue). Thus, the observers' criterion for saying a particular color was the same for all the primes.

The second important change that Cheesman and Merikle introduced was the calculation of several prime-detection thresholds for each subject. Using the method of limits, they varied the interval between the prime and mask so that forced-choice detection of the prime was 25 percent, 55 percent, or 90 percent. Chance level of detecting the prime in choosing among four alternatives is 25 percent. Thus, the lowest threshold they calculated was chance detection. The 55 percent level of responding was approximately equal to the threshold used by Marcel. The 90 percent threshold yields near-perfect performance. At all levels of detection, the mask was usually effective in eliminating verbal awareness of the prime. That is, even though the subjects could differentially detect the color words, depending on the prime-mask interval, they claimed not to be aware of what the words were—they claimed to be guessing.

In the Stroop portion of the experiment, Cheesman and Merikle followed Marcel's procedure (see figure 7–14), except that they had four conditions instead of two. The four conditions were the three prime-mask intervals, which yielded 25 percent, 55 percent, and 90 percent detection, as well as a no-mask condition. As in Marcel's experiment, the prime bore a neutral, congruent, or incongruent relation to the color patch.

The results of the Cheesman and Merikle experiment are shown in figure 7–15. The standard Stroop effect was obtained in each condition, except when the prime was detected at a chance level. Even though the observers claimed to be unaware of the primes in the 55 percent and 90 percent conditions, their behavior showed that they were sensitive to the meanings of the primes. At a very short prime-mask interval that leads to chance detection (the 25 percent condition), the subjects were not sensitive to the meaning of the primes.

If we take the chance detection threshold as the one indicating no awareness of the prime, then we can interpret the results of Cheesman and Merikle as providing no evidence for perception of meaning without awareness. On the other hand, behavior at the 55 percent and 90 percent prime-detection levels (where subjects say they are unaware of the prime) shows that there is perception of meaning. Cheesman and Merikle (1984; 1986) theorized that their data are congruent with the idea that there are two thresholds. One is an *objective threshold*, where the level of discriminative

FIGURE 7–15.

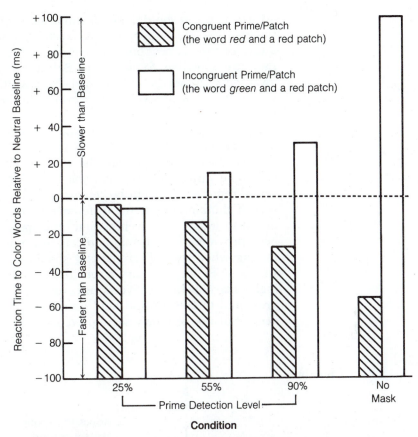

Results of Cheesman and Merikle (1984), showing reaction times to congruent and incongruent primes relative to the neutral primes in each of the four conditions. The Stroop effect is seen in all conditions except the 25 percent prime detection condition.

responding is at a chance level of performance. The other is a *subjective threshold*, where the level of discriminative responding is above the chance level, but the observers *claim* that they cannot detect or recognize the perceptual information. Thus, they are hypothesizing that discriminative response thresholds require a weaker synchronous event (e_i) than do verbal response thresholds.

To test this theory directly, Cheesman and Merikle (1984) conducted a second experiment in which they varied the intensity (energy level) of the prime to determine the two thresholds. At the objective threshold, observers detected at a chance level and were verbally unaware of the words. At the subjective threshold, observers detected the words 66 percent of the time, but claimed to be unable to identify them. Then, the Stroop test was repeated, and the Stroop effect was found for primes presented at the subjective threshold—but not for primes presented at the objective threshold.

The two-threshold theory is illustrated in figure 7–16. Between the two thresholds, people make verbal reports that they are unaware of the primes, but their responses to stimuli indicate that they are sensitive to meaning. Below the objective threshold, awareness cannot be determined, because the subjects both respond at a chance level and are verbally unaware. According to this way of viewing the masked-prime Stroop effect, Marcel had determined in his experiments the subjective threshold, not an objective one.

The theory derived from the work by Cheesman and Merikle has some important implications for understanding the role of verbal reports in perceptual research. In the first place, a coherent way of thinking about the difference between verbal reports believed to indicate awareness and other perceptual responses has been provided. For normal subjects, we now have ways of determining when such discrepancies should occur, and for patients such as D.B., we now have a sensible way of thinking about seemingly bizarre behavior. Weiskrantz reports that very strong stimuli presented to D.B.'s blind field produced some feelings of awareness—but not ordinary seeing. We can conclude that one conse-

FIGURE 7–16.

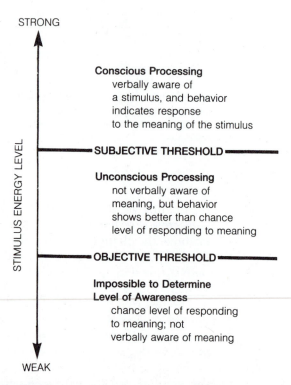

STRONG

Conscious Processing
verbally aware of
a stimulus, and behavior
indicates response
to the meaning of the stimulus

SUBJECTIVE THRESHOLD

Unconscious Processing
not verbally aware of
meaning, but behavior
shows better than chance
level of responding to meaning

OBJECTIVE THRESHOLD

**Impossible to Determine
Level of Awareness**
chance level of responding
to meaning; not
verbally aware of meaning

STIMULUS ENERGY LEVEL

WEAK

The two-threshold theory developed by Cheesman and Merikle (1984; 1986). Between the subjective and objective thresholds, people claim they are unaware of the stimulus, but their behavior shows otherwise. Below the objective threshold, people are unaware and their behavior is at a chance level. Above the subjective threshold, people are verbally aware of the stimulus and their behavior is sensitive to meaning.

quence of damage to the visual part of the brain is a marked elevation of the subjective threshold (as noted below, there are additional factors as well).

A second implication of the two-threshold theory is that there is not necessarily anything special about a verbal report. At each threshold level in the research by Cheesman and Merikle, the verbal report provided little information beyond that given by forced-choice discriminative responses. This suggests that such indexes of perception are perfectly adequate, and the premium that people place on the veracity of and necessity for verbal reports of awareness may be misplaced. In many instances, all that is needed to understand a perception is an indicator response: statements of awareness are not essential.

Nevertheless, the strong phenomenological component of perception remains, and people are aware of some things and not of others. The threshold of awareness cannot be the objective threshold. So Cheesman and Merikle (1986) conclude, "Given that perceptual awareness or consciousness is a subjective state, we propose that the subjective threshold, or the threshold for *claimed* awareness, better captures the phenomenological distinction between conscious and unconscious perceptual experiences and that the subjective threshold, therefore, provides a better definition of the boundary between conscious and unconscious processes than is provided by the objective threshold" (p. 344, emphasis in the original).

Cheesman and Merikle have offered an operational definition of awareness (see the discussions of operational definitions in chapters 6 and 12). Simply defining awareness does not allow us to distinguish conscious from unconscious processes and to determine the validity of a verbal report. At face value, Cheesman and Merikle simply allow each subject to use his or her own subjective confidence to establish the awareness threshold. They point out that this is a serious problem, because subjective confidence cannot be distinguished from response bias. If we have only the subjective threshold as a measure of the awareness threshold, then we are nearly back where we started: we have an unverifiable report. To solve this problem adequately, we need to use converging operations, a topic to which we now turn.

7.2 Experimental Topics and Research Illustrations

Topic: Converging Operations
Illustration: Perceptual Defense and Perception
Without Awareness

The distinction between the experience of perceiving and responding to stimuli, discussed in the preceding section, was a major impetus for applying the ideas of the physicist Bridgman to the psychological concept of perception. In a classic article entitled "Operationism and the Concept of Perception," Garner, Hake, and Eriksen (1956) showed that perception was more than just a response. This may seem obvious to you after reading the preceding section, so we must take a step backward in time.

Thirty years ago, experimental psychology was barely starting to recover from the throes of a rigidly applied framework of Watsonian behaviorism. Observers made responses that discriminated one stimulus pattern from another; for many psychologists, such responses were equivalent to perception. We now realize, largely owing to Garner, Hake, and Eriksen, that such a limited concept of perception arises from a very literal and incomplete interpretation of operationism. You will recall that, according to operationism, concepts are defined by the operations used to measure and produce them. If weight were defined as the movement of a meter located in a small rectangular box on your bathroom floor, then the response indicated on the scale dial when you stepped on the scale would define weight. If perception were defined as an observer's saying one stimulus looks different from another, then that response would be perception.

Garner, Hake, and Eriksen pointed out that this was only part of operationism. Equally important was the need for a *set* of operations to define each concept. They cited Bridgman (1945) to emphasize this neglected aspect:

> Operational definitions, in spite of their precision, are in application without significance unless the situations to which they are applied are sufficiently developed so that *at least two* methods are known of getting to the terminus. Definition of a phenomenon by the operations which produced it, taken naked and without further qualification, has an entirely specious precision, because it is a description of a single isolated event. (p.248, emphasis added)

Operationally defining perception as a discrimination response— that is, a response of *A* or *B*—is not enough. At least two operations are required. When only a single operation is used, it is impossible to distinguish between limitations of the perceptual system and those of the response system. Since perceptual and response systems are to some extent independent, two or more operations are required to separate the limitations of each system.

Converging operations are a set of two or more operations that eliminate alternate concepts that might explain a set of experimental results. This abstract definition is best understood through several examples. We start with an example used by Garner, Hake, and Eriksen (1956).

Perceptual defense. Let us take the so-called perceptual defense experiment mentioned earlier, in which taboo or vulgar words are presented to an observer. *Perceptual defense* refers to the fact that vulgar words must be presented for long durations before people will report seeing them. Presumably, some perceptual device prevented the observer from seeing the vulgar words—the observer is defended against seeing something obnoxious. Garner and his coworkers suggested using four words, two ordinary and two vulgar. The exposure time needed for an observer to report these words by pronouncing them to the experimenter turned out to be greater for the vulgar words. Does this mean that perception of vulgar words takes longer? Without any converging operations, it is impossible to tell. The alternate explanation, that the response system inhibits overt vocalization of vulgar words, cannot be eliminated. The results could be owing to either the perceptual system or the response system.

What converging operation might allow us to conclude which system is responsible for this effect? Garner and his colleagues suggested keeping the stimuli the same, but switching the responses so that ordinary words would be pronounced when vulgar words were the stimuli, and vice versa. So when the observer saw a vulgar word, the correct response would be an ordinary word. Vulgar words would have to be pronounced only when ordinary words were the stimuli. If vulgar responses still required more exposure time when paired with ordinary stimuli, we could conclude from both experiments that the response system, and not the perceptual system, was responsible for the effect.

Such an experiment was performed by Zajonc (1962). He used a paired-associate technique, in which taboo words could be paired with either neutral words or vulgar words. Results showed no perceptual effects. Greater exposure time was required when the response was a taboo word, not when the stimulus was vulgar and the response was neutral. This converging operation supported the response system as the locus for "perceptual defense."

This second experiment by itself no more provides converging operations than does the first experiment alone. Only the combination of *both* experiments yields converging operations. If only the results of the second experiment were known, it would be logically possible to argue that ordinary-word stimuli need longer exposure times when vulgar responses are used because either (1) ordinary stimuli take longer to be perceived than vulgar stimuli—that is, vulgar stimuli are somehow more potent, or (2) vulgar responses are inhibited. As is the case with the first experiment considered by itself, it would be impossible to choose between perceptual and response systems as the cause of the effect. However, when results of both experiments are jointly considered, only one conclusion can be drawn.

Perception without awareness. In the experiments by Cheesman and Merikle (1984), the phenomenological claims of unawareness to stimuli occurring below the subjective threshold cannot be distinguished from a response bias to withhold a verbal report of awareness. To bolster our confidence in the distinction between perception with awareness and perception without awareness, a converging operation is needed to show that perceptual processing under the two levels of awareness is qualitatively different. Otherwise, all we can say about the results is that the Stroop effect is sometimes accompanied by reports of awareness of the prime and sometimes not accompanied by awareness. Later experiments by Cheesman and Merikle (1986) provided the converging operations by showing that an independent variable (the frequency with which congruent prime-color patch trials occurred) had a qualitatively different effect on unconscious perceptual processing than it did on conscious perceptual processing. In addition to the subjective threshold, another variable distinguished between aware and unaware perception.

Cheesman and Merikle (1986) decided to vary the frequency with which congruent prime-color patch combinations occurred. Earlier research using different forms of the Stroop test had shown that the facilitation and inhibition of reaction time on congruent and incongruent trials (see the no-mask condition of figure 7–15) increased with increases in the frequency of congruent trials (Glaser and Glaser, 1982). The congruent trials (the word *red* and red ink) occurred twice as often as mismatches between the word and ink color. Observers had a strong tendency to say the color named by the word, and this anticipation speeded up responding on congruent trials. Since this anticipation would lead to an incorrect response on incongruent trials, reaction time was very slow on trials having a mismatch between word and color (for example, the word *yellow* and blue ink color). Frequency effects such as this represent a voluntary strategy on the part of the observers (Lowe and Mitterer, 1982). When congruent trials occur with high frequency, the subjects become biased toward making the most frequent response, based on their identification of the relative frequency of various types of trials. This results in a facilitation of reaction time on the majority of trials (the congruent ones), and a disruption of reaction time on only a small subset of trials (the incongruent ones).

Since the congruent, incongruent, and neutral primes each occurred on one-third of the trials in their earlier work, Cheesman and Merikle reasoned that the effects of increasing the frequency of congruent-prime trials (to two-thirds of the trials) would depend on whether the primes were above or below the subjective threshold. They argued that if the frequency effect resulted from the observers' identification of the most frequent type of trial, then when the primes were presented below the subjective threshold and could not be consciously identified, the frequency effect would not occur. If the primes were above the subjective threshold and could be consciously identified, then the frequency effect would be observed.

After showing that congruent primes presented on two-thirds of the no-mask trials enhanced the Stroop effect, Cheesman and

Merikle then varied the frequency of congruent-prime trials: they occurred on one-third or two-thirds of the trials. They also had primes either below the subjective threshold or well above it.

The results of this experiment are shown in figure 7–17. Just as in their earlier work (see figure 7–15), the Stroop effect did not depend on whether the primes were above or below the subjective threshold. However, the frequency of congruent trials had an effect only when the primes were above the subjective threshold and were consciously identified. Observers can use strategies only when they are consciously aware of the stimuli as defined by the subjective threshold. Thus, converging operations indicate that conscious and unconscious perceptual processing are qualitatively different, and the phenomenological distinction between different levels of awareness in perception is on firm experimental ground. These conclusions required two sets of observations: the determination of different awareness thresholds and demonstration of the differential effect of congruent trial frequency across levels of awareness. Both sets of observations converge on the adequacy of the distinction between perception with awareness and perception without it.

FIGURE 7–17.

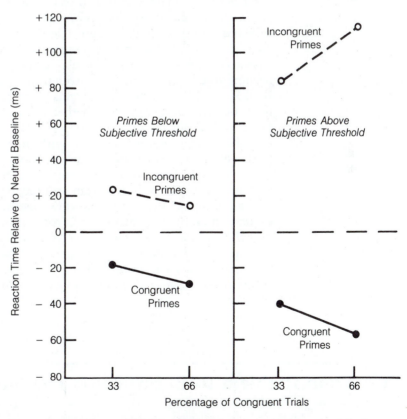

Results of Cheesman and Merikle (1986), showing an enhancement of the Stroop effect for primes above subjective threshold when the frequency of congruent trials is increased. The magnitude of the Stroop effect for unaware primes is not influenced by the frequency of congruent trials.

Blindsight reviewed. Our analysis of D.B.'s perception is incomplete. Converging operations are needed to verify the claim that he could not see objects in his blind field, despite his ability to accurately detect and localize them. To provide converging operations to show that D.B.'s perception of objects in his blind field was qualitatively different from that in his good field, Weiskrantz used a tactic similar to the one used by Cheesman and Merikle.

The procedure used by Weiskrantz to provide converging operations is called *double dissociation of function* (Milner, 1970). In this procedure, opposite behaviors are elicited by two different tasks from different areas of functioning. Specifically, Weiskrantz wanted to find a set of conditions under which detection and localization were *poorer* in the good field than in the blind one, while at the same time demonstrating that recognition and identification still were absent in the blind field and present in the good one. If there were opposite perceptual deficits in the two fields under these conditions, then Weiskrantz could be sure that the kind of vision in the blind field was qualitatively different from that in the good field and that the blindness was not just a poorer version of normal vision.

Weiskrantz presented an *x* or a triangle to the periphery of the good field; for brief and dim presentations, detection there was poorer than detection in the center portion of the blind field. Despite the poor detection in the good field, D.B. could still say whether an *x* or a triangle had been presented on these trials. As was the case in other experiments, accurate detection in the blind field was accompanied by blindness for the identification of the stimuli. That is, D.B. could tell when the targets were presented to the blind field, but he could not tell whether an *x* or a triangle had been presented. From his experiments on D.B., Weiskrantz concluded that the dissociation is consistent with the idea that there are two visual systems. As mentioned earlier, one is a "what" system that concerns identification and recognition. The other is a "where" system that deals with detection and localization. In the absence of brain damage, these systems work together, so that detection is accompanied by recognition and, in adult humans, verbal awareness. Except for verbal awareness, Weiskrantz (1977) has observed similar dissociations of the "where" and "what" functions in animals, upon surgical removal of parts of their visual systems. Thus, an additional converging operation, a controlled procedure on animals, adds to an understanding of visual perception as comprised of two functional systems.

 # From Problem to Experiment: The Nuts and Bolts

Problem: The color-distance illusion

It is well known in the visual arts that warm colors (yellow, orange, red, and transitions between these colors) give the appearance of moving toward the viewer, whereas cool colors (blue, green) seem to recede from the viewer. A two-dimensional picture can be made to look three-dimensional by such artistic devices as having blue backgrounds and warm-colored foregrounds. This illusion can be quite convincing. One of us remembers viewing an exhibition of stained glass in which one work of art had several deep blue panes of glass surrounding a red circle. The illusion of three dimensions was so strong that the circle looked as if it floated about ten centimeters in front of the blue background. The author had to go up and touch the glass to convince himself that the red and blue pieces of glass were in the same plane.

Let us imagine that an experimental psychologist wishes to investigate this warm–cool color illusion. The problem can be simply stated.

Problem: *Why do warm colors appear to come forward and cool colors appear to recede?*

Before trying to answer this question in any detail, a careful experimental psychologist would first attempt to demonstrate the phenomenon in controlled laboratory circumstances. He or she would want to rule out the possibility that the illusion occurs because of other artistic devices such as perspective or variations in brightness, both of which can create an appearance of distance. So a general hypothesis that color serves as a cue to depth would first be advanced. As is always true, several more specific testable versions of this general hypothesis can be formulated.

Hypothesis: *When pairs of color patches are presented in the same plane, the warmer color will be judged closer by a person viewing these stimuli with one eye (monocularly).*

The major independent variable is, of course, the color (or, more technically, the hue) of the visual test patches. Another independent variable that would probably be manipulated at the same time is the distance between the eye and the stimuli. This variable would be included because the experimenter would have no prior reason to select some particular viewing distance. Since there is nothing special about the viewing distance, you might think that this independent variable is unnecessary. Any distance selected at random would do. Although this reasoning is correct if the assumption that distance does not matter is true, this is only the experimenter's best guess. Since it is easy and inexpensive to use three or four viewing distances instead of only one, most experimenters would go ahead and manipulate distance. Data showing that viewing distance has no effect on the depth cue of color, although a null finding, is still of interest, since it would allow ruling out certain explanations of the illusion. Finally, the experimenter's guess might be wrong, and the two independent variables (hue and viewing distance) might interact.

How many hues should be tested in this experiment? If all possible pairs of hues are to be presented to the observer, we find that the number of stimuli (a stimulus is one pair of color patches) increases dramatically with the number of hues to be tested. The minimum experiment would have three hues: one warm, one cool, and one neutral gray. This would require a total of three stimuli to present all possible pairs. Although this total is most reasonable in terms of demanding experimental effort, three stimuli (and only two real colors) are too few to establish the generality of the effect. The next number of hues is five: two warm colors, two cool colors, and one gray. This would require ten stimuli. Seven colors would require twenty-one stimuli, and nine colors thirty-six stimuli. To keep the experiment to a reasonable time, we might select five colors and four viewing distances.

The dependent variable is a forced-choice judgment, with the observer being required to state which of the two color patches appears closer. (Actually, they are both the same distance from the observer.) This would be scored by creating a matrix, with all the hues listed down the columns and also across the rows. Each cell in the matrix specifies a combination of two colors. The main diagonal would not have any entries, since the same color would not be presented twice within a stimulus. Cell entries would be the number of times (or the percentages) that color X was judged to be closer than color Y.

As with any perceptual experiment, many control variables are required. What the person in the street calls color is actually composed of three independent attributes: hue, saturation, and brightness. *Hue* is the frequency of the light and corresponds to shade of color—red, green, etc. *Saturation* corresponds to the strength of color—that is, whether it is pale and washed-out or deep and strong. *Brightness* refers to the amount of light reflected from a surface. Since our experiment has hue as its major independent variable, both saturation and brightness must be controlled. Brightness especially is an important cue to depth, with brighter objects being perceived as closer to the viewer, all other things being equal. So we must be extremely sure that all our stimuli are of equal brightness. Another of the control variables has already been given in the hypothesis, which specified monocular (one eye) viewing conditions. Because each eye sees external objects from a slightly different location, binocular vision (both eyes) is an important cue for depth perception. Since we are primarily interested in color as a possible depth cue, all other cues to distance must be eliminated from the experiment.

We do not know what the results of this experiment would be. However, for purposes of further discussion, let us pretend that warm colors were judged as closer. We would then formulate another hypothesis, trying to provide a converging operation to bolster the results and interpretation of this first experiment.

Hypothesis: *When an observer is asked to move an adjustable colored stimulus so that it appears in the same plane as a fixed colored stimulus, the distance between the two stimuli will be set so that the*

*adjustable stimulus will be closer to the observer if it is a cool color
and the fixed stimulus is a warm color, and vice versa.*

This hypothesis is more complicated than the first, so let us explain
it in more detail. Imagine two colored circles in front of you, with
one of them sitting on a pulley so that it can move forward and
backward. The other circle cannot be moved. Your task is to adjust
this pulley until both stimuli appear equally distant from you. The
hypothesis predicts that, since warm colors will appear closer to
you, a cool color (which appears farther away) placed on the pulley
must be moved closer in order to appear even with the fixed warm
color. Similarly, if the fixed color is cool, it will appear farther
away, so that a warm color (which will appear closer) on the pulley
must be moved farther away from you than the fixed color.

The independent and control variables are as before. The dependent variable is now the distance between the observer and the
adjustable stimulus. However, in scoring this distance, we probably would take the position of the fixed stimulus as zero and record
a negative number if the adjustable stimulus is closer to the viewer
and a positive number if it is farther away. Whereas the first experiment yielded a qualitative assessment of the warm – cool illusion, this experiment gives a number based on perceived distance. Thus, it provides an indication of how strong or weak the
illusion might be for different combinations of colors. If we were
bold enough, this hypothesis could be made even more specific by
predicting that the size of the illusion would depend on the difference in frequency between the hues of each pair of stimuli. As
stimuli were further apart in the visual spectrum, greater distance
settings would result.

So far, our two experiments have been aimed more at establishing the replicability and reliability of the (hypothetical) finding
that warm colors move forward and cool colors recede than at
explaining why this happens. The converging operations provided
by the two experiments are weak, since they are quite similar and
differ only in the precision with which the dependent variable is
measured. In particular, the judgments made by the viewer are
relative judgments concerning two colors viewed simultaneously.
One next step toward explaining our (hypothetical) result would
be to provide a stronger converging operation by requiring an
absolute judgment about a single stimulus.

Hypothesis: *When an observer, using both eyes, is required to estimate the distance of a single colored stimulus chip, warm colors will
be judged to be closer than cool colors.*

Our independent variable is unchanged, as are the control variables. The dependent variable is a direct estimate of distance. There
are several scaling techniques that could be used, but for the sake
of simplicity we shall let our observer make a judgment in distance
units that are familiar to him, such as inches or centimeters. Of

course, it is unlikely that, even for a neutral-gray stimulus, such estimates will be highly accurate, but that is not the issue we wish to investigate. All we care about in this experiment are the relative values of the distance estimates for warm versus cool colors. If results agree with those hypothesized for the first two experiments, we have learned that there is some absolute property of color that serves as a cue for distance. If no differences are found—that is, if distance estimates are the same for all colors—there remain two possibilities. You have probably noticed that the hypothesis states that normal binocular vision (both eyes) was to be tested. This is another converging operation. If results were negative, a careful experimenter would replicate this third experiment, using monocular vision, as before. If results still were negative with monocular vision, then we would be forced to conclude that the warm—cool distance illusion was a property of relative judgments and that a contrast between two stimuli was necessary to produce it. This would be a major step in explaining the effect, but still only a beginning. The remaining steps are left as exercises for future experimenters. (If you want to find out more about this, look up *chromatic aberration* in a perception text, such as Kaufman, 1979).

SUMMARY

1. Perception is often described as the interpretation of sensation. Issues in the study of perception include the role of direct and indirect processes in perception (often referred to as bottom-up and top-down processes); the ways native and experiential factors influence perception; and the part played by awareness.

2. Illusions illustrate that perception is not always verifiable (accurate). Impossible figures and illusions of perspective show how perception depends on past experience. People try to interpret perceptual data in a meaningful way, even if the actual stimulus contains ambiguities. Thus, they can be tricked by certain stimuli because of expectations about the way the world is organized.

3. Verbal reports allow the psychologist to study another person's perceptual and phenomenological experiences. However, care is needed to make sure that the verbal reports are adequate dependent variables. Examples of perceptual issues that have been studied by verbal reports are blindsight and perception without awareness.

4. In the Stroop effect, work by Cheesman and Merikle indicates that there is a difference in verbal awareness for items presented above a subjective threshold and for those presented below the subjective threshold and above the objective threshold.

5. Converging operations allow inferences about perceptual operations that are stronger than inferences from a single experiment or experimental condition. Converging operations have allowed psychologists to have a better understanding of blindsight and perception without awareness.

KEY TERMS

awareness
blindsight
bottom-up processing
conceptually driven processing
converging operations
data-driven processing
direct perception
double dissociation of function
dynamic perimetry
empirical theory
hallucination
illusion
impossible figure
indirect perception
masking
objective threshold

nativistic theory
perception
perceptual defense
perspective
phenomenological experience
priming
scotoma
sensation
size constancy
Stroop effect
subjective threshold
tachistoscope
top-down processing
unconscious inferences
verbal report

DISCUSSION QUESTIONS

1. It has been found that the threshold to identify a letter is lower when that letter appears in a word than when it is presented alone or in a nonword. So, if subjects are briefly shown the word *bird* and then are asked whether there was an *r* or an *l* in it, they do so more accurately and at a briefer presentation time than when *r* is presented alone or in a nonword such as *dirb*. This is called the *word-superiority effect,* and McClelland and Rumelhart developed their theory to account for it. See if you can use the information in figure 7–11 to account for the word-superiority effect.

2. If you have ever taken prescription drugs to alleviate surgical or dental pain, you may have experienced a dissociation between the feeling or pain (the hurt) and your ability to localize the source of pain. Relate this to blindsight and perception without awareness.

3. Consult Garner (1974), and discuss how converging operations are used to bolster the concepts of dimensional integrality and separability.

4. Design your own experiment to further investigate the warm-cool color distance illusion.

5. Consult a perception text (such as Coren and Girgus, 1978; Kaufman, 1979), and discuss additional examples of illusions and phenomenological reports. The rotating trapezoid is one of many relevant illusions you will find appropriate for discussion.

The Stroop Effect

YOU CAN EASILY TRY the Stroop test for yourself. All you need are some index cards, colored markers, and a watch with a second hand or, even better, a stop watch. Take sixteen index cards, and using your markers, write the name of the color in its color—that is, with a green marker, write GREEN, etc. If you have eight markers, each color will be repeated twice. If you only have four markers, repeat each color four times. Take another sixteen index cards and write color names that do not correspond to the ink—that is, with a green marker, write RED, etc. Your stimuli are now completed. Pick one of the two decks; for each card, name the color of the ink. Time how long it takes you to go through all sixteen cards. Do the same for the other deck. Were you faster for the deck that had compatible color names and inks?

Another way that you can study the Stroop effect is to use number stimuli. Determine how quickly your subjects can read through a long column of digits in which the numbers 1 through 4 are repeated several times. Then determine how long long it takes them to count the numbers of arbitrary symbols in a column. The column should be as long as the first one, and you should use a symbol such as a dollar sign in such a way that there are 1, 2, 3, or 4 of them on a line. Now, you are ready to try the Stroop conflict condition. Work up a column as long as the previous two in which you have stimuli such as *2 2 2 2*, *1 1*, *3*, and *4 4 4*. The subjects' task is to name the number of digits; that is, to say "four" when they see *2 2 2 2*, and so on.

For your last experiment, have your subjects read all the stimuli when they are presented upside down. This will make reading more difficult and slow down the rate of responding. What happens to the magnitude of the Stroop effect? Why?

CHAPTER

Attention and Reaction Time

The great tragedy of Science—the slaying of a beautiful hypothesis by an ugly fact.

—T. H. HUXLEY

THERE ARE MANY INSTANCES IN life in which a small amount of time has a crucial effect. A jet airplane traveling at seven hundred miles per hour will cover almost two miles in ten seconds. The few seconds it takes the pilot to notice another plane on a collision course and make an appropriate correction can mean the difference between life and death. The time it takes a driver of an automobile to notice that the car he or she is following is stopping and to step on the brake pedal determines whether an accident or a safe stop will occur. The time required for a child to pull down his or her pants could spell the difference between making a big mess and reaching the potty quickly enough to prevent a minor disaster. The familiar adage "time is money" shows how important a role time plays in American life.

Psychologists, too, are much concerned with the time needed to accomplish different mental operations. By measuring this time, they are able to make inferences about the structure and organization of mental events: events that by their nature cannot directly be observed. Studying *reaction time*—that is, the time between the occurrence of a particular stimulus and a response to that stimulus—gives psychologists a window into the mind. As we shall see, this window is often streaked and clouded, but use of good methodology and experimental principles can clean up the window somewhat and improve our view of mental operations.

A topic closely related to reaction time is that of attention. Paying attention to something can often speed up your reaction time. If you expect the car in front of you to stop, you will react more quickly than if you were not ready. Attention also plays a role in how many different things you can do at the same time. A drummer in a rock band can keep playing in rhythm while having a conversation, perhaps with an attractive listener, at the same time. But does the conversation force the drummer to play more poorly (or the drumming force him or her to converse more poorly) than if only one task were being performed at a time?

The ABC of Reaction Time

The psychologist's interest in reaction time began in the eighteenth century, when an assistant at the Royal Observatory was fired because his reaction times did not agree with his employer's reaction times. Today, of course, labor unions would prevent such misfortune, but back in those days employees did not have much in the way of job security. Although history has duly noted the mistake of the Royal Observatory, experimental psychology came too late to help the poor assistant. Here is how it happened.

Astronomers in those days recorded the time and position of astral events by observing when some celestial body crossed a hairline in the eyepiece of their telescope. A nearby clock ticked every second, and the observer was expected to note the crossing time to the nearest tenth of a second. When Kinnebrook, the unfortunate assistant at the Royal Observatory, had his crossing times checked by his boss, they were always too great. Kinnebrook was warned, but was unable to shorten his observation times—and so was booted out of the Observatory.

This would have been the end of the tale, except that the astronomer Bessel heard of the incident from some of his friends and began to wonder whether the systematic difference between Kinnebrook and his boss was caused by something other than incompetence. He suspected that each person might observe the same crossing with slightly different reaction times. Indeed, when astronomers began to compare their measurements of crossing times, systematic differences among astronomers were found consistently. This phenomenon was named the *personal equation,* and one can imagine astronomers of the day busily comparing personal equations at the annual meeting of the Royal Astronomical Society.

The personal equation remained only a problem in astronomy until the Dutch physiologist Donders realized he could use it to calibrate the time required for various mental operations. Donders established three kinds of reaction-time situations that are still known as *Donders A, B,* and *C reactions.* In the *A* reaction shown in figure 8–1, sometimes called *simple reaction,* a light goes on and the observer responds by pressing a key or button. There is only one stimulus and one response. When you turn off your alarm clock in response to a loud signal, the time between the onset of the sound and your depression of the alarm button is called simple reaction time. Donders believed that simple (or *A*) reaction time was a baseline that took into account factors (such as speed of nerve conduction) that were components of more complex reaction

FIGURE 8–1.

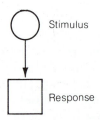

Stimulus

Response

The Donders *A* (or simple) reaction task. One stimulus is linked to one response.

times. These more complicated reaction situations he called *B* and *C* reactions. In a *B* or *choice reaction* situation, as shown in figure 8–2, there is more than one stimulus and more than one response. Each stimulus has its own unique response. When your car is at a traffic light, you are faced with a choice (or *B*) reaction. If the light is green, you step on the accelerator; if it is red, on the brake pedal. What mental operations are necessary for such a choice reaction? First, you must identify which light, red or green, has been illuminated. Then you must select which pedal, accelerator or brake, you should press down. A choice reaction, therefore, involves the mental operations of stimulus identification and response selection. To estimate the time required for these two mental operations, we must study yet a third kind of reaction: the Donders *C* reaction, shown in figure 8–3. Here, as in the *B* reaction, there are several stimuli. However, unlike the *B* reaction, only one stimulus is linked with a response. If any other stimulus occurs, the correct behavior is to withhold responding and to do nothing. Waiting in line at a takeout restaurant would be an example of a *C* reaction. Until your number is called, you should not respond. What mental operations are necessary to perform a *C* reaction? As in the *B* reaction, you must identify your number when it is called. However, once this is accomplished, there is no need to select a response, since only one response is appropriate. So the *C* reaction requires stimulus identification, but no response selection.

We can now estimate the time required for the mental operations of identification and selection by subtracting appropriate pairs of reaction times. The *C* reaction measures identification plus assorted baseline times (nerve-conduction time, etc.). Therefore, subtracting the *A* reaction time from the *C* reaction time tells us

FIGURE 8–2.

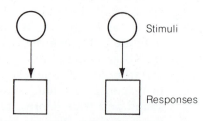

Stimuli

Responses

The Donders *B* (or choice) reaction task. Two stimuli are linked to two responses.

FIGURE 8–3.

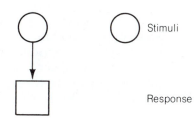

The Donders *C* reaction task. There are two stimuli, but only one of them is linked to a response.

how long identification takes. Similarly, subtracting the *C* reaction time from the *B* reaction time estimates selection time, since the *B* reaction includes identification, selection, and baseline times, while the *C* reaction includes only identification and baseline times. These relationships are shown in figure 8–4.

You would think that such an important discovery—the ability to measure mental events—would have made Donders a famous man in his time, that he would have received many awards, and perhaps even the nineteenth-century equivalent of a ticker-tape parade down Wall Street. At first, Donders' method was considered very promising; when Wundt (see appendix A) opened his psychology laboratory in 1879, his students devoted much effort to studying reaction time. But they were not able to obtain firm estimates of the times needed to perform different mental processes. Early in the next century, introspectionists mounted a fierce attack on the *subtractive method*, and it was discredited.

FIGURE 8–4.

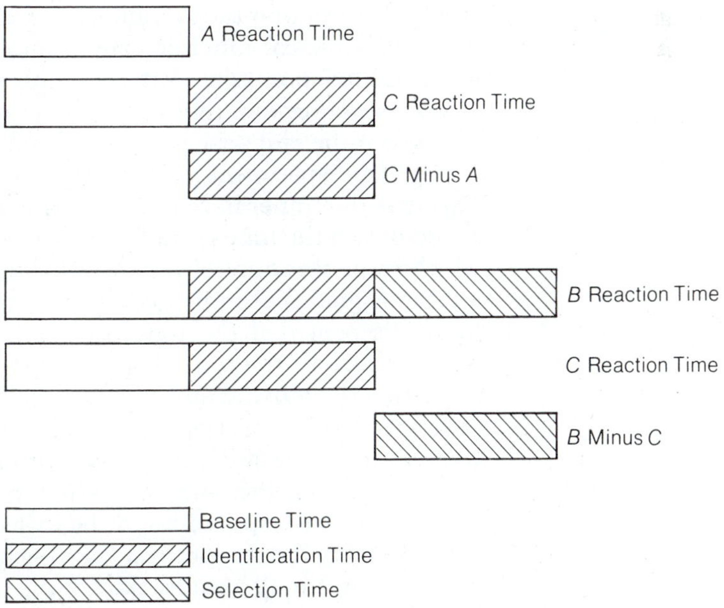

	A Reaction Time
	C Reaction Time
	C Minus *A*

	B Reaction Time
	C Reaction Time
	B Minus *C*

☐ Baseline Time
▨ Identification Time
⧄ Selection Time

Illustration of Donders' subtractive method.

Donders' subtractive method predicted that when the three kinds of reactions are ordered, the *B* reaction should take the longest, then the *C* reaction, then the *A* reaction. This prediction comes about because the *A* reaction has only basic mental components (baseline time), the *C* reaction two components (baseline and identification), and the *B* reaction three components (baseline, identification, and selection). Indeed, when data are acquired, this prediction is completely confirmed. Nevertheless, despite a promising beginning, Donders' subtractive method was scorned for much of the last century. To understand this rejection of method and supporting data, we must realize that the dominant mode of psychological inquiry in the early twentieth century was the method of introspection (see appendix A). Although psychology later rejected this method, at that time it was all-powerful. Trained introspectionists performed *A*, *B*, and *C* reactions and reported that a *C* reaction did not feel like an *A* reaction plus something else, nor did a *B* reaction feel like a *C* reaction plus something else. Instead, the three reactions all felt completely different. Strange as it may seem now, at that time this was enough to discredit Donders' subtractive method. It did not feel right and so, much like the hapless assistant Kinnebrook, it was booted out.

Today, of course, Donders holds a respected position in experimental psychology, and his method (and more sophisticated extensions of it) are widely used. Indeed, even now Donders' method has "never been discredited on any basis other than introspective report" (Taylor, 1976, p. 179).

Donders' subtractive method is more than a historical footnote in modern experimental psychology. Researchers are still exploring the validity of its assumptions today. Gottsdanker and Shragg (1985) realized that the stimulus in a reaction-time task carries out two psychological functions simultaneously. First, there is an informative function; that is, the stimulus tells which response should be executed. Second, there is an imperative function: the stimulus tells when the response should be made.

In their experiment, an auditory tone occurred on half the trials. This was the imperative stimulus. Subjects were instructed to respond only if the tone occurred. However, the tone did not indicate which response should be made. This knowledge was conveyed by a visual signal that indicated whether a left or right response was to be performed if the tone occurred. The visual signal always occurred before the tone. The visual signal conveyed advance information (Kantowitz and Sanders, 1972); if processed, this should have speeded up reaction time relative to the (standard) condition where imperative and informative stimuli occurred together (since they are usually the same stimulus). In other words, knowing in advance which response might be called for allows the subject to start planning the response and getting it ready. This should reduce RT (reaction time), because part of the mental work in responding has already been completed by the time the imperative stimulus (the tone) is heard.

The time between the informative and imperative stimuli varied between 0 and 150 ms. Gottsdanker and Shragg (1985) were interested in how this advance processing time would be used for simple and choice reactions. In the choice-reaction task, there should be an advantage of presenting the informative stimulus early. However, in the simple-reaction task, there is only one response possible; the informative stimulus is not useful, because the response is already known. Thus, plotting RT as a function of the interval between informative and imperative stimuli should yield a horizontal line for simple reactions. But for choice reactions, RT should be high at the 0 interval and gradually decrease and asymptote at the RT for simple reactions. This prediction was verified. Another prediction concerned the hypothetical latency between the onset of the informative stimulus and the onset of the response. Since the onset of a response is a hypothetical mental event that cannot be observed directly, subtractive logic must be used to estimate this mental latency. Gottsdanker and Shragg predicted and found that mental latency was constant for short intervals between informative and imperative stimuli, and then increased for longer intervals. These results are strong support for the validity of Donders' subtractive method.

The most popular extension of Donders' subtractive method is the *additive factors* method proposed by Sternberg (1969). The mathematics of this new method is beyond the scope of this text, but we can give an approximate verbal description. The method of additive factors takes a total reaction time and breaks this down into successive stages of information processing. The definition of a stage was left vague, but it roughly corresponded to one complete subunit of processing. There are two important differences between the subtractive method and the additive-factors method (Taylor, 1976). First, Sternberg used experimental manipulations to alter the durations of stages. The experimental independent variables used to accomplish this were called *factors*. Second, Sternberg provided a way to infer a relationship between factors and stages. Factors that influenced different stages would cause additive (noninteracting) influences on reaction time. Factors that influenced the same stage (or stages) would interact. So by doing factorial experiments and looking for patterns of interaction and additivity, psychologists could discover how processing stages were related.

Biederman and Kaplan (1970) used the method of additive factors to determine if two independent variables, stimulus discriminability and stimulus-response compatibility, influenced the same or different stages of mental processing. Their stimulus display was a set of four lights arranged in a rectangle: two left lights forming the left vertical axis of the rectangle and two right lights forming the right vertical axis. The response set was two pianolike keys. On any trial all four lights would go on with different intensities. In the high stimulus-response compatibility condition, the correct response was pressing the key on the same side as the brightest light. In the low stimulus-response compatibility condition, the correct response was the key on the opposite side; for example, if the top left light was brightest, the correct response for the low compatibility condition would be to press the right key versus pressing the left key for the high compatibility condition. Stimulus discriminability was varied by altering the luminance (brightness) of the set of four lights. In the low discriminability condition, luminances were closer together than in the high discriminability condition. Since the high discriminability condition had a greater range of luminance, it was easier to see which light was brightest.

Results of this experiment are shown in figure 8–5. The parallel lines indicate that the factors of stimulus discriminability and stimulus-response compatibility are additive. Thus, each factor influences a separate stage of information processing.

The method of additive factors does not estimate the time required by a processing stage. It only tells us how to discover these stages. Donders was a hundred years ahead of his time; it is only recently that the rest of psychology has caught up with him.

FIGURE 8–5.

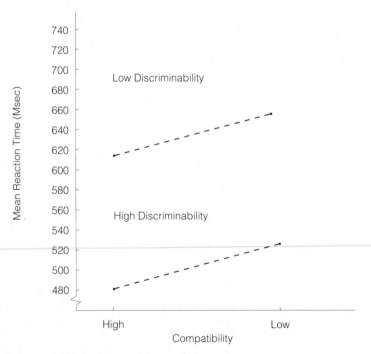

Mean correct RT as a function of stimulus discriminability and S-R compatibility. (Adapted from Biederman and Kaplan, 1979)

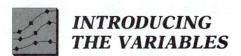

INTRODUCING THE VARIABLES

Dependent Variables

In studies of attention, the range of dependent variables is considerably more restricted than that of independent variables. Reaction time is by far the preferred variable and is extensively used. Percentage of correct responses is also used, especially in studies of attention in which memory plays a role. When an experiment is framed within the context of a particular model, such as the theory of signal detection (see chapter 6), derived statistics such as d' and beta are also used as dependent variables. Another common statistic is amount of information in bits, where one bit is the information present in the toss of a fair coin that can come up either heads or tails. These derived statistics may be combined with reaction time to yield measures of the rate of performance, such as bits/sec or d'/sec.

Independent Variables

Although studies of attention and reaction time have used an impressive variety of independent variables, these variables center around the need for the human to make decisions and the rate at which such decisions can be made. Thus, varying the number of alternatives in a choice-reaction task increases the number of decisions that must be made to identify the correct stimulus and select its associated response. Varying the presentation rate of a series of stimuli limits the amount of attention that can be devoted to processing each stimulus and is a common technique used to study the upper bounds of attention. Another way of increasing the attention demanded by some task is

to increase its complexity; thus, a simple version of a task may require naming a visually presented digit, whereas a more complex decision may require subtracting the digit from nine.

The key point in manipulating attention is to gradually increase task demands until the person is hard pressed to keep up with them. The use of *overload* as a diagnostic device has been borrowed from engineering, where it is quite common. For example, the strength of materials is tested by placing them in a hydraulic press and gradually increasing the pressure until the material fails. This gives the metallurgical engineer information about the material that could not be easily gained from the intact structure. Although a far gentler method of imposing overload is required for the study of human attention, the underlying goals and techniques are similar to those of the engineer. By discovering how the human system reacts to overloads of information, the psychologist gains an insight into human performance and information processing with more reasonable attentive loads.

Control Variables

Research in attention and reaction time is usually quite carefully controlled. Perceptual factors such as the intensity and duration of stimuli are often under the control of a computer or other automated equipment that conducts the experiment. Even speech sounds can be presented in exactly the same way trial after trial by using a "talking computer." This precise control is necessary if psychologists are to interpret small changes in reaction time on the order of tens of milliseconds (one millisecond being equal to one one-thousandth of a second).

8.1 Experimental Topics and Research Illustrations

Topic: Confounding
Illustration: Dichotic Listening

One of the most frequently performed tasks in the study of attention is derived from the difficulties encountered by air traffic controllers, who must direct several airplanes at once. Radio communication between controllers and airplane pilots occurs often, as the controllers give directions and the pilots acknowledge their instructions. This is a trying and stressful task for the controller, and indeed the Federal Aviation Administration has instituted a special early-retirement plan because the job is so demanding. Psychologists studying this task wondered if it could be made easier by having spatially separated loudspeakers so that the voices of different pilots would appear in different locations. This research has continued, and now there is a large body of data concerning attention and listening.

In a *dichotic listening* task, two separate and independent messages are presented, with each message heard in a different ear. This differs from stereo high fidelity, in which both ears hear both messages, although with different intensities. Dichotic stimuli are usually arranged so that each word arrives simultaneously in both ears. For example, the right ear might receive the message "One, Red, Jump" while the left ear hears "Quick, Tango, Fox." The words in each pair "One-Quick," "Red-Tango," "Jump-Fox" would occur at the same time. This task is illustrated in figure 8–6. The difficulty of the dichotic-listening task depends on the rate at which word pairs are presented. At a very slow rate, say, one pair every two seconds, it is easy to attend to both words. Of course, if the list of words is even moderately long, there may be problems in remem-

FIGURE 8–6.

The dichotic-listening task. Separate words are presented in each ear at the same time.

bering all the words. Psychologists studying attention try to separate difficulties resulting from inability to pay attention from difficulties caused by excess memory load. One way to accomplish this goal is to use extremely short lists, for example, only one word pair presented at a time. Most people have little difficulty remembering only two words, so that problems can usually be traced to deficits in attention rather than memory. If, however, longer lists are used, then it becomes quite possible (and even likely for lists of more than four or five pairs) that attention and memory can be mixed up together. In more technical terms, the processes of attention are *confounded* with those of memory.

This use of the term *confounding* differs slightly from our earlier use, where confounding referred to independent variables rather than psychological processes. But we shall see that saying processes are confounded really means that independent variables have been confounded. Since certain variables—for example, delay of recall—are theoretically associated more with memory than with attention, it is a small step to speak of confounding processes when in actuality variables are confounded. Operationally, confounding must always be traced back to independent or uncontrolled variables, but it is often more convenient to speak of confounded processes in addition to confounded variables. When experimental procedures are inadequate, so that more than one independent variable (or more than one psychological process) can account for obtained results, we say that the variables (or processes) have been confounded.

A monitoring experiment. An example of confounded memory and attentional processes is provided by an experiment performed by Broadbent and Gregory (1963). They used a dichotic-listening task in which digits were presented to one ear and a signal-detection task was presented to the other ear. The signal-detection task consisted of a burst of white noise that might or might not contain a pure tone. The tone was present in half of the noise bursts and absent in the remaining half. The sequence of tones was randomized, so that on any one trial the listener did not know in advance whether the tone would be present. Thus, listeners in this experiment had to perform two tasks simultaneously: they had to try to detect a tone if one occurred, and they had to try to hear the digits.

Listeners were asked to perform (at different times, of course) under two sets of instructions. In the concentrated-attention condition, they were asked to devote all their attention to detecting the tone. In the divided-attention condition, they were required to detect the tone and to report the digits after they occurred. So in the concentrated-attention condition, subjects ignored the digits and reported the presence or absence of the tone at the end of each trial. In the divided-attention condition, they first reported as many digits as they could remember from the original list of six digits and then reported the presence or absence of the tone.

The results of this experiment can be found in figure 8–7. Tone detection was better in the concentrated-attention condition; that is, d′ (see chapter 6) was greater. Therefore, Broadbent and Gregory concluded that paying attention to only one task is more effective and causes better performance than paying attention to two tasks.

But this conclusion may be in error, since the procedures used by Broadbent and Gregory confounded memory and attention. Did you notice the defect in experimental design? In the concentrated-attention condition, listeners reported the presence or absence of the tone immediately. But in the divided-attention condition, they first reported the digits. This meant that the tone report was delayed until they had finished naming all the digits they could remember. Since delay affects memory, the possibility exists that listeners could have correctly reported the presence or absence of the tone in the divided-attention condition if the report had been immediate, as was the case in the concentrated-attention condition, but simply forgot whether they had heard the tone while they were busy reporting digits.

The concentrated- and divided-attention conditions were intended to be alike in every respect except the requirement to pay

FIGURE 8–7.

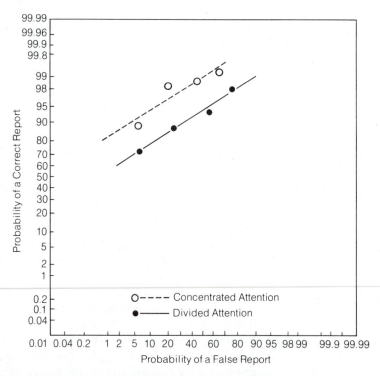

Effects of concentrated and divided attention on signal detection. Better performance (higher d′) is indicated when the line is closer to the upper left-hand corner of the graph. Thus the figure shows that the concentrated-attention condition is superior to the divided-attention condition. (Data from Broadbent and Gregory, 1963)

attention to one versus two ears. If this had been accomplished, any different results, such as those in figure 8–7, could be reasonably assigned to differences in attention. But the two conditions also differed in the amount of time from the end of a trial until the tone report was made. So it is equally possible that the observed differences in figure 8–7 could be caused by this unequal delay across experimental conditions. In short, it is impossible to conclude which of these two factors, attentional instructions or delay of report, is responsible for the results, because these two factors have been confounded in the experiment.

How could we alter the experimental procedures to remove this unpleasant confounding? This could be accomplished quite simply by requiring listeners in the divided-attention condition to first make the tone report and then report the digits. With this slight alteration in procedure, both conditions would have the tone report occurring at the same time. When the experiment is done this way (Kantowitz, 1974, p. 121), results are the same as those of figure 8–7. Broadbent and Gregory were lucky, since their confounding did not alter the correct conclusion. But science cannot depend on good fortune as a substitute for good experimental design. Different results might have occurred, and until the experiment was repeated without confounding memory and attention, it was impossible to interpret the results obtained by Broadbent and Gregory.

A shadowing experiment.   The Broadbent and Gregory experiment required listeners to monitor messages, that is, to simply listen and make no attempt at repeating the message until it had ended. One problem with this procedure is that the experimenter has no direct way of checking that the listeners are indeed monitoring and not thinking about something completely unrelated to the experiment. A more common procedure in studies of dichotic listening is to require that the listener repeat aloud each word as it occurs in one of the ears. As in monitoring experiments, the listener is then required to recall as much of the message as possible at the end of the list. But because the experimenter has heard the listener repeat each word, the experimenter knows that attention has been devoted to at least one ear. This procedure is called *shadowing* a message, and the ear that is shadowed is called the attended ear. You might expect that listeners do relatively well at recalling the words from the attended ear and so may wonder why psychologists bother to test them at all. The main purpose of shadowing experiments relates to the fate of the message in the unattended ear. Since the shadowing procedure guarantees that attention is devoted to the attended ear, theoretical questions focus on the listener's ability to attend to messages in the other ear. The usual finding is that the unattended message is recalled poorly compared with the shadowed or attended message. This may seem obvious to you, but the interesting point for psychologists is that the unattended message can be recalled at all. Although we shall not go into any theoretical detail (see, for example, Broadbent, 1971, chapter 5), the bare fact of any correct recall from the unattended channel forces psychologists to postulate attentional mechanisms like a filter that can rapidly switch back and forth between the two ears, or an attenuator that weakens but does not completely eliminate the unattended message, or one of several other alternate models.

Although the shadowing technique has been widely used since the early 1950s, it was almost fifteen years before the possibility of a basic confounding in the paradigm was suggested and tested. Norman (1969) believed that the relatively poorer performance on the unattended message was not caused by the listener's inability to attend to the message, but instead could be attributed to the interference produced by the overt vocalization of the attended message during shadowing. It is well known that any overt vocalization—for example, counting backward by threes—will interfere with memory and rehearsal (see chapter 10). So Norman argued that the unshadowed message could be attended as well as the shadowed message, but that its poor recall was caused by prevention of rehearsal. Thus, memory, and not attention, would be the proper locus of this deficit. Norman hypothesized that rehearsal— a memory process—was blocked by the overt vocalization of the shadowed message.

To test his hypothesis, Norman had to create a situation in which vocalization of the shadowed message stopped. This would remove the source of interference blocking rehearsal of the unshadowed message and should result in greatly increased recall of the unshadowed message. The main experimental conditions required that listeners shadow a verbal message and memorize a list of digits simultaneously presented in the other ear (Condition MS— Memorize and Shadow). The test of memory for these digits was either immediate—as soon as the digit list ended—or delayed for twenty seconds. The memory task was also tested by itself, with no concurrent shadowing (Condition M). A memory interference condition (MI) required shadowing only after the digit list had been presented. Results for the tests of digit memory are shown in figure 8–8.

In the immediate-recall conditions, memory was always better than in delayed recall, indicating that if listeners stopped shadowing, the digit list was available in short-term memory. But the digit list was not maintained (or transferred to long-term memory) if recall was delayed and shadowing continued. So even though the digit list was available immediately, continued shadowing wiped it out.

Memory was always better when no shadowing was required. In the delayed-recall conditions, memory was poor. This was equally true in the MI condition, where no shadowing was required during the presentation of the digit list. Here, any memory decrement must have been caused by interference, and not attention, just as counting backward interferes with memory. So Norman concluded

FIGURE 8–8.

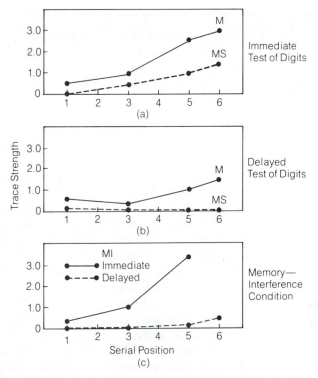

Memory performance for immediate and delayed tests with (**MS**) and without (**M**) shadowing. Trace strength is a derived dependent variable similar to d′. The top and middle panels show that memory is better when shadowing is not required (**M**), regardless of whether the test is immediate (top panel) or delayed (middle panel). Memory is better when tested immediately. The bottom panel for condition **MI** shows a similar finding, even though no shadowing was required during the presentation of the digit list in this condition. (From Norman, 1969)

that the decrement in memory that occurred when listeners were required to shadow was *not* caused by their inability to attend to two messages (digit list and verbal message) simultaneously.[1]

This type of confounding is more subtle and difficult to spot than the direct confounding of independent variables. However, confounding of psychological processes is a more serious (and more likely) error in psychological research because it can go unnoticed, at least for a while. In attention research it is difficult to separate effects caused by limitations on the listener's ability to attend to more than one stimulus at a time from those caused by an inability to remember more than one item at a time.

[1]It could be argued that listeners might have shifted attention to the memory task at the expense of shadowing, thereby improving memory performance and decreasing shadowing performance. However, memory was still better when no shadowing was required. Furthermore, Norman properly included a shadowing-only condition to test this possibility: shadowing performance was, for the most part, the same whether or not listeners were required to remember digits.

8.2 Experimental Topics and Research Illustrations

Topic: Interaction
Illustration: Dichotic Listening

An *interaction* occurs when the effects of one independent variable are not identical over different levels of other independent variables. As we mentioned in chapter 3, the search for interaction is a major reason for including more than one independent variable in an experiment.

Knight and Kantowitz (1975) presented five pairs of dichotic words to listeners. These pairs were presented at either a fast rate (two pairs/ sec) or a slow rate (one pair/sec). The dichotic list was immediately followed by a probe word—that is, one of the words previously contained in the list. The listener was to respond with the word that followed the probe word in the same ear as the probe word (see table 8–1). This procedure may at first seem rather more complicated than the usual procedure of asking the listener to recall as many words as possible, but it has the distinct advantage of minimizing interference among words during output, since only a single item must be recalled. Knight and Kantowitz were interested in (among other things) the relationship between rate of presentation (slow or fast) and the serial position of the probe. *Serial position* is the item's location in an ordered list. The first item has serial position one, the second item has serial position two, etc. If the probe came from the first dichotic word pair, it had serial position one; if from the second pair, serial position two; and so on. However, the probe word could never come from the last (fifth) dichotic word pair, since it would then be impossible for the listener to report the following word—that is, there were no more words after the last word. So probe serial position could only assume the values one through four as an independent variable. Serial position is a very common independent variable, especially in

TABLE 8–1.   Dichotic Word List

Serial Position	Left Ear	Right Ear
1	Quick	One
2	Tango	Red
3	Fox	Jump
4	Boy	Blue
5	Bird	Help

Probe Word: Red
Correct Response: Jump

memory research (see chapter 10), and it has become customary to plot dependent variables as a function of serial position. Figure 8–9 shows the number of correct responses in this experiment as a function of serial position of the probe word and also of presentation rate.

It is clear from figure 8–9 that the two curves are far from parallel and that a strong interaction between serial position and presentation rate has occurred. Without going into any details about theoretical models of attention, let us merely state that this sort of interaction suggests a joint effect of attentional and memory processes. Indeed, because the interaction is so strong—it is a so-called crossover interaction—researchers would have great faith in the conclusion that slow and fast items are either represented in, or retrieved from, memory differently. In general, as was stated earlier in this chapter, interactions indicate shared or common stages of information processing, whereas additivities (no interactions) indicate separate processing of information.

Now look at figure 8–10, where the same data are presented, except that the scale has been changed for the independent variable. Instead of probe serial position being plotted, recall delay has been calculated for each serial position. *Recall delay* is the time between presentation of an item within a dichotic pair and presentation of the probe word. The lower the serial position of an item—that is, the earlier it was presented—the greater the recall delay. As figure 8–10 clearly shows, measuring recall delay instead of serial position completely eliminates the interaction with presentation rate: the two curves are parallel. The interpretation of figure 8–10 is rather different from the interpretation of figure 8–9. Using recall delay as the dependent variable, we would say that regardless of presentation rate, all items are affected the same

FIGURE 8–9.

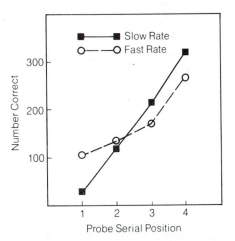

Number of words correctly recalled as a function of presentation rate and serial position of probe word. The crossing lines indicate a strong interaction. (From Knight and Kantowitz, 1974)

FIGURE 8–10.

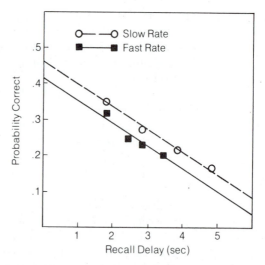

Probability of correct recall as a function of presentation rate and recall delay. These data are the same as in the preceding figure. (Plotting probability correct instead of number correct does not change the shape of the data.) The parallel lines show no interaction. (From Knight and Kantowitz, 1974)

way in memory. We might even go so far as to suggest that the rate of loss or decay in memory (related to the slope of the parallel lines in figure 8–10) is the same for items presented both at the fast rate and at the slow rate.

Which of these two interpretations is correct? In other words, which of the two figures is the right way to plot the relationship between the two independent variables? Figure 8–9 shows the traditional method of plotting these data and so has history on its side. However, serial position is scaled only on an ordinal metric (see chapter 6). In figure 8–10, recall delay is measured on a ratio scale (see chapter 6). Since ratio scales represent a higher order of measurement, this suggests that figure 8–10 should be preferred. The main point to remember is not so much that one figure is better, but that interactions cannot be interpreted without first giving considerable thought to the measurement scale used for variables.

Scale Attenuation. Interactions can be misleading even when the dependent variable is scaled correctly. The following fictitious example shows how this could happen in a dichotic-listening experiment. Paying people more money to perform a task usually helps them do better. This result is attributed to motivational processes—that is, the worker tries harder and is more attentive to the task. So an industrial psychologist who knows something about dichotic listening designs an experiment to discover whether paying more attention and improving motivation by a monetary reward are related. One independent variable is the amount of money paid for each correct recall of a dichotic word: either one cent or fifty cents. The other independent variable is the number of dichotic word pairs presented in each auditory list: either five or ten pairs. The results of this hypothetical experiment are shown in figure 8–11. As expected, paying listeners more money improved their performance. Also, people did better on the shorter word list, recalling a higher percentage of words. But most important of all, the two independent variables show a clear interaction, since the lines are far from parallel. Increasing the payoff caused a large improvement in recall for the long ten-word list, but very little improvement for the short five-word list. This interaction would suggest that what experimental psychologists call attention and what industrial psychologists call motivation are closely related.

But there is a serious flaw that prevents this experiment from supporting such a conclusion. Recall of the short list was quite good even when the payoff was only one cent per word. For recall of the short list to improve as much as recall for the long list—that is, for the two lines in figure 8–11 to be parallel—recall would have to exceed 100 percent. This is, of course, impossible. Recall of the shorter list has bumped into the top of the measurement scale for the dependent variable: this may be the explanation for the interaction. This type of problem is called scale attenuation (ceiling and floor effects) and is discussed in detail in chapter 10. For now, merely note that it is another instance where an interaction cannot be trusted. This experiment would have to be repeated with longer lists—say, ten and fifteen dichotic pairs—to avoid the ceiling effect in figure 8–11.

The search for interactions is an important part of psychological research and explains much of the popularity of analysis of variance as the major statistical technique used by psychologists. But a graph showing nonparallel lines does not always mean that

FIGURE 8–11.

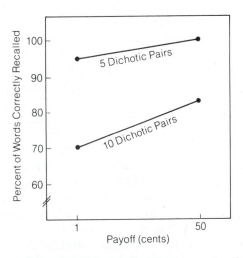

Percent of words correctly recalled in dichotic listening as a function of payoff and list length. Increasing payoff has a greater effect on the longer list. (Fictitious data)

a legitimate interaction is portrayed. The scale of measurement used in the dependent variable must be carefully examined before any conclusion about the presence or absence of an interaction can be reached. Transformations of the scale can create or eliminate interactions. Scale attenuation also can alter patterns of interaction.

8.3 Experimental Topics and Research Illustrations

Topic:　　　Selection of Dependent Variable
Illustration: Speed-Accuracy Tradeoff

As discussed in chapter 3, the experimenter must select one dependent variable from a host of possible dependent variables. An extremely popular dependent variable used in research on attention and information processing is reaction time. Indeed, this variable is so popular that the study of reaction time has become virtually a content area in itself. When experimental psychologists get together, it is quite common for some of them to identify their research interests by stating, "I'm in reaction time." This may sound odd to you, since a psychologist studying memory would not say, "I'm in percent correct," but it does indicate that a dependent variable may become so important that it is studied not only as a means of investigating specific content areas, but also as an object of study in its own right.

At first, one might think that reaction time would be a poor topic to illustrate selection of a dependent variable, since by naming reaction time we have already made the selection. It is true that some psychologists routinely measure reaction time with little thought about the implications of this selection decision. Right now, reaction time is "in." The speed with which a task can be performed is often taken as an indication of the attentional requirements of the task. Things that can be done quickly are interpreted as having small attentional requirements. This logic is not always correct, since attention can be operationally defined in ways that need not involve reaction time. In this section, we shall see that an even simpler use of reaction time, in which no assumptions about attention are made, can be misleading, because not enough thought is given to selection of the dependent variable.

There is an inverse (backward) relationship between the speed and accuracy of performance. When you try to do something very fast, you make more mistakes than if you do it slowly. Conversely, if you try to do something, such as type a term paper, very accurately, you must go more slowly to achieve the desired accuracy. Psychologists call this relationship the *speed-accuracy tradeoff*. It has important implications for studies that measure reaction time as the dependent variable.

This can be illustrated by an experiment conducted by Theios (1975), in which the task of the participant was quite simple. A digit was presented visually: the participant only had to name the digit. The independent variable was the probability (relative frequency) of the digits, which varied from .2 (a particular digit was presented 20 percent of the time) to .8. Reaction-time data from this experiment are shown in figure 8–12. Theios concluded that stimulus probability had no effect on reaction time.

This conclusion appears quite reasonable when errors are ignored. But when the error data also shown in figure 8–12 are considered, another interpretation emerges (Pachella, 1974). The average error rate of 3 percent may not seem very high to you, but stop and think about how simple the task was. All that was required was to name a digit—hardly a mind-blowing task for college students. Even worse, the error rate varied systematically according to stimulus probability, the independent variable. The highest error rate (6 percent) occurred with the lowest stimulus probability; as the probability increased, error rate decreased. What would the reaction times have been if the error rates were equal for all levels of stimulus probability? According to the speed-accuracy tradeoff, reaction times in the low stimulus-probability conditions would have to increase in order to decrease the error rate. Pachella (1974) has suggested that to lower error rates to 2 percent, reaction time

FIGURE 8–12.

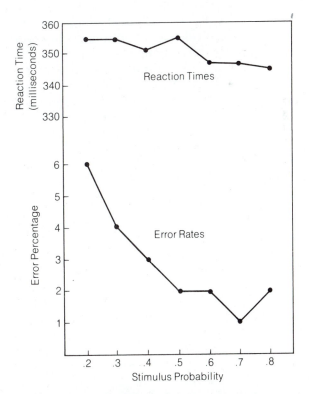

Reaction time and error rate as a function of stimulus probability. Although reaction time is fairly constant, error rate declines as stimulus probability increases. (Data from Theios, 1975 and Pachella, 1974)

in the .2 stimulus-probability condition might have to be increased as much as 100 milliseconds. So the conclusion that stimulus probability does not affect reaction time must be questioned once error rates are considered.

The basic problem here lies with the selection of reaction time as the *only* important dependent variable. Since reaction time depends in part on the error rate, we must consider both speed and accuracy as dependent variables. In short, reaction time is not a univariate dependent variable, but a multivariate variable. It may reduce to a single dependent variable in some cases where error rate is constant across all levels of the independent variables; but in general, two dependent variables—reaction time and error rate—must be jointly considered.

This point will be illustrated one more time by reference to an attention experiment conducted by Knight and Kantowitz (1974). They presented two stimuli separated by a very short time period, called the *interstimulus interval.* This was the independent variable. The dependent variables were reaction time and error rate. Previous research had shown that under conditions similar to those investigated by Knight and Kantowitz, reaction time was constant for different interstimulus intervals. Such a finding is similar to that of Theios, where stimulus probability was held to have no influence on reaction time. But when Knight and Kantowitz plotted error data as a function of interstimulus interval (see figure 8–13), a definite relationship was found. Error rates were higher at shorter interstimulus intervals. Again we could ask: what would the reaction times have been if error rates were equal at all interstimulus intervals? According to the speed-accuracy tradeoff, reaction times at shorter interstimulus intervals would have been greater. So the earlier conclusion of previous investigators that reaction time was not influenced by interstimulus interval was shown to be misleading. Correctly selecting two dependent variables would have allowed them to reach a more accurate conclusion.

FIGURE 8–13.

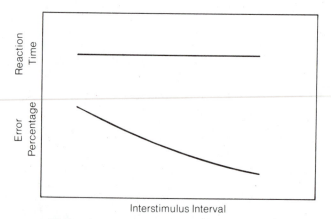

Reaction time and error rate as a function of interstimulus interval. Although reaction time is constant, error rate decreases for longer interstimulus intervals. (Adapted from Knight and Kantowitz, 1974)

From Problem to Experiment: The Nuts and Bolts

Problem: Measuring Attention

Some of the things we do seem to proceed fairly automatically, and others seem to require great concentration. Motor skills such as walking do not require much mental effort, whereas doing mental arithmetic can be quite taxing. To study the attentional requirements of various tasks, we must have some way to measure attention.

Problem: *How can we determine the amount of attention or mental effort that any arbitrary task might require?*

As is usually the case, this problem must be refined further: some hypotheses must be formulated before any meaningful solution can be attempted.

Hypothesis: *Increased attentional demands will be accompanied by increased stress, which will show up as a change in some physiological measure of body function.*

This hypothesis is a little vague, because it fails to specify the dependent variable precisely. There are many physiological correlates of behavior, and it is not clear from the hypothesis whether the experimenter should record heart rate, galvanic skin response, or brain waves, or perform a chemical analysis of breathing exhalations. This difficulty could be bypassed by deciding to record every physiological measure that could be conveniently instrumented. Use of several dependent measures is indeed quite common in studies that investigate physiological correlates of attention, and this approach, although not terribly efficient, would strike some psychologists as a reasonable one. Although some of the dependent variables might prove to be useless, presumably they could be thrown out and only the "good" physiological measures retained.

Let us arbitrarily select three dependent variables: heart rate, brain wave (EEG), and pupil (a part of the eye, not a student) diameter. We hope that one or more of these will be correlated with attention. Now we must choose an independent variable. To do this, we need first to select a task for which we are fairly certain that (a) attention is required and (b) the amount of attention required can be varied by changing task difficulty. This is not as easy as it first appears; to do this properly, we must search the available literature to find converging operations (see chapter 7 or 14), where the same task has been used in different situations. Without going into the details of how this can be accomplished, let us assume that one task that meets this requirement is the dichotic-listening task discussed earlier in this chapter. We will further assume that attentional requirements of dichotic listening can be controlled by varying the presentation rate of dichotic lists, with faster rates calling for more attention. So our independent variable will be the presentation rate of a series of dichotic lists that are to be shadowed (repeated aloud). How many different presentation rates should be used? Clearly, at least two, since we cannot manipulate attention required with only a single presentation rate. The actual number selected would be a compromise between having as many different presentation rates as possible and the limitations of time, money, and so forth. Let us say that four presentation rates will be used: one word pair every 4 seconds, every 2 seconds, and every 1 second; and two pairs every 1 second.

What about control variables? First, we need to make sure that the only difference among the various dichotic lists is the blank interval between successive pairs of words and that the duration of the words does not change with presentation rate. This means that we cannot simply use a tape recorder with someone speaking in time with a metronome, since, as people speak more quickly to generate faster presentation rates, the word durations also change. We should use a computer to generate our dichotic lists. We will also need to control for variables that are likely to influence heart rate, EEG, and pupil diameter. This list of variables is quite extensive, and our present discussion will illustrate control on only two dependent variables. Heart rate is known to change with respiration (breathing) rate. It is difficult to control someone's breathing rate without resorting to unpleasant chemical and mechanical treatments. Most experimenters would not take this kind of risk and would simply monitor breathing rates. Technically, this kind of control adds another dependent variable. The control achieved is statistical rather than experimental—in this case, the correlation of heart and breathing rates. Pupil diameter is very sensitive to amount of illumination, with bright light causing the pupil to contract. So the experimenter would take care to keep the level of illumination constant throughout the study. Control would then be experimental rather than statistical, unlike the control of heart rate.

If we actually did this kind of experiment, we might expect only EEG to be related to attention. However, there are data (see Kahneman, 1973) suggesting that all three of our dependent variables are related to attention and amount of mental effort. It is often important to have more than one dependent variable because some dependent variables may be more sensitive to manipulation than others.

Hypothesis: *The amount of attention required by some task can be measured by reaction time for a simultaneous Donders B reaction task.*

Here, the dependent variable is specified precisely. It is choice-reaction time. The logic behind this hypothesis is that the choice-reaction task requires attention, so that attention devoted to the other task (usually called the primary task) must be diverted away from the reaction task, leading to increased reaction time. A further assumption is that both the primary task and the choice-reaction task draw on a common source of attention or capacity.

Let us use the same independent variable as in the previous example: dichotic presentation rate. Our listener must shadow a dichotic list and at the same time respond to a choice-reaction signal. Since the dichotic list occupies the auditory modality, a visual reaction signal should be used. Similarly, a motor reaction response such as a keypress should be used, since the speech mechanism is occupied by shadowing. If the hypothesis is correct, longer reaction times will occur when faster presentation rates are used.

Control variables would be computer control of the dichotic list, control of the intensity of the visual signals, and timing of the visual signals. The most important control would be instructions (or payoff), to guarantee that performance on the dichotic lists was not changed by adding the reaction task. So we would have a control condition (not a control variable), where only one task was required, and an experimental condition, where both tasks had to be done together. Unless performance on the primary task was the same in both control and experimental conditions, we could not reach any conclusions about the attention demands of shadowing. For example, if listeners did much better when no reaction task was required, this could indicate a shift of attention from shadowing to reaction task, when both were performed together. The logic of the hypothesis demands that the same amount of attention always be devoted to the listening task within any one presentation rate. The reaction-time task measures the surplus attention left over from shadowing. If the listener voluntarily diverts attention away from the shadowing task to do the reaction task, the experiment is spoiled.

SUMMARY

1. Interest in reaction time began with the personal equation, a systematic difference in reaction times found among eighteenth-century astronomers. This phenomenon led Donders to formulate his subtractive method.

2. The Donders *A* reaction time, when subtracted from the C reaction time, yields identification time. Similarly, Donders *B* reaction time minus *C* reaction time yields an estimate of selection time.

3. The current descendant of Donders' efforts is the method of additive factors. It uses factorial combinations of independent variables to reveal internal processing stages.

4. In dichotic listening experiments, two independent messages are presented simultaneously, one to each ear. The shadowing technique requires that a listener repeat one of the messages aloud, whereas the monitoring task requires that a subject only listen and not vocalize.

5. Confounding occurs when a factor that covaries with an independent variable may account for observed changes in behavior. Both the shadowing and monitoring tasks in dichotic listening can be misused to confound factors related to attention and memory.

6. Interactions occur when the effect of one independent variable differs for levels of other independent variables manipulated in the same experiment. Mathematical transformations of data can remove (or create) interactions. Altering the way a dependent variable is scaled or measured can also change interactions.

7. Dependent variables must be carefully selected. Studies that measure reaction time must also record error rate. Speed can be traded off for accuracy, as when a task is completed more rapidly but at the expense of a higher error rate. Thus, reaction time is only one component of a multivariate dependent variable. Error rate is the other component.

KEY TERMS

additive factors
attention
bit
choice reaction
confounding
dichotic listening
Donders *A* reaction
Donders *B* reaction
Donders *C* reaction
factors
interaction

interstimulus interval
overload
personal equation
reaction time
recall delay
serial position
shadowing
simple reaction
speed-accuracy tradeoff
subtractive method

DISCUSSION QUESTIONS

1. What arguments could Kinnebrook have used to keep his job at the Royal Observatory?

2. Read the articles by Sternberg and by Taylor, cited in this chapter. What are the critical differences between the subtractive method and the method of additive factors? What are some of the problems with the method of additive factors?

3. What variables are confounded in the following experiment?
   An experimenter who believes that women talk much more than men suspects that women will do better in a shadowing task than men, especially at faster presentation rates. Two groups of subjects, one consisting of ten men and the other of ten women,

are formed. The women shadow dichotic messages at a rate of ten pairs per second for twenty trials. Each trial consists of one minute of dichotic messages. Then the women listen to twenty additional trials at a rate of five pairs per second. So that the effects of presentation rate are counterbalanced, the men start with the slower rate (five pairs per second) and then shadow the faster dichotic messages.

How would you improve this experimental design?

4. List five samples of speed-accuracy tradeoff that occur in everyday life outside the laboratory. Select two of your examples and design a laboratory experiment that will measure speed-accuracy tradeoff. Plot graphs of hypothetical results for each experiment.

PSYCHOLOGY IN ACTION

Speed-Accuracy Tradeoff

THE FOLLOWING DEMONSTRATION REQUIRES a pencil, a newspaper, and a watch with a second hand. It helps if you have a friend to time you, but a photographic timer with a buzzer can be used instead. Set your timer (or your friend) to thirty seconds. Now, going at a comfortable speed, work your way through a newspaper article, crossing out every letter *e* that occurs. Stop after thirty seconds and count the number of lines that you have completed. This number is your baseline figure. (Enter it in table 8–2.) Next, keep the time constant at thirty seconds, but try to increase the number of lines that have crossed-out letter *e*'s by 10 percent. Third, repeat this process with 10 percent fewer lines than your baseline—that is, go slower this time. Then, repeat with 15 percent more lines (go faster); finally, with 15 percent fewer. Now take a well-deserved rest. When you have recovered, go back over each of the five passages you have crossed out and count the number of letter *e*'s you should have crossed out and the number you actually crossed out. Dividing the number crossed out by the total number gives you your error rate or percentage. Did you systematically make more errors as you tried to go faster and include more lines, thus revealing a tradeoff between speed and accuracy?

TABLE 8–2. Empirical Determination of Speed-Accuracy Tradeoff

	Number of Lines	Number e's Crossed Out Correctly (1)	Number e's Missed (2)	Total e's (1) + (2)	Percent (2) ÷ [(1) + (2)]
Baseline (B)					
B + 10%					
B − 10%					
B + 15%					
B − 15%					

CHAPTER

9

Conditioning and Learning

We should be careful to get out of an experience only the wisdom that is in it—and stop there; lest we be like the cat that sits down on a hot stove-lid. She will never sit down on a hot stove-lid again—and that is well; but also she will never sit down on a cold one anymore.

—MARK TWAIN

THE ABOVE WARNING BY MARK Twain refers to some important characteristics of one kind of conditioning, called *classical conditioning*. In classical conditioning, the experience, as Twain indicates, is usually not under control of the organism. The cat does not seek out a hot stove-lid to sit on; rather, the stove just happens to be hot when she sits on it; there is nothing she can do about it. Twain also notes that the effects of conditioning can be far-reaching—the cat will not choose to sit on any stove-lid again, regardless of whether the lid is hot. This sort of conditioning is a prominent part of our lives. Some of the more unfortunate cases of it have been studied by Rozin (1986).

Rozin has catalogued instances of disgust and distaste leading to conditioning of the sort undergone by Twain's cat. Some of you are likely to have had conditioning experiences resulting from disgust or distaste. For example, Rozin writes of one person who had a very strong aversion to rye bread. Apparently, the person began to eat the bread in the dark, and then turned on the lights, only to notice mold on the bread. The mold was disgusting to the person, who now reports feeling ill just by thinking about rye bread. An accidental event had far-reaching consequences for this individual, much the same as for Twain's cat.

Not all conditioning involves events that simply happen to the organism. In *instrumental conditioning*, the behavior of the organism is instrumental in producing consequences, often called rewards and punishments, which alter the rate of the behaviors that have produced the consequences. Let us examine an example of instrumental conditioning in a horse.

In the early 1900s, the German public was introduced to the feats of Clever Hans, a remarkable horse that belonged to Herr von Osten, a mathematics teacher. Von Osten would read arithmetic problems to Clever Hans, and the horse would tap out the correct answer with his forefoot. When asked to add "eight plus three," Hans tapped his foot eleven times. The horse was about equally adept at addition, subtraction, multiplication, and division; he was also able to answer simple questions about spelling, reading, and musical harmony.

Needless to say, many Germans found Clever Hans's talents hard to believe. Yet von Osten seemed earnest, and he did not try to profit from his horse's notoriety. So that the skeptics would be satisfied, the horse was tested in the absence of von Osten. Surprisingly, Hans performed his tasks about as well as ever.

Could Hans really understand language and do arithmetic? Two psychologists, Pfungst and Stumpf, performed a series of experiments that finally convinced everyone that although Hans was in some ways a very clever horse, his talents did not extend to mathematics. Pfungst (1911) reported that Hans actually accomplished his feats by detecting subtle nonverbal signals that the questioners provided unconsciously. The researchers noted that when Hans tapped he would go quickly at first, then slow down, then stop at the right place (or sometimes miss by a number or two). They discovered that the questioners tended to incline their heads as they gave Hans a problem, then straighten up as he neared the correct answer. Hans also seemed to be sensitive to each questioner's eyebrow movements, dilation of nostrils, and tone of voice. When prevented from seeing or hearing his questioners while he tapped, Hans was no longer able to perform. The horse had simply learned covert signals from von Osten indicating when he should stop tapping.

Although Hans could not understand mathematics, he at least had the horse sense to outwit his human observers for a long while. Actually, the process of instrumental conditioning by which Hans learned his trick is as interesting as the trick itself. From a cue, Hans learned to perform a response that was rewarded with attention and food. The same learning techniques are used by animal trainers to teach animals a variety of marvelous acts. Elephants stand on their front paws, dolphins caper about performing a long series of tricks, and killer whales even "kiss" their trainers. In these cases, animals are explicitly trained to perform, whereas Hans mastered his trick on his own.

In this chapter, we consider two fundamental types of learning—classical and instrumental conditioning—in order to illustrate several methodological issues. Before discussing these issues, we will describe the two fundamental types of conditioning.

Types of Conditioning

Classical Conditioning: Does the Name Pavlov Ring a Bell?

Early in this century, some fundamental psychological discoveries were made by Ivan P. Pavlov (1849–1936). The basic discovery that he made—which is now called Pavlovian, respondent, or *classical conditioning*—is well known today, even by those outside psychology—but the fascinating story of how it came about is not. Pavlov was not trained as a psychologist (there were no psychologists in Russia, or elsewhere, when he received his education), but as a physiologist. He made great contributions in physiology concerning the measurement and analysis of stomach secretions accompanying the digestive process. He was able to carefully measure the fluids produced by different sorts of food, and he regarded the secretion of the stomach juices as a physiological reflex. For his important work on the gastric juices in the digestive process, he was awarded the Nobel prize for medicine in 1904.

It was only after he had won the Nobel prize that Pavlov turned to some more or less incidental discoveries he had made in the course of his work, which led to the ones for which he is so well known today. In one type of physiological experiment, Pavlov cut a dog's esophagus so that it would no longer carry food to the stomach (see figure 9–1). But he discovered that when he placed food in the dog's mouth, the stomach secreted almost as much gastric juice as it did when the food went to the stomach. The reflexive action of the stomach seemed to depend on stimuli located in other places besides those in direct contact with the stomach lining. But then Pavlov made an even more remarkable discovery.

FIGURE 9–1.

Ivan Pavlov and his staff are shown here with one of the dogs used in his experiments. The dog was harnessed to the wooden frame shown in the picture. Saliva was conducted by a tube to a measuring device that could record the rate and quantity of salivation.

He found that it was not even necessary to place food in contact with the mouth to obtain salivary and gastric secretions. The mere sight of food would produce the secretions—or even the sight of the food dish without the food—or even the sight of the person who usually fed the animal! Obviously, then, secretion of the gastric juices must be caused by more than an automatic physiological reflex produced when a substance comes into direct contact with the stomach lining. A physiological reflex is one that is shown by all physically normal animals of a certain species; it is "wired" into the nervous system. Pavlov had discovered a new type of reflex, one that he sometimes called a psychic reflex and sometimes a conditioned reflex. The standard paradigm for studying Pavlovian conditioning in the laboratory is outlined in figure 9–2.

The importance of Pavlov's discovery is that any stimulus in the environment that normally is neutral (that is, has no specific effect on behavior) can be made to control certain responses by being paired with other stimuli that produce an automatic physical reaction. For example, if a person is subjected to a stressful event in a particular situation (say, his or her office or room), then the body will respond with defensive reactions: the heart may race, blood pressure increase, adrenalin flow, and so on. These responses might become conditioned to the situation, so that even without a stressful event, a person may show all these physiological changes in the situation. Some researchers in the field of behavioral medicine have argued that many disorders so prevalent today—hypertension, gastric ulcers, headaches—may be caused by conditioned reactions that occur when people are in situations where they have repeatedly experienced stress. As indicated by the case in which the discovery of mold led to extreme dislike of rye bread,

FIGURE 9–2.

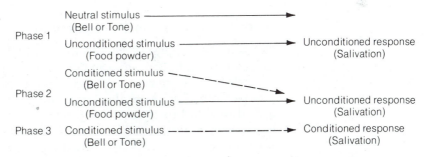

An outline of the stages in classical conditioning. A neutral stimulus such as a bell or a tone that elicits no salivation when presented by itself is delivered to the organism slightly before an unconditioned stimulus (US), such as food powder, that produces an unconditioned response (UR), salivation. After a number of such pairings (Phase 1), the neutral stimulus becomes associated with the UR, as indicated by the broken line in Phase 2. The response becomes conditioned to the neutral stimulus, which is now called the conditioned stimulus (CS). Eventually (Phase 3), the CS will elicit salivation (now called the conditioned response, CR, in absence of the US). If the CS is repeatedly presented without the US, the CR will grow weaker and eventually extinguish altogether.

Pavlovian conditioning also seems to play a role in the development of other important human behaviors, including phobias (irrational fears) and other aversions.

Pavlovian conditioning does not, however, indicate that you are entirely at the mercy of arbitrarily paired events. Research has shown that although contiguous pairing of events (say, an office and stress) may be necessary for classical conditioning to occur, such pairing may not be sufficient. Several years ago Kamin (1969) showed that it is important for the CS to *predict* the US and not just coincide with it. Kamin first demonstrated that rats could easily learn to associate CSs that were a light, a noise, or a combination of light and noise with a mild electric shock (the US). Then he showed that if a rat first learned that one CS was associated with shock (say, the noise), the rat would not learn much at all about the light-US relation when the light was subsequently presented with the noise CS in combination with the shock. Kamin reasoned that the rat first learned that noise predicted shock. Then when the noise and light appeared together, the light was redundant to the noise and the animal did not learn to associate it with the shock. According to these results, a person who showed a stress reaction to his or her office would not learn to associate stress to a new piece of office furniture because the office itself would be a good predictor of stress. When one event predicts another, a *contingent* relation (or a *contingency*) is said to exist between the two events.

Although processes of classical conditioning are of importance, other psychologists (particularly B. F. Skinner) argue that many types of learning do not occur by these processes. They suggest that a different form of learning—usually called instrumental or operant conditioning—is the prototype for much learning.

Instrumental (Operant) Conditioning

The earliest examples of the second type of conditioning were experiments by E. L. Thorndike at Columbia University, who put cats in puzzle boxes from which they were to escape. These experiments were performed at about the same time as Pavlov's. They are described in detail in chapter 11; briefly, the primary point is that the experiment concerned learning from the consequences of some action. Thorndike's cats performed some response that allowed them to escape from the puzzle box; then, when they were replaced in the box, they tended to perform the same response again. The consequences of a behavior affected how it was learned. Since the behavior was instrumental in producing the consequence (the reward), this form of learning was called *instrumental conditioning*. It was seen as obeying different principles from those of Pavlovian conditioning (what is the US?, the UR?, the CS?, the CR?) and was also viewed as a more general type of learning.

Over the years, a great number of American psychologists have devoted much effort to understanding instrumental conditioning.

In fact, this was perhaps the central topic in experimental psychology from 1930 to 1960, with the involvement of such prominent psychologists as Clark Hull, Edward Tolman, and Kenneth Spence. But perhaps the most famous investigator and popularizer of the study of this type of conditioning is B. F. Skinner, whose importance is unparalleled in psychology today.

Skinner calls this type of conditioning *operant conditioning*, because the response operates on the environment. This is distinguished from what he called *respondent conditioning*, the classical conditioning studied by Pavlovians, in which the organism simply responds to environmental stimulation. The primary datum of interest in the study of operant conditioning is the rate at which some response occurs. The primary responses that have been studied are those of lever pressing by rats and key pecking by pigeons in operant-conditioning apparatuses (or, more colloquially, in Skinner boxes). A Skinner box is simply a small, well-lit little box with a lever or key that can be depressed and a place for dispensing food (see figure 9 – 3).

In operant conditioning, the experimenter waits until the animal makes the desired response; he or she then rewards it, say,

FIGURE 9–3.

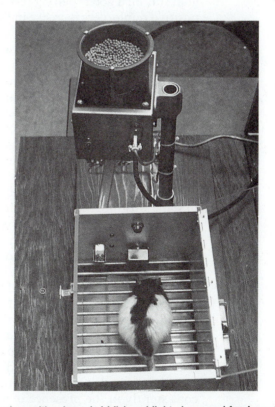

Typical Skinner box with a lever (middle) and light above and food cup to the left. The top of the picture shows the pellet dispenser with 45-mg precision food pellets. When the animal makes a correct response, a pellet of food rolls down the clear tube between the dispenser and the box and falls into the cup. All of this machinery is controlled by programming equipment that allows the experimenter to set different tasks for the animal.

with food. If the entire response is not performed, the experimenter must reinforce successive approximations to it until the desired response occurs. For example, if you want to teach a pigeon to walk around in figure-eights, you must first reward quarter-circle turns, then half-turns, and so on. This procedure of reinforcing greater and greater approximations to the desired behavior is called shaping the behavior; in principle it is the same as the "getting warmer" game played by children. Operant conditioning works on the principle of the law of effect: If an operant response is made and followed by a reinforcing stimulus, the probability that the response will occur again is increased. What will serve as a reinforcing stimulus is not specified ahead of time, but must be discovered for each situation. Using this straightforward principle, Skinner and many others have undertaken the experimental analysis of numerous behaviors.

A reinforcing stimulus is one that strengthens the response that it follows. Generally, two different classes of reinforcing stimuli are identified: *positive reinforcing stimulus* and *negative reinforcing stimulus*. Positive reinforcers are the familiar rewards that are given following a particular response: food pellets in the Skinner box, a gold star on a good spelling test, and so on. Behaviors that produce positive reinforcers increase in likelihood. Negative reinforcers are aversive events, and responses that remove or avoid them are strengthened. For example, a rat can learn to press a bar in a Skinner box to terminate a shock or to postpone it. In a similar fashion, you are reinforced on a bitterly cold day for putting on a warm coat and avoiding getting uncomfortably chilly.

Do not confuse negative reinforcement with *punishment*. Behaviors that produce aversive events are said to be punished. Punished behaviors decrease in frequency. If a rat has been positively reinforced with food for pressing a lever and is now punished for each lever press with a mild electric shock, the rate of pressing the lever will decrease. Likewise, the young child who is reprimanded in some way for snitching cookies will decrease his or her thievery.

The role of stimuli other than the reinforcing stimulus is also important in the study of operant conditioning. A *discriminative stimulus* signals when a behavior will be followed by a reward. For example, a pigeon might be trained to peck a button for food only in the presence of a red light. If any other light is on, pecking will not be followed by food. Animals learn such contingencies between stimuli and responses quite readily. A discriminative stimulus (or S^D) may be said to "set the stage" or "provide the occasion" for some response. One of the primary tasks of operant conditioning is to bring some response "under stimulus control." An organism is said to be under stimulus control when it responds correctly and consistently in the presence of a discriminative stimulus, and not in its absence. Clever Hans was under stimulus control when he responded to the subtle cues by tapping, which resulted in reinforcement.

Recall that effective CSs in classical conditioning are those that are contingently related to the US (the CS predicts the US). Operant conditioning also has important contingent relations; namely, the relation between the response and the reinforcing stimulus. In operant conditioning, organisms can learn that there is a positive contingency between behavior and reinforcement, which is the standard Skinner box arrangement. Organisms can also learn that there is a negative contingency between behavior and reinforcement, such that if they respond, reinforcement will not occur. One way of examining this contingency is to use a procedure called *experimental extinction*, in which reinforcement is withheld after an organism has learned to make a particular response. After several times of having reinforcement fail to follow the response, the organism ceases to make the response (see the *Nuts and Bolts* section at the end of this chapter for an additional discussion of extinction). Finally, organisms can learn that there is a null contingency between their behavior and reinforcement. A *null contingency* is one in which the reinforcer is independent of behavior—sometimes a behavior leads to reinforcement, and sometimes the reinforcement occurs in the absence of a particular behavior. When organisms learn that no matter what they do aversive events will happen, they tend to become helpless and show various signs of depression (Seligman, 1975). Likewise, when positive events occur independently of behavior, organisms tend to become lazy (Welker, 1976). It is tempting to generalize the latter effect to "spoiled brats" who receive substantial numbers of noncontingent positive reinforcers and then fail to work hard to get them when it becomes necessary to do so.

Both operant- and classical-conditioning procedures are actively investigated by contemporary psychologists interested in learning. We will discuss both procedures in the context of specific experimental issues later in the chapter.

INTRODUCING THE VARIABLES

Dependent Variables

One important dependent variable in animal-learning research is the rate of responding, often plotted over time. Another important dependent variable commonly used in classical conditioning is the amplitude of the response. Rather than just noting whether or not a dog salivates to a conditioned stimulus, we can measure the amplitude of the response by seeing how much saliva is produced. Another commonly measured characteristic of responses is their latency, or the time it takes the animal to accomplish the response. This measure is widely used in maze-learning experiments, where the time it takes an animal to complete the maze is recorded. Often results are plotted in terms of speed rather than latency, speed being the reciprocal of latency (l/latency).

A derived measure of learning is resistance to extinction. After a response has been learned, if the experimenter no longer applies reinforcement when the animal executes the response, the response gradually grows weaker or extinguishes. Resistance to extinction, then, can be used as an index of how well the response was learned in the first place. It is considered a derived, rather than basic, measure, because what is still being measured is frequency, amplitude, or speed of response. These all decline during extinction, but they may decline at different rates after different manipulations of the independent variable. Thus, resistance to extinction is a derived measure of the effectiveness of some independent variable on learning.

Independent Variables

A great many independent variables may be manipulated in studies of animal learning and conditioning. Many have to do with the nature of reinforcement. Experimenters can vary the magnitude of reinforcement in Pavlovian and instrumental conditioning. Experimenters can also vary the schedule by which reinforcement is administered. They can also vary the delay after the response, before they present the reinforcing stimulus to the subject. (Typically, longer delays produce less learning.) Another popular variable is the drive level, or motivation, of the animal. This can be manipulated by varying the amount of time the organism

has been deprived of the reinforcing stimulus (say, food or water) before the experiment. These are, of course, a small sample of the possible independent variables.

Control Variables

Control of extraneous variation is typically quite sophisticated in basic animal-learning research, but even here there are subtle problems. One of these is the problem of pseudoconditioning in classical-conditioning experiments. Pseudoconditioning refers to a temporary elevation in the amplitude of the conditioned response that is not caused by the association between the CS and US. Thus it is not true conditioning, but only mimics conditioning. It is recognized by being relatively short-lived and variable in nature and is usually caused by the general excitement of the experimental situation for the animal, including the presentation of the CS and US. The appropriate control for pseudoconditioning is to have one group of animals in the experiment exposed to the same number of CS and US presentations as the animals in the conditioning group, but to have the presentations unpaired and presented randomly. Both the experimental and the pseudoconditioning control groups should be affected by the general excitement induced by the experimental situation; any difference between the two groups should be due to the learning produced by the CS – US pairings in the case of the experimental group (Rescorla, 1967).

9.1 Experimental Topics and Research Illustrations

Topic: Within- and Between-subjects Designs
Illustration: Stimulus Intensity

One fundamental question about classical conditioning is how the intensity of a neutral stimulus affects the conditioning process. For example, if a tone is paired with food given to dogs, will the intensity of the tone affect how quickly the dog becomes conditioned, so that the tone alone (now called the conditioned stimulus) produces salivation? A reasonable hypothesis is that the stronger the stimulus, the more quickly conditioning will occur. Animals should be very sensitive to more salient stimuli, and thus better associate them with unconditioned stimuli. We might predict that the stronger the conditioned stimulus, the faster and stronger conditioning will occur.

Many researchers have investigated this question over the years; the surprising finding from most of the early research was that stimulus intensity did not seem to have much effect on Pavlovian conditioning. Relatively weak stimuli seemed to produce just as good conditioning as did strong stimuli (Carter, 1941; Grant and Schneider, 1948). Since most theories of the time predicted that conditioning should be affected by the intensity of the stimulus (Hull, 1943), the failure to find the effect constituted something of a puzzle. The researchers who did these experiments on stimulus-intensity effects in conditioning typically used between-subjects designs, so that different groups of subjects received different stimulus intensities. Before discussing the reason for their doing this, let us consider some of the general advantages and disadvantages of between-subjects and within-subjects experimental designs.

Between-subjects versus within-subjects designs. Perhaps the simplest sort of experimental design is the case in which there are two conditions, experimental and control, with different groups of subjects assigned to each. In a *between-subjects design*, a different group of subjects is usually assigned to each level of each independent variable. One potential problem in using a between-subjects design is that a difference obtained on the dependent variable might be caused by the fact that different groups of subjects are used in the two conditions. That is, subjects may be confounded with the independent variable of interest. To overcome this potential problem, experimenters randomly assign subjects to conditions in between-subjects designs. Thus, *on the average*, the groups should be of equal ability in the two conditions. In all between-subjects designs, then, the subjects should be randomly assigned to the different conditions to ensure that the groups are equivalent prior to the manipulation of the independent variable. This is absolutely crucial, since otherwise any difference observed between the groups on the dependent variable might be merely because subjects in the different groups differed in ability. If we have a large number of subjects and randomly assign them to groups, then we can minimize the possibility of this sort of confounding and be more confident that any difference we find on the dependent variable is actually owing to the independent-variable manipulation. When subjects are randomly assigned to conditions in a between-subjects design, this is referred to as a *random-groups design*.

There are two primary drawbacks to between-subjects or random-groups designs. One is that they are wasteful in terms of the number of subjects required. When a different group of subjects is assigned to each condition, the number of subjects required for an experiment can quickly become quite large—especially if the experimental design is at all complex. Thus, between-subjects designs are impractical when, as is often the case, there is a shortage of subjects available for an experiment.

The second problem is more serious; it has to do with the variability introduced by using different groups of subjects. One basic fact of all psychological research is that subjects differ greatly in their abilities to perform almost any task (on almost any dependent variable). When numerous subjects are used in between-subjects designs, some of the differences in behavior in the experimental conditions will be owing to differences among subjects. This can have the unfortunate effect of making it difficult to determine whether subject differences or the independent variable determined the results. Thus, subjects are confounded with groups, and in between-subjects designs, this variability caused by subject differences cannot be estimated statistically and taken into account.

Both the problems with between-subjects designs can be reduced by using *within-subjects designs*, in which all subjects are given treatments at every level of the independent variable. Within-subjects designs use fewer subjects than between-subjects designs, because each subject serves in all conditions. Also, there are statistical techniques for taking into account the variance that is produced by the differences between subjects. This is because each subject serves as his or her own control—another way of saying that subjects are *not* confounded with groups, as is the case in a between-subjects experiment. A within-subjects design is usually more effective than a between-subjects design in detecting differences between conditions on the dependent variable, because this variance due to subject differences can be estimated statistically and taken into account. The exact statistical techniques for analyzing within-subjects experiments will not be discussed here. In general, the within-subjects design is more powerful—more likely to allow detection of a difference between conditions if there really is one—than the between-subjects design. This advantage makes the within-subjects design preferred by many investigators whenever it is possible to use it.

Although there are advantages to using within-subjects designs, new problems are introduced by them. Unfortunately, within-subjects designs simply cannot be used in investigating some types of experimental problems, and even when they can be used, they have requirements that between-subjects designs do not. Within-subjects designs cannot be used in cases where performing in one condition is likely to completely change performance in another condition. This problem is usually called *asymmetrical transfer*, or a *carryover effect*. If we want to know how rats differ in learning a maze with and without their hippocampuses (a part of the brain related to learning and memory), we cannot use a within-subjects design, since we cannot replace a hippocampus once it is removed. The same problem occurs any time the independent variable may provide a change in behavior that will carry over until the subject is tested under the other condition.

If we want to test people on a task either with or without some specific training, we cannot test them first with training and then with no training. And we cannot test them always in the reverse order (no training and then training), because then we have confounded conditions with practice on the task. For example, if we want to see if a specific memory-training program is effective, we cannot teach people the program (the training phase), test them, and then test them again with no training. Once a person has had the training, we cannot take it away; it will carry over to the next part of the experiment. We cannot test people in the other direction, either, with a memory test, a training phase, and then a second memory test. The reason is that if people improved on the second test, we would not know whether the improvement was a result of training or merely practice at taking memory tests. In other words, training and practice would be confounded. A between-subjects design is appropriate in this case. One group of subjects would have their memories tested with no training; the other group would be tested after having been trained with the memory program.

Within-subjects designs are also inappropriate in cases where subjects may figure out what is expected of them in the experiment, and then try to cooperate with the experimenter and produce the desired results. This is more likely to happen with within- than between-subjects designs, because in the former case, the subjects participate in each condition. This problem makes within-subjects designs all but nonexistent in certain types of social psychological research.

Even when these problems do not eliminate the possibility of using a within-subjects design in some situation, there are additional problems to be considered. In within-subjects designs, the subjects are always tested at two or more points in time; thus, the experimenter must be on guard for factors related to time that would affect the experimental results.

The two primary factors that must be considered are *practice effects* and *fatigue effects*, which tend to offset one another. Practice effects refer to subjects performing better in the experimental task simply because of practice, and not the manipulation of the independent variable (as in the memory experiment just discussed). Fatigue effects refer to decreases in performance over the course of the experiment, especially if the experimental task is long, difficult, or boring. The effects of practice and fatigue may be taken into account and minimized by systematically arranging the order in which the experimental conditions are presented to subjects. This is referred to as *counterbalancing* of conditions and is discussed later in the chapter.

As we have said, when appropriate, within-subjects designs are generally preferred to between-subjects designs, despite the fact that they involve a number of additional considerations. The primary advantage, once again, is that within-subjects designs are typically more powerful or more sensitive, because the possibility of error resulting from subject variability is reduced relative to that in between-subjects designs.

A third sort of design, the *matched-groups design*, attempts to introduce some of the advantages of a within-subjects design to a between-subjects comparison. The matched-groups design attempts to reduce subject variability among groups by matching the subjects in the different groups on other variables. Thus, in a human memory experiment, subjects might be matched on the basis of I.Q. before they were randomly assigned to conditions. (Each subgroup of subjects matched for I.Q. is randomly assigned to a particular group.) Matching on relevant variables can help reduce the variability caused by the simple random assignment of subjects to each group (the random-groups design). Also, it is very important that assignment to conditions still be random within matched sets of subjects; otherwise, there is the possibility of confounding and other problems, especially regression artifacts (see chapters 2 and 12). In many situations, matching tends to involve much work, since subjects must be measured separately on the matching variable.

One matching technique used in animal research is the *split-litter technique*. This involves taking animals from the same litter and then randomly assigning them to groups. Since the animals in the different groups are genetically similar, this helps reduce variability resulting from subject differences that occurs in random-groups designs.

Stimulus intensity in classical conditioning. Let us now return to the problem we considered earlier. How does the intensity of the conditioned stimulus affect acquisition of a conditioned response? Common sense, as well as some theories, led to the prediction that more intense stimuli should lead to faster conditioning than less intense stimuli. However, as mentioned earlier, the first research on this topic failed to find such effects. For example, Grant and Schneider (1948) varied the intensity of a light as a conditioned stimulus in an eyelid-conditioning experiment. In such experiments, people are attached to an apparatus that delivers puffs of air to the eye and records responses (eye blinks). The unconditioned stimulus is the air puff, the unconditioned response is the blinking, and the conditioned stimulus is a light that precedes the air puff. Originally the light does not cause a subject to blink; but after it is repeatedly paired with the air puff, eventually the light by itself causes the blinking, which then is the conditioned response. Grant and Schneider asked simply whether more intense lights would cause faster conditioning. Would a bright light cause subjects to develop a conditioned response faster than a dim light? They tested different groups of subjects in the two cases, one with each intensity of light, and discovered that, contrary to expectations, conditioning was just as fast in the condition with the dim light as it was in the condition with the bright light. Other researchers obtained similar results when they examined the effects of stimulus intensity on conditioning in between-subjects designs, even when they used different stimuli (such as tones instead of lights).

The use of between- or within-subjects designs is usually determined by the nature of the problem studied, the independent variables manipulated, the number of subjects available to the researcher, and other considerations described in the preceding section. Rarely do researchers consider the possibility that the very outcome of their research could depend on the type of design they choose. However, this is exactly the case in the issue of the effects of stimulus intensity on conditioning, as was discovered after Grant and Schneider's (1948) research.

Years later, Beck (1963) again asked the question of whether the intensity of the stimulus affected eyelid conditioning. She was also interested in other variables, including the intensity of the unconditioned stimulus (the air puff) and the anxiety level of her subjects. For our purposes, we will consider only the effect of the intensity level of the conditioned stimulus, which was varied within subjects as one factor in a complex experimental design. Beck used two intensity levels and presented them in an irregular order across 100 conditioning trials in her experiment. She found a large and statistically significant effect of stimulus intensity on development of the conditioned response, contrary to what other researchers had found.

Grice and Hunter (1964) noticed Beck's effect and wondered if she had found an effect where others had found none because she had used a within-subjects design, whereas most others had used between-subjects designs. To discover this, they tested three groups of subjects: in two groups, the variable of intensity of the conditioned stimulus was varied between subjects, and for the remaining group it was varied within subjects. They used a soft tone (50 decibels) or a loud tone (100 decibels) as the conditioned stimuli in an eyelid-conditioning experiment. Subjects in each group participated in 100 trials. On each trial, subjects heard a buzzer that alerted them that a trial was beginning. Two seconds later, they heard a tone (soft or loud) that lasted .5 seconds, and then after another half-second they received a puff of air to the eye. The tone was the conditioned stimulus, the air puff the unconditioned stimulus. The Loud Group received the 100-decibel tone on all 100 trials, whereas the Soft Group received the 50-decibel tone on all 100 trials. These two groups represent a between-subjects comparison of stimulus-intensity level in eyelid conditioning. Subjects in the third group (the Loud/Soft Group) received 50 trials with the loud tone (*L*) and 50 trials with the soft tone (*S*). The trials occurred in one of two irregular orders, such that one order was the mirror image of the other. In other words, if the order of the first ten trials was *L, S, S, L, S, L, L, L, S, L,* the other order would be *S, L, L, S, L, S, S, S, L, S.* In the Loud/Soft Group, half the subjects received each order.

Grice and Hunter reported the results of their experiment in two ways. One was the percentage of the last 60 trials on which subjects showed a conditioned response, that is, blinking to the tone before the air puff came. These results are shown in figure 9–4. One line represents the between-subjects comparison, in which each subject had experience with only the loud stimulus or the soft stimulus. As you can see, the percentage of trials on which subjects responded did not vary as a function of stimulus intensity in the one-stimulus, between-subjects case. (The slight difference seen is not statistically reliable.) On the other hand, when stimulus in-

FIGURE 9–4.

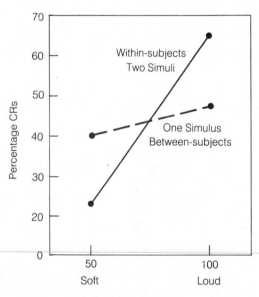

Results of Grice and Hunter's (1964) experiment. When stimulus intensity was varied between subjects so that every subject had experience only with the loud or soft stimulus, no reliable effect of stimulus intensity was found. However, when there was a within-subjects manipulation of stimulus intensity so that every subject experienced both intensities, a large effect was obtained. (The measure was the percentage of the last 60 trials on which a conditioned response occurred.) The results show that the type of experimental design can affect the results obtained in an experiment.

tensity was varied within subjects in the Loud/Soft Group, a large effect of stimulus intensity was found. Subjects responded just slightly more than 20 percent of the time to the soft stimulus, but almost 70 percent of the time to the loud stimulus, a difference that proved reliable.

The conditioning performance is plotted somewhat differently in figure 9–5, where the percentage of conditioned responses to the stimuli is shown for each successive block of 20 trials so that you can see how quickly the conditioned response was acquired. (Recall that performance in figure 9–4 showed the percentages for only the last 60 trials.) In figure 9–5 you can see that the difference between the loud and soft stimulus occurs in the very first block of trials for the Loud/Soft Group, and holds over all five blocks of 20 trials. However, for the between-subjects comparison, there is not even a hint of a difference between the loud and soft stimuli in producing conditioned responses on the first 40 trials, and only a slight (and not statistically significant) difference after that.

The results of Grice and Hunter's experiment show that the choice of a between-subjects or within-subjects design can have far-reaching effects. In this case, the actual outcome of experiments designed to examine the effects of stimulus intensity was determined by the choice of design. When subjects experienced both stimuli, they reacted to them differently; but when they experienced only one stimulus or the other, they showed no difference in responding. Grice (1966) reports other situations in which a

FIGURE 9–5.

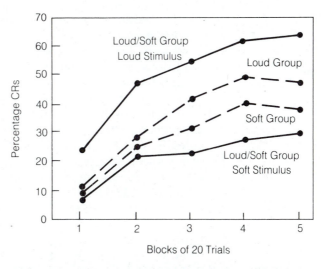

Learning of the conditioned response in Grice and Hunter's (1964) experiment. The graph shows the percentage of trials in which subjects produced a conditioned response, in blocks of 20 trials. In the between-subjects manipulation (the comparison between the Loud and Soft groups), there was no difference over the first 40 trials in responding to the loud and soft tones, and only a slight difference on the last 60 trials. However, when the same comparison between tones was made within subjects (the Loud/Soft Group), a large difference was revealed on the first 20 trials; it then increased throughout the 100 conditioning trials.

similar pattern of results occurs. In many experimental situations, researchers cannot tell whether their findings would be changed by switching from a between-subjects to a within-subjects design (or vice versa), because it is impossible to ask the experimental question with the other design, for reasons discussed earlier. However, Grice and Hunter's (1964) research reminds us that the choice of an experimental design can have ramifications beyond mundane considerations of the number of subjects used and the like. The actual outcome of the research may be affected.

In this instance, the different results obtained with the two designs may be owing to a sort of carryover effect in the within-subjects version of the experiment. As compared with subjects in the between-subjects (one-stimulus) design, people in the within-subjects design may have perceived the loud stimulus as louder and the soft stimulus as softer because they experienced both intensities and could contrast them. In the next section, we will examine another sort of contrast that can occur in conditioning.

9.2 Experimental Topics and Research Illustrations

Topic: Counterbalancing
Illustration: Simultaneous Contrast

Whenever a within-subjects design is used, one needs to decide with care the order in which the conditions should be presented to the subjects. The arrangement must be such that on the average the conditions are presented at the same stage of practice, so that there can be no confounding between the experimental conditions and stage of practice. Counterbalancing is also necessary to minimize the effect of other variables besides time that might affect the experiment. Often, it is necessary to counterbalance across variables in which the experimenter is not interested, even in between-subjects designs, so that these extraneous variables do not affect the conditions of interest. An example of this problem should make it clearer.

In learning an instrumental response, the particular magnitude of the reward used greatly influences performance. Typically, performance is greater as the magnitude of reward is increased. However, the particular magnitude of reward used does not have an invariable effect on performance, but depends on the experience that the organism has had with other reinforcement conditions. One example of this effect is provided by an experiment done by Bower (1961) on *simultaneous contrast*, in which some subjects experienced two contrasting magnitudes of reward.

Bower's experiment consisted of three groups of ten rats, each of which received four trials a day in a straight-alley maze for thirty-two days, for a total of 128 trials. The independent variable was the magnitude of reward used. One group of rats received eight food pellets in the goal box on their four trials. Since they received a constant eight pellets on each trial, this condition is referred to as Constant 8. Another group received only one pellet after each trial (Constant 1). These two groups can be considered as controls for the third (Contrast) group. Subjects in this group received two trials each day, in two different straight alleys. The two alleys were quite discriminable, one being black and one being white. In one alley they always received a one-pellet reward; in the other alley, they always received eight pellets. Bower was interested in seeing how the exposure to both levels of reinforcement would affect running speed, as compared with exposure to only one level all the time. Would rats run at a different speed for a one- (or eight-) pellet reward if they had experienced another level of reward, rather than having had constant training at one particular level?

Before examining the results, let us consider some design features that Bower had to face for the contrast subjects. Since magnitude of reward was varied within subjects in this condition, there were two problems to consider. First, it was important to ensure that not all subjects received the greater or lesser reinforcement in either the black or white alley, since then alley color would be confounded with reward magnitude, and rats may simply have run faster in black alleys than white (or vice versa). This was easily accomplished by having half the animals receive eight pellets in the black alley and one pellet in the white, and having the other half of the animals receive the reverse arrangement. For the control subjects that received only one reward magnitude, half would be tested in a white alley and half in a black alley. All of this may sound rather complicated, so we have outlined the design scheme in figure 9–6.

The second problem was in what order the rats in the Contrast group should be given the two conditions on the four trials each day. Obviously, they should not first be given the two large-reward trials followed by the two small-reward trials (or vice versa), since time of testing would be confounded with reward magnitude. Perhaps a random order could be used for the 128 trials. But random orders are not preferred in such cases, since there can be, even in random orders, long runs in which the same occurrence appears. So it would not be surprising to find cases where there were two trials in a row of the same type (large or small magnitude of reward), although across all subjects there would be no confounding with practice. It is preferable in cases such as this to counterbalance the conditions, rather than vary them randomly. *Counterbalancing*, you will remember, refers to any technique used to systematically vary the order of conditions in an experiment to distribute the effects of time of testing (such as practice and fatigue), so that they are not confounded with conditions.

When there are two conditions to be tested in blocks of four trials, there are six possible orders in which the conditions can

FIGURE 9–6.

Group	Number of Rats	Alley Color	Number of Trials (per day)	Number of Pellets
Constant 8	5	black	4	8
	5	white	4	8
Constant 1	5	black	4	1
	5	white	4	1
Contrast	5	black	2	8
		white	2	1
	5	black	2	1
		white	2	8

An outline of the design of Bower's experiment, showing some of the features used to minimize confounding. Alley color is not confounded with group or magnitude of reward (number of pellets). For the Contrast group, additional counterbalancing is needed to balance the order of one- vs. eight-pellet trials within the daily session (see text).

occur within trials. In the present case, if S stands for a small (one pellet) and L for a large (eight pellet) reward, then the six orders are *SSLL, SLSL, SLLS, LLSS, LSLS, LSSL*. Bower's solution to the counterbalancing problem was to use each of these orders equally often. On a particular day of testing, he would pick a particular order for the trials for half the subjects (for example, *LSSL*), and then simply test the other half of the subjects using the other order (*SLLS*). On the next day, he would pick another order for half the rats, while the others received the reverse order, and so on. Thus there was no confounding between order and conditions, and all the orders were used equally often, so that the experiment did not depend on just one order. We shall return to this point in a moment.

Bower's results are presented in figure 9–7, where the mean running speed for each of the four conditions is plotted across blocks of two days (eight trials). First, notice that for the rats that received constant reward, those rewarded with eight pellets performed better after the first few days than those rewarded with only one. It was not exactly big news, of course, that rats ran faster for more, rather than for less, food. The real interest was in how fast rats in the contrast conditions ran for one- and eight-pellet rewards. Although there was no statistically reliable effect between speeds of the Constant-8 and Contrast-8 conditions in figure 9–7, the Contrast-1 rats ran reliably more slowly for the reward than did the Constant-1 rats, at least toward the end of training. This is referred to as a *negative contrast effect*, since the contrast subjects ran more slowly for the small reward than did the rats that always

FIGURE 9–7.

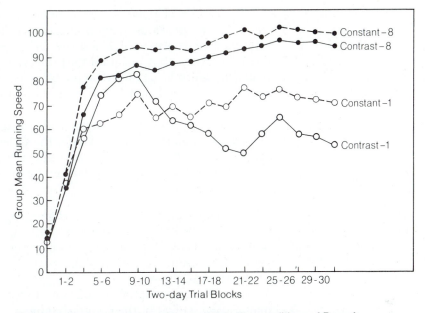

These are the group mean running speeds for the conditions of Bower's experiment, averaged over blocks of eight trials (two days). The rats that received both one-pellet and eight-pellet trials ran more slowly for the one-pellet reward than rats that always received one pellet. This is referred to as a negative contrast effect. (After Bower, 1961, Fig. 1)

received the small reward. One interpretation of this phenomenon considers emotional states induced in the contrast rats owing to their experience in the situation. Since the contrast rats were familiar with both levels of reward, when placed in the distinctive alley that told them that they would receive a small reward, they were annoyed or frustrated at having to run down the alley for only one crummy pellet.

It is an interesting question as to why Bower did not find a *positive contrast effect*, or faster running for the Contrast-8 subjects relative to the Constant-8 subjects. Why weren't the Contrast-8 rats happy or elated to learn, when placed in the distinctive alley signaling a large reward, that they would get eight pellets rather than only one? One possibility is that they *were* more elated, but that a ceiling effect prevented this from being reflected in their running speeds. Perhaps performance was already so good in the Constant-8 condition because of the large reward that there was no room for improvement in the Contrast-8 condition. The rats in the control (Constant-8) condition were already running as fast as their little legs would carry them, so no matter how much more elated the Contrast rats might be, this could not be reflected in their performance. Although this ceiling-effect interpretation of the present data is bolstered somewhat by other reports of positive contrast effects (Padilla, 1971), negative contrast effects seem more easily obtained than positive ones. The problem of ceiling effects in data analysis is discussed more fully in chapter 10.

The results of Bower's experiment should remind you of the lesson in the previous section contrasting between- and within-subjects designs. As in Grice and Hunter's experiments on stimulus-intensity effects, Bower found that the effect of a reward of a particular magnitude depended on the type of design used. In a within-subjects design, in which the animals had experience with both reward magnitudes, the effect on behavior was greater than in the between-subjects comparison, in which a different group of animals received constant rewards over the series of trials. Once again, the nature of the design used can affect the conclusion reached about how strong an effect is produced by the independent variable.

Further considerations in counterbalancing. There is a great variety of counterbalancing schemes that can be used in various situations. Some of these become very complex. Here we discuss only some of the simpler counterbalancing designs, to provide you with a few tricks of the trade.

The case represented by Bower's (1961) contrast group is in many ways typical of the counterbalancing problem as it usually arises. There were two conditions to be tested within subjects, and thus they had to be counterbalanced so as not to be confounded with stage of practice. One solution to this problem, and the one most psychologists would pick, would be to use an *ABBA* design, where *A* stands for one condition and *B* stands for the other. This would unconfound particular conditions with time of testing, since each condition would be tested at the same time on the average (1 + 4 = 5 for *A*, and 2 + 3 = 5 for *B*, where the numbers refer to the order of test). But perhaps the specific order of testing might also matter. For example, let us assume that there is a very large practice effect on the dependent variable, but that it occurs very early in training, on the first *A* trial. Then, it would contribute to the *A* condition but not to the *B* condition, so that the *ABBA* design would not eliminate the confounding of conditions with practice.

Two solutions to this problem of large effects of practice early in training can be suggested. One is to give a number of practice trials in the experimental situation before the experiment proper begins. Thus the subjects are given practice, and performance on the dependent variable is allowed to stabilize before the experimental conditions of interest are introduced. Another solution is to employ more than one counterbalancing scheme. For example, half the subjects might get the reverse of the scheme that the other half receives. So half the subjects would get *ABBA* and the other half would get *BAAB*. Bower's solution to the counterbalancing problem was the ideal extension of this logic, since he used every possible counterbalancing scheme equally often. But when more than two conditions are involved, this becomes unwieldy. In most situations, an adequate solution to the problem of practice effects at the beginning of a testing session would be to give subjects practice and then use two counterbalancing schemes, one of which is the reverse of the other. Grice and Hunter (1964), in the experiment on stimulus intensity described earlier, did just this.

For situations in which there are more than two conditions, there is one particular scheme for counterbalancing that we would like to recommend as generally desirable. This is the *balanced Latin square design.* Suppose there were six conditions in a particular experiment, and you wanted subjects to receive all six conditions in a counterbalanced order, so that practice effects would not confound the results. For example, in a simultaneous contrast experiment such as Bower's, six different reward magnitudes could be used rather than only two. A balanced Latin square design would ensure that when each condition was tested, it would be preceded and followed equally often by every other condition. This last feature is very useful in minimizing carryover effects among conditions and makes the balanced Latin square preferred to other counterbalancing schemes.

Constructing a balanced Latin square is easy, especially if there is an even number of conditions in the experiment. Let us number the six conditions in an experiment from one to six. A balanced Latin square can be thought of as a two-dimensional matrix in which the columns (extending vertically) represent conditions tested, and the rows represent the subjects. A balanced Latin square for six conditions is presented in table 9–1. The subjects are labeled *a* through *f*, and the order in which they receive the conditions is indicated by reading across the row. So subject *a* receives the conditions in the order 1, 2, 6, 3, 5, 4. The general formula for constructing the first row of a balanced Latin square is 1, 2, *n*, 3, *n* − 1, 4, *n* − 2, and so on, where *n* stands for the total number of conditions. After the first row is in place, just number down the columns with higher numbers, starting over when you get to *n* (as in table 9–1). When a balanced Latin square is used, subjects must be run in multiples of *n*, in this case six, in order to appropriately counterbalance conditions against practice.

When an experimental design has an odd number of conditions, it becomes a bit more complicated to use a balanced Latin square. In fact, two squares must be used, the second of which is the reverse

TABLE 9–1.   Balanced Latin square for six experimental conditions (1–6) presented to each subject. Rows indicate the order in which subjects *a* through *f* receive the experimental conditions.

| Subjects | Order of Testing Conditions | | | | | |
	1st	2nd	3rd	4th	5th	6th
a	1	2	6	3	5	4
b	2	3	1	4	6	5
c	3	4	2	5	1	6
d	4	5	3	6	2	1
e	5	6	4	1	3	2
f	6	1	5	2	4	3

TABLE 9–2. Balanced Latin square for five experimental conditions (1–5) presented to each subject. Rows indicate the order in which subjects a through e receive the experimental conditions. When there is an odd number of subjects, each condition must be given to each subject twice for a balanced Latin square.

| Subjects | Square 1 Order of Testing | | | | | Square 2 | | | | |
	1st	2nd	3rd	4th	5th	1st	2nd	3rd	4th	5th
a	1	2	5	3	4	4	3	5	2	1
b	2	3	1	4	5	5	4	1	3	2
c	3	4	2	5	1	1	5	2	4	3
d	4	5	3	1	2	2	1	3	5	4
e	5	1	4	2	3	3	2	4	1	5

of the first, as seen in table 9–2, where once again letters indicate subjects and numbers stand for conditions in the experiment. When a balanced Latin square is used with an unequal number of conditions, each subject must be tested in each condition twice. The case represented in table 9–2 is for five conditions. In general, the first square is constructed in exactly the same manner as when there is an even number of conditions, and then the second square is an exact reversal of the first.

The balanced Latin square is an optimal counterbalancing system for many purposes, since each condition occurs, on the average, at the same stage of practice, and each condition precedes and follows every other equally often. This latter feature is not true of other counterbalancing schemes, and thus there is more concern that testing in one condition may affect testing in another condition.

9.3 Experimental Topics and Research Illustrations

Topic: Small-*n* Design
Illustration: Behavior Problems in Children

A child, seemingly quite happy while playing by herself, begins to whine and cry. At first, the whines are rather soft and are ignored by the parent, who continues to talk on the telephone. Soon the whines accelerate to cries, and the parent must discontinue the conversation to look after the unhappy child. Some time later, the parent is once again talking to a neighbor who is in the home. The child at first plays quietly in another part of the house, but soon begins whining. The whines accelerate to cries, and the parent eventually interrupts the conversation again to deal with the child. The next day as the parent is involved with housework, the child begins to whine and cry. This time the parent is determined to ignore it, because it is obviously a mistake to encourage this type of behavior. The child continues crying, and then suddenly begins shrieking and wailing. The parent ignores this for as long as possible, but this is none too long, because of his worry that something serious might be the matter.

Later, the parents decide to seek psychological help for their child. She is now having temper tantrums quite frequently, and often also banging her head on the floor. Sometimes her head even bleeds. The parents are, of course, quite concerned with these problem behaviors exhibited by their child.

The psychological therapist, perhaps a clinical psychologist, now sees the child for the first time. What conclusions is he or she to draw? What caused this behavior? What can the therapist do to remove it and return the child to a more normal existence? The parents describe the child's problem as best they can, but of course they have forgotten the original mild crying episodes. The interpretation and proposed cure for the child's problems will depend critically on the psychologist's interpretation of the problem, and the therapy will depend on the supposed cause.

Behavior therapists would seek to discover the learning history of the child, which has produced such seemingly maladaptive behavior. In particular, the behavior therapist would attempt to discover the contingencies of reinforcement that produced and maintain the child's crying, tantrums, and head banging. What is reinforcing the child's behavior? The proposed therapy would be designed to change the contingencies of reinforcement, so that the child is rewarded for appropriate, and not maladaptive, behavior.

One potent source of reinforcement for all children is parental attention. Young children will go to great lengths to attract the attention of parents. The behavior therapist's interpretation might go something like this. Once, when the child was feeling alone and neglected, she began to whine and cry. The parent dropped what he or she was doing, attended to her, and thus reinforced the behavior. The next time the child felt neglected, she again tried the crying gambit—and was again reinforced. Before long, the child found that she had to cry more loudly for attention, both because the parents were becoming somewhat used to it, and also because they were consciously trying to ignore it in hopes that the child would stop. The parents realized that they should not reward the crying with attention, but every time the child increased the extremity of the behavior, the parents would once again start paying attention, at least for a while. Thus the problem behavior increased in intensity and frequency, until the parents were forced to see the therapist. The parents unwittingly shaped the child's behavior by reinforcing increases in intensity. Just as a pigeon can be trained to walk around in figure-eights by first being rewarded for approximations to the figure-eight, so can a child be reinforced for head banging and temper tantrums by being rewarded for successive steps along the way.

At this point, the behavior therapist's interpretation of the child's behavior is that it has been sustained by an unfortunate set of reinforcement contingencies. Therapy will involve changing the contingencies, so that the positive behavior is rewarded and the negative behavior is not. The therapist's job, in large part, is to treat the parents to become effective behavior therapists themselves. The parents should, of course, start paying attention to the child when she is behaving normally. If the tantrums persist, they should try to reinforce the child for lessening their intensity. If the child is throwing a tantrum to which the parents must pay attention, they should wait for a momentary lull in the tantrum before attending in order to try to reward the lessening intensity and gradually shape the tantrums to be less severe. Best of all would be to entirely ignore the tantrums, if possible, to try to extinguish them.

The AB design. In behavior therapy, as in all therapies, research as to the effectiveness of the therapy should be incorporated into the treatment whenever possible. This seems like a fairly simple matter: measure the frequency of behavior that needs to be changed; then institute the therapy and see if the behavior does change. We can call this an *AB design*, where *A* represents the baseline condition before therapy is applied, and *B* represents the condition after the therapy (the independent variable) is introduced. This design is used in much medical, educational, and other applied research, where a therapy or training procedure is instituted to determine its effects on the problem of interest. However, the *AB* design (Campbell and Stanley, 1966) is quite poor and should be avoided. The reason is that whatever changes occur while the treatment is being applied during the *B* phase may be caused by any number of other factors that may be confounded with the factor of interest. The treatment might produce the change in behavior, but so might any number of other sources that the experimenter is not aware of or has failed to control. Remember, confounding occurs when a second variable is inadvertently varied with the primary factor of interest, in this case, the therapy. So, it is very important to control carefully secondary variables to ensure that the primary one is producing the observed effect. This cannot be done in the *AB* design, since the therapist-experimenter may not even be aware of the other factors.

The usual solution to this problem is to compare two groups to which subjects have been randomly assigned. One, the experimental, receives the treatment; the other, the control, does not. Then if the experimental condition improves with therapy, and the control does not, we may conclude that it is the treatment and not some extraneous factor that produces the result.

Let us take a practical example of the *AB* design. If one were to ask a therapist how she knows that her therapy works, she may well reply, "Because I have seen it help people." This is reasoning employing an implicit *AB* design: the therapist sees patients when they are at rock bottom; a great percentage of the time, patients improve. But does therapy really help, or would the patients improve anyway? In 1952, H. J. Eysenck created a brouhaha in the therapeutic world when he reviewed twenty-four articles comparing traditional psychoanalytic therapy to two control situations. When patients underwent psychoanalysis, an average of 44 percent improved: the typical *AB* result of improvement relative to baseline. But 64 percent of patients treated by other techniques improved, and about the same percentage of patients only given custodial care or treated by general practitioners improved! So, sure enough, psychotherapy "improved" patients when observed in the *AB* design, but compared with appropriate control groups it actually seemed to hurt. Eysenck's conclusions have sparked a long debate, and it seems likely from more recent evidence that the results of psychotherapy are beneficial. In a carefully reasoned review of work in this area, Bergin (1971) concludes that psychotherapy has "an average effect that is moderately positive" (p. 263). To determine this, though, we must use appropriate control groups and not simply an *AB* design.

The studies just discussed are based simply on a global measure of "improvement" under some conditions and are often not particularly analytical. A number of psychological disturbances are lumped together, and such research is not too specific about a particular problem. In the case of therapy on an individual, such as the case of the little girl we discussed, there is no potential control group, and only one subject in the experimental "group." The usual comparison between control and experimental conditions depends on having a large number of subjects to assign randomly among conditions to introduce experimental control and eliminate the possibility of confounding. Thus such designs are called *large-n designs* (*n* being the designation for number of subjects). Large-*n* designs are inappropriate for most sorts of clinical research because the problems being dealt with are to some degree unique, such as the case of the child throwing temper tantrums. It is too much to ask that large numbers of such children be found, randomly assigned to an experimental (treatment) or control condition, and then compared in outcome. It may also be unethical to withhold treatment from the control group. Rather than attempt to employ the traditional large-*n* designs in such research, special techniques known as *small-n designs* have been developed.

Small-n designs. Large-*n* research designs have become the norm in psychological research because of the powerful statistical techniques that are now routinely applied in psychological research (see appendix B). Most psychologists have accepted these methods and the brand of research that they promote, namely, large-*n* designs. There have been two primary areas within experimental psychology that have successfully resisted the trend to this type of research. One is psychophysics (see chapter 6); the other is the experimental analysis of behavior in terms of operant conditioning, fathered by B. F. Skinner. Research in both these traditions is based on the intensive analysis of very few subjects, rather than a few observations of behavior in a great many subjects. Small-*n* designs are, then, within-subjects designs, in which the subjects serve in each condition. The logic developed for the study of operant conditioning by Skinner and others is especially amenable to the clinical applications of behavior modification, since such applications are based, in large part, on operant analyses of behavior.

Skinner has argued for years against the traditional large-*n* designs called for by sophisticated statistical techniques. In a paper called "The Flight from the Laboratory," he argues that the use of statistics is one of several factors that has made experimental research less attractive to many students, or as he puts it, less reinforcing. "What statisticians call experimental design (I have pointed out elsewhere that this means design which yields data to which the methods of statistics are appropriate) usually generates a much more intimate acquaintance with a calculating machine than with a behaving organism" (Skinner, 1963, p. 328). Today we might replace "calculating machine" with "computer program," but the point remains the same.

The logic of small-*n* design in operant-conditioning research has been detailed in Sidman's (1960) book, *Tactics of Scientific Research*. The experimental control usually achieved in traditional research with large numbers of subjects randomly assigned to conditions is achieved in small-*n* research by very carefully controlling the experimental setting and by taking numerous and continuous measures of the dependent variable. One powerful design commonly used in this research is the *ABA design*, or *reversal design* (Wolf and Risley, 1971).

The ABA or reversal design. The *AB* design, as we have already discussed, involves measuring the dependent variable of interest to establish a baseline in the *A* phase, before the intervening variable or treatment is applied in the *B* phase. The baseline period should be extended, of course, until the frequency of occurrence of the dependent variable becomes stable; otherwise, it would be difficult to know what to make of changes observed when the treatment variable is applied. If there is a change in the dependent variable when the treatment is administered in the *B* phase, we cannot conclusively establish that it has been caused by the treatment variable because of a lack of control comparisons. The change in the dependent variable might have occurred anyway, without the treatment variable being applied, because of variation in some uncontrolled secondary variable that might have been unobserved by the experimenter. The second *A* phase in the *ABA* design serves to rule out this possibility by returning the conditions of the experiment to their original, baseline level, with the independent variable no longer applied. If behavior in the second *A* phase returns to its baseline level, then we can conclude that it was the independent variable that effected the change during the *B* phase. This generalization would not apply if a secondary variable not detected by the experimenter happened to be perfectly correlated with the independent variable of primary interest. Such a situation is unlikely.

In our previous example of the child throwing tantrums, the therapist would instruct the parents to get a baseline measure on the number of crying episodes, tantrums, and head bangings when they reacted just as they normally would. Then the therapist would instruct them to alter their behavior by rewarding the child with attention when she engaged in good behavior and by trying to extinguish the tantrums and other behavior by ignoring them altogether. If this produced a change in the frequency of the tantrums over a period of several weeks, then the therapist might ask the parents to reinstitute their old pattern of behavior, just to ensure that it was their attention to the child at inappropriate moments that was really controlling the child's behavior, and not something else. (If the therapist were not interested in research, of course, he or she might just leave well enough alone after the successful *B* phase.) If the original treatment produced no effect on the dependent variable, the frequency of tantrums, it would be necessary to try something else. The techniques of behavior modification based on operant analysis have met with great success in the treatment of certain sorts of psychological problems. Here we consider an example.

Conditioning of crying. In an interesting study, Hart and coworkers (1964) investigated the excessive crying of a four-year-old nursery-school pupil, Bill, who otherwise seemed quite healthy and normal. The crying often came in response to mild frustrations that other children dealt with in more effective ways. Rather than attribute his crying to internal variables such as fear, lack of confidence, or regression to behavior of an earlier age, the investigators looked to the social learning environment to see what reinforcement contingencies might be producing such behavior. They decided, with reasoning similar to that already discussed in the case of our hypothetical little girl, that adult attention was the reinforcer for Bill's crying behavior. Hart and colleagues set about testing this supposition with an *ABA* (actually *ABAB*) design.

First, it was necessary to gain a good measure of the dependent variable, crying. The teacher carried a pocket counter and depressed the lever every time there was a crying episode. "A crying episode was defined as a cry (a) loud enough to be heard at least 50 feet away and (b) of 5 seconds or more duration." At the end of each nursery-school day, the total number of crying episodes was recorded. We could, perhaps, quibble some with this operational definition of a crying episode (did the teacher go 50 feet away each time to listen?), but let us assume it is valid and reliable.

FIGURE 9–8.

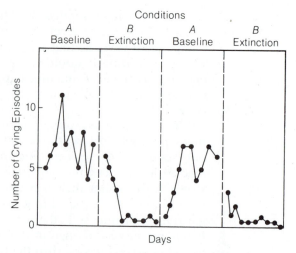

The number of crying episodes exhibited by Bill, a nursery-school student, during the four phases of an *ABAB* design initiated to control his problem crying. (From Wolf and Risley, 1969, p. 316).

During the initial baseline of phase *A*, Bill was treated as he normally had been, with attention being given by the teacher to his crying. During the ten days of the first baseline period, the number of crying episodes was between 5 and 10 a day, as shown in the left-most panel of figure 9–8, where the frequency of crying episodes on the ordinate is plotted against days on the abscissa. For the next ten days (the first *B* phase), the teacher attempted to extinguish the crying episodes by ignoring them, while rewarding Bill with attention every time he responded to minor calamities (such as falls or pushes) in a more appropriate way. As can be seen in figure 9–8, the number of crying episodes dropped precipitously, so that there were between 0 and 2 during the last six days of the first *B* phase. This completes the *AB* phase of the design; once again, we cannot be certain that the reinforcement contingencies were responsible for Bill's improved behavior. Perhaps he was getting along better with his classmates, or his parents were treating him better at home. Either of these things (or others) could have improved his disposition.

To gain better evidence that it was actually the reinforcement contingencies that changed Bill's behavior, the investigators returned to the baseline: Bill was again reinforced for crying. At first, he was rewarded with attention for approximations to crying (whimpering and sulking); after crying had been established again, it was maintained with attention to each crying episode. As the third panel in figure 9–8 shows, it took only four days to reestablish crying. This led to the conclusion that the reinforcement contingencies, and not any number of other factors, were responsible for the termination of crying in the first *B* phase. Finally, since this was a therapeutic situation, the investigators instituted a second

B phase similar to the first, in which Bill's crying was once again extinguished.

In this investigation, no inferential statistics were employed to justify the conclusions drawn. Rather, with good control of the independent variable and repeated measures on the dependent variable, the differences between conditions in this experiment were striking enough to decrease the need for inferential statistics. Use of *ABA* small-*n* designs can allow powerful experimental inferences.

From Problem to Experiment: The Nuts and Bolts

Problem: The Partial Reinforcement Extinction Effect

To produce instrumental learning (operant conditioning), we follow the behavior that we are interested in having the animal learn with a reinforcement stimulus. The animal soon learns that the reward is forthcoming in the situation if the appropriate response is emitted. For example, suppose we want to teach an animal to learn a maze. The simplest sort of maze is the straight alley, which is composed of a start box where the animal is placed, an alley through which the animal runs when the start box door is opened, and the goal box where the animal is reinforced. The reinforcement is typically food, and usually the animal has been deprived of food prior to the experiment. The dependent variable is running speed or time to run the straight-alley maze. Often the animal's speed in each section of the runway is measured, so that the experimenter finds speeds for its leaving the start box, traversing the alley, and approaching the goal. Learning is indicated by the fact that after a number of trials the rat's speed increases (the latency decreases). At first the rat dawdles along, but on later trials it really hustles.

Problem: *How is learning affected by the amount of reinforcement?*

Suppose we now wanted to ask a straightforward question about learning in this situation: How is learning affected by the amount of reinforcement? Intuitively, you might expect that learning would increase as the amount of reinforcement increases. But if you read the first part of this chapter carefully, you should realize that this depends on how "amount of reinforcement" and "learning" are defined. We could vary the amount of reinforcement by varying the percentage of trials on which subjects receive reward or by varying the magnitude of reward after each trial. We could also measure learning in at least two ways: one might be running speed, the other resistance to extinction. The latter measure is found by seeing how long after training an animal will continue running a maze when it no longer receives reinforcement.

Problem: *What is the effect of percentage of reward on resistance to extinction?*

Let us confine our interest to the case in which we vary the percentage of rewarded trials. Our experiment has now become more manageable. We vary the percentage of trials on which the animals receive rewards for running the maze (the independent variable), and we measure the time it takes the animals to run the maze and their resistance to extinction (or running speeds during extinction training).

In many experiments such as these, researchers have found that resistance to extinction is generally greater the *smaller* the percentage of trials during which the animal receives reinforcement during training. If an animal receives continuous reinforcement (that is, is reinforced after every trial), its running behavior will extinguish much more rapidly when reinforcement is withdrawn than will animals that receive reinforcement on only some percentage of the acquisition trials. In general, the smaller the percentage of reinforced trials, the greater will be the resistance to extinction (that is, the faster the animal will run when reinforcement is withdrawn). This fact, that infrequent reinforcement will lead to greater persistence in responding than continuous reinforcement, is called the *partial reinforcement extinction effect.* Several explanations of it have been proposed (Amsel, 1962, 1971; Capaldi, 1966, 1971).

A number of variables may contribute to the typical partial reinforcement extinction effect. When rats are rewarded on only some proportion of trials, a number of factors may vary simultaneously. One factor is the number of nonrewarded trials (or *N*-trials) that precede a rewarded (or *R*) trial. Another factor is the number of transitions from nonrewarded to rewarded trials (or *N-R* transitions) during the course of partial reinforcement training. A third factor is the number of different *N*-lengths (or number of different sequences of nonrewarded trials preceding a rewarded trial) during partial reinforcement. All these variables could be (and have been) examined; let us consider the first by way of an experiment in animal-learning research.

Hypothesis: *Resistance to extinction will increase with increases in the number of nonrewarded trials that precede a rewarded trial (the N-length).*

Basically, we want to design an experiment in which the number of nonrewarded trials would be varied before a rewarded trial. There could be three *N*-lengths of one, two, and three nonrewarded trials before a rewarded trial, with the hypothesis being that resistance to extinction should increase with *N*-length. The greater the number of nonrewarded trials, the faster the rats should run during extinction.

A simple straight alley is used as the training apparatus, and the time for the rat to run the maze is the dependent variable. Do we want to use a within-subjects or between-subjects design? If we use a within-subjects design, we have to counterbalance the three schedules of reinforcement. But even if we do this, there is a serious problem of carryover effects, or the effect that training rats under one schedule has on training them on the next. It is probably wiser to use a between-subjects design, especially since with animal subjects there is less problem of variability resulting from individual differences. Stable results in the partial reinforcement situation could probably be achieved with only fifteen subjects in each of three groups.

Before the experiment is begun, it is usual to pretrain the animals to get them used to the experimental situation. This reduces the amount of within-subjects variability caused by extraneous factors, such as fear of being handled by the experimenter. Thus, for several days the animals are handled for an hour or so each day by the experimenter. The rats should also be placed in the goal box with food pellets in the food dish to ensure that they will eat the pellets. Otherwise, as you might readily suppose, the pellets are unlikely to serve as a reinforcer. Finally, the rats should be placed in the straight alley and allowed to explore it for a few minutes on each of several days before actual testing. This is to ensure that it will not be frightening when they are placed in it for testing.

On each trial of the experiment proper, the experimenter takes the rat from its home cage and places it in the start box. The start-box door is opened, which starts a timer, and the rat moves down the alley to the goal box. Near the goal box, the rat passes through a photoelectric beam, which stops the timer. When the rat enters the goal box, the goal-box door is closed, so that the rat cannot return to the alley. Typically, the rat is confined to the goal box for a constant period of time in all conditions, say, thirty seconds. Then the rat is placed in a separate cage to await the next trial.

In this experiment, the independent variable is the number of nonrewarded or N-trials (1, 2, or 3) preceding a rewarded or R-trial. This is straightforward, since it is easy either to provide or not to provide food when the rat runs the maze. The only tricky aspect is that the experimental procedure confounds the number of nonrewarded trials with the amount of reward trials that the rats receive during a series of tests. The rats with greater N-lengths receive less reward. One way to correct this confounding is to provide subjects in conditions with N-lengths of two and three with intertrial reinforcements. These are simply periods when rats are given rewards between trials in the neutral cage. The rewards are not dependent on the instrumental response.

The rats should be given a number of days of training, perhaps ten, to ensure that they learn their particular schedule of reinforcement. Twelve trials per day would be an appropriate number. After ten days of learning, extinction training is introduced. This consists of simply running the rats at twelve trials per day for perhaps four days with no reward at all and measuring the time taken for the rats to run the maze. This phase of the experiment is critical, since we want to ascertain the effect of the training schedules on resistance to extinction. But a problem enters here. It is common during extinction for at least some rats to simply stop running. Either they refuse to leave the start box or they stop halfway down the alley. What happens to our dependent measure in cases such as this? The convention adopted to avoid this problem is to allow the rats a fixed amount of time to traverse the alley and to remove them and begin the next trial if they fail to beat the cutoff. A limit of 90 seconds is often used; if a rat has not made it a few feet down the maze in 90 seconds, it is unlikely that it will make it at all. Thus, the experimenter simply removes the animal, records its time as 90 seconds, and places it in the neutral cage in preparation for the next trial. Since different schedules of training sometimes produce lopsided or skewed distributions of running times, it is often necessary to use the median time for each animal rather than the mean to eliminate the effect of a few extremely long times (see appendix B for a discussion of medians).

The basic purpose of the experiment is to see whether the number of nonrewarded trials produces greater resistance to extinction. In other words, if subjects receive greater N-lengths, will they run faster when given no reward during extinction? In an experiment very similar to the one described here, Capaldi (1964) found that greater N-lengths were associated with greater resistance to extinction.

SUMMARY

1. The study of animal learning and behavior has identified two basic types of conditioning. In classical (or Pavlovian or respondent) conditioning, a neutral stimulus such as a light or tone precedes an unconditioned stimulus that produces an automatic or unconditioned response. After a number of such pairings, the originally neutral stimulus produces the response if there is a contingent (predictive) relation between the neutral stimulus and the unconditioned stimulus.

2. In instrumental (operant) conditioning, a particular behavior that is followed by a reinforcing stimulus will increase in frequency. A positve reinforcing stimulus (the familiar rewards) increases the frequency of the response that produces it. A negative reinforcing stimulus increases the frequency of the response that removes it. A response that is followed by a punishing stimulus decreases in frequency.

3. In all experimental research, whether with humans or other organisms, a fundamental question is whether to use the same

organisms in each condition of the experiment (a within-subjects design) or to use different organisms in the different conditions (a between-subjects design).

4. Within-subjects designs are preferred when they can be used, because they minimize the amount of variability caused by differences among subjects. Also, within-subjects designs employ fewer subjects than between-subjects designs, though of course it is necessary to test each individual for longer periods of time.

5. The primary danger in within-subjects designs is that of carry-over effects, the relatively permanent effect that testing subjects in one condition might have on their later behavior in another condition. In such cases, it is necessary to use between-subjects designs, even though more subjects will be needed and there is less control of subject variability.

6. The choice of an experimental design may in some instances strongly affect the outcome of an experiment. For example, stimulus intensity appears to play little role in classical conditioning when manipulated between subjects, but a great role when manipulated within subjects. Thus, the type of experimental design chosen can sometimes be critical.

7. In within-subjects designs, it is necessary to counterbalance conditions, or to vary the conditions in a systematic way so that they are not confounded with time of testing. If conditions are not counterbalanced, then time-related effects such as fatigue or practice rather than manipulation of the independent variable may account for the results. It is also necessary to counterbalance in between-subjects designs across variables that are not of central interest, such as black or white arms in an experiment using a T-maze. One quite useful counterbalancing scheme is the balanced Latin square design, in which each condition precedes and follows every other one equally often.

8. The traditional large-n research methodology is often inappropriate in applied settings, where there is only one subject. Often an *AB* design is used as a small-n design. A baseline of behavior is established (the *A* phase) and then some treatment is imposed (the *B* phase). The conclusion that changes in behavior during the *B* phase resulted from the treatment is faulty because other variables may be confounded with the treatment (such as practice or fatigue effects).

9. The *ABA* design is a powerful alternative to the *AB* design. The second *A* phase introduced after the *B* (treatment) phase removes the treatment to determine whether any changes observed during the *B* phase were caused by the independent variable or by confounding factors.

KEY TERMS

AB design
ABA (reversal) design
ABAB design
ABBA design
asymmetrical transfer
balanced Latin square design
between-subjects design
carryover effect
classical conditioning
conditioned response (CR)
conditioned stimulus (CS)
contingency
counterbalancing
discriminative stimulus
experimental extinction
fatigue effect
instrumental conditioning
large-*n* designs
matched-groups design

negative contrast effect
negative reinforcing stimulus
null contingency
operant conditioning
partial reinforcement
   extinction effect
positive contrast effect
positive reinforcing stimulus
practice effect
punishment
random-groups design
respondent conditioning
simultaneous contrast
small-*n* designs
split-litter technique
unconditioned response (UR)
unconditioned stimulus (US)
within-subjects design

DISCUSSION QUESTIONS

1. Discuss the advantages of within-subjects designs. What complications and problems are entailed by using a within-subjects design?

2. Discuss the advantages and disadvantages of using a between-subjects design.

3. In each of the following cases, tell whether it would be best to examine the independent variable in a within-subjects or a between-subjects design. Justify your answer in each case.

   (a) a social psychological study of helping, in which the researchers are interested in how group size affects whether or not an individual will help someone else in the group.

   (b) a study of the effect of varying loudness of a tone in measuring how quickly people can respond to the tone.

   (c) an experiment designed to answer the question of whether the color of a woman's hair affects the likelihood that she will be asked out for dates.

   (d) a study in which three different training techniques are compared as to their effectiveness in teaching animals tricks.

4. Tell what a balanced Latin square is and explain why it is a preferred counterbalancing scheme in many situations. Draw up two balanced Latin squares similar to those in tables 9–1 and 9–2, for cases in which there are (a) three conditions, and (b) four conditions.

5. The results of two experiments described in this chapter showed different effects of an independent variable when it was manipulated between and within subjects. Make a list of three variables for which you think between- and within-subjects designs would show the same effects, and provide two further instances in which you think the two types of designs would produce different results. Justify your reasoning in each case.

6. Discuss the sorts of confoundings that may arise from the use of an *AB* design.

Transfer of Contingencies

ONE ASPECT OF INAPPROPRIATE reinforcement contingencies that has been studied in great detail is the effect of learning one contingency on learning another. For example, a series of noncontingent aversive events can lead to depression and feelings of failure. That is, when a person has experienced a long series of failures and then is put in a situation where avoidance of failure is possible, the person often does not try to succeed. Likewise, a person who has experienced a substantial number of noncontingent positive outcomes often fails to work for rewards when it becomes necessary to do so.

You can investigate the negative transfer of one contingency on another fairly easily. However, you do not want to produce spoiled brats or depressed people, which means that your experiment should be benign and have short-lived effects. The general procedure is to have some people repeatedly fail to solve problems and others to succeed at them very easily. Then both groups of people are tested on a common set of solvable problems. The dependent variable is the time it takes each group to solve the common set of problems.

One way that this experiment could be implemented is to have people solve anagrams. Some people are given a long series (say, fifteen) of four-letter anagrams that are easy to solve, and the solution is always by the same rule: *lirg → girl; tenb → bent; eret → tree;* and so on. A second group of people would receive the same set of anagrams as the first group, but the anagram arrangement would be random rather than always having the same moves provide a solution. A third group of people are told to solve fifteen anagrams under time pressure. The time period that you allow will depend on the difficulty of the anagrams that you choose, so you might have to do some preliminary testing (so called pilot work) to determine a time period that is too short to permit successful completion of the anagrams. One way to generate very difficult anagrams is to use longer words (say, more than six letters). Also use words that are likely to be unfamiliar to most of your subjects.

The study manuals for the Graduate Record Examination are a good source for such words. Some examples are: *oathncie* → *inchoate; emednci* → *endemic; bytirop* → *probity;* and so on.

After the initial portion of the experiment, all subjects receive the same set of twenty moderately difficult anagrams, say, five-letter words (you could gather your materials from *Jumbles*, which appears in many newspapers), and then determine how long it takes them to solve the anagrams, as well as the total number solved. You will probably want to set a time limit of five or ten minutes in all conditions.

Compared with the group that initially solved moderately difficult anagrams, the other two groups would be expected to have difficulty during the criterion test because the prior experience with very easy or very difficult anagrams made them less sensitive to the contingency available on the criterion task.

As an ethical researcher, you will need to debrief your subjects carefully by apprising them of the purposes of the experiment and the methods that were used.

Since this is necessarily a between-subjects design, you will want to collaborate with your classmates in collecting data. To ensure that each class member treats the subjects the same way, a protocol detailing all procedures should be made out before any testing is undertaken.

CHAPTER 10

Remembering and Forgetting

The whole of science is nothing more than refinement of everyday thinking.

—ALBERT EINSTEIN

WHAT EXPERIENCES CAN YOU RECALL from your year in the eighth grade? Think of them for a moment. You learned many facts there; lots of things happened to you. Probably you will never recall even a small fraction of the facts you learned or experiences you had then. What has happened to these memories? Are they lost forever? Or are the memories still stored somewhere but never actively recalled, since you never have an appropriate situation to bring them to mind? There are some things you will never forget, even if you want to; but others you cannot recall, no matter how urgent the need. If a budding romance had a catastrophic ending, this memory from your days in the eighth grade may stick with you long after other events have been relegated to the dim recesses of the past. Why?

The humorist Robert Benchley, in an essay called "What College Did to Me," attempted to recall the things he had learned in college years before and to classify these by the year in which they were learned. There were thirty-nine items in the list. He remembered twelve things from his freshman year; this decreased to only eight things recalled from his senior year. A selective sampling from Benchley's list appears in table 10–1. It is selective only with regard to the number of pieces of information included, so that it does give a fair representation of the depth and range of the lasting knowledge acquired in college. You should, of course, be happy and proud to know that you too may soon have a college degree,

---

TABLE 10–1.   Selected Items Robert Benchley Recalled from His Years in College

---

Things I Learned—Freshman Year

1. Charlemagne either died or was born or did something with the Holy Roman Empire in 800.
2. By placing a paper bag inside another paper bag you can carry home a milkshake in it.
3. There is a double *l* in the middle of "parallel."
4. French nouns ending in "aison" are feminine.
5. Almost everything you need to know about a subject is in the encyclopedia.
6. A tasty sandwich can be made by spreading peanut butter on raisin bread.
7. The chances are against filling an inside straight.
8. There is a law in economics called *The Law of Diminishing Returns*, which means after a certain margin is reached returns begin to diminish. This may not be correctly stated, but there *is* a law by that name.

Sophomore Year

1. A good imitation of measles rash can be effected by stabbing the forearm with a stiff whiskbroom.
2. Queen Elizabeth was not above suspicion.
3. You can sleep undetected in a lecture course by resting the head on the hand as if shading the eyes.
4. The ancient Phoenicians were really Jews, and got as far north as England where they operated tin mines.
5. You can get dressed much quicker in the morning if the night before when you are going to bed you take off your trousers and underdrawers at once, leaving the latter inside the former.

Junior Year

1. Emerson left his pastorate because he had some argument about communion.
2. Pushing your arms back as far as they will go fifty times each day increases your chest measurement.
3. Marcus Aurelius had a son who turned out to be a bad boy.
4. Eight hours of sleep are not necessary.
5. Heraclitus believed fire was the basis of all life.
6. The chances are you will never fill an inside straight.

Senior Year

1. There is as yet no law determining what constitutes trespass in an airplane.
2. Six hours of sleep are not necessary.
3. Bicarbonate of soda taken before retiring makes you feel better the next day.
4. May is the shortest month of the year.

---

a certificate that proclaims your knowledge of certain basic facts such as these.

Is this all Benchley really remembers from his college days? If you made a list from your days in the eighth grade, it would probably be similarly brief. This leads to an interesting question: How can we study memories that cannot be recalled? If a person cannot recall an experience, can we assume that the memory trace representing that experience has vanished?

Ebbinghaus's Contribution—When Memory Was Young

The experimental investigation of human memory was begun by a German psychologist, Hermann Ebbinghaus (figure 10–1). Ebbinghaus was a true scientific pioneer. He believed, unlike his famous contemporary, Wilhelm Wundt (see appendix A), that experimental psychology could be developed to study the higher mental processes and not just the organs of sense. His main achievement was demonstrating how empirical research could be done to answer interesting questions about the topic of memory. This research was published in 1885 in a remarkable book, *Memory: A Contribution to Experimental Psychology*. One of the first questions Ebbinghaus faced was the one we have just been considering: how to measure memory. Ebbinghaus served as the only subject in all his experiments; the materials he invented to be memorized are called *nonsense syllables*. He used meaningless syllables that contained a vowel sandwiched between two consonants (therefore called *CVC* syllables), such as *ZOK*, *VAP*, and so on. By using these syllables, he hoped to minimize the influence of linguistic associations that would have been present had he used words, sentences, or (as he sometimes did) passages of poetry as materials to be remembered. (Later research has shown that "nonsense" syllables is a misnomer, because a few items he used were words. Also, in learning even nonsense words, people imbue them with meaning.)

Ebbinghaus selected these syllables at random from a master set of 2,300 and placed them into lists that varied in length. If the list contained, say, thirty nonsense syllables, Ebbinghaus would read the syllables out loud to himself at a uniform rate. Immediately afterward, he would cover up the list and then try to repeat it back to himself or write it down. Obviously, on the first trial this feat was impossible, but he could measure the number of syllables

FIGURE 10–1.

Hermann Ebbinghaus began the experimental study of verbal learning and memory (the Bettmann Archive).

he was able to recall correctly. Then he would read the list aloud a second time, attempt recall, and so on. One measure that Ebbinghaus used of the difficulty of recalling a list is the number of such study/test trials (or the amount of time) needed for one perfect recitation of the list. This is called a *trials to criterion* measure of memory; it was widely used in memory research for years, though it is rare now.

Suppose Ebbinghaus wanted to test his memory for a list a month after learning it. He might, as an initial cue, provide himself with the first nonsense syllable in the list. But suppose this did not help him recall the list and that, try as he might, he could recall nothing further. Would this mean that the series he had memorized a month earlier had left no lasting impression? How could we ever know? Ebbinghaus invented an ingenious method of answering this question. In measuring memory for a series of nonsense syllables, Ebbinghaus attempted to *relearn* the series, just as he had learned it in the first place, by repeatedly reading it aloud and then attempting to recite it or write it. Once again, he could measure the number of trials (or amount of time) necessary to learn the list. The memory for the list at the time of relearning could be measured by the *savings* in terms of the smaller number of trials or less time needed to relearn the list; this measure of memory would be obtainable even when a person could remember nothing of the material (when nothing could be recalled before relearning). Ebbinghaus found that even when he could recall none of the nonsense syllables in a list, he often still exhibited a considerable savings in the number of trials or amount of time it took him to relearn the list, indicating that memory for the list could exist without active recall.

One of Ebbinghaus's best-known findings is presented in figure 10–2. The graph shows the relation between the amount of savings and the time since original learning, or how forgetting is related to time. As you can see, Ebbinghaus found that forgetting is rapid soon after learning, but then slows. The *savings method* is still used today to ask important questions about memory (e.g., MacLeod, 1988).

Even though Robert Benchley may have exhibited poor recall for information he learned in college, if he had been required to retake his courses, he probably would, like Ebbinghaus, have exhibited considerable savings. (He tells us that these courses included such gems as Early Renaissance Etchers, the Social Life of Minor Sixteenth-Century Poets, and the History of Lace Making.) Perhaps you may recall little of your geometry course in high school (or chapter 2 of this book, for that matter), but presumably you would find the course much easier were you to take it again.

You may wonder whether Ebbinghaus's findings are representative of human memory in general, since he studied only one subject (himself), repeatedly, a method that is rarely acceptable in modern research. However, his findings have been replicated many times with larger groups of subjects and are still considered

FIGURE 10–2.

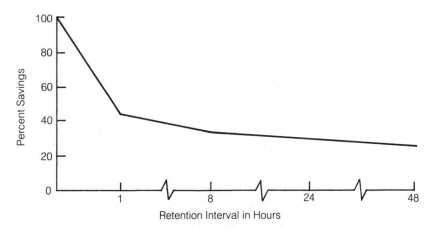

The forgetting curve. Ebbinghaus measured the savings in relearning a list of nonsense syllables after various periods of time had elapsed since original learning. Notice that forgetting is rapid at first and then levels off.

valid today. (The importance of "replicability," or repeatability of experimental results, is discussed in chapter 11.)

Ebbinghaus's work in memory was truly original. But besides his seminal memory research, his other achievements include an interesting discussion of the problem of experimenter bias, production of one of psychology's earliest mathematical models, one of the earliest examples of explicit hypothesis testing, and an advanced (for the time) discussion of statistical problems in research. He also wrote an interesting psychology text and designed an early intelligence test.

Varieties of Memory

The term *memory* is quite broad and covers many different kinds of skills and abilities. All have in common the properties that something is learned, retained over time, and then used in some particular situation, but beyond that types of memory may differ considerably. You have doubtless had the experience of looking up a telephone number, repeating it correctly to yourself, and then utterly forgetting it by the time you walked across the room to the telephone. This spectacularly fast forgetting seems quite different from the slower forgetting studied by Ebbinghaus (see figure 10–1). Remembering information such as a telephone number over a brief interval reflects *short-term memory*, and some psychologists believe that it has different properties from *long-term memory* (the kind Ebbinghaus studied) and should properly be considered a distinct memory system or store. One way of defining short-term memory is the recovery of information shortly after it has been perceived, before it has even left conscious awareness (James, 1890). Long-term memory, then, refers to retrieval of memories that have disappeared from consciousness after their initial perception.

This general definition of long-term memory today seems too broad to most psychologists, who make further distinctions among types of memory. These will be discussed more fully later in the chapter when we illustrate how memory is studied in different ways. One basic distinction that guides much research today is between explicit memory and implicit memory (Graf and Schacter, 1985; Schacter, 1987). *Explicit memory* (sometimes called *episodic memory*) refers to the conscious recollection of events (or episodes) in one's life. People may be asked to recall what they learned in a particular time or place, or to recognize things that happened to them from plausible distractors. Examples of explicit remembering would be in answering the question of what you did last Saturday night, what you learned in your introductory psychology course, or what you have done thus far today. Tasks typically used to measure both short-term and long-term memory would be classified as explicit memory tests, because people are explicitly told to retrieve information from their past.

Implicit memory, on the other hand, refers to the expression of past learning in which a person need not make any conscious effort to retrieve information from the past (Schacter, 1990). It just happens, more or less automatically. For example, when you bend over to tie your shoelaces, you need not say to yourself 'How do I do this?'' When did I learn to do this? Can I remember how?'' Instead, the behavior runs off relatively effortlessly, and if you stop to reflect on exactly how you are doing it, you may actually do worse. Of course, information expressed implicitly was learned, but the crux of the distinction is that, unlike explicit remembering, implicit expressions of memory do not require people consciously to retrieve information from their past. In fact, as we shall see later in the chapter, patterns of performance on explicit and implicit tests of memory are often quite different (Roediger, 1990).

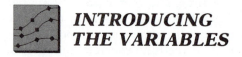

INTRODUCING THE VARIABLES

Dependent Variables

Remembering may be measured in numerous ways; these often involve either *recall* or *recognition*. In recall tests, reproduction of material is required, whereas in recognition tests, material is presented to people and they are required to judge whether or not they have seen it previously. Three popular recall tests are *serial recall, free recall,* and *paired-associate recall*. In serial recall, people are required to recall information in the serial order it was presented, whereas in free recall, the order of recall is irrelevant. In paired-associate recall, people are presented with pairs of items, such as *igloo-saloon;* at recall, they are given one member of the pair (igloo, referred to as the stimulus) and are asked to produce the other member (saloon, the response).

Recognition tests are generally of two types. In *yes/no recognition tests*, people are given the original material they studied, such as words, mixed in with a number of new but generally similar items (words). Subjects respond yes or no to each word, depending on whether they believe it was in the original list. *Forced-choice recognition tests* are multiple-choice tests. Several alternatives are presented, only one of which is correct, and the subject in the experiment is forced to choose the correct alternative. Forced-choice tests are preferred to yes/no tests because correcting for guessing is less of a problem.

Recall and recognition tests are not dichotomous; rather, they may be viewed as lying on a continuum, with the dimension being the amount of information given about the material, or the power of the retrieval cues presented. If *GRA* is presented as a cue for the word *GRAPH*, which appeared in the list, is this a test of recall or recognition?

In each case, the dependent measure in tests of recall and recognition is the number or proportion of items correctly recalled or recognized in different conditions, or the number of errors, which amounts to the same thing. Sometimes a derivative measure is used, such as d' from the theory of signal detection (see chapter 7). Recently, investigators concerned with recognition have used reaction time as a dependent measure, as discussed in chapter 8.

Recently, the study of implicit memory tests has intrigued cognitive psychologists (Schacter, 1987). Although these tests do not require people to consciously remember the material they have studied, performance on these tasks is influenced or "primed" by previous exposure to the material. That is, implicit memory tests are tasks that can be performed without specific reference to the previous experiences in the laboratory, such as filling in a fragmented word such as "s_r_w_e_r_." On these types of tasks, "memory" is reflected by the fact that performance on the test is primed or

biased by the previous study episode. For example, your ability to complete the above word fragment as "strawberry" would be greatly enhanced if you had read the word "strawberry" earlier, even though you were not explicitly asked to remember having done so. These tests are especially interesting because they behave very differently from traditional explicit memory tests such as recall and recognition. In some sense, the "laws of memory" are different when examined with these implicit tests rather than standard explicit memory tests. Later in the chapter, we will examine these implicit tests more closely.

Independent Variables

Many types of variables are manipulated in experiments on human memory. One of the most popular variables historically has been the nature of the material presented for memory. It can be letters, digits, nonsense syllables, words, phrases, sentences, paragraphs, or long passages of prose text; the characteristics of each of these types of material can also be varied. For example, words that refer to concrete objects (cigar, rhinoceros) are better recalled than abstract words (beauty, dread), when other relevant factors such as word length are held constant (Paivio, 1969). Several other important independent variables will be considered in the experiments discussed in this chapter. One is quite obvious: the retention interval between presentation of material and test. How fast does forgetting occur? What are its mechanisms? Another variable attracting much attention is modality of presentation. Is information better remembered if it comes in through the ears or the eyes, or is there no difference? Study strategy is also important, such as how a person tries to learn (or encode) the material. A final variable under consideration is the nature of the memory test given to people. For example, do recall tests show results different from recognition tests? How are implicit memory tests different from explicit tests? This is just a sample of the variables that are investigated in memory studies.

Control Variables

Memory experiments are typically quite well controlled. Important variables that are usually held constant across conditions are the amount of material presented and the rate of presentation, though of course these can be interesting variables in their own right. The modality of presentation is another factor that must not vary, unless it is a variable of major interest. If some characteristic of the material is being varied, then it is necessary to hold constant other factors. If a researcher is interested in varying the concreteness or abstractness of words, then other characteristics, such as word length and frequency of occurrence, must be held constant across the different conditions.

10.1 Experimental Topics and Research Illustrations

Topic: Scale Attenuation
Illustration: Modality Differences

The first topic we are considering here is important, but is often overlooked in psychological research. The general problem is how to interpret performance on some dependent variable in an experiment when performance is either very nearly perfect (near the "ceiling" of the scale) or very nearly lacking altogether (near the "floor"). These effects are called *scale-attenuation effects* (or, more commonly, *ceiling* and *floor effects*). As usual, we shall embed our discussion in the context of an actual research problem.

One subject in memory research that has attracted a great deal of attention is that of modality differences. Do we remember information better if it comes through our eyes or through our ears? Or is there no difference? Is information better remembered if it is presented to both the ears and the eyes simultaneously than if it is presented to only one or the other? These questions are not only of theoretical importance, but also of practical import. When you look up a phone number and need to remember it while you cross the room to the telephone, is it sufficient to simply read the number silently to yourself as you usually do, or would you be better off to also read the number aloud so that information entered both your ears and your eyes?

The eyes have it: Scarborough's experiment. One attempt to answer these questions was reported by Scarborough (1972). He used a short-term memory task called the *Brown-Peterson technique* after its inventors (Brown, 1958; Peterson and Peterson, 1959). Here, people are presented with information to remember for a short period of time and then are distracted from rehearsing (repeating it to themselves) by being required to perform some other task until they are later asked to recall the information. Typically, subjects are given a single *CCC* trigram (three consonants, for example, *NRF*). They are then required to count backward by threes from a three-digit number (464, 461, 458, etc.) for varying periods of time (the retention interval) up to about thirty seconds before attempting recall. Try it yourself. Three letters and a three-digit number will appear after the next sentence. Read the letters and the number out loud, look away and then count backward by threes from the number for about thirty seconds before you try to recall the letters.

XGR 679

How did you do? Chances are you recalled the trigram perfectly. People almost always do on the first trial in experiments using this task. However, recall drops off when multiple trials are used with a different trigram on each trial, so that after four or five trials, subjects are typically recalling trigrams correctly only 50 percent of the time, with an eighteen-second retention interval (see figure 10–3). This phenomenon is named *proactive interference*, since the early trials in this task interfere with recall on later trials.

In Scarborough's (1972) experiment, all subjects received thirty-six consonant trigrams presented for .7 second in the Brown-Peterson technique. There were three groups of six subjects; the method in

FIGURE 10–3.

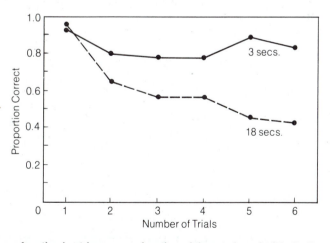

Retention of a stimulus trigram as a function of the number of trials (1–6) and the retention interval on each trial (3 or 18 seconds). On the first trial, there is very little forgetting of the trigram, even with an 18-second retention interval. However, after a number of trials, recall becomes poorer due to the prior tests, especially with the 18-second retention interval (Keppel & Underwood, 1962). This phenomenon is known as proactive interference.

which the trigrams were presented differed for each group. One group of subjects *saw* the trigrams (Visual Only condition), one group *heard* the trigrams (Auditory Only), and a third group both saw and heard the trigrams (Visual + Auditory). Presentation time was carefully controlled by having the trigrams presented over a tape recorder or a tachistoscope, a device for quickly exposing and removing visual information. One second after presentation of the trigram, subjects heard a three-digit number, except in one condition where subjects were requested to recall the trigram immediately (the zero-second retention-interval condition). Subjects in each condition were required to retain the letters during retention intervals of 0, 3, 6, 9, 12, or 18 seconds. Once the three-digit number was presented, subjects were required to count backward by threes aloud at the rate of one count per second (in time with a metronome). At the end of the retention interval, the metronome stopped and two green lights came on, signaling the ten-second recall period. So each trial consisted of a warning signal (two yellow lights and a tone) indicating that the trigram was about to be displayed; presentation of the trigram; presentation of the three-digit number (with the one exception just noted); the retention interval during which the subjects counted backward by threes; and finally the recall period. A typical trial is exemplified in figure 10−4. This procedure was repeated thirty-six times (six trials at each of the six retention intervals, in a counterbalanced order), with different trigrams. In summary, three between-subjects conditions (Visual Only, Auditory Only, Visual + Auditory) were combined with six within-subjects conditions (retention intervals of 0, 3, 6, 9, 12, or 18 seconds) in the experiment.

The results of Scarborough's experiment are reproduced in figure 10−5, where the percentage of times a trigram was correctly

FIGURE 10−4.

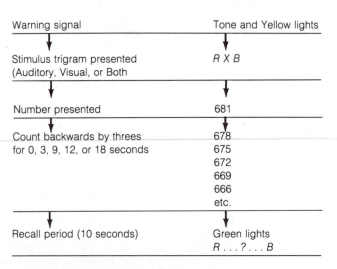

Schematic overview of a typical trial in the Brown-Peterson short-term memory procedure, as used in Scarborough's experiment.

FIGURE 10–5.

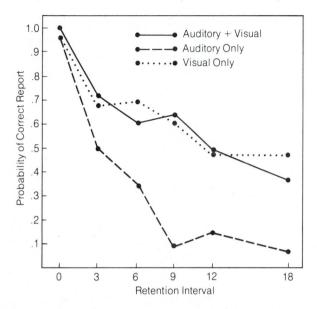

The probability of correctly recalling a stimulus trigram as a function of the three presentation conditions and the duration of the counting task. Notice that (a) visual presentation is generally superior to auditory presentation, and (b) simultaneous auditory and visual presentation is no better than only visual presentation. (Scarborough, 1972)

reported is plotted as a function of retention interval. This figure (and the statistics that Scarborough reports back this up) shows that subjects who received only visual presentation of the trigrams generally recalled them a greater percentage of the time than did subjects who received only auditory presentation. Furthermore, receiving information in both modalities simultaneously did not produce any better recall than presenting the information only visually; the percentage correct at each retention interval is roughly the same for Visual Only and Visual + Auditory subjects. So far so good. But what else can we conclude from figure 10–5? In particular, can we conclude anything about the rates of forgetting for information that is presented auditorily and visually? Is the rate of forgetting the same or different in the two cases?

Scarborough (1972) was quite careful on this score. Although the Auditory Only and Visual Only functions appear to diverge increasingly as the retention interval becomes longer, he did not draw the conclusion that the rate of forgetting is greater for information presented through the ears than through the eyes. However, consider what Massaro (1975) said about this experiment in his textbook:

> The figure shows that the curves intercept the Y ordinate at roughly the same point and diverge significantly. The intercept value at zero sec. provides a measure of the original perception and storage of the stimuli, since it measures how much infor-

mation the subject has immediately after the presentation of the stimuli, when no forgetting has taken place. The rate of forgetting can be determined from the slopes of the forgetting functions. According to this analysis, Figure [10–5] shows that the items presented auditorily are forgotten much faster than the items presented visually. (pp. 530–531).

Unfortunately, although it seems reasonable, this conclusion must be called into question. The reason is that performance at the zero-second retention interval is very nearly perfect in all conditions. When performance is perfect, it is impossible to tell whether there are any "real" differences among conditions because of scale attenuation—in this case, a ceiling effect. If the scale of the dependent measure were really "long" enough, it might show differences between auditory and visual presentation even at the zero-second retention interval. So Massaro's conclusion that the rate of forgetting is greater for auditory than for visual presentation cannot be accepted on the basis of the argument we just quoted, because the assumption of equivalent performance at the zero-second retention interval may not be correct.

All this may be a bit confusing at first, so let us take a clearer case and demonstrate the same thing. Suppose two obese men decided to make a bet as to who could lose the greatest amount of weight in a certain amount of time. One man looked much heavier than the other, but neither was sure what he actually weighed, since they both made a point of avoiding scales. The scale they decided to use for the bet was a common bathroom scale which runs from 0 to 300 pounds. On the day they were to begin their weight-loss programs, each man weighed himself while the other watched. To their great surprise, both men weighed in at exactly the same value, 300 pounds. So despite their different sizes, the two men decided that they were beginning their bet at equal weights.

The problem again is one of ceiling effects in the scale of measurement. The weight range of the bathroom scale simply did not go high enough to record the actual weight of these men. Let us imagine that one would be found to actually weigh 300 and the other 350, if their weights had been taken by a scale with a greater range. After six months of their weight-loss program, let us further suppose, both men had actually lost 100 pounds. They would both reweigh themselves at this point and discover that one now weighed 200 pounds, and the other 250. Since they believed that they both had started from the same weight (300), they would reach the erroneous conclusion that the person who presently weighed 200 had won the bet (see figure 10–6).

The problem here is really the same as that in interpreting the results of Scarborough's experiment as evidence that information presented auditorily is forgotten at a greater rate than information presented visually. There is no better way for us to know the rate of forgetting in the two conditions of interest in that experiment than there is for the two men to know the rate of weight loss in

FIGURE 10–6.

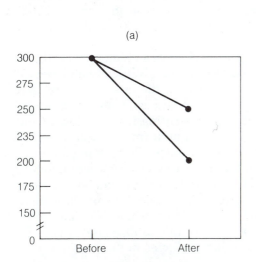

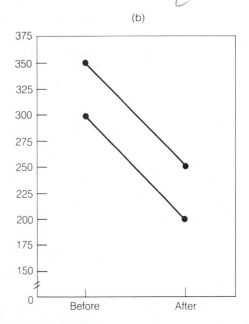

Panel (a) illustrates the situation as the fat men believed it to be: they started at the same weight, and one lost twice as much as the other. Panel (b) reveals the actual case, with the ceiling effect in the scale of measurement removed. In fact, both men lost 100 pounds. Scale attentuation (ceiling and floor effects) can hide actual differences that may exist between conditions in an experiment.

judging who won their bet. In neither case can we assume equivalent initial scores before the measurement of loss begins.

One way to avoid this problem in Scarborough's experiment would be to ignore the data points at the zero-second retention interval and ask whether the rate of forgetting is greater between 3 and 18 seconds for auditory than for visual presentation. This could be done by computing an interaction between presentation and retention interval over the range of 3 to 18 seconds; but by simply inspecting figure 10–5, you can get some idea as to whether the Auditory Only and Visual Only points are diverging increasingly. They are between 3 and 9 seconds, but after that the difference between them remains constant. However, this lack of an increasingly larger difference over the last three points may be caused by a floor effect in the Auditory Only condition, since performance is so poor, especially on the last point (only 7 or 8 percent correct). One must be very careful in interpreting data when there are ceiling or floor effects present. A prudent investigator would hesitate to draw any conclusion from the data in figure 10–5 about rates of forgetting: Scarborough's approach exactly. But we should also note that over the retention intervals where there are neither ceiling nor floor effects (3, 6, and 9 seconds), there seems to be greater forgetting with auditory than with visual presentation, in agreement with Massaro's conclusion quoted earlier.

How can problems of ceiling and floor effects be avoided in psychological research? Unfortunately, no hard-and-fast rule can be given. Researchers usually try to design their experiments such that they avoid extremes in performance; then, they often test their intuitions about performance on the task by testing small groups of pilot subjects. If these subjects perform near the ceiling or floor of the scale, then it will often be necessary to revise the experimental task. For example, if performance in a memory experiment is too good, the amount of material being given can be increased so as to lower performance. Similarly, if the task is so hard that people hardly remember anything, the task can be made easier by reducing the amount of material, presenting it more slowly, and so on. The idea is to design tasks and performance scales so that people typically score in the middle ranges. Then, as the independent variables are manipulated, improvements or decrements in people's performance can be observed. The prudent investigator will usually make the effort to test pilot subjects before launching into an experiment that may turn out later to have been flawed by ceiling or floor effects. The testing of pilot subjects also permits the researcher to learn about other problems in the design or procedure of the experiment.

10.2 Experimental Topics and Research Illustrations

Topic: Generality of Results
Illustration: Levels of Processing

We mentioned in chapter 3 that there are many ways to test a hypothesis and that single experiments which test a hypothesis, although informative to a certain extent, need to be viewed against a background of other experiments designed to test the same hypothesis in other ways. Ideally, researchers would like experiments that test a particular hypothesis in a variety of situations to converge on one conclusion, but in reality this is often not the case. The issue is one of *generality of results:* often the conclusion drawn from one experimental situation does not generalize to other situations. This is frustrating, but inevitable. It is also important. We should always ask these questions after some experiment has shown an effect of some independent variable on some dependent variable: To what subject populations does this effect generalize? (Just because an effect holds for rats does not necessarily mean that it will hold for people; see chapter 15.) Under what settings, either experimental or extraexperimental, does this conclusion hold? Will the conclusion hold when the independent and dependent variables are operationalized or defined in a slightly different way than they are in the original experiment? The question of generality crops up, of course, in all types of research. If huge doses of some drug produce cancer in laboratory mice, should this drug be banned from human consumption, even when the dosage level is much smaller and the organism entirely different?

To illustrate the issues surrounding the problem of generality of results, we consider experiments bearing on the *levels of processing approach* to memory. Craik and Lockhart (1972) proposed that memory could be viewed as a by-product of perception and, further, that perception could be conceived as progressing through various stages or levels. For example, consider your perception and comprehension of the word *YACHT*. Craik and Lockhart (1972) noted that a person pays attention to features at different cognitive "levels" when reading such a word. A first level is that of surface features of appearances: the word has five letters, includes one vowel, is in uppercase type, and so on. Perception of the word's letters is a first step in reading it; a *graphemic* (letter) level of analysis is required. Second, the reading of many words is accompanied by translating the written form into some common (phonemic) code that is shared with words that are heard. The code is called *phonemic* (or *phonological*) because it is assumed to be based on phonemes, the basic sound patterns of a language. We would rely on a phonemic code when we decide that *yacht* rhymes with *hot*, even though the words do not look alike. A third stage, or level, of processing is the determination of a word's meaning. The purpose of reading is to derive the meaning of the words, to know what a yacht is. This is referred to as a *semantic* level of analysis.

Craik and Lockhart (1972) proposed that perceiving words (or anything else) involved progress through the stages from appearance (shallow levels in the cognitive system) to meaning (deep levels in the cognitive system). Further, they argued that later memory for experiences was directly tied to their depth of processing during initial perception: The deeper the level of processing during initial perception, the better should be memory for the experience.

An experiment reported by Craik and Tulving (1975) illustrates the type of evidence supporting the levels of processing approach to memory. They presented undergraduate subjects with 60 words and had them answer questions about each word. The questions were designed to control the level of processing of the words. For example, the subjects might see the word *BEAR* on a screen and be asked one of the following three questions: Is it in uppercase letters? Does it rhyme with *chair*? Is it an animal? In each case the subject should answer *yes*, but in doing so should process the word to different levels. In the first case, only superficial (graphemic) characteristics of the word must be checked to answer the question about typeface. In the second case the sound of the word (or its phonemic code) must be consulted. Finally, in the third case the subject must access the word's meaning, or process it semantically. The researchers predicted, in line with the levels of processing theory, that words processed to deeper levels should be better remembered than those processed to shallower levels (semantic > phonemic > graphemic).

Craik and Tulving's (1975) results confirmed those predictions impressively. They tested memory by a recognition test on which their subjects were given the 60 old words (those about which they had answered questions) along with 120 new words. The subjects were told to try to pick out and circle exactly 60 words that they had seen in the earlier phase of the experiment. Because subjects had to pick out 60 words, chance performance (that is, the level expected for people who had never seen the words) would have been 33 percent (60 of 180). The results are shown in figure 10–7 for those words receiving a *yes* response during the study phase. Recognition increased from just above chance with superficial, graphemic processing of the word's appearance to nearly perfect with a deep, semantic level of processing. The only difference among the three conditions during the study phase was the very brief mental process that occurred when the person answered the question, so this experiment shows the power of even very rapid encoding processes on memory. The results conformed nicely to the predictions from levels of processing theory.

The levels of processing approach and the experiments designed to test it have greatly excited experimental psychologists and have produced a large amount of research (see Lockhart and Craik, 1990; Cermak and Craik, 1979). Our concern here is with the generality of the basic experimental results as seen in figure 10–7, rather than with the theory itself. The theory has been criticized as being circular and untestable, because there is no inde-

FIGURE 10–7.

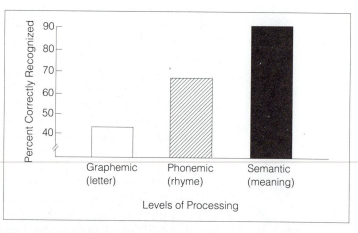

Results of Craik and Tulving (1975). Subjects answered questions about words that were designed to effect different levels of processing: graphemic (Is it in uppercase letters?), phonemic (Does it rhyme with _____?), and semantic (Is it in the _____ category?). In line with the levels of processing approach, the deeper the level of original processing, the more accurate was recognition on the later test. (After Craik and Tulving, 1975)

pendent way of assessing depth or level of processing except for performance on a memory test (Nelson, 1977). Without converging operations (see chapters 7 and 14) on the construct of levels of processing, the theory does run the risk of being circular: processing that produces good retention is deep processing, and vice versa. Despite this difficulty, the levels of processing framework has generated a massive amount of research, in part because the basic experimental effects are so strong. Few variables in the study of memory take performance from almost chance levels to almost perfect, with all other variables held constant.

The Craik and Tulving (1975) results are powerful, but how general are they? The subjects in the experiment were highly selected college students; the materials were single words about which questions were asked; the test was recognition, with subjects forced to respond with a fixed number of words (so they had to guess); and levels of processing was operationalized (manipulated) in a particular way. Were any or all of these features critical in producing Craik and Tulving's (1975) results? As we discussed in chapter 3, every experiment involves many choices in deciding how a particular theory or hypothesis is tested. Further research is necessary to determine the generality of the findings.

Jenkins (1979) has proposed an interesting way to think about the issue of generalizability of results, as represented in his *tetrahedral model of memory experiments* shown in figure 10–8. (A tetrahedron has four faces, hence the name.) Jenkins (1979) noted that any researcher exploring memory must make choices along four dimensions, whether or not that particular dimension is of interest in the experiment (i.e., even if it is a control variable). These are (1) the subjects being tested, (2) the material used for learning and testing, (3) the orienting tasks (or the features of the setting in which subjects are tested), and (4) the type of test used. In the Craik and Tulving (1975) experiment, the researchers were interested in how the orienting task (the questions orienting the subjects to process the words in particular ways) affected retention. The other three were not of interest and so these potential variables were controlled: all subjects were college students; the memory test was recognition, and the materials used were words. Jenkins' (1979) framework points out that any experimental result should be viewed in the context of other potential variables that could have been manipulated. The issue of generality of results can then be framed as follows: if the other control variables were manipulated, would the same results hold? If the independent variable was operationally defined in a different way, would the result replicate? We turn now to research that helps answer this question about the levels of processing effect. (The coverage below is not complete, but illustrates the points by selective use of examples.)

Subjects. Do people other than college students show the levels of processing effect (better memory for material processed meaningfully)? In general, the answer here to date is *yes*. For example,

FIGURE 10–8.

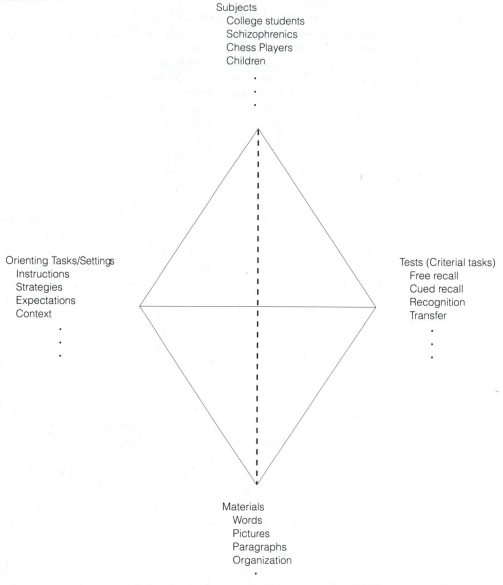

Jenkins' (1979) tetrahedral model of memory experiments. Each corner represents a cluster of factors in which memory researchers may be interested. Even if only one factor (say, type of material) is of interest in an experiment, the outcome of the experiment may still be influenced by the values selected on the other dimensions as control variables.

Cermak and Reale (1978) tested patients with Korsakoff's syndrome, a brain disorder suffered by some chronic alcoholics due to a vitamin deficiency. One hallmark of Korsakoff's syndrome is a severe memory deficit on explicit memory tests such as recall or recognition. Nonetheless, Cermak and Reale (1978) discovered that

Korsakoff patients did show a level of processing effect when tested in a manner similar to Craik and Tulving's (1975). Although performance was much lower overall for Korsakoff patients than for normal control subjects, the patients still showed somewhat better retention following meaningful encoding than following shallow encoding.

Other experiments have been directed at the variable of age. Murphy and Brown (1975) tested preschool children (under 5) by giving them sixteen pictures and having different groups judge them on three different dimensions. One group was asked if the pictures belonged to a particular category. A second group was asked if the pictures represented something nasty or nice. The children in a third group were asked to name the dominant color in the pictures. This last task was judged to involve shallow encoding, whereas the first two were thought to be deep. The results came out just this way: Children who had named pictures' colors during the study phase recalled 18 percent of the pictures later, but those who had performed the more meaningful encoding tasks recalled about 40 percent. At the other end of the lifespan, elderly subjects also show strong levels of processing effects (Craik, 1977). In short, the levels of processing effect is relatively robust across those subject variables studied thus far.

Materials.   Can levels of processing effects be found with materials other than lists of words? Obviously, the effect would be of little interest if it does not generalize beyond this restriction. Smith and Winograd (1978) showed people faces at the rate of one every eight seconds. One group was told to decide whether or not each person had a big nose (a superficial judgment). Another group was told to judge whether each person was friendly (a deep judgment). On a later recognition test, subjects who judged the faces on friendliness recognized them better than those who judged them on nose size, confirming the basic levels of processing effect with faces.

As mentioned in the preceding section, Murphy and Brown (1975) tested preschool children with pictures in a levels of processing paradigm and replicated the basic effect, too. Lane and Robertson (1979) also found a levels of processing effect in chess players' memory for positions on chess boards.

In general, evidence exists that the levels of processing ideas can be extended to nonverbal material, although it is certainly true that the great bulk of levels of processing research has used verbal material. However, Intraub and Nicklos (1985) have reported an exception to this pattern. They had people look at pictures and answer either physical questions (Is this horizontal or vertical?) or questions requiring access to meaning (Is this edible or inedible?). Later they asked subjects to recall the pictures by writing a one- or two-sentence descriptive phrase. Surprisingly, they found that physical questions led to better retention than did meaningful questions, a reverse of the usual pattern. The outcome cannot be dismissed as a fluke, because they replicated the finding in six experiments under various conditions. The unusual finding by Intraub and Nicklos (1985) represents something of a mystery; as yet no one has satisfactorily explained why they found a reverse levels of processing effect (physical judgments superior to meaningful judgments) in retention of pictures. But exceptions to a general pattern can lead to opportunities for theoretical advancement, as we shall see below.

Orienting tasks and settings. This category of variables refers to the many aspects of the particular experimental context, including the instructions subject are given, the particular version of the experimental task, the strategies subjects use, whether the independent variable is manipulated within subjects (so each subject receives each condition) or between subjects (so each subject receives only one condition), and so on.

The basic levels of processing effect (deep encoding producing greater retention than shallow encoding) has been shown to hold over a wide variety of changes in experimental setting. For example, one dimension often considered in memory experiments is whether subjects know their memories are to be tested when they are exposed to material. When subjects are told that their memories will be tested, it is referred to as intentional learning; when they are given material with no such warning (but think they are performing some other task), it is called incidental learning (because learning the material is perceived, by the subject, to be incidental to the purpose of the experiment). Craik and Tulving (1975) tested subjects under both incidental and intentional learning conditions and showed that the levels of processing effect occurred in both cases.

Another dimension of interest in the levels of processing experiment is the particular questions (or the orienting tasks) used to induce shallow and deep processing. Craik and Tulving (1975) had subjects judge the typeface of words (upper or lower case) for the shallow, physical dimension and judge whether or not the word belonged to a particular category (animal?) for the deep level. But many other types of questions could be used to direct subjects' attention to superficial or meaningful aspects of the words. For example, Hyde and Jenkins (1969) asked subjects whether words contained particular letters (an e?) as the shallow task and to rate the words' pleasantness as the deep task. This manipulation also produced a robust levels of processing effect. In general, numerous manipulations with verbal materials converge on the same conclusion: retention is poorer after physical (shallow) orienting tasks than after meaningful (deep) orienting tasks. Thus the levels of processing effect is generally robust over many variations on the basic experimental paradigm with verbal materials and with recall or recognition as the memory tests.

Type of test. The fourth dimension in Jenkin's (1979) model of memory experiments is the type of test used to assess memory.

The standard measures of memory have been variations on recall and recognition tests. Levels of processing effects have been found repeatedly with both types of test. However, researchers have found other kinds of tests on which levels of processing has no effect (Fisher and Craik, 1977; Jacoby and Dallas, 1981; McDaniel, Friedman, and Bourne, 1978) or even a reverse effect (Morris, Bransford, and Franks, 1977). This discovery has helped refine ideas about levels of processing and led to a new approach, *transfer appropriate processing*. The basic idea guiding this research is that the form of a test—what kind of knowledge it taps—may determine what encoding activities are useful for the test.

Morris et al. (1977) conducted an experiment similar in many ways to the original Craik and Tulving (1975) experiment. They used college students as subjects and asked them to make judgments about words. The questions about the words (e.g., EAGLE) were designed to induce a phonemic level of processing ("_____ rhymes with legal?") or a semantic level ("_____ is a large bird?"). Subjects answered phonemic questions for half the words and semantic questions for the other half, with the correct answer *yes* half the time and *no* half the time. According to the levels of processing view, the meaningful questions should produce deeper encoding and better retention. This prediction was upheld in a standard recognition test (such as that used by Craik and Tulving) in which studied words were mixed with nonstudied words and the subjects' task was to pick out the studied words. As shown in the left panel of figure 10–9, subjects recognized words 84 percent of the time following semantic encoding, but only 63 percent of the time following phonemic encoding.

But Morris et al. (1977) gave a second group of subjects a different test, called a rhyme recognition test. The subjects' job in this test was to examine a list of words and to pick out words that rhymed with words they had studied earlier. So if *beagle* were on the test list, they should pick it because it rhymes with the studied word *eagle*. (None of the words on the test list had appeared on the study list, just words that rhymed with them.) Subjects performed better on the rhyme recognition test if they had studied words in the phonemic condition (49 percent correct) than in the semantic condition (33 percent correct), a reversal of the usual finding. Thus Morris et al. (1977) argued that one type of processing is not inherently superior or inferior to another type, but that effects of encoding manipulations depend on how the information will be used or tested. Instead of a fixed levels of processing, they argued for *transfer appropriate processing:* performance on a test will benefit to the extent that the knowledge acquired (or the operations performed) during study match the knowledge or operations required by the test. On a recognition test that required use of phonemic (rhyme) knowledge, prior phonemic encoding led to superior performance than did semantic encoding.

Although levels of processing effects are robust across many variables, they do not generalize to all types of tests. For tests that

FIGURE 10–9.

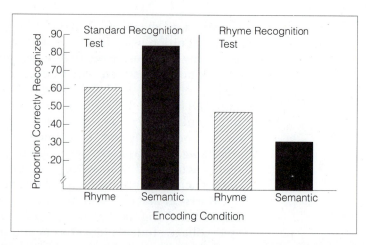

Results of Morris, Bransford, and Franks (1977). After answering questions about words designed to make them think about the word's sound (phonemic coding) or meaning (semantic coding), subjects took either a standard recognition test (left panel) or a rhyme recognition test in which they had to select words that rhymed with the original studied words (right panel). The usual levels of processing effect was found with the standard recogniton test, but phonemic coding produced better performance than semantic coding on the rhyme recognition test. Thus types of processing are not inherently shallow or deep, but depend on the way the information must be used. Poor processing for one type of test may be good processing for another test.

require access of meaningful information, standard levels of processing effects are found. However, this is not so for other types of tests (see Jacoby and Dallas, 1981; Graf, Mandler, and Haden, 1982).

This section has been oriented around Jenkins' (1979) model of memory experiments shown in figure 10–8, but his model also can be broadened to apply to all psychology experiments. That is, in any line of inquiry one should ask if the results will generalize across types of subjects, across research settings, across different dependent measures, and across different ways of manipulating the independent variables.

Whenever an experimental result does not generalize across some variable, noting this fact is only the first step. The real problem is to find out why. Scientists often tend to disbelieve or ignore exceptions to firmly held beliefs, at least until the exception has been replicated enough time to be made salient. Changing one's mind about strongly held beliefs is always uncomfortable, but one way science sometimes progresses by leaps is when an empirical exception to a widely accepted theory becomes understood. Often, understanding the exception causes us to discard or greatly modify our theory. So failures of generalization are not necessarily to be lamented; they can be great opportunities. The finding that levels of processing effects do not hold on all tests has thus led to a new theoretical approach named transfer appropriate processing, which has been applied in other domains, too (see Blaxton, 1989, Roediger, 1990).

10.3 Experimental Topics and Research Illustrations

Topic: Interaction Effects
Illustration: Implicit and Explicit Memory Tests

The term *interaction effect* is a statistical term that arises from the use of analysis of variance in evaluating multifactor experiments. Interaction effects are more commonly referred to as *interactions;* they have been discussed previously in chapters 3 and 8. (The analysis of variance is described in appendix B.) However, because the concept of interactions is so important, we consider it again in somewhat more detail. Also, we have discovered that it is a concept that is somewhat bothersome to students, so repeated treatments should provide a better grasp of the topic.

Multifactor experiments, you will recall, are those in which two or more independent variables are manipulated at the same time. An interaction effect occurs when the effect of one independent variable changes, depending on the level of the other independent variable. You have already been exposed to interaction effects several times in this chapter, although we did not refer to them as such. For example, Scarborough's (1972) results seen in figure 10–5 show that the superiority of visual to auditory presentation in his short-term memory paradigm depended on the retention interval used. Similarly, the results of Morris et al. (1977) shown in Figure 10–9 show an interaction between the level of processing during study and the type of test taken. The examples used below are similar to those of Morris et al. (1977).

Implicit and explicit tests. We will use differences between implicit and explicit memory tests to illustrate various types of interactions. The distinction between these types of tests was described briefly at the beginning of the chapter, but will be amplified here.

Explicit memory measures are those that require a person to consciously recollect the material that he or she studied during an earlier part of the experiment. Examples of such tests are free recall, cued recall, and recognition; in each case, people are told to recollect previous experiences. Thus, these tests are explicitly provided as tests of memory.

In contrast, implicit memory tests are tasks that can be performed without specific reference to the previous experiences in the laboratory. One example of an implicit test is the *word fragment completion task.* In this task, subjects see words that have letters missing from them and are required to fill in the blanks to form complete words (e.g., _l_p_a_t for elephant). People are typically told just to produce whatever word fits the frame as quickly as possible and are not told that some of the fragments are made from previously studied items. The fragments are quite difficult, and a person can typically complete only 20 to 35 percent of them if he or she has not seen them recently. (The proportion of fragments that can be completed without a subject's ever having studied the items is the control condition, often called the "nonstudied baseline.") However, if the person has read the words that complete the fragments at some time prior to performing the fragment completion test, he or she can complete many more of the fragments: typically, about 25 percent more of them. This occurs even when people are not told that the fragments come from the words studied earlier. Memory is said to be tested implicitly, because even though the subjects do not have to try to remember the studied words in order to perform the task, their performance is spontaneously improved by the prior exposures.

This improvement in performance is called *priming*. To measure priming, researchers test subjects on a random mixture of fragments for both words they studied and words they did not study. Each person's priming score can then be computed by subtracting the proportion of nonstudied items that were solved (the nonstudied baseline) from the proportion of studied items completed. For example, suppose you have studied ten words. Later, you receive a fragment test with fragments for the ten words you have studied, plus ten other fragments for words you have not studied, randomly mixed together. If you solve fragments for five out of the ten studied words (50 percent), but only two out of the ten nonstudied words (nonstudied baseline of 20 percent), then your priming score would be $.50 - .20 = .30$. (To make sure that the difference between studied and nonstudied words is not simply due to the studied items being easier, the items are counterbalanced across subjects. That is, half the subjects study one half of the items, whereas the other subjects study the other half of the items. Thus, during the course of the experiment, each item appears as a studied and as a nonstudied item. See chapter 9.)

Another example of an implicit memory test is the word stem completion test. On this test, people see word stems that are the first three letters of a word, such as ele_____, and are told to complete the stem with the first word that comes to mind. What word did you think of to complete this stem? Most likely, you thought of "elephant" instead of "element" or "elegant," etc., because you were primed with that word in a previous paragraph. The same priming occurs when people study a list of words before taking the word stem completion test.

Several other types of implicit memory tests have also been used, but we will not describe them here (see Schacter, 1987). The critical feature of these tests is that they can all be performed without people's necessarily being aware that they are remembering the prior study episode, even though their answers are influenced or "primed" by the material they have seen earlier. These tests are sometimes said to reflect "memory without awareness" (Jacoby and Witherspoon, 1982), because improved performance does not require that people be aware of the relation between the test and study materials.

Amnesia. Interest in the distinction between implicit and explicit memory measures originally arose out of research with amnesics (e.g., Warrington and Weiskrantz, 1970). Patients with *amnesia* have brain damage from any one of a number of sources, such as chronic alcoholism (Korsakoff's syndrome), anoxia (loss of oxygen to the brain), surgery, or head injury; they show severe memory deficits on explicit retention measures. Typically, they can recall or recognize very little about recently presented information, even though their other cognitive functions are intact. Some cases are so profound that the patient's doctors must reintroduce themselves each time they meet with the patient! The following excerpt is taken from a book by Wayne Wickelgren (1977), who has worked with amnesic patients.

> Once in the course of testing one of these people, I had a rather eerie experience. The patient was a young man in his twenties who had recently suffered brain damage because of an unusual fencing accident. Suzanne Corkin introduced me to the patient saying something like, "This is Wayne Wickelgren." The young man replied 'Wickelgren, that's a German name isn't it?" I said, "no." Then he said "Irish?" Again I said "no." Then he said "Scandinavian?" and I answered "yes." I talked with him for perhaps five minutes, and then I had to leave to make a telephone call. When I returned, everyone was standing in approximately the same locations as before. Sue, realizing that the patient would have no knowledge of ever having met me before, reintroduced me to him. After she said, "This is Wayne Wickelgren," he proceeded to say, "That's a German name, isn't it?" I replied, "no." Then he said, 'Irish?" I said, "no," and he said "Scandinavian?"—exactly the same series of questions he had asked the first time he met me. (p. 326)

Thus, amnesics' explicit recollection is severely impaired, as compared with that of normal subjects. It was often hypothesized in the past that amnesics lacked the ability to learn and to store new verbal information.

In 1970, Elizabeth Warrington and Lawrence Weiskrantz decided to test amnesics' memory in a different way and made a discovery that has greatly changed the way scientists think about amnesia, in particular, and memory functioning in general. Warrington and Weiskrantz asked amnesics and control subjects (patients with neurological disease) to study lists of 24 words and then tested their memories in several different ways. (They studied different lists for each memory test.) We will discuss two of the tests here. The first test was a traditional explicit free recall test, in which the subjects were simply instructed to recall as many of the words as possible. As expected, the amnesics recalled many fewer items (33 percent) than did the controls (54 percent). The second test was an implicit test, in which subjects saw perceptually degraded words (pieces of each letter were obliterated, so that none of the words could be identified by the subjects before the test); they were simply instructed to try to figure out and name the word. (All the words had been presented previously during the study phase.) The interesting question was whether amnesics would show their typical poor performance on this implicit memory task, or whether something different would happen.

To introduce the concept of interactions, in the following section we will examine several possible outcomes that might have been obtained in this experiment.

Interactions. *In general, two variables are said to interact when the effect of one variable changes at different levels of the other variable.* We have chosen to illustrate this concept with our discussion of implicit and explicit memory tests because they exhibit many interesting interactions. That is, implicit and explicit memory tests respond differently to manipulations of certain independent variables. Variables that have a large effect on an implicit test may have no effect—or even the opposite effect—on explicit tests. We will now illustrate interactions involving implicit and explicit memory tests by examining some different patterns of results that might have been obtained in the Warrington and Weiskrantz experiment, described in the preceding section.

Figure 10–10 (on pages 320 and 321) contains four sets of hypothetical data illustrating different patterns of results that Warrington and Weiskrantz might have observed in their experiment comparing implicit and explicit memory in amnesic and control subjects. The data in the tables on the left are illustrated in corresponding bar graphs (in the middle panels) and line graphs (on the right). We will discuss each display in turn. As we discuss each example, examine the pattern of data in the table and then look at how the data appear when plotted on the graphs.

Example A is included as the starting point to demonstrate how data might look when there is no interaction between the variables. Here, the controls perform better than the amnesics on both the explicit and the implicit tests, showing a *main effect* of the subject group. That is, subjects whose memories are intact (controls) have better memories than amnesics, regardless of how memory is tested. Thus, there is no interaction between memory group and test type in this example. Main effects are generalizations; they tell us that at each level of one variable (here, test type), the same effect was observed on the other variable (here, controls performed better than amnesics).

Example B illustrates one possible type of interaction that might be obtained. In this case, controls perform better than amnesics on the explicit free recall test, but amnesics perform as well as controls on the word identification task. In other words, the traditional difference between amnesic and normal memory disappears when memory is measured implicitly. Thus, the effect of one independent variable (the presence or absence of a memory deficit) changes, depending on the level of the other independent variable (test type). This is one example of what is meant by an interaction between two variables.

Example C illustrates a type of interaction that researchers typically find very interesting, known as a *crossover interaction*. The reason for this name is best illustrated in line graph C (on the far right). In our example, the control subjects show better memory than amnesics on the explicit test, but the amnesics show better memory than the controls on the implicit test. Thus, in a crossover interaction, the first independent variable has one effect at one level of the second independent variable, but it has the opposite effect at the other level of the second independent variable. If we obtained the data in Example C in our experiment, we would conclude that amnesics have better memory than normals if memory is measured implicitly (at least on this test), but that the reverse occurs on the explicit test.

Although many other types of interactions exist, we will end our illustrations with the interaction depicted in Example D. If these data were obtained in our experiment, we would conclude that the amnesic deficit is more pronounced on the explicit test than on the implicit test. That is, although control subjects perform substantially better than amnesics on the implicit test, the superiority of controls' to amnesics' memory is even greater on the explicit test. These data would suggest that the implicit test is a less sensitive measure of amnesic deficits than is the explicit test.

We will not keep you in suspense any longer. It turns out that Warrington and Weiskrantz obtained the results depicted in Example B. They found that although amnesics performed very poorly on the explicit recall test, the amount of priming they showed on the word fragment identification task was identical to performance of normal controls! (Recall that no subjects could identify any of the fragmented words before they started the experiment, so the proportions of items identified are priming scores.) That is, the amnesic deficit disappears when memory is tapped implicitly, with tests that can be performed without referring to the prior learning episode.

Since Warrington and Weiskrantz's important discovery, many other experimenters have obtained similar results with a variety of implicit tasks (Shimamura, 1986). That is, although amnesics perform poorly on explicit tests, they show preserved priming on implicit tests. The reasons for these interactions are not entirely understood, but they certainly dispel the notion that amnesics preserve no memorial record of recent experiences. At least part of the amnesics' problem seems to lie in gaining conscious access to these stored experiences.

One interesting outgrowth of the work comparing performance on explicit and implicit tests is the examination of normal people's memories. Can interactions between these measures be found in

FIGURE 10–10.

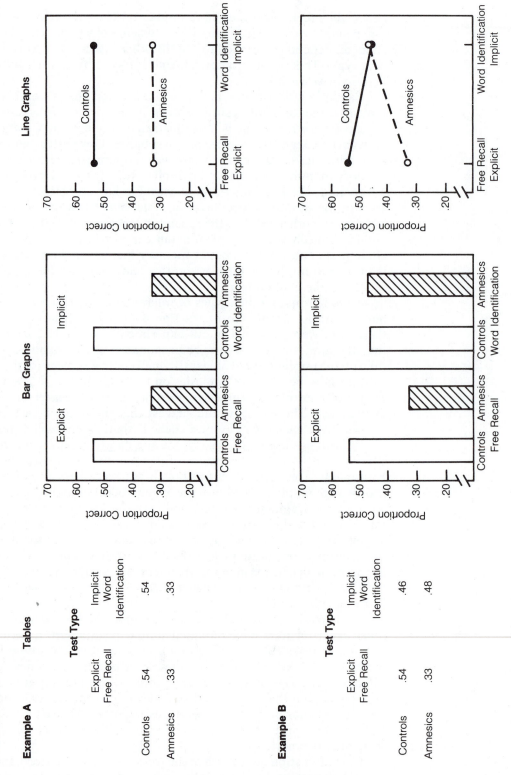

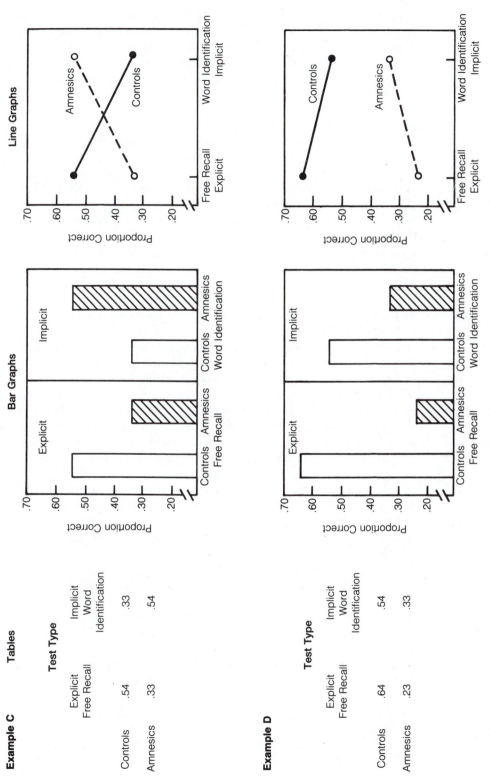

Example C

Tables

Test Type

	Explicit Free Recall	Implicit Word Identification
Controls	.54	.33
Amnesics	.33	.54

Example D

Test Type

	Explicit Free Recall	Implicit Word Identification
Controls	.64	.54
Amnesics	.23	.33

Bar Graphs

Line Graphs

Hypothetical interactions between test type (explicit free recall vs. implicit word identification) and memory deficit (amnesics vs. controls). The data in the tables on the left are illustrated with bar graphs (middle panels) and line graphs (right panels). Categorical variables, such as those illustrated here, should be plotted with bar graphs. Variables with ordinal, interval, and ratio scales of measurement can be plotted with line graphs. Note that, technically, the variables represented here should not be plotted on line graphs; they are plotted this way here only to facilitate the comparisons of the different formats for presenting the data.

normals? If so, this would argue that the explicit/implicit contrast generalizes to other subjects. In this case (unike the previous levels of processing instance) we ask whether findings obtained with an unusual population (amnesic patients) generalize to more typical groups. Many experiments have indeed shown interactions between independent variables and the type of test in normal subjects (Roediger, 1990); we consider here one reported by Weldon and Roediger (1987).

Weldon and Roediger (1987) were interested in the picture superiority effect, the finding that pictures are remembered better than words. However, this effect has typically only been studied with explicit memory tests (recall and recognition), and Weldon and Roediger (1987) wanted to extend the study of picture/word differences to implicit tests. (They suspected, for various reasons, that the picture superiority effect would not be found on implicit tests such as those used by Warrington and Weiskrantz, 1970). In their experiment, college student subjects studied a long series of pictures and of words in anticipation of a later memory test, the nature of which was unspecified. There were three sets of items, and subjects studied one set as pictures, one set as words, and did not study the third set. The item sets were counterbalanced across subjects, so that if subjects in one group saw a picture of an elephant, those in another group saw the word elephant, and those in a third group did not see the item in either form.

After studying the words and pictures, subjects took either an explicit free recall test or an implicit word fragment completion test. In the free recall test, subjects were given a blank sheet of paper and asked to recall the names of the pictures and words as well as possible (i.e., they recalled pictures by writing down their names, not by trying to draw them). Despite the fact that the response mode was always verbal, pictures were better remembered than were words, as shown in the left side of figure 10–11. The picture superiority effect was not large in this experiment, but it was statistically significant and replicates many other reports (Madigan, 1983).

In the word fragment completion test, subjects were given a long series of fragmented words (e.g., _l_p_a_t) and told simply to complete each one with a word, if possible. In this case the measure of interest was priming—the advantage in completing a fragment when its prior presentation was either a picture or a word, relative to the case when neither form has been studied. When subjects did not study the concept, they completed 0.37 of the fragments. The data in the right side of figure 10–11 show the priming from prior study of pictures and words over this level. Unlike the results on the left and the entire prior literature, words produced more priming than pictures on the implicit word fragment completion test. The pattern in figure 10–11 shows an interaction between *explicit* and *implicit retention* in normal subjects. In some ways, this interaction is even more striking than the interaction between tests shown in amnesics, because it represents a crossover interaction.

FIGURE 10–11.

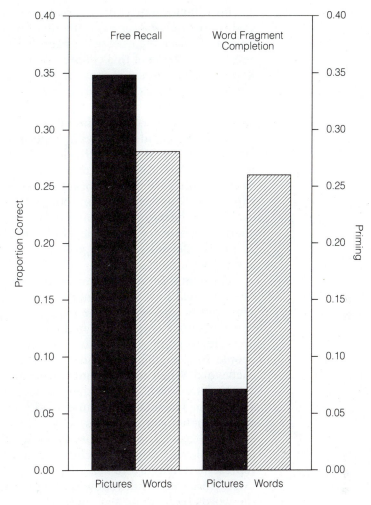

Results of Weldon and Roediger (1987). Pictures were better remembered than words in the explicit free recall tests, but words produced more priming than pictures on the implicit word fragment completion test. The overall pattern reveals a crossover interaction.

The topic of interactions is also related to the first problem considered in the chapter, that of scale attenuation. Often, ceiling and floor effects make the interpretation of interactions hazardous. Look back at the results of Scarborough's experiment, shown in figure 10–5. An interaction is pictured there between modality of presentation and retention interval. Modality of presentation has an effect, but only at the longer retention intervals. But we decided that this interaction could not be meaningfully interpreted, since it might have been produced by a ceiling effect at the zero-second retention interval. Now we can state a general rule: extreme caution should be used in interpreting interactions where performance on the dependent variable is at either the floor or the ceiling at some level of one of the independent variables.

Multifactor experiments are extremely useful and much preferable to single-factor experiments, for the very reason that they help us answer the question of generality. As we discussed in the preceding section of this chapter, one thing we very much want to know about the effect of some independent variable on a dependent variable is the conditions under which it holds. By independently varying a second (or even a third) variable in the same experiment, we can gain at least a partial answer to this question.

We have considered cases in which two factors are manipulated simultaneously. However, this logic can be extended to design experiments that involve simultaneous manipulation of three, four, or even more variables. (In practice, researchers hardly ever design experiments with more than four independent variables of interest.) When the nature of an interaction effect between two variables changes depending on the level of some third variable, the interaction is referred to as a *higher-order interaction*, since it involves several variables.

For example, suppose an investigator designs an experiment in which test type and memory deficit are manipulated, as in the Warrington and Weiskrantz experiment; but in this experiment levels of processing is also manipulated. People in one condition are told to count the number of vowels in each word, whereas people in the other condition are told to form a sentence using each word. When people count vowels, they are encoding the words at a shallow level, because they are focusing their attention on the surface, or graphemic, features of the words. On the other hand, when people form sentences, they are focusing on the meaning, or semantic, aspects of the words and are thus processing words at a deeper level. If the researcher were to find the pattern of results represented in figure 10–12, then a higher-order interaction would exist. Here, the results show that when the control subjects study the words by forming sentences, they recall many more words on the explicit recall test than when they simply count the vowels. However, the amnesics do not show this improvement in performance on the explicit test. On the implicit test, however, there is no change in performance for either the controls or the amnesics when they study the words by forming sentences. Therefore, manipulation of a third variable (level of processing) changes the nature of the interaction between the other two variables. (Note that the data in figure 10–12 are hypothetical.)

Many other intriguing interactions involving implicit versus explicit memory tests have been obtained; they are opening a whole new area of research (Schacter, 1987). To date, this research has generated many new insights and theories about human memory. Thus, interactions between implicit and explicit tests not only have revealed interesting things about memory disorders such as amnesia, but also are providing a wealth of new information about normal memory.

FIGURE 10–12.

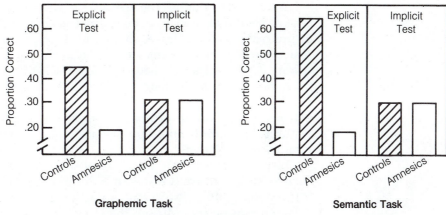

A hypothetical higher-order interaction involving test type, memory deficit, and level of processing (graphemic vs. semantic).

Graphing the data. During the above discussion, you probably figured out that the easiest way to detect interactions is to graph the data and then examine the patterns in the graphs. When the patterns of the effect of one variable are consistent across the levels of the other variable (e.g., Example A in figure 10–10), then the two variables do not interact. When the patterns change at different levels of the independent variables (i.e., the means converge, cross over, or diverge), then interactions between the variables probably exist. Of course, appropriate statistical tests must be performed to determine the degree to which the interactions are real effects and are not simply due to chance variation.

Different types of graphs are appropriate for plotting different types of variables. Bar graphs should be used when the independent variable is categorical or qualitative: that is, when the levels of the independent variable bear no quantitative relation to one another. Examples of categorical variables are one's major in school; modality of stimulus presentation; type of study material (e.g., pictures vs. words); and the two variables used in Warrington and Weiskrantz's experiment: test type and memory impairment. Categorical variables should not be plotted with line graphs, because a continuous line implies that the underlying variable is continuous, or at least ordered in a meaningful way. How would you order study materials, for example? Are pictures "more" or "less" than words? Obviously, they are simply different types of items. Strictly speaking, the line graphs in the right-hand panels of figure 10–10 are inappropriate for graphing the data in the example, because categorical dimensions are plotted on the abscissa (x-axis). The proper modes for presenting these variables are bar graphs or tables.

To use line graphs, the variable plotted along the abscissa (x-axis) should at least have an ordinal scale, and preferably have an interval or ratio scale (see chapter 6). An example of an ordinally scaled variable is the rank order of items according to some attribute (e.g., unpleasant, neutral, pleasant). Different levels of ordinal variables imply "more" or "less" of some attribute, but the magnitude of the difference is not known. Because the distances between points on an ordinal scale are not meaningful, ordinal variables are often more appropriately plotted with bar graphs than with line graphs.

Interval scales have meaningful distances between points, such as temperature (Celsius or Fahrenheit) or IQ, but have arbitrary zero points. Ratio scales also have meaningful distances between points; in addition, they have true zero points, so that the ratios between measures are meaningful. Examples are distance, weight, retention interval (the elapsed time between study and test), and drug dosage. Both interval and ratio scales are continuous; independent variables that have these properties can be plotted on line graphs. Of course, tables can always be used to present such data, too.

From Problem to Experiment: The Nuts and Bolts

Problem: Is Reading Better than Listening?

We have discussed the problem of modality differences in memory tasks that involve a short string of stimuli, such as three letters. A question of more general interest is whether there are differences in the comprehension and memory of information that is read as opposed to that which is heard. If the same information were presented by a lecturer or were read in a book, which would be more effective? Reading might allow us to go quickly over material we understand well and to tarry over difficult ideas. But while reading, we may be more apt to just glide our eyes over the page and daydream; a lecturer moving about and talking might better capture our attention.

Problem: *Is reading better than listening?*

Numerous hypotheses can be formed and operationally defined in different ways to answer this question. One such hypothesis will be considered here.

Hypothesis: *Subjects who read a long passage of material will be better able to answer multiple-choice questions about the material than will subjects who listen to another person reading the material.*

Even though this hypothesis is fairly specific, there are still a great many matters open to interpretation in actually performing the experiment. The variables need to be given operational definitions. How long is a "long passage"? What should be the subject matter of the passage? Should we use more than one passage? How should the passage to be read be presented? How long should the presentation take? Who should read the passage—or should we vary that? What kinds of questions should we ask on the multiple-choice (forced-choice recognition) test? Should we use a between-subjects or within-subjects design? These are only some of the questions that must be answered in translating the hypothesis into an actual experiment. How we decide these matters may affect the outcome of the experiment.

Let us consider the last question first. Should we use each subject in both the reading and listening conditions, or should we use different groups of subjects in the two conditions? In general, it is best to use the same subjects in each condition, since in that case we do not have to worry about differences between conditions being caused by differences between subjects in the two conditions. As long as we counterbalance the conditions for practice effects by testing half the subjects in the Read condition before the Listen condition, and the other half in the reverse order, there is nothing to prevent us from using the advantageous within-subjects design.

This decision helps determine the answer to another question. Since we are using each subject in two different conditions, we should obviously use at least two passages of test material, one for one condition and one for the other. We might even use more passages, since we would like to have some confidence that our results generalize to other reading material besides the particular passages used in the experiment. This issue of the generality of results over materials is an important one, especially since it is widely overlooked in certain types of research, with the result that statistical tests are often misapplied (see Clark, 1973).

What kinds of passages should be used? Presumably, material that is relatively unfamiliar to the subjects would be the best choice, since we want to test knowledge they gain during the reading of the passage, and not that which they acquired before the experiment. If subjects could answer almost all the questions on the multiple-choice test before coming into the experiment, there would be no chance for our independent variable (reading versus listening to the passage) to exert any influence over our dependent variable (recognition), since we would have a ceiling effect in the recognition test (close to 100 percent performance). In attempting to avoid familiar materials, researchers investigating memory for "naturalistic" prose passages have often chosen passages that contain so many words and concepts foreign to the subjects that we might wonder how "natural" these bizarre stories are. We would probably be better off using passages with mostly familiar words, but new information. Passages might be taken from parts of articles from *Scientific American* or other magazines at a similar level of difficulty.

How long should the passage be? This is closely tied in with how long the presentation should take. Suppose we decide that the recognition tests should take about seven minutes in each case. We might then want to limit time of presentation of each passage to fifteen minutes in order to make the experiment last only an hour. (There should be about fifteen minutes allotted for instructions, handing out and picking up tests, and explaining the experiment when it is finished.)

Perhaps the trickiest aspect of designing this experiment is deciding exactly how the passages are to be presented during the fifteen minutes in each presentation condition. Suppose we pick passages that take fifteen minutes to be read out loud in the Listen condition. In the condition in which subjects read the passage, should we also simply allow them fifteen minutes to read it? Then they could quite likely have more actual presentation time, since most people can read silently faster than they can read aloud. Thus subjects who read the passage could spend more time on the difficult material. Do we want to try to eliminate this in some way, for example, by instructing subjects to read the passage once straight through? Or do we want to leave it in as one of the natural differences between reading and listening that we are trying to investigate? If we somehow remove or minimize regression (reading back over the material) in the Read condition and then find listening to be better than reading, we may be open to the criticism that our conclusion holds only in artificial laboratory situations and not in the "real world." So, to maximize the possibility for generalizable results, let us allow subjects in the Read condition fifteen minutes to read the material—the same amount of time as is allowed for oral presentation—and then see what differences occur. If reading is superior to listening (or vice versa), we will have to do further research to see exactly what aspects of the process are important.

The same problem arises with oral presentation of the passage. Should we vary who reads it? The sex of the person? His or her attractiveness? Should it be read in a monotone, or with zest and enthusiasm, such as a lecturer might really try to convey? Let us decide to have one person read it with normal intonation as much as possible, and not in a monotone.

Designing the multiple-choice test is also important, especially with regard to making it neither too hard nor too easy, to avoid ceiling and floor effects. Should the test tap only surface-level questions (was _____ discussed in the third paragraph?), or more meaningful questions about the text? Or should we vary this? We could probably agree to use meaningful questions. Or why not use a recall test in the first place? (Because it is more difficult to derive quantitative measures of recall of prose, though, of course, it is possible.)

There are even more choices and difficulties than we have discussed here, even though we have only a 2 × 2 within-subjects design with two types of presentation (read versus listen) and two passages, (passage is a variable we are not primarily interested in). Since it is obvious that we could have operationalized the basic conditions differently and used a different dependent variable, it would be important to consider results of the present experiment against a background of other experiments in which the variables are operationalized differently. A series of such converging experiments is necessary if we are to gain some idea as to the generality or limitation of any particular experimental result.

This area of research examining modality differences in long-term retention of prose materials has received surprisingly little attention. However, two relevant references are King (1968) and Kintsch and Kozminsky (1977).

SUMMARY

1. Ebbinghaus was the first psychologist to study learning and memory systematically. He solved the problem of how to study unrecallable memories by relearning material and measuring the savings in the number of relearning trials compared with those needed for original learning. Although savings methods are still used today, most researchers measure memory in other ways: typically, with some variation of recall (production) and recognition (discrimination of studied from nonstudied material) tests.

2. Scale attenuation in psychological research refers to situations in which a measurement scale is too restricted to measure differences between conditions that may actually exist. When performance is nearly perfect, the problem is referred to as a ceiling effect, since performance is bumping into the top or roof of the scale. When performance is nearly absent altogether, the problem is referred to as a floor effect.

3. It is an error to assume that performance in two conditions is equivalent when it is at the ceiling or floor of a measurement scale. Although subjects in two conditions may score equivalently on the dependent variable (near either 0 percent or 100 percent), there may be a true difference between conditions, but the measurement scale of the variable may be too restricted (too "short") to show the real difference. Recall the case of the two men weighing themselves on a bathroom scale that only registers up to 300 pounds. The examples in this chapter illustrate ceiling effects, but floor effects are as common and as important. If the mean recall in a memory experiment involving two- and three-year-old children is 2 percent for each age group, are we justified in concluding that memory capacity is the same for both groups of children? Similarly, there can be errors in in-

terpreting interactions when performance in some conditions is constrained by ceiling and floor effects.

4. A critical issue about any experimental result is its generalizability beyond the conditions under which it was discovered. Jenkins' tetrahedral model of memory experiments provides four dimensions across which such generality can be assessed. (1) Would the finding hold with different subject populations? (2) Would the finding be obtained with different experimental materials? (3) Would the finding occur with different types of memory tests? (4) Would be same results occur with a different experimental setting and different ways of operationalizing the independent variables?

5. Researchers are interested in whether a particular result will generalize across several dimensions: subject populations, materials, situations, dependent measures, and so on. Multifactor experiments, or those in which more than one variable is manipulated simultaneously, are extremely important in determining generality of results. Such experiments tell us whether the effect of an independent variable on a dependent variable is the same or different when other variables are manipulated at the same time.

6. When an independent variable has an effect that is the same at all levels of the second independent variable, this is referred to as a main effect. Two independent variables are said to interact when the effect of an independent variable on the dependent variable is different at different levels of a second independent variable. Main effects can be thought of as allowing generalizations to be made across other conditions, because the independent variable has the same effect at all levels of the other independent variable. Interactions indicate that simple generalizations about an independent variable are not safe; the effect of this independent variable depends on the level of the second independent variable in the multifactor experiment.

7. Implicit and explicit memory tests interact with a variety of independent variables. For example, even though amnesics perform poorly on explicit tests such as free recall, they show just as much priming as control subjects on implicit tests such as priming in word identification. By studying the way these types of tests interact with other variables, scientists are gaining a new understanding of both normal and abnormal memory function.

KEY TERMS

amnesia

Brown-Peterson technique

ceiling effect

crossover interaction

episodic memory

explicit memory

floor effect

forced-choice recognition test

free recall

generality of results

graphemic code

higher-order interaction

implicit memory

interaction

levels of processing

long-term memory

main effect

nonsense syllables

paired-associate recall

phonemic (phonological) code

priming

proactive interference

recall

recognition

savings method

scale-attenuation effects

semantic code

serial recall

short-term memory

tetrahedral model of memory experiments

transfer appropriate processing

trials to criterion

word fragment completion task

yes/no recognition test

DISCUSSION QUESTIONS

1. Identify two situations, besides those presented in the chapter, in which ceiling and floor effects would probably make interpreting experimental observations difficult. How could problems caused by these effects be overcome in the experiments?

2. Researchers often lament the discovery that some result does not generalize to a new setting. Discuss why failures of generalization can often lead to progress in understanding a phenomenon. Can you think of discoveries in science sparked by an anomalous result when past knowledge failed to generalize to a new situation?

3. What are the advantages of multifactor experiments that make them so popular among researchers, despite their complexity? Discuss the relation of multifactor experiments to the problem of generality of results.

Can You Improve Your Memory?

AT ONE TIME OR another, you have probably witnessed an incredible feat of memory, such as the ability of a guest on a talk show to recall the first and last names of a few hundred audience members he or she has met just before the show. Many people marvel at the ability of others to remember names, faces, events, and statistics, while rueing their own poor memories. One of the most interesting and famous accounts of extraordinary memory has been reported by the Russian psychologist Luria, who extensively studied a mnemonist known as "S." (for Shereshevski). S. seemed to be incapable of forgetting anything—he could perfectly remember lists of nonsense syllables fifteen years after he had learned them! (Luria's fascinating account of his findings from thirty years of studying S.'s memory were published in 1968 in a book called *The Mind of a Mnemonist*.)

Are people born with good memories, or do we all have the capacity for excellent memory? Although most of us could never develop memorial skills as powerful as S.'s, we can substantially improve our memories by employing *mnemonic techniques*, which are mental operations for successfully learning and retrieving information.

One of the oldest mnemonic devices is the *method of loci*, which has been credited to Simonides of ancient Greece. When he was called away from a banquet to receive a message, the roof of the banquet hall collapsed, killing everyone inside. Although the dead were mutilated beyond recognition, Simonides was able to identify the bodies by remembering where the people had sat. Subsequently, he capitalized on his observation that locations can serve as effective retrieval cues and developed the technique for more general use.

You can easily demonstrate the benefits of mnemonic devices by instructing people to learn lists of words in different ways. Different groups of subjects can be taught the different mnemonic techniques described below. Proper control groups are also needed.

The method of loci simply requires that each person select a series of distinct locations along a familiar route. For example, one might imagine a path to school, selecting a particular mailbox, house, tree, shop window, etc. Have each person select twenty locations along a well-known route and practice this route several times. Then present a list of twenty words and instruct your subjects to mentally walk along the path as you present the list, placing each subsequent word in the subsequent locations, in the order in which they are presented. For example, if the first word in the list is *butter*, and the first memory location along the route is a mailbox, the subject should imagine a stick of butter in the mailbox. The second word in the list should be imagined in the second location, etc.

A second group of people can be taught the *peg-word method*. In this scheme, your subjects must first learn a list of peg words that rhyme with the numbers from 1 to 20, such as "One is a gun," "Two is a shoe," etc. A commonly used peg-word rhyme system is presented in Table 10–2. After your subjects have memorized these rhymes and practiced them, present the list of twenty words and tell your subjects to imagine each subsequent word interacting with the appropriate peg word. For example, for the first word *butter*, one could form an image of a gun shooting a large stick of butter. If the second word is *caterpillar*, one can imagine a caterpillar crawling into a shoe.

TABLE 10–2. Peg-word rhymes that can be used as a mnemonic device. Each rhyme associates an object or *peg word* with a number. After you have learned them, you can remember a series of items (or points in a speech) by forming an image of each item and imagining it interacting with the peg word.

One is a gun
Two is a shoe
Three is a tree
Four is a door
Five is knives
Six is sticks
Seven is an oven
Eight is a plate
Nine is wine
Ten is a hen
Eleven is "penny-one," hotdog bun
Twelve is "penny-two," airplane glue
Thirteen is "penny-three," bumble bee
Fourteen is "penny-four," grocery store
Fifteen is "penny-five," big bee hive
Sixteen is "penny-six," magic tricks
Seventeen is "penny-seven," go to heaven
Eighteen is "penny-eight," golden gate
Nineteen is "penny-nine," ball of twine
Twenty is "penny-ten," ballpoint pen

A third group can be told to form an image of each word as it is presented, but be given no further instructions on how to use the image. Control groups for the mnemonic conditions should receive the same lists at the same rate as the mnemonic groups, but should receive different study instructions ahead of time. For example, a fourth group can be instructed simply to repeat each word over and over during list presentation until the next word is presented.

After you have presented the list of items, give your subjects a piece of paper with lines numbered 1 to 20 and tell them to try to recall all the words you presented. Instruct them to recall the words in order if they can remember them; if they cannot remember the position in which an item occurred in the list, they should write it anyway at the bottom of the page.

You can score your results in two ways. First, count the total number of items each person recalled, regardless of whether or not he or she recalled it in the correct order of presentation. Second, count only the items recalled in the correct position. Which mnemonic devices do you think will produce the best recall on each of these two scoring systems?

You will probably find that simple rehearsal produces the worst recall. This is because rehearsal does not require elaboration or thinking about the meaning of the words, and so the information is easily lost. Unfortunately, this is the technique many students use to study for exams.

Imagery will produce better recall than rehearsal when total recall is scored, because images convert the words into a format that is typically easier for people to remember. That is, in general, people can remember pictures (even "mental pictures") much better than words. However, when you count the number of items recalled in the correct order, the imagery instructions probably will not have helped very much, because simply forming the images does not help a person remember their order.

The people who will recall the most items and the most items in the correct positions will be those who used the method of loci and the peg-word method. First, these two mnemonic techniques employ interactive imagery—that is, the images of the objects are imagined to interact—which significantly boosts recall as compared with simple imagery (Bower, 1972). Furthermore, these two methods also incorporate information about the order of events into their schemes, and subjects associate this order information with each item to be remembered. For example, a person who uses the peg-word method might think of the number two, remember that it rhymes with shoe, and then remember the image of the caterpillar crawling into the shoe. Thus, these two methods are quite powerful not only for helping people remember information, but also when it is important to remember the order of the information (Roediger, 1980).

People who have excellent memories typically use a wide variety of mnemonic techniques. A book full of such methods, called *The Memory Book,* has been published by Harry Lorayne and Jerry Lucas. You might find this book helpful for learning mnemonic devices for memorizing information of all sorts, from peoples' names to playing cards to foreign vocabulary words. Further information is available in Kenneth Higbee's, *Your Memory: How it Works and How to Improve It.*

CHAPTER 11

Thinking and Problem Solving

Life does not consist mainly—or even largely—of facts and happenings. It consists mainly of the storm of thoughts that is forever blowing through one's head.

—MARK TWAIN

I N CASE YOU DO NOT have any problems at the moment, let us give you one. Read the following problem carefully and examine its representation in figure 11–1. Give the problem some careful thought before you continue reading the text.

> Two train stations are 100 miles apart. At 2 P.M. one Saturday afternoon the two trains start toward each other, one from each station. One train travels at 60 miles per hour, the other at 40 miles per hour. Just as the trains pull out of their stations, a bird springs into the air in front of the first train and flies ahead to the front of the second train. When the bird reaches the second train it turns back without losing any speed and flies directly toward the first train. The bird continues to fly back and forth between the trains at a rate of 80 miles per hour. How many miles will the bird have flown before the trains meet?

Were you able to solve the problem? Most people have a great deal of difficulty with it, but some people solve it almost immediately. They must be very good mathematicians, you might be thinking. Not at all.

Let us consider how most people try to solve this problem. Because of the way it is stated and the way the picture in figure 11–1 is drawn, most people begin worrying immediately about how long it will take the bird to go from the first to the second train,

FIGURE 11–1.

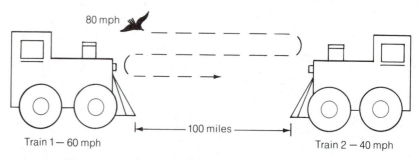

An illustration of the bird-and-train problem.

how far the second train will have moved by the time the bird arrives, then how long it will take the bird to trek back to the first train and how far that train will have moved, and so on. The general strategy is to try to figure out how long it will take the bird to make each trip between the trains, then add these times together to find out how many miles the bird will have flown before the trains meet. This is a quite reasonable strategy and it will give you the answer, provided you have plenty of time, a good calculator, and knowledge of calculus.

Since it is quite likely that you do not have one or more of these three resources, you might need to find a simpler solution. *Thought* can be defined as "the achievement of a new representation through the performance of mental operations" (Posner, 1973, p. 147). We can say that thought is necessary in order to find a simpler solution to the bird-and-train problem. To solve the problem, you must reconceptualize it. In fact, after you make an appropriate reconceptualization, the solution to the problem is simple. What you need to focus on is how long the trains will be traveling before they meet. Since one is traveling at 60 miles per hour and the other at 40 miles per hour and they are 100 miles apart, they will meet in an hour. Once you think of recasting the problem in this way and using one other piece of information, the solution is obvious. Since the trains will meet in an hour and the bird is flying at 80 miles per hour, the bird will have flown 80 miles before the trains meet. Not much time is needed; nor is a calculator; nor is higher mathematics. Just thought.

Just thought? That is simple enough to say, but the process is very complicated. What happens mentally while a person is trying to discover a solution to a problem? How does a person go about discovering a simpler solution to the problem (thinking)? Can we find general psychological laws of thought? How can we even study this hidden process? These are among the difficult questions that we will be considering in this chapter.

The experimental topics covered in this chapter include the issue of *reliability of results* (or replicability), the problem of *extraneous variables* and *experimental control*, and the use of *verbal reports* in psychological research. The first concern is the reliability of results: if we were to perform an experiment a second time, how likely would we be to obtain data that would allow us to reach the same conclusion as in the first experiment? This problem exists in all research, but, for reasons to be discussed later, may be heightened in research on thinking and other complex processes. Second, the topic of problem solving and thought is so complicated that great ingenuity is needed to perform interesting and useful experiments in this area. How can we gain control over some independent variable while controlling the extraneous variables, since there are so many that might influence the thought process? The final issue is one of subjective report and its value in psychological research. In an area such as problem solving and thinking, people are quite willing, usually, to tell how they think they set about solving a problem. Are we to accept their reports as useful evidence on the nature of the processes involved?

Two Approaches to Thinking

Historically, there have been two primary approaches to the study of problem solving that have different emphases. Both have been very influential on the study of thinking and the study of learning. The two approaches represent a bottom-up (data-driven) analysis and top-down (conceptually driven) analysis analogous to the ways of examining perception that were discussed in chapter 7.

Thorndike's Trial-and-Error Learning

In some interesting early experiments Thorndike (1898) studied problem solving in cats. He placed them in specially constructed puzzle boxes with food placed outside. The cats' problem was how to escape from the box and obtain the food. In some cases, the appropriate solution was simply clawing down a rope, but sometimes there were as many as three different solutions the cat could use. Thorndike observed the cats' performance on successive trials in the puzzle box and measured the amount of time it took them to escape on each trial. On the first trial, the cat would try a variety of strategies in attempting to escape the box and would strike out in an undirected manner at nearby objects. Eventually, the cat would claw at the rope that released it from the cage. It apparently learned by trial and error. Its success in escaping from the box seemed completely accidental, at least at first. On successive occasions, though, the cats began to escape from the box more quickly and systematically each time. Nonetheless, the guiding principle that seemed to govern the cats' solution attempts was one of trial-and-error learning.

In his analysis of trial-and-error learning, Thorndike was particularly concerned with success. It seemed obvious that the success of a correct movement caused it to be impressed or learned. The effect of the movement was to lead to success, which "stamps in" the movement, as Thorndike put it. These early experiments led to the *law of effect* and the concept of reinforcement (see chapter 9). The historical impact of this bottom-up research has been much greater in the field of animal learning, where its importance is overwhelming, than in research concerned with thinking and problem solving. The emphasis in research on human thinking and problem solving has been much more on higher-level conceptually driven processes, in the tradition to be discussed next. Nonetheless, there have been attempts to analyze human thought processes in terms of trial-and-error learning, or operant conditioning (see Skinner, 1957, chapter 19).

Insight in Köhler's Chimpanzees

Wolfgang Köhler, a German psychologist, was posted by his country to the island of Tenerife (a part of the Canary Islands) during 1913 to study anthropoid apes. Soon afterward, World War I broke out, and Köhler remained on Tenerife. While there, he conducted research on the problem-solving capacities of chimpanzees. Many of the problems he used could not be solved in a simple, direct way, as could Thorndike's puzzle-box problem, in which the cat merely had to claw at a rope. Instead, solutions required a more roundabout approach. Köhler discussed his research in a book published in German in 1921 and translated into English as *The Mentality of Apes* (1927).

In one problem, Köhler dangled a banana out of reach of the chimpanzees. It was too far above them for them to reach it, even with the aid of a stick placed within their enclosure. A more indirect solution to the problem was required. Köhler describes in detail attempts of the chimps to obtain the banana. Usually, they would first try out various direct strategies of obtaining it, like reaching and poking at it with the stick. Failing with these methods, they would then seem to engage in various random acts, or often apparently give up on the problem altogether. Somewhat later, however, a chimp would suddenly implement the appropriate solution to the problem. The solution in this case was to stack some crates (that were in the enclosure) on top of one another and then climb up them to reach the banana (figure 11–2).

Köhler emphasized the importance of *insight* in solving the problem. After a period of random activity or no activity at all, the chimp (presumably) suddenly conceived of the boxes as related to the problem. Once this insight was achieved, implementing the solution was quite simple.

Köhler's top-down approach to problem solving emphasized its structured, planned, and conceptual nature, rather than its trial-and-error aspect. Köhler was a member of the Gestalt school of psychology (see appendix A), which in general was opposed to the more elementary type of analysis of behaviorism that grew, in part, from work such as Thorndike's. Both behavioristic and Gestalt approaches have been tremendously influential in psychology. Cur-

FIGURE 11–2.

One of Köhler's chimpanzees stacking boxes on top of one another to reach the bananas. (From Köhler, 1927, Plate V)

rent research and theory concerning the psychology of thinking and problem solving probably reflect the Gestalt influence to a greater extent, but the two approaches have been combined into a model similar to the word recognition model outlined in chapter 7 (Holyoak, 1990).

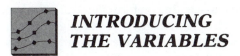

INTRODUCING THE VARIABLES

Dependent variables

There are three primary ways to measure the process of problem solving. Let us assume that we either do or do not present an illustration along with the train-and-bird problem. One group of subjects attempts to solve it with figure 11–1 present, and one group attempts to solve it without the illustration. What do we measure? The first and most obvious thing to measure is the number or proportion of subjects in the two conditions that are

able to solve the problem within a time limit (say, forty-five minutes). But most problems chosen for study are likely to be fairly easy, or at least solvable within the time limit. What if everyone in both groups solves the problem? Then it is impossible to tell whether the independent variable had any effect, because of a ceiling effect in performance (see chapter 10). It is, of course, improper to conclude that the variable had no effect just because the percentage of people solving the problem is equivalent, since the problem was too easy to reveal any possible differences. What we can do is look at a second measure of performance in solving the problem: latency, or the time taken to solve the problem. Even though all subjects in both groups solved the problem, they might have taken different amounts of time to do this in the different conditions. So although there may be no differences in percentages of people solving the problem, measurement of the time taken to solve the problem may prove a more sensitive index of problem difficulty in the two conditions (picture versus no picture). In fact, even if there were no ceiling effect, but the percentages of people solving the problem were still equivalent at (say) 60 percent, differences in performance might still be revealed by latencies. Therefore, we can say that latencies are likely to be a more sensitive dependent variable than percentage correct, since this measure is more likely to indicate an effect of the independent variable in most situations. (It would be very unusual to find the reverse: an effect on percentage correct, but not on latency.) Of course, we would normally expect a high negative correlation between percentage correct and latency, such that in conditions where fewer subjects are able to solve a problem, they also take longer to do so.

A third measure that can be used in some problem-solving situations where more than one solution is possible is the quality of the solution. It must be possible to rank the solutions on an ordinal scale; in other words, it must be possible to order them from best to worst. Then, even if percentage correct and latency measures indicate no difference between subjects solving problems under two conditions, subjects in one condition may still achieve more satisfactory solutions than subjects in another condition.

One might want to use all three measures of problem solution as converging operations of some problem-solving construct, but there may well be no straightforward relationship among them. For example, subjects in one condition may take much longer to solve a particular problem than subjects in another condition, and perhaps a smaller percentage of subjects will solve the problem in the first condition, but the solutions the subjects achieve in this condition might be superior to those in the other. In other words, variation in the independent variable might allow subjects in one condition to frequently produce a poor solution in a relatively short period of time, as opposed to subjects in another condition who may less frequently produce a better solution and take a longer time doing so. So there may be no simple relation among measures. This problem is a variant of the speed-accuracy tradeoff problem discussed under reaction-time measures in chapter 8.

Independent variables

The primary independent variable in the study of problem solving is the manner in which the problem is presented. This can be varied in several different ways. Let us consider the problem concerning how long it takes the bird to fly between the two trains before the trains meet, which was presented at the beginning of the chapter. One thing we could vary is the order and prominence of the information needed to solve the problem. The critical fact that the bird was flying at 80 miles per hour is buried in the description of the problem. If it were made more prominent, subjects might get the idea of using this fact earlier in their attempts to restructure the problem. A second factor that might be varied is the amount of irrelevant information presented. For example, the information that the trains began at 2 P.M. on a Saturday is completely irrelevant to solving the problem and should be ignored. It may well be that the more irrelevant information presented along with the few relevant facts, the longer it will take to solve the problem. Whether or not an illustration is presented and the nature of the illustration could also be varied. Presenting or not presenting an illustration with the problem may aid or hinder its solution, depending on the nature of the problem. Other sorts of psycholinguistic variables could be studied too, such as whether active or passive sentences are used in describing the problem. Besides those dealing with how the problem is presented, other variables of interest might be whether there is time pressure (or some other sort of stress) that people are working under when attempting to solve the problem; whether the magnitude of a reward offered affects the solution; and whether there are individual differences among classes of people (for example, high versus low I.Q.) solving the problem.

Control Variables

Experiments concerned with problem solving and thinking are often more complicated than others in human experimental psychology, and thus this area (along with others, such as social and environmental psychology, that deal with complex processes) requires a great deal of care to produce experimental control. Since it is typical in this field to use between-subjects designs (independent groups of subjects are assigned to different conditions), care must be taken to ensure that subjects in the different conditions are statistically equivalent, either by randomly assigning them to conditions or by matching them on some dimension such as I.Q. Similarly, one must make certain that all other extraneous variables (such as the way the problem is stated or how it is presented) are held constant.

11.1 Experimental Topics and Research Illustrations

Topic: Reliability and Replication
Illustration: Analogical Reasoning

The basic issue of reliability of experimental results is simply this: If an experiment were repeated, would the results be the same as those found the first time? Obviously, this is a crucial topic in psychological research, for an experimental outcome is worthless if we cannot have reasonable certainty that the results from it are reliable.

The key to insuring the reliability of our observations is the number of observations we make. The greater the number of observations, the more confident we can be that our sample statistics approximate the true population parameter values. If we take a random sample of persons in the United States and ask them survey questions (for example, about their preference in an upcoming presidential election), we can be more confident that the results accurately represent the population if the sample consists of 100,000 people than if it consists of only 100.

The thing to keep in mind, then, is that our confidence in the reliability of a particular result increases with the number of observations on which the result is based. So, in general, we should attempt to maximize the number of observations in the conditions of our experiments. This increases not only our confidence in the reliability of the result, but also the *power* of the statistical tests we employ, or the ability of the tests to allow rejection of the null hypothesis if it is in fact false.

Reliability involves not only sample size and statistics, but also different types of experimental replicability. The key to experimental replicability is the identification of the relevant variables, because they must be systematically manipulated or controlled in order to produce consistent results. In general, in the study of more complex processes, there should probably be greater concern with reliability of results than in the study of simpler processes. One reason is that in research concerned with complex processes, it is often necessary to use between-subjects designs, or designs in which a different group of subjects serves in each experimental condition, because of the carry-over effects that would occur from within-subjects designs (see chapter 9). The use of between-subjects designs rather than within-subjects designs tends to increase variability of observations, since differences among individual subjects are not as well controlled.

But there is another reason that experimental reliability can be a problem in researching complex cognition. Typically, for practical reasons, it is difficult to obtain many observations per condition in the study of complex processes with between-subjects designs. This is because it is often necessary to test subjects individually, which takes a great amount of time. In experiments on complex processes such as problem solving, it might take an hour to test an individual subject. Thus, even if there were only four conditions in the experiment and we wanted only twenty-five observations in each condition, that would still amount to up to one hundred hours of testing of subjects. Because of these practical considerations, then, we often find very few observations per experimental condition in the study of complex processes, even though this means we will have less confidence in the reliability of the results, and our statistical tests will have less power.

Analogical reasoning. We will illustrate some further points about reliability of research by discussing problem solving by *analogy*. When people comprehend some point by analogy, they understand one thing in terms of another. If you were told in high-school physics that the structure of the atom was similar in some ways to the organization of the solar system, or in chemistry that molecules of gas bumped off one another like billiard balls on a pool table, or in psychology that human memory could be compared to a giant library or dictionary, your teacher was employing analogical reasoning. She or he was trying to get you to understand something unfamiliar in terms of something you already understood. Psychologists interested in thinking have long recognized the importance of analogies in thinking and making discoveries. The art of discovery often lies in perceiving a resemblance between two items in different domains of knowledge (Hadamard, 1945). For example, in the seventeenth century William Harvey developed a hydraulic model of blood circulation after he conceived of the heart as a pump.

The study of reasoning by analogy is, of course, quite difficult. Problem solving, thinking, and discovery are topics that have long resisted understanding by psychologists. However, in the last twenty years or so, some real gains have been made in this area on numerous fronts (Mayer, 1983). Here we consider examples from experiments by Gick and Holyoak (1980, 1983) to illustrate how interesting research can be done on these topics and to show the importance of determining reliability of experimental phenomena.

Gick and Holyoak were interested in the effects of analogical reasoning on problem solving. Before discussing this research, let us give you the problem they used, to let you mull it over before reading on. It is called the radiation problem and was first used by Duncker in 1945. It can be stated as follows:

> Suppose you are a doctor faced with a patient who has a malignant tumor in his stomach. It is impossible to operate on the tumor, but unless the tumor is destroyed the patient will die. There is a kind of ray that can be used to destroy the tumor. If the rays reach the tumor all at once at a sufficiently high intensity, the tumor will be destroyed. Unfortunately, at this intensity the healthy tissue that the rays pass through on the way to the tumor will also be destroyed. At lower intensities, the rays are harmless to healthy tissue, but they will not affect the tumor either. What type of procedure might be used to destroy the tumor with the rays, and at the same time avoid destroying the healthy tissue? (Gick and Holyoak, 1980, pp. 307–308)

Shut your book and think about how to solve this problem before you read on. Do not read ahead until you have thought of at least one solution to the problem.

How did you do? Many students have difficulty solving the problem, given all the constraints placed on them. Many "solutions" depend on advanced technology, such as immunizing the healthy tissue with some drug and then passing the ray through it to the cancerous tumor. A more practical solution is to operate on the patient and insert a tube into the affected area or otherwise expose the tumor, so that the radiation can be directly applied to the diseased organ. However, perhaps the most creative and effective solution to the problem would be to aim several weak rays at the tumor from different directions, so that they converged on it. Each of the rays would be weak enough not to hurt the tissue through which it passed, but the strength of all the rays when they converged would be sufficient to destroy the tumor. This solution is generated by very few students; in the original studies of this problem by Duncker (1945), only two out of forty-five subjects (4 percent) came up with this solution.

Gick and Holyoak (1980, 1983) were interested in seeing whether they could get more people to solve this problem by giving them an analogous problem and solution before the radiation problem. The idea is that people will abstract the guiding principle from the first problem and then be able to apply it to the second. With this in mind, Gick and Holyoak developed other "analog stories" that embodied the same principle as that which applied to the most effective solution to the radiation problem.

In one story, called The Commander, the leader of a tank corps needed to mount an attack on an enemy headquarters. By attacking with many tanks he had a good chance of winning, but he had to attack across narrow, rickety bridges that would permit only a few tanks to pass. An assault with such a small force across one bridge would be easily repulsed. To achieve victory, the tank commander hit on the plan of sending a few tanks to each of the small bridges that circled the headquarters. All the tanks were then able to attack across the bridges at once and overtake the enemy headquarters.

The similarity between the tank-attack problem and the radiation problem should be apparent. In both cases, it is necessary for the problem solver to forgo a direct attack on the headquarters (or cancerous tumor) and disperse forces (or radiation) for a simultaneous converging attack from different directions. But would subjects in an experiment use the principles derived from reading a story such as The Commander to solve the radiation problem? Gick and Holyoak (1980) performed a series of experiments in which subjects attempted to solve the radiation problem either after reading a story similar to The Commander, or after reading no story (or an irrelevant story). They found in several experiments that subjects who were given no story or an irrelevant story before the radiation problem solved the problem with the most effective solution only about 10 percent of the time. However, when subjects were given an analog story before the radiation problem, about 75 percent of the people solved it within the time limit. Since this result was obtained in several experiments, the basic phenomenon was replicated several times. Obviously, people can profit from analogy in solving problems.

The results of one of their experiments led Gick and Holyoak (1980) to consider more closely the processes involved in reasoning by analogy. In Experiment 4 of their series, they gave all subjects the analog story to read and then the radiation problem to solve. However, in the Hint condition of Experiment 4, subjects were told, after they had read the story but before they got the radiation problem, to use the story as a hint on how to solve the problem. (This instruction had also been included in all of Gick and Holyoak's prior experiments in the series.) For subjects in the No-Hint condition, no mention was made about the relation between the story they had just read and the problem-solving task ahead. The results revealed that the hint was indeed a critical component to solving the problem by analogy. When the hint was given, 92 percent of the subjects solved the problem; when the hint was not given, only 20 percent of them solved it. The results seem to show that it is not enough to have been exposed to the analogy; one must be led to make active use of it during the attempt to solve the later problem. (The higher percentage of students solving the problem in Experiment 4 relative to earlier experiments—92 percent to about 75 percent—was likely due to somewhat different stories being used across experiments.)

This fact may not seem surprising: telling people to use a source of knowledge does indeed lead them to do so. But what is surprising is how few subjects (20 percent) came upon the solution spontaneously, without the hint. The first question we ask ourselves about a surprising discovery in any experimental field is this: Is it real? This brings us back to the question of reliability: if the experiment were repeated, would the same result be obtained?

One way to answer this question is to compute inferential statistics, the logic of which is described in appendix B. Briefly, inferential statistics are used to determine whether a difference obtained between conditions is due to operation of the independent variable or to chance factors. If the difference between the conditions is great enough so that it would occur by chance in fewer than one case in twenty, then the researcher rejects the possibility that chance factors produced the result, and instead accepts the result as evidence for a real effect of the independent variable— in this case, the presence or absence of the hint. In fact, Gick and Holyoak (1980) performed the appropriate inferential statistics and concluded that the difference in the percentage of solutions between the two groups was not a result of chance factors, but was caused by the presence or absence of the hint. Thus, we can conclude on the basis of such a test that the difference has *statistical reliability*.

Statistical reliability is a necessary condition for taking seriously an experimental result, but many researchers prefer to see an experimenter also establish *experimental reliability*. If the experiment is repeated under essentially the same conditions, will the results be the same as they were before? An adage among researchers is that "one replication is worth a thousand *t* tests." (The *t* test is a well-known statistical test used to evaluate the statistical reliability between two conditions.) The gist of the adage is that many researchers are more convinced by repetitions of the experiment than by inferential statistics applied to the original outcome. Although an outcome may be deemed statistically reliable, the possibility remains that it could have occurred by chance (statistical reliability still allows a 5 percent error rate) or because of some unintentional confounding or error on the part of the experimenter. For example, perhaps smarter subjects happened to be assigned to one condition rather than another. Although these possibilities might seem unlikely, they do sometimes occur. In some experiments, subjects are randomly assigned to conditions, and then, prior to the main experiment, the various groups are given a pretest to determine whether the groups are actually equivalent (on the average) in ability. Occasionally, pretests of this sort turn up differences, before the independent variable has been introduced (see, for example, Tulving and Pearlstone, 1966). Since such problems can occur even in well-controlled research, researchers encourage replication of experiments, even when inferential statistics indicate that some effect is reliable.

There are three types of experimental replication: *direct replication*, *systematic replication*, and *conceptual replication*. Direct replication, as the name implies, is the attempt to repeat the experiment as closely as is practical, with as few changes as possible in the original method. If Gick and Holyoak (1980) had attempted to repeat their fourth experiment as precisely as possible with the exception of testing new groups of subjects randomly assigned to conditions, this would have constituted a direct replication of their experiment.

A more interesting type of replication is systematic replication. In systematic replications, the experimenter attempts to vary factors believed to be irrelevant to the experimental outcome. If the phenomenon is not illusory, it will survive these changes. If the effect disappears, then the researcher has discovered important boundary conditions on the phenomenon being studied. Actually, Experiment 4 of the Gick and Holyoak series might itself be considered a systematic replication that led to important new information. In their first three experiments, Gick and Holyoak had compared conditions in which subjects solved the radiation problem either after studying a story that embodied an analogous solution (the experimental condition) or after studying one that did not (the control condition). As previously discussed, they found that a greater percentage of subjects solved the radiation problem with the "convergence solution" (aiming the rays from various sides) when tested in the experimental condition than when tested in the control condition. They replicated this observation several times. However, in each of the first three experiments, subjects in the experimental condition were told that they should use the story in attempting to solve the problem. In Experiment 4, Gick and Holyoak attempted to repeat the experiment, but vary this one (seemingly small) feature; this allowed the experiment to be considered a systematic replication. They discovered that this hint was actually a critical part of the experimental manipulation; simply having subjects study the story and then try to solve the radiation problem without the specific hint produced a much lower percentage of subjects solving the problem than instructing them to use the hint.

In a conceptual replication, one attempts to replicate a phenomenon, but in a way radically different from the original experiment. In later experiments that followed up the ones already described, Gick and Holyoak (1983) attempted to determine conditions that would promote positive transfer of analog stories to problem solutions. In three experiments with the radiation problem and another problem, Gick and Holyoak had subjects process the analog story in different ways (the experimental conditions) to see whether the amount of positive transfer could be increased, as compared with the case in which the analogy was simply presented by itself with no special instructions (the control condition). They found that the amount of positive transfer (indexed by a greater percentage of subjects solving the problem in the experimental conditions) did not improve when (1) subjects were told to summarize stories rather than study them for a test of recall (Experiment 1), or (2) subjects were given or not given a verbal principle along with the story that captured the essence of the strategy (Experiment 2), or (3) subjects were given diagrams along with the story (Experiment 3).

Gick and Holyoak (1983) did manage to uncover conditions that produced positive transfer of the story analogs to solving the radiation problem. When subjects studied two analogs and then described their similarities (before being given the problem), greater positive transfer occurred than when subjects studied only one analog. Gick and Holyoak argued that subjects who processed two analogs and thought about their similarities could generate a better underlying idea (or schema, in their terms), which could then be spontaneously applied to solving new problems.

Although the experiments reported by Gick and Holyoak (1983) were not direct or systematic replications of their earlier experiment indicating that subjects had difficulty spontaneously using analogies to solve problems, they converged on the same conclusion that it is difficult to improve reasoning from analogies. Thus, these later experiments may be considered conceptual replications, in the sense that they reproduced the essence of the phenomenon of the difficulty of reasoning from analogies without overt direction to do so, even though the experimental techniques were not exact replicas of those used in the original experiment.

The problem of replicability is interwoven with the topic of generality of results. In the case of systematic and conceptual replications, a researcher is not repeating an experiment exactly, but really asking whether the phenomenon of interest generalizes in one way or another. In systematic replications, the variables manipulated (and across which generality is sought) are typically not dramatically different from those of the original experiment, whereas in conceptual replications the differences in procedure are usually much greater. In a certain sense, it is best if the researcher eventually finds conditions under which the phenomenon *cannot* be replicated.

For example, Spencer and Weisberg (1986) replicated Gick and Holyoak's (1983) condition, in which subjects were given two analog stories before solving the radiation problem. They added an interesting twist, however, by changing the pretext under which the two initial training stories and the radiation problem were administered. In the "same-context" condition, subjects were led to believe that all three stories were part of a pilot experiment, and were tested on all three by an experimenter who came into their classrooms. In the "different-context" condition, the subjects were told that only the first two stories were part of an experiment. After they performed the training stories, the experimenter left the classroom, and then their instructor gave them the radiation problem to solve as part of a "class demonstration." In addition, the radiation problem was given either immediately or 45 minutes after the training problems. Different classrooms of subjects participated in the four different combinations of conditions, and no subjects received hints that the radiation problem was related to the first two problems.

The results are presented in figure 11–3. When there was no delay between the first two problems and the radiation problem, there were equal amounts of transfer in the same- and different-context groups. However, when there was a 45-minute interval between the training and radiation problems, only subjects who tried to solve the radiation problem in the same context showed transfer. Subjects in the different-context condition showed no transfer after the 45-minute interval. Subjects did not see that the radiation problem was like the first two problems when the apparent relation among them was destroyed by changing the pretext for performing the radiation task. These results support the notion

FIGURE 11–3.

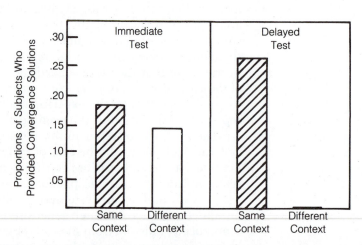

Proportion of subjects in Spencer and Weisberg's (1986) experiment who showed transfer when solving similar types of problems. When the test problem was given 45 minutes after the two training problems, subjects in the different-context condition, who were told that the training problems were part of an experiment but that the test problem was part of a class demonstration, showed no transfer from having previously solved the training problems. Subjects in the same-context condition, who were told that all three problems were part of an experiment, showed transfer with both the immediate test and the long delay.

that analogical reasoning is not readily generalized to new problems and situations. They also help define the conditions under which analogical transfer will and will not be obtained.

Given the research we have just described, a reasonable question to ask is, "What conditions allow a person to use analogies to solve problems in an efficient way?" Holyoak (1990; Holyoak, and Thagard, 1989) has developed a theory that describes the conditions under which successful analogical transfer will occur. According to Holyoak, having experience with the fortress problem will help a person solve the tumor problem only if the person finds the best set of correspondences between the original problem and the transfer problem. Holyoak calls the ways in which a person relates the elements of one problem to another *mapping*. In the fortress/tumor case, for example, the person trying to solve the problem needs to recognize that the goals of capturing the fortress and destroying the tumor correspond. Further, the person needs to realize that the rays' capacity to destroy corresponds to the army's ability to capture.

According to the theory, the correspondences that are noticed must be considered in a unified fashion. That is, the mapping or correspondence between the original problem and the target problem must have *structural consistency*, which means that the elements that correspond in the two problems need to be related to each other in a way that is consistent with other mappings.

Consider the structural mappings that are illustrated in figure 11–4. Holyoak assumes that if the perceived relationship of one pair of elements in the two problems is consistent, then the relationships among other elements also have to be consistent. If the problem solver notices the analogy between the fortress and the tumor, then capturing would have to correspond to destroying, and the destroyer (rays) would have to map onto the capturer,

FIGURE 11–4.

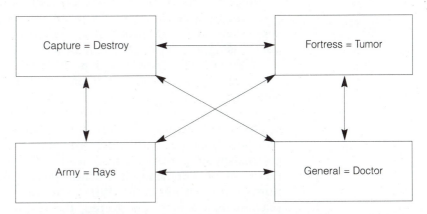

An outline of Holyoak's model of analogical correspondences between the tumor problem and the fortress problem.

which would be the army in this instance. The pattern of such analogical mappings would be structurally consistent.

The correspondences among the components of the two problems shown in figure 11–4 form a coherent set and thus support each other. Holyoak notes that his theory of structural consistency is similar to the model of word recognition by McClelland and Rumelhart (1981). As noted in chapter 7, their theory of word perception assumes a parallel examination of letters within a word such that knowing one letter increases the likelihood that other letters would be activated. That is, the activated letters would be consistent with what a person knows about the structure of particular words. The analogous process in a problem-solving task would be that the correspondence between elements of the two problems, say, army is the same as rays, increases the likelihood that a particular element will map onto another, such as the general corresponding to the doctor.

This part of Holyoak's model also is analogous to the word perception theory in another way. Holyoak assumes that being able to map a structure such as the army onto rays decreases the possibility that rays would be mapped onto the fortress. Likewise, the word perception theory notes that words can only have one first letter. Having a *t* as a first letter means that the word cannot have *k* as the first letter. In the current example, the correspondence between army and rays means that rays cannot correspond to the fortress or that the tumor cannot equal the army.

Holyoak believes that his theory of structural consistency helps to specify the conditions under which analogous solutions are easy or difficult. If a person is able to recognize one or two mappings, then the other consistencies will fall into place, and the problem should be solved. It is interesting to note that Holyoak's theory is itself an analogue of another theory; namely, the one devised by McClelland and Rumelhart (1981). Holyoak used analogical reasoning to solve a problem.

Recent experiments by Novick (1990) show that the amount of generalization depends on how problems are represented or conceptualized. If general problem-solving strategies, such as thinking about using a two-dimensional matrix as an aid to solution are valuable in solving one type of problem, then people will use the technique again on other problems that do not have analogous solutions.

If a researcher cannot find variables that control the presence or absence of the phenomenon, then an understanding of the topic will be hampered. Performing systematic and conceptual replications should permit a researcher to delineate the *boundary conditions* of a phenomenon: the conditions outside of which the phenomenon does not hold. When the variables that control a phenomenon can be discovered, the researcher can construct a better theory about it, for the relevant factors are known.

11.2 Experimental Topics and Research Illustrations

Topic: Experimental Control
Illustration: Functional Fixity

The topic of experimental control runs throughout this book, as it should, since it is crucial to all types of experimental research. The purpose of any experiment is to observe the effect of manipulation of certain variables—the independent variables—on the measurement of dependent variables. For a conclusion about the effect of an independent variable on a dependent variable to be sound, it is necessary that we gain a sufficient amount of experimental control over the situation to ensure that no other factor varies with the independent variable. In this book, these other variables are usually called control variables, although they are also referred to as extraneous variables, or even nuisance variables. If an extraneous variable is allowed to vary at the same time as the independent variable of interest, we cannot know whether the effect on the dependent variable is caused by variation in the independent variable, the extraneous variable, or both operating together. In such cases, we say that the two variables are confounded.

In the study of complex processes, there are often greater problems of experimental control than in other types of research. In the study of topics such as problem solving, there is frequently a great deal of variation in the measures taken on the dependent variable. We have already discussed some of the reasons for this. Since it is necessary to use between-subjects designs in much of this research, individual differences among subjects contribute greatly to the uncontrolled variation, or "error variance." Also, it may not be possible to tightly control all the nuisance variables that may affect a situation. Instead, they may be left to vary in an unsystematic way, since unsystematic variation will not affect one experimental condition more than another. Still, these randomly varying factors may serve to increase the variability of measurements.

Because of the effect of these variations on the dependent variable, detecting a reliable effect of the independent variable may be more difficult. One other reason for experimental control, then, is to reduce these extraneous sources of variation on the dependent variables. But given that they do occur and may be more prevalent in the study of problem solving and other complex processes, it becomes necessary to increase the number of observations in experimental conditions to get reliable results. For practical reasons that we have already discussed, this is not always possible. Therefore, employing as much experimental control over extraneous variables as can be mustered in these situations becomes even more important and desirable.

Our intent in discussing all these considerations is not to imply that solid research on interesting, complex processes is practically impossible. However, it is necessary to keep firmly in mind the difficulties one encounters in such research. Some experimental psychologists view research in these complex areas as relatively "sloppy," since it often lacks tight experimental control and employs relatively few observations in experimental conditions (leading to the possibility of unreliable results). It is as though some researchers in this area believe that the greater difficulty in studying complex psychological processes somehow justifies lesser, rather than greater, experimental control. But it is quite obvious that the problems inherent in studying complex processes can be overcome: we have instances of exemplary research in this area.

A good example is the research on *functional fixity* in problem solving. This work was begun in an important series of studies by Karl Duncker (1945, pp. 85–101). The general idea behind the concept is that if an object has recently been used in one particular way in a given situation, its use in a second, different way to solve a new problem is likely to be overlooked. Duncker invented a number of problems that he used to test this general idea; we will focus on only one, the well-known "box" problem.

Duncker's box problem. In the box problem, subjects were told that their task was to affix three small candles onto a door at eye level. The materials they were to use were placed on a table. Among other objects were several crucial ones: some tacks, matches, three small pasteboard boxes about the size of a matchbox, and, of course, the candles. The appropriate solution to the problem was to tack the boxes to the wall and use them as platforms on which the candles could be attached with some melted wax. In the control condition, the boxes were empty; but in the functional-fixity condition, the boxes were filled with the needed material. There were several candles in one, tacks in a second, and matches in a third. Thus in the latter condition, the function of the box as a container was to be "fixed" in the subjects' minds. This should have been less the case in the control condition, since the boxes were not used as containers. Duncker also employed a third condition, which we will refer to as the neutral-use condition. Here the boxes were also used as containers, but they contained neutral objects (such as buttons) not needed as parts of the solution.

A between-subjects design was necessary in this experiment, since once subjects had been exposed to the problem, they could not, for obvious reasons, be tested again in a different condition. In this particular experiment, Duncker employed only seven subjects in each condition. The results for the three conditions are reported in figure 11–5 as the percentage of subjects solving the problem in each condition. All seven subjects in the control condition solved the problem, but only 43 percent of the subjects in the functional-fixity condition (3 out of 7) were able to do so. In

FIGURE 11–5.

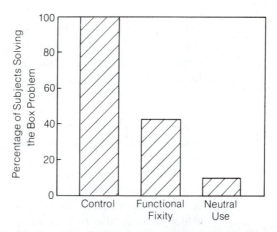

Percentage of subjects solving Duncker's box problem in three different experimental conditions. When subjects were given the boxes that contained material (the functional-fixity and neutral-use conditions), a smaller percentage was able to solve the problem than when the boxes were given to them empty (control). Presumably, in the former cases the function of the box was "fixed" as a container, and thus subjects did not as readily think of the boxes as potential platforms for the candles.

the neutral-use condition, only one subject (14 percent) was able to solve the problem. Of course, these differences among conditions were not evaluated statistically, but the difference between the control and functional-fixity conditions was replicated with four other problems. The difference between the functional-fixity and neutral-use conditions was replicated with two independent groups solving one other problem. The functional-fixity effect has since been replicated a number of times, so we can be assured it is reliable, despite the small number of subjects used in the original studies.

Duncker's findings can be interpreted within the framework of Gestalt principles of problem solving, discussed earlier in this chapter. Recall that Gestaltists believed that many problems are solved through insight, or a sudden restructuring of the problem in a way that leads to the correct solution. In Duncker's experiment, subjects in the functional-fixity condition seemed unable to overcome the bias induced by seeing all the objects serving their ordinary functions and could not restructure their perceptions to see different uses for the objects.

Adamson's replication. A study by Adamson (1952) is interesting in this regard. He sought to replicate Duncker's original experiment by comparing subjects in the functional-fixity and control conditions on the solution to three problems. These included the box problem we have already discussed, as well as two others, referred to as the paper clip problem and the gimlet problem. (The exact nature of these problems need not concern us.) In each situation, the comparison was between subjects who had previous experience with an object (and who thus should have been thinking of the function of the object as fixed) and control subjects for whom this was not the case. Adamson was primarily concerned about how few subjects were used in Duncker's original experiment, so he used between twenty-six and twenty-nine subjects in each of his six separate conditions (3 problems × 2 experimental conditions). The dependent measures he used were the percentage of subjects who were able to solve the problem in the twenty-minute period and the amount of time it took successful subjects to solve the problem.

The results are quite instructive. When Adamson used Duncker's dependent measure of percentage of subjects who were able to solve the problem, he was able to replicate the functional-fixity effect in only the box problem. A full 86 percent of the control subjects, but only 41 percent of the subjects in the functional-fixity condition, were able to solve the box problem. However, performance on the other two problems was impossible to interpret with this measure, because of *ceiling effects* in both conditions. That is, almost all subjects in both conditions solved the problem, so performance did not differ; for both problems, it approached 100 percent in each condition. This problem is discussed in the "Introducing the Variables" section in this chapter (see also chapter 10); once again, we are not justified in concluding that there was no difference between the two conditions under these circumstances. The conclusion, rather, is that the dependent variable was not sufficiently sensitive to allow detection of any possible differences between conditions.

Fortunately, Adamson also used a second dependent measure. He also measured how long it took to solve the problems; what is usually called *latency*. The results, in terms of mean time to solution for subjects in the two conditions, are presented in figure 11–6 for both the gimlet and the paperclip problems. Only data concerning subjects who actually solved the problems are included. Although almost all subjects were able to solve the problems, the amount of time it took to do so varied greatly in the two conditions, as is apparent from figure 11–6. In each case, subjects in the control condition solved the problem much faster than subjects in the experimental (functional-fixity) condition. Thus, having the function of the objects fixed by the way the problem was presented slowed, but did not prevent, solution to the problem. The important point is that functional fixity was demonstrated in all three of Adamson's problems, but in two of them it was necessary to use a latency measure that was more sensitive than simply the percentage of subjects solving the problem.

Why was Adamson unable to replicate Duncker's results with the gimlet and paperclip problems, when the percentage of subjects solving the problem was the dependent measure? Adamson suggests that he simply may have had more able subjects, which is certainly a possibility. But another real possibility is that Adamson allowed twenty minutes for his subjects to solve the problem, whereas

FIGURE 11–6.

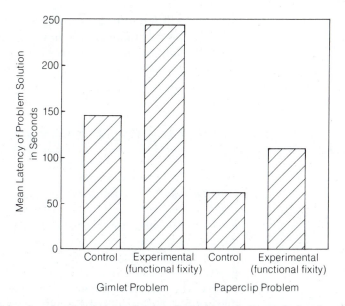

Time taken to solve the gimlet and paperclip problems in the control and experimental (functional-fixity) conditions of Adamson's (1952) experiment. It took subjects in the functional-fixity condition longer to solve the problems than the controls.

Duncker seems to have allowed much less time, though it varied somewhat from individual to individual, depending on the progress of each toward a solution.

The Adamson study is an excellent example of a systematic, well-controlled replication that served to clean up an original demonstration of an interesting phenomenon. Such replications are quite valuable, especially since they often lead to new knowledge on the generality of the phenomenon in question. However, after a novel phenomenon has been replicated once or twice in independent laboratories, further research effort directed at simple replications is to be discouraged. (The chances are excellent that journal editors would not see fit to publish further studies of direct or even systematic replications at this point.) The research effort must turn to developing an understanding of the factors that influence the phenomenon and developing a theory or model of the psychological processes involved.

In the area of functional fixity, Glucksberg and his associates have provided systematic research on the effect of verbalization and labeling on functional fixity (Glucksberg and Weisberg, 1966; Glucksberg and Danks, 1967, 1968). For example, it has been found that when objects in the candle problem are given verbal labels (candle, tacks, box, matches) when shown to the subjects, the problem is solved by more subjects than when no labels are given. The trick is to have the subjects think of the box not merely as a container of tacks, but as a separate object capable of being used to solve the problem. Labeling the objects aids this process. As Glucksberg has pointed out, "It is not the way the world *is* that influences what we do as much as it is *how we represent* that world symbolically" (1966, p. 26: italics are Glucksberg's).

11.3 Experimental Topics and Research Illustrations

Topic: Verbal Reports
Illustration: Overconfidence in Judgments

Early in the history of experimental psychology, there was an emphasis on the use of introspective reports as a method for discovering the structure of the mind. As is discussed in appendix A, introspection was not a casual, moody reflection on the contents of the mind during some experience or other, but a rigorous, methodical technique of describing experience. Its basic problem was one of reliability: investigators who used introspection in different psychology laboratories often arrived at different conclusions about the structure of the mind. The method would probably have fallen into disuse for this reason alone, but its departure from psychology was hastened by Watson's (1913) attack on the entire enterprise of structural psychology and by the subsequent rise of behaviorism. Since introspection has a technical meaning in the vocabulary of structural psychology, we will use the term *verbal report* to refer to the use of subjects' reports in psychological experiments (see chapter 7 also). These are sometimes called *subjective reports,* as well.

Despite the success of behaviorism in sweeping away the structural approach, the use of the subjective report has kept its place in psychology. In fact, the use of verbal report is quite in accord with the scientific rules of behaviorists, since verbal reports are, of course, overt behavior. In fact, Watson, the founder of behaviorism, states this quite clearly in a section called "The Behaviorist's Platform" in *Behaviorism:*

> The behaviorist asks: Why don't we make what we can *observe* the real field of psychology? Let us limit ourselves to things that can be observed, and formulate laws concerning only those things. Now what can we observe? We can observe *behavior—what the organism does or says.* And let us point out at once: that *saying* is doing—that is, *behaving.* Speaking overtly or to ourselves (thinking) is just as objective a type of behavior as baseball. (1925, p. 6: italics are Watson's)

The use of verbal report, then, was endorsed by the founder of behaviorism. But as Spence (1948) pointed out, the use of verbal report is very different for structuralist and behaviorist psychologists. For the former, introspective reports are facts or data about internal mental events that are thought to directly mirror these events. For behaviorists, on the other hand, verbal reports are simply one type of behavior that may be worth studying as a dependent variable. They are to be considered no more nor less worthwhile or "real" a priori than any other type of response or dependent variable (see chapter 7). If one wants to use verbal reports as evidence for some particular mental construct, they are to be considered as only one of several needed converging operations. Verbal reports are, of course, more likely to be useful in certain areas of psychology than others. Research on thinking is one area in which extensive use is made of verbal reports.

One critical component in thinking is the ability to evaluate one's knowledge. A number of experiments have explored the *feeling-of-knowing* phenomenon, first studied systematically by Hart (1965). A representative experiment is one by Freedman and Landauer (1966). Subjects were given a long series of general-knowledge questions (What is the capitol of Ecuador? Who was the fifth president of the United States?) and asked to provide answers. For each question for which subjects could not provide an answer, they were asked to rate on a four-point scale how confident they were that they could recognize the answer if it were presented with similar alternatives. The four judgments were "definitely know" the answer; "probably know" it; "probably don't know" it; and "definitely don't know" it. After making these feeling-of-knowing judgments, subjects were given the questions again and asked to pick the correct answer from among six alternatives.

The subjects recognized 73 percent of the items that they had judged they would definitely know; 61 percent they had said they would probably know; and 51 percent and 35 percent of the answers to questions they had thought they either probably or definitely did not know. The fact that the ratings are generally correlated with later recognition performance may be taken as an indication that people's subjective feelings of what they know (following a failure of recall) are fairly accurate. Other experiments have revealed a similar feeling-of-knowing effect (for example, Schacter, 1983). However, one other interesting feature of the data is that even when people were convinced they knew the answer to a question, they were able to respond correctly only 73 percent of the time. Obviously, the ability to monitor the state of one's knowledge is rather imperfect. Often we seem overly confident that we know something when in fact we do not, or at least cannot remember it at the time we are tested.

Other studies using slightly different techniques have shown that people have this tendency to be overly confident of their knowledge. One technique is to ask people to answer questions with two alternative answers, and then ask them to rate the probability of their having answered them correctly. Suppose you were given the following item: "Bile pigments accumulate as a result of a condition known as (a) jaundice (b) gangrene." After choosing the answer you believed to be correct, you would then be asked to estimate the probability from .50 to 1.00 that you are in fact correct. (Since there are two alternatives, .50 is chance.) Lichtenstein and Fischhoff (1977) reported that although there was a general correlation between judgments of confidence and accuracy, subjects were generally much more confident than warranted by their knowledge. For example, for items that subjects estimated they would answer correctly 80 percent of the time, the actual accuracy was only .70. This overconfidence does not seem to result from subjects' not taking the task very seriously, for other studies have reported the same tendency even when subjects are given elaborate instructions emphasizing accuracy, and when they are given the opportunity to bet on their answers with the possibility of losing money as a result (Fischhoff, Slovic, and Lichtenstein, 1977).

These studies show that although verbal reports of our factual knowledge are generally correlated with that knowledge, they are by no means perfect reflections of what we know. This points out a shortcoming of retrospective verbal reports of cognitive processes. The vagaries of memory may produce an inaccurate or biased judgment of what we thought while performing some act. Many factors—motivational, emotional, social—may lessen the accuracy of verbal reports. Indeed, researchers in some areas have long been leery of accepting verbal reports at face value.

Nisbett and Wilson (1977) reviewed many experiments that related individuals' verbal reports to their behavior in experimental situations and reached the rather startling conclusion that "there may be little or no direct introspective awareness to higher order cognitive processes" (p. 231). They used many lines of evidence to draw this conclusion; one general type involves experiments comparing performance of people in between-subjects designs. Some experimental variable is manipulated and shown to have a strong influence on behavior; later, subjects in the different groups are asked why they responded the way they did. If subjects are consciously aware of the forces guiding their behavior, they should report the influence of the independent variable as a critical determinant of their performance. In many cases reviewed by Nisbett and Wilson, subjects could not do this and, in addition, often denied that the independent variable could have affected them, even when the experimenter suggested it as a possibility.

Research on bystander intervention also illustrates this phenomenon (see chapters 3 and 13). The question asked in this research is this: Under what conditions will an individual help another person who is in distress? In experimental studies by social psychologists, an "emergency" is standardized and subjects are exposed to it under varying conditions. The primary dependent measures are the percentage of subjects helping the victim in each condition and the speed with which they help. One of the most startling effects in such studies is seen when the experimenter varies the number of other people present in the emergency situation. As the number of other people increases, the subject becomes less likely to help the victim.

Many hypotheses have been put forth to account for this fact, but the interesting point for present purposes involves the responses that subjects give when asked about their behavior in the situation. Latané and Darley, who were responsible for the early work in this area, systematically asked their subjects whether they thought the presence of other people had influenced their behavior in the situation.

> We asked this question every way we know how: subtly, directly, tactfully, bluntly. Always we got the same answer. Subjects persistently claimed that their behavior was not influenced by the other people present. This denial occurred in the face of results showing that the presence of others did inhibit helping. (Latané and Darley, 1970, p. 241)

Nisbett and Wilson (1977) used such reports as the basis for their claim that people have no direct introspective access to the cognitive processes that mediate behavior. A corollary of this position would seem to be that subjective reports are generally inaccurate as descriptions of cognitive events. (Nisbett and Wilson argue that even when such reports are accurate, they may be based on general knowledge and not on some special self-knowledge.) Others argue that Nisbett and Wilson's position is too extreme (see Ericsson and Simon, 1979; Smith and Miller, 1978). They maintain that under many conditions people can be shown to have generally accurate access to their mental states. After all, the feeling-of-knowing studies discussed earlier showed that subjects are generally accurate in judging whether they know information, even when they cannot recall it. Many of the studies described by Nisbett and Wilson had features such as between-subjects designs and reports from subjects after the task was completed. Subjects likely would show better awareness if they participated in experiments that used within-subjects designs, since they would be exposed to the full range of the independent variable. Similarly, if subjects were asked to make reports during the actual performance of a task (for example, by reporting out loud to the experimenter), reports might be more accurate. Using retrospective reports rather than ones taken "on line" makes subjects rely on fallible memory; perhaps they knew what they were doing at the time they were doing it, but then forgot (or distorted) their reasons later.

Janet Metcalfe (1986) conducted an experiment in which she obtained such on-line reports. Metcalfe wondered whether people who are trying to solve certain types of problems experience premonitions that they are approaching the solution, or the solution comes to them suddenly. Notice that this question relates to the issue of trial-and-error versus insight learning, discussed at the beginning of this chapter. Metcalfe asked subjects to solve a variety of problems, such as anagrams (unscrambling the letters in scrambled words, such as *valert* for *travel*) and other brainteasers. As they worked on the problems, a click sounded every 10 seconds; at each click, subjects rated how close they thought they were to solving the problem by writing a number from 0 to 10. A 0 meant they were very "cold" and had no idea what the solution was; intermediate values meant they felt they were getting "warm"; and a 10 meant they had solved the problem, at which point they wrote the solution.

Metcalfe reasoned that if problem solving proceeds in a gradual trial-and-error fashion, people will achieve the solutions step by step, and their "feeling-of-warmth" ratings will get increasingly high as they approach the solution. On the other hand, if people solve problems through a sudden insight, then their feelings of warmth should stay relatively low and constant during the intervals preceding the solution and then jump to a 10 when they solve the problem. Finally, if people can accurately assess whether they are reaching a correct solution, then the "feeling-of-warmth" judgments should be higher preceding correct than preceding incorrect answers.

To summarize, the experiment addressed two interesting questions. First, do people have the subjective feeling that they solve problems gradually, or do they discover the answers in a flash of insight? Second, do people have accurate subjective premonitions that they are successfully reaching a problem solution? That is, do they know when their line of reasoning is leading to a correct solution?

The results of Metcalfe's experiment were quite interesting. First of all, the "feelings-of-warmth" ratings that subjects gave tended to follow an insight pattern. That is, while trying to solve the problems, subjects felt relatively "cold" and did not indicate that they were getting warmer or closer to the solution until the interval in which they solved the problem. Therefore, for the type of problems she used, people tended to achieve the solutions with rather sudden insights. The most surprising result, however, was that the subjects' feeling-of-warmth judgments were very inaccurate. That is, when subjects indicated that they thought they were very close to a solution (i.e., their warmth ratings were relatively high), they actually were more likely to give an incorrect than a correct solution! Thus, Metcalfe's experiment shows that people's subjective intuitions about whether they will solve a problem may not be reliable. Again, subjective reports must be interpreted cautiously (see chapter 7, as well).

Where do all these considerations leave us in evaluating the use of subjective verbal reports as a research tool? Although the issue is complex, we can venture a few summary statements. First, it is probably unwise in many instances to place too much emphasis on verbal reports, by using them, for example, as the sole dependent measure in an experiment. Some psychologists have suggested that for experiments that might be impractical or unethical to conduct, researchers should describe the procedure and various conditions to subjects and have subjects say how they would react (for example, Brown, 1962; Kelman, 1966). However, the assumption that one's predictions while role-playing always (or even usually) accurately reflect how one will behave when placed in an actual situation seems risky. Second, verbal reports may very well be useful in some situations, but a researcher will have to analyze each situation carefully to determine the potential for error in using verbal reports. Most researchers consider subjective reports as useful extra sources of information in experiments, but not as the primary dependent variable of interest. However, Ericsson and Simon (1979) detail conditions under which they believe verbal reports can serve as primary data. Finally, we believe that verbal reports can serve as interesting dependent measures, whether or not such reports accurately reflect cognitive states of the individual. Even if Nisbett and Wilson are correct in asserting that people have little or no accurate introspective awareness of the causes of their behavior, studying people's beliefs and reports about those causes would be of interest in itself.

From Problem to Experiment: The Nuts and Bolts

Problem: Incubation in Problem Solving

Many writers on the subject of thinking and problem solving have described a rather mysterious process that seems to aid in solving problems. Consider the following account of the French mathematician, Henri Poincaré. (The mathematical terms in the quotation should not dismay you; just examine the passage for the psychological principle involved.)

> Just at this time I left Caen, where I was then living, to go on a geologic excursion under the auspices of the school of mines. The changes of travel made me forget my mathematical work. Having reached Coutances, we entered an omnibus to go some place or other. At the moment when I put my foot on the step the idea came to me, without anything in my former thoughts seeming to have paved the way for it, that the transformations I had used to define the Fuchsian functions were identical with those of non-Euclidean geometry. I did not verify the idea; I should not have the time, as, upon taking my seat in the omnibus, I went on with a conversation already commenced, but I felt a perfect certainty. On my return to Caen, for conscience's sake I verified the result at my leisure.
>
> Then I turned my attention to the study of some arithmetical questions apparently without much success and without a suspicion of my connection with my preceding researches. Disgusted with my failure, I went to spend a few days at the seaside, and thought of something else. One morning, walking on the bluff, the idea came to me, with just the same characteristics of brevity, suddenness, and immediate certainty,

that the arithmetic transformations of indeterminate ternary quadratic forms were identical with those of non-Euclidean geometry. . . .

I shall limit myself to this single example; it is useless to multiply them. In regard to my other researches I would have to say analogous things. . . .

Most striking at first is this appearance of sudden illumination, a manifest sign of long, unconscious prior work. The role of this unconscious work in mathematical invention appears to me incontestable. (Poincaré, 1929, p. 388)

There are many reports of similar experiences from writers, mathematicians, and scientists. Koestler (1964) cited several examples of a problem's being solved in a sudden flash of illumination after all apparent progress on it had ceased, and in fact the solver had turned to other matters. (Recall the similar appearance in Köhler's chimps.) But what are we to make of these reports? How are they to be evaluated? Can we accept them as useful evidence on the nature of thought? If so, then apparently the search for problem solutions can proceed without conscious attention; the mind may inexorably grind away at solving a problem without any conscious direction on the part of its owner.

Experimental psychologists are unlikely to be convinced by these reports that such a process is central to thought, rather than representing a more or less rare and curious accident. Instead, they are likely to consider such reports as hypotheses in need of experimental tests. On the basis of his own intuitions, Poincaré outlined four stages in the thought process. First is *preparation*, during which a person becomes immersed in trying to solve a problem and learns the numerous relevant facts and considerations. Second is *incubation*, during which a person turns to other matters after failing to solve the problem. The problem is said to incubate, much as eggs do while a hen sits on them. (The same idea is expressed when you say "Let me sit on it a while.") Next comes the stage of *illumination* (which Köhler calls *insight*), when the idea is hatched. Finally comes the stage of *verification*, when the solution to the problem must be carefully checked. These stages were identified on the basis of intuition and have thus been given only loose verbal definitions.

Although Poincaré collected many instances that seemed to confirm his theory of problem solving—and in particular the incubation process—as we all know, an example or two can be found to support almost any idea or theory, no matter how silly. And surely we can find many counterexamples in which problems are solved without incubation and sudden illumination. Instead of providing anecdotes, we must subject the concept of incubation to experimental test.

Problem: *Can we find evidence for the concept of incubation?*

At present, this concept is rather fuzzy. We need to provide it with a more precise operational definition, so we will know exactly what we are looking for. Let us examine a definition by Posner (1973): "*Incubation* refers to an increase in the likelihood of successfully solving a problem that results from placing a delay between the period of intense work which initiates the problem solution and another period of conscious effort which finalizes the solution" (p. 171). This is somewhat precise, but a number of points still must be specified. In fact, it is a rather curious operational definition, since we do not even know if the defined phenomenon exists at this point! What we have done, really, is to suggest a hypothetical operational definition that can serve as the hypothesis of an experiment in search of the concept.

Hypothesis: *Subjects who are allowed a break between two periods of work on solving a problem will be more likely to eventually find a solution (or to find one faster) than subjects not provided a break.*

Further, the longer the break, the more likely that the subjects will find the solution (and find it faster), at least up to some limit.

There remain, as always, a host of considerations to which we must turn our attention. How long should we allow subjects to solve the problem? Two 15-minute periods, or a total of 30 minutes, might be appropriate. The primary independent variable is the delay that is to be introduced between the two periods of work on the problem. At a minimum, we would want three independent conditions, so appropriate delays might be 0, 15, or 30 minutes between the two work periods. (Of course more conditions with a wider range of delay intervals might be appropriate, too.) The experiment should probably employ a between-subjects design, since the amount of time required for subjects to serve in all three conditions would be prohibitive. The number of subjects to serve in each condition would depend on the available resources, but should be as great as possible. A minimum of 20 may be sufficient, but the power of statistical tests based on this small a sample would not be great. It would be much better to have 75 or 100 subjects per condition. Since groups of subjects could be tested rather than individuals, the amount of effort in testing 300 subjects would not be prohibitive, if this many people were available. The length of the entire procedure would vary from perhaps 45 minutes in the zero-delay condition to 75 minutes in the 30-minute delay condition.

Another important consideration is the type of problem to be used. It would probably be best to test subjects in the three conditions on more than one problem to ensure that the phenomenon, if found at all, is not specific to only one problem. If 75 subjects were used in each condition, 25 could be tested on each of three problems. It would be necessary to pretest the problems on subjects similar to those to be used in the experiment to ensure that (1) very few subjects could solve the problems in 15 minutes, or before the independent variable is introduced; and (2) around half (at least) could solve the problem in 30 minutes with no delay. The latter requirement is to guard against floor effects, or performance too poor to allow manipulation of the independent variable to reveal any effect. A sample problem might be the following:

> A man had four chains, each three links long. He wanted to join the four chains into a single closed chain. Having a link opened cost 2 cents, and having a link closed cost 3 cents. The man had his chains joined into a closed chain for 15 cents. How did he do it?

Another consideration is what subjects should be doing during the delay intervals. Obviously, they should not simply be allowed to sit there and mull over the problem, since then they are essentially not given a delay at all. Subjects should be occupied with mental arithmetic problems or the like; it might even be wise to lead them to believe, at the beginning of the break, that they are going on to a new phase of the experiment and will not be returning to the problem they have failed to solve. This would ensure that subjects would not be trying to devote some attention to the problem while working on the filler activity.

The primary dependent measures would be the percentage of subjects in each condition who solved the problem and the amount of time it took them to do so. If the problems were selected carefully enough so that there were several solutions, the quality of solutions might also be evaluated. Even if the problems did not have this feature, subjects could be asked at the end of the second 15-minute period to write out how they were attempting to solve the problem, and the quality of these attempts could be evaluated to see whether the different conditions affected the quality of the terminal-solution attempts. The evaluations, of course, should be made by someone who does not know the conditions of the subjects (that is, someone who is blind with respect to conditions).

These are the essentials, then, for an experiment on incubation. The predictions are that subjects who experience a delay between the two 15-minute periods of working on the problem will solve the problem more often (and will do so faster) than subjects who work on the problem continually for 30 minutes. Also, subjects who have a 30-minute break should achieve a solution more often (and do so faster) than those who have the shorter, 15-minute break.

Experiments such as this can make real contributions to the understanding of incubation. Perhaps the best evidence for incubation comes from a doctoral dissertation by Silveira (1971), which is a somewhat more complicated version of the type of experiment we have just outlined here. It is discussed briefly in Posner's book (1973, pp. 169–175). However, a similar experiment by Olton and Johnson (1976) failed to find any evidence for incubation.

If the phenomenon of incubation has been established experimentally, this is only the beginning of our attempts to understand it. What factors influence incubation? What kind of psychological theory could explain it? Saying that it is caused by "unconscious thought processes" is as bad as saying nothing at all. Actually, it might even be worse, since it gives the illusion of providing an explanation when, in fact, it does nothing of the kind. Can you think of explicit, testable hypotheses that could account for incubation? This is the path we must take to even begin to understand the phenomenon.

(By the way, to solve the chain problem, the man opened all the links in one of the chains—3 × 2 cents = 6 cents—and then used the three open loops to join the remaining three chains together—3 closed at 3 cents each, for 9 cents.)

Summary

1. Studies of complex psychological processes, such as thinking and problem solving, have special problems in terms of reliability of results and experimental control. One main problem concerns the relatively great variability that is likely to occur in observations under different experimental conditions. The individual differences that people exhibit in performing a complex task, such as solving a problem, are apt to be much greater than in performing simpler tasks.

2. In complex experiments, it is often necessary to use between-subjects designs, in which an independent group of subjects serves in each experimental condition. Unfortunately, less control over variance introduced by differences between subjects is possible than in within-subjects designs. A partial solution to these problems is to obtain as many observations per condition as possible to produce stable results, and to control as tightly as feasible all extraneous variables, so they will not increase the variability within conditions.

3. Reliability of results from a single experiment can be assessed through the logic of statistical inference by employing appropriate statistical tests. Such tests allow us to assess how likely it is that the effect of some experimental variable is actually caused by the operation of that variable and not random (chance) factors.

4. Experimental reliability, which is preferred to statistical reliability by many psychologists, refers to actual replicability of experiments. Three types are identified. In direct replications, the attempt is to repeat the experiment as exactly as possible to see whether the same results will be obtained a second time. Systematic replications involve changing variables not thought to be critical to the phenomenon under consideration to make sure it survives such changes. Conceptual replications attempt to demonstrate the phenomenon with a wholly new paradigm or set of experimental conditions.

5. Systematic and conceptual replications are also concerned with generality of results. Do results of an experiment generalize

across the rather slight changes in procedure in systematic replications and the greater changes in procedure in conceptual replications? Often, advances in understanding a phenomenon are enhanced when researchers are able to find conditions under which the phenomenon does not replicate. When such boundary conditions are established and the researcher understands what factors control the presence or absence of the phenomenon, better theories can be constructed.

6. Subjective reports are verbal reports about people's awareness of their cognitive processes. They are sometimes used in the study of thinking, but caution must be exercised in their use. In some instances, people are overly confident in judgments of their knowledge. In experiments on various complex judgments, people provided erroneous subjective impressions regarding the influence of particular variables which were shown to actually control their behavior. Verbal reports are sometimes useful in psychological research, but their trustworthiness will likely vary with the topic being studied.

KEY TERMS

analogy
boundary conditions
ceiling effect
conceptual replication
direct replication
experimental control
experimental reliability
extraneous variables
feeling of knowing
functional fixity
incubation

insight
latency
law of effect
mapping
reliability
statistical reliability
structural consistency
systematic replication
subjective report
thought
verbal report

DISCUSSION QUESTIONS

1. A researcher in the biology department of your university has just demonstrated extrasensory perception (ESP) in rats. The rats were placed in a maze, where they had to choose between two possible runways, one of which led to food. The rats could not see or smell the food at the place in the maze where they had to make their decision, and the runway in which the experimenter put the food varied randomly from trial to trial. Over a series of fifty trials, the researcher found that there were two rats out of one hundred tested that seemed to perform better than would be expected on the basis of chance. One picked the correct runway 64 percent of the time; the other picked it 66 percent of the time (with chance being 50 percent). Which of the two following tests would be more convincing to you as confirmation of these rats having ESP? (a) The researcher performs statistical tests showing that the two rats had indeed performed better than chance in making their choices; or (b) a

different researcher tests the two rats on several hundred more trials and does succeed in replicating the first researcher's findings. Defend your choice. If you were the second researcher, what safeguards would you introduce into the experiment to ensure that the rats were not using sensory cues to solve the problem (assuming the rats again performed above chance)?

2. After seeing the results of the first experiment (namely, two out of a hundred rats apparently scored better than chance on the test of extrasensory perception), we ask the experimenter how many of the rats scored *below* chance by 10 percent or more. The researcher reports that three did, and says he is fascinated by this new discovery, which seems to indicate that some rats have "negative extrasensory perception." What do you, as a dispassionate observer, conclude about these claims?

3. Distinguish among direct replications, systematic replications, and conceptual replications. Should the three types be considered as qualitatively different, or do they lie on a continuum? If they lie on a continuum, what dimension underlies it?

4. The reward system in science discourages replications of other people's work. Researchers are rewarded much more for novel contributions than for "merely repeating" the work of others. Some have argued that this reward system tends to create fragmentation and disarray in many areas of psychology, because people are rewarded for going their own way and (sometimes) ignoring progress in other closely related areas. Thus, basic phenomena will often be unreplicated. Do you think replication should be more strongly encouraged? If so, how?

5. Many psychological journals are encouraging researchers to report a series of experiments about some phenomenon, rather than a single experiment. Do you think this is a good idea? If so, why? What dangers might be inherent in requiring that research reports contain numerous experiments?

6. Verbal reports are likely to be more useful in some areas of psychology than in others. For each of the following topics, discuss the pros and cons of using verbal reports. In those cases which you think verbal reports cannot be used, suggest better methods: (a) studying strategies by which people remember their childhood experiences when asked to do so; (b) studying sexual behavior of college students; (c) studying people's mental processes that occur when they decide to buy one product rather than another; (d) studying the reasons that one person likes another; and (e) studying what factors affect visual illusions.

Missionaries and Cannibals

TRY TO SOLVE THE following problem, which is called *The Missionaries and Cannibals Problem.*

> Three missionaries and three cannibals want to cross from the left side of a river to the right. The boat they have can carry only two people at a time. Both the missionaries and the cannibals can use the boat. At no time can the number of cannibals be greater than the number of missionaries on either side of the river, because if the missionaries are outnumbered they will be eaten. Your problem is to find the fewest number of crossings that will allow the missionaries and the cannibals to cross the river safely. You will find it helpful to number your crossings on a piece of paper. Each move should indicate who is on each bank of the river, and who is travelling in the boat. Before reading on, work at solving this problem.

This problem has been analyzed by many cognitive psychologists, in particular, Newell and Simon (1972). The minimum number of moves to solve this problem is eleven crossings, but most people take many more moves than this. The optimal sequence of moves is illustrated in figure 11–7, and we expect that you started to have real difficulty around move number 6. This is because most people are reluctant to move a missionary and a cannibal back to the left bank of the river in move 6.

The reluctance to return people to the original side of the river reflects the general tendency in problem solving to constantly strive toward the goal and not backtrack. This general strategy of constantly moving toward the goal is called *means-ends-analysis* and with some important modifications has been implemented in a computer program called the *General Problem Solver* or *GPS* by Newell and Simon. The major important tactic written into GPS was to allow subgoals. Instead of always trying to reduce the difference between the current state of affairs and problem solution (as in a strict means-ends strategy), GPS generated subgoals. In the missionaries-and-cannibals problem, the problem can be solved

FIGURE 11–7. Optimal solution to the missionaries (m) and cannibals (c) problem.

Move	People on Left Bank	Procedure	People on Right Bank
	mmm		
	ccc START		
1	mmm	cc	
	c	→	cc
2	mmm	c	
	cc	←	c
3	mmm	cc	
		→	ccc
4	mmm	c	
	c	←	cc
5	m	mm	mm
	c	→	cc
6	mm	mc	m
	cc	←	c
7		mm	mmm
	cc	→	c
8		c	mmm
	ccc	←	
9		cc	mmm
	c	→	cc
10		c	mmm
	cc	←	c
11		cc	mmm
		→	ccc GOAL

by getting all of the cannibals across the river first. If that subgoal is attained, then the main goal of having everyone on the right bank might be easier to see. Similarly, you might have guessed that if you made it to move 8, where all the missionaries are on the right bank of the river, then the solution is at hand.

When subgoals were programmed into GPS, it was able to solve the missionaries-and-cannibals problem as well as several other types of problems. GPS is often viewed as an important step in developing artificial intelligence and understanding natural intelligence, topics that are examined in the next chapter.

12

Individual Differences and Development

Don't let us forget that the causes of human actions are usually immeasurably more complex and varied than our subsequent explanations of them.

—DOSTOEVSKY

As THIS IS BEING WRITTEN (1990), Balamurati Krishna Ambati is a third-year student at New York University. He is a premedical student who enjoys chess, basketball, and various kinds of biological research. What distinguishes Balamurati from other undergraduates? Well, for one thing, he is twelve years old. For another, he hopes to become the youngest graduate of a medical school. Balamurati is a child prodigy who mastered calculus at age four. His grade point average and his test scores indicate that he should graduate from medical school prior to his eighteenth birthday (Stanley, 1990).

Clearly, Balamurati is different from most students, who might begin medical school at age twenty-two and finally finish in their mid-twenties. Why is Balamurati nearly ten years ahead of the typical medical school student? How and why did he develop so quickly that he is now going to school with students much older than he? These sorts of questions are addressed by psychologists interested in individual differences and development. In this chapter, we will examine some methodological issues relevant to undertaking research on how people differ and develop.

The study of individual differences began because of important practical decisions that had to be made about people, but it is a topic that has been relatively ignored by experimental psychologists, who are primarily interested in finding general laws and explanations for behavior. Investigation of individual differences is really just getting under way by psychologists who employ experimental methods, though it has long been a topic of concern for psychologists with more practical and applied interests.

The experimental investigation of individual differences illustrates the need for *reliability* of measures of individual characteristics. If individuals' decisions concerning future action are to be based on their particular mental abilities, interests, and ways of responding to events, then measures of these must yield similar results on different test occasions. In addition, the characteristics in which a psychologist is interested need to be defined in a way that can be communicated to others. It would be unreasonable to expect consistent measures of intelligence if everyone who measured it used a different definition of intelligence. The most useful kind of definition, because it is the most easily communicated, describes a procedure for producing and measuring the characteristic of interest. Such procedures are called *operational definitions* and are a necessary component of all research. When people are separated into classes on the basis of the operational definitions and then these classes of people are studied in experimental settings, they are referred to as *subject variables*. Examples of subject variables are age, intelligence, sex, degree of neuroticism, or any characteristic of people that can be specified in a precise manner. Age is a subject variable of particular interest to developmental psychologists, who study changes in behavior across the life span. Later in the chapter, we consider problems associated with studying age-related changes.

Once an investigator has operationally defined an individual characteristic and found the measure to be reliable, she or he may then wish to change that characteristic through some type of learning experience. One of the hazards in interpreting such a change is known as *regression to the mean*, which may lead an investigator to believe a change has been produced when in fact it has not, or vice versa. In this chapter, we will discuss reliability, operational definitions, subject variables, and regression in the context of research on individual differences and development.

Analytical Versus Empirical Approaches to Individual Differences

A general issue in science, and particularly in the psychology of individual differences, concerns the best method for deriving predictions of future events. Two methods of approaching the problem of prediction are the analytical and the empirical, which are equivalent to the deductive and inductive approaches discussed in chapter 1. Analytical approaches attempt to predict events on the basis of a theoretical understanding or model of the causes of those events. Empirical approaches attempt to achieve predictive power not by specifying a causal model, but by carefully observing the events that tend to accompany those events they wish to predict. Thus, the appearance of large cumulus clouds could lead one to predict rain, if one understands that such clouds contain moisture and knows that the conditions are right for condensing that moisture into drops heavy enough to be pulled to earth by gravity (an analytical approach to meteorology). The same clouds could lead one to predict the same thing if one observes that rain often falls when large cumulus clouds are present in the sky (an empirical approach to meteorology).

The Empirical Approach

The *empirical approach* aims to achieve the greatest degree of predictive precision possible by any means available. This usually involves a search for any measure or combination of measures that will predict the events in question. The traditional intelligence test given to groups of schoolchildren is an example of this approach to prediction. As noted in chapter 1, the French government early in this century commissioned Alfred Binet and Theodore Simon to devise tests that would determine which children could profit from an education and which could not. Thus, the original basis for intelligence tests, and the one still used today, is how well the tests can predict performance in school. As normal children develop, they should be able to handle more difficult problems. So, younger children who do well on questions devised for older ones are thought to be intelligent; those who do not perform up to their age level are considered to be duller than average. Binet and Simon employed tests of memory, comprehension, attention, and the like, but the logic is the same for all tasks. If children's success in school were most highly correlated with the number of birthday candles they could blow out and how well they liked spinach on a 1 to 7 scale, then these measures would *operationally define* intelligence: the ability to succeed in school. Children would be assigned to fast or slow classes, and directed toward trade schools or colleges, on the basis of these measures. If you were to object to the proposition that these measures reflect intelligence, the test designers would probably reply, "Call it whatever you like, but what it does is accurately predict success in school."

Intelligence tests were first devised to solve a specific problem in prediction. School administrators wanted to know which children would profit most from what sorts of education. These tests have become highly popular because they accomplish what they set out to do—in fact, correlations between intelligence and measures of academic success generally run in the neighborhood of + .60. When a test predicts a criterion behavior well, it is said to have *predictive validity* (sometimes called *criterion validity*). Predictive validity means that the test provides useful, sound measures of the behavior in question. In addition, the tests may have considerable *face validity*—that is, they may seem to measure something we would be willing to call intelligence. This would be the case if success in school were better predicted by test items that appeared to measure mental ability than by tests that measured candle-blowing prowess and taste for spinach. Knowing *what* works in science can often lead to a better understanding of *why* and *how* something works. For this reason, empirical solutions to specific problems often precede theoretical and analytical understanding of those problems.

The Analytical Approach

An *analytical approach* towards measuring intelligence involves a theoretical analysis of what produces the effects we attribute to intelligence. If productive thinking and successful problem solving are thought to result from high intelligence, then the processes involved in these mental activities constitute intelligence. Once we have analyzed the components of the concept, we can proceed to measure them. Sir Francis Galton, in nineteenth-century England, proposed that the ability to form mental images and the ability to respond quickly to a stimulus should be components of intelligence. When he compared these abilities in scientists and statesmen with those of common workers, he was surprised to find no differences. Thus, he concluded, these abilities do not contribute heavily to intelligence, even though certain theories of his day held that they were important in thinking and problem solving.

Contemporary researchers have had better success in breaking down intelligence into its mental components. The information-processing approach to mental performance (see chapter 8) has produced measures that offer some promise as predictors of academic success (Hunt and Lansman, 1975). These include measures of the speed and capacity of various memory systems, for example. However, we are still some distance from being able to predict scholastic performance as well with these techniques as with the empiricists' intelligence tests. Researchers pursue the analytical approach because it offers understanding and flexibility in addition to predictive power. Knowing what specific skill or capacity a child is lacking could allow for remediation through special training or compensation through special learning aids.

Theoretical and Empirical Approaches

We have discussed the distinction between theoretical and empirical approaches with regard to intelligence, but the same two approaches can be applied to all areas in which individual differences are a concern. Personality tests have been devised to attempt to categorize people on the basis of different personality traits—aggressive versus friendly, depressed versus not depressed, and so on; the tests are often used to assess differences across the life span. Is it better first to construct a model of personality and test it to gain some theoretical understanding of the underlying processes? Or is it better simply to try to construct a test of some sort and then give it to people already classified as depressed or not by some other method to see which items on the test discriminate between the two types of people? The same issue crops up in the study of individual differences in personnel, such as the development of tests designed to fit people to appropriate jobs.

Analytical (theoretical) and empirical approaches to individual-difference research should be seen as complementary rather than antagonistic. Each approach is able to improve its methods by the other's advances. A theoretical understanding of moral development can be furthered by examining the items that distinguish between children of different ages. Similarly, better test items can be constructed when the empiricist has some notion of how children of different ages differ in their underlying mental structures and processes.

An outstanding example of the effectiveness of combining the two approaches can be seen in the work of Jean Piaget, the eminent developmental psychologist. Piaget (1932) spent many years observing children (primarily his own). From the empirical regularities that he observed in cognitive and social development, Piaget developed a comprehensive theory of development (Piaget and Inhelder, 1969). The theory, in turn, has become the guiding force behind a substantial portion of the research in developmental psychology. Thus, as we noted in chapter 1, individual scientists may focus on a particular approach toward understanding. However, a combination of empirical and analytic work will best lead to scientific progress.

INTRODUCING THE VARIABLES

We will consider here just one type of individual difference, intelligence, but the general principles also hold for other individual differences.

Dependent Variables

The dependent variables in the study of intelligence are the *measures* of intelligence used by each experimenter. Since notions of what intelligence really is differ widely among experimenters, it is difficult to devise a single measure that would be acceptable to all. Empirical approaches are generally based on the observation that, as children grow older, they are able to perform more complicated and more difficult tasks. For individuals of any given age, an average level of performance on certain tasks can be determined by testing a large and representative sample. The particular tasks or test items will be selected on the basis of their correlations with objective criteria of success in school, such as grades and reading level, and possibly also with subjective criteria, such as teacher ratings. At any particular age level, there will be some average number of items that children can pass. If a seven-year-old child can pass the same number of items as the average nine-year-old, we would say that this child has a *mental age* of nine. The Intelligence Quotient, or I.Q., is defined as mental age divided by *chronological age* × 100, or (in this case) 9/7 × 100 = 129. By definition, a score of 100 means that an individual scored the average for others his or her age, and every 15-point variation from this average represents one standard deviation (see appendix B) from this mean. Variants of the I.Q. are used as an index of intelligence.

A purely analytic intelligence test (none is currently in general use) would contain many subtests designed to measure specific properties of a person's information-processing system. Examples of these properties might be short-term memory capacity and scanning rate, long-term memory organization and access time, maximum information-transmission rates in various types of tasks, and ability to allocate attention. Performance on these tasks could be compared with normative performance, as with empirical tests. A combined score computed from all the separate task results may possibly be used as a predictor of scholastic performance.

Independent Variables

All individual differences, including intelligence, are subject variables and not true independent variables. Studies of human intelligence are often aimed at determining the relative importance of genetic, as opposed to environmental, factors in producing intelligence. One of the techniques employed in this research has been to examine monozygotic (identical) twins, dizygotic (fraternal) twins, other siblings, and unrelated children who are reared in the same household or in different households. Genetic similarity varies in these studies as follows: identical twins (of course) have the same genetic inheritance, fraternal twins and other siblings are genetically similar to a lesser degree than identical twins, and unrelated children have the least degree of genetic similarity. Environmental similarity varies in that children reared in the same household have more similar experiences than children reared in separate households.

A number of objections to the definition of environmental similarity can be raised. In the first place, it seems unreasonable to assume that all pairs of children in the same household have equally similar experiences. Twins, and particularly identical twins, are often treated more alike than other pairs of children, if for no other reason than that they are at the same age when various family events occur. Also, foster children and natural children may be treated somewhat differently even when they are of the same age. A second objection is based on the fact that foster children enter the family at later ages than natural children, even if by only a few weeks or months. Although this difference may appear trivial when intelligence is measured at ages of ten to fifteen years or more, many studies have shown that early experiences are quite important in the development of intelligence. A third objection is based on the potential influence of experiences that occur even earlier than those of the first few weeks in the home, namely, those which occur in the prenatal environment. As with genetic inheritance, these prenatal experiences will generally be most similar for twins, less similar for siblings, and least similar for unrelated children. Similarity of prenatal and early postnatal experience may thus be correlated with genetic similarity, making it risky to intepret correlations of one or the other with measured intelligence.

Control Variables

In studies of intelligence, it is difficult to define an exhaustive set of control variables. The single most important factor to control, however, is generally thought to be specific learning that could affect test performance. If certain individuals have learned answers to a number of the test questions, rather than having to "reason out" the answers, they will appear more intelligent than other individuals who have not previously learned these particular facts, words, or relations. Although many items have been deleted from modern intelligence tests in order to make them more "culture-fair," or less influenced by particular learning experiences, it is impossible to eliminate all the effects of learning, language usage, motivation, cultural knowledge, testing experience, and other factors that are known to affect intelligence measures. This is not a problem if intelligence is interpreted simply as probability of success in school, since these other factors no doubt influence school performance. But if intelligence is interpreted as "mental capacity" or some such construct, the effects of these extraneous variables must be minimized.

12.1 Experimental Topics and Research Illustrations

Topic: Reliability of Measures
Illustration: Intelligence and Developmental Research Designs

When psychologists speak of reliability, they are referring to the consistency of their measures of some quantity. You might suppose that several attempts to measure the same thing would all yield the same numbers, unless of course someone had made an error. In fact, there is nearly always some variability in a group of measures; the amount of variability determines the reliability of the measuring instrument and procedure. The "error" to which psychologists refer is meant to imply not that someone goofed, but merely that certain unavoided factors caused unpredictable variability in the data. Psychologists try to reduce this variability, hence increasing the reliability of their measures, by taking their measures under the same conditions on successive occasions.

If identical conditions could be insured, then variability in measurement would have to be caused by a real change in the measured quantity. If your height is measured on two occasions, with the results 5′8″ and 5′10″, is this variability owing to error or to a real change in your height? The answer could be either, or both. But the more similar the conditions—shoes worn, posture— the less likely you would be to attribute the difference to error. Also, the closer the two measures were in time, the less likely you would be to attribute the difference to a real change in stature. You have some notion of how quickly stature can change, or of the stability of a person's true stature.

Intelligence is more difficult to measure than stature, however. It is also more difficult to develop a notion of its stability. Does intelligence vary at all, or does it remain fixed throughout life? If it changes markedly, can it do so within a week, a month, a year, or ten years? If it changes, can we determine those factors that produce the change? These are questions that psychologists would like to answer; the answers require measurement of intelligence. But the alert reader will realize that we have now reasoned ourselves into a logical circle. Let us go around again, and try to get out.

Several measures of the same quantity will not, in general, exactly agree. This variability may be a result of error or of real change in the measured quantity. We cannot tell, without some additional assumptions, how much error there is in our measurement. Thus, how can we ask if intelligence changes? A useful assumption—one that allows the logical circle to be broken—is that the measured quantity is stable over relatively short periods of time. (If a researcher measures your intelligence in the morning and then again in the afternoon, any change can be assumed to be caused by measurement error rather than a real change in intelligence.) With this assumption, a psychologist can estimate measurement error and attempt to improve and specify the reliability of the measuring instrument. Then questions concerning the stability of the underlying quantity, in this case intelligence, can be answered.

We will first review some of the techniques that test developers use to assess the reliability of their measures. Then we will review a study that attempted to determine the stability of intelligence over many years.

Test reliability. We noted previously that the concept of intelligence is not well defined theoretically. Some theorists postulate a number of separate mental abilities, perhaps more than a hundred (Guilford, 1967). Others believe that there is one primary mental ability and that although other more specific abilities may be isolated, they are less important. This primary ability has been described as "a capacity for abstract reasoning and problem solving" (Jensen, 1969, p. 19). To test for this ability, we assemble collections of problems or tasks and present them to individuals to solve, generally within a specified time period. The score that an individual achieves is then compared with scores obtained by others. Before placing much confidence in an individual's score, however, we need to know how reliable it is. Would the individual achieve about the same score if we were to test him or her again the next day, or a week later? Because we do not believe that the underlying ability changes appreciably during so short a time, we attribute a large change in scores to measurement error, indicating unreliability in our test. This procedure of giving the same test twice in succession over a short time interval is used to determine what is called the *test-retest reliability* of a measure. It is generally expressed as a correlation between first and second scores obtained from a large sample of subjects.

A slightly different procedure can be employed to avoid problems such as specific practice effects. This technique involves giving alternate or *parallel forms* of the test on the two testing occasions. Again, if correlations between first and second scores are high, they indicate reliability of the tests. Also, the equivalence of the two forms of the test can be determined in this way.

A third procedure can be used to evaluate reliability with a single test presentation. This technique provides *split-half reliability;* it involves dividing the test items into two arbitrary groups and correlating the scores obtained in the two halves of the test. If these correlations are high, the test reliability is confirmed. In addition, the equivalence of the test items is established.

Stability of intelligence measures. Modern intelligence tests are usually found to yield quite high test-retest reliabilities (correlations of about .95). If we accept these tests as reliable, we can then proceed to ask how stable measured intelligence remains over an individual's lifetime. A number of longitudinal studies have been initiated to examine this question, and reports are published every ten years or so to bring the results up to date. One report (Kangas and Bradway, 1971) includes data on a group of subjects tested with the Stanford-Binet test in 1931, at a mean age of a little over four years, and then tested again in 1941, 1956, and 1969. The original sample consisted of San Francisco Bay Area children who were part of a nationwide standardization population for a revision of the Stanford-Binet scale. Scores were obtained on two alternate forms of the test. In 1941, 138 of these subjects were retested with the same form of the test, and in 1956, 111 received the Wechsler Adult Intelligence Scale and the Stanford-Binet test. In 1969, 48 individuals agreed to be retested yet again.

Before we examine the results of this study, we should recall that these results will be descriptive of the population of subjects from which the data were gathered. They will also, one hopes, be representative of data from similar subjects. They may or may not be representative of subjects who differ in important respects from the subjects in this study.

Kangas and Bradway provided data to show that the 48 subjects tested in 1969 did not differ from the larger group of 111 subjects tested in 1956. They provided means and standard deviations for both chronological age and I.Q. as assessed by the Stanford-Binet test at each age and found no differences between the two samples.

The authors reported correlations between scores obtained at each pair of test administrations, with scores from the parallel forms administered in 1931 averaged. The tests used at each age were the Stanford-Binet (S-B) intelligence tests and, for the 1956 and 1969 tests only, the Wechsler Adult Intelligence Scale (WAIS). The results are presented in table 12–1. Notice that the WAIS has a verbal component and a performance component, which together give the full score. As you look from left to right across the table, you see that correlations between successive testings decrease with the amount of time between testings. The drop is especially pronounced when preschool intelligence, taken when the children's mean age was 4.1, is correlated with the other scores (the top row of the table). The correlations are much higher when adult scores are correlated. However, all the correlations in table 12–1 are statistically significant; scores obtained when children are about four years old can be said to predict to some extent (a correlation of .41) how well they will do much later, at age 41.6. (We should also note that intelligence tests given to four-year-olds are quite different in types of questions from those given to older children; this may help account for the low correlations.)

The increase in correlation between the 1969 measures and previous ones as the subjects' ages increase is reflected as one looks from the top of the table to the bottom. The correlations are higher when S-B scores are correlated with each other rather than with WAIS scores, and vice versa. Since the Stanford-Binet test is verbal, it does not correlate too highly with the performance part of the

TABLE 12–1.

Correlations between I.Q. test scores at four administrations, from 1931–1969.

Test	1941 (N = 138) S-B (Form L)	1956 (N = 109 – 111[a])				1969 (N = 48)			
		S-B (Form L)	WAIS			S-B (Form L-M)	WAIS		
			Full	Verbal	Per-formance		Full	Verbal	Per-formance
1931 S-B									
(Forms L & M)	.65	.59	.64	.60	.54	.41	.39	.28	.29
1941 S-B (Form L)		.85	.80	.81	.51	.68	.53	.57	.18
1956 S-B (Form L)			.83	.89	.46	.77	.58	.68	.14
1956 WAIS									
Full				.87	.84	.72	.73	.69	.41
Verbal					.59	.73	.63	.70	.20
Performance						.36	.67	.47	.57
1969 S-B									
(Form L-M)							.77	.86	.36
1969 WAIS									
Full								.87	.74
Verbal									.38

Note: S-B is the Stanford-Binet test, given at all ages, and WAIS is the Wechsler Adult Intelligence Scale, given in 1956 and 1969. All correlations are significant beyond the .01 level. (From Kangas and Bradway, 1971, table 2. The 1931–1956 portion of the table is reprinted from an article by Katherine P. Bradway and Clare C. Thompson published in the February 1962 *Journal of Educational Psychology*. Copyright 1962 by the American Psychological Association. Reprinted by permission.

[a]Because of incomplete data for two of the subjects, the number of total subjects on which any one correlation is based varies from 109 to 111.

WAIS. The results presented in table 12–1 indicate that intelligence is fairly stable across thirty-seven years for this sample.

Another interesting finding of the Kangas and Bradway study is that the test scores increased at each testing age from 4.1 to 41.6. This increase was examined separately for males and for females (twenty-four of each), and these groups were further separated into high, medium, and low scoring groups by taking the top eight, middle eight, and bottom eight subjects of each sex. The results are presented in figure 12–1, where gains in Stanford-Binet I.Q. are plotted for the high- and low-scoring men and women. As already mentioned, continual gains were recorded for all groups, including the medium groups, which are not shown. But one group seemed to gain much less than the others: the high-scoring group of women. This result may not be caused by a ceiling effect (see chapters 10 and 11), because the men with high scores show a substantial increase. Since we do not know whether the men and women scoring highly were equivalent initially, and since the low-scoring women improved dramatically, a ceiling effect is a possibility.

Although this study cannot be considered conclusive in itself, it is in general agreement with others in showing that measured intelligence does remain *relatively* stable over a large portion of one's life, from early childhood to middle age. This also means that early measures of mental development can predict later intelligence, which has been confirmed in an important longitudinal study by Bornstein and Sigman (1986).

Age as a variable. In the Kangas and Bradway study, the primary variable of interest was age. As discussed previously, age is a subject variable. Subject variables, by definition, cannot be experi-

FIGURE 12–1.

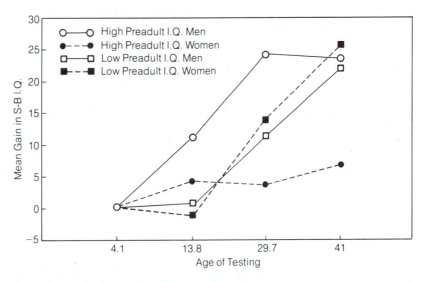

Mean gains in Stanford-Binet I.Q. at successive mean ages for men and women of differing pre-adult I.Q. levels. (From Kangas and Bradway, 1970, Figure 1) Copyright 1970 by the American Psychological Association. Reprinted by permission.

mentally manipulated. Instead, a researcher can only select instances that satisfy different categories and study those. Thus, research with subject variables is largely correlational in nature; researchers can identify dependent variables that change with variations in a subject variable, but it is difficult to pin causation on the subject variable and not on some possibly confounded factor that varies with the subject variable. This is clearly seen in studies with age as a subject variable.

The most typical experimental design in which age is varied is called a *cross-sectional design*. In this design, a researcher takes a cross-section of the population and tests the subjects in the experiment or procedure of interest. If a researcher were interested in how intelligence varied with age, she or he might test people who were 5, 10, 15, 20, 25, 30, 35, 40, 45, 50, 55, 60, 65, 70, and 75 years old. If 25 people were tested at each age, then 375 people would need to be tested. In fact, this is a quite common research design, although the large number of ages sampled is atypical. This design for developmental research has been faulted on important grounds. It has been argued that many other factors are likely to be confounded with age in this sort of design. For example, people who are 25 in 1990 are likely to differ from people who are 65 and 75 on a number of important dimensions: the older subjects will have been raised differently, have been educated differently, be more likely to have immigrated to the United States, be more likely to have served in the armed forces, and so on. These kinds of confoundings have been called *cohort effects*, to refer to effects of the different sorts of people (the *cohorts*) that grow up with people of differing ages. Your cohorts, such as your classmates, are necessarily different from the cohorts of your grandparents. Another crucial difference in many studies of intellectual performance is that older people are likely to have had fewer years of formal education than younger people. Thus, if in using a cross-sectional research design researchers discover differences among people of different ages, they will have difficulty showing that age is responsible for the difference, rather than any number of confounded factors.

Many cross-sectional studies of intelligence have been conducted that show a common pattern of performance: intelligence (as measured on a standard test) increases steadily to the early twenties, then drops gradually until about age sixty, and then declines more quickly thereafter. The conclusion, then, is a rather gloomy one, since many researchers inferred that intelligence leveled off or even dropped after people turned twenty. However, in retrospect and with evidence from other studies, it seems that a more likely conclusion is that cross-sectional studies of intelligence are flawed by all the factors just mentioned, particularly differences in education over the decades. In fact, as we have just seen, when Kangas and Bradway used a different research design to ask the question of how age affects intelligence, they concluded that intelligence continually *increased* across the ages in the study.

Kangas and Bradway used a *longitudinal design*. In these designs, the same group of subjects is tested repeatedly over time. In this way, all the confoundings inherent in the cross-sectional design are avoided. Thus, a researcher may be more confident in some cases that age rather than confounded subject variables is responsible for whatever changes are observed in performance. However, the longitudinal design is not without problems, either. Imagine that a researcher in 1950 was interested in how age affected people's attitudes toward war and whether the United States should have a strong military capability. If people were measured in 1950, their attitudes might generally have been quite favorable, since the United States had recently experienced the success of World War II. However, if these people were tested twenty years later, at the height of the unpopular Vietnam War, their attitudes might have been much less favorable. Obviously, a researcher would be rash to conclude that people's attitudes toward war and defense grow less favorable as the people age. Other confoundings in the longitudinal design include the time of measurement, which by definition is a confound, and the fact that across time people will drop out of the experiment (from death or moving away), and this drop-out rate will increase across time. In general, longitudinal designs will not lead to sound conclusions about how age alters behavior when experiential changes during the period between tests may have produced the change.

Given these problems of cross-sectional and longitudinal designs, how can psychologists perform sound research on developmental differences? In fact, many of the developmental studies on which psychologists depend have employed cross-sectional and longitudinal studies (with the former predominating). However, Schaie (1977) advocated other research designs that allow more unambiguous assessments of age changes in performance. One of these, the *cross-sequential design*, is illustrated in figure 12–2, which

FIGURE 12–2.

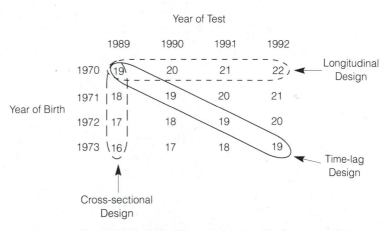

The cross-sequential research design for investigating developmental differences. People born in 1970–1973 are tested repeatedly in 1989–1992. The number in each cell is the age of the person when tested.

shows how people born in four successive years (1970 through 1973) might be tested later in four successive years (1989 to 1992). Each column of the figure represents a cross-sectional design, since people of different ages are being tested in one year. Similarly, each row represents a longitudinal design, since people of the same age are tested repeatedly as they age. In addition, a third type of design is shown in the diagonal in the figure. This is the *time-lag design*, which aims at determining the effects of time of testing while holding age constant. Age at testing is held constant at nineteen in the time-lag design, so that any changes observed may be attributed to the changing eras in which people are tested. However, age in this design is confounded with both the year of birth and the year of test. In the entire cross-sequential design, if both the longitudinal and cross-sectional components show some dependent variable changing with age, and the time-lag component shows no change with time of testing while holding age constant, then a researcher may safely attribute the observed changes to age itself and not some confounded factor.

12.2 Experimental Topics and Research Illustrations

Topic: Operational Definitions
Illustration: Artificial Intelligence

Consider the following game, which is called the *imitation game*. The imitation game is a hypothetical experiment devised by Turing (1950) in an article titled "Computing Machinery and Intelligence." Turing's purpose was to devise a situation that would allow one to assess whether a machine could think.

> It is played with three people, a man (A), a woman (B), and an interrogator (C) who may be of either sex. The interrogator stays in a room apart from the other two. The object of the game for the interrogator is to determine which of the other two is the man and which is the woman. He (the interrogator) knows them by labels X and Y, and at the end of the game he says either "X is A and Y is B" or "X is B and Y is A." The interrogator is allowed to put questions to A and B thus:
>
> C: Will X please tell me the length of his or her hair?
>
> Now suppose that X is actually A, then A must answer. It is A's object in the game to try to cause C to make the wrong identification. His answer might therefore be
>
> "My hair is shingled, and the longest strands are about nine inches long."
>
> In order that tones of voice may not help the interrogator the answers should be written, or better still, typewritten. The

ideal arrangement is to have a teleprinter communicating between the two rooms. Alternatively the question and answers can be repeated by an intermediary. The object of the game for the third player (B) is to help the interrogator. The best strategy for her is probably to give truthful answers. She can add such things as "I am the woman, don't listen to him!" to her answers, but it will avail nothing as the man can make similar remarks.

We now ask the question, "What will happen when a machine takes the part of A in this game?" Will the interrogator decide wrongly as often when the game is played like this as he does when the game is played between a man and a woman? These questions replace our original, "Can machines think?" (Turing, 1950, pp. 433–434)

The imitation game is usually called the *Turing test*. Presumably, the test could determine whether any machine, computer or otherwise, had intelligence. The criterion for intelligence in machines is specified in Turing's test: A machine would be called intelligent if an interrogator physically separated from a machine and a person could not distinguish between their typewritten answers to questions. More bluntly, a machine whose output is capable of imitating a human has intelligence.

Turing argued that, in principle at least, a machine would be taken for a human in the imitation game. To many psychologists and computer scientists, the Turing test is a valid one for determining intelligence. On the basis of the arguments supporting the Turing test, the belief in the possibility of *artificial intelligence (AI)* has become widespread. There are two general views about AI (Searle, 1980). The first is called *strong AI*, and it is the belief, following Turing, that machines can have intelligence. Put another way, the strong AI position states that it is possible for machines to possess a cognitive state that would be called intelligence if a person possessed that cognitive state. The cognitive state is realized in the program that runs the machine. Intelligence in this view is simply the manipulation of the formal symbols in the program. The second type of AI is called *weak AI*, which involves using computer programs to model human intelligence; it tests theories of cognition by means of computer programs. The weak AI approach has not generated much disagreement, and we will not consider it here. Instead, we will focus on the strong AI position, because it has generated a substantial amount of controversy.

Operational definitions. The Turing test has been considered positively by many because it has two important features. The first of these is that evaluation of machine intelligence by means of the imitation game involves an experiment: whether an interrogator believes a machine is equivalent to a person. The second feature is more important for our purposes. The experiment described by Turing yields an *operational definition*.

Operational definitions were discussed in chapter 6, using the concept of threshold as an example. Recall that an operational definition is a formula for building a construct, such as intelligence, in a way that other scientists can duplicate, by specifying the operations used to produce and measure it. An operational definition of hunger might specify withholding food from a dog for a period of time and then measuring how much the dog eats. Likewise, according to Turing's operational definition of intelligence, we specify the production of intelligence, a machine program that answers questions, and we measure intelligence by the amount of deception that the answers produce. This seems to be a perfectly acceptable operational definition, so why has it generated so much debate?

The primary reason that the Turing test is controversial is that operational definitions are reliable in principle, but they are not necessarily valid. The major value of an operational definition is to facilitate communication. In this case, if someone claims that machines are intelligent, it refers to the fact that the machine passed the Turing test and, presumably, nothing more.

In terms of clarity of expression, the Turing test appears to be adequate. The conditions necessary for consistently (that is, reliably) producing what Turing calls intelligence are precisely given. However, the debate about strong AI centers on the issue of whether the Turing test adequately captures what we would call intelligence in humans. Thus, there are disagreements as to the validity of the Turing test as a definition of intelligence. *Validity* in the current context refers to the truth or soundness of the definition. Is the Turing test defining intelligence or is it defining something else? Does the amount of deception produced by the computer reflect intelligence?

Operational definitions nearly always are limited in their applicability, which means that their validity will suffer. Reconsider the operational definition of hunger that was presented earlier: withhold food for a period of time and observe the amount eaten. Does this adequately specify what we mean by hunger? Probably not. Humans eat for a variety of reasons, only one of which has to do with food privation. Sometimes we eat to be sociable, sometimes we eat because we desire a particular type of food, and sometimes we eat because we have not eaten for several hours. Furthermore, the above operational definition is not symmetrical, because not eating does not mean that our stomachs are full. Sometimes we do not eat because we have an upset stomach, sometimes we do not eat because we are trying to lose weight, and sometimes we do not eat because we have just eaten. To characterize the concept of hunger in a way that accounts for these kinds of observations, we need to have multiple operational definitions that fit together in a coherent theory. We have to use converging operations (see chapter 7 and 14).

Much of the criticism against strong AI is of the sort that could be leveled against our definition of hunger. "Machines are not human. But can a computer talk? Can it write sonnets?" Turing anticipated some of these criticisms and believes that they can be answered in time—yes, a computer program can do those things in such a fashion that an observer (interrogator) would not know that they were produced by a machine. As Turing (1950) said, "The question and answer method seems to be suitable for introducing almost any one of the fields of human endeavor that we wish to include. We do not wish to penalize the machine for its inability to shine in beauty competitions, nor to penalize a man for losing in a race against an airplane. The conditions of our game make these disabilities irrelevant. The 'witnesses' can brag, if they consider it advisable, as much as they please about their charms, strength or heroism, but the interrogator cannot demand practical demonstrations" (p. 435). Some of the critiques and Turing's rebuttal may be empirical questions that could be resolved by observation and experiment, but, even if machines were developed that could do these things, there are additional criticisms, and we now address a criticism of the validity of the Turing test.

The Chinese room. A major argument against the possibility of strong AI was developed by the philosopher Searle (1980, 1990), and his objections relate to the fundamental validity of the Turing test. Searle also uses a hypothetical experiment to bolster his argument. He asks us to imagine a person who does not know the Chinese language. For purposes of the following, let us suppose that the person is you. You are isolated in a room, and in it you have a complete instruction book written in your native language that specifies what you are to do when a piece of paper comes into the room with certain squiggles on it. The instructions tell you to match those squiggles to certain cards that you have in the room with you. These cards have different patterns of lines on them as well. When you have found the card or cards you were instructed to find, you then put them in a slot that drops the card(s) outside of the room.

Unbeknownst to you, the cards have Chinese characters on them, and also unbeknownst to you, you are actually answering questions in Chinese that were asked to you in Chinese. The thought experiment assumes that your instructions are detailed enough to allow you to answer the questions adequately even though you do not understand any Chinese—you do not even know that you are manipulating Chinese symbols. Thus, you are taking part in a version of the Turing test, because people are asking "the room" questions in Chinese (hence the name *Chinese room*), and the interrogators should not be able to distinguish your answers from those given by a person who speaks Chinese. You are adequately manipulating a set of formal symbols, but these symbols have no meaning for you.

Searle believes that you would pass the Turing test in a real Chinese room competition. Does that mean you are intelligent in Chinese? Searle's answer is no. You do not understand any Chinese yet you pass the Turing test. You are functioning just the same as a computer that fools an interrogator into believing that a human rather than a machine is answering questions. The computer program, like you in the Chinese room, manipulates symbols, and, like you, the computer does not attach meaning or understanding to the symbols. According to Searle, this must mean that the Turing test is an invalid way to show that machines have intelligence.

Searle adds to his argument by suggesting that true understanding apparently requires a brain that has causal powers in the situation under examination. You do not understand Chinese in the same way that you understand your native language, because you cannot produce it. All you can do with Chinese, and presumably all a computer can do in any "intelligent" activity, is follow the instructions on how to manipulate symbols. To produce intelligent behavior, the symbols that are manipulated must have content or meaning. Since human minds have meaningful contents and computer programs do not, programs cannot be intelligent. Searle (1990) contends that biologically based machines such as our brains may not be the only things that can think, but he regards the possibility of creating artificial thinking devices as "up for grabs."

Searle's Chinese room argument and his position about brains have not gone unchallenged (see Churchland and Churchland, 1990). The basic issue seems to be: what counts as an adequate test for intelligence? Is the behavior of a device that simply manipulates symbols enough to count as intelligence? The strong AI answer is yes. Searle's reply is no—a program that simulates a speaker of Chinese does not understand Chinese, just as a program that simulates digestion does not digest food.

Defining intelligence. A question you might now ask is, "Aren't there other operational definitions of intelligence that are generally accepted?" The short answer is no. Here we will examine some other definitions of intelligence and some additional problems associated with operationally defining concepts.

You may have noticed that we did not define intelligence when we discussed reliability in the first section of this chapter. This is because test developers usually have a pragmatic problem at hand. Binet merely wanted to determine the appropriate grade level for students in French schools. In these pragmatic circumstances the validity of the test is determined by some criterion, such as success in school. In fact, the Stanford-Binet and Wechsler tests do a good job of predicting academic performance. So, you might be tempted to say that intelligence is what tests measure if they have good criterion validity (the tests predict academic performance). The problem here is twofold. On the one hand, most intelligence tests focus on mathematical and verbal abilities, which means that they ignore other kinds of important intellectual activities, including musical ability and the ability to understand other people. On the other hand, intellectual ability in an academic sense is often viewed as a limited and culturally biased way of defining intelligence. The typical I.Q. test does not measure one's ability to succeed in life or adapt to the environment. The I.Q. tests are, according to some critics, a reflection of white upper middle class values and do not reflect what intelligence means for society as a whole. So, the argument goes, the I.Q. scores of people may have nothing to do with common sense or leading a productive life. Furthermore, even if people were productive and had common sense, their I.Q. scores would not predict their success in another context, such as surviving on a desert island or fending well in the jungle.

Thus, accepting the definition of intelligence as what intelligence tests measure does not solve many problems. It is limited in its range of expertise, and the definition is one that is likely to be contested by the general public's conception of what intelligence is all about.

Let us briefly consider a contemporary attempt to define intelligence operationally. The theory is called a theory of *multiple intelligences* and was developed by Gardner (1983). His goal was to broaden the standard academic definition of intelligence to include intelligences (to use his phraseology) that are less tied to Western cultural values than those associated with the standard intelligence test. Gardner presents cross-cultural, psychological, psychometric, developmental, and neurological evidence for the existence of seven facets of intelligence. These multiple intelligences are bodily-kinesthetic, linguistic, logical-mathematical, musical, self understanding, social success, and spatial. Of these, only linguistic, logical-mathematical, and spatial are tested on standard I.Q. tests. For each of the seven intelligences, Gardner tries to show that there are separate neural structures associated with them, that each has a separate developmental history, that a person can be very good in one area and poor or mediocre in others, and that cross-culturally each of the areas can be shown to play prominent roles, though in different ways.

Rather than examine each of the intelligences, let us consider how Gardner analyzes one: music. First, Gardner, shows that the underlying neural structures for music are different from those associated with other intelligences. Musical ability is associated with the right hemisphere of the brain unlike linguistic ability, which is associated with the left hemisphere. People with damage to the left hemisphere are often *aphasic*, which means they have a disorder of language. Interestingly, although aphasics often have trouble speaking, they can usually sing, and, even if in the rare case that they cannot sing words, their musical abilities are otherwise undisturbed. Contrariwise, people with damage to the right hemisphere often suffer from *tonal agnosia*. Tonal agnosics are unable to sing, and their ordinary vocal inflections are diminished. Otherwise, the language facility of people suffering from tonal agnosia is intact.

The next thing that Gardner notes is that there are tremendous individual differences in musical intelligence. This can be assessed by special tests (that is, psychometrically), but it is also obvious in everyday observation. Mozart was obviously a musical genius. At an early age this prodigy was composing elegant symphonic music, and he was performing before the royal courts of Europe prior to entering adolescence.

Gardner presents further evidence for a separate musical intelligence, which we need not consider here. The point is that for each of the intelligences he proposes he tries to operationally define them along several dimensions. This means that he is using converging operations to refine his concept of intelligence. Is he successful in defining intelligence? Is Gardner's theory of multiple intelligences *the* definition of intelligence? As you might expect, the answer to those questions is no, or at least the answer is no for some psychologists.

One of the nay sayers of Gardner's theory is the psychologist Robert Sternberg, who has taken the information-processing approach to defining intelligence (the most accessible treatment of Sternberg's work is *The Triarchic Mind*, 1988). Sternberg's major criticism of Gardner's approach is that the processes underlying the seven intelligences are not specified. Sternberg suggests that Gardner simply names the intelligences without specifying exactly what they are and what they are not. A second criticism that Sternberg makes is that intelligence is general, but Gardner's intelligences are specific. According to Sternberg, Gardner has identified talents rather than intelligences. Lacking musical talent should not be too damaging to a person and may go unrecognized. However, a person who could not plan or reason, which are important components of intelligence for Sternberg, could not function in the world.

Sternberg's criticisms are taken into account in his own theory of intelligence, which emphasizes the ability to process information, synthesize information in novel ways, and adapt to new situations. Sternberg's operational definition of intelligence suggests that intelligent behavior reflects the ability to solve problems established in a social context (see Sternberg and Salter, 1982). This view is a prominent one and is accepted by many psychologists interested in the information-processing approach (see Kantowitz, 1989).

But is this adaptive problem solving intelligence? In this view, would writing a poem or composing a symphony be a manifestation of intelligence or simply a talent? Answers to these questions require a cogent theory bolstered by confirming data based on converging operations derived from many operational definitions. Although operational definitions clearly play an important role in the development of scientific theories, using operational definitions has both advantages and disadvantages. On the plus side, operational definitions can facilitate scientific communication and, hence, the reliability of scientific research. Such reliable work sets the stage for elaboration and refinement of concepts. On the minus side, operational definitions can be controversial definitions of the concepts in question. Although they can be valid, their meaning is often subject to debate. The definitions need to fit into a network of other concepts that lead to the description and prediction of behavior. Certainly, progress in understanding both natural and artificial intelligence depends on a satisfactory definition of what is entailed by the concept of intelligence.

12.3 Experimental Topics and Research Illustrations

Topic: Regression Artifacts
Illustration: Educational Assessment

An issue related to the study of intelligence and individual differences revolves around attempts by psychologists and educators to improve the performance of individuals, and the importance of evaluating such attempts. As you might suspect, accurate measurement lies at the heart of assessing change. Whenever there is measurement error, there is also the possibility of wrongly concluding that some sort of change has occurred or has failed to occur. Although this statement may appear less than profound to you, a number of psychological studies have been faulted for failing to take adequate account of its truth.

Certain designs or procedures for gathering data are particularly susceptible to bias caused by measurement error. Those designs, remember, are termed *quasi-experimental*, because subjects are not assigned to treatment and control groups on a random basis (Campbell and Stanley, 1966). Subjects in these groups may be matched on a number of factors by a researcher, but it is difficult to ensure that important differences between the groups did not exist prior to the start of the treatment. This problem is amplified when the experimental (treatment) group and control (no treatment) group are not matched prior to the study on the variable they will be tested on at the end of the study. For example, a group of children from one neighborhood might be selected as an experimental group to test a new training course for teaching running. A second group of children might be chosen from the same neighborhood to serve as a control group. Following six weeks of training by the experimental group, both groups might be tested for running speed. This would be a quasi-experimental design, because the children were not assigned randomly to one of the two groups. Even if the experimenter reported that the two groups had been of the same average height, weight, and age, we would not know for certain that the average running speed of the two groups had been the same prior to the treatment. In fact, even if control subjects had been picked to match the running speeds of the experimental group, we could not be sure that group differences following training were owing to the effects of training. This is because the possibility would remain that the two groups had been sampled from populations that differed prior to the study. When population differences exist, there is the possibility of being misled by what are known as *regression artifacts,* or experimental effects produced by "statistical regression" rather than by experimental manipulations. You will remember that we talked about regression artifacts in chapter 2.

Perhaps an example will help here. Suppose that you are an *A* student and that your neighbor is a *C* student, although you both have similar backgrounds. On one particular assignment, you both receive a *B.* In an effort to improve, your neighbor decides to attend a series of help sessions. Your instructor decides to evaluate the effectiveness of the help sessions by comparing the future grades of help-session students with future grades of non-help-session students who are similar in background and received the same grades on the previous assignment. You are selected as the matched student to be compared with your friend. On the next assignment, you receive an *A*−, and your friend receives a *C*+. The course of events in this evaluation program is illustrated in figure 12–3. Note the changes in the criterion grade as a function of the person's mean grade. Should the instructor conclude that help sessions are harmful because your friend went from a *B* to a *C*+, whereas you went from a *B* to an *A*−? Probably not, since both of you merely regressed toward your mean grades. The effect seen in this little study is probably not a true treatment effect, but rather a regression artifact caused by the fact that you and your friend were not truly equivalent students. The help session may even have benefited your friend, since her or his grade was higher than the usual grade of *C.* If *B* students on the first assignment had been randomly assigned to help-session or non-help-session groups, and then compared on the basis of grades on the second assignment, accurate assessment of the effect of help sessions on students' grades could have been obtained.

The reason for the phenomenon of regression to the mean is that all psychological measures are subject to a certain amount of unreliability. With any measure that is not perfectly reliable, the group of subjects obtaining the highest scores contains not only

FIGURE 12–3.   Illustration of regression to the mean confusing the interpretation of the outcome of a quasi-experiment. Although both people were matched as B students, their performance, with or without the help session, regressed towards their actual average grade. Did the help session help?

Person	Mean Grade	Matching Grade	Help Session	Criterion Grade
You	A	B	no	A−
Neighbor	C	B	yes	C+

those who really belong in the highest category, but also others who were placed in this category due to chance errors of measurement. On a retest, these chance measurement errors will not necessarily occur in the same direction. Thus the scores of the highest group will tend to average lower on a retest. Similarly, a group selected for poor performance on an original test will tend to average higher on a retest. The Psychology in Action section at the end of this chapter is intended to give you a better understanding of this point through a simple demonstration of regression to the mean.

The importance of regression artifacts such as this in quasi-experimental studies of compensatory education has been the subject of much debate. One influential study of the effects of the Head Start program of the 1960s (Cicirelli et al., 1969) received particular attention. In this study, called the Westinghouse-Ohio study, children completing their Head Start experience were randomly selected for evaluation. A control population of children from the same area, who had been eligible for the program but had not attended, was then defined. Control children were selected at random to be matched with experimental children on the basis of sex, racial-ethnic group membership, and kindergarten attendance. Note well, the children were selected from two different groups: one that did attend Head Start and one that did not. After the final selection of experimental and control subjects was made, additional measures of socioeconomic status, demographic status, and attitude were compiled and compared for the two groups. Differences were reported to be slight. Measures of experimental (Head Start) and control (no Head Start) children's academic achievement and potential were then computed and compared. The general conclusion from this large study was that Head Start was not effective in removing the effects of poverty and social disadvantage.

Other psychologists (Campbell and Erlebacher, 1970a) were quick to criticize this study on several grounds. First, it was pointed out that the results of the study were undoubtedly caused partially by regression artifacts. Worse, the magnitude of the artifacts could not be estimated, casting doubt over the entire set of findings.

The basic problem is one of matching (see chapter 2 for a similar example). Cicirelli and coworkers laudably tried to match a sample of disadvantaged children who had been in the Head Start program with others from the same area who had not been in the program. Later differences between the two groups should have been due to the program. Right? Not necessarily. It is right only if the two samples came from the same underlying population distributions, which is unlikely. What is likely is that the two populations differed, with the disadvantaged "treatment" children coming from a population that was poorer in ability than the "control" children. The "treatment" children who attended Head Start were usually preselected to be from a disadvantaged background (which is why they were included in the program), whereas the "controls" who were not in the program were likely to be from a different population that was greater in ability. The basic problem is that subjects were not randomly assigned to conditions, so the researchers had to try to match control subjects with experimental subjects. To match two samples from these different populations, the experimenters would have had to select children *above* the population mean for the disadvantaged treatment group, and *below* the mean for the control group. But when this is done, the dreaded regression artifact will always be introduced. When each group is retested, the performance of individuals will tend to regress to the mean of the group; in other words, the disadvantaged group will tend to perform worse in this example, and the control group will tend to perform better.

This regression to the mean will happen in the absence of any treatment being given to either group and despite matching. The effect is the same as that in the previous example of the grades of the superior student increasing to $A-$ from B and the other's decreasing from B to $C+$, when the two students were erroneously "matched" as B students. Since we already expect a difference between the groups (favoring the control) in this situation because of regression to the mean, how we do evaluate the outcome of our study? Cicirelli and coworkers found no difference between the groups. Since we might expect the treatment (Head Start) group to actually be worse owing to regression artifacts, does this mean the group actually improved owing to Head Start?

It is impossible to answer this question, because in the Westinghouse-Ohio evaluation of Head Start the direction or magnitude of regression artifacts could not be assessed. In the preceding paragraph, we made reasonable suppositions concerning regression artifacts in this type of study. But the conclusion that Head Start had no effect cannot be drawn from the Westinghouse-Ohio study. More properly, no conclusion can be drawn on the basis of that study, since it is not known how regression artifacts affected the results.

In general, then, regression artifacts of a difficult-to-estimate magnitude are highly probable in this type of study, and this fact is acknowledged by all. Why, then, would such studies be conducted, particularly when very important political, economic, and social decisions might be based on their results? This question was raised by Campbell and Erlebacher (1970a, b) and Cicirelli and his supporters (Cicirelli, 1970; Evans and Schiller, 1970). Their answers were quite different, and they represent the type of issue that frequently confronts scientists, but that science can never resolve. Campbell and Erlebacher proposed that bad information was worse than no information at all; that if properly controlled experiments could not be performed, then no data should be gathered. On the other side of the issue, Evans and Schiller replied, "This position fails to understand that every program *will* be evaluated by the most arbitrary, anecdotal, partisan and subjective means" (p. 220). Campbell and Erlebacher concurred, but stated, "we judge it fundamentally misleading to lend the prestige of science to any report in a situation where no scientific evaluation is possible" (1970b, p. 224). As an ultimate solution, they proposed that a commission "composed of experts who are not yet partisans in this controversy" be convened to decide the matter.

This issue may not be decidable on strictly rational grounds, but we can all agree that a research study should be conducted according to the best scientific procedures available. How could the Westinghouse-Ohio study have been done appropriately? The best way would have been to randomly assign participants to either the no-treatment or the treatment (Head Start) condition in the beginning. There is no substitute for random assignment in eliminating confounding factors. But it seems unfair to give half the children who seek the help of a remedial program no training whatsoever. Of course, there is no guarantee at the outset that the program will do them any good; that is what the study is intended to discover. The same issue occurs in medical research when a control group with a disease is given a placebo rather than a treatment drug. The argument could be made in both cases that in the long run more people will be aided by careful research into the effectiveness of treatments than may be harmed because treatment is withheld.

There are other solutions besides random assignment. One would be to randomly assign all the children to different groups and put them in different programs, to pit the effectiveness of the programs against one another. One difficulty here would be that the training programs might turn out to be equally effective. Then one could not know if any of them were better than no program at all.

What happens when children are randomly assigned to treatment and no-treatment conditions? Let us examine a 4½-year longitudinal experiment conducted by Breitmayer and Ramey (1986). The subjects in their work were 80 children from disadvantaged families in a large U.S. city. At birth, half of the children were randomly assigned to be in the no-treatment control group. The control children attended a day-care center until the end of the experiment, but they did not receive any special educational treatment. The other half of the children were randomly assigned to the treatment group. Their day-care center included a Head Start-type program that was designed to prevent mental retardation. All subjects in the experiment had a normal birth and weighed at least five pounds. In the first minute after birth, the neonates were assessed for their biological responsiveness on a scale similar to the one devised by Brazelton that was described in chapter 2. The results of this testing indicated that just over half of the babies in the control and experimental groups were not biologically optimal immediately after birth. So, we wind up with four groups in this experiment: experimental (educationally enriched day care)/optimal; control (ordinary day care)/optimal; experimental/nonoptimal; and control/nonoptimal.

Measures of intelligence at 4½ indicated three important findings. First, the children who were biologically optimal in the first

FIGURE 12–4.

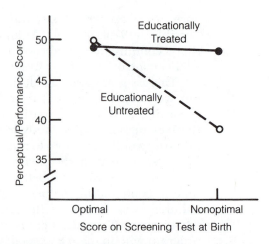

Score on Screening Test at Birth

The results of Breitmayer and Ramey (1986), showing an interaction of educational treatment and health at birth on the perceptual/performance score obtained at age 54 months. Similar, though not as pronounced, interactions were seen for scores on the verbal and quantitative portions of the intelligence test.

minute after birth scored higher on the intelligence tests than did the children who were biologically nonoptimal. Second, the educationally treated children fared somewhat better than controls on the verbal portion of the test, and the experimentals far exceeded the controls on the performance component. Finally, most of the effect of education was owing to an interaction: the nonoptimal control subjects did especially poorly on all aspects of the intelligence test. Illustrative results are shown in figure 12–4. This interaction is similar to the example of synergism mentioned in chapter 2. Since after-the-fact examination revealed highly similar home situations for the two groups, Breitmayer and Ramey were able to safely conclude that early education has some important benefits—especially for children who are not biologically optimal at birth.

From Problem to Experiment: The Nuts and Bolts

Problem: What Roles Do Motivation and Emotion Play in Intellectual Performance?

Many of you, we suspect, are math phobic—you simply detest math courses, math homework, and math tests. Others of you may simply not like certain kinds of tests, such as essay exams or multiple-choice quizzes. If you fall into either of those groups, or if you have particular intellectual likes or dislikes that can influence your performance on tests and exams, then you are showing the effects of motivation and emotion on intellectual performance. Such likes and dislikes should be particularly important for elementary-school teachers to identify, because once a student starts to dislike something a snowball effect could arise. For example, suppose a young student begins to dislike math for some reason. That student not only will find math tests aversive, but also will find learning about match aversive. Not learning newer math concepts will lead to poor test performance, which will increase the aversion, and so on.

The emotional views toward cognitive pursuits need not be specific. Dweck and her associates have identified two general goals that children seem to have when undertaking intellectual activities, and these goals are manifest in the primitive theories that children have about intelligence (Dweck and Bempechat, 1983; Dweck and Elliott, 1983). Some children adopt what are called *performance goals.* These children seem to be motivated by not looking foolish; they want to look smart and not receive negative evaluations from their peers or their teachers. Children who adopt performance goals have what Dweck calls an *entity theory* of intelligence. These children believe that the fixed intelligence that they have is best assessed by how well others evaluate them and how well they do on intellectual tasks. Other children tend to be motivated by *learning goals,* in which they try to become smarter by learning new skills and knowledge. Children who are motivated by learning goals believe in what Dweck calls an *instrumental incremental theory,* which refers to their belief that intelligence is a set of skills and knowledge that can be increased through hard work and effort. How do these goals affect the youngster's performance? Are the goals beneficial under some circumstances? These are the issues addressed here.

Problem: *How do the motivational goals of a child influence his or her intellectual performance?*

We might expect that how the children's goals influence their performance would interact with the task demands (Hetherington and Parke, 1986). If the situation demands quick, accurate, and correct performance, then we might expect the entity theorists to perform better than if the situation requires new learning and substantial effort. For the instrumental incremental theorists, on the other hand, better performance should occur in the latter situation, which requires effort and new learning.

Hypothesis: *The nature of the task and the child's motivational goals will interact such that intellectual performance will be best in those situations that place emphasis on goals congruent with the child's, and intellectual performance will suffer in those situations in which the task demands and motivational goal are in conflict.*

One experimental design to test this hypothesis calls for two groups of children: Entity and Instrumental Incremental. Each of these groups should be tested under two conditions: Performance Goals and Learning Goals. Thus, the design would be a mixed one with subject group as a between-subjects variable and test condition a within-subjects variable.

The primary reason for including these two variables is to look for the interaction between them. This is very important when one of the variables is a quasi-independent variable, as subject variables are. Since the subject variable must be selected and not manipulated, it is important to look for the differential effect of a real independent variable on the different levels of the subject variable.

The first thing that must be done in this research is to select subjects in the two groups. Unfortunately, there are no published tests that serve this purpose. However, Dweck has provided a rather straightforward way of distinguishing between entity theorists and instrumental incremental ones. Children are asked to choose one of two statements about intelligence, where one statement reflects performance goals and the other reflects learning goals. So, you would have to make up a number of such pairs of statements (say, 16). A child's score on this test would be the number of times a particular type of statement was selected. An entity score could range from 0 to 16 in this example. Some examples of the types of statements you might generate are:

1. (a) You can learn new things, but how smart you are stays pretty much the same.
   (b) Smartness is something you can increase as much as you want to.

2. (a) I feel smart when I don't make mistakes.
   (b) I feel smart when I figure out how to do something.

3. (a) I like school work when I can hand in my papers first.
   (b) I like school work when I learn something new.

4. (a) I feel smart when I get easy work.
   (b) I feel smart when I'm reading a hard book.

The easiest way to determine to which group a child belongs is to calculate the median entity score (that is, the middle one) for all of the children who took the test. Then you assign children to the Entity group who scored above the group median, and you assign the rest of the children, those who scored below the median, to the Instrumental Incremental group.

Devising a reliable and valid test could be extremely difficult and time consuming. You may also find it difficult to get a wide spread in scores on your test. To ensure that you obtain many children who score very high and many who score very low, you may need to revise your set of test questions until you find a set that yields a good spread of scores.

After determining the group membership of a number of children (about 15 in each group would be a good minimum number), you will need to devise test situations. Here, the previous work of Dweck and her associates may be of some help. Dweck and Bempechat (1983) describe several kinds of tasks that they asked Entity and Instrumental children to choose between and to make estimates as to how well they would do. These tasks differed in their difficulty and in the performance goals (learning or looking smart). After making their choices, all children were given the same task, which was of moderate difficulty. So, they manipulated the children's perception of the task by prior instructions. The same sort of procedure could be done in the present experiment. We could use instructions similar to those used by Dweck and then have the children engage in some task. For purposes of testing most children, it is often useful to suggest to them that the test procedure is a game of some sort. This is done to maintain their motivation and interest. For the learning-oriented task, children could be told the following: "In this game you'll probably learn some new things, but you'll also make some mistakes. You might get confused and feel dumb, but you should learn some neat stuff." For the performance-oriented task, the instructions might be: "This game is a lot of fun because it is easier than some. Although you won't learn a lot, it will really show me just how much kids can do." You will then need two tasks, one for each set of instructions. To maintain the children's interest, the two tasks should not be too similar. But with two different tasks you will have to counterbalance the tasks across instructions for the two groups of children. Selecting tasks could be difficult, but the most straightforward way to find them would be to elicit help from a teacher who has children in her or his class of the same age as your test subjects. The teacher should be able to help you select two intellectual tasks that the typical third-grader, for example, would find to be of moderate difficulty. Let us call the two tasks you select A and B. Adequate counterbalancing and an overview of the design are illustrated in table 12–2.

TABLE 12–2. Design and counterbalancing for the combinations of two tasks (A and B) and two types of instructions (Performance and Learning). The numbers in the table indicate the number of subjects in each condition. The total number of subjects in each group is assumed to be 16.

Group	First Test	Second Test
Entity	(4) Task A/Performance	Task B/Learning
	(4) Task B/Performance	Task A/Learning
	(4) Task A/Learning	Task B/Performance
	(4) Task B/Learning	Task A/Performance
Instrumental Incremental	(4) Task A/Performance	Task B/Learning
	(4) Task B/Performance	Task A/Learning
	(4) Task A/Learning	Task B/Performance
	(4) Task B/Learning	Task A/Performance

It is predicted that Entity subjects will do more poorly on the task preceded by Learning instructions than on the task preceded by Performance instructions. On the other hand, we expect the Instrumental Incremental subjects to do better on the task preceded by the Learning instructions and more poorly on the task preceded by the Performance instructions.

This research project seems to be manageable, with the possible exception of developing the Entity theory test. However, research on subject variables, especially with children, poses many difficulties for the researcher. One problem has to do with ethics. Since it is unlikely that a child can give true informed consent to participate in an experiment, the children's parents must be allowed to indicate whether they want their child to participate. This means that you would have to approach an elementary-school teacher, elicit his or her consent to test the students, and then have the parents sign a consent form. Your professor will be able to help you devise a consent form that would be acceptable for these purposes.

Another issue that must be resolved is the age of the children. Most earlier work has used children in the primary grades, and that would be a safe bet here. If the children are too young, say of preschool age, they may not have a well-developed idea of what it means to be smart. On the other hand, high-school students may be too sophisticated in their beliefs about intelligence to allow you to generate different groups of subjects.

Still another issue has to do with gender. Do you want to test just boys, just girls, or a mixture? Dweck has found that boys and girls respond differently to Learning and Performance situations, so at the very least you would like to make sure that you had the same proportion of each sex in each of your test groups, such as 45 percent boys in each group. On the other hand, if you are interested in the ways in which boys and girls might differ in your situation, you might consider including gender as an additional subject variable.

Research on subject variables is often particularly interesting, and it often concerns questions that have practical importance. However, do not lose sight of the fact that subject variables are selected and not manipulated. The conclusions you draw must recognize that you are not working with a true independent variable.

1. The two general approaches to the study of individual differences are empirical and analytical. Empirical approaches are based on finding correlates of the individual difference in question, such as intelligence tests designed to predict school grades. Empirical approaches generally provide the most predictive power and are useful for this reason. In addition, a good empirical relationship may offer clues to understand the under-

lying mechanisms of interest. Analytical theories of individual differences attempt to provide explanations for the differences in behavior by pointing to differences in underlying psychological processes. Such theories may allow greater flexibility in generalizing results to new situations.

2. Reliability of measuring instruments and devices is crucial to all scientific investigation, including the study of individual differences. Devising reliable measures of complicated mental abilities such as intelligence is difficult, but if reliable measures are derived, they can be used to investigate such interesting questions as the stability of the quantity, measured over long periods of time.

3. The most common design used in developmental research is the cross-sectional design, in which people of different ages (a cross-section of the population) are tested. Unfortunately, any differences found may be owing to factors confounded with age, such as differences in education or other particular life experiences. In the longitudinal design, the same group of people is tested repeatedly as they age, thus eliminating much of the confounding that occurs in the cross-sectional approach. Unfortunately, in some cases the longitudinal design can also be misleading, when the observed changes are not owing to age *per se*, but to life experiences that just happen to be correlated with age. The cross-sequential design embeds multiple cross-sectional and longitudinal designs within it and permits evaluation of variation caused by changing times or eras (rather than age), through examination of the time-lag design built into it. In the time-lag design, people of the same age are examined over different eras, thus revealing the effect of era rather than age. The cross-sequential design allows stronger inferences to be made about the effects of age, unconfounded with other factors, but unfortunately such designs are difficult to implement in practice. Most developmental research still relies on the cross-sectional approach, with attempts made to match people on other factors, such as socioeconomic status.

4. Operational definitions of psychological constructs involve specifying the construct in terms of the experimental operations used to study it. The Turing test defines intelligence in such a way that machines could possess intelligence. The controversy raised by this test points to the problem of the validity of operational definitions.

5. When individual differences such as intelligence, weight, or age are examined in experiments, they are referred to as subject variables. By their nature, subject variables preclude random assignment of subjects to conditions; one must avoid concluding that experimental effects are produced by subject variables, because some confounded factor may have produced the effect.

6. In studies in which subjects in two groups (a treatment and a control) are matched on some criterion rather than being randomly assigned to the two groups, there is a great likelihood that statistical regression will affect the results and conclusions drawn. When extreme groups of subjects are selected (extreme on one dimension), their scores upon retesting will tend toward the mean of the group. This occurs despite matching on other criteria. This can materially affect the outcome of a study, because we expect the scores of the groups to change even without any intervening treatment. Therefore, it becomes difficult or impossible to evaluate the effect of the treatment in studies employing such ex post facto quasi-experimental designs. The only sure way to avoid the problem is to randomly assign subjects to conditions in the first place.

KEY TERMS

AI (artificial intelligence)
analytical approach
Aphasic
Chinese room
chronological age
cohort
cohort effects
cross-sectional design
cross-sequential design
empirical approach
face validity
intelligence
longitudinal design
mental age
multiple intelligences
operational definition

parallel forms of a test
predictive (criterion) validity
quasi-experimental designs
regression artifact
regression to the mean
reliability
split-half reliability
strong AI
subject variables
test-retest reliability
time-lag design
tonal agnosia
Turing test
validity
weak AI

DISCUSSION QUESTIONS

1. Often, psychological tests are constructed to measure some psychological construct, such as intelligence, depression, or dietary restraint. One prime requirement is that such tests be reliable. What is reliability? Discuss three different ways of assessing reliability in a psychological test.

2. Discuss reasons that operational definitions are necessary in psychology. Provide two operational definitions for each of the following constructs: (a) thirst, (b) intelligence, (c) memory capacity, (d) sexual satisfaction, and (e) fear of snakes. Does it worry you that there can be more than one definition of the "same" construct?

3. Discuss the advantages and disadvantages of each of the following research designs for developmental research: (a) cross-sectional, (b) longitudinal, and (c) cross-sequential.

4. Discuss the strong AI approach to intelligence. Are computers intelligent?

5. A psychotherapist is interested in evaluating the effectiveness of the new therapy she has invented. It is called Pet Therapy and involves convincing depressed people to keep a dog as a pet, with the hope that in caring for the dog, the person will cheer up. To evaluate the therapy, the therapist gives each of her patients a dog from the Humane Society to care for. She measures depression using a written test (which has been shown to be reliable) a week before they get the pets and then two months later. She discovers that patients are much less depressed when assessed the second time and thus concludes that Pet Therapy is a success. Discuss several things wrong with this piece of research and the conclusion drawn from it. How are regression artifacts likely to have played a part? How could the research have been done better?

6. Discuss the following statement: "All experiments involving subject variables are quasi-experiments; the results obtained are always correlational in nature and possibly contaminated by confoundings." Is this statement true? Can you think of exceptions to it? In trying to do so, make a list of all the subject variables you can think of that might be of interest to psychologists.

A Demonstration of Regression Artifacts

A SERIOUS PROBLEM IN many areas of research is known as statistical regression to the mean, or the regression artifact. You can better appreciate this phenomenon by allowing yourself to become a victim of it. Try the following experiment, proceeding through the steps as given:

1. Roll six dice on a table in front of you.

2. Place the three dice showing the lowest numbers on the left, and the three dice showing the highest numbers on the right. In case of ties, randomly assign the dice to the two groups.

3. Compute and record the mean number per die for each group of three dice.

4. Raise both hands over your head and loudly proclaim, "Improve, in the name of Science."

5. Roll the three low-scoring dice and compute a new mean number per die for the low group.

6. Roll the three high-scoring dice and compute a new mean number per die for the high group.

7. Compare the pre- and posttreatment scores for both groups. Combine your data with those of your classmates, if possible.

On the average, this procedure will produce an increase in the performance of the low group and a decrease in the performance of the high group. You might be tempted to conclude that invoking the name of Science has a beneficial effect on underachieving dice and that overachieving dice require more individualized attention to maintain their outstanding performance. Such conclusions, however, fail to consider the effects of regression, which reflect the tendency for many types of measures to yield values close to their mean. You know that the roll of a fair die can yield values from 1 to 6, but that the average value from many rolls will be about 3.5.

The likelihood of the average of three dice being close to 3.5 is higher than the likelihood of this average being close to 1 or 6. Thus, when you select three dice that give you a low average and roll them again, they will tend to yield a higher average value (a value closer to the mean of 3.5). In the same way, the three dice in the high group should yield a lower value when rolled again.

In determining the effects of experimental treatments, you must subtract the regression effect from the total observed change. In the dice experiment, for example, control groups of dice that showed the same values on the first roll but received no "treatment" should be rolled again. Only if the change from pretest to posttest is significantly larger in the experimental group than in the control group can an effect caused by the treatment or independent variable be concluded. Studies that fail to control for regression, including many involving educational enrichment and psychotherapy, are difficult or impossible to evaluate.

Social Influence

We know more about the atom than ourselves, and the consequences are everywhere to be seen.

—CARL KAYSEN

T HE BEHAVIOR OF EVERY HUMAN is potentially determined by a web of complex social and cultural influences. Many of the acts we perform every day are determined by the culture and society into which we are born and raised. Our experience is limited by our culture, so that we are exposed to only a very small set of the potential actions humans might perform. Most people in our society will never speak Hottentot, sail outrigger canoes, or hunt wildebeest, for the very good reason that these activities are not part of our culture. In each society, the individual's behavior conforms to a large extent to that of his or her "significant others," that is, family, peers, teachers, and so on.

The psychological study of how society affects the individual is part of the field of *social psychology*. This is a large subject: a tremendous variety of research topics falls under the general rubric of social psychology. Among other things, it is concerned with how people are influenced to change their attitudes, beliefs, and behavior; how they form impressions of other people; why they like one another; the roots of aggression and violence; and the conditions determining altruism and helping. The list could easily be doubled. But with few exceptions, the topics studied by social psychologists have to do with the impact of society (other people) on the behavior of the individual.

Social psychologists generally are concerned with less global sorts of social influence than the influence of an entire cultural system on behavior, and so usually study more circumscribed topics. For example, a more direct form of social influence has to do with compliance or *obedience* to authority. How might one person or a group of people in authority induce others to follow commands, especially when those commands may be to perform antisocial or immoral acts? The most ghastly case of this in the twentieth century occurred in Nazi Germany, where a small cadre of fanatic Nazis instituted a program for the systematic murder of a large portion of the populace of Germany and of the countries it had conquered. The people who developed this plan were by far too few in number to implement it, so it was necessary for them to elicit the direct obedience of a large number of German citizens to carry out the murder of about six million Jews and five million others. They also had to receive the tacit acceptance of the bulk of the German population. Presumably, this heinous program was carried out by many otherwise normal people.

Much more recently, the issue of the unthinking obedience to authority has been brought to public attention by other tragic events. In 1978, the Reverend Jim Jones, founder of Jonestown, Guyana, ordered hundreds of his followers to commit suicide by drinking poison. They obeyed. A dozen years earlier, the issue of blind obedience was raised by the My Lai massacre during the Vietnam War. A portion of an interview between one of the participants and CBS reporter Mike Wallace went as follows:

Q. How many people did you round up?

A. Well, there was about forty, fifty people that we gathered in the center of the village. And we placed them in there, and it was like a little island, right there in the center of the village, I'd say . . . And . . .

Q. What kind of people—men, women, children?

A. Men, women, children.

Q. Babies?

A. Babies. And we huddled them up. We made them squat down and Lieutenant Calley came over and said, "You know what to do with them don't you?" And I said yes. So I took it for granted that he just wanted us to watch them. And he left, and came back about ten or fifteen minutes later and said, "How come you ain't killed them yet?" And I told him that I didn't think you wanted us to kill them, that you just wanted us to guard them. He said, "No, I want them dead." So.—. . .

Q. And you killed how many? At that time?

A. Well, I fired them automatic, so you can't—You just spray the area on them and so you can't know how many you killed 'cause they were going fast. So I might have killed ten or fifteen of them.

Q. Men, women, and children?

A. Men, women, and children.

Q. And babies?

A. And babies . . .

Q. Why did you do it?

A. Why did I do it? Because I felt like I was ordered to do it, and it seemed like that, at the time I felt like I was doing the right thing, because, like I said, I lost buddies . . .

Q. What did these civilians—particularly the women and children, the old men—what did they do? What did they say to you?

A. They weren't much saying to them. They (were) just being pushed and they were doing what they was told to do.

Q. They weren't begging, or saying, "no . . . no," or . . .

A. Right. They were begging and saying, "no, no." And the mothers was hugging their children, and . . . but they kept right on firing. Well, we kept right on firing. They was waving their arms and begging. (*New York Times*, Nov. 25, 1969)

Why do otherwise normal people perform such terrible acts when ordered to? Stated differently, what are the social psychological forces that operate in determining obedience to authority? Later we shall discuss research that explores this issue.

The Origins of Social Psychology

The enterprise of scientific psychology is only about a hundred years old, and the application of scientific method to the study of the interesting and complex phenomena of social psychology is even younger. The first two texts on social psychology appeared in 1908; one was written by William McDougall, a psychologist, and the other was written by E. A. Ross, a sociologist. In both books, the treatment of social psychology is very different from the approach used today. However, McDougall's book had a great impact in the field of psychology as a whole. He argued strongly that social behavior is largely determined by a variety of instincts that are inborn and relatively unaffected by either the history of a particular person or her or his present social situation. This view was thoroughly discredited, and even though the concept of instinct has made something of a comeback in psychology (Mason and Lott, 1976), no one today believes that it can explain complex human social behavior in the way McDougall tried to apply it.

Social psychology became established as an independent field of empirical study during the 1920s and 1930s. Many significant advances were made during this time, including the excellent early work of Muzafer Sherif (1935) on *social norms* (the generalized rules of conduct that tell us how we ought to behave) and the surprisingly powerful impact these rules have on our behavior. Sherif examined the influence of social norms and their development through studying a perceptual illusion, the autokinetic phenomenon. When a person is placed in a room that is completely dark and a single spot of light is shown on one of the walls, the light appears to move. This apparent movement occurs despite the fact that the light is actually stationary. The light seems to "move itself," thus giving rise to the name of the phenomenon.

Sherif was interested in how other people's judgments would affect those of a person perceiving the light. Would other people's judgments produce social norms that would affect the perceptions that an individual reported in this situation? What Sherif discovered from a number of experiments was that a person's judgments of how the spot of light moved were greatly influenced by reports of other participants. If the experimenter (or another subject) led a subject to expect the light to move in a wide arc, then the subject would usually report that in fact it did seem to move in a wide arc. These experiments indicated that a person's perceptual reports could be manipulated by social influence in a dramatic way and that this process could be studied experimentally. Thus Sherif's experiments helped provide the impetus for an experimental social psychology.

In Sherif's experiments, subjects were in quite an ambiguous situation. Perhaps they were easily influenced by others because they were so unsure of their own perceptions. Could we still find evidence for such great effects of social influence on perception and behavior if we made the situation less ambiguous? Solomon Asch (1951, 1956, 1958) asked this interesting question in his landmark experiments on conformity. Asch (1956) remarked on the importance of the problem as follows: "Granting the great power of groups, may we simply conclude that they can induce persons to shift their decisions and convictions in almost any desired direction, that they can prompt us to call true what we yesterday deemed false, that they can make us invest the identical action with the aura of rightness or the stigma of grotesqueness and malice?" (p. 2). The answer to this question provided by his experiments was a qualified yes, which has led many social psychologists to become interested in the topic of *conformity*.

The basic procedure Asch used is as follows. A group of students was gathered into a room to take part in what was described as a study of visual discrimination. They were shown a single line and then three comparison lines: their task was to say which of the three comparison lines matched the standard. An example appears in figure 13–1. There were seven people in the group in one experiment, but there was only one real subject. The other six were confederates of the experimenter, or assistants. The situation was arranged so that the real subject always responded with his or her answer next to last, after five other "subjects" had already given their judgments. Everyone gave his or her answers out loud, so that the rest of the group knew each person's response.

FIGURE 13–1.

Subjects in the perceptual discrimination task used by Asch were asked to decide
which of the comparison lines (*B*) was the same length as that of the standard (*A*).
How do you think you would respond if five people before you had all said that
comparison line 3 was the correct answer?

There were eighteen trials; in each case, one comparison line
was equal to the standard. The confederates were instructed to
give the correct answer on six of the trials, but to give a consistently
wrong answer on twelve trials. The question of interest was whether
the real subject in the procedure would conform to the group judgment and go against his or her own perception. A very large percentage of the subjects (about 70 percent—see table 13–1) did conform to the erroneous judgments of the group on one or more of
the twelve trials. A control group was also used, in which the
confederates did not make any errors; under these conditions, only
5 percent of the real subjects made an error.

These experiments indicate that group judgments can have
much power over the individual. However, later research has un-

TABLE 13–1. The distribution of conforming responses in the original Asch study.
Of 50 subjects, 37 conformed by picking the same (incorrect) line
that the confederates did on one or more trials. (From Wrightsman and
Deaux, 1981)

Number of Conforming Responses	Number of True Subjects Who Gave This Number of Conforming Responses
0	13
1	4
2	5
3	6
4	3
5	4
6	1
7	2
8	5
9	3
10	3
11	1
12	0
Total 78	50 subjects
Mean 3.84	

covered many factors that can lessen the influence of the group. For example, if just one confederate responding before the subject does not go along with the group but answers correctly, then the subject will usually fail to follow the lead of the majority, too, and respond with the correct answer.

At about the same time Sherif was writing about social norms, Kurt Lewin was also writing extensively about social psychology. Lewin provided a theoretical account of social behavior, known as field theory, as well as some interesting experiments. He was also quite concerned with applying the knowledge social psychologists were gathering to the solution of social problems. He helped found the Research Center for Group Dynamics (now at the University of Michigan) for the study of such topics as leadership and group productivity. He also played a major role in establishing "sensitivity training" and the T-group as a method of coping with complex human relationships.

Today, social psychology is one of the fastest-growing subdisciplines within psychology. Social psychologists employ experimental methods in attempting to understand many issues that are of interest to most individuals, such as aggression, attraction, and altruism and helping. But because most people are interested in social psychology and have probably given some thought to the topics it includes, they sometimes tend to regard its phenomena and theories as mere common sense. Worse yet, some people even believe this area is one that should not be approached in a scientific way with the logic of experimental method. Lewin (1948) argued against this sort of reasoning some years ago:

> For thousands of years man's everyday experience with falling objects did not suffice to bring him to a correct theory of gravity. A sequence of very unusual, man-made experiences, so-called experiments, which grew out of the systematic search for the truth were necessary to bring about a change from less adequate to more adequate concepts. To assume that first-hand experience in the social world would automatically lead to the formation of correct concepts or to the creation of adequate stereotypes seems therefore unjustifiable. (pp. 60–61)

 ## INTRODUCING THE VARIABLES

Dependent Variables

The dependent variable in social psychological research is often a measure of preference (or liking, or belief, etc.) obtained by having subjects fill out a questionnaire after experiencing some experimental treatment. For example, subjects might be asked to judge on a seven-point scale how much they liked or disliked the other subjects in the experiment, or how much they agree with the position that abortion is murder. These measures would usually be taken only after an experimental treatment was designed to influence the judgments in some way. Although much useful information has been gained through the questionnaire technique, social psychologists are increasingly turning to techniques by which overt behavior, rather than verbal report of covert preference, is measured. Though rating scales remain an important dependent measure in social psychological research, many experimenters try to also include behavioral measurement. Instead of asking a person how much animosity he or she feels toward another subject in an aggression experiment, the experimenter might set up the situation so that the subject had an opportunity to deliver mild electric shocks to the other subject, in the guise of a learning experiment. Thus, aggression could be measured in terms of how many shocks were delivered. (Actually, the confederate would receive no shocks.) Similarly, rather than ask a male subject how attracted he is to a female confederate in the experiment, the experimenter might measure how much he talks to her or smiles at her, or whether or not he asks her out. These are behavioral measures of aggression and attraction. Generally, the more converging measures we can obtain of the same hypothetical entity (aggression, attraction, and so on) that agree, the more faith we can place in the relation discovered in the experiment.

Independent Variables

Independent variables in social psychology experiments usually are character-

istics of a social situation or of the people in a situation that can be manipulated. In an experiment on attitude change, the persuasiveness of a message might be varied by manipulating the number of arguments used in support of the position being argued (for example, that abortion is murder). In an experiment testing the hypothesis that aggression increases as the temperature rises, the experimenter might vary the temperature of the room in which an aggressive activity might occur between a subject and a confederate. In an experiment on conformity, an investigator might vary the number of people who disagree with some judgment that a subject has made to see whether the subject will be more likely to change his or her mind. Variables concerning the characteristics of the subjects in the experiment, such as sex and race, also can be manipulated. Are people more likely to help (or show aggression against, or like, or agree with) people of their own sex or race?

Control Variables

The introduction of experimental control in social psychological research is quite tricky, since the situations dealt with are usually complex. It is often very difficult to vary one or several factors while keeping all others constant, the prerequisite for providing firm inferences about the relation between independent and dependent variables in experiments. The next section deals with this issue.

13.1 Experimental Topics and Research Illustrations

Topic: Experimental Control
Illustration: Obedience to Authority

Psychologists perform experiments to discover the causes of behavior. First, the investigator selects a problem of interest: Why does some behavior occur? Second, a hypothesis is suggested that provides a tentative understanding of the behavior. Usually the hypothesis will specify factors that cause or determine the behavior. The researcher will then try to create experimental conditions to test the hypothesis. If one factor has been pinpointed by the hypothesis as the alleged cause of the behavior, will the behavior in fact be affected when the factor is manipulated in a systematic way? In the experiment, the factor that is manipulated is called the independent variable, and the behavior measured is called the dependent variable. *Experimental control* has to do with the researcher's gaining control over other factors in the situation, so that he or she can be certain that the change in behavior is caused by the independent variable and not some other factor. The more complex the behavior of interest, the harder it is to gain control over all other relevant aspects of the situation.

Experimental error occurs when a change in the dependent variable—the behavior of interest—is produced by some factor other than the independent variable. Experimental control attempts to minimize or eliminate experimental error. One main source of experimental error is *confounding*, which occurs when a second variable is unintentionally varied along with the independent variable of interest. When this happens, the researcher cannot be certain whether the independent variable or the second, confounded variable has produced the change in the dependent variable.

There are several ways of reducing experimental error caused by confounding. The most direct is to control all other variables of interest, so that only the independent variable is manipulated. The other factors that are kept constant are referred to as *control variables*, as we have discussed previously (see chapter 3).

Sometimes it is not possible to rigidly control a variable across all conditions of an experiment; at such times, other techniques must be used. This problem occurs, for example, when a between-subjects experimental design is used. If there are two conditions, an experimental and a control condition, which differ in the manipulation of the independent variable, a researcher does not want to have any second variable on which the two groups also differ. However, in a between-subjects design, there is at least one other difference in conditions, which is built in: different groups of subjects are tested in the two conditions.

When it is not possible to control a variable, as with subjects in a between-subjects design, the experimenter randomizes the variable to discount its influence. Thus, if a between-subjects design is used, the researcher randomly assigns subjects to conditions. (The assignment is based on some scheme that guarantees true randomization, such as the random-numbers table, described in appendix C at the end of the book in table F). As subjects arrive for the experiment, the researcher could use the numbers in the table's rows to assign subjects to the conditions. If there are two conditions, odd numbers would indicate subjects in one condition, and even numbers would represent those in the other condition.

Randomization guarantees that even though the variable cannot be controlled, its influence will not affect the outcome of the experiment by being confounded with the independent variable. Although different subjects are assigned to the two conditions, the researcher can rest assured that on average, the subjects in the two conditions are equal in all important respects. Thus, if there is a statistically reliable difference in behavior between the two conditions, it could be safely attributed to the operation of the independent variable, and not to the fact that there were different subjects in the two conditions.

In social psychological research, investigators are interested in situations that are generally more complex than those considered thus far in the book. In social situations, many factors may influence people's behavior, such as the number of other people present, the behavior and attitudes of these other people, interpersonal dynamics, and other events or social interactions that may occur in an uncontrolled or unpredictable manner. That is, in social situations, there are many variables besides the independent variable that must be controlled or randomized before the researcher can be certain that any change in a dependent variable is caused by the independent variable.

How do we go about studying a complex social phenomenon in a controlled setting? Consider, for example, the problem of obedience to authority discussed at the beginning of this chapter. Obviously, there are a great number of factors to consider, such as the perceived power of the authority figure, the behavior the subject is expected to perform, the perceived consequences of disobedience, the effects of peer pressure, the political or ideological issues involved, etc. And how do we measure obedience? Obedience is an important topic that should be considered carefully and thoroughly understood. But how can we bring such a complex phenomenon into a controlled setting to study the critical factors underlying it, while holding the others constant?

Stanley Milgram answered this question in a fascinating series of experiments that culminated in a book on the topic (Milgram, 1974). We will consider these experiments as a case history of bringing a complicated social psychological topic into the lab for close scrutiny. The original experiments (Milgram, 1963, 1964a, 1965) all used a common methodology to establish obedience to authority in a controlled experimental setting. In the first study, Milgram (1963) used male subjects who responded to advertisements to participate, for pay, in a study of memory and learning at Yale University. When a subject appeared at the laboratory, he met another subject (actually a confederate of the experimenter) who was a 47-year-old accountant specially trained for his role. The confederate appeared rather mild-mannered and likable (figure 13–2). Subjects were told that very little was known about the effects of punishment on memory and that one of them was to be the teacher and one the learner in a scientific study of this topic. The subjects drew slips of paper from a hat to determine who was to appear in which role, but in actuality the drawing was rigged so that the naïve subject was always the teacher and the confederate was always the learner. The experimenter was played by a rather severe 31-year-old biology teacher who wore a white lab coat. The learner was strapped into an electric chair to prevent excessive movement, and electrodes were placed on his wrists with paste "to avoid blisters and burns." In response to a question by the learner the experimenter said, "Although the shocks can be extremely painful, they cause no permanent tissue damage" (Milgram, 1963, p. 373).

The teacher-subjects were required to read a paired-associate list to the learners (see chapter 10) and then later to test them on the list by presenting a stimulus and four alternatives, one of which was correct. The learner-confederate was required to pick the cor-

FIGURE 13–2.

The learner (or victim) in Milgram's original study on obedience to authority. Would you risk seriously harming this man in an experiment if someone told you to? Milgram's findings suggest that you would. (From Milgram, 1974, p. 17)

rect response from among the four alternatives and say it aloud. If he made an error, the teacher-subject was instructed to give him an electric shock by pressing a switch on an imposing shock generator. Although the confederate actually received no shocks, the subject had been given a mild sample shock at the beginning of the experiment to convince him that the generator was real. During the course of the experiment, subjects were required to increase the amount of shock every time the learner made an error. The primary dependent measure was the amount of electric shock the naïve subject was willing to give. The shock generator consisted of thirty lever switches, clearly labeled as proceeding from 15 to 450 volts. There were seven switches (in each of four groups), and they were given the following verbal descriptions (from left to right): Slight Shock, Moderate Shock, Strong Shock, Very Strong Shock, Intense Shock, Extreme-Intensity Shock, and Danger: Severe Shock. Two other switches at the far right were marked XXX.

From the beginning, the learner-confederate made errors; thus, the subject-teacher was supposed to administer ever-increasing electric shocks. In the original study, the confederate was out of sight of the subject, but he could be heard. His responses were standardized on tape. "Starting with 75 volts the learner begins to grunt and moan. At 150 volts he demands to be let out of the experiment. At 180 volts he cries out that he can no longer stand the pain. At 300 volts he refuses to provide any more answers. . . . The experimenter (then) instructs the naïve subject to treat the absence of an answer as equivalent to a wrong answer, and to follow the usual shock procedure" (Milgram, 1965, p. 61).

All subjects who participated in this procedure appeared very nervous and upset and frequently asked the experimenter what they should do next. Whenever subjects seemed unwilling to continue the experimenter had a series of statements (which accelerated to commands) which the subject was to obey. The first was rather gentle: "Please go on." Next was "The experiment requires that you continue," which progressed to "It is absolutely essential that you continue." Finally the experimenter said "You have no other choice. You *must* go on."

Milgram's (1963) results are truly remarkable. Of the 40 subjects originally tested in this situation, 26 (65 percent) "went all the way" and gave the confederate the full series of shocks, whereas the other 14 broke off the experiment by refusing to continue at or after the 300-volt level. The results are portrayed in figure 13–3. The subjects here were not impassive, cruel torturers. They were (just like you and me) normal people who felt a great deal of conflict in this situation. One chapter of Milgram's (1974) book contains transcripts that show that many subjects felt anguish but nonetheless continued under the directions of the experimenter. Most were sweating profusely and many were trembling. Another symptom of their discomfort was the occurrence of nervous laughter, which became uncontrollable in several subjects. One viewer of the experiment commented:

FIGURE 13–3.

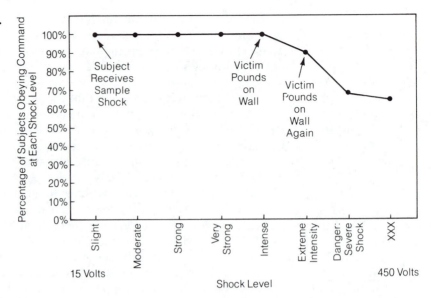

Percentage of subjects who obeyed commands to continue shocking the victim at various levels of shock intensity. Even when the victim reacted as if in pain and stopped responding to the memory task, almost two-thirds of the subjects obeyed the experimenter and administered shocks at the level of "danger" and beyond. (From Baron and Byrne, 1977, p. 292)

I observed a mature and initially poised businessman enter the laboratory smiling and confident. Within 20 minutes he was reduced to a nervous, stuttering wreck, who was rapidly approaching a point of nervous collapse. He constantly pulled on his earlobe and twisted his hands. At one point he pushed his fist into his forehead and muttered: "Oh God, let's stop it." And yet he continued to respond to every word of the experimenter, and obeyed to the end. (Milgram, 1963, p. 377)

It is interesting to note that Milgram's demonstration may actually *underestimate* people's willingness to obey. Because Milgram wanted to study obedience in a controlled laboratory setting, one source of obedience was lacking: genuine power over the subject's behavior. That is, the subject could have simply walked out of the experiment and never have suffered any negative repercussions for disobedience. However, in most real-world situations, an authority figure has the power to inflict harm if his or her orders are not followed. Parents, teachers, and law enforcement officials can punish those who disobey. Therefore, Milgram's study did not capture all the essential components of obedience as it naturally occurs. This difference between real-world settings and Milgram's laboratory setting does not devalue his contribution, however. Rather, it makes his demonstration all the more astonishing, when one realizes that he obtained such high levels of obedience *without* the threat of punishment for disobedience. We might predict that subjects would have been even more obedient if the experimenter had possessed any real power over them.

Conditions encouraging obedience. You might have noticed something lacking in the description of Milgram's study, something crucial to an experiment. There was no variation of an independent variable in the experiment. Thus, no information was gained about the conditions that enhance or diminish obedience to authority in this situation. Although Milgram employed a controlled setting to produce laboratory obedience, his first study is better referred to as a demonstration rather than an experiment, since there was no manipulation of an independent variable. Milgram, of course, realized this, and made no claims to the contrary. In the original report he outlined areas in which systematic variations in the procedure might lead to useful new information about conditions necessary for obedience; he also provided some of these variations in later experiments.

One factor that could have encouraged obedience in the original study was its setting; it was conducted at Yale University, an institution presumably held in high regard by the subject (at least before the experiment). Perhaps the general Yale aura helped foster obedience, since presumably this well-known institution would not allow its premises to be used for shady purposes. Milgram (1965) reported a later study similar to the original in most details, except that it was done in an old office building in a rather sleazy part of Bridgeport, Connecticut, under the auspices of Research Associates of Bridgeport, a fictitious company. Although compliance was somewhat reduced in the Bridgeport study (48 percent delivered the maximum shock, versus 65 percent in the original Yale sample), the difference was apparently not statistically significant; Milgram concluded that Yale's reputation was not responsible for the original high level of compliance. Since this conclusion is based on a failure to reject the null hypothesis, it is suspect (see chapter 3), especially since there was a rather large absolute difference between the two studies (17 percent). But it does seem safe to conclude that the Yale setting was not the critical factor in producing obedience.

It is of interest to ask what conclusions Milgram could have reached from this study if there had been a significant reduction in obedience in Bridgeport relative to the original Yale study. Could he have concluded that it was the nature of the setting (Yale versus a dilapidated office building) that produced the results? The answer is *no*, or at least *not strictly*, since many other conditions varied between the two situations besides the setting (for example, the city and the time of year). Thus, at least several variables were potentially confounded. It may have been that the different settings produced the result, since the experimenter and the confederates were the same in the two studies. But, in general, conclusions drawn from a comparison of conditions across different experiments is hazardous, since one can never be certain that all other conditions were held constant and that no confounding occurred. What could Milgram have concluded if the Bridgeport volunteers responding to his advertisement had turned out to differ in occupation or socioeconomic status from the Yale sample? (In fact, the two samples did not differ in any obvious way.) To determine the reasons for the differences in obedience, he would have had to conduct additional experiments. First, he could have formulated reasonable hypotheses regarding which factors were causing the differences (e.g., socioeconomic status, age, occupation). Then, he could have conducted a series of experiments in which he manipulated each factor, until he had identified the ones that affected obedience. In other words, when a variety of uncontrolled factors change across experiments (i.e., are confounded), and different results are found in those experiments, then the confounded factors must be isolated and varied independently to determine which ones produce the differences in behavior.

In more tightly controlled experiments, other variables have been found to have a great effect on obedience. When other people serve in the experiment as subjects who are supposed to provide shocks (though they are actually confederates), their behavior markedly affects that of the naïve subject. In one case Milgram (1965) had the two confederates refuse to continue at predetermined levels of shock. The results are portrayed in figure 13–4, which indicates that the naïve subjects were much better able to refuse to continue when others did. On the other hand, in another experiment when there were two conforming peers who encouraged the subject to increase the shock level, subjects administered much greater shock than when they determined the shock level themselves (Milgram, 1964a).

FIGURE 13–4.

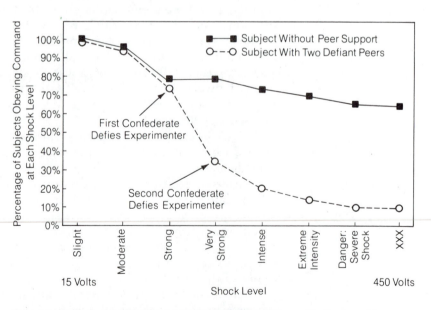

Group pressure as an influence in defying authority. When subjects do not have peer support, 65 percent continue to obey the experimenter's commands to give stronger and stronger shocks throughout the experiment. When subjects are with peers who defy the experimenter, only 10 percent continue to obey the experimenter's commands. (From Baron and Byrne, 1977, p. 297)

Another interesting manipulation Milgram (1965) tried was to vary the closeness of the victim, so that in one condition the subject could only hear the victim moan and complain; in another condition he was in the same room so he could also see the victim; and in yet another condition the subject was actually instructed to force the learner's arm down onto the metal shock plate on each trial (figure 13–5). Although obedience decreased with closeness of the victim, from 74 percent to 40 percent to 30 percent obeying the experimenter's instructions to the end in the different conditions, it is still remarkable that almost one-third of the subjects continued to give the shocks even when they had to hold down the person's hand.

Milgram's research on obedience allows us to see how an interesting and complicated problem concerning social influence can be investigated in the relatively controlled setting of the social psychology laboratory. Although not all aspects of obedience are transported into the lab (for example, the person issuing commands had no real power over the subject), the situation was still compelling enough to produce a dramatically high level of compliance.

Before leaving this topic, we should briefly mention three more issues. Many people who encounter Milgram's research say "I wouldn't do that." The point is that, given the appropriate setting, you probably would. Yale college students were tested in the original situation; their results were no different from those of the "real people" in the New Haven community. Perhaps after reading this you would not participate in a situation exactly like Milgram's,

FIGURE 13–5.

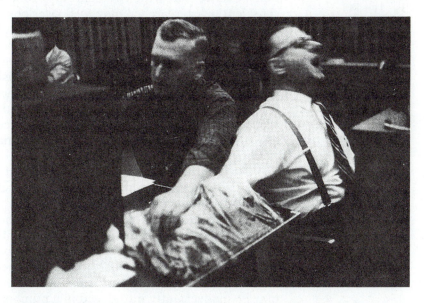

An obedient subject shocking a subject while forcing his arm onto the metal plate. (From Milgram, 1974, p. 37)

but you would probably do similar things without giving them much thought.

A second aspect of Milgram's studies that often provokes comment is whether or not it was (and is) ethical to put subjects through this procedure, since their cooperation is obtained under false pretenses and the procedure is quite stressful. These issues have been debated by Baumrind (1964) and Milgram (1964b) at some length, so we will simply refer the interested reader to these articles and Appendix I of Milgram's (1974) book for comment on the ethical issues involved in this research. (We considered the problem of ethics in chapter 4.)

Finally, as Milgram points out repeatedly in his writing, obedience in itself is not necessarily bad. In fact, if almost all of us did not obey the numerous laws and persons in authority in our society, life would be all but unthinkable. It is only when one is asked to obey commands that produce harm that the issue arises.

13.2 Experimental Topics and Research Illustrations

Topic: Demand Characteristics and Experimenter Bias
Illustration: Hypnosis

Psychological experiments typically employ as much experimental control as can be mustered by the prudent investigator. This section is concerned with two sources of bias that even the most conscientious researcher may well overlook: bias introduced by the experimenters and by the subjects themselves. The problem of *experimenter bias* is potentially prevalent in all sciences. The most blatant form of bias is the deliberate faking of data. The social pressures that exist to be productive, to publish many articles, and to find spectacular results so as to receive more money from granting agencies have led some investigators to fake results. Broad and Wade (1982) consider a number of documented cases of such fraud and discuss the problem at length. Unfortunately, nothing much can be done by scientists to reduce this sort of fraud, except to be vigilant and to punish offenders whenever they are caught. Such frauds may be uncovered when other researchers try to replicate and confirm the work.

Experimenter bias refers not only to the conscious cases of fraud, but also to the much more subtle influences that experimenters may unknowingly exert on the outcome of their research. That such effects do occur has been established by much research, as well as by anecdotal observations. This more covert form of bias may be inadvertently introduced in a number of ways. The experimenter may interact with the subjects in the different conditions in slightly different ways; the tone of voice and emphasis may change when the instructions are read; and, similarly, facial cues, gestures, and so forth may differ. The experimenter may not even be aware of such effects, but expectations of the way the subjects should behave in the different conditions may change her or his behavior very slightly to help produce the expected effect.

Rosenthal (1966, 1969) reviewed work (much of it his own) on the influence of experimenter expectancies and discussed various solutions to the problem. One of the most effective solutions is for the experimenter to keep himself or herself insulated in some way from knowing either the hypotheses being considered or the particular conditions of the subject being tested. In such a case, the experimenter is said to be *blind* with respect to conditions. Unfortunately, it is difficult or impractical to satisfy this condition in much research, because the experimenter must administer the conditions.

The problem of experimenter bias, although potentially dangerous, may not be as serious as is sometimes assumed. Barber and Silver (1968) exhaustively analyzed the research on experimenter expectancy effects and argue that there is still not enough evidence to conclude that such effects are proven phenomena. Regardless of the validity of this claim, other factors make us believe that the importance of experimenter effects is often exaggerated. We have emphasized repeatedly throughout this book that the results of any individual experiment need to be viewed in the context of other, similar experiments before one can make a generalization. If a particular experimental result is considered important, one can rest assured that much future research will be directed toward discovering the conditions under which it holds, explicating the mechanisms involved, and so on. In the course of such research, there will be many occasions for the basic phenomenon to be replicated by experimenters with many different views on the subject, some hoping to find it, some hoping not to. If the phenomenon is replicated by all, then we can assume that it is not produced by experimenter bias; if not, we can suspect experimenter bias of being responsible for part of the difficulty. The important point is that experimenter bias, or even the blatant dishonesty of an isolated investigator, will be discovered in the normal course of scientific inquiry. Such effects should still be guarded against with all possible caution, of course. It is simply that in the long run, effects of experimenter bias will likely be winnowed out in the scientific process.

A potentially more powerful source of bias, which is unique to the social sciences, has to do with the subject and what she or he expects to occur in a psychological experiment. Martin Orne (1962, 1969) pioneered in making psychologists aware of this problem. He pointed out that subjects entering an experiment have some general notions of what to expect and are probably trying to figure out the specific purpose of the experiment. They are likely to believe that reasonable care will be taken for their well-being and that whatever the experimenter asks them to do will serve a useful purpose. They will also want to know this purpose and seek clues in the experimental situation. Because many psychological experiments, especially ones in social psychology such as Milgram's obedience studies, would provide uninteresting results if the true purpose of the study were known (everyone would soon refuse to obey the experimenter), elaborate deceptions are often involved to mask the true purposes of the experiment. But, as Orne points out, these might sometimes be rather transparent. At any rate, the general problem exists as to how the subject's expectations affect or determine her or his behavior in an experiment. As Orne (1969) notes:

> Insofar as the subject cares about the outcome, his perception of his role and of the hypothesis being tested will become a significant determinant of his behavior. The cues which govern his behavior—which communicate what is expected of him and what the experimenter hopes to find—can therefore be crucial variables. Some time ago I proposed that these cues be called "demand characteristics of an experiment." . . . They include the scuttlebutt about the experiment, its setting, implicit and explicit instructions, the person of the experimenter, subtle cues provided by him, and, of particular importance, the experimental procedure. (p. 146)

If results of an experiment are produced by *demand characteristics* of the experimental situation, they will not generalize to other situations. It is well known that people's awareness of being part of an experiment will greatly affect their behavior. In Psychology in Action at the end of the chapter, we suggest an exercise you can carry out to demonstrate this point.

In all laboratory experiments, subjects realize that they are being observed and that their behavior is being carefully monitored. The subjects' expectations of how they are supposed to behave may greatly determine their performance in the experiment. Another phenomenon of this sort is well known to medical researchers; it is called the *placebo effect*. This refers to the fact that when patients in medical research are given a chemically inert substance and told that it is medicine that should help them, they often show an improvement in the illness or find relief from their pain. Thus, when a drug is evaluated in medical research it is not enough to compare a group of patients that receives the drug with a group that does not, because the patients who receive the drug may improve simply because of the placebo effect (see chapter 6). Instead, the drug group is also compared with a placebo group, so that the effect of the drug can be measured in relation to the placebo effect. Usually the doctors administering the drugs are also blind to the condition of the patients, so that their expectations of improvement cannot affect the results.

In one line of laboratory research, Orne (1962) sought to find a task that was so meaningless and boring that normal subjects would refuse to perform it. He was interested in finding such a task because he then wanted to see whether or not subjects under the influence of hypnosis would perform the task when instructed to do so. One experiment involved giving subjects two thousand sheets of paper filled with rows of random digits. The subjects were instructed to add together the many pairs of digits in each row on all the sheets. Clearly, it was an impossible task; Orne assumed that the control subjects would quickly realize this and refuse to go on. But instead, the subjects, who were deprived of their watches, kept at the task for hours on end, with little decrement in performance. Subjects in a later study (that aimed at making the task even more onerous and meaningless) were told that after each sheet was completed, they were to pick up a card and follow the direction written on it. Each card instructed the subject to tear up the sheet of paper into a minimum of thirty-two pieces and continue on to the next sheet. Still subjects persisted for hours. When questioned, they explained their behavior by saying that since they were in an experiment, they figured there must be a good reason for the request (an endurance test, or the like).

Investigators have asked subjects under hypnosis to do all sorts of things, often with notable success. One apparently well-established finding is that subjects under hypnosis can be led to perform various antisocial and destructive acts, such as throwing acid in someone's face and handling venomous snakes (Rowland, 1939; Young, 1952). Orne and Evans (1965) suspected that this behavior might have been owing more to the demand characteristics of the situation than to the effects of hypnosis. They asked subjects to perform a series of seemingly dangerous acts, such as grasping a venomous snake, taking a coin from fuming acid, and throwing nitric acid in the experimenter's face. (The procedures were designed to appear threatening, but the acts were really safe for the subjects.) There were several treatment conditions: (1) subjects who were under deep hypnosis; (2) subjects who were told to simulate or pretend that they were under hypnosis; (3) awake control subjects who were not asked to simulate hypnosis, but who were pressed by the experimenter to comply with the requests; (4) awake control subjects who were not pressed to comply; and (5) people who were asked to perform the tasks without being made part of an experiment. The experimenter in this study was blind to the conditions of the subjects, so as not to affect their behavior. The results are summarized in table 13–2. As would be expected, people not in the experimental setting refused to carry out the antisocial tasks, but as other investigators had reported, a high percentage of hypnotized subjects did carry out the tasks as instructed. However, *all* simulating control subjects also performed the tasks; even the nonsimulating controls performed them to a large extent if they were pressed to comply, which demonstrates the power of the experimental situation.

The conclusion to be drawn is that hypnosis is not necessarily responsible for subjects' performance of the antisocial acts. Rather, demand characteristics of the experimental situation, including

TABLE 13–2.   Percentage of subjects who performed dangerous tasks in response to requests by the experimenter. (Adapted from Orne and Evans, 1965)

Subject Group	Grasp Venomous Snake	Take Coin from Acid	Throw Acid at Experimenter
Real hypnosis	83	83	83
Simulating hypnosis	100	100	100
Waking control— press to comply	50	83	83
Waking control— without press to comply	50	17	17
Nonexperimental	0	0	0

the setting, the instructions, and the way subjects think they are supposed to behave while under hypnosis, are sufficient to produce the antisocial acts. Perhaps people can be induced to perform antisocial acts under deep hypnosis, but studies currently available do not offer reliable evidence to support the idea that hypnosis is responsible for the behavior.

The use of *simulating control subjects,* as in the Orne and Evans experiment, is one way of attacking the problem of demand characteristics. The logic is essentially the same as that for using a placebo condition in medical research. The demand characteristics of the situation are assumed to be the same for subjects in both the experimental condition and the simulating control condition. If the experimental manipulation (say, hypnosis) is truly effective, then the behavior of the experimental subjects should differ reliably from that of the simulating controls. One problem with this logic, of course, is the implication that because no difference was found, no difference exists. This is an example of the logical error of accepting the null hypothesis (appendix B). However, the failure to find a difference between the hypnotized and simulating control subjects does not prove that hypnosis has no effect on behavior. Rather, Orne and Evans's experiment simply makes the point that there is an alternative explanation of hypnotized subjects' compliance with requests to perform dangerous acts: subjects may be responding to the demand characteristics of the situation, rather than demonstrating a unique effect of hypnosis.

The problem of demand characteristics is a thorny one, especially in social psychological research. As Orne (1969, p. 156) points out, these concerns are less important in those experimental studies that do not involve deception and that encourage subjects to respond as accurately as possible. But in studies where optimal performance may not be encouraged for various reasons and where deception is often involved, results may be contaminated by demand characteristics. In the hypnosis study, subjects in all experimental conditions said they performed the acts because they were in an experiment and felt assured, despite rather convincing pretenses to the contrary, that the experimenter had taken precautions against harming them and himself. (They were correct.) Interestingly, Orne and Holland (1968) argued that Milgram's results on obedience may have largely been produced by similar demand characteristics in the experimental situation. Subjects might have seen through Milgram's deceptions and, at any rate, assumed that no one would really be harmed in the experiment, since the experimenter himself never became concerned. Milgram (1972) replied, and criticized their argument on various grounds. He argued that if his subjects were just doing what they thought the experimenter expected of them and were not really concerned about the safety of the person they were shocking, they would not have shown signs of nervousness and conflict, such as perspiration, trembling, and uncontrollable laughter.

13.3 Experimental Topics and Research Illustrations

Topic: Field Research
Illustration: Bystander Intervention

The problems of demand characteristics in laboratory settings, along with other factors, have caused many social psychologists to turn to *field research* in recent years. Rather than attempting to bring some phenomenon into the laboratory for study in a controlled setting, the researcher instead attempts to introduce enough control into a setting (in "the field") to allow inferences to be made about how variations in an independent variable affect a dependent variable. In such cases, there is no problem of generalizing to the real world, since the experiment is conducted in the real world to begin with. However, in some ways, field research in social psychology is even more difficult to conceive and carry out than laboratory research. We shall discuss some of these problems before examining a field study.

The crux of experimental method in laboratory research is to abstract relevant variables from complex situations in nature and then reproduce parts of these situations, so that by varying different factors we may determine their contribution to the behavior of interest. By bringing the phenomenon into the laboratory, we gain control over the situation. The main problems in field research have to do with this issue of control. How can we gain control over and manipulate the independent variable in a field setting? Presuming we can do this, how do we then simultaneously go about controlling or randomizing all the other factors that are likely to be varying willy-nilly in complex situations? And what do we measure, anyway, in a naturally occurring setting? What should our dependent variable be? There are all sorts of things we could measure, but how directly related are they to the phenomenon of interest? These are very difficult questions; the answers will depend to a great extent on the problem investigated and the ingenuity of the individual researchers in providing control in a complex situation.

The issue of specifying dependent variables is treated systematically by Webb, Campbell, Schwartz, and Sechrest in a book called *Unobtrusive Measures: Nonreactive Research in the Social Sciences* (1966). The authors are concerned with the problem of people's changes in behavior when they know they are being observed or studied. They discuss a number of "unobtrusive" measures that can be taken on behavior without the subject's knowledge and that are thus suitable for use in field research in psychology and other social sciences (see chapter 2). Although their book contains many clever and ingenious suggestions, most of the unobtrusive measures they describe have little bearing on many psychological problems under active investigation by psychologists. The primary problem in obtaining a good dependent measure, or providing a good operational definition of whatever underlying construct one is trying to measure, is ensuring that a plausible link exists between the construct and what is measured. This is a problem in all research, as is that of finding converging operations on a construct, but in field research these problems are magnified. The dependent measure seems often only tangentially related to the underlying construct, as when, say, a standard mortality ratio is used as an index of social pathology (see chapters 2 and 14).

Another problem in field research is the question of ethics. Can we justify involving people in research in the name of science when they do not volunteer and are in fact unsuspecting? Should we allow ourselves to manipulate our fellow citizens (via the independent variable) and then record their reactions (the dependent variables)? This is especially a problem when the manipulation involves inducing stress or embarrassment or some other undesirable state. In the lab, psychologists can (and are required to) debrief participants after the experiment and tell them why they were placed in this uncomfortable situation, but in the field this is usually not done, since the participants are not even aware that they are being manipulated and observed by psychologists. Psychologists have decided, not without a certain amount of self-interest, that field research is allowable as long as no great stress or harm is occasioned on the "subjects." Whether citizens themselves will agree with this judgment when (if) the legitimacy of field research ever becomes an issue is another matter. Certainly we do not tolerate manipulation and eavesdropping by government agencies, and it seems unlikely that the public at large will find psychologists' scientific motives any more acceptable. The issue has not yet arisen to a great extent, but when it does, it may spell the death knell for field research.

Before discussing a field study concerned with *bystander inter-*

vention, let us examine how social psychologists became interested in this topic. Consider the following actual incidents.

> Kitty Genovese is set upon by a maniac as she returns home from work at 3 A.M. Thirty-eight of her neighbors in Kew Gardens come to their windows when she cries out in terror; none come to her assistance even though her stalker takes over half an hour to murder her. No one even so much as calls the police. She dies.
>
> Andrew Mormille is stabbed in the stomach as he rides the A train home in Manhattan. Eleven other riders watch the 17-year-old boy as he bleeds to death; none come to his assistance even though his attackers have left the car. He dies.
>
> An 18-year-old switchboard operator, alone in her office in the Bronx, is raped and beaten. Escaping momentarily, she runs naked and bleeding to the street, screaming for help. A crowd of 40 passersby gathers and watches as, in broad daylight, the rapist tries to drag her back upstairs; no one interferes. Finally, two policemen happen by and arrest her assailant.

These vignettes are taken verbatim from a fascinating book by Bibb Latané and John Darley called *The Unresponsive Bystander: Why Doesn't He Help?* (1970, pp. 1–2), in which they describe their research in trying to answer this question. Although there are potentially many reasons the bystander may not help in such crisis situations, one that cropped up early in this research had to do with the number of bystanders. The more people who observe a crisis and who are potential helpers, the *less* likely any one bystander is to help the victim. In one laboratory experiment (Darley and Latané, 1968), subjects were led to believe that they were participating (via an intercom system) in a discussion on personal problems in college life, with either one, two, or five other students. The experimenter left the scene after the subject had been given instructions. The discussion began with the students introducing themselves, but suddenly one of the students started to act, in a very convincing way, as though he were undergoing an epileptic seizure. (Actually only one subject participated at a time; the other voices heard were recorded.) The interest was in seeing how the subjects would behave when they thought there were zero, one, or four other bystanders. The results are shown in table 13–3, where it can be seen that the percentage of subjects trying to help the stranger decreased as the number of other bystanders increased. Even when subjects did respond to the emergency, they were slower when they thought others were also present in the situation. There is apparently a "diffusion of responsibility," so that the more people present (and the more people there are to potentially witness one's making a fool of oneself), the less any individual feels responsible to intervene. A student in a class with a hundred other students feels less responsible for answering an instructor's question than a student in a class with five others.

TABLE 13–3. Both the percentage of people who help a person having an epileptic seizure and the speed with which they respond are affected by the number of others in the situation. As the number increases, fewer individuals try to help and more time passes before help is given. (From Darley and Latané, 1968)

Number of Bystanders	Percentage of Subjects Trying to Help Stranger	Number of Seconds Elapsing before Subject Tries to Help
1	85	52
2	62	93
5	31	166

An interesting field study on bystander intervention was conducted on a New York City subway by Piliavin, Rodin, and Piliavin (1969). (We discussed another bystander intervention study by these researchers in chapter 3.) They picked an express run between two stations that lasted 7.5 minutes and produced an emergency in order to observe who responded and how fast. Four teams of students conducted the experiment, which involved the collapse of one person (the victim) on the train about seventy seconds after it left the station. The independent variables were the race of the victim and whether the victim appeared to be ill (he carried a cane) or drunk (he carried a liquor bottle wrapped in a brown paper bag and also smelled of liquor). Two other experimenters served as observers and recorded the dependent measures, which were whether help was offered and the time that elapsed before help was offered. In addition, they recorded the race of the helper, the number of helpers, and the number and racial composition of the group of bystanders or observers.

Some of the predictions were that people would be more likely to help a person of their own race than of another race, that help would more likely be given when the victim was perceived as ill rather than drunk, and that the tendency to help would decrease with the number of observers. Interestingly, these predictions (which seem to accord with common sense) were only partially verified. There was a clear tendency for help to be offered more readily to ill than drunk victims (on 95 percent of the trials for the ill victim versus 50 percent for the drunk victim). But in both of these conditions, the number of observers did not in any way affect the likelihood that help would be offered or the speed with which it was offered. Also, the race of the ill victim did not affect whether one or the other race helped. However, when the victim was drunk, people of the same race helped the victim more than did people of a different race.

Let us consider again the diffusion-of-responsibility theory. This hypothesis was developed by Darley and Latané when they analyzed factors that might have influenced bystanders who failed to respond to crises in natural settings. They tested this idea in a laboratory situation by systematically varying the number of bystanders and found support for it. But then when the idea was tested in the natural circumstances of the field (where the phenomenon was first noticed), no evidence was found for it! Presumably, the results differed not because of any great difference between field and laboratory research, but because of other subtle factors that influence helping in such complex situations.

How can we determine what these factors are? First, the researcher would have to formulate hypotheses to answer this question: Under what circumstances does an increased number of bystanders reduce other people's willingness to intervene? After deciding which variables may be important, the experimenter must systematically vary them to see which influence bystander intervention when different numbers of bystanders are present. In this case, the experimenter would be searching for an *interaction* (chapter 3) between the number of bystanders and some other factor that he or she is trying to discover.

One other lesson to be drawn from bystander-intervention studies is that the responses of others greatly determine what we perceive as the social reality of a situation. If forty other people stand around watching a murder, you and I will, too. Such behavior is seen as appropriate, since everyone else is doing it. Why risk our necks, when all these others could help? Where are the police when you need them? Research has shown that if people are made to feel responsible for a crisis or see someone else intervene, they are more likely to intervene (Moriarity, 1975). These facts may help explain why Milgram's subjects did not intervene to help the victim: the only other person in the situation (the experimenter) remained cool and unconcerned. Also, the subject was told that the experimenter was responsible if anything happened to the victim.

The examples of social psychological research presented in this chapter fall under the rubric of social impact. Latané (1981) has developed an interesting theory of social impact that seems to account for obedience on the one hand and diffusion of responsibility on the other. His theory focuses on the impact associated with the number of social forces (typically other people) that are present. Latané presents a substantial amount of data consistent with the idea that people conform or obey according to a power function: *Impact = Number of People^t,* where the exponent t is less than one. The equation is usually presented as $I = N^t$, and it is the same sort of relationship that Stevens thought existed between psychological judgments of intensity and the physical intensity of a stimulus (see chapter 6). So, the more people demanding obedience, the greater the obedience, but each additional person has less impact.

Latané cleverly adapted this equation to describe diffusion of responsibility. He reasoned that the impact of any one person decreases as you add other people, and data from numerous experiments show that further additions of others has less and less negative influence on impact. This relationship also describes a power function, but in this case there is a negative exponent: *Diffusion = Number of People*$^{-1}$ ($I = N^{-1}$). The data from studies concerned with diffusion of responsibility fit the equation very well. Thus the two equations specify the effects of the presence of others when a person is the target of social influence ($I = N^{1}$) and when a person and other people are attempting to apply social impact ($I = N^{-1}$).

The field experiments concerned with bystander intervention serve as good examples of well-conducted field research. Although it is not possible to control variables as tightly as could be done in a laboratory setting, the independent variables can be manipulated without being confounded with other variables. This is achieved by randomizing over the other variables. For example, on each train run in the Piliavin, Rodin, and Piliavin study, the condition of the experiment was randomly determined. Thus, other variables—such as differences among the particular people riding on the trains—were randomized across the conditions, which greatly reduced the probability that they affected the conclusions drawn from the study. However, we can ask if there was an ethical problem in conducting this research, since the "subjects" did not know they were in the experiment. Suppose one of the bystanders had fainted (or had had a heart attack) while observing the crisis that was staged repeatedly in the course of the experiment. Would the knowledge gained from the experiment be worth the ordeal of the subjects? This issue confronts anyone who chooses to investigate problems through field research.

 # From Problem to Experiment: The Nuts and Bolts

Problem: How Does the Presence of Other People Affect an Individual's Performance on a Task?

The presence of other people can affect our behavior in many ways. Certainly, when we know someone is watching us, we behave differently than when we believe we are unobserved. One example of this effect is known as *social facilitation*, which is the phenomenon that the presence of others can facilitate an individual's performance on a task. You may have noticed this effect yourself when you are exercising at a gym or playing a sport, for example. When spectators are present, you probably exert just a bit more effort and perform a little better. From this observation, we might predict that when people work together on a task, they will actually do better than when they work alone.

Problem: *Do people perform better when they work on a task with other people?*

This is an important consideration in industry, for example. Should jobs be designed so that people work alone or in groups? Are there conditions under which individual performance may be helped or hindered by others? What are those conditions?

Hypothesis: *When a person shares responsibility for a task with others, she or he will perform better on the task than if she or he performs it alone.*

To test this hypothesis, we must first find an appropriate task for our subjects to perform in the laboratory. We must select something that can be performed both alone and with a group of people. Furthermore, the task must have an outcome that is measurable and comparable in both the individual and group situations. For example, suppose the task were to design a better telephone for the handicapped. Naturally, we would expect most group designs to be better than most individuals' designs (with the exception of an occasional genius, perhaps). But how would we compare the performance of each individual working in the group to his or her performance working alone? When working alone, the individual is solely responsible for the product. When working in a group, the individual is a member of a team and contributes only partially to the final product. It would be difficult to determine how much the individual contributes to the group product relative to his or her individual product. What we need is a task that is essentially the same whether performed alone or in a group, and that also reflects the effects of group effort, while still allowing us to assess the individual's relative contribution.

A potential candidate for this task is one involving physical exertion, such as the force with which one can pull on a rope, a task discussed in research described in chapter 1. Let us see if this task meets the criteria outlined above. First, the performance measure is easily quantified. The rope can be attached to a mechanism that measures the amount of force exerted when a person pulls on it. Second, the measure is meaningful whether one or several people pull the rope, since the metric of performance, i.e., force, is the same in both situations. Finally, individual performance can be easily compared with group performance. We can ask each subject to pull on the rope alone as hard as posible, then add up all the subjects' force scores. This sum would represent the potential contribution of each individual to the group effort and would serve as a baseline for comparing the effect of group performance. Next, we could have all the subjects pull on the rope together and compare the force exerted by the group to the sum of the individual's forces. If the group's total is greater than the sum of the individuals' scores, we would conclude that people's individual performance improves when they perform this task with others. We would know that in general the subjects exerted more effort in the group than when alone.

One interesting question that arises in connection with this experiment is whether the size of the group affects individual performance. For example, if we believe that other people's presence will facilitate performance, then maybe the more people present, the more performance will be facilitated.

Hypothesis: *The larger the group working together, the greater will be the improvement in the individuals' performance.*

We can easily test this hypothesis with our rope-pull task. We can simply vary the size of the groups that we test: say, groups of two, three, five, and eight subjects.

Now, let us summarize the experimental variables so far. We have two independent variables, group size (two, three, five, or eight) and social environment (alone versus with the group). Group size will be a between-subjects factor; we cannot manipulate this within subjects because the groups are of different sizes, so by definition, we must have different subjects in each group. Social environment will be compared within subjects: each subject will perform the rope-pull task alone and also with a group.

Our dependent variable will be the *total* force exerted by the group members. In the alone condition, the individuals' scores will be summed to obtain the total score. There is one difficulty with this measure, now that we have decided to compare groups of different sizes. The total forces will be much greater in the larger than in the smaller groups, since more scores contribute to the total in the large groups. To make the groups comparable, we can convert the group scores to ratios. That is, we can measure the total force exerted by the group, and then divide this by the sum of the individual forces of the members of this group. For example, if a group exerted 500 pounds of tension on the rope when they pulled together, and a summed total of only 400 pounds when they pulled alone, the ratio would be 5/4. If we predict that the group will facilitate individual performance, these ratios should be larger than 1.00: the group force (the numerator) should be larger than the sum of the individual forces (the denominator). Furthermore, if we predict that larger groups produce more facilitation, the ratio should increase as group size increases (for example, 5/4 for a group of three subjects vs. 6/4 for a group of eight subjects).

What other factors must we consider? First, we must test more than one group in each condition. Even though a few subjects will participate in each group, each group will only provide two data points, the sum of the force exerted by the members alone and the total force exerted by the group pulling together. Obviously, we cannot make meaningful comparisons if we have only one observation in each group-size condition. Ideally, we should test 20 to 30 groups in each condition. Second, we should counterbalance the order of the pulling conditions. For each group-size condition, the individuals in half the groups should perform the individual pull first; the other half of the subjects should perform the group pull first. Third, subjects should have an adequate rest between their individual and group pulls, so that their muscles are not more fatigued in one condition than in the other.

Now let us think back over our experiment. First, do you think that we will find evidence for social facilitation? That is, do you think that people will exert more effort when they pull with the group than when they pull alone? Second, do you think that people in the larger groups will exert more effort than people in the smaller groups? Can you think of any reason that we might actually predict that the opposite will happen, that is, that the group situation will actually produce *poorer* performance? Recall that in the last section (and in chapter 1) we introduced the idea of *diffusion of responsibility* to explain bystander apathy. That is, in many settings it has been observed that the more people who witness an emergency, the *less* likely it is that any one person will intervene, perhaps because individuals feel personally less responsible when others are around to help. Interestingly, we can invoke this theory to predict that sharing the work with other people will actually *reduce* individual performance: the opposite prediction to that made by our social facilitation hypothesis. Therefore, our proposed experiment provides a test of two competing theories, a desirable situation from a scientist's point of view.

As you will recall from chapters 1 and 3, experiments very similar to the one we have proposed have been conducted: the research indicates that, in fact, people work *less* hard in a group than when alone. The earliest such study (by Ringelmann, reported in Kravitz and Martin, 1986) suggested that groups of two work at only 93 percent of their total individual capabilities, and groups of four and eight dropped to 77 percent and 49 percent, respectively. Thus, contrary to our original predictions (social facilitation), individuals' performance is lower in groups, and becomes lower still as the group size increases. This phenomenon has been called *social loafing* (Latané, Williams, and Harkins, 1979) and seems consistent with the notion that responsibility diffuses among the members of a group, reducing individual effort ($I = N^{-1}$).

Does our experiment disprove the hypothesis of social facilitation? Not at all. As further research has shown, the critical variable determining whether the presence of other people facilitates or impairs an individual's performance is whether the individual's behavior can be uniquely observed in the situation. That is, when people know that their personal performance can be assessed, they are likely to work harder when others are present. However, if a person can "fade into the crowd," then he or she is likely to expend less effort. ("After all, why should I knock myself out when nobody notices, anyway?")

The advice to the business manager would seem to be that work groups should be designed so that a person's output can be observed by others (to produce social facilitation) and also so that each individual's efforts can be assessed independent of those of the group (to prevent social loafing).

SUMMARY

1. Social psychological research is in many ways more difficult to perform than other types of research discussed in this book, because the situations examined are often quite complex, with many variables affecting behavior. Thus, introducing experimental control into the situation so that sound inferences can be made about the effects of different experimental treatments on the dependent variable often requires great effort.

2. Experimental control combats the problem of experimental error, or any variation in the dependent variable that is not caused by the independent variable. Such extraneous factors should be controlled as much as possible by equating them across conditions. If control is not possible, then these factors should be randomly distributed over conditions.

3. The expectations of both the experimenter and the subjects can create problems in social psychological (and other) research. The experimenter may subtly bias results in several ways, for example, by treating subjects slightly differently in the different conditions. A solution to this problem is for the experimenter to be blind with respect to the subject's condition at the time of test—but often, this is not feasible, since the experimenter must provide the experimental manipulation in some way. Experimenter-bias effects are likely to be discovered in the normal course of scientific research.

4. The problem of subjects' behavior being shaped by the demand characteristics of the experimental setting is potentially more dangerous than that of experimenter bias, because demand characteristics are likely to be common across experiments in different laboratories. Demand characteristics include subjects' expectations of how they should perform in the experiment. Orne developed some ingenious techniques for evaluating the effect of demand characteristics. He used quasi-control groups such as simulating subjects, which often enable investigators to assess whether demand characteristics affect a particular experiment, but not what the outcome of the experiment would be were the demand characteristics removed.

5. One way to avoid the problem of demand characteristics is to conduct an experiment "in the field," or in a natural setting. Demand characteristics are then excluded, since the subjects are not even aware that they are in an experiment. Many social psychologists are turning to field research, since generality of results is no longer a problem, as it is in laboratory research. However, severe problems are involved with field research, too. It is often difficult to effectively manipulate an independent variable while controlling extraneous "nuisance" variables, and it is also difficult to know what to measure, since participants do not even know they are in an experiment and cannot be asked to perform some task, or rate how they feel, etc. Even if these

problems are overcome, we are left with an important ethical problem, even harder to solve, as to whether psychologists are justified in experimenting on unsuspecting members of society.

KEY TERMS

blind
bystander intervention
conformity
confounding
control variables
demand characteristics
diffusion $(I = N^{-t})$
experimental control
experimental error
experimenter bias

field research
impact $(I = N^t)$
obedience
placebo effect
randomization
simulating control subjects
social facilitation
social loafing
social norms
social psychology

DISCUSSION QUESTIONS

1. Why is experimental control often more difficult to achieve in social psychology experiments than in other sorts of research? To illustrate, make a list of variables that would have to be controlled (or randomized) in a typical bystander-intervention study that is done (a) in a laboratory situation, or (b) in a field experiment.

2. Evaluate the following statement: "If an extraneous variable is in danger of being confounded with the independent variable of interest in an experiment, it is better to randomize the influence of the variable across conditions than to control it so that it cannot vary between conditions." Explain why you think this statement is true or false.

3. Do you think that the deliberate faking of results is a threat to the cumulative progress of science over long periods of time? How might the short-term effects of deliberate fraud differ from the long-term effects?

4. Discuss the problem of unintentional experimenter bias and the problem of demand characteristics of the experimental situation. How can the influence of these problems be minimized in experimental situations? Are these problems equally likely to occur in all types of research?

5. Discuss the advantages and disadvantages of field research. Would you mind being the unwitting subject in an experiment on bystander intervention if you later found out that your reactions in the situation had been recorded?

6. Make a list of topics that you think could best be studied (a) in laboratory experiments, and (b) in field experiments. Explain why you choose the topics you do in each case.

PSYCHOLOGY IN ACTION

The Power of Being in an Experiment

PEOPLE'S KNOWLEDGE THAT THEY are participating in an experiment often strongly affects their behavior. People do things when they are in an experiment that they would not do under other circumstances. You can demonstrate this by performing a simple experiment with your friends. Make a list of ten friends and randomly assign them to one of two conditions, either the experimental condition or the control condition. The independent variable for the two groups is the statement you make at the beginning of the experiment. Say to the experimental subjects, "I would like you to do some things for me as part of a psychology experiment for one of my courses." Say to the control group, "I would like you to do me a favor." Then tell each friend that you have a request; you would like the person to do five jumping jacks, six sit-ups, four push-ups, and make a paper airplane as fast as possible.

Of course, the small number of subjects in the experiment makes it difficult for you to draw any strong conclusions. But you will probably discover that the friends who are asked to help you out with a psychology experiment are likely to be much more cooperative. They probably will do more of the activities, do them faster, and ask fewer questions. People in the control group will probably think you have been studying too hard.

The point of this demonstration is to show that psychology experiments do not just provide neutral surveys of behavior; they also can create the behaviors that are studied. When people know they are being observed in an experiment, they may react differently. Thus, the psychologist is in danger of studying behavior produced in the laboratory that may bear little relation to behavior occurring in the outside world. The cues in the experiment that guide subjects' behavior in this way are called demand characteristics.

CHAPTER

14

Environmental Psychology

Science is built up with facts, as a house is with stones. But a collection of facts is no more a science than a heap of stones is a house.

J. H. POINCARÉ

THE PROBLEM DISCUSSED IN GREATEST depth in this chapter is *generalization of results*. One study of noise (Cohen, Glass, and Singer, 1973) showed that children who lived on the lower floors of an apartment building that was built directly over a busy freeway were poorer readers than those children living higher up, where the noise of passing traffic was less intense. As a result of this study, the building occupants demanded that a roof be built over the freeway (figure 14–1). Did the problem justify this demand? Investigators must be able to show—as did Cohen and his colleagues—that the conclusions drawn from their data can be meaningfully generalized.

A second problem that environmental psychologists share with other social scientists involves *converging operations*. To establish that a theory or model of behavior is correct, we must approach it from several angles. An example that will be discussed in some detail later on is the topic of personal space. How do psychologists know there is such a thing as a space bubble that we carry around? We cannot see the bubble, or smell it, or feel it. The bubble is a theoretical construct, since it is not directly observable. We must aim for converging operations to prove that certain behavior is affected by personal space.

A third problem, one that is perhaps more troublesome for environmental and social psychologists, involves *ethical issues* in research. The scientist has a responsibility to ensure that individ-

FIGURE 14–1.

These apartments are built over the approach to the George Washington Bridge in New York City. Highway noise is a severe problem for the residents.

uals are not harmed in the search for knowledge. Often, however, some degree of risk is involved. How, then, can the psychologist ensure that research complies with established ethical principles?

Is Science the Only Path To Truth?

Our society has placed a high value on science and technology. The landing of astronauts on the moon symbolizes the power and prestige of American science, as does the orbiting Hubble space telescope. Many citizens believe that our high standard of living, directly attributable to such technological devices as automobiles, televisions, and computers, will continue to increase as science advances. Hence, the quest for scientific knowledge is widely justified—on the practical grounds that science creates better lives for people, as well as on the philosophical grounds that science, rather than art, religion, literature, and so on, offers the best chance for finding truth (figure 14–2).

Psychology has yet to achieve the stunning successes of older sciences such as physics and chemistry. Therefore, it is more difficult to justify the scientific benefits of psychology on purely practical grounds. However, some people claim that our understanding of physical processes such as those related to nuclear energy has so far outstripped our understanding of human processes that we have become captives of our science, rather than beneficiaries. As pollution, crowding, and related environmental problems decrease the quality of life, the importance of social science becomes more and more obvious. Environmental psychology deals with issues that directly affect our everyday lives.

Since physical scientists have built up impressive accomplishments, both theoretically and practically, it seems reasonable for

FIGURE 14–2.

Reprinted by permission of UFS, Inc.

Although science is not the only path to knowledge, it is one of the most effective methods available. Unlike grass, science will not believe anything you tell it.

social scientists to emulate their more established colleagues. Virtually all social scientists believe that powerful truths can and will be discovered by applying the scientific methods used by physical scientists. Science will grant us a better theoretical understanding of the nature of human activity, and this will eventually lead to a technology capable of improving the quality of life.

Not all scientists are aware of the limitations of science, despite brief exposure to these points as part of their education. The practicing scientist may eventually discard assorted philosophical points as being of only limited value in his or her daily work (Medawar, 1969, chapter 1). Nevertheless, it is appropriate to present the other side of the coin and to discuss these limitations. Science focuses on only certain questions and ignores other issues. It would be extremely difficult to answer the question "Does God exist?" scientifically, so most scientists are content to pursue other matters. Similarly, psychologists tend to concentrate on the study of behavior rather than on other kinds of human experience. Aldous Huxley (1946) comments on this aspect of science:

> Pragmatically [scientists] are justified in acting in this odd and extremely arbitrary way; for by concentrating exclusively on the measurable aspects of such elements of experience as can be explained in terms of a causal system they have been able to achieve a great and increasing control over the energies of nature. But power is not the same thing as insight and, as a representation of reality, the scientific picture of the world is inadequate for the simple reason that science does not even profess to deal with experience as a whole but only with certain aspects of it in certain contexts. All this is quite clearly understood by the more philosophically minded men of science. But some scientists . . . tend to accept the world picture implicit in the theories of science as a complete and exhaustive account of reality; they tend to regard those aspects of experience which scientists leave out of account, *because they are incompetent to deal with them,* as being somehow less real than the aspects which science has arbitrarily chosen to abstract from out of the infinitely rich totality of given facts. (pp. 35–36, emphasis added)

Weizenbaum (1976) makes this same point using an anecdote about a drunkard looking for lost keys. The drunkard, kneeling under a lamppost, is approached by a police officer. The drunkard explains he is looking for his keys, which he lost somewhere over there in the darkness. When the police officer asks why he isn't looking over there, the drunkard replies that the light is better here under the lamppost. Science is somewhat like the drunkard, since it looks where its tools provide the best illumination.

Environmental psychology is particularly hard-pressed when this criticism of science is applied. The real world, as distinct from the somewhat artificial world of the carefully controlled laboratory studies of the experimental psychologist, is chock-full of problems outside the circle of light given off by a lamppost. Psychologists know that scientific progress comes about, slowly but surely, if they stay within the rays of the lamppost until a new breakthrough yields a more powerful lamp. But this traditional approach offers small hope for the rapid solution of pressing environmental problems. If environmental psychologists move slowly and traditionally, they are open to the criticism that their research is irrelevant to the needs of society. This is a serious charge, since ultimately society pays the price for this research, through federal research grants and such. On the other hand, the unwary psychologist who immediately rushes in to solve the ills of society runs a high risk of obtaining results that may later prove to be inadequate. And if public policy is formulated on the basis of such incomplete research (or no research at all), the price to society may be quite high (see figure 14–3).

FIGURE 14–3.

Demolition of part of the Pruitt-Igoe housing project in St. Louis. These buildings, although physically sound, were rendered unfit for occupation because of vandalism. Since then, research conducted by environmental social scientists has revealed how to prevent such tragedies.

Discovering the Truth About City Life

All of us, whether we dwell in large metropolitan areas or in rural communities, have opinions about the quality of urban life. For some, the city represents the height of culture and achievement. For others, the city is a cesspool of violence, pollution, and noise. How can we discover the truth about city life?

One of the most insightful views of city life can be found in a fascinating book, *Death and Life of Great American Cities*, by Jane Jacobs (1961). As one example of her insight, we will briefly discuss Jacobs's views on the functions of the sidewalk. For most of us, the sidewalk exists to get us from one place to another. Most of us, including psychologists, have not given much thought to the psychological functions of the common sidewalk. Jacobs shows that the sidewalk makes a great contribution to social interaction within the city. Owners of small shops that line local streets—tailors, drugstores, candy stores—provide a multitude of social services for the neighborhood street users. These services go beyond the nature of each individual business. Thus, a tailor might keep an eye out for children running into the street and warn their parents; the candy store owner might let children use his toilet facilities so they won't have to run upstairs; the delicatessen owner might receive mail for a customer who is out of town for a few days. Each such service by itself is small. But when added together, they form the basis for positive feelings about a neighborhood as a good place to live.

Anyone who has lived on such an old-fashioned city street intuitively accepts the truth of Jacobs's statements. Yet, her conclusions are based only on naturalistic observation. Although observation is an important origin for science (see chapter 2), a better method would add credibility to her statements. There is nothing experimental about the way Jacobs collected her data. No systematic attempts were made to manipulate independent variables and record dependent variables; no replications were conducted; no control variables enter her descriptions of behavior. Although no scientist would reject her conclusions outright, few would accept them. Most scientists would claim that an adequate test of her suggestions or "hypotheses" has yet to be accomplished. Until the formal procedures required by science are duly performed, Jacobs's conclusions cannot be sanctified as scientific truth, but only regarded as interesting possibilities.

The problem takes us back to our example of the lamppost. Jacobs is operating outside of the light. This makes scientists reluctant to accept her truths. Yet to many people, her conclusions seem obviously correct. Why is the scientific method any better than astute observation? The answer to this important question is given in chapter 1, where we discuss the fixation of belief. You will recall that the great advantage of the scientific method is that it is self-correcting. If a different observer reached different conclusions about the functions and value of sidewalks, how could you decide which view was correct? So far we do not have a better way than science to decide such issues. Science as a method of fixing beliefs is much like democracy as described by Winston Churchill: "Democracy is the worst system of government except for all the others." Accepting the scientific method does not imply that any other method of arriving at truth—such as Jacobs's observations of city life—is necessarily invalid. Indeed, psychological research has confirmed many of Jacobs's suggestions. There most certainly is more than one path to truth. But when we must agree on some particular truth over which there is some dispute, then the scientific method, with all its limitations, offers the best long-term solution.

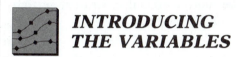

INTRODUCING THE VARIABLES

Dependent Variables

Environmental psychologists often record feelings and emotion in addition to observable behavior. Such internal states are inferred from rating scales. Thus, a study on crowding might ask persons to rate such things, as their opinion of the other people involved in the study, the pleasantness of the experience, the perceived size of the room. Merely labeling a scale with some descriptive title, however, does not guarantee that the scale measures that, and only that, particular facet of human experience. Consider a rating question such as the following, for which the reader must circle a number from 1 to 5:

In terms of physical attractiveness my partner was

Extremely good looking				A real dog
1	2	3	4	5

The subject's response could well be influenced by nonphysical behavioral characteristics. A partner who was helpful and cooperative might be judged more physically attractive than the same partner (in a different experimental condition) who was insulting and rude.

Independent Variables

Studies of crowding manipulate *density*, which is most often defined as the number of people per unit area—for example, six people in ten square meters (or feet). Since we can count the number of people and can measure area, density so defined satisfies our requirements for a clear operational definition. Since density has two components, we can manipulate it in two ways. First, we can hold the number of people constant and vary the size of the room that contains them. Second, we can hold room size constant and vary the number of people in the room. Although these two kinds of density manipulation may at first appear equivalent, it turns out that they have different effects on behavior and feelings (for example, see Marshall and Heslin, 1975). So the usual operational definition, although precise and clear, is inadequate, because it confounds two separate variables: number of people and amount of space. For example, if density is manipulated by increasing the number of people and holding room size constant, we do not know if observable differences are best attributed to density effects or to the effects of numbers of people. The issue is further complicated by the fact that psychological density often is not the same as physical density. The feeling of being crowded depends not only on physical density but also on social context (Rapoport, 1975). A crowded discotheque has far more pleasant associations than an equally crowded subway car.

Another set of independent variables studied by environmental psychologists falls into the category of stressors: those agents that produce stressful situations. Loud noise, high temperatures, and air pollution are examples of this kind of independent variable.

in more rigorous areas of experimental psychology. Although gross physical features of the environment, such as room temperature, are controlled, more finely grained variables, for example, the relative position of participants (side by side or face to face), are often neglected. This defect is particularly evident in field studies that by their very nature do not offer the experimenter much control over the situation. Environmental psychologists who conduct field studies are aware of this problem, but think that the greater reality of the field situation as opposed to the more artificial laboratory setting is ample recompense.

Control Variables

Studies in environmental psychology often lack the elegant control variables found

14.1 Experimental Topics and Research Illustrations

Topic: Generalization of Results
Illustration: Crowding

No experiment is an end in itself. Experiments are steps along the way to the psychologists's ultimate goal of predicting and explaining behavior. Unless results of past experiments can be applied to new situations, the experiments are of little value. Thus, models explaining the flow of electricity are designed to deal not only with the small number of electrons that have been studied in the laboratory, but also with the electrons living in the wall sockets of your house.

An important criterion for judging the utility of an experiment is its *representativeness*. Experiments that are representative allow us to extend their findings to more general situations. When it was discovered that cigarette tars caused cancer in laboratory beagles, many cigarette smokers felt that such research demonstrated only that dogs should not smoke. In short, they doubted the representativeness of the findings and did not believe that the results could be generalized to humans. However, later studies confirmed these earlier findings; now, the Surgeon General is so convinced of the dangers of cigarette smoking that all cigarette packages must be labeled with a warning to the user.

The preceding cigarette-beagle experiment is one example of the problem of generalizing results from one sample to a different sample, or to a different population. We shall term this *sample generalization*. It occurs in many forms. The most studied human organism is the college student taking an introductory psychology class who, as part of the educational process, is often required to participate in several experiments. Let us pretend that we have just completed a study about different methods of improving reading speed and comprehension, using a small sample of Rice students enrolled in introductory psychology. If such a study yields appropriate results, it could have important implications for education. But first, before these implications can be made, several questions about sample generalization need to be answered. First, are these results typical or representative of all Rice students taking introductory psychology? If our sample consists of only male subjects, clearly the answer is no. Even if our sampling procedure enables us to answer yes to this first question, we are not yet out of the woods. Are these results representative of Rice undergraduates in general? Again, if our sample consists only of Rice freshmen, we cannot be sure that Rice seniors would yield the same results. And even if our results generalized to all Rice undergraduates, it would probably not be worthwhile to institute a drastic change in reading methodology, unless it could be demonstrated that college students across the country could benefit. Even then, we might ask if high-school and grade-school students could use this new reading method. Clearly, a single experiment will seldom generalize to every population of interest.

Similar problems about generalization of independent and dependent variables also exist. Environmental stress can be induced by such diverse means as increasing temperature, increasing noise level, and depriving a person of sleep the night before the experiment. To the extent that our concern is with environmental stress in general, rather than specific effects of noise, temperature, and sleep deprivation, we must ensure that these different manipulations of related independent variables allow us to make representative statements about stress. We shall term this *variable representativeness*. Let us say we are concerned with the effects of temperature on urban riots: Does the long, hot summer lead to aggression? When this is studied in the laboratory (Baron and Bell, 1976), we find that high temperatures do not necessarily lead to increased aggression. But before we can reject this explanation of summertime urban problems and advance to other hypotheses (for example, more young people are idling in the streets during the summer months), we must ensure that independent and dependent measures generalize from the laboratory to the urban scene. Most of us would be willing to accept the assertion that a temperature of 95°F in the laboratory is equivalent to the same temperature in the city street. But this equivalence is less clear when we consider

FIGURE 14–4.

A typical shock machine used in laboratory studies of aggression. The buttons control the (hypothetical) shock intensity. (© 1983 Text-Eye)

common laboratory measures of aggression. The most widely used technique calls for the subject to administer an electric shock to a confederate, as used in Milgram's work that was outlined in chapter 13 (see figure 14–4). (In reality, no shock is delivered, but the experimenter hopes that the subject thinks he or she is controlling an electric shock.) Higher shock intensities and longer shock durations are interpreted as evidence for greater aggression. Is the aggression involved in pushing a button the same aggression involved in hurling a brick through a storefront window or sniping at police and firefighters with a rifle (figure 14–5)? Although the ultimate effect—harming someone else—appears to be the same

FIGURE 14–5.

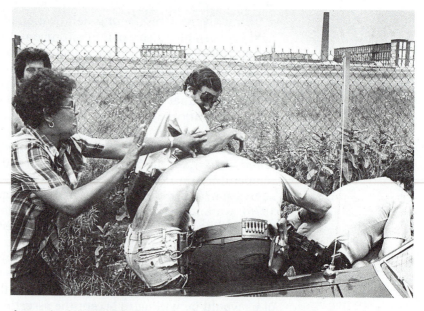

Aggression in a nonlaboratory situation. Do you think this is the same kind of aggression tested in figure 14–4?

in aggression inside and outside the laboratory, civil disorder may add another dimension to aggression. Establishing a physical analogy in the laboratory—as when rats are trained to "hoard" money—does not necessarily imply a psychological identity. Indeed, it is this considerable difficulty in establishing variable representativeness that has turned many environmental psychologists away from laboratory studies and toward field studies, despite the fact that there is considerably less experimental control.

In this section, we will discuss four studies on crowding and carefully examine how their results might be generalized. The first study uses animal subjects, whereas the rest use humans. The three human studies differ in that one is based on demographic data correlated by sociologists, one uses field-study techniques with experimental control instead of post hoc statistical control, and one is a laboratory experiment.

Crowding in animals: Toocloseforcomfort.

A long series of studies conducted by John Calhoun (1962, 1966, 1971) at the National Institute of Mental Health produced some astonishing findings about the long-term effects of crowding in rats. Calhoun placed his rats in a "rat universe" (see figure 14–6) with four compartments. Since compartments 1 and 4 were not connected (see figure 14–6), they became dead ends and the rats congregated in compartments 2 and 3. This overcrowding caused several pathological types of behavior to develop. The mortality rate for infant rats was as high as 96 percent in pens 2 and 3. Female rats were unable to build proper nests and often dropped infant rats. These infants died where they were dropped and often were eaten by adult rats. The high mortality rates had the greatest implications for the rat universe. There was also odd sexual behavior exhibited by male rats. The strangest rats were called "probers" by Calhoun. Instead of engaging in normal rat courtship, these probers would pursue female rats into their burrows, where they would eat dead infant rats. Probers were also homosexual and hyperactive. Thus, the independent variable (high density) caused strange maternal and sexual behaviors (dependent variables) to evolve.

These results are frightening, to say the least; if generalized to human crowding, they strongly imply that overcrowding will eventually destroy society as we know it today. But before we forsake our high-rise apartments for the wide-open spaces, let us first examine some studies conducted with humans.

Crowding in humans: A correlational demographic study.

Calhoun's studies with rats imply that high density causes pathological behavior. Since it would be highly unethical for an investigator to crowd people for long periods of time in the way Calhoun crowded rats, a direct experimental test analogous to Calhoun's experiments is impossible. However, there are parts of our big cities where society has created high densities, and it is certainly ethical to observe the effects of these densities in the real world. The advan-

FIGURE 14–6.

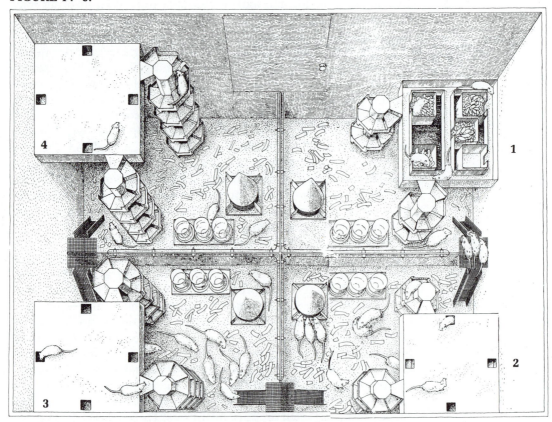

The rat universe studied by Calhoun. Note that the pens are not all joined together by ramps, so that two of them become deadends. *(Scientific American)*

tage of studying such real-life situations is that there is less difficulty in generalizing results, for example, from one city to another, than from a laboratory to a city. The disadvantage is that there is virtually no experimental control over the independent variable and possible extraneous variables. One solution often used when experimental control is not feasible is after-the-fact statistical control. This is the approach taken by sociologists Galle, Gove, and McPherson (1972), who studied crowding and social pathology in the city of Chicago.

These sociologists found five types of *social pathology* for which data were available. Their first index was the standard mortality ratio, which is the age-adjusted death rate of a specific community, expressed as a ratio of the death rate for the entire Chicago population. Their second index of social pathology was general fertility rate, defined as the number of births in a specific community per 1,000 women between the ages of 15 and 44 in the same community. These two indexes are essentially biological and are quite similar to those studied by Calhoun.

The remaining three indexes of social pathology were public-assistance rate, defined as number of persons under 18 years of age receiving public-assistance payments; juvenile delinquency rate, defined as the number of males appearing before family court; and last, an age-adjusted rate of admissions to mental hospitals. Sociological indexes are limited, of course, to those for which data have been compiled. To determine if these five social pathologies are more frequent in high-density areas, the investigators had to operationally define density. They first used only one measure of *density:* number of persons per acre.

The statistical technique used by Galle and coworkers was correlation. You will recall from our discussion of correlation in chapter 2 that it is often difficult to reach conclusions about causation with only correlational data. Thus, we must be extra careful in interpreting the demographic data of this study. Their results are shown in figure 14–7. Correlations ranged from +.28 to +.49. Although this at first appears to support a relationship between density and social pathology, we know that other factors might account for the relationship—that is, a third "unknown" factor might correlate highly with both density and social pathology, and thus be responsible for the correlations in figure 14–7. What kinds of unknown factors might operate in urban areas? Two factors that come immediately to mind are social class and ethnicity (percentages of blacks, Puerto Ricans, and foreign-born in the com-

FIGURE 14–7.

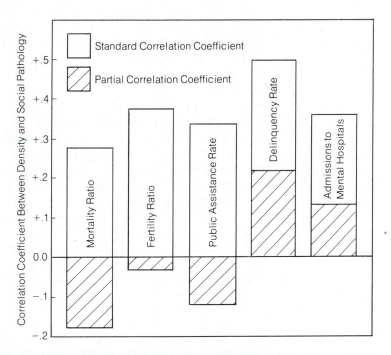

The relationship between density and social pathology, when density is defined as number of people per acre. (Adapted from Galle et al., 1972)

munity). The investigators developed two crude indexes for social class and ethnicity, and then used the statistical technique of partial correlation to introduce after-the-fact control. The partial-correlation technique allows us to remove the influence of these factors from our overall correlation coefficient. These data are also shown in figure 14–7. It is clear that with this statistical control, correlation coefficients drop dramatically. In fact, the partial correlation coefficients shown do not differ significantly from zero. This means that there is no relationship between density and social pathology once social class and ethnicity are (statistically) controlled.

Although these data fail to support any relationship between density and social pathology, Galle and workers were not ready to throw in the towel. They decided that their measure of *density*, number of people per acre, was inadequate. Too many other components of population density could be combined to yield equivalent numbers of people per acre. So they broke number-of-people-per-acre into four smaller density components: number of persons per room, number of rooms per housing unit, number of housing units per structure, and number of residential structures per acre. Then they recalculated their correlation coefficients. (Since these new correlations are based on four measures of density instead of a single measure, technically they are called multiple-correlation coefficients. The technique of multiple correlation allows us to combine several measures into a single multiple-correlation coefficient.) These results, shown in figure 14–8, now show a correlational relationship between density and social pathology, even when effects of social class and ethnicity are removed statistically by using partial-correlation coefficients. So, Galle and co-workers concluded that Calhoun's results were directly generalizable to humans living in Chicago.

This conclusion, although reasonable given their data, must be accepted with caution. The possibility remains that some unknown variable in addition to social class and ethnicity should have been removed or partialled out as well. This is the basic difficulty with correlational studies: one can never reach conclusions about causation. Although we can state that high density and social pathology are related, we cannot state that social pathology is a result of high density. Even the statistical control introduced by the method of partial-correlation coefficients is not without its problems. (The major difficulty arises when the extraneous variables to be partialled out are themselves correlated. If this is the case, portions of the variance may be removed more than once, especially if several extraneous variables have been considered. This artifact will cause an inflated partial-correlation coefficient, yielding misleading results.)

Crowding in humans: A field study in a railroad station. Only a study that manipulates independent variables permits statements about causation. Saegert, Mackintosh, and West (1975) took their

FIGURE 14–8.

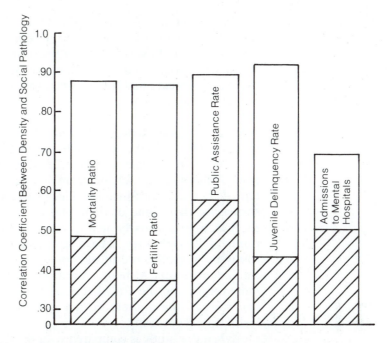

The relationship between density and social pathology, with a complex index of density. Unlike the preceding figure, partial-correlation coefficients (shaded bars) are all statistically reliable. (Adapted from Galle et al., 1972)

subjects to Manhattan's Pennsylvania Railroad Station to test effects of crowding on performance and affect (feelings). Density, the most important independent variable, was manipulated by choosing the time at which the station was visited: either 10–11:30 A.M. or 5–6 P.M. (at the height of rush hour). This manipulation confounds time of day with density, but the experimenters felt that time of day would not have any significant effects on the tasks. However, this assumption was not tested empirically. The experimenters were careful to make some population counts to ensure that the number of persons actually present was within the desired ranges.

The subjects were given a list of forty-two tasks that they were to perform inside the station: things such as looking up a telephone number, finding the ticket counter, buying something at the newsstand, and so forth. They were given thirty minutes to complete as many tasks as they could; this was one dependent variable. Then subjects filled out a Mood Adjective Checklist. This is a rating scheme that permits people to describe their feelings.

The main finding was that "crowding did seem to interfere somewhat with tasks requiring knowledge and manipulation of the environment," since in the high-density condition subjects completed about twenty-five tasks, versus about twenty-nine for the low-density condition. Statistically, however, this effect was significant only at the .10 level, which means it could have occurred by chance in one experiment out of ten. The conclusion drawn by Saegert and co-workers is not very representative. The tasks required subjects to walk back and forth through the crowds in the railroad station. Even if no cognitive demands had been made, that is, if subjects had merely been asked to walk back and forth as many times as possible, we would expect crowds to have slowed them down. It is harder to move around in a dense crowd than in an empty station. Hence, it does not seem reasonable to generalize these results, as do the authors, to mean that cognitive functioning is impaired in crowded situations. However, the rating scales confirmed that subjects felt more anxious and more skeptical in the crowded condition. Since the checklist has eleven scales, it is not surprising that some of them showed an effect of density. This shotgun approach is typical of many studies in social and environmental psychology, where large numbers of rating scales are routinely administered in the hopes that some of them will yield significant results. Although it is quite reasonable that subjects felt more anxious in the crowded condition where they were bumped and shoved, the authors do not interpret the finding of greater feelings of skepticism.

When this study is compared with the Galle demographic study, one conclusion is obvious. Although studies that manipulate independent variables should generally be preferred to studies that only correlate variables, this does not necessarily mean that any experimental study is automatically superior to any correlational study. Good research, even of the correlational variety, is always preferable to poor research, even of the experimental variety.

Crowding in humans: A laboratory study. We noted earlier that density can be manipulated in two ways. A study conducted by Marshall and Heslin (1975) used both techniques in a combination of two amounts of space (4 versus 18 square feet per person) and two group sizes (4 versus 16 persons). This means that a total of four experimental treatments were administered: 4 people in a 16-square-foot space; 4 people in a 69-square-foot space; 16 people in a 69-square-foot space; and 16 people in a 288-square-foot space. Additional independent variables were the sex of the people (a common independent variable in social and environmental psychology, since it is easy to manipulate) and the group composition (all the same sex, or half males and half females). The investigators were interested in how members of these different groups would feel about one another, so several rating scales were used to measure such things as interpersonal attraction, liking for the group as a whole, and feelings in general. These ratings were the dependent variables. Control variables were physical characteristics of the two rooms, such as wall color, carpeting, and ceiling height, which remained constant over all experimental treatments.

The subjects were asked to perform different kinds of problem-solving tasks together. The experimenters were not particularly interested in how well problems were solved, but used these tasks as a pretext to get the members of the groups involved with one another. This type of "cover" task is fairly common in social and environmental psychology.

Results of this study were complicated, with many interactions between independent variables. Only some of the findings will be discussed here. Figure 14–9 shows that feelings toward the group have no simple relation with group size. Females liked large groups more than small groups only if the group was of mixed sex. If the group was all female, females preferred the small group. Males, however, although preferring mixed-sex groups, did not care too much about group size.

Females showed similar results for feelings about individuals in the group as a function of amount of space (figure 14–10). Crowded groups were preferred if they were of mixed sex but not if they were all female. Males generally preferred crowded groups regardless of sexual composition.

Note how much more complicated it is to generalize these laboratory results. Effects of crowding depend not only on your sex, but also on the sex of the other people in your group. This kind of detail, typical of experimental studies, is missing in the other studies of human crowding we have examined. Although you might be tempted to draw the conclusion that you should avoid laboratory studies if you want life to be simple, a better way of regarding these results is to realize that the complexities of life can be studied most precisely in highly controlled laboratory situations.

Comparison of crowding studies. We have examined effects of crowding on four studies: an animal study, a correlational demographic study, a field study, and a laboratory experiment. The kinds of generalizations we can draw from each study differ substantially. You are probably wondering which study is the best.

FIGURE 14–9.

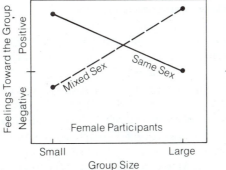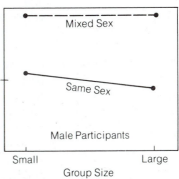

Feelings about the group according to the sex of participant, group size, and group composition. The effects of group size are quite different for male and female participants. (Adapted from Marshall and Heslin, 1975)

FIGURE 14–10.

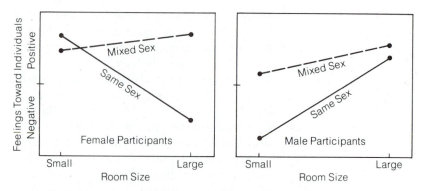

Feelings toward individuals in the group according to room size, sex of participants, and group composition. As in the previous figure, males and females differ in the effect of size. (Adapted from Marshall and Heslin, 1975)

There is no straightforward answer to this question: psychologists do not agree on which is best, although experimental psychologists tend to prefer laboratory studies. The purpose of this section is to acquaint you with the difficulties in generalizing results of any study, regardless of type. By now, you may feel that these difficulties are so great that it hardly seems worthwhile to do research at all. But this conclusion is unduly pessimistic. Although it is difficult to generalize from any single study, a set of studies may indeed lead us to representative conclusions. This is especially true when researchers design the studies to come together by approaching the same problem from related, but not identical, viewpoints. The next section, on converging operations, explains this more fully.

14.2 Experimental Topics and Research Illustrations

Topic: Converging Operations
Illustration: Personal Space

An excellent way to increase the representativeness and generality of a scientific concept is to perform more than one experiment relating to that concept. This gives the concept more than one leg to stand on, so that it is not totally dependent on any single experimental procedure. We call this technique of using slightly different types of experiments to jointly support a single concept use of *converging operations* (Garner, Hake, and Eriksen, 1956; Garner, 1974).

How might we define converging operations for the concept "success"? One way to define a successful person, at least in American society, is by a high income. So anyone earning more than

$100,000 a year could be called successful. Another attribute of success might be to have a charming family. Still another characteristic of success might be to be respected in the community. Each of these characteristics of success is independent, in the sense that their definitions are unrelated. Yet it is quite likely that a successful person has all three attributes. These characteristics all converge to define the common concept "success."

Now that you have the general idea of converging operations, we will illustrate two experimental procedures that converge on the common concept of *personal space*. This concept implies that you are surrounded by an invisible bubble designed to protect you from a wide variety of social encroachments. How do psychologists know that such a bubble exists? Since it cannot be directly sensed by vision, smell, touch, etc., the concept must be indirectly evaluated. The two experiments to be discussed demonstrate that there is a personal-space bubble; they use two different kinds of spatial invasion and yield similar results.

Personal space: Help, there's someone in my bubble! It is ironic that the personal-space bubble that helps you maintain privacy is best studied by invasions that violate the privacy it affords. A simple experiment conducted by psychiatrist August Kinzel (1970) shows one operation that defines personal space. Kinzel was interested in the personal-space bubbles surrounding violent and nonviolent prisoners. Thus, one independent variable—more precisely a subject variable (see chapter 2), since it was not manipulated—in his study was classification of prisoners as violent (having inflicted physical injury on another person) or not. Each prisoner stood in the center of an empty room that was 20 feet wide and 20 feet long. The experimenter then approached from one of eight directions (the second independent variable) until the prisoner said "stop" because the experimenter was too close. The dependent variable was the distance between prisoner and experimenter when the prisoner said "stop." If there is no personal-space bubble, the experimenter should have been able to walk right up to the prisoner (distance = 0). Control variables were the room itself and the experimenter, who was the same person throughout the experiment. The results of this experiment, shown in figure 14–11, clearly show that violent prisoners have larger personal-space bubbles than nonviolent prisoners.

This experiment may not have entirely convinced you that there really is a personal-space bubble. A concept based on only one experiment is just a restatement of that particular experimental finding. Also, you may feel that there is something strange about a person's walking right up to you without saying anything. Certainly, if this happened to you on the street, you would think it unusual, to say the least. The next experiment avoids this potential difficulty.

FIGURE 14–11.

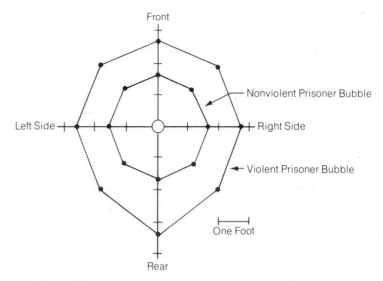

Looking down on the personal-space bubble of violent and nonviolent prisoners. (After Kinzel, 1970)

Personal space: Oops, pardon my bubble. To avoid actively invading someone's personal-space bubble, Barefoot, Hoople, and McClay (1972) gave subjects the opportunity to invade the experimenter's bubble. The experimenter sat near a water fountain and pretended to read a book. Anyone getting a drink of water had to invade the experimenter's personal space. The independent variable was the distance between the experimenter and the water fountain. This was either one foot, five feet, or ten feet. This last distance is large enough so that it exceeds the bounds of the experimenter's personal space, and thus is a control condition. A confederate kept track of the number of persons passing by the fountain in each of the three experimental conditions. The dependent variable was the percentage of passersby who drank from the fountain. When the experimenter was one foot away, only 10 percent drank; when the experimenter was five feet away, 18 percent drank. Finally, at an experimenter distance of ten feet, 22 percent drank from the fountain.

These results agree with those of the active-invasion paradigm used by Kinzel. The single concept of a personal-space bubble explains findings of both experiments. Hence, the experiments provide converging operations supporting the personal-space concept.

14.3 Experimental Topics and Research Illustrations

Topic: Ethical Issues
Illustration: Deception and Concealment

Psychologists are extremely concerned with the ethics of research with human participants. Although some of this concern is pragmatic, caused by fear of restriction of research funds and loss of access to subject populations, most psychologists are ethical persons who have no desire to inflict harm on anyone. The mad researcher who will do anything to obtain data is largely a myth.

Since it is difficult for an experimenter to be completely impartial and objective in judging the ethical issues concerning his or her own research, most universities and research institutions have peer committees that judge whether the proposed research is ethical. Indeed, all federally funded research must be approved by such a committee before any funding is granted. These committees are guided by several principles advocated by the American Psychological Association (1973). One important principle is the right of *informed consent*. This means that every potential participant in an experiment is given both an explanation of all salient features of the research before the experiment is conducted and the opportunity to decline to participate in the research. Thus, the experimenter has a clear ethical obligation to inform participants of any possible harmful effects of the experiment. For example, if an environmental psychology experiment calls for loud noises as stressors, participants must be told this in advance, so that anyone with a history of sensitivity to sound, resulting perhaps from a childhood illness, can decline to participate. (Even with informed consent, no ethical researcher would use extremely loud sounds that might cause permanent hearing loss.)

It is extremely difficult for many proposed studies in environmental psychology to comply with the principle of informed consent. There are many situations in which, if people knew they were being observed, they might not behave normally. In such cases, the researcher would like to conceal the fact that an experiment is under way, only informing or debriefing participants after the study has ended. Clearly, this procedure violates the principle of informed consent, since the person has neither been informed nor given consent: such research could be banned outright. However, many psychologists think that such a severe restriction would seriously impair their ability to design studies aimed at understanding human behavior in real-life environments—that is, it would greatly reduce the ability to generalize research. They argue that the potential worth of the research must be balanced against the potential harm to participants.

Imagine that you are serving on an ethics committee. Decide whether or not you would allow the following examples of proposed research:

1. An environmental psychologist sits in a crowded library and keeps detailed records of seating patterns.

2. An environmental psychologist takes videotapes of seating patterns in a library. These tapes are maintained indefinitely; library patrons do not know they have been filmed.

3. An experimental psychologist tells students that she is inter-

ested in their reading comprehension, when in reality she is recording the speed of their responses rather than their comprehension.

4. A social psychologist is studying bystander intervention in a liquor store. Permission has been obtained from the store manager. In clear view of a patron, an experimenter "steals" a bottle of liquor. A second experimenter approaches the patron and asks, "Did you see him steal that bottle?"

5. A social psychologist connects surface electrodes to male participants, with their prior approval. These participants are told that the electrodes are connected to a meter in front of them that measures sexual arousal. In reality, the meter is controlled by the experimenter. Participants are then shown slides of nude males and females. The meter gives high readings for pictures of males, leading the participants to believe they have latent homosexual tendencies.

There are no absolutes in ethics, and we cannot state that some of these examples are clearly ethical and others are clearly not. However, informal discussions with our colleagues revealed that only number 1 was unequivocally considered ethical. Since the psychologist is merely observing and does not know the people (they are represented only by symbols on the data sheet), informed consent is not deemed necessary. Any individual, psychologist or not, could easily observe these same people in the library. The potential harm to participants is negligible.

You may be astonished that objections were raised to every other example. Number 2 was thought to invade personal privacy, since the tapes were not erased after data had been abstracted. Number 3 would be acceptable only if the experimenter carefully debriefed participants by explaining the nature and reasons for this minor deception. Number 4 was actually performed; a patron denied seeing the theft, and then called the police as soon as she left the store. The investigator had to go down to the police station to bail out the experimenters. Number 5 was considered unethical, even with debriefing. It is not clear that the potential psychological harm of the participant's thinking he had hidden homosexual tendencies could be removed by even immediate debriefing, especially if the person did indeed have latent homosexual tendencies that until the experiment had been successfully suppressed.

These examples should show that there is no clear answer as to what is ethical. The responsibility rests with the experimenter and the review committees. Although deception and concealment may be justified in limited instances, great caution is demanded in such experiments.

From Problem to Experiment: The Nuts and Bolts

Problem: Is Exposure to Noise Bad for You?

An issue that concerns environmental psychologists and citizens alike is the psychological effect of noise on humans. Airports, factories, and city streets expose citizens to long-term noisy environments. How might we evaluate possible effects of such exposure to noise?

Problem: *Does noise cause psychological harm?*

As always, several hypotheses can be derived from this vague problem. First, we will try a laboratory approach by formulating a hypothesis that can be tested under highly controlled circumstances.

Hypothesis: *Exposure to loud (110 dB SPL) continuous white noise will cause decreases in the number and accuracy of arithmetic problems that can be performed in 25 minutes.*

How did we arrive at some of the variables specified in the hypothesis? The independent variable, noise intensity (set at 110 dB, roughly as loud as a riveter), is close to the limit for safe exposure to 25 minutes of noise. Any louder noise might be harmful, and any softer noise might not yield experimental effects: that is, if no effects of noise on performance were obtained with noise much less than 110 dB, we might be tempted to conclude that our noise just was not loud enough. White noise (which is roughly similar to the sound you hear when your radio is tuned between stations) contains all frequencies of sound and is a convenient noise source often used in the laboratory.

Why 25 minutes of exposure to the noise? Since we expect to use college students as participants, we know that they find it most convenient if an experiment takes roughly one hour—that is, about the same time as a class. Since our hypothesis implies a no-noise control condition, we have divided our hour experiment into two 25-minute segments, one with noise and one without. This leaves 10 minutes for instructions and debriefing.

Our dependent variable is performance on an arithmetic task. This task was chosen because it is a simple task that college students are familiar with, so that no training is needed during the experiment. Performance—number of correct and number of incorrect problems—is easy to measure. Since there may be practice or fatigue effects, we will also be careful to counterbalance our experiment by having half the participants start in the quiet condition and half start in the noise condition. Since all participants complete all conditions, this is a within-subjects experimental design, offering greater experimental precision than a between-subjects design. In a within-subjects design, each person is compared to herself or himself, so that differences among people do not increase the error in an experiment. However, if we are concerned that performance following noise might be different from performance following quiet, that is, that noise effects might linger on even after the noise is no longer physically present, a better experimental design would be to use separate groups of participants for each 25-minute segment, giving us a between-subjects design.

Although our experiment is well controlled, we have several problems when we attempt to generalize results. If no effects of noise were obtained (if arithmetic performance was the same for noise and quiet segments), it could be argued that a 25-minute sample of life is far too short to tell us about a worker who has been exposed to 90-dB noise eight hours a day for many years. On the other hand, if effects of noise were obtained (if arithmetic performance was worse in noise segments), it could still be argued that eventually a worker adapts to noisy environments, so that if we had tested participants for several days or weeks, our initial effect might have disappeared. We will now formulate another hypothesis, so that results can be more easily generalized.

Hypothesis: *Residents of a noisy city street will (a) move more frequently and (b) score lower on a rating scale for residential satisfaction than residents of a quiet street.*

Since this hypothesis deals with the long-term effects of permanent residence, it avoids the problems of generalization seen in the preceding experiment. However, this hypothesis is not nearly so precise as the other hypothesis. Sound levels for noisy and quiet streets are not specified in advance, but have to be measured during the experiment. The experimenter has to decide whether to measure sound levels only at certain times, for example, during rush hours, or to take a 24-hour average. The independent variable is not completely under the experimenter's control. Furthermore, it may be confounded with things such as income and status, since persons with lower socioeconomic status are more likely to reside on noisier streets.

The dependent variables are not entirely satisfactory, either. Even if residents desire to move more often from noisy streets, economic factors may prohibit them from accomplishing this. On the other hand, the turnover in an area is an objective number that can be reliably measured. The second dependent variable depends to a great extent on the validity of the rating scale used to assess residential satisfaction. The experimenter will attempt to find a scale that has already been used in several studies and previously validated. If the experimenter is forced to construct a scale, then the scale must first be validated—a time-consuming and difficult process. Thus, the price of the greater ease of generalization in this study is a considerable loss of experimenter control.

When we compare both studies as solutions to the problem posed at the start of this section, it is clear that neither is perfect. This is always true with research. No single experiment can answer a question. The scientist is forced to focus on a more specific hypothesis, thus answering only a small part of the problem. This is a major source of frustration for all psychologists, since no general answers are possible until many tiny pieces, each corresponding to a specific hypothesis, are put together. An environmental psychologist could easily spend an entire career trying to understand the problem of noise and its psychological effects. For more information about the psychology of noise, see Kantowitz and Sorkin (1983), chapter 16.

SUMMARY

1. Science is not the only path to truth, and only certain portions of human experience are presently open to scientific analysis. However, the scientific method is self-correcting, whereas other methods of fixing belief are not. Therefore science is preferable wherever its tools are appropriate.

2. Experiments are steps along the way to the psychologist's ultimate goal of predicting and explaining behavior. This goal can be most rapidly achieved by having experiments that are *representative* and that can be *generalized* to related situations. Two types of representativeness are *sample generalization* and *variable representativeness*. Four studies of crowding are discussed; the kinds of generalizations we could draw from each differ substantially.

3. The generality of a concept can be considerably bolstered through the use of *converging operations*. Two different experimental procedures that converge on the concept of personal space illustrate converging operations.

4. Psychologists are extremely concerned with the ethical aspects of participation in research. The right of *informed consent* cannot always be granted in research. In such cases, the potential harm to participants must be balanced against the potential worth of the research. Experiments involving deception and concealment must be conducted only with great caution, if at all.

KEY TERMS

converging operations
crowding
deception
density
ethical issues
generality of results

informed consent
personal space
representativeness
sample generalization
social pathology
variable representativeness

DISCUSSION QUESTIONS

1. A priest, a rabbi, and a scientist were walking along the beach, discussing whether it was possible to walk on water. As an empirical test, the priest and the rabbi waded into the ocean while the scientist watched in amazement from the beach. Soon the priest was up to his chin, while the rabbi was dry from his knees up. "How are you managing to stay dry?", asked the priest. "Easy," replied the rabbi, "I walk on the rocks." What did the two clerics say about empiricism to the scientist when they returned to the beach, and what was his reply?

2. Select two areas in which science is *not* the appropriate path to truth. Discuss why the tools of science are irrelevant or inapplicable in these two fields. Will it be possible for science to handle these areas in the distant future?

3. Rush to the library and read the latest issues of *Environment and Behavior* and *Human Factors*. These are two journals that specialize in applied research. Discuss whether the articles you read can be more readily generalized than articles published in the *Journal of Experimental Psychology*.

4. Devise four potential indexes of social pathology. For how many of these indexes can you find existing data?

5. Design an experiment that provides a converging operation (different from those discussed in this chapter) for the concept of personal space. Find two reasons that your proposed experiment should not be conducted.

6. Make up a short list of unethical experiments you would like to do. Visit faculty members who specialize in the research areas of your experiments and ask them if they would be willing to supervise the experiments. How many faculty members tell you that they refuse because your experiment is unethical? Is this assignment ethical?

Mapping
Personal Space

THIS EXERCISE ALLOWS YOU to replicate the Kinzel (1970) and the Barefoot, Hoople, and McClay (1972) studies discussed in the text. If you are really ambitious, go to the library and obtain the original articles. You then can go ahead and plan your replication, without needing to read any further. If you cannot get to the library (or if the articles cannot be found there), read on.

Stand in the middle of a room. Have a friend approach you from about fifteen feet away. (This actually works better if a stranger approaches you. But if you are not sure how to obtain a friendly stranger, go ahead with one of your friends.) Say "stop" when you start to feel uncomfortable, and then note the distance between you. Repeat this operation several times, from different starting directions. Then draw your bubble on graph paper.

There are several variations you can try with this technique. One is to have people draw their space bubbles by imagining that someone is approaching them. Then verify their drawing with an empirical test. You can also try this with a person of the other sex. Do men and women have different-sized bubbles?

You can also do this experiment by hanging around a water fountain. Vary the distance between you and the fountain. Have a colleague count the number of people passing by, while you keep track of how many people actually drink from the fountain. (Hint: For the condition where you sit adjacent to the fountain, you will keep drier if you sit on the side of the fountain away from the spray direction.) But before you perform this experiment, you must first decide if keeping people from drinking water is ethical.

CHAPTER

15

Human Factors

When our sciences of human nature and human relations are anything like as developed as are our sciences of physical nature, their chief concern will be with the problem of how human nature is more effectively modified. The question will not be whether it is capable of change, but how it is to be changed under what conditions.

—JOHN DEWEY

THE MAJOR JUSTIFICATION FOR LABORATORY research is its ability to provide precise statements about causality. Once some effect or phenomenon is understood from laboratory research, the applied psychologist then can use this information to improve some aspect of the world outside the laboratory. This applied enterprise serves a scientific function, in addition to solving some practical difficulty. If an important effect has been correctly identified inside the laboratory, then the behavioral laws and relationships that describe or explain this effect should also operate outside the lab. Indeed, if they do not, serious doubts about the validity of the original laboratory research can be raised. To be useful, knowledge must be applied; laboratory research is thus a beginning, not an end (see chapter 1).

In this chapter we show how some findings, originally discovered and refined in the experimental psychology laboratory, can be applied usefully and meaningfully to practical human factors problems. Solving practical problems sometimes means additional laboratory work. At other times, the researcher must go outside the laboratory to seek solutions. We do not intend these few human factors examples to be interpreted as the ultimate justification for experimental psychology, since it is far too early to determine how basic research findings will shape our lives in the future. The lesson to be learned in this chapter is the generalization of basic experimental psychology principles; the specific applications discussed are intended to illustrate this point.

Human Factors and Human Behavior

Definition

Human factors is defined as "the discipline that tries to optimize the relationship between technology and the human" (Kantowitz and Sorkin, 1983, p. 4). Technology can be something small and commonplace, such as a can opener, or something large and esoteric, such as a space station. The common denominator of technology is people; all systems large and small must be used by people. If we had sufficient understanding of how the human operates, we could in principle design all technology to better interface with people.

The central role of the person in human factors explains why experimental psychology has had such a strong influence on human factors research. More than half of the members of the Human Factors Society were trained as psychologists. A substantial portion of the articles published in the journal *Human Factors* can be considered applied experimental psychology. Understanding how the human functions in applied settings is a crucial aspect of human factors research.

Honor Thy User

The first commandment of human factors is "Honor Thy User." If there is one thing you should remember twenty-five years from now about human factors, it is "Honor Thy User." Everything else merely embellishes this dominant theme.

Before you can honor the user, you must first know who the user will be. Different user populations have different human factors requirements. When Japan first started manufacturing automobiles, it designed cars for Japanese citizens. This created a problem when the cars were exported to the United States. American men were unable to depress the brake pedal without simultaneously depressing either the clutch or accelerator pedals. In hindsight, the reason for this design error was clear. Americans are physically larger than Japanese and have bigger feet. Although pedal spacing was satisfactory for the smaller Japanese foot, the pedals were too close together for the larger American foot. Since American feet had not been specified in the original design characteristics, the first commandment of human factors had been violated.

This same error can occur in more sophisticated ways. A large American telecommunications company, highly regarded for its human factors efforts, was designing a system for presenting recorded messages by telephone at times specified by the user. Since the hardware for this effort was specified, the human factors designers had to come up with the equivalent of a miniature computer language where the user could enter appropriate commands. So computer scientists were selected to create this new minilanguage. After several months of effort, they came up with a powerful language that could efficiently control recorded messages. Furthermore, being prudent designers they tested their new system by using secretaries as test subjects. Since this device was intended for use by secretaries, this was the ideal test population. Alas, none of the secretaries were able to master the new language. After some thought, the designers decided they needed a greatly improved instruction manual and so spent several more months perfecting a tutorial manual with many examples and illustrations. A second test found a few secretaries able to use the device but most were still baffled. The designers were very unhappy and questioned the successful secretaries carefully. It turned out that all of them had prior experience with computer programming. Now the problem was clear. The designers, being computer programmers themselves, had created a system that was optimal for anyone who could think like a computer programmer. But the typical user lacked computer skills. The designers created a new inefficient language that required many more instructions to complete any given recording schedule. But this new language was easy to learn and easy to use. A final test showed that the great majority of secretaries could now accomplish the task. The designer's training, which had stressed efficiency in minimizing the length of a program, had tricked them into violating the first commandment. They had designed for themselves rather than for the user. But disaster was prevented because the designers were wise enough to test their product before sending it out the door. So an important aspect of honoring the user is to test using the same population that will eventually operate the system.

The last violation to be discussed is the design of a lathe (figure 15–1). Here the user population is known. But, as figure 15–1 shows, the lathe was designed for a human with a very short trunk and extremely long arms. No humans have these body dimensions. This example demonstrates that it is easier to change the machine than to change the person who must operate it.

The Value of Life

One important, but often neglected, topic in human factors is the value of life. It may seem crass to place an economic value on death, but this is done all the time whenever manufacturers decide how much safety equipment should be built into systems and what kinds of safety warnings are needed. No product is ever perfectly safe. Even a small button could prove fatal if swallowed by an infant. How could one evaluate the economic utility of a recent decision by an American automobile manufacturer to include air bags in all its 1990-model cars?

A presidential address to the Human Factors Society (Parsons, 1970) discussed life and death. The value of a human life has been

FIGURE 15–1.

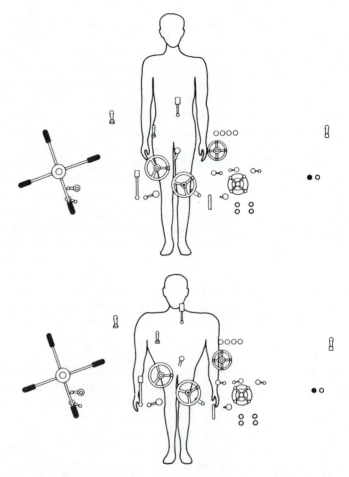

The controls of a lathe in current use are not within easy reach of the average person. They are placed so that the ideal operator should be 1372 mm (4½ ft) tall, 640 mm (2 ft) across the shoulder, and have a 2348 mm (8 ft) arm span. Butterworth Heinemann, Ltd.

assessed many ways, ranging from a few cents corresponding to the value of chemicals that comprise the human body to thirty pieces of silver to million-dollar insurance policies on the lives of corporate executives. Parsons estimated that choosing to return the apollo astronauts to earth, instead of allowing them to expire in space, cost the U.S. taxpayer about half a billion dollars per astronaut. Although Parsons was not advocating a kamikaze Apollo mission, it is clear that not all lives are valued equally.

Human factors research advocated by Parsons takes the value of life and death into account. By studying warning labels and signs, the researcher can improve safety. By eliminating human causes of aircraft accidents and explosions in chemical plants, lives are saved. The potential to improve human life is an important reward for researchers working in human factors.

Is Controlling Behavior Ethical?

Applications of psychology hit closer to home than applications of any other science. For some, the specter of a cadre of applied psychologists controlling behavior conjures up Orwellian images of a Big Brother watching over us. Of course, people have always attempted to control your behavior ever since you were an infant. Your parents wanted you to eat good food instead of ice cream and candy, wanted you to become toilet trained, and may well be responsible for your present occupation as a student. Since this control lies in the bosom of the family, society has raised no objection. But society also tolerates control of your behavior by complete strangers. Corporate giants solicit your trade by expensive advertising on television, on radio, and in print. Although society occasionally objects to the poor taste exhibited by some of these commercial messages, or to their high frequency of occurrence, few have objected to the principle of advertising that is generally seen as a First Amendment constitutional right in the United States. The university controls your behavior by giving grades and demanding your physical presence in class. Business controls your behavior at work by specifying hours of employment and pay schedules. You would have to be a hermit isolated from all other people before none would attempt to control your behavior; indeed, even then society might try to demand payment of a property tax on your cave. With all these examples of behavior control, why then do people get so uptight whenever psychologists attempt to control behavior?

One answer might be that psychologists are better at controlling behavior than are the various social institutions, whose control is seen as hit-or-miss, and so is less resented. You have the option of turning off your television if a commercial offends you, driving faster than 55 miles per hour if you wish to violate the law, and cutting class if it is a nice spring day. Although you probably do not violate these rules often, it still is comforting to believe that you can ignore them if you so wish. In short, you have freedom of action and can do whatever you want to do, regardless of the rules.

The control of behavior that is technically possible through psychology is seen by many as a gross limitation of this freedom. Indeed, for many it appears directly counter to the most treasured principles of our democratic society. In a well-known article entitled "Freedom and the Control of Men," B. F. Skinner (1955) has addressed this issue directly. He argues that it is the end, not the means, that is of primary importance. If control of behavior is used to achieve ends we all admire and consider praiseworthy, then it should be used. Skinner cites T. H. Huxley on the automatic attainment of virtue:

> If some great power would agree to make me always think what is true and what is right, on condition of being a sort of clock and wound up every morning before I got out of bed, I should close instantly with the offer.

Doubtless, some of you do not agree with Huxley and Skinner. The price of being an automatic clock may seem too high to justify the end. But you do not object to an airplane being bound by the laws of physics or to a moth being attracted by a flame. That humans are subject to behavioral laws in the same way that machines are governed by physical laws has been discussed in chapter 1 and now reappears in a slightly different guise. Each of us already is a "sort of clock," whether we like it or not. If this is accepted, Skinner's point that control should be used to further good ends becomes more palatable. It would be unfortunate not to use behavioral control to increase the quality of life for everyone and to further the aims of humanitarian action.

The danger, not discussed much by Skinner, is that control of behavior can be used to achieve evil ends as well as good ends. In this regard, psychology is in the same position as any other science. Should nuclear energy be used for war or peace—or not used at all? Scientists in every discipline have recently become far more sensitive to the possible applications of their findings, and psychology is no exception (Bevan, 1976). Although psychologists surely have moral and ethical obligations to ensure that their science is used to improve life, you as an educated consumer of psychological research share this obligation. For you to bear this responsibility wisely, however, you must first know how psychology can be applied and the methodological problems that such applications involve. The rest of this chapter is directed to this aim.

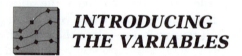

INTRODUCING THE VARIABLES

Dependent Variables

The most common dependent variable in human factors research is error rate. This is an obvious choice since decreasing human error is a major goal of human factors as a discipline. Time is also an important dependent variable. Total time to complete a task is often measured as well as component times such as reaction time and movement time. In practical situations excessive response time can be equivalent to an error. For example, if you correctly decide to step on the brake pedal of your car but delay your response until just before your vehicle goes over a cliff, the outcome would be the same as not stepping on the brake pedal.

Independent Variables

Human factors has a scope greater than that of experimental psychology. Thus, although many independent variables are the same as used by experimental psychologists, in general a wider range of independent variables is studied.

A human factors researcher interested in the role of visual illusions in aircraft crashes would study the same independent variables as an experimental psychologist interested in perception. Similarly, a researcher interested in training would manipulate some of the same independent variables, for example, practice, distribution of practice, and presentation modality, as a memory researcher. A human factors scientist studying mental workload would use some of the same independent variables as an experimental psychologist involved in attention research.

However, a human factors specialist interested in such complex systems as nuclear power plants or military command, control, and communication systems might manipulate communication pathways in small groups similar to ways social and organizational psychologists or sociologists might use. Environmental independent variables such as noise, temperature, and vibration are of interest in applied settings. Subject variables,

such as people with different leadership styles, might be selected. Schedules for shift work and time of day are also manipulated in human factors research.

Control Variables

Although not altogether absent, control variables are minimal in much of applied research. The field settings in which most of this research is conducted prevent the kind of experimental control we would demand inside the laboratory. The success of applied psychology is even more impressive when we stop to consider that in the typical applied setting, many potential independent variables cannot be held constant.

15.1 Experimental Topics and Research Illustrations

Topic: Small-*n* Design
Illustration: Dynamic Visual Acuity

Many practical situations require the detection and recognition of a moving target. A center fielder running to catch a long fly ball must find the target (baseball) in his visual field before he can predict where the ball will land. An airplane pilot operating in a crowded terminal area under visual flight rules must detect and avoid oncoming aircraft. An astronaut attempting to dock a space shuttle must judge relative motion between her craft and the docking gate. An automobile driver passing another car on a highway must detect oncoming traffic to decide if it is safe to pass. All these situations are examples of dynamic visual acuity at work.

Dynamic visual acuity is defined as the ability to perceive detail in moving objects. It is usually compared to static visual acuity, the ability to perceive detail in a fixed object. Visual acuity is often measured by presenting a letter C (called a *Landolt C*) with a small gap (see figure 15–2). If the gap is large, it is easy to notice. If the gap is very small, the letter C may be perceived as the letter O. The size of the gap that will allow you to reliably discriminate between the letter C and an apparently closed letter O is an index

FIGURE 15–2.

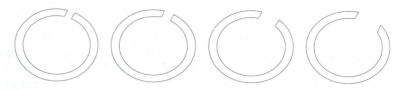

Landolt Cs

of your visual acuity. If the Landolt C does not move, we are measuring static acuity. If the Landolt C has a trajectory, we are measuring dynamic acuity. When you try to read a Snellen eye chart at the optometrist's office, your static visual acuity is being determined.

Although static and dynamic visual acuity are related (Scialfa, Garvey, Gish, Deering, Leibowitz, and Goebel, 1988), using static acuity to predict dynamic acuity can result in technical problems. Thus, for determining a person's ability to perform successfully in occupations that demand good dynamic acuity, the prudent researcher measures dynamic visual acuity directly. Furthermore, dynamic visual acuity has important design implications for complex systems. The designer would like to choose values that make it easier for a human to detect and recognize moving targets.

Effects of target wavelength on dynamic visual acuity. As with all interesting human factors problems, the effect of color on the resolution of a moving target has both practical and theoretical import. Design decisions involving such disparate items as computer display screens and street signs would be influenced by the knowledge that some particular color was easier to perceive. From a theoretical viewpoint, the blue cone color receptors are known to differ from the other color receptors having lower static acuity and being more sluggish (Long and Garvey, 1988). Thus, Long and Garvey (1988) had both practical and theoretical reasons for studying the effect of wavelength (color) on dynamic visual acuity.

Only two male observers were used in all experimental conditions. Both observers had static acuity of 20/20 when wearing eyeglasses, which of course were worn during the experiment. Although this is a small number of subjects, each observer participated in more than forty 40- to 60-minute sessions over a twelve-month period. Small-n designs are not used to minimize experimental effort. Instead, they are appropriate in highly-controlled experimental situations where data can be easily replicated. The psychophysical study (see chapter 6) of dynamic visual acuity meets this requirement for small-n design.

Landolt C targets were projected onto a white screen. The gap in the targets had four possible locations: upper left, upper right, lower left, lower right. The position of the gap varied randomly from trial to trial. The observer, in order to be correct, had to report the position of the gap. The size of the gap varied from 2.3 to 43.2 minutes of arc. The psychophysical technique used was the *method of limits* (see chapter 6). A trial run always started with a large target gap. Following a correct response, gap size was decreased. This continued until an incorrect response was made. Then gap size was increased to that of the preceding trial and the procedure was repeated. When the observer erred for the second time with a given gap size, testing under those conditions was stopped. The threshold was recorded as the next larger size gap. Long and Garvey (1988) do not explain why the method of limits was always used with descending gap sizes. Logically, one could also have used an ascending series starting with a small gap and increasing gap size until the gap was correctly detected.

Another important independent variable was adaptation level of the observer's eye. In night viewing conditions, vision is controlled by the rods; this is called *scotopic vision*. In brighter day viewing conditions, vision is controlled by the cones; this is called *photopic vision*. Rods and cones have different sensitivities to wavelength (color). Even though the rods cannot recognize color, they still respond with different sensitivity to various wavelengths. So it was prudent to study effects of wavelength under scotopic conditions where rods dominate versus photopic conditions where cones dominate vision. In this study a low background luminance level (0.03 candelas/meter squared) was used to produce scotopic vision and a higher luminance (34.26 candelas/meter squared) was used to produce photopic vision.

Finally, the last independent variable we shall discuss was target velocity. Three values of angular velocity were studied: 60 degrees/second, 90 degrees/second, and 120 degrees/second. These values were selected to bracket velocities used in earlier studies and because a deleterious effect of target motion on acuity was expected for this range of velocities.

Results are shown in figure 15–3. Each observer is represented by his own graph, because small-n research does not generally average data from different observers. As target velocity increases, threshold (size of gap) also increases. Faster-moving targets are harder to perceive. Blue targets are easier to perceive (lower threshold) for scotopic vision, but not for photopic vision.

These results have some interesting practical implications. For example, red illumination is customarily used to maintain human dark adaptation, but this practice might be harmful if people are required to detect moving targets.

15.2 Experimental Topics and Research Illustrations

Topic: Field Research
Illustration: Pilot Mental Workload

Eastern Airlines flight 401 was approaching Miami International Airport when the pilot realized that the indicator light for the nose wheel was not illuminated. He therefore diverted and flew over the

FIGURE 15–3.

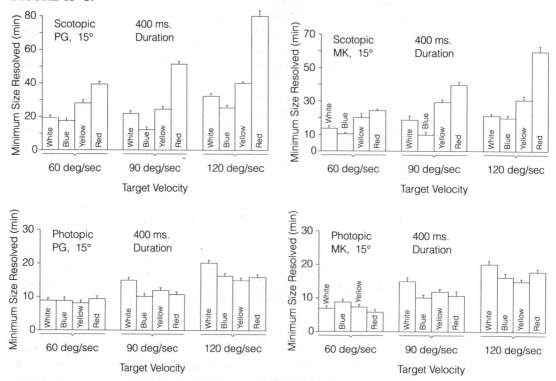

Dynamic visual acuity as a function of target velocity and target color. (From *Human Factors*, copyright 1988, by the Human Factors Society, Inc., and reproduced by permission.)

Everglades at a low altitude while the crew tried to determine if the problem was the signal light itself, or if the nosegear was not down and locked in its landing position. Although landing a plane with a failed nose wheel is not a very dangerous procedure, the crew naturally wanted to lower the wheel manually if the signal light correctly showed a nosegear failure.

The plane was flying on autopilot while the entire three-man crew tried to determine if the light bulb was defective and if the gear was down. However, unknown to the crew, the autopilot had been accidentally disengaged, and the plane had begun a gradual descent. The crew's attention was focused on the signal light; it was quite a while before the copilot noticed the altimeter reading. In the eight seconds remaining before flight 401 crashed into the ground, the crew made no attempt to increase altitude. The mechanical cause of this accident that killed 99 people was a burnt-out light bulb. The psychological cause was the mental process of attention. The crew was so mentally locked into solving the problem of the signal light that no one paid attention to the more important problem of flying the airplane and monitoring altitude.

Basic research on divided and focused attention provides models and data that bear directly on this kind of practical problem (see chapter 8). But the practical utility of the research cannot be evaluated in the laboratory. *Field studies* are needed to determine if the so-called ivory tower laboratory research performed in universities works in the real world. In aviation, it is expensive and possibly dangerous to conduct field studies in airplanes in actual flight. Thus, most research is performed in flight simulators. These simulators so closely duplicate the reality of flight that they are approved by the Federal Aviation Agency for training and recertification of professional pilots. In aviation, the flight simulator provides a "halfway house" between the carefully controlled laboratory and the airways. For safety reasons, most field studies are conducted in flight simulators. We will review a series of studies conducted in flight simulators at the National Aeronautics and Space Administration's Ames Research Center in California, and then conclude with a field study from the flying observatory stationed at Ames. Our goal is to explain how to measure and evaluate the attentional requirements of flight: the effects of *workload* on the pilots' ability to control the simulators.

The NASA GAT experiments: measuring workload in a simulator. Starting in 1983, a series of experiments was carried out in the General Aviation Trainer (GAT) at NASA. This is a relatively inexpensive flight simulator that trains pilots to fly a generic single-engine airplane. It is mounted on a base that allows the entire cockpit to move according to the pilot's actions. It is most often used with the cockpit window covered over, so that the pilot must depend on instrument readings to guide flight. The experience can be quite realistic; pilots have even been known to become airsick inside the GAT.

The goal of this research effort, expressed in a general way, was to provide objective workload measurement methods, especially using secondary-task methodology, that would work in a flight simulator. A *secondary task* is an extra task inserted with the important task (called the primary task) under investigation. Often, performance on the secondary task can be interpreted as an index of attention required by the primary task. If secondary-task performance is poor, this might indicate high attention demands for the primary task. The problem was how to utilize the large body of attention research to help solve a practical predicament in a field setting.

Many studies completed in the laboratories of experimental psychologists studying attention suggested that secondary tasks were useful indicants of attentional load (Kantowitz, 1985). The challenge was to utilize this basic research knowledge, most of which was not aimed at solving any practical problems in the near future, in a more realistic setting. The GAT environment was a reasonable compromise between the rigor and control of the experimental psychology laboratory and the high validity of a real aircraft. Simulators are widely used in aviation for training; they offer the substantial advantages of safety, economy, and a higher degree of experimental control than can be obtained in flight.

Field research in pilot workload uses both *objective* and *subjective* dependent variables. Objective measures include variables, such as reaction time and percent correct, that can be easily verified by the experimenter. Subjective measures are introspective reports given on rating scales: for example, a pilot could be asked to judge workload on a scale of 1 to 10. Subjective ratings cannot be directly verified by the experimenter. In the early 1980s, investigators studying workload in flight simulators were having trouble finding satisfactory objective measures. The typical study would investigate many objective and subjective measures. It was commonplace to find subjective measures that yielded statistical significance, but useful objective measures were rare. A study that found one objective measure out of perhaps a dozen to yield reliable statistical results was state of the art. Therefore, investigators began to prefer subjective measures to objective measures. This preference is quite understandable, since no one wants to waste resources studying effects that do not meet appropriate statistical criteria.

The general inability to find useful objective indexes of workload was disturbing for several reasons. First, as discussed previously, there is some uncertainty associated with the interpretation of subjective ratings, especially when each laboratory uses different rating scales. Being able to confirm the subjective results with objective results would increase our faith in both kinds of measures. Second, it was not clear if this failure to find reliable objective measures was due entirely to deficiencies in these measures, or at least in part to an inability to program flight scenarios that really did require different levels of pilot workload. In other words, the failure to find reliable objective measures in some cases might simply reflect the reality that the underlying missions actually did not differ in pilot workload. Finding significant subjective effects in such cases might be an artifact of pilot expectations about missions; pilots might be reporting what they thought the workload should be, rather than what it actually was. This type of (well-intentioned) pilot error is always a potential hazard with studies of subjective impressions.

Finally, the large body of laboratory research on attention so strongly suggested that objective measures should be successful in simulated flight that the general difficulty in obtaining success implied that either (a) laboratory behavioral research is useless in guiding practical research, or (b) investigators were doing something wrong. Because of prior public statements that rejected the first explanation (Kantowitz, 1982), the first author was highly motivated to believe explanation (b). However, the proof of the pudding is in the eating: a mere suspicion about possible deficiencies in workload experiments would not be at all convincing unless the skeptic could provide hard experimental data that demonstrated the utility of objective workload measurement techniques.

So Kantowitz, who at the time was blissfully ignorant about both aviation and the special difficulties associated with simulator research, gamely agreed to put his money where his mouth was and spend a summer at Ames obtaining the necessary data.

Thus did our hero leave his pristine laboratory amidst the corn fields of Indiana and head west to laid-back California to search for truth in a GAT. The good people at Ames did all in their power to aid this search. After a thirty-minute lecture on the theory of flight, our protagonist was popped into the GAT, where, without any prior experience, he immediately made a successful simulated landing on the roof of the San Jose Civic Center. But with practice, and lots of help from colleagues at Ames, eventually he became familiar with the rudiments of aviation. The remainder of this section details the experimental results he obtained.

Theoretical assumptions. A major problem in the human factors of aviation is the absence of meaningful theoretical frameworks to help guide research and practice. Much of the psychological literature seems irrelevant to the practitioner; therefore, most of the previous workload studies did not rely on any theoretical viewpoints. A kind of loose engineering approach was taken, based on the notion that if enough objective measures were studied, sooner or later a winner would emerge. Although some consideration was given to copying the methods used in laboratory studies of attention, little effort was devoted to understanding the theoretical implications of these methods.

One common secondary-task technique uses a reaction-time (RT) probe as the secondary task. Most laboratory studies have used a simple reaction probe task, in which the human observers in an experiment must press a key as soon as they hear an auditory tone. The tone is the secondary task; some other experimental task is the main focus of interest. Increased RT to the tone is interpreted as revealing attention requirements of the primary (main) task.

To reach a valid conclusion, insertion of the secondary task must not change performance on the primary task. If performance is degraded on the primary task when it is performed together with the secondary task, this implies that attention has been diverted away from the primary task to the secondary task. This prevents us from drawing any conclusions about the attentional demands of the primary task. For the secondary-task technique to be effective, performance on the primary task must remain constant, with no attention being siphoned away to the secondary task. This strong constraint leads laboratory researchers to favor very simple secondary tasks, as less likely to draw attention away from the primary task. The simplest probe reaction task is simple RT with only one stimulus (the tone) and one response.

When the secondary task was moved into the flight simulator, it was quite natural to carry along the simple probe task. Most results showed that the probe task was not an indicant of pilot workload. Therefore, many workers became discouraged and abandoned secondary tasks. However, applying models of attention raises another possible interpretation. The secondary probe task may have shown no effect because it was too simple. It required so little capacity that in a flight simulator, where the world is less controlled than in an experimental-psychology laboratory, it was swamped by the noise (variance) in the environment. The solution was to substitute a choice-reaction task for the simple probe.

In choice reactions, there are several possible stimuli (e.g., tones of different frequencies); each one has its own unique response. Since choice reaction requires more capacity, there is an increased danger of violating the requirement that the primary task remain unaffected by the secondary task. Indeed, performing such an experiment with college sophomores, the typical subjects of experimental psychology, might very well fail. But pilots have a tremendous advantage over college sophomores. Pilots are extremely well trained. They have learned that no matter what else happens, their first responsibility is to fly the airplane. So Kantowitz hoped that his strategy of using a more complex secondary task would be safe: pilots would first fly the plane, and then—and only then—pay attention to the tones. As you shall see, the experimental results justified this hope.

Before moving on to the results, let us stress an important point once again. The difference between a choice-reaction and a simple-reaction task may seem almost trivial, especially to those unfamiliar with the reaction-time literature. Many other differences among experiments would appear equally important. But a theory of attention provides a lens for the close examination of experiments. Theory suggests that this difference is vital. This, of course, does not mean that the theory is correct; for verification, we must obtain data. But without theory, we do not know where to look for critical parts of an experiment. This leads to the generally unsuccessful "shotgun" procedure described earlier, in which experimenters throw in lots of variables, in hopes that some will work. The experiments described below were unusual in that only a single secondary task, that of choice reactions, was used. Even sympathetic colleagues at Ames had their doubts about putting all the eggs into one basket with only one secondary task. To many, such brazen faith in theory was *hubris* and would undoubtedly lead to *nemesis*. Waiting for the slow accumulation of data that would tell the tale made for an exciting summer.

Experiment 1.0. The main goals of this first experiment were (1) to discover if a choice-reaction secondary task could meet the assumption of noninterference with the primary flying task; and, if it could, (2) to see if results were an index of pilot workload. Not all results will be discussed here; the interested reader is directed to the published report by Kantowitz, Hart, and Bortolussi (1983).

The secondary task consisted of either two or four auditory tones. (Reasons for using both two- and four-choice tasks are related to theoretical issues that are beyond the scope of this chapter; see Kantowitz and Knight, 1976.) Pilots responded to the tones by pushing a switch, mounted under the pilot's left thumb, in the appropriate direction, depending on the pitch of the tone. Tones occurred every 22 seconds during simulated flight.

Each pilot flew one Hard and one Easy flight scenario, lasting 22 minutes each. Scenarios were constructed based on earlier rating data (Childress, Hart, and Bortolussi, 1982). Each scenario was flown three times: once alone as a control condition, once with a two-choice secondary task, and once with a four-choice secondary task.

Figure 15–4 shows error on the flying task as a function of level of the secondary task. The Hard scenario showed greater error, as expected; this confirmed predictions based on the rating data used to construct the flight scenarios. Of greater importance is the effect of secondary task. Appropriate statistical analysis shows that the two curves in figure 15–4 are flat. There is no statistical difference between no secondary task (labeled None in the figure) and either two- or four-choice secondary tasks. Thus, the key assumption that pilots first fly the plane and do not let secondary tasks interfere with the primary flying task was validated.

Figure 15–5 shows performance on the secondary tone task as a function of flight segment. The vertical axis shows transmitted information in bits/sec. This is a measure that takes both speed and accuracy of responding into account. Higher scores indicate better performance. There are reliable statistical differences among these points. In particular, the last flight segments showed the lowest scores. This means that attention and workload was greatest during this segment. There was relatively less attention available for the secondary task during this segment, and so the bits/sec score is low. This result makes intuitive sense to pilots, who believe that

FIGURE 15–4.

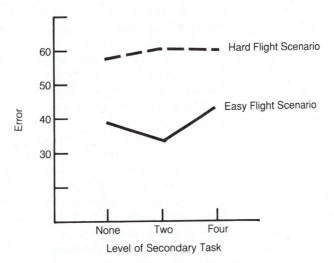

Primary task (flying) error as a function of levels of secondary task.

FIGURE 15–5.

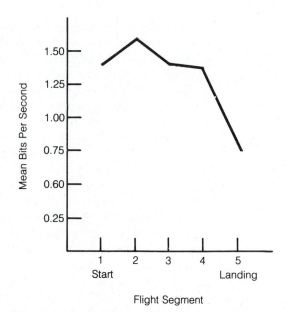

Flight Segment

Transmitted information on the secondary task as a function of flight segment.

workload is highest during landing. However, their opinion is subjective. The objective results of figure 15–5 are not based on opinion. The convergence of both objective and subjective measures
increases our faith in the result that landing causes high workload.

Experiments 2.1 and 2.2. Experiment 1 demonstrated the feasibility of using an objective choice-reaction secondary task to measure pilot workload in a GAT simulator. Experiment 2 used this
tool to attack a serious problem facing workload researchers: how
to construct valid flight scenarios. Failure to obtain workload effects could mean that either (a) the secondary task was inadequate,
or (b) the flight scenarios tested do not differ in workload. Since
different laboratories use different secondary tasks as well as different flight scenarios, it is often quite difficult to compare results.
Some kind of standardization was badly needed. Now that we had
a tool (from Experiment 1) that worked, we could go on to evaluate
the workload of different components of simulated flight. Once this
workload was known, researchers would be able to build standardized scenarios of known relative workload. So we called this
experiment "Building Levels of Workload."

   Flight tasks were divided into three levels of complexity: Base,
Paired, and Complex. Base tasks were single subtasks; paired tasks
were combinations of two base tasks; and complex tasks were made
up of three base subtasks. In Experiment 2.1, very simple base
tasks were chosen. Irrelevant task dimensions in the simulator
were frozen to prevent pilots from trying to control more than the
desired sub-task. More realistic flight tasks were used in Experiment 2.2.

Detailed results are presented by Kantowitz, Hart, Bortolussi, Shively, and Kantowitz (1984). Here we note only that both experiments were successful in building levels of workload. Both secondary tasks and subjective ratings showed higher levels of workload to be associated with the progression from base to complex flight tasks. Figures 15–6 (Experiment 2.1) and 15–7 (Experiment 2.2) are representative; they show that secondary-task per-

FIGURE 15–6.

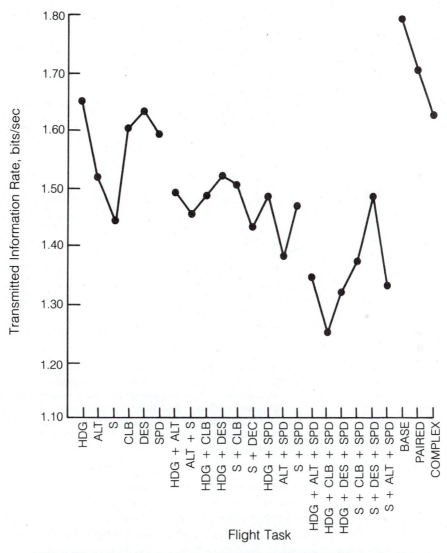

Transmitted information on the secondary task in Experiment 2.1 as a function of flight task. The flight tasks were: maintaining a constant heading (HDG), holding a constant altitude (ALT), making an S-turn (S), climbing (CLB), descending (DES), and keeping a constant speed (SPD). The figures on the right labeled Base, Paired, and Complex are control data from single stimulus reaction times. (From *Proceedings of the Human Factors Society 27th Annual Meeting,* Vol. 30, No. 1, 1983. Copyright 1983 by the Human Factors Society, Inc., and reproduced by permission.)

FIGURE 15–7.

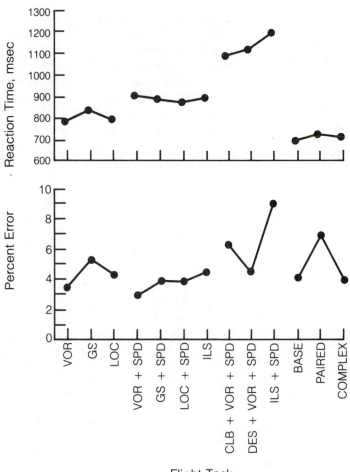

Reaction time and percent error on the secondary task in Experiment 2.2 as a function of flight task. The flight tasks were: approaching a signal beacon (VOR), maintaining a glide slope on landing (GS), using an aerial localizer (LOC), and using the instrument landing system (ILS). The three points at the right of the figure represent control data from single stimulation conditions. (From *Human Factors*, copyright 1988, by the Human Factors Society, Inc., and reproduced by permission.)

formance was worst for the complex flight tasks. Subjective ratings, especially those based on a weighting procedure in which individual pilots rated the factors that they found important in estimating workload, were in agreement with objective results.

Experiment 3.0. This experiment (Bortolussi, Hart and Kantowitz, 1986) compared four methods for measuring pilot workload: choice-reaction secondary task with visual stimuli (versus the tones used in previous experiments); a time-estimation secondary task; retrospective subjective ratings; and in-flight verbal workload estimates. Choice reactions provided the most successful objective measure. Time estimation was less sensitive; although partially successful, it did not reveal subtle workload differences captured by the choice-reaction secondary task. Subjective ratings confirmed the objective results with in-flight ratings more sensitive than the retrospective ratings used in earlier experiments.

Summary and implications. The three years of experimentation briefly described above have been successful enough to exceed the researchers' expectations. They have shown that theory is indeed a practical tool. In the GAT simulator, an environment that is at least an order of magnitude less controlled than the laboratory settings that created the theory, we were still able to find an objective measure of pilot workload by using choice reactions. Furthermore, we now have a workload data base that will permit contruction of standardized flight scenarios.

Measuring pilot workload in the air. The NASA Kuiper Airborne Observatory (figure 15–8) is a "flying telescope" that permits astronomers to get above much of the atmosphere by flying at high altitudes—over 40,000 feet, with 85 percent of the earth's atmosphere below it—thereby getting better images of astral events. In conjunction with the observatory's regular mission, workload researchers were able to go along to monitor four measures of pilot workload: communications analysis, subjective ratings of workload, subjective ratings of additional factors related to workload, and heart rate (Hart, Hauser, and Lester, 1984).

Because the workload research could not interfere with normal flight procedures, the researchers had to accept several limitations on the research design. For example, no measures (except for heart rate) were taken during takeoffs and landings, for safety reasons.

FIGURE 15–8.

The NASA Kuiper Airborne Observatory

It was also not practical to obtain objective measures by introducing a secondary task. Nevertheless, some useful information was still obtained. The most interesting result was a difference in mean heart rate between pilots and copilots. The pilots, who were responsible for flying the plane, had higher mean heart rates than the copilots, who were responsible for navigation and communication. This difference could not be attributed to differences in training, because all of the pilots were fully qualified; indeed, it was often the case that a man who had functioned as a copilot on one flight would be the pilot for another flight. However, practical scheduling difficulties prevented a complete experimental design by which all pilots could be tested in both pilot and copilot jobs. Similarly, it was not possible to obtain nonflying baseline heart-rate data. There was a large difference in heart rate (72 to 87 beats per minute) for the pilot; no such increase was obtained for the copilot. However, subjective workload estimates, although differing significantly across flight segments, did not differ between pilots and copilots.

As with most in-flight studies of workload, these results are not as easy to interpret as laboratory or simulator studies. Heart rate is very sensitive to amount of physical effort: the higher heart rate for pilots could reflect physical activity more than mental activity. Heart-rate variance is a measure of mental workload that is less affected by physical effort, but the researchers did not report variance results. The best approach seems to be a combination of objective, subjective, and physiological measures conducted in laboratories and simulators. The objective measures can be used to calibrate the other kinds of measures that are more appropriate for in-flight tests. Future progress in measuring pilot mental workload depends on linking present results to theories of attention. This is not an easy task and will require better cooperation between basic and applied researchers (Kantowitz, 1982).

From Problem to Experiment: The Nuts and Bolts

Problem: Measure Pilot Mental Workload in Flight

Field research almost always has limitations that prevent the straightforward application of laboratory methods and solutions. Although we can measure mental workload in the laboratory and in flight simulators with some degree of success (see Kantowitz and Casper, 1989, for a review), there at present is no universally accepted in-flight technique for continuous monitoring of pilot mental workload. This is the problem discussed here.

Problem: *Find an unobtrusive way to measure pilot mental workload in flight.*

The key word here is unobtrusive. This means that our method cannot interfere with normal flight procedures. So the best laboratory technique, using an objective secondary task, must be ruled out. Under high workload, the extra attention that might be diverted to a secondary task could present a safety hazard. The same argument could be made against having pilots continuously report subjective workload ratings.

This suggests that a physiological measure might be most suitable as a dependent variable. Pilots would not be bothered if painless electrodes could be attached to record heart rate or brain waves, to name two possible physiological measures. Independent variables could be phase of flight and pilot versus copilot.

Hypothesis: *Brain waves index pilot mental workload in flight.*

This hypothesis is far more complex than it appears to be at first. The major experimental problem is how to score brain waves. The technology for recording brain waves (called evoked potentials) from surface electrodes attached painlessly to the scalp is well established, but the interpretation of these signals is quite another matter. There are many components inside the evoked potential; sophisticated computer programs are needed to distinguish true components from electrical noise. Even once components are correctly identified and scored, they must still be related to pilot workload.

For the sake of discussion, let us assume we have been able to locate some specific evoked potential component and have a small but powerful computer system in the airplane that can continuously process the brain waves of the pilot and copilot. We would like to demonstrate that the magnitude of the evoked-potential component increases with increasing pilot workload. We might also predict that the pilot would exhibit a larger magnitude than the copilot.

The details of our experimental design would probably depend on the flight requirements of the mission. Field researchers usually do not have the luxury of designing missions to fit their research needs. Instead, the research problem must be piggybacked onto some existing mission. This greatly limits experimental design. Hopefully, we would be able to identify different phases of flight (landing, cruising, etc.) that provided different levels of pilot workload. Of course, we would have to use published results from prior experiments to relate workload and phase of flight.

If our experiment worked, the greatest brain wave components would occur during the most difficult phases of flight. If, however, this was not the case, there could be many sources of potential error in this field of study that could prevent the desired outcome—even if our hypothesis were correct. Perhaps the phases of flight did not differ sufficiently in pilot workload. Perhaps the wrong brain wave component was selected. Perhaps we could not obtain sufficient data to create a powerful statistical test of our results.

Perhaps our sample of pilots was much too small. Perhaps the skill level of our pilots was so high relative to a mission that was at the low end of the workload continuum that no overload occurred. Many other problems could be listed here.

The bottom line is that field experiments are always more frustrating for the experimenter than laboratory research. However, this does not necessarily imply that field research is bad and laboratory research is always good. Ultimately, the success of the experimental psychologist, as evaluated by the society that supports psychological research, is related to how well the knowledge created is translated into practical benefits to society. Practical problems will be solved by applying research concepts developed in the laboratory. But the utility of these concepts in improving human productivity, safety, and quality of life can be assessed only in field settings.

SUMMARY

1. Human factors is the discipline that tries to optimize the relationship between people and technology. Many human factors researchers and practitioners were originally trained in experimental psychology. However, the scope of human factors includes more than experimental psychology.

2. The main principle of human factors is "Honor thy user." Since people are the common element in various technological systems, we cannot improve system performance and quality without understanding how the human functions as part of the system.

3. In many human factors settings, the traditional large-n research methodology of psychological research cannot be employed. Dynamic visual acuity is one research topic in human factors where psychophysical research techniques are most appropriate. Color and movement velocity affect dynamic visual acuity.

4. Experiments in human factors can be conducted in the laboratory, in simulators, or in the field on working systems. For reasons of safety and economy, simulator research is used in areas such as aviation and nuclear power.

5. Both objective and subjective measures are used to study mental workload. Subjective measures are easier to obtain, whereas objective measures are easier to verify by researchers.

6. Theories are as important in guiding human factors research as they are in basic research. Models of color vision have been applied to studying dynamic visual acuity. Models of attention are useful in directing simulator studies of mental workload.

KEY TERMS

dynamic visual acuity
field research
human factors
Landolt C
large-*n* design
method of limits
objective measures

photopic vision
secondary task
scotopic vision
small-*n* design
subjective measures
workload

DISCUSSION QUESTIONS

1. What ethical factors must a human factors researcher consider when undertaking an investigation that has the potential to alter people's work environments?

2. How might a system designer take into account safety features that add cost to the system but can protect human lives?

3. List some practical situations in which object color might be an important aspect of dynamic visual acuity.

4. Discuss some of the difficulties inherent in field research. Can you think of methods to combat these problems?

5. Compare the advantages and disadvantages of studying pilot mental workload in a flight simulator rather than in an airplane during flight.

Population Stereotypes

POPULATION STEREOTYPES ARE LEARNED relationships and habits common to specific populations. For example, in the United States we have learned to throw a light switch up to turn a light on. However, in England the population stereotype is to throw the switch down. Population stereotypes are of great concern to the human factors designers who wishes to create compatible relationships (Kantowitz, Triggs, and Barnes, 1990). Population stereotypes in human factors were first applied to relationships between controls and displays, but the concept is easily extended to other areas such as verbal labels and pictures (Smith, 1981). Take the following short quiz. Then compare your answers to those of a sample of 92 male engineers, 80 women who were friends or relatives of these engineers, and 55 (mostly male) human factors specialists tested by Smith (1981).

Population Stereotype Quiz
(from Smith, 1981)

1. Knob turn

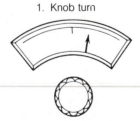

1. To move the arrow-indicator to the center of the display, how would you turn the knob?

____ clockwise
____ counterclockwise

2. Quadrant labels

2. In what order would you label the four quadrants of a circle? Write in the letters A, B, C, and D, assigning one letter to each quadrant.

492

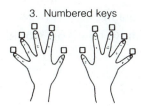

3. Numbered keys

3. A worker is required to duplicate numbers as they appear on a screen, by pressing 10 keys, one for each finger.

Label the diagram to show how you would assign the 10 numerals to the 10 fingers.

4. Cross faucets

4. Here are two knobs on a bathroom sink, looking down on them.

Put an arrow on each dotted line, to show how you would operate these knobs to turn the water on.

5. *"Pressure High"*

Working with a fire crew, the hoseman yells "Pressure High."

What should be done to the water pressure?

_____ Lower the pressure
_____ Raise the pressure

6. River bank

6. Here is a river, flowing from east to west.

Is the church on the
_____ left bank?
_____ right bank?

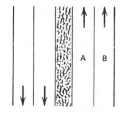

7. Highway lanes

7. On the four-lane divided highway pictured here, which is the outside line?

_____ A
_____ B

8. Lever control

8. To move the arrow-indicator to the right of the display, how would you move the level?

_____ push
_____ pull

9. Lever faucets

9. Here are two knobs on a bathroom sink, looking down at them. Put an arrow on each dotted line, to show how you would operate these knobs to turn the water on.

10. Digital counter

Knob

10. To increase the number displayed in the window, how would you turn the knob?

____ clockwise
____ counterclockwise

Answers

1. Counterclockwise: Engineers (%)   97%
Women (%)   94%
HF (%)   91%

2.

	Engineers (%)	Women (%)	HFS (%)
Clockwise from upper right	33	26	45
Clockwise from upper left	19	11	5
Counterclockwise from upper right	34	3	5
"Reading" order	14	54	43
Other		6	2

3.

	Engineers (%)	Women (%)	HFS (%)
Ascending left to right	70	70	84
Ascending outwards from thumbs	18	16	5
Other	12	14	11

4.

Left faucet	Right faucet	Engineers (%)	Women (%)	HFS (%)
C	C	17	34	22
C	CC	23	20	13
CC	C	13	26	16
CC	CC	47	20	49

5.

	Engineers (%)	Women (%)	HFS (%)
"Lower the pressure" (Error)	66	48	78
"Raise the pressure" (Command)	34	53	22

6.

	Engineers (%)	Women (%)	HFS (%)
Left bank	18	16	13
Right bank	82	84	80
Other (not answered)			7

7.

	Engineers (%)	Women (%)	HFS (%)
A outside	50	51	20
B outside	50	49	80

8.

	Engineers (%)	Women (%)	HFS (%)
Push	76	59	71
Pull	24	41	25
Other (not answered)			4

Note: Only 70 engineers and 63 women received this question.

9.

Left faucet	Right faucet	Engineers (%)	Women (%)	HFS (%)
Back	Back	25	33	16
Back	Forward	3	3	5
Forward	Back	10	4	7
Forward	Forward	62	60	71

10.

	Engineers (%)	Women (%)	HFS (%)
Clockwise	87	79	95
Counterclockwise	13	21	5

Note: Only 46 engineers and 43 women received this question.

Experimental Psychology: A Historical Sketch

Psychology has a long past, but only a short history.
—HERMANN EBBINGHAUS

CURIOSITY AND WONDER ARE THE prime motivations for science, and there are few topics that people have found more interesting than the workings of their own minds. Many of the writings of the great philosophers, from Aristotle's time to the present, have been concerned with what can be called psychological problems. How do we perceive and know the external world? How do we learn about it and remember what we learn? How do we use this information to build concepts of the world and solve the problems that the world presents us? What are the roots of abnormal behavior? Are there laws that govern social and political behavior? Is there meaning to dreams?

Although such topics have been discussed for centuries, the methods of science were not applied to the study of the human mind and behavior until three or four hundred years after they found a solid place in physics (thus Ebbinghaus's quote). In fact, psychology today is to be compared, perhaps, with sixteenth-century physics. As many students of psychology realize (to their dismay), we still have much to learn about many important areas of human behavior.

This appendix provides a brief and very rough sketch of the intellectual history of experimental psychology. Full histories can be found in Boring (1950), the classic in the field, and in a more recent and readable work by Schultz and Schultz (1987).

Origins of Experimental Psychology: Philosophy and Physiology

An important issue in the history of philosophy is the mind-body problem. Are the mind and body essentially the same or different in nature? A once-popular position on this issue, which probably greatly retarded the development of a scientific psychology, is that the mind and body are separate entities and operate according to different principles. According to this theory, often called *dualism*, the body is governed by physical laws, as are inanimate objects, but the mind is not governed by such laws, since it possesses free will. It makes no sense to apply scientific methods in an attempt to discover laws of mental life if one is a dualist and believes that such laws do not exist. Early dualists argued that although the mind could control the body, there was little influence in the opposite direction.

The influential philosophical writings of René Descartes (1596–1650) helped weaken the belief that the body and mind do not interact. Descartes advanced the idea of mutual interaction: the body could affect the mind, and the mind could affect the body. Although the dualist position remained, and the mind was still regarded as immortal and as possessing free will and a soul, the body could be studied as a mechanical system by rational, scientific means. And since animals were regarded as not possessing souls, they too could be studied by the methods applied to the inanimate objects of physical science. Thus, the application of the scientific method began to expand beyond the study of purely physical systems to the study of organic systems.

Over the years, the idea became more prevalent that even the human mind could be treated as something that could be profitably studied to discover mental laws. The British empiricist philosophers (Locke, Berkeley, Hume, Hartley) were impressed by the power of mechanistic models for explaining physical systems (e.g., astronomy and physics). They believed that the mind could be modeled in a similar fashion, that is, in terms of elements (ideas) and forces (associations) that act upon those elements in lawful ways. The empiricists emphasized the mechanical nature of mental phenomena; they discussed the "laws" of association in thought and the physical basis of the perception of the external world. The idea was beginning to take hold that for scientific study, the mind could be treated as a machine.

The British philosophers also emphasized the importance of learning in our understanding of the world. Descartes had argued that some ideas are innate, or develop without information from the external world impinging on the senses. Kant expanded on this position, and aspects of it were later incorporated into the Gestalt school of psychology. The British empiricists received their name by rejecting this idea (*empiric* comes from the Greek *empeiria*, meaning experience). John Locke wrote thus in *An Essay Concerning Human Understanding:*

> Let us suppose the mind to be, as we say, white paper, void of all characters, without any ideas:—How comes it to be fur-

nished? Whence comes it by that vast store which the busy and boundless fancy of man has painted on it with an almost endless variety? Whence has it all the *materials* of reason and knowledge? To this I answer, in one word, from EXPERIENCE. In that all our knowledge is founded. (Book II, chapter I).

Philosophers were preparing the way for a scientific psychology by treating the mind as subject to natural laws, but their method of study was simply one of anecdote and reflection. No matter how brilliant, these methods were likely to advance our knowledge little past the careful reflections of Plato and Aristotle centuries before. What was needed was application of the experimental methods and logic of science to the study of the mind and behavior. As Boring observed, "The application of the experimental method to the problem of mind is the great outstanding event to which no other is comparable." This method came to psychology by way of physiology.

German physiologists in the middle of the nineteenth century were interested in what is today considered sensory physiology: the physiology of the sense organs, (the eyes, ears, etc.) and the transmission of information from these organs to the brain via the nervous system. Many of the German physiologists hoped that physiology could be reduced ultimately to physics, and, as they became interested in the physiology of the human nervous system, they came increasingly close to treating the mind as a physical machine. The Berlin Physical Society was formed in the 1840s with an overriding commitment to the belief that ultimately all phenomena could be explained in terms of physics. Four of the radical young scientists in the society, all in their twenties, signed in blood (so the story goes) an oath stating their belief that all forces in the human organism were chemical and physical ones.

The Contribution of Helmholtz

One of these young scientists was Hermann von Helmholtz (1821–1894). He was primarily a physicist and physiologist and was not concerned with establishing psychology as an independent discipline, but his research is given much credit in having had this effect. His work in vision and audition was overwhelmingly important, but what we should emphasize here is his role in conducting what may be considered transition experiments between physiology and experimental psychology.

One famous case was his use of what is now known as a *reaction-time experiment* to study the speed of neural impulses. Johannes Müller, a famous German physiologist, had argued that transmission of nervous impulses was instantaneous, or perhaps approached the speed of light. If you pinch your hand, do you notice any time elapse between the time you see yourself do the pinching and the time you feel the pinch? Probably not. At any rate, Müller also stated that we could probably never calculate the speed of nervous impulses. Only a few years later (in 1851), Helmholtz measured the speed experimentally. The basic idea was ingeniously simple: Stimulate a nerve at two different distances from the brain and measure the difference in time it takes for the organism to respond to the stimulation. If one knows the distance between the two points of stimulation and the difference in time taken to respond, then one can calculate the rate of the nervous impulse, since rate equals distance divided by time. Helmholtz stimulated blindfolded people on either the shoulder or the ankle and measured how fast they could react with their hand (by pushing a lever) in each case. Since he could measure approximately how much farther the impulse would have to travel to the brain from the ankle than from the shoulder, he was able to estimate the speed of nervous impulses at the relatively slow rate of 50 meters per second—not even the speed of sound, much less that of light! Helmholtz's most careful experimental work on this issue was with frogs (where of course the technique, but not the logic, was different), and the estimates were not too different. In fact, the estimates have more or less withstood the test of time, though we know today that the speed of the nervous impulse depends on the diameter of the nerves involved.

An interesting footnote is that Helmholtz so despaired of the great variability (or differences) in the reaction times that he found among subjects, and even within the same subject on different trials, that he gave up altogether on this line of research (Schultz and Schultz, 1987). Many psychologists since Helmholtz have also lamented the variability one finds in psychological research, although most have not given it up for this reason. Much of this book is concerned with the problem of variability in measures of animal or human behavior and how to overcome this problem.

Early Scientific Psychology

Scientific psychology had its birth and early life in Germany. In this section, we will mention the contributions of four early pioneers: Weber, Fechner, Wundt, and Ebbinghaus.

Ernst Weber

Ernst Weber (1795–1878) was an anatomist and physiologist at Leipzig whose research centered on cutaneous sensation, or the sense of touch. His most important contribution to psychology grew out of some experiments he conducted to investigate whether active engagement of one's muscles affected one's judgment of the weights of objects (see chapter 6). He had people compare two weights, one of which was called a standard. In one case, blindfolded subjects picked up first a standard weight and then a comparison weight, and indicated to the experimenter whether the two weighed the same amount. In another case, the subjects were passive; they simply had the weights placed in their hands successively, and then made their decisions.

Weber discovered that judgments were more accurate when subjects actively engaged their muscles; but more important, he noted something interesting in subjects' abilities to detect a difference between the standard and comparison weights. The greater the weight of the standard, the greater the difference between the standard and comparison weight had to be before the difference could be noticed by the subjects. When the standard weight was small, only a small difference between the standard and comparison was necessary for subjects to detect a difference. But when the weight was large, the difference necessary for detection (called the *just-noticeable difference* or *jnd*) was correspondingly larger. Weber further discovered that for any of the senses, the ratio of the amount of difference necessary to produce a jnd to the standard was a constant. Thus, not only does the amount of difference necessary to produce a jnd increase with the size of the standard, but it does so in a quite systematic way. This fact has come to be known as *Weber's law* (see chapter 6).

Gustav Fechner

Weber thought that his finding was an interesting and useful generalization, but he was by no means staggered by its importance. Gustav Fechner (1801–1887) was. Fechner was eccentric, in many ways, but his importance to psychology was great. He was trained as a physicist, but also made contributions to philosophy, religion, aesthetics, and psychology. Among numerous other academic ventures, he wrote one book on life after death and another (antedating a recent revival of interest in this topic) which argues that plants have a "mental life." In the 1830s, his interests turned to the psychological topics of color vision and afterimages. He badly injured his eyes while staring at the sun through colored lenses; this, combined with severe depression and strain from overwork, forced him into retirement in 1839.

Fechner recovered, however, to the lasting benefit of psychology. In 1850, he was worrying about the fundamental problem of whether there were laws that governed the translation of physical energy into its psychological or mental representation. He began searching for laws that would relate the intensity of physical stimuli to the subjective impression of these stimuli. While grappling with this problem, he came upon Weber's work and greatly celebrated the principle Weber discovered, naming it Weber's law. Fechner elaborated on it somewhat; as we discuss in chapter 6, this extension is called *Fechner's law.* To Fechner, this was the fulfillment of his hope that exact quantitative relationships exist between the physical and mental worlds. Thus we say that Fechner founded the important discipline of *psychophysics*, which we consider in chapter 6.

Wilhelm Wundt

Perhaps the first person to consider himself primarily a psychologist, although late in his career, was Wilhelm Wundt (1832–1920). Trained in physiology and medicine (by Helmholtz, among others), he gradually became interested in psychology. In 1874 his *Principles of Physiological Psychology* was published; the eminent historian Boring called it the most important book in the history of experimental psychology. In it he systematically reviewed everything known about psychology at the time and also presented his system of psychology, which later came to be called the *structural school* of psychology (discussed below). The book went through six editions and helped lay the groundwork for a systematic psychology. Wundt's contributions were primarily in organizing psychology and helping to establish it as an independent discipline, more than in making important scientific discoveries. Wundt trained many people who were later to make important contributions in their own right. He also is given credit for establishing the first laboratory of experimental psychology in 1879 at Leipzig and for establishing the first psychology journal.

Although Wundt was instrumental in establishing experimental psychology as a separate discipline, he did not believe that the higher mental processes such as memory, thought, and creativity could ever be studied experimentally. Experimental method, he claimed, could only be applied to the study of sensation and perception. He thought that the higher mental processes should be studied through the examination of the works of civilization over the centuries in various cultures, or through cultural history or cultural anthropology. Wundt contributed ten volumes of research to this latter pursuit.

Hermann Ebbinghaus

In the same year (1879) that Wundt was establishing his laboratory, work was being done to discredit his belief about the extreme limits of experimental method in psychology. In this year, Hermann Ebbinghaus (1850–1909) initiated his pioneering experiments on human learning and memory, which culminated in his important book, *On Memory*, in 1885. This text showed that interesting experimental work could be done on more complex psychological topics, such as memory. His investigations spawned the critical area of inquiry concerning human learning and memory, and are considered more fully in chapter 10.

Schools of Psychology

It is customary to divide psychology into a number of schools when considering the years 1890 to 1940 or so, though this does some damage to certain trends in psychology that resist being neatly fit into these pigeonholes. Nonetheless, we shall briefly describe here some of the main features of the schools of *structuralism, functionalism, behaviorism,* and *Gestalt psychology*.

Structuralism: The Structure of Mental Life

Wundt was the originator of the structural school of psychology, although the school is also closely associated with the name of Edward Bradford Titchener (1867–1927). Titchener was one of Wundt's students who brought this view to the United States and advanced it from his lab at Cornell University. Though these men differed on some particulars, we can treat their views together.

As its name implies, structural psychology was primarily concerned with uncovering the structure of the mind. According to the structuralists, the three primary questions for psychology were these: (1) What are the elements of experience? (2) How are they combined? and (3) Why? What is the cause? The basic elements of experience were considered to be *sensations:* sights, sounds, tastes, smells, and so forth. The other two elements of experience were *images* or *ideas,* which represented experiences not actually present; and *affections,* which were emotional reactions such as hatred, joy, and love. Each element of experience could also be evaluated as to its attributes of duration, intensity, quality, and clearness.

The work of structural psychology was to break down complex mental experiences into their components, in the belief that by understanding the fundamental elements of conscious experience, one could understand how they combine into complex mental phenomena. Thus it was elementaristic, since it sought the basic elements of mental experience. Elementary sensations and images were thought to be compounded through principles of association to become complex mental events. The method of decomposing these mental events was *introspection.* For structural psychologists, introspection did not refer to casual reflection, or even to critical reflection, but rather to a specific, technical method of viewing experience. To naïve observers (that is, all of us), consciousness seems to be all of one piece, or a stream, as William James described it. Trained introspectionists were weaned from this view. They were to report the conscious contents of an experience, instead of the focal object under consideration. A trained introspectionist would not report seeing a table in the environment, but rather would report seeing a particular spatial pattern, color, brightness, and so on. In other words, introspectionists were trained to see the elements of the experience of seeing a table. If one naïvely reported seeing a table, this was considered to be a case of committing the *stimulus error.*

Introspection was a rigorous and difficult method which people outside the structural camp felt to be sterile. It was also unreliable; introspectionists in different laboratories were not able to agree on the contents of the same experience. Titchener believed that the structural program set the pattern for the way psychology should develop, and what remained was simply to fill in the details. He railed against the newer trends in psychology, trends that eventually pushed the structural school from the scene after 1920. Nonetheless, Wundt and Titchener trained many psychologists who were later to become prominent, and structuralism served an important function, since the other schools were, in part, a reaction against it.

Functionalism: The Uses of Mind

Just as the structuralists were concerned with the structure of mental life, the functionalists were concerned with the functions of mental processes and structures. During the late 1800s, Darwin's theory of evolution swept through intellectual circles in both England and the United States. Thus, it was quite natural that people began asking about the adaptive significance of psychological processes. What is the function of psychological processes? What differences do they make?

John Dewey (1859–1952) initiated functionalism at the University of Chicago after his arrival in 1894. Arriving at about the same time were George Herbert Mead, James Rowland Angell, and A. W. Moore. Dewey was greatly influenced by Darwin's concept of natural selection. In 1896, he published a paper called "The Reflex Arc Concept in Psychology," in which he criticized the trend toward elementarism in psychology, which is the breaking down of psychological processes into their supposed elementary parts. Interestingly, he did not attack Titchener in the paper, but was more concerned with other issues. He argued that psychological processes were continuous, ongoing events and that psychologists should be careful to remember that distinctions they introduced to study the process were to some extent artificial and not part of the act itself. Dewey emphasized studying behavior in its natural context to determine its functions.

The functionalist school was more vague and amorphous than Titchener's tight little band of structuralists. The functionalists had little use for introspection, thought it was impossible to study mental processes devoid of their context and function, and they were much more prone to endorse practical or applied programs in psychology. Yet the functionalists had no specific program for psychology, as did Titchener, and the closest they ever came to providing a manifesto was Angell's presidential address to the American Psychological Association (1907). Besides emphasizing applied activities such as mental tests and education (the field to which Dewey migrated), functionalism helped introduce the study of lower organisms into psychology. This naturally followed from its emphasis on evolution and the developmental function of psychological processes.

Functionalism spread from Chicago in numerous directions, especially to Columbia University. Its position, never too systematic or dogmatic, was simply absorbed by psychology at large. And while functionalism was enjoying its heyday at the University of Chicago, a young psychologist named John Watson received his degree there in 1903.

Behaviorism: Rejecting Mental Explanations

In 1913, John Watson published a paper called "Psychology as the Behaviorist Views It." Thus began the behaviorist revolution in psychology. Watson's ideas about what was later to be called behaviorism had begun to take shape during his days at the University of Chicago, but were not fully developed until some years later, when he was teaching at Johns Hopkins University. In his 1913 paper, Watson sharply attacked structural psychology and introspectionism, with its emphasis on consciousness and mental contents. Watson argued that we should sweep away all this nonsense, which could not even be reproduced from one lab to another, and study something that all reasonable people could agree on: behavior. He endorsed a statement by Pillsbury that "psychology is the science of behavior" and continued:

> I believe we can write a psychology, define it as Pillsbury, and never go back upon our definition: never use the terms consciousness, mental states, mind, content, introspectively verifiable, imagery, and the like. It can be done in terms of stimulus and response, in terms of habit formation, habit integration, and the like. Furthermore, I believe it is really worth while to make this attempt now (1913, pp. 166–167).

Watson's clear, concise statement of the position of behaviorism was quite influential. For many psychologists, it justified throwing out a lot of the murky nonsense that had occupied the field for so long. Watson's flair for straightforward, interesting writing was evident also in his other works, among which is his notable book *Psychology from the Standpoint of a Behaviorist* (1919).

The behaviorists were intent on establishing psychology as a natural science, a status they felt it lacked in 1913. Its subject matter was to be behavior. There was no need to become engaged in complicated arguments about terms such as consciousness, imageless thought, and apperception, whose meanings were unclear. Watson and the other behaviorists attacked both structuralism and functionalism on the grounds of vagueness. The behaviorists did not say that consciousness, imagery, etc. did not exist; they just maintained that such terms were not useful scientific constructs.

Behaviorists considered that most important behaviors were learned, so the study of learning became the central focus of interest. The pioneering studies of Pavlov and Thorndike, reviewed in chapters 9 and 11, indicated the possibility of an objective psychology of learning, and the focus of behavioral psychology has been on learning ever since.

The issues of behaviorism brought on a revolution within psychology, a revolution that is still with us. Much of the behaviorist point of view has by now been absorbed into the mainstream of psychology, though there are still debates over many particulars. There is, indeed, no one position that today can be called behaviorism, except the general one that endorses the study of behavior as the appropriate subject matter of psychology. (Presumably, all experimental psychologists subscribe to this view today, since all are observing behavior.) Rather, there are a number of different behaviorist positions identified with a number of different people. Some of Watson's most prominent successors in the behaviorist line are E. B. Holt, Karl Lashley, E. C. Tolman, E. R. Guthrie, Clark Hull, Kenneth Spence, and B. F. Skinner. These psychologists all have considered themselves behaviorists, though they have differed widely on a number of issues regarding how psychology should be approached. For example, Lashley and Hull were quite concerned with the physiological bases of behavior, whereas Skinner has shunned such inquiries. Critics these days who argue against behaviorism usually are arguing against the position of B. F. Skinner, who has attracted much attention for the extremity of some of his views as a radical behaviorist. But, of course, Skinner's position is not to be identified as the only form of behaviorism in psychology, since there are numerous other behaviorist positions.

It is popular to say these days that behaviorism is on the decline. Mental constructs (such as attention) have been reintroduced in psychology, even in the study of animal behavior. But these mental constructs are closely tied to observable responses. (We discuss in chapters 7 and 14 how to find evidence for unobservable psychological constructs.) Behaviorism has had a wide impact on all areas of experimental psychology and thrives today in many forms.

Gestalt Psychology: Perception of the Whole

Functionalism and behaviorism developed in the United States partly as a reaction to structuralism. Another revolt against structuralism developed on its home ground, in Germany. The structural view of perception can be characterized as a brick-and-mortar view: sensations (the bricks) are held together by associations (the mortar). Gestalt psychologists argued against this elementaristic position and claimed that perception of objects was of wholes, not complicated sums of parts. In the terms of Gestalt psychology, people perceive the world in unitary wholes.

Max Wertheimer (1880–1943) and the other Gestalt psychologists produced many demonstrations of the unity of the perceptual process that seemed incompatible with the structuralist position. One of these was the phenomenon of *shape constancy*. If you stand in front of a table with a book on it, a rectangular image may be produced on your retina, but if you move sideways several feet in one direction or the other, the retinal image may become trapezoidal. Despite this change in the retinal sensations, you perceive the book as being the same and having the same shape in both cases. The shape remains constant in your perception. There are similar constancies of size and brightness, as well as numerous other perceptual phenomena, demonstrating the same point. Perception appears to have qualities of wholeness independent of the changing sensations projected on the receptors.

Gestalt psychology began, as did behaviorism, as a successful protest against structural psychology, but soon found itself competing with behaviorism. The Gestaltists found the same unsatisfactory elementarism in the behaviorists' descriptions of behavior as they had in the structuralists', but now the elements were stimuli and responses. The behaviorists in turn found the Gestaltists' constructs every bit as fuzzy and ill-defined as they had the structuralists' and functionalists'. In addition, the Gestaltists were often content to make some point or other through simple demonstrations, without devising clear theories and testing them experimentally. To some extent, Gestaltists and behaviorists were investigating different areas, with the Gestaltists concerned primarily with perception and the behaviorists with learning. But the later Gestalt psychologists, the most notable of whom were Kurt Koffka and Wolfgang Köhler, began applying Gestalt constructs to other areas of psychology, such as the study of learning, memory, and problem solving. Thus behaviorists and Gestaltists often have come into conflict, with the experimental battles usually ending in draws. It may well be that Gestalt theorists were describing behavior at a more general level than behaviorists and that their seemingly disparate accounts of the same psychological phenomena might not be as incompatible as they seemed at the time.

Gestalt psychology has not been as integrated into the mainstream of psychology as have functionalism and behaviorism, but its influence in certain areas of psychology has been overwhelming. This is certainly true of modern cognitive psychology, especially in the areas of perception, problem solving, and thought.

Some Modern Trends

The era of schools of psychology declined around 1940 or so, and this way of strictly dividing the field of psychology is no longer profitable. The influence of the schools lives on in contemporary research, but the organization of the field lies along different lines. Very little has been written about the history of psychology since 1940, as there are few unifying themes yet apparent. We will sketch here some modern trends, however.

World War II and the Extension of Psychology

During World War II, psychologists were employed in such diverse occupations as studying public opinion and propaganda, aiding race relations in the armed services, training animals to aid in combat situations, designing cockpits of complicated aircraft, constructing tests for personnel selection, and dealing with clinical problems of battle fatigue, depression, and so forth. Psychologists were forced from their scholastic retreats and encouraged to apply their knowledge to the numerous problems at hand. In many cases, this contact with real-world problems allowed them to see the inadequacy of their concepts and provided them the opportunity to develop new and better ideas. Thus, the war had a healthy influence on many areas of psychology. It was during this period that human factors, then called human engineering, came into its own as a discipline.

Another trend occurring at about the same time was the extension of experimental method to problem areas to which it had not previously been applied. Experimental social psychology and experimental child psychology received considerable attention during the 1930s and 1940s.

Cognitive Psychology: The Return of Mind

Behaviorism dominated American psychology through the 1930s and 1940s, and because the study of unobservable events was eschewed, the study of mental processes was virtually abandoned during this time. However, several developments in the 1950s reinstated the scientific study of higher mental processes as a legitimate and feasible (albeit difficult) endeavor.

First, psychologists showed that many mental operations are difficult to explain in terms of conditioned associations between environmental stimuli and responses. Humans are actively involved in controlling mental activity, and the variety and complexity of many interesting human behaviors (e.g., language, problem solving, creativity) cannot be entirely and satisfactorily explained by simple behavioristic mechanisms. Richer theories of mental mechanisms provide more powerful means of explaining the complexities of mental life. The current challenge is to study these unobservable mental events with objective, scientific methods that tie mental constructs to observable responses. Many clever inferential techniques have been developed to do so (see chapters 7 and 14).

Cognitive psychology also has benefited from modern technology. The principles of *information theory*, which were borrowed from engineering in the late 1940s, allowed the quantification of concepts previously measured poorly, if at all (e.g., the amount of "information" in a stimulus). Although the approach did not solve many of the traditional problems in psychology, it was influential in the development of information-processing models, which represent human cognitive processes in terms of information flow through the system. These models have stimulated much research.

Another major influence from outside psychology has been computer science. Because computers are capable of performing complex computational tasks, many scientists have suggested that the computer may provide a model for the way the human mind encodes, stores, processes, and retrieves information. The field of artificial intelligence is aimed at exploring the relation between human and machine intelligence, and computer science has inspired many precise and testable cognitive models.

Specialization

Perhaps the most notable recent trend in psychology is specialization. The schools of psychology tended to be all-encompassing; they had something to say about every phase of what they considered psychology. For example, behaviorists did not just concern themselves with learning, though this was their primary interest; they also applied their concepts to the areas of thought, language, and child development. Now psychologists no longer identify themselves by schools, but by areas of interest. Most psychology departments are organized along these lines, as are chapters 6 through 15 of this book.

Psychologists may be social psychologists, or animal-learning psychologists, or developmental psychologists, or cognitive psychologists (sensation, perception, memory, language, thinking, information processing, etc.), or personality psychologists, and so forth. Or psychologists may specialize in psychobiology, clinical psychology, or organizational or industrial psychology. And all these areas have subareas, such as those just listed for cognitive psychology. Workers within these fields are often quite likely to know little about the other areas. This trend toward specialization is often decried as unfortunate, but there seems little alternative. Such specialization is simply the mark of a maturing science, for there seems little possibility for a psychologist to be knowledgeable in all the areas of psychology today.

Experimental psychology is only one of the forty-five divisions of the American Psychological Association. However, many psychologists belonging to most of the other areas employ experimental method in their work. (On the other hand, members of some fields may oppose the use of experimental method in psychology.) The listing in table A–1 gives you some idea of the great diversity and specialization found among present-day psychologists.

In addition to the American Psychological Association, there are two other societies of great importance to experimental psychologists. The Psychonomic Society was founded in 1958. Full membership is restricted to scientists who have already made scholarly contributions by publishing articles in scientific journals. The Psychonomic Society publishes several influential journals of experimental psychology and sponsors an important annual meeting where scientists can exchange information. The American Psychological Society, founded in 1988, is the newest society. Its goals are to advance the discipline of psychology, to preserve the scientific base of psychology, to promote public understanding of psychological science and its applications, to enhance the quality of graduate education, and to encourage the "giving away" of psychology in the public interest.

TABLE A–1. The Divisions of the American Psychological Association

APA Division Number	APA Division Name
1.	Division of General Psychology
2.	Division on the Teaching of Psychology
3.	Division of Experimental Psychology
5.	Division on Evaluation and Measurement
6.	Division on Physiological and Comparative Psychology
7.	Division on Developmental Psychology
8.	The Society of Personality and Social Psychology—A Division of the APA
9.	The Society for the Psychological Study of Social Issues— A Division of the APA
10.	Division of Psychology and the Arts
12.	Division of Clinical Psychology
13.	Division of Consulting Psychology
14.	The Society for Industrial and Organizational Psychology, Inc.—A Division of the APA
15.	Division of Educational Psychology
16.	Division of School Psychology
17.	Division of Counseling Psychology
18.	Division of Psychologists in Public Service
19.	Division of Military Psychology
20.	Division of Adult Development and Aging
21.	The Society of Engineering Psychologists—A Division of the APA
22.	Division of Rehabilitation Psychology
23.	Division of Consumer Psychology
24.	Division of Theoretical and Philosophical Psychology
25.	Division for the Experimental Analysis of Behavior
26.	Division of the History of Psychology
27.	Division of Community Psychology
28.	Division of Psychopharmacology
29.	Division of Psychotherapy
30.	Division of Psychological Hypnosis
31.	Division of State Psychological Association Affairs
32.	Division of Humanistic Psychology
33.	Division on Mental Retardation
34.	Division of Population and Environmental Psychology
35.	Division of Psychology of Women
36.	Psychologists Interested in Religious Issues (PIRI)—A Division of the APA
37.	Division of Child, Youth, and Family Services
38.	Division on Health Psychology
39.	Division on Psychoanalysis
40.	Division of Clinical Neuropsychology
41.	Division of Psychology and Law

TABLE A–1 *(Continued)*.	**The Divisions of the American Psychological Association**

APA Division Number	APA Division Name
42.	Division of Psychologists in Independent Practice
43.	Division of Family Psychology
44.	The Society for the Psychological Study of Lesbian and Gay Issues
45.	Society for the Study of Ethnic Minority Issues
46.	Division of Media Psychology
47.	Division of Exercise and Sport Psychology

Note: There are no division numbers 4 or 11.

SUMMARY

1. Scientific psychology dates from a century ago, give or take a decade. The roots of psychology are in the questions asked by philosophers for thousands of years. The original techniques for studying psychology experimentally were devised by physicists and physiologists who became interested in psychological topics, particularly those concerned with reception of stimuli by the senses.

2. Four early pioneers of psychology were Helmholtz, Weber, Fechner, and Ebbinghaus. In an early reaction-time experiment, Helmholtz measured the speed of the nervous impulse, thus showing how experimental techniques could provide information about psychological topics.

3. Weber examined how much a stimulus had to change in order for an observer to notice the difference. He discovered that the amount of change needed for a just-noticeable difference was a constant proportion of the magnitude of the standard stimulus, a fact that became known as Weber's law. Fechner continued Weber's work and coined the term psychophysics for the field, which was concerned with how changes in the physical world are related to a person's perception of the changes.

4. Ebbinghaus performed the first systematic experiments on memory. His research methods and findings had tremendous impact on the field, because they showed that even higher mental processes could be studied experimentally.

5. A number of different schools of psychology came into being between 1890 and 1940. Four primary ones were structuralism, functionalism, behaviorism, and Gestalt. A summary of their primary characteristics is presented in table A–2. The influence of the schools lives on today, but contemporary psychology is divided along lines of various subject matters of interest to researchers. As psychology has matured, the focus of most psychologists has become increasingly specialized.

TABLE A–2.   Summary of Four Primary Schools of Psychology

School	Subject Matter	Research Goals	Research Methods
Structuralism	Conscious experience	To break down conscious experience into its basic components: sensations, images, affections	Analytic introspection
Functionalism	The function of mental processes and how they help people adapt	To study mental processes in their natural contexts; to discover what effects they have	Objective measures; informal observation and introspection
Behaviorism	Behavior: how it is changed under different conditions, with emphasis on learning	Description, explanation, prediction, and control of behavior	Objective measures of behavior; formal experiments
Gestalt Psychology	Subjective experience, with emphasis on perception, memory, and thinking	To understand the phenomena of conscious experience in terms of the whole experience (not to break down experience into arbitrary categories)	Subjective reports; some behavioral measures; demonstrations

KEY TERMS

affections
behaviorism
cognitive psychology
dualism
Fechner's law
functionalism
Gestalt psychology
ideas
images
information theory

introspection
just-noticeable difference (jnd)
psychophysics
radical behaviorism
reaction-time experiment
sensations
shape constancy
stimulus error
structuralism
Weber's law

APPENDIX  B

Statistical Reasoning: An Introduction

Statistical thinking will one day be as necessary for efficient citizenship as the ability to read and write.

—H. G. WELLS

MANY PSYCHOLOGY STUDENTS ARE FRIGHTENED by statistics. It seems to them a hopeless jumble of complicated jargon having little to do with the interesting aspects of psychology. The purpose of this appendix is to give you some idea as to why an understanding of statistics is actually crucial to the conduct and interpretation of psychological research. We will also give some attention to how statistical reasoning is used in psychological research, even though we can hardly hope to turn you into an expert statistician from reading this one section. This appendix will serve as a review for those of you who have already taken statistics. Students new to statistics may need to read the chapter several times very carefully, since there will be quite a bit of new information. You should probably be aware by now that if you were to complete graduate work for the Ph.D. in psychology, you would probably be required to take a minimum of three courses in statistics.

Many aspects of the world we live in can be treated in terms of probabilities. We do not always know with complete certainty that events will occur given prior conditions, but only that they will happen some proportion of the time, or with a certain probability. A common example is that of weather forecasting. Meteorologists say there is an 80 percent chance of rain or a 20 percent chance of snow, given certain prior conditions. Even when the prior conditions are known, it is impossible to predict perfectly the future weather. Much of human behavior is probabilistic in the same sense. Statistics are useful in helping psychologists estimate the probability of whether differences in groups of observations between two conditions have been produced by random, or chance, factors. The branch of statistics used for this purpose is *inferential statistics*. The other primary type of statistics, which helps psychologists summarize or describe observations, is *descriptive statistics*. We shall first examine descriptive statistics, and then turn to inferential statistics.

Descriptive Statistics: Telling It Like It Is

Psychologists typically conduct experiments in their quest for an understanding of behavior. Usually there are at least two conditions, an experimental and a control, which differ in the presence or absence of an independent variable. Measures are taken of the dependent variable in each condition. Numbers are produced. What are we to do with them? First, we need to systematize and organize them. We do not have to look at the whole array of numbers produced by subjects in the different conditions of the experiment; instead, we can look at a briefer version. By summarizing the data, we may see general trends that are otherwise hidden by the large array of numbers. Descriptive statistics provide this systematizing and summarizing function. The two main types are measures of *central tendency* (the typical score) and measures of *dispersion* (the spread of the data).

Let us take a hypothetical experimental situation. A drug company has sponsored a test of the effects of LSD on behavior of rats, so we decide for starters to see how the drug affects the rats' running speed. Forty food-deprived rats have been trained to run a straight-alley maze for a food reward. We randomly assign them to two groups. To one group, we administer LSD by injection and observe the effect on the speed with which they run the alley for food thirty minutes after the injection. The other group is tested in a similar manner thirty minutes after receiving an injection of a placebo (an inert substance). The following are the running times for the twenty control subjects in seconds: 13, 11, 14, 18, 12, 14, 10, 13, 13, 16, 15, 9, 12, 20, 11, 13, 12, 17, 15, and 14. The running times for the subjects receiving the LSD injections are 17, 15, 16, 20, 14, 19, 14, 13, 18, 18, 26, 17, 19, 13, 16, 22, 18, 16, 18, and 9. Now that we have the running times, what do we do with them? One thing we might want is some sort of graphical representation of the numbers, as in the two *histograms* in figure B–1. Here, the running speeds in seconds appear along the abscissa (*X*-axis) and the frequency with which each speed occurred in the two conditions is displayed along the ordinate (*Y*-axis). Running times for the control subjects are in the top histogram; those for the experimental subjects are represented in the bottom one. Another way to represent the same information is by using a *frequency polygon*. Its construction is equivalent to that of the histogram; you can visualize this type of graph by connecting the midpoints of the bars in the histogram. Examples of frequency polygons appear later in

FIGURE B–1.

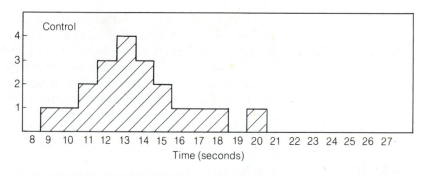

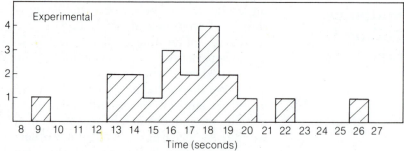

Histograms representing scores for twenty subjects in the control and experimental conditions of the hypothetical LSD experiment.

the appendix (in figure B–2). In both conditions in figure B–1, the greatest number of scores occurs in the middle; they tend to tail off toward the ends. This is more obvious for the control than for the experimental subjects. Also, the times for the experimental group tend to be greater than those for the control group. Both the histogram and the frequency polygon are types of *frequency distributions*. They help systematize the data somewhat, but there are more efficient summary descriptions.

Central Tendency

The most common summary description of data is some measure of central tendency which, as the term implies, indicates the center of the distribution of scores. By far the most typical measure of central tendency in psychological research is the *arithmetic mean*. The mean $(\bar{X})$ is simply the sum of all the scores (ΣX) divided by the number of scores (n), or $\bar{X} = \Sigma X/n$. It is what most people think of as the average of a set of numbers, although the term *average* technically applies to any measure of central tendency. The sums of the running times for the experimental and control conditions of our hypothetical experiment were 338 and 272 seconds, respectively. Since there were 20 observations in each condition, the means are 16.9 seconds for the experimental condition and 13.6 for the control.

The mean is the most useful measure of central tendency, and almost all inferential statistics, which we come to later, are based on it. Therefore this statistic is used whenever possible. However, another measure of central tendency is sometimes used: the *median*. It is the score above which half of the distribution lies and below which the other half lies. The median, then, is the midpoint of the distribution. When there is an odd number of scores in the distribution, such as 27, the median is the 14th score from the bottom or top, since that score divides the distribution into two groups of 13 scores. When the number of scores *(n)* is an even number, the median is the arithmetic mean of the two middle scores, if the scores are not tied. So the median of the scores 66, 70, 72, 76, 80, and 96 is (72 + 76)/2, or 74. When, as often happens, the two middle scores are tied, as in the distribution of scores from the hypothetical LSD experiment, the convention is to designate the median as the appropriate proportion of the distance between the *limits* of the particular score, where the limits are a half score above and below the tied score. This will be clearer with an example. Consider the distributions of scores from our experiment. If you arrange the 20 control running times from lowest to highest, you will discover that the 8th, 9th, 10th, and 11th scores are all 13. Under such conditions, the 10th score is considered the median. It is considered to lie three-quarters of the distance between the limits of 12.5 and 13.5. So the median would be 12.5 + .75, or 13.25, for the control subjects. By the same reasoning (and you should try it yourself), we find that the median for the experimental subjects is 17.

Why is the median used? The primary reason is that it has the (desirable) property of being insensitive to extreme scores. In the distribution of scores of 66, 70, 72, 76, 80, and 96, the median of the distribution would remain exactly the same if the lowest score were 1 rather than 66, or the highest score were 1,223 rather than 96. The mean, on the other hand, would differ widely with these other scores. Often this benefit can be extremely useful in summarizing data from the real world. In our LSD experiment, suppose that one of the rats given LSD had stopped halfway down the alley to examine a particularly interesting feature of the runway before continuing on its way to the goal box, and thus its time to complete the runway was 45 minutes, or 2,700 seconds. If this score replaced the 26-second score in the original distribution, the mean would go from 16.9 seconds to 150.6, or from 3.30 seconds greater than the control mean to 137.0 seconds greater. This would be only because of one very deviant score; in such cases, researchers frequently use the median score rather than the mean to represent the central tendency. Using the mean seems to given an unrepresentative estimate of central tendency because of the great influence of the one score. However, using the median often limits severely any statistical tests that can be applied to the data.

Measures of Dispersion

Measures of central tendency indicate the center of the scores, whereas measures of dispersion indicate how the scores are spread out about the center. The simplest measure of dispersion is the *range*, which is the difference between the highest and lowest score in the distribution. For the control rats in the LSD experiment, the range is 11 (20 − 9), and for the experimental rats it is 17 (26 − 9). Since the range indicates only the extreme scores, it is rarely used.

In deciding on a measure of dispersion, we want to provide a number that reflects the amount of spread that the scores exhibit around some central-tendency measure, usually the mean. One such measure that would be appropriate is the mean deviation. This is calculated by taking the difference between the mean and every score in a distribution, summing these differences, and then dividing by the number of scores. However, it is actually necessary to take the mean absolute difference (that is, to ignore the sign of the difference: whether the score is greater or less than the mean). The reason is that the sum of the deviations of scores about the mean is always zero, a defining characteristic of the mean (see table B–1). Thus, the mean deviation must be the *absolute mean deviation*. The mean deviations for our hypothetical experimental conditions in the LSD experiment are calculated in table B–1. The symbol | | indicates the absolute value of a number: $|-6| = 6$.

The absolute mean deviation of a set of scores is an adequate measure of dispersion and is based on the same logic involved in finding the mean of a distribution. However, the standard deviation and variance (defined on the following page) are preferred to the mean deviation, because they have mathematical properties that make them much more useful in more advanced statistical computations. The logic behind their calculation is quite similar to that of the mean deviation, which is why we have considered the mean deviation here. In calculating the mean deviation, we had to take the absolute value of the difference of each score from the mean, so that these differences would not add up to zero. Instead of taking the absolute difference, we could have gotten rid of the troublesome negative numbers by squaring the differences. This is exactly what is done in calculating the variance and standard deviation of a distribution.

The *variance* of a distribution is defined as *the sum of the squared deviations from the mean, divided by the number of scores*. In other words, each score is taken, subtracted from the mean, and squared; then, all these values are summed and divided by the number of scores. The formula for the variance is:

$$s^2 = \frac{\Sigma(X - \overline{X})^2}{n},$$

(B–1)

where s^2 represents the variance, X the individual scores, $\overline{X}$ the mean, and n the number of scores or observations. The *standard deviation* is simply *the square root of the variance*, and is therefore represented by s.

$$s = \sqrt{\frac{\Sigma(X - \overline{X})^2}{n}}$$

(B–2)

TABLE B–1. Calculation of the mean deviations and absolute mean deviations from two sets of scores. The sum of the deviations (differences) in calculating the mean deviation is zero, which is why it is necessary to use the absolute mean deviation.

Control group			Experimental group		
X	$(X - \bar{X})$	$|X - \bar{X}|$	X	$(X - \bar{X})$	$|X - \bar{X}|$
9	−4.60	4.60	9	−7.90	7.90
10	−3.60	3.60	13	−3.90	3.90
11	−2.60	2.60	13	−3.90	3.90
11	−2.60	2.60	14	−2.90	2.90
12	−1.60	1.60	14	−2.90	2.90
12	−1.60	1.60	15	−1.90	1.90
12	−1.60	1.60	16	− .90	.90
13	− .60	.60	16	− .90	.90
13	− .60	.60	16	− .90	.90
13	− .60	.60	17	+ .10	.10
13	− .60	.60	17	+ .10	.10
14	+ .40	.40	18	+1.10	.10
14	+ .40	.40	18	+1.10	1.10
14	+ .40	.40	18	+1.10	1.10
15	+1.40	1.40	18	+1.10	1.10
15	+1.40	1.40	19	+2.10	2.10
16	+2.40	2.40	19	+2.10	2.10
17	+3.40	3.40	20	+3.10	3.10
18	+4.40	4.40	22	+5.10	5.10
20	+6.40	6.40	26	+9.10	9.10

$\Sigma X = 272$ Total = 0.00 Total = 41.20 $\Sigma X = 338$ Total = 0.00 Total = 52.20
$\bar{X} = 13.60$ $\bar{X} = 16.90$

Absolute mean deviation $= \dfrac{41.20}{20} = 2.06$ Absolute mean deviation $= \dfrac{52.20}{20} = 2.61$

Calculation of the standard deviations for the control and experimental conditions from the LSD experiment by the mean-deviation method is illustrated in table B–2.

The formulas for the variance and standard deviation of a distribution given in equations B–1 and B–2 are rather cumbersome; in practice, the equivalent computational formulas are used. The standard-deviation computational formula is

$$s = \sqrt{\frac{\Sigma X^2}{n} - \bar{X}^2}, \qquad \text{(B–3)}$$

where ΣX^2 is the sum of the squares of all the scores, $\bar{X}$ is the mean of the distribution, and n is the number of scores. Similarly, the computational formula for variance is

$$s^2 = \frac{\Sigma X^2}{n} - \bar{X}^2. \qquad \text{(B–4)}$$

The standard deviations for the experimental and control scores are calculated with the computational formula in table B–3. The value in each case is the same as that obtained when the definitional formula is used.

TABLE B–2.   Calculation of the standard deviation, s, for the control and experimental conditions by the mean-deviation method.

Control group			Experimental group		
X	$(X-\bar{X})$	$(X-\bar{X})^2$	X	$(X-\bar{X})$	$(X-\bar{X})^2$
9	-4.60	21.16	9	-7.90	62.41
10	-3.60	12.96	13	-3.90	15.21
11	-2.60	6.76	13	-3.90	15.21
11	-2.60	6.76	14	-2.90	8.41
12	-1.60	2.56	14	-2.90	8.41
12	-1.60	2.56	15	-1.90	3.61
12	-1.60	2.56	16	$-$ .90	.81
13	$-$ .60	.36	16	$-$ .90	.81
13	$-$ .60	.36	16	$-$ .90	.81
13	$-$ .60	.36	17	$+$ .10	.01
13	$-$ .60	.36	17	$+$ .10	.01
14	$+$ .40	.16	18	$+1.10$	1.21
14	$+$ .40	.16	18	$+1.10$	1.21
14	$+$ .40	.16	18	$+1.10$	1.21
15	$+1.40$	1.96	18	$+1.10$	1.21
15	$+1.40$	1.96	19	$+2.10$	4.41
16	$+2.40$	5.76	19	$+2.10$	4.41
17	$+3.40$	11.56	20	$+3.10$	9.61
18	$+4.40$	19.36	22	$+5.10$	26.01
20	$+6.40$	40.96	26	$+9.10$	82.81

$\Sigma X=272$ Total$=0.00$ $\Sigma(X-\bar{X})^2=138.80$ $\Sigma X=338$ Total$=0.00$ $\Sigma(X-\bar{X})^2=247.80$

$\bar{X}=13.60$ $\bar{X}=16.90$

$$s = \sqrt{\frac{\Sigma(X-\bar{X})^2}{n}}$$ $$s = \sqrt{\frac{\Sigma(X-\bar{X})^2}{n}}$$

$$s = \sqrt{\frac{138.80}{20}}$$ $$s = \sqrt{\frac{247.80}{20}}$$

$s = 2.63$ $s = 3.52$

In describing an array of data, psychologists typically present two descriptive statistics, the mean and the standard deviation. Although there are other measures of central tendency and dispersion, these are most useful for descriptive purposes. Variance is used extensively, as we shall see, in inferential statistics.

A Note on Calculation

Throughout this appendix, we will illustrate statistical procedures with detailed calculations, as is done in table B–3. We do this in the hopes that the logic behind the calculations will become clear. However, it is entirely possible that you will never have to work through a statistical procedure step by step. Many calculators and computers will directly calculate statistics for you. Often, all that you need to do is to enter the data into the calculator or computer; with a few additional commands, the results will be determined.

TABLE B–3. Calculation of the standard deviation, s, for the control and experimental conditions by using the computational formula (also called the raw-score method). The same values are obtained as when the definitional formula is used (see table B–2), but the calculations are much easier to perform.

X	X^2	X	X^2
9	81	9	81
10	100	13	169
11	121	13	169
11	121	14	196
12	144	14	196
12	144	15	225
12	144	16	256
13	169	16	256
13	169	16	256
13	169	17	289
13	169	17	289
14	196	18	324
14	196	18	324
14	196	18	324
15	225	18	324
15	225	19	361
16	256	19	361
17	289	20	400
18	324	22	484
20	400	26	676
$\Sigma X = 272$	$\Sigma X^2 = 3838$	$\Sigma X = 338$	$\Sigma X^2 = 5960$

$$\overline{X} = 13.60 \qquad\qquad \overline{X} = 16.90$$

$$\overline{X}^2 = 184.96 \qquad\qquad \overline{X}^2 = 285.61$$

$$s = \sqrt{\frac{\Sigma X^2}{n} - \overline{X}^2} \qquad\qquad s = \sqrt{\frac{\Sigma X^2}{n} - \overline{X}^2}$$

$$s = \sqrt{\frac{3838}{20} - 184.96} \qquad\qquad s = \sqrt{\frac{5960}{20} - 285.61}$$

$$s = 2.63 \qquad\qquad s = 3.52$$

Computers are popular for statistical analyses, because they are fast and do not make mistakes unless you enter the data incorrectly or select the wrong program. Later, when we examine the correlation coefficient, we will illustrate one use of computers in calculating statistics.

The Normal Distribution

The graphs of the scores of the hypothetical LSD experiment in figure B–1 show that the scores pile up in the middle, but tail off toward the extremes (tails) of the distribution of scores. Although these numbers are hypothetical, this sort of distribution has a property that occurs for most measures of behavior: that is, for most phenomena that are measured, scores cluster in the center of the distribution. This configuration is called the *normal curve,* an example of which is presented in figure B–2 (the curve labeled *B*). When put on a graph, psychological data typically are most numerous in the middle of the set of scores; they decline in frequency with distance from the middle in a roughly symmetrical way. A score ten points below the center of the distribution occurs about as frequently as a score ten points above the center.

The three curves shown in figure B–2 are all symmetrical. In such distributions of scores, the mean and median of the distribution both fall at the same point or score. Curves with the same mean and median may differ in their variability, as do the curves in figure B–2. The tall, thin curve labeled *A* would have a smaller standard deviation than the other two. Similarly, the broad, flat curve (*C*) would have a greater standard deviation than the other two.

The normal curve has a very useful property. It turns out that a specific proportion of scores falls under each part of the normal curve. This feature is illustrated in figure B–3. On each side of the normal curve in figure B–3, there is a point at which the curve slightly reverses its direction; it starts bending outward more. This is called the *inflection point.* The inflection point in the curve is always one standard deviation from the mean. In fact, the normal curve has the useful property that specific proportions of the distribution of scores it represents are contained within specific areas of the curve itself. About 68 percent of all scores are contained within one standard deviation of the mean (34 percent on each

FIGURE B–2.

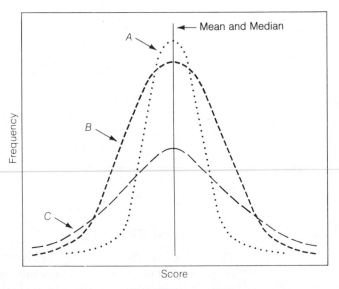

Three examples of the normal curve that differ in variability. *C* has the greatest variability and *A* the least. The normal curve is a symmetrical distribution in which the mean and median have the same value.

side). Similarly, almost 96 percent of the scores are contained within two standard deviations of the mean, and 99.74 percent of the scores are within three standard deviations. The percentage in each area is shown in figure B–3.

This property of normal curves is extremely useful: if we know an individual's score and the mean and the standard deviation in the distribution of scores, we also know the person's relative rank. For example, most I.Q. tests are devised so that the population mean is 100 and the standard deviation is 15. If a person has an I.Q. of 115, we know that he or she has scored higher than 84 percent of all people on the test (50 percent of the people below the mean and 34 percent above). Similarly, a person with an I.Q. of 130 has scored higher than almost 98 percent of all people, and a person with an I.Q. of 145 has scored higher than 99.87 percent of the population.

Many distributions of scores in psychological data are, or at least are assumed to be, normal. (Often, with small samples, as in our hypothetical data in figure B–1, it is difficult to tell whether the distribution is normal.) It is common to compare scores across normal distributions with different means and variances in terms of *standard scores*, or *z scores*. This is simply the difference between an individual score and the mean, expressed in units of standard deviations. So an I.Q. of 115 translates to a *z* score of 1.00, that is, [115 − 100]/15, and an I.Q. of 78 translates to a *z* score of − 1.47, that is, [78 − 100]/15. Standard scores are useful since they allow comparison of the relative ranks of scores for people, across distributions in which the means and standard deviations vary greatly. Grades in courses should be calculated in terms of *z* scores if the means and standard deviations of the scores vary widely from one test to the next. Thus, a person's eventual rank in the class is calculated more faithfully by finding the mean of the *z* scores than by finding the mean of the raw scores of the tests.

When it is said that data in some experiment or other are *normally distributed*, it means that if they are graphed, they will

FIGURE B–3.

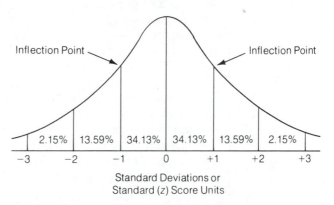

Proportions of scores in specific areas under the normal curve. The inflection points are one standard deviation from the mean.

tend to form a normal distribution. Thus, *normal,* as it is used in psychological research, usually refers to a type of distribution: not to a value judgment as to the goodness or badness of the scores.

Correlation Coefficient

In chapter 2, correlational research is described. The purpose of correlational research is to see how two or more attributes of an organism vary together. The strength and direction of a correlation is determined by the calculation of a correlation coefficient. We will consider just one: *Pearson product-moment correlation coefficient* or *r.* Shown in box B–1 is the calculation formula for *r,* using the hypothetical data relating head size to memory performance discussed in chapter 2. Box B–2 repeats this analysis, using the computerized statistical package called MINITAB.

Regardless of how you calculate *r,* you should read the appropriate sections of chapter 2 that discuss the use and interpretation of a correlation coefficient.

BOX B–1.   **Computing Pearson *r***

Let us call one set of numbers in table B–4 *X* scores and the other set *Y* scores. For example, head sizes might be *X* scores and words recalled *Y* scores. The formula for computing Pearson *r* from the raw scores in panels (a), (b), or (c) of table 2–1 is

$$r = \frac{n\,\Sigma XY - (\Sigma X)(\Sigma Y)}{\sqrt{[n\,\Sigma X^2 - (\Sigma X)^2][n\,\Sigma Y^2 - (\Sigma Y)^2]}} \qquad \textbf{(B–5)}$$

The *n* refers to the number of subjects on which observations are taken (here, 10); the terms ΣX and ΣY are the totals of the *X* and *Y* scores, respectively; ΣX^2 and ΣY^2 are the sum of all the *X* (or *Y*) values after each is squared; and the $(\Sigma X)^2$ and $(\Sigma Y)^2$ are the total of all the *X* or *Y* values with the entire total or sum squared. This leaves the value ΣXY, or the sum of the cross products. This is obtained very simply by multiplying each *X*-value by its corresponding *Y* and then summing these products. You may see other formulas for calculation of Pearson *r* besides the raw-score formula in equation B–5, but these will be equivalent (in general) to the one presented here. An illustration of how Pearson *r* is calculated using this raw-score formula is presented in table B–4 using the data from the (a) column of table 2–1 (chapter 2 page 41). You should try to work out the values for Pearson *r* for the (b) and (c) panels yourself, to make certain you understand how to calculate the values and to gain an intuitive feel for the concept of correlation. The values of *r* are given below the appropriate columns in table 2–1.

TABLE B–4. | Calculation of Pearson r for the data in the first (a) column of table 2–1, by the raw-score formula (equation B–5).

Subject number	X Head size (cm.)	X^2	Y Words recalled	Y^2	$X \cdot Y$
1	50.8	2580.64	17	289	863.60
2	63.5	4032.25	21	441	1330.50
3	45.7	2088.49	16	256	731.20
4	25.4	645.16	11	121	279.40
5	29.2	852.64	9	81	262.80
6	49.5	2450.25	15	225	742.50
7	38.1	1451.61	13	169	495.30
8	30.5	930.25	12	144	366.00
9	35.6	1267.36	14	196	498.40
10	58.4	3410.56	23	529	1343.20
$n =$ 10	$\Sigma X =$ 426.70	$\Sigma X^2 =$ 19,709.21	$\Sigma Y =$ 151	$\Sigma Y^2 =$ 2451	$\Sigma XY =$ 6915.90

$$r = \frac{n\Sigma XY - (\Sigma X)(\Sigma Y)}{\sqrt{[n\Sigma X^2 - (\Sigma X)^2][n\Sigma Y^2 - (\Sigma Y)^2]}}$$

$$r = \frac{10(6915.90) - (426.70)(151)}{\sqrt{[(10)(19,709.21) - (426.70)^2][(10)(2451) - (151)^2]}}$$

$$r = \frac{69,159.00 - 64,431.70}{\sqrt{[197,092.10 - 182,072.89][24,510 - 22,801]}}$$

$$r = \frac{4727.30}{\sqrt{[15,019.21][1709]}} = \frac{4727.30}{\sqrt{25,667,829.89}}$$

$$r = \frac{4727.30}{5066.34}$$

$$r = +.93$$

BOX B–2. Calculation of r by a Computer

One popular statistical package on many large computers is called MINITAB. The MINITAB program will compute r, as well as many other statistics. We have outlined a typical session on a computer in which MINITAB is used to calculate r for the data in box B–1. The entries shaded are what you type into the computer, and the other information is what the computer presents to you. After you have signed on to the computer, you need to gain access to MINITAB, which in this case is done by typing MINITAB. (However, different computer systems may have other ways of accessing MINITAB; check with your computer center before trying to run MINITAB.) Then, you are likely to see some information about the MINITAB program, followed by "MTB." MTB means that you should enter the appropriate

MINITAB command, and it is here that you need to tell MINITAB that you are entering data to be "read" for analysis. So, the appropriate command is: "READ INTO C1, C2." This tells MINITAB that you are entering two columns of data (C1 and C2). Then MINITAB asks for the two columns by printing "DATA," next to which you enter the two scores for a particular subject. You continue to enter pairs of scores until the data for all subjects have been entered (ten pairs in this case), after which you type "END." You then enter the command "CORRELATION BETWEEN C1 AND C2," which tells MINITAB to compute the r between the ten pairs of scores. MINITAB tells you that ten rows of data were read (a handy check that you have entered the correct number of pairs of scores), and then prints out the correlation. The correlation computed by MINITAB is identical to the one in table B–4. Next, MINITAB asks for additional commands. When you enter "STOP," you leave the MINITAB program. You are now ready to sign off the computer. (You could have entered another MINITAB command besides "STOP" if you had additional statistical computations to perform.)

```
MINITAB RELEASE 82.1 *** COPYRIGHT - PENN STATE UNIV. 1982
APRIL 25, 1984 *** CONVERTED AT U. OF WISC. WAISMAN CENTER
STORAGE AVAILABLE  41099

MTB > READ INTO C1, C2
DATA> 50.8 17
DATA> 63.5 21
DATA> 45.7 16
DATA> 25.4 11
DATA> 29.2 9
DATA> 49.5 15
DATA> 38.1 13
DATA> 30.5 12
DATA> 35.6 14
DATA> 58.4 23
DATA> END
   10 ROWS READ
MTB > CORRELATION BETWEEN C1 AND C2

   CORRELATION OF      C1 AND C2     = 0.933

MTB > STOP

*** MINITAB *** STATISTICS DEPT * PENN STATE UNIV. * RELEASE
82.1 * STORAGE AVAILABLE   41099
```

The results of a computer session with MINITAB. MINITAB has calculated the r for the data presented in box B–1. Shaded entries are typed in by the user, and the other information is printed by the computer program.

There are several other statistical packages for computers (for example, SPSS and BMD) that may be available to you; whichever one is available, we recommend you become familiar with it. Computer analysis is faster and more accurate than doing statistical work by hand or step by step on a calculator.

Inferential Statistics

Descriptive statistics are concerned with describing or summarizing data. The results from our hypothetical experiment can be summarized by the statement that the control group's mean running time was 13.6 seconds, with a standard deviation of 2.63, whereas the experimental subjects injected with LSD had a mean of 16.9 seconds and a standard deviation of 3.52. The experimental rats ran more slowly than the controls; the difference between the means was 3.3 seconds. But should we take this difference seriously? Perhaps it is owing merely to chance factors, such as measurement error or a few rats in the control group having a particularly good day, and thus feeling like running a bit faster. How can we judge the likelihood that the difference between the two conditions is "real" or reliable—that it is not a fluke? How large must the difference be for us to conclude that it is unlikely to have occurred merely by chance alone? Inferential statistics are used to answer this question.

In actual practice, the procedure is not too complicated. We choose an appropriate statistical test for the experimental situation, perform a few straightforward computations on a calculator (or computer), and then consult a special table. The table informs us of the probability that the difference we have found between our conditions is a result of random factors. If it is sufficiently unlikely to have occurred by chance, we conclude that the difference is statistically significant, or reliable. But although the actual computational procedures followed are often quite simple, the logic behind them needs to be understood so that you will appreciate how statistical inferences are made.

Sampling

A *population* is a complete set of measurements (or individuals or objects) having some common observable characteristic. Examples of populations are all U.S. citizens of voting age; all albino rats that have had injections of LSD; or all people asked to remember a list of fifty words. These are all populations we might be interested in for one reason or another, but of course it is impossible to study the entire population in any of these cases. If we could measure the entire population of rats for running speed after either an injection of LSD or an injection of a chemically inert substance, then we would better know what the effects of LSD were, since we would have measured the entire population. (Any difference could still, of course, be attributable to measurement error.) But since it is almost always impractical to measure an entire population, we must *sample* from it. A *sample* is a subset of a population: this is what we are almost always examining when we compare experimental conditions. We make statistical inferences, then, when we draw a conclusion that is based on only a sample of observations about an entire population. We really want to know about the effects of LSD and the inert substance on rats in general, but we hope to draw this conclusion from a sample of, say, twenty rats in each condition.

Samples should always be as representative as possible of the population under study. One way of accomplishing this is *random sampling*, by which members are picked from the population by some completely arbitrary means. (Random sampling is often carried out by using a random-numbers table, such as the one in table G in appendix C). Technically, we can only generalize to the population from which we have sampled, although if taken literally, this would make experimental research hardly worth doing. If we received fifty rats from a supply house for our hypothetical experiment, selected a sample of forty, and randomly assigned them to the two conditions of the experiment, then would our conclusions be true only of the population of fifty rats? Well, perhaps technically, but no one would care about the result if this were so, and no one would have wasted the time doing the experiment. We would at least want to assume that the results are characteristic of that strain of rats. In practice, psychologists assume that their results generalize more widely than the limited population from which they sampled for their experiment. We consider the problem of generality of results and the basis of this assumption more fully in chapters 10 and 14.

BOX B–3.   Statistical Notation

Characteristics of a population of scores are called *parameters*, whereas characteristics of a sample of scores drawn from a larger population are *statistics*. The mean of an entire population of scores is a parameter, and the mean of a sample is a statistic. So that these distinctions are maintained, different symbols are used for population parameters and sample statistics. Some of the most frequent symbols are listed here. Some have been explained; the others will be discussed in the next few pages.

N = number of scores in a population

n = number of scores in a sample

μ = population mean (μ is pronounced mu)

$\bar{X}$ = sample mean

σ^2 = population variance (σ is pronounced sigma)

s^2 = sample variance $\dfrac{\Sigma(X - \bar{X})^2}{n}$

$\hat{s}^2$ = unbiased estimate of population variance $\dfrac{\Sigma(X - \bar{X})^2}{n - 1}$

σ = population standard deviation

s = sample standard deviation

$\hat{s}$ = sample standard deviation based on the unbiased variance estimate

$\sigma_{\bar{x}}$ = standard error of the mean, $\dfrac{\sigma}{\sqrt{N}}$

$s_{\bar{x}}$ = estimated standard error of the mean, $\dfrac{s}{\sqrt{n}}$ or $\dfrac{s}{\sqrt{n - 1}}$

The distribution of sample means. One way we could ask about the reliability of our hypothetical experiment would be to perform it repeatedly with new groups of rats. Of course, it would be very unlikely for us to get exactly the same mean running times for the experimental and control conditions in these replications. The means in seconds for the experimental and control conditions in four replications might be 17.9 and 12.5, 16.0 and 13.4, 16.6 and 14.5, and 15.4 and 15.1. Since the experimental rats which receive the LSD always run more slowly than the control rats which do not, this would increase our confidence in the original finding, although the difference is rather small in the last replication. If we repeated the experiment like this and plotted the distribution of the sample means obtained in the two conditions, these distributions would tend to be normal. Thus they would have all the characteristics of the normal distribution, such as a certain proportion of the scores falling under a certain part of the curve. We could also find the difference between the two means in each experiment and plot the distribution of the differences between the sample means. These differences would also be normally distributed.

To give you a better idea of the concept of the *distribution of sample means*, let us borrow an example from a class demonstration by Horowitz (1974, pp. 179–182). Horowitz manufactured a population of 1,000 normally distributed scores so that the mean and standard deviation of the entire population would be known. This is almost never the case in actual research situations, of course. His 1,000 scores ranged from 0 to 100 with a mean of 50 and a standard deviation of 15.8. The scores were listed on 1,000 slips of paper and placed in a container. Horowitz had 96 students take samples of 10 slips from the container and calculate the mean. On each draw from the container, a slip was taken out, its number was noted, and then the slip was replaced. The slips were then mixed up somewhat in the container, and another slip was drawn, and so on. After each student calculated the mean of the 10 scores in her or his sample, Horowitz collected all 96 and plotted the distribution of sample means, which is represented in table B–5. The intervals between which means might fall are on the left; the number of means falling within each interval is on the right. The distribution is almost perfectly symmetrical, with almost as many scores in any interval a certain distance below the true mean of the population (50) as above it. Also, the mean of the 96 sample means (49.99) is quite close to the actual mean of the population (50). But the main thing that table B–5 shows is the great variability among the sample means. Although each sample of 10 was presumably random and not biased in any way, one sample had a mean of 37.8, while another had a mean of 62.3. Obviously, these are very disparate means, even though they were sampled from the same population. If you were doing an experiment and found two very different sample means, and you were trying to decide whether they came from the same underlying distribution or two different distributions, you might think that such a large difference would indicate that they came from different distributions. In other

TABLE B–5.   The distribution of sample means for the 96 samples taken by students in Horowitz's class. Each sample mean was based on 10 observations. (After Horowitz, 1974, table 8.1)

Interval	Frequency
62.0–63.9	1
60.0–61.9	1
58.0–59.9	3
56.0–57.9	7
54.0–55.9	9
52.0–53.9	12
50.0–51.9	15
48.0–49.9	15
46.0–47.9	13
44.0–45.9	9
42.0–43.9	6
40.0–41.9	3
38.0–39.9	1
36.0–37.9	1
	96 samples

Mean of sample means = 49.99
Standard deviation (s) of sample means = 5.01

words, you would think that the experimental treatment produced scores reliably different (from a different distribution) from the control scores. Usually this is a good rule—the larger the difference between means in the conditions, the more likely the means are to be reliably different—but as we have seen here, even random sampling from a known distribution can produce sample means that differ greatly from each other and from the true population mean, which is known in this case. This is a lesson that should be kept in mind while pondering small differences between means. Is the 3.3-second difference between experimental and control means in our hypothetical LSD experiment really reliable?

The standard error of the mean. The *standard error of the mean* is the standard deviation of a distribution of sample means. In the data in table B–5, it is 5.01. The standard error of the mean gives us some idea as to the amount of variability in the distribution of sample means, or how likely it is that the value of any particular sample mean is in error. Large standard errors indicate great variability, whereas small ones tell us that any particular sample mean is likely to be quite close to the actual population mean. Thus, the standard error of the mean is a very useful number.

You might be wondering why we bother to tell you about the standard error of the mean if, in order to calculate it, you must repeat an experiment numerous times to get the distribution of sample means, and then calculate its standard deviation. Fortunately, you do not have to do this. The formula for finding the standard error of the mean (represented by $\sigma_{\bar{x}}$) is simply the standard deviation of the population (σ) divided by the square root of the number of observations ($\sqrt{N}$).

$$\sigma_{\bar{x}} = \frac{\sigma}{\sqrt{N}} \qquad\qquad \textbf{(B–6)}$$

Now, if you are still with us, you might well be thinking, "Terrific. What good does this do me, since the standard deviation of the population, the numerator in equation B–6, is never known?" That has occurred to statisticians, too, so they have devised a method for estimating the standard deviation of the population from the standard deviation of a sample. If you look back at equation B–2, where the formula for the standard deviation of a sample (s) appears, and simply replace the n in the denominator by $n - 1$, then you have the formula for getting an unbiased estimate of σ, the standard deviation of the population. The equation for finding the standard error of distribution of sample means (called the standard error of the mean or $s_{\bar{x}}$) is

$$\text{Estimated } \sigma_{\bar{x}} = s_{\bar{x}} = \frac{s}{\sqrt{n - 1}} \qquad\qquad \textbf{(B–7)}$$

Obviously, we want the standard error of the mean to be as small as possible, since it represents the error we have in assuming that our sample mean represents the population mean. Equations B–6 and B–7 tell us how to do this: Increase the size of the sample, n, which increases the denominator in the equations. The greater n is, the sample size, the smaller will be the standard error of the mean, $s_{\bar{x}}$. This should be no surprise. If the population involves 1,000 scores, the sample mean should be closer to the population mean if there are 500 observations in the sample than if there are only 10.

Horowitz drove this point home to the 96 students in his class by having them repeat the exercise of drawing slips from the population of 1,000 scores and calculating the mean again; but this time, he had them sample 50 slips, rather than only 10. The resulting distribution of sample means is in table B–6. This time, with larger samples, there is much less variability in the sample means the students obtained. They are much closer to the actual population mean of 50. The standard deviation of the distribution of sample means, or the standard error of the mean, is 2.23, as opposed to 5.01 when the sample size was only 10. If $n = 100$ in a sample from the 1,000 scores, the standard error of the mean would be 1.59; with a sample of 500, it would be .71; and with 1,000 scores in a sample, it would be only .50. (These were calculated from equation B–6, since the standard deviation, σ, is known for the entire population.) The reason we might not get the population mean even with a sample of 1,000 is that the sampling was done with replacement; that is, after a slip was drawn, it was returned to the container; thus, it might have been drawn more than once, while some slips were never drawn.

TABLE B–6. The distribution of sample means for the 96 samples taken by students when sample size (n) = 50. The distribution is again normal, as in table B–5, but when each sample is based on a larger sample size, as it is here, the variability of the distribution (represented by the standard error of the mean) is much smaller. (After Horowitz, 1974, table 8.2)

Interval	Frequency
55.0–55.9	1
54.0–54.9	3
53.0–53.9	5
52.0–52.9	9
51.0–51.9	13
50.0–50.9	17
49.0–49.9	16
48.0–48.9	14
47.0–47.9	9
46.0–46.9	6
45.0–45.9	2
44.0–44.9	1
	96 samples

Mean of sample means = 49.95
Standard deviation (s) of sample means = 2.23

The lesson to be learned is that we should always try to maximize the number of observations—the sample size—in experimental conditions, so that the statistics obtained will be as close as possible to the population parameters.

Testing Hypotheses

Scientists set up experiments to test hypotheses. The conventional statistical logic for testing hypotheses runs something like this. An experimenter arranges conditions, such as the experimental (LSD) and control (placebo) in our experiment with rats, in order to test an *experimental hypothesis*. The experimental hypothesis in this case is that LSD will have some effect on running speed. This is tested by pitting it against the *null hypothesis*, which maintains that the two conditions do not differ in their effects on running speed. Stated another way, the experimental hypothesis is that the samples of running speeds come from two different underlying populations (that is, populations with different distributions); the null hypothesis is that the two samples come from the same distribution.

A critical assumption is that it is impossible to prove the alternative hypothesis conclusively, since there is always some chance that the two samples come from the same population, no matter how different they appear. What inferential statistics allow us to do, though, is to determine how confident we can be in rejecting the null hypothesis. The alternative hypothesis is thus tested indirectly; if we can be quite confident in rejecting the null hypothesis, then we assume that the alternative hypothesis is correct, and that there is a real difference between scores in the different conditions. Psychologists have agreed, by convention, that if calculations from a statistical test show that there is less than a .05 probability (a 5 percent chance) that the null hypothesis is correct we can reject it and accept the alternative hypothesis.

We will describe the concept of probability briefly in this context. Consider the following problem: What is the probability that if we randomly draw a card from a deck of 52 cards, it will be a spade? Since there are 13 spades in a deck, the probability of drawing a spade is 13 divided by 52, or $\frac{1}{4}$ = .25. In general, if there are r ways that an event can occur and a total of N possibilities, then the probability of the event is r/N. What is the probability that a fair coin will come up heads when flipped? There are two ways a coin can come up, so $N = 2$. One of them is heads, so $r = 1$. So the probability of heads is $\frac{1}{2}$, or .50.

Now we can more precisely describe what the conventional level of .05 for statistical significance means. If the null hypothesis were actually true, a researcher would obtain such a large difference between conditions less than 5 times in 100. If the chances are this slight in making an error by rejecting the null hypothesis, then it is deemed safe to do so and to opt for the alternative hypothesis. The .05 criterion is referred to as the .05 *level of confidence,* since a mistake will be made only 5 times in 100. When the null hypothesis is rejected, researchers conclude that the results are reliably different, or statistically significant. In other words, the researchers can be quite confident that the difference obtained between the conditions is trustworthy and that if the experiment were repeated, the same outcome would result.

The logic of pitting an experimental hypothesis against the null hypothesis has come under attack in recent years for several reasons. Some argue that it gives a misleading idea as to how scientists operate. For one thing, not many researchers wander about the world losing any sleep over or investing any thought in the null hypothesis. In general, experiments are set up to test our theories; what is of primary concern is how the results of the experiments can be interpreted or accounted for in the light of our theories. Of special interest is the case in which important experimental results seem irreconcilable with the major theories of a phenomenon. So experiments are important because of what they tell us about our theories and ideas—this is why we designed them in the first place— and not about whether or not the null hypothesis is rejected. But the null-hypothesis testing logic is widely used as an introduction, however oversimplified, of the way scientific inference proceeds. Thus, we present it here. Do not be misled, though, into thinking that psychologists spend their days dreaming up experimental hypotheses to pit against the null hypothesis. This is so in part, but the processes of scientific inference are fortunately much more varied and complicated than the logic of using the null hypothesis would lead us to believe (see chapter 1).

Testing hypotheses: Parameters known. The logic of testing hypotheses against the null hypothesis can be aptly illustrated in cases in which the parameters of a population are known and we wish to determine whether a particular sample comes from the population. Such cases are quite unusual in actual research, of course, since population parameters are rarely known.

Suppose you were interested in whether the members of your experimental psychology class were reliably above the national mean in intelligence as measured by I.Q. tests (or reliably below, as the case may be). We know the population parameters in this case; the mean is 100, and the standard deviation is 15. You could test your class easily enough by giving them the short form of some intelligence test, such as the Wechsler Adult Intelligence Scale developed for group testing. Suppose you randomly sampled 25 people from your class of 100 and found the mean I.Q. of the sample to be 108, with a standard deviation of 5.

How do we go about testing the experimental hypothesis that the class is reliably brighter than the population as a whole? First, let us consider the hypotheses. The experimental hypothesis is that the students are brighter than people in the nation as a whole, or that the I.Q. scores of the students sampled come from a different population than randomly selected people. It is not exactly an exciting hypothesis, one in the vanguard of psychological research, but it will do for our purposes. The null hypothesis is, of course, that there is no reliable difference between our sample and the national mean, or that the students in the class are a sample from the same national population. If the null hypothesis were actually the case, the difference between the sample mean of 108 and the population parameter mean (μ) of 100 would be due to random factors. And certainly this is not implausible, because we have seen from our discussion of the sample distribution of means how much a sample mean can differ from a population parameter, even when the sample is selected in an unbiased manner. Remember Horowitz's classroom demonstration, the results of which are portrayed in tables B–5 and B–6.

The normal curve, the distribution of sample means, and z scores can be used to help us determine how likely it is that the null hypothesis is false. When unbiased samples are taken from a larger population, the means of these samples are normally distributed. With normal distributions, we can specify what proportion of the distribution falls under each part of the curve, as seen in figure B–3. Finally, also remember that z scores are the calculation of any score in a normal distribution in terms of standard deviation units from the mean.

All this is by way of review. Now, how does this help us? What we do in testing the hypothesis that the sample is actually from a population with a mean I.Q. greater than the population at large is to treat the sample mean as an individual score (in terms of our earlier discussion) and calculate a z score on the basis of the deviation of the sample mean from the population mean. In this case, we know the population mean is 100 and the class mean of the randomly selected students is 108. To calculate the z score, we also

r raw scores gathered
n the z score just cal-
with a distribution of
ood that such a value
were in fact true. This
bility our result can be
bability is less than 5
we say that the null
y is sometimes called
nologists prefer values
ectively), so that they
the null hypothesis is

ice you very briefly to
First, let us consider
plying statistical tests
ypothesis testing logic.
errors, so that students
ssible. A *type I error* is
actually true, and the
indexed by the alpha
hall mistakenly reject
illustrates the proba-
not absolutely certain
ly reasonably certain.
nploy in determining
nave of making a type
ility of a *type II error*,
hypothesis when it is
fferent points, we sys-
types of errors. They

such matters, so the α
ts as .05 or .01 (rather
error of rejecting the
g a difference in our
e, though, we increase
ve statistical test min-
atistical tests increase
that of a type II error.
e in our experimental
I or type II errors. We
al replications of our
calculating the *power*
test is the probability
ually false; obviously,
r statistical tests. This
of tests is calculated,
nfluence power. Look
Whatever would make

of the mean: the standard devia-
e means. So the equation for the

(B–8)

$\sigma_{\bar{x}}$) is found by dividing the stan-
, σ (which we know in the case of
s the sample size of the class, or
om equation B–6.) The σ is thus
100/3, or 2.67.

obtaining a z score of 2.67? This
hypothesis with reasonable con-
f the alternative hypothesis, that
the population at large in terms
ig this question: How likely is a z
nple mean is drawn from a larger
e population is actually 100? The
.0038 of the time, or 38 times in
is was calculated in the next par-
g the null hypothesis is that if it
chance, we would reject it, so the
ean is reliably different, or signif-
of the population.

emarkable conclusion is reached,
cial property of the normal curve,
on of cases falls under each part of
hat a z score of ±2.00 is highly
ther direction occur only 2.15 per-
, the probability of such an occur-
ow the 5 percent or .05 level of
e), so any mean score two or more
pulation mean is considered, using
, to be reliably (significantly) dif-
n. In fact, the critical z value for
he .05 level of confidence is ±1.96.
(1) z scores from zero to four, with
n the mean and z, and (3) most
beyond z. The amount of area be-
ling a score that distant from the
one. Once again, when this proba-
with z scores of ±1.96 (or more),
With a z of 2.67, as in our I.Q. ex-
a rare occurrence is only .0038.

have just considered—comparing
parameter to see whether the sam-
n—is rather artificial, since popu-
own. But this example does exhibit
i statistical tests. In all tests, some

computations are performed on the data
from an experiment; a value is found, a
culated; and then this value is compare
values so that we can determine the like
could be obtained if the null hypothesis
distribution tells us, then, with what prob
attributed to random variation. If the p
cases in 100 ($p < .05$), then by conventi
hypothesis can be rejected. This probabi
the *alpha* (α) *level*. As mentioned, some ps
of .01 or even .001 (1 in 100 or 1,000, re
can be more certain that the rejection c
made correctly.

Our z-score test can also serve to intro
some other important statistical concept
two types of errors that can be made by
to experimental data, according to the null
Some dullard named them type I and type
could henceforth confuse them whenever
rejection of the null hypothesis when it i
probability that this error is being made
level. If the alpha level is $p = .05$, then we
the null hypothesis in 5 cases in 100. Th
bilistic nature of inferential statistics; we a
that a null hypothesis can be rejected—c
Thus the lower the α level or p level we
statistical significance, the less chance we
I error. However, this increases the proba
which occurs when we *fail* to reject the nu
actually *false*. Thus, by setting α levels at
tematically decrease and increase the tw
trade off against one another.

Scientists are generally conservative i
level is usually kept fairly small, at such po
than, say, .10 or .15). Thus, we minimize t
null hypothesis when it is true, or claim
results when it is not there. As a consequen
the probability of type II errors. A *conserva*
imizes type I errors, whereas more *liberal* s
the probability of type I error, but decrease

Unfortunately we can never know for s
situations whether we are committing typ
find this out primarily through experime
results. However, we can also find this out b
of a statistical test. The power of a statistica
of rejecting the null hypothesis when it is a
we always want to maximize the power of o
is not the place to describe how the powe
but we can note the two main factors that
back to the z score formula in equation B–8

the z score larger would increase the power of the statistical test, or the likelihood of rejecting the null hypothesis. The value μ, the population mean, is fixed. Thus, only two changes in the values of equation B–8 can affect z. One is the difference between the sample mean and the population mean ($\bar{x} - \mu$) and the other is n, the size of the sample. If the discrepancy between μ and $\bar{x}$ is increased (or in other cases, if the difference between sample means in an experimental comparison is increased), the probability of rejecting the null hypothesis is also increased.

But there is nothing we can do about the size of the difference between means; it is fixed. What we can do to increase the power of our statistical tests is to increase the sample size. The reason for this, in brief, is that with larger samples, we can be more confident that our sample means represent the means of the populations from which they are drawn, and thus we can be more confident that any difference between a sample mean and a population mean (or between two sample means) is reliable. Sample size can have a great effect on the power of a test, as shown in table B–7. Presented there are the z scores and p values for our difference between a sample mean of 108 I.Q. points and the population mean of 100, as the sample size varies. Obviously, as the sample size varies, so will our conclusion as to whether the sample

---

TABLE B–7. How varying sample size (n) affects the power of a statistical test; or, how likely it is that the null hypothesis can be rejected when the test is used. The example is from the z score (calculated in the text) on a mean sample I.Q. of 108, where

$$z = \frac{\bar{X} - \mu}{\sigma_{\bar{x}}}.$$

If the mean difference remains the same but n increases, z increases because

$$\sigma_{\bar{x}} = \frac{\sigma}{\sqrt{n}}.$$

n	$\bar{X} - \mu$	$\sigma_{\bar{x}}$	z	p[†]
2	8	13.14	.61	.2709
5	8	6.70	1.19	.1170
7	8	5.67	1.41	.0793
10	8	4.74	1.69	.0455*
12	8	4.33	1.85	.0322*
15	8	3.88	2.06	.0197*
17	8	3.64	2.20	.0139*
20	8	3.35	2.38	.0087*
25	8	3.00	2.67	.0038*
50	8	2.12	3.77	.0001*
75	8	1.73	4.62	<.00003*
100	8	1.50	5.33	<.00003*

* All these values meet the conventional level of statistical significance, $p < .05$ (one-tailed);

† p values are one-tailed.

comes from a national population or a more restricted, high-I.Q. population. If we assume that the null hypothesis is actually false here, then by increasing sample size, we decrease the probability of a type II error, or increase the power of the test we are using.

One final issue to be considered is specification of *directionality* of statistical tests. According to conventional logic involved in testing an alternative hypothesis against the null hypothesis, the alternative hypothesis may be *directional* or *nondirectional*. If there are an experimental and a control group in an experiment, a nondirectional alternative hypothesis would simply be that the two groups would differ in performance on the dependent variable. But a directional hypothesis would state in addition the predicted direction of the difference; for example, the experimental group might be predicted to do better than the control.

This distinction is important, because if the alternative hypothesis is directional, a *one-tailed* (or *one-sided*) *statistical test* is used, but if the alternative hypothesis is nondirectional, a *two-tailed (two-sided) test* is used. One versus two "tails" refers to whether in looking up a p level associated with some determined value of the statistical test (say, $z = 1.69$), we consider one or both tails of the distribution (see figure B–4).

This should be clearer with reference to our earlier example. We took a sample ($n = 25$) of students, determined that the mean I.Q. of the sample was 108, and calculated a $z = +2.67$ in testing to see whether this was different from the mean population I.Q. of

FIGURE B–4.

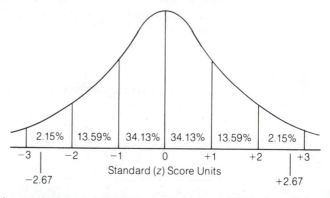

This is the standard normal distribution which is presented in figure B–3. There are two sides or tails to the distribution: positive and negative. If an experimenter simply asserts that there should be a difference between an experimental and a control condition, but does not specify the direction of the difference, this is called a nondirectional hypothesis. If a $z = 2.67$ is found, it is necessary to look up the probability that this will occur in both the positive and negative tails of the distribution and add the two, since the experimenter has not specified whether the difference should be positive or negative. When the experimenter has specified the direction of difference, one need only look up the probability in one tail. Since the distribution is symmetrical, the probability that the null hypothesis can be rejected is half as great with a one-tailed as with a two-tailed test. The less certain one is about the outcome of an experiment, the greater the difference between conditions must be for it to be decided that it is not due to chance.

100. If we had no prior expectation of how the sample I.Q. should deviate from the normal population—if we thought it could be either greater or lower—this would have been a nondirectional hypothesis. In fact, we did expect the sample I.Q. to be greater than 100, so we were testing a directional hypothesis, and thus used a one-tailed test. This means that we looked up the resulting z score in only one tail of the normal distribution: that greater than zero. A $z = +2.67$ leads to a one-tailed p value of .0038. If the hypothesis were nondirectional, then we would have no a priori right to expect the resultant z score to be greater instead of less than zero. The z could fall in the positive or negative tail. Since the difference could have occurred in either direction, we use a two-tailed test. In practice, since the two tails of the distribution are symmetrical, we simply double the p level for the one-tailed test. In our example, if the hypothesis had been nondirectional, p would equal $2 \times .0038$, or .0076, still well below .05.

Two-tailed tests are more conservative and less powerful than one-tailed tests; it is harder to reject the null hypothesis. If we are uncertain about the outcome of an experiment, we need a greater value of the statistic to allow us to declare a difference. In practice, most investigators prefer to use the more conservative two-tailed test, with sufficient power ensured by fairly large sample sizes.

Tests for Differences between Two Groups

There is a bewildering variety of statistical tests for almost every purpose. At present, we are interested in discussing tests that assess the reliability of a difference between two groups or conditions. How do we pick an appropriate test from all those available? There is no hard-and-fast rule. Tests vary in the assumptions they make, their power, and the types of situation for which they are appropriate. Perhaps the most popular test for the difference between two means in psychological research is the t test. Since the t test provides the same estimate of reliability as does the simple analysis of variance (to be discussed soon), we will first concentrate on two other tests, the *Mann-Whitney U test* and the *Wilcoxon signed-ranks test*. These tests also are useful in introducing yet another type of statistical test.

The Mann-Whitney and Wilcoxon tests are *nonparametric tests,* as opposed to *parametric tests*. Parametric statistical tests are those that make assumptions about the underlying population parameters of the samples on which the tests are performed. Common assumptions of parametric tests are that the variances of the underlying populations being compared are equivalent and that the underlying distributions are normal. If these assumptions are not met, then the test may be inappropriate. But how can we ever know whether the assumptions underlying the test are met, since we do not know the population parameters? Usually we cannot, except by estimating population parameters from sample statistics. However, if we turn to nonparametric statistics, the problem does not arise, because these tests make no assumptions about the underlying population parameters. Since the parameters cannot be known anyway, this provides an important reason for using nonparametric tests. Another reason is that these tests generally are very easy to calculate and can often even be done by hand. However, nonparametric tests are usually less powerful than parametric tests employed in the same situation; that is, they are less likely to provide a rejection of the null hypothesis.

The Mann-Whitney U test is used when we wish to compare two samples to decide whether they come from the same or different underlying populations. It is used when the two samples are composed of different subjects, or in between-subjects designs. The underlying rationale for the Mann-Whitney test will not be discussed here. In general, the logic is the same as in other statistical tests in which a value is computed from the test and compared with a distribution of values to determine whether the null hypothesis should be rejected. The way in which the Mann-Whitney test is applied to actual data is outlined in box B–4; thus, the reliability of the difference between the two samples in our hypothetical LSD experiment is tested.

The Wilcoxon signed-ranks test is also used in testing for the difference between two samples, but in this case the design must be a *related measures design.* In other words, either the same subjects must serve in both the experimental and control groups (a within-subjects design), or the subjects must be matched in some way. Of course, precautions must be taken in within-subjects designs to ensure that some variable such as practice or fatigue is not confounded with the variable of interest (see chapter 3). But as long as the experiment has been done well, the Wilcoxon signed-ranks test is an appropriate tool for analysis of the results.

Before considering the signed-ranks test, we will examine its simpler cousin, the *sign test*, which is also appropriate in the same situations. The sign test is the essence of simplicity. Suppose we have 26 subjects serving in both conditions of an experiment in which we are predicting that when subjects are in the experimental condition, they will do better than when they are in the control condition. Now suppose that 19 subjects actually do better in the experimental condition than in the control, while the reverse is true for the other 7. Is this difference reliable? The sign test allows us to answer this question without our needing more information about what the actual scores were. In terms of the null hypothesis, we might expect 13 subjects to perform better in the experimental condition and 13 in the control. The sign test allows us to compute the exact probability that the null hypothesis is false when there are 19 cases in the predicted direction, but also 7 reversals or exceptions. It turns out that the null hypothesis can be rejected in this case with a .014 confidence level (one-tailed). With a nondirectional prediction, p equals .028 (two-tailed). Once again, we cannot delve into the details of how this is computed, but in table C in appendix C we present the α levels (one-tailed) for cases of

BOX B–4. Calculation of a Mann-Whitney *U* Test on Hypothetical Experimental Data from Figure B–1.

Step 1. Rank all the numbers for *both* groups together, beginning with the smallest number. Assign it the lowest rank.

Control (Placebo)		Experimental (LSD)	
Latency (sec.)	Rank	Latency (sec.)	Rank
9	1.5	9	1.5
10	3	13	11.5
11	4.5	13	11.5
11	4.5	14	17
12	7	14	17
12	7	15	21
12	7	16	24.5
13	11.5	16	24.5
13	11.5	16	24.5
13	11.5	17	28
13	11.5	17	28
14	17	18	32
14	17	18	32
14	17	18	32
15	21	18	32
15	21	19	35.5
16	24.5	19	35.5
17	28	20	37.5
18	32	22	39
20	37.5	26	40,
	Σ rank$_1$ 295.5		Σ rank$_2$ 524.5

Note: When scores are tied, assign the mean value of the tied ranks to each. Thus, for both 9-second times in this example, the rank 1.5 is assigned (the mean of 1 and 2).

Step 2. The equations for finding *U* and *U'* are as follows, where n_1 is the size of the smaller sample, n_2 is the size of the larger sample, ΣR_1 is the sum of the ranks of the smaller sample, and ΣR_2 is the sum of the ranks of the larger sample. Obviously, the subscripts are important only if the sample sizes are unequal, which is not the case here.

$$U = n_1 n_2 + \frac{n_1(n_1 + 1)}{2} - \Sigma R_1$$

$$U = (20)(20) + \frac{(20)(21)}{2} - 295.5 \qquad \textbf{(B–9)}$$

$$U = 400 + 210 - 295.5$$

$$U = 314.5$$

$$U' = n_1 n_2 + \frac{n_2(n_2 + 1)}{2} - \Sigma R_2$$

$$U' = (20)(20) + \frac{(20)(21)}{2} - 524.5 \qquad \textbf{(B–10)}$$

$$U' = 85.5$$

Actually, it is necessary to compute only either U or U', because the other can be found according to the equations

$$U = n_1 n_2 - U'$$

or

$$U' = n_1 n_2 - U.$$

Step 3. Take U or U', whichever value is *smaller*, and look in table B in appendix C to see whether the difference between the two groups is reliable. The values in table B are recorded according to different sample sizes. In this case both sample sizes are 20, so the critical value from the table is 88. For the difference between the two groups to be judged reliable, the U or U' from the experiment must be *less than* the appropriate value in table B. Since 85.5 is less than 88, we can conclude that the difference between the two groups is reliable at the .001 level of confidence.

Note: Table B is only appropriate for situations which the sizes of the two samples are between 8 and 21. For other cases, you should consult an advanced text.

sample sizes from 3 to 42, when there are x number of exceptions to the predicted hypothesis. So, for example, when there are 16 subjects in the experiment (remember, in both conditions), and 13 show the predicted pattern of results while 3 exhibit reversals, we can reject the null hypothesis at the .011 level of confidence (one-tailed).

The sign test uses very little of the information from an experiment: just whether the subjects performed better or worse in one condition than in another. For the sign test, it does not matter whether the difference in performance is great or small; the direction of the difference is all that matters. The sign test therefore wastes much of the information gathered in an experiment and is not a very powerful statistical test. The Wilcoxon signed-ranks test is like the sign test in that it is used in situations where the same (or matched) subjects are employed in two conditions, and the direction of the difference is taken into account. However, in the Wilcoxon signed-ranks test, the size of the difference is taken into account, too. For this reason, it is also called the sized sign test. An example of how the Wilcoxon signed-ranks test is used is in box B–5.

BOX B–5. **Calculation of the Wilcoxon Signed-Ranks Test**

Imagine an experiment testing whether Professor Humboldt von Widget's memory course, "How to Constipate Your Mind by Remembering Everything," really works. First, a group of thirty subjects is presented with fifty words to be remembered. Then the subjects are randomly separated into two groups, and a check indicates that the groups do not differ reliably in the mean number of words recalled. The experimental group is given Professor von Widget's three-week course, whereas the control group is not. Then all thirty subjects are tested again on another fifty-word list. The controls show no improvement from one list to another. The question we ask here is whether the experimental subjects' memories were reliably improved. (Note: We could—and should—also compare the experimental subjects' performance on the second test with that of the controls. The Mann-Whitney test is appropriate for this comparison. Do you know why?) We employ the Wilcoxon signed-ranks test to assess whether the experimental subjects improved reliably from the first test to the second.

Step 1. Place the data in a table (such as the one presented on the facing page) in which both scores for each subject (before and after the memory course) are paired together. Find and record the difference between the pairs.

Step 2. Rank the values of the differences according to size, beginning with the smallest. *Ignore the sign.* Use the absolute values of the numbers. For tied ranks, assign each the mean value of the ranks. (See the right-hand column of the table here.)

Step 3. Add the ranks for all the difference values that are negative (5.5 + 2.5 + 8.5 + 5.5 = 22.0) and positive (14 + 15 + 2.5 + 8.5 + 8.5 + 2.5 + 13 + 2.5 + 11.5 + 8.5 + 11.5 = 98.0). These are the signed-rank values.

Step 4. Take the signed-rank value that is smallest (22 in this case), and go to table D in appendix C. Look up the number of pairs of observations (listed as *n* on the left). There are 15 in this case. Then look at the number under the desired level of significance. Since the direction of the outcome was predicted in this case (we expected the memory course to help rather than hurt recall of words), let us choose the value under the .025 level of significance for a one-tailed test. This value is 25. If the smaller of the two values from the experiment is *below* the appropriate value in the table, then the result is reliable. Since 22 is below 25, we can conclude that Professor von Widget's course really did help memory for words.

Note: Remember that the controls showed no improvement in performance from one test to the other. This is a crucial bit of information, for otherwise we could not rule out two plausible competing hypotheses. One is that the improvement on the second list was simply owing to practice on the first, and the other is that the second list was easier than the first. Actually, if Professor von Widget's course were as effective as numerous memory courses currently on the market, results from an actual experiment would show (and have shown) more spectacular improvement than the hypothetical results here. Memory-improvement courses, all of which embody the same few principles, really work for objective materials such as word lists.

Mean number of words recalled

Subject	Before	After	Difference	Rank
1	11	17	+6	14
2	18	16	−2	5.5
3	9	21	+12	15
4	15	16	+1	2.5
5	14	17	+3	8.5
6	12	15	+3	8.5
7	17	16	−1	2.5
8	16	17	+1	2.5
9	15	20	+5	13
10	19	16	−3	8.5
11	12	13	+1	2.5
12	16	14	−2	5.5
13	10	14	+4	11.5
14	17	20	+3	8.5
15	6	10	+4	11.5
	$\bar{x} = 13.80$	$\bar{x} = 16.07$		

t Test

In boxes B–6 and B–7, we present the corresponding *t* tests for the analyses presented in the previous two boxes. The *t* test is a parametric test; this means that we assume that the underlying distributions are roughly normal in shape. Furthermore, the *t* test and other parametric tests were designed to be used on data that are at least interval in nature. The U test and the sign test require only ordinal data. The *t* tests are essentially based on z scores having to do with the standard error of the difference between means. Thus, even if the computational formulas appear unusual at first, the underlying logic is the same as that discussed earlier in this appendix.

BOX B–6.   Calculation of a Between-Subjects *t* Test

These are hypothetical experimental data previously discussed (see box B–4). The calculation formula is

$$t = \frac{\bar{X}_1 - \bar{X}_2}{\sqrt{\left[\frac{\Sigma X_1^2 - \frac{(\Sigma X_1)^2}{N_1} + \Sigma X_2^2 - \frac{(\Sigma X_2)^2}{N_2}}{N_1 + N_2 - 2}\right]\left[\frac{1}{N_1} + \frac{1}{N_2}\right]}} \quad \text{(B–11)}$$

$\bar{X}_1$ = mean of group 1 $\qquad$ ΣX_1^2 = sum of squared scores in group 1

$\bar{X}_2$ = mean of group 2 $\qquad$ ΣX_2^2 = sum of squared scores in group 2

N_1 = number of scores in group 1 $\quad$ $(\Sigma X_1)^2$ = square of group-1 sum

N_2 = number of scores in group 2 $\quad$ $(\Sigma X_2)^2$ = square of group-2 sum

Control (placebo)				Experimental (LSD)			
X	X^2	X	X^2	X	X^2	X	X^2
9	81	13	169	9	81	17	289
10	100	14	196	13	169	18	324
11	121	14	196	13	169	18	324
11	121	14	196	14	196	18	324
12	144	15	225	14	196	18	324
12	144	15	225	15	225	19	361
12	144	16	256	16	256	19	361
13	169	17	289	16	356	20	400
13	169	18	324	16	356	22	484
13	169	20	400	17	289	26	676

$\Sigma X = 272$
$\bar{X} = 13.60$ $\qquad$ $\Sigma X^2 = 3838$ $\qquad$ $\Sigma X = 338$
$\bar{X} = 16.90$ $\qquad$ $\Sigma X^2 = 5960$

Step 1. After calculating ΣX, ΣX^2, and $\bar{X}$ for each group (by the way, there is no need to rank order our data), we need to calculate $(\Sigma X)^2/N$ for each group: $(272)^2/20 = 3699.20$ and $(338)^2/20 = 5712.20$. Then we need to determine $\Sigma X^2 - (\Sigma X)^2/N$ for each group: $3838 - 3699.2 = 138.8$ and $5960 - 5712.2 = 247.8$.

Step 2. Now we add the two group figures we obtained in the last step: $247.8 + 138.8$, and divide this sum by $N_1 + N_2 - 2$: $386.6/38 = 10.17$.

Step 3. The quotient obtained in Step 2 (10.17) is multiplied by

$$\left[\frac{1}{N_1} + \frac{1}{N_2} \right]: (10.17)(2/20) = 1.02.$$

Step 4. We now take the square root of the product obtained in Step 3: $\sqrt{1.02} = 1.01$.

Step 5. We find the absolute difference between the mean scores of the two groups (by subtracting one from the other, and ignoring the sign): $16.90 - 13.60 = 3.30$.

Step 6. t = the difference between means (Step 5) divided by the results of Step 4: $3.30/1.01 = 3.27$. So, our $t = 3.27$. To evaluate this, we look in the tabled values of t in table E in appendix C. We enter this table with the number of degrees of freedom (df) in our experiment, which means the number of scores that are free to vary. For a between-subjects t, the degrees of freedom are $N_1 + N_2 - 2$—in this case, $df = 38$. For $p = .05$ and $df = 38$, the critical value of t is 2.04 in our table (always take the next lowest df to calculate the critical value). Since our obtained *t* exceeds the critical value, we can reject the hypothesis that our two groups have the same running scores; that is, we can say that LSD had an effect on the behavior of our subjects.

BOX B–7. **Calculation of a Within-Subjects *t* Test**

The hypothetical data are from Professor von Widget's experiment (see box B–5). The computational formula for the within-subjects *t* test is

$$t = \sqrt{\frac{N - 1}{[N\Sigma D^2/(\Sigma D)^2] - 1}},\qquad \textbf{(B–12)}$$

where N = number of subjects; and D = difference in the scores of a given subject (or matched subject pair) in the two conditions.

Subject	Mean Number of Words Recalled Before	After	Difference	D^2
1	11	17	+ 6	36
2	18	16	− 2	4
3	9	21	+12	144
4	15	16	+ 1	1
5	14	17	+ 3	9
6	12	15	+ 3	9
7	17	16	− 1	1
8	16	17	+ 1	1
9	15	20	+ 5	25
10	19	16	− 3	9
11	12	13	+ 1	1
12	16	14	− 2	4
13	10	14	+ 4	16
14	17	20	+ 3	9
15	6	10	+ 4	16
	$\bar{X} = 13.80$	$\bar{X} = 16.07$	$\Sigma D = 35$ $(\Sigma D)^2 = 1,225$	$\Sigma D^2 = 285$

Step 1. After you arrange the scores for each subject in pairs as shown in this table, record the difference between each pair; then, square each of these difference scores.

Step 2. Add the difference scores across subjects, which yields ΣD, then square this sum to get $(\Sigma D)^2$: $\Sigma D = 35$; and $(\Sigma D)^2 = 1,225$.

Step 3. Calculate the sum of the squared difference scores to get $\Sigma D^2 = 285$.

Step 4. Multiply ΣD^2 (Step 3) by the number of subjects: $285 \times 15 = 4,275$.

Step 5. Divide the product found in Step 5 by $(\Sigma D)^2$: $4,275/1,225 = 3.49$, and then subtract 1 from the result: $3.49 − 1 = 2.49$.

Step 6. Divide the number of subjects less 1 ($N - 1$) by the result of Step 5: 14/2.49 = 5.62.

Step 7. $t = \sqrt{5.62} = 2.37$.

Step 8. To evaluate t, compare it to the critical values shown in statistical table E. Enter the table with $N - 1$ *df*, and for this study *df* = 14. With *df* = 14, the critical value of t is 2.145 for p = .05. Since the obtained t exceeds the critical value, we can conclude that von Widget's course really did affect word recall.

The Analysis of Variance

Most psychological research has progressed beyond the stage at which there are only two conditions, an experimental and a control, that are compared to one another. Rather than varying only the presence or absence of some independent variable, researchers often systematically vary the magnitude of the independent variable. In our example of the effects of LSD on running speed of rats, it may be quite useful to vary the amount of LSD administered to the rats. Perhaps effects are different at low dosages than at high ones. We could not determine this from the two-group design in which one group received LSD in some amount and the other did not. To evaluate the results of such an experiment with multiple groups, we must employ the *analysis of variance*, in particular *simple analysis of variance*. Simple analysis of variance is used in situations in which one factor or independent variable (such as amount of LSD) is varied systematically. Thus, it is also called one-factor analysis of variance. Often, researchers are interested in more complex situations. They may be interested in varying two or more factors simultaneously. In such two-factor or multifactor experimental designs, the analysis of variance is also appropriate, but it is more complicated. In this section, we introduce you to the logic of simple and two-factor analysis of variance (abbreviated ANOVA). However, in our examples and discussion, we stick to the case of between-subjects experimental designs. Calculations for within-subjects designs are different.

At the heart of the analysis-of-variance procedure is a comparison of variance estimates. We have already discussed the concept of variance and its estimation from one particular sample of observations. You should refer back to the section on measures of dispersion if the concept of variance is hazy to you at this point. Recall that the equation for the unbiased estimate of the population variance is

$$\hat{s}^2 = \frac{\Sigma(X - \overline{X})^2}{n - 1}$$

(B–13)

and that when the deviation of scores from the mean is large, the variance will be great. Similarly, when the deviations from the mean are small, the variance will be small.

In the analysis of variance, two independent estimates of variance are obtained. One is based on the variability *between* the different experimental groups: how much the means of the different groups vary from one another. Actually, the variance is computed as to how much the individual group means differ from the overall mean of all scores in the experiment. The greater the difference among the means of the groups, the greater will be the *between-groups variance.*

The other estimate of variance is the *within-groups variance.* This is the concept that we have already discussed previously in considering estimates of variance from individual samples; now we are concerned with finding an estimate of within-groups variance that is representative of all the individual groups, so we take the mean of the variances of these groups. The within-groups variance gives us an estimate of how much subjects in the groups differ from one another (or the mean of the group). In short, two variance estimates are obtained: one for the variance within groups and one for the variance between groups. Now what good does this do?

The basic logic of testing to see whether the scores of the different groups or conditions are reliably different is as follows. The null hypothesis is that all the subjects in the various conditions are drawn from the same underlying population; the experimental variable has no effect. If the null hypothesis is true and all the scores in the different groups come from the same population, then the between-groups variance should be the same as the within-groups variance. The means from the different groups should vary from one another no more nor less than do the scores within the groups. For us to be able to reject the null hypothesis, then, the means of the different groups must vary from one another more than the scores vary within the groups. The greater the variance (differences) between the groups of the experiment, the more likely the independent variable is to have had an effect, especially if the within-groups variance is low.

The person who originated this logic was the eminent British statistician R. A. Fisher; the test is referred to as an *F test* in his honor. The *F* test is simply a ratio of the between-groups variance estimate to the within-groups variance estimate:

$$F = \frac{\text{between-groups variance}}{\text{within-groups variance}} \tag{B–14}$$

According to the logic we have just outlined, the *F* ratio under the null hypothesis should be 1.00, because the between-groups variance should be the same as the within-groups variance. The greater the between-groups variance is than the within-groups variance, and consequently the greater the *F* ratio is than 1.00, the more confident we can be in rejecting the null hypothesis. Exactly how much greater the *F* ratio must be than 1.00 depends on the *degrees of freedom* in the experiment, or how free the measures are to vary. This depends both on the number of groups or conditions in the experiment and on the number of observations in each group. The greater the number of degrees of freedom, the smaller need be the value of the *F* ratio to be judged a reliable effect, as you can see from examining table F in appendix C. You should follow the computational example in box B–8 carefully to gain a feel for the analysis of variance.

If the simple analysis of variance indicates that there is reliable variation among the conditions of an experiment, this still does not tell us all we would like to know. In particular, it is still of great interest to know which of the individual conditions vary among themselves. This is especially important in cases where independent-variable manipulation is qualitative in nature. *Quantitative variation* of an independent variable refers to the case in which the quantity of an independent variable is manipulated (for example, amount of LSD), whereas *qualitative variation* is the case of conditions that vary, but not in some easily specified quantitative manner. An example of qualitative variation is an instructional manipulation in which the different conditions vary in the instructions that are given at the beginning of the experiment. In such cases, it is not enough simply to say that the conditions vary reliably from one another. It is of interest to know which particular conditions differ. To answer this question, we need to perform tests after the simple analysis of variance. In these follow-up tests, the conditions of the experiment are taken two at a time and compared, so that we can see which pairs are reliably different. There is a great variety of statistical tests that can be used for this purpose. We could perform analyses of variance on groups taken as pairs, which is equivalent to performing *t* tests, but usually other tests are performed. These include the Newman-Keuls test, the Scheffé test, Duncan's multiple-range test, Tukey's HSD (Honestly Significant Differences) test, and Dunnett's test. These vary in their assumptions and their power. You should consult statistical texts when you need to use a follow-up test.

BOX B–8.   Computing Simple Analysis of Variance

Imagine that you have just performed an experiment testing the effects of LSD on the running speeds of rats, but that there were three levels of LSD administered, rather than only two, as in our earlier example. Ten rats received no LSD, ten others received a small amount, and yet a third group of ten received a great amount. Thus, the experiment employs a between-subjects design, in which amount of LSD (none, small, large) is the independent variable and running time is the dependent variable. First, calculate the sum of the scores (ΣX) and the sum of the squared values of the scores (ΣX^2).

	Amount of LSD		
	None	Small	Large
	13	17	26
	11	15	20
	14	16	29
	18	20	31
	12	13	17
	14	19	25
	10	18	26
	13	17	23
	16	19	25
	12	21	27
ΣX	133	175	249
$\overline{X}$	13.30	17.50	24.90
ΣX^2	1819	3115	6351

A basic quantity in calculation of analysis of variance is the *sum of squares*, which is an abbreviated form for the term *sum of squared deviations from the mean*. If you look back to equation B–1, which defines the variance of a sample, you will see that the sum of squares is the numerator. There are actually three sums of squares of interest. First is the total sum of squares (SS_{total}), which is defined as the sum of the squared deviations of the individual scores from the grand mean, or the mean of all the scores in all groups in the experiment. Second is the sum of squares between groups ($SS_{between}$), which is the sum of the squared deviations of the group means from the grand mean. Third, the sum of squares within groups (SS_{within}) is the mean of the sum of the squared deviations of the individual scores within groups or conditions from the group means. It turns out that $SS_{total} = SS_{between} + SS_{within}$, so that in practice only two sums of squares need be calculated; the third can be found by subtraction.

These sums of squares could be calculated by taking the deviations from the appropriate means, squaring them, and then finding the sum, but such a method would take much time and labor. Fortunately, there are computational formulas that allow the calculations to be done more easily, especially if the values of ΣX and ΣX^2 have been found for each group, as in the present data. The formula for finding the total sum of squares is

$$SS_{total} = \Sigma\Sigma X^2 - \frac{T^2}{N}, \qquad \text{(B–15)}$$

where $\Sigma\Sigma X^2$ means that each score within each group is squared (X^2) and all these squared values are added together, so ΣX^2. There are two separate summation signs, one for summing the squared values within groups and one for then summing these ΣX^2 across the different groups. The T is for the total of all scores; N here is the total number of scores in the experiment. So SS_{total} in our example is calculated in the following way:

$$SS_{total} = \Sigma\Sigma X^2 - \frac{T^2}{N}$$

$$SS_{total} = 1819 + 3115 + 6351 - \frac{(133 + 175 + 249)^2}{30}$$

$$SS_{total} = 11{,}285 - \frac{310{,}249}{30}$$

$$SS_{total} = 11{,}285 - 10{,}341.63$$

$$SS_{total} = 943.37$$

The between-groups sum of squares is calculated with the following formula:

$$SS_{between} = \Sigma\frac{(\Sigma X)^2}{n} - \frac{T^2}{N} . \qquad \textbf{(B-16)}$$

The first part of the formula means that the sum of the values for each group is squared and then divided by the number of observations on which it is based or $(\Sigma X)^2/n$; then, these values are summed across groups, so $\Sigma(\Sigma X)^2/n]$. The second part of the formula is the same as for the SS_{total}:

$$SS_{between} = \Sigma\frac{(\Sigma X)^2}{n} - \frac{T^2}{N}$$

$$SS_{between} = \frac{17{,}689}{10} + \frac{30{,}625}{10} + \frac{62{,}001}{10} - 10{,}341.63$$

$$SS_{between} = 11{,}031.50 - 10{,}341.63$$

$$SS_{between} = 689.87$$

The sum of squares within groups can be found by subtracting $SS_{between}$ from SS_{total}, so $SS_{within} = 943.37 - 689.87 = 253.50$. But as a check, it is also worthwhile to compute it directly. This is done by computing an SS_{total}, as in equation B–15 for each group, and summing all these sums of squares for the individual groups. Unless you have made an error, this quantity should equal SS_{within} obtained by subtraction.

After we have obtained the various sums of squares, it is convenient to construct an analysis-of-variance table such as the one that follows. In the far left column appears the source of variance, or source. Keep in mind that there are two primary sources of variance we are interested in comparing: between groups and within groups.

In the next column are the number of degrees of freedom (df). These can be thought of as the number of scores that are free to vary, given that the total is fixed. For the degrees of freedom between groups, if the overall total is fixed, all groups are free to vary except one. So the between-groups *df* is the number of groups minus one. In our example, then, it is $3 - 1 = 2$. The within-groups *df* is equal to the total number of scores minus the number of groups, because there is one score in each group that cannot vary if the group total is fixed. So within-groups *df* is $30 - 3 = 27$. The total $df =$ between-groups *df* + within-groups *df*.

The third column is for the sum of squares (*SS*), which have already been calculated. The fourth column is for the mean squares (*MS*), which are found by dividing the *SS* for each row by the *df*. Each mean square is an estimate of the population variance, if the null hypothesis is true. But if the independent variable had an effect, the between-groups mean square should be larger than the within-groups mean square.

As already discussed in the text, these two values are compared by computing an *F* ratio, which is found by dividing the $MS_{between}$ by the MS_{within}. Once the *F* value is calculated, it is necessary to determine whether the value reaches an acceptable level of statistical significance. By looking in table F in appendix C, we can see that for 2 and 26 degrees of freedom (the closest we can get to 2 and 27), an *F* value of 9.12 is needed for the .001 level of significance. Our *F* value surpasses 9.12, so we can conclude that the groups varied reliably in running speed because of variation in the independent variable, amount of LSD injected.

Source	df	SS	MS	F	p
Between groups	2	689.87	344.94	36.73	<.001
Within groups	27	253.50	9.39		
Total	29	943.37			

Note: If you compute analyses of variance yourself with the aid of a calculator, you must guard against errors. If you ever come up with a negative sum of squares within groups (by subtracting $SS_{between}$ from SS_{total}), you will know you have made an error. You cannot have a negative sum of squares. You should compute SS_{within} both by subtraction and directly, anyway, as a check. One common error is to confuse ΣX^2 (square each number and then sum the squares) with $(\Sigma X)^2$, which is the square of the total (ΣX) of the scores.

Multifactor analysis of variance. A frustrating aspect to the study of behavior is that there are hardly ever any simple or one-factor explanations. Even the simplest behaviors studied in laboratory situations turn out to be affected by multiple factors. To discover these multiple determinants of behavior and how they interact, we must perform experiments in which more than one factor is varied simultaneously. The appropriate procedure for analyzing results of such experiments is *multifactor analysis of variance.* This may involve analysis of experiments in which any number of factors are concerned, but in practice it is rare to find more than four variables of interest manipulated simultaneously. When there are two factors, the analysis is referred to as a two-way ANOVA; where there are three factors, it is a three-way ANOVA; and so on.

The importance of such complex designs involving more than one factor is that they allow us to assess how different factors may interact to produce an experimental result. Recall that an interaction occurs when the effect of one experimental variable is affected by the level of the other experimental variable (see chapter 3). If we performed a 2×2 experiment (this refers to two different factors with two different levels of each factor) on interpersonal attraction involving sex of the subject (male versus female) and sex of the experimental confederate whom the subject was to evaluate, we might discover an interaction effect. If the distance the subject stands from the confederate were one of the dependent variables, then we might find that male subjects tend to stand closer to female confederates, and female subjects closer to male confederates. This is an example of an interaction. There is no simple generalization as to how close male or female subjects will stand to a confederate in an experiment; it depends on the sex of the confederate.

When performing a complex analysis of variance, we find out the separate effects of each factor in the experiment (called *main effects*), and also how the variables affect one another (called *interaction effects,* or simply interactions). If women tended to stand closer to the confederate than did men, regardless of the sex of the confederate, this would be a main effect of sex of subject on interpersonal distance. And, again, an interaction would be the different effect of sex of subject, depending on sex of the confederate.

Unfortunately we cannot devote space here to explaining completely how these complex analyses of variance are performed. Briefly, the $SS_{between}$ is found as it is in the simple or one-way analysis of variance, but here it is further decomposed into the main effects of the independent variables and their interactions. Then, mean squares are computed on the basis of these sums of squares by dividing by the appropriate number of degrees of freedom, and F ratios are obtained as before. An example appears in box B–9.

The analysis of variance is a parametric statistical test; thus, assumptions are built into the test about the population parameters underlying the samples. The two most important assumptions in the type of analysis of variance we are considering (the fixed-effects model) are that the observations in each condition are normally distributed and that the within-groups variances of the different conditions are equivalent. This latter assumption is called the *homogeneity of variance* assumption. It is assumed that manipulation of the independent variables should affect the variance between groups, but not the variance within groups. In practice, investigators do not worry much about these assumptions. The

BOX B–9. Calculation of a 2 × 2 ANOVA on the Data from a Memory Experiment

In this experiment, there were forty subjects. They were divided up into four groups of ten, each group representing a different condition. Two groups were given high-imagery words to learn, or words that refer to concrete objects that are easily visualized (for example, elephant, chair, automobile). The other two groups received low-imagery words, or ones that are abstract and hard to form images of (such as beauty, democracy, truth). The two groups that received each type of word differed in the learning instructions they were given. One group of subjects in each of the two imagery conditions was told to repeat each word until they saw the next word appear on the screen. These subjects were in the Rote Rehearsal condition. Subjects in the Elaborative Rehearsal condition were instructed to create mental images or meaningful associations between the words as they were learning them. Thus, the experiment represents a 2 × 2 factorial design, with one factor being the type of material studied (high- or low-imagery words) and the other being the instructions subjects were given (rote- or elaborative-rehearsal instructions). The design is between subjects, since a different group of subjects participated in each of the four conditions. The number of words recalled by each subject appears in the following table. Then the steps involved in the analysis of variance, which allow us to appropriately analyze the results of the experiment, are outlined.

	High-Imagery Words		Low-Imagery Words	
	Rote Rehearsal	Elaborative Rehearsal	Rote Rehearsal	Elaborative Rehearsal
	5	8	4	7
	7	8	1	6
	6	9	5	3
	4	7	6	3
	4	10	4	5
	9	10	3	6
	7	8	4	2
	5	9	4	4
	5	8	5	5
	6	9	3	4
$\Sigma X =$	58	86	39	45
$\overline{X} =$	5.8	8.6	3.9	4.5
$\Sigma X^2 =$	358	748	169	225

$\Sigma\Sigma X^2 = (358 + \ldots + 225) = 1500$ $\Sigma\Sigma X = 228$

Step 1. Square the grand sum ($\Sigma\Sigma X = 228$) and divide by the total number of scores (40). $(\Sigma\Sigma X)^2/N = (228)^2/40 = 1299.6$. This is the correction term.

Step 2. SS Total $= \Sigma\Sigma X^2 - (\Sigma\Sigma X)^2/N$. Subtract the results of Step 1 from 1500. SS Total $= 200.4$.

Step 3. SS Imagery. Get the sum of all scores in each imagery condition, square each sum, then divide each sum by the number of scores yielding each sum, add the two quotients, and then subtract the results of Step 1 from the last sum.

$$SS \text{ Imagery} = (58 + 86)^2/20 + (39 + 45)^2/20 - \text{Step 1}$$

$$= \frac{144^2 + 84^2}{20} - 1299.6$$

$$= 1389.6 - 1299.6$$

$$= 90$$

Step 4. *SS* Rehearsal. This is calculated in the same manner as Step 3, except that you base your calculations on the grand sum of each type of rehearsal.

$$SS \text{ Rehearsal} = \frac{(86 + 45)^2 + (58 + 39)^2}{20} - \text{Step 1}$$

$$= 1328.5 - 1299.6$$

$$= 28.9$$

Step 5. *SS* Imagery X Rehearsal. Square each group sum and add the squares. Then divide each sum by the number of scores in each sum. From the last result, subtract the *SS* Imagery (Step 3), *SS* Rehearsal (Step 4), and Step 1.

$$SSI \text{ X R} = \frac{58^2 + 86^2 + 39^2 + 45^2}{10} - \text{Step 1} - \text{Step 3}$$

$$- \text{Step 4}$$

$$= 14306/10 - 1299.6 - 90 - 28.9$$

$$= 12.1$$

Step 6. *SS* Error. Subtract each of your treatments *SS* from *SS* Total.

$$SS \text{ Error} = 200.4 - 90 - 28.9 - 12.1$$

$$= 69.4$$

Step 7. Determining degrees of freedom.

Step 8. Summary table. Calculate mean squares (*MS*) by dividing *SS* by the number of *df*. Then calculate the *F* ratios by dividing the treatment *MS* by the *MS* Error.

Summary Table of a 2 × 2 ANOVA

Source	SS	df	MS	F	p
Imagery	90.	1	90.	46.6	<.05
Rehearsal	28.9	1	28.9	15.0	<.05
Imagery X Rehearsal	12.1	1	12.1	6.3	<.05
Error	69.4	36	1.9		

> *Step 9.* To determine the significance of the *F* ratio, enter statistical table F with the *df* for the numerator (in this case it is always 1), and with the *df* for the denominator (*df* Error), which is 36, for any effect you are interested in.
>
> We can conclude that the type of words and type of rehearsal both influenced recall. But we should note that the effects of word type were dependent on the type of rehearsal (that is, we obtained an interaction). Elaborative rehearsal produced better recall than rote rehearsal, but the effect was larger on high-imagery words than on low-imagery words.

reason is that statisticians have shown that the analysis of variance is a *robust* statistical test, or one in which violations of its assumptions are unlikely to lead to erroneous conclusions. Most investigators do not even check for violations of the assumptions, but even if they do and they find that the assumptions are violated, the best solution is simply to employ a more conservative level of confidence (say, .01 instead of .05). The fact that a manipulation has influenced the variance of the different experimental conditions may be quite interesting in its own right, because it indicates that the subjects in the condition with the high variance were differentially influenced by the treatment. Understanding this fact may be a clue to understanding behavior in the situation.

Misuses of Statistics

Statistics are used so often that it seems possible to bolster any argument with them. They are employed by politicians, economists, advertisers, psychologists, and many others to support various views, so it is little wonder that people have gained the impression that statistics can be bent to any purpose. But an old adage has it that "Statistics don't lie, statisticians do." Actually, there is probably little to fear from statisticians themselves, because their sophistication permits them to differentiate a true argument based on statistics from a false one. Nonetheless, statistics can be misused to create a false impression. You should be aware of some common misuses, so that you will not be misled by them.

Use of Small or Biased Samples

Many television commercials implicitly mislead us with small and/or biased samples. Viewers see a woman who is asked to test two brands of detergent on her family's greasy and grass-stained clothes. She is pitting her usual product, BAF, against new Super Crud Remover (SCR). BAF goes into one washer, Super Crud Remover goes into the other, and later the woman is shown exclaiming over the better job that SCR did. Announcer: "Are you convinced?" Woman: "Why, yes. I will always use Super Crud Remover from now on. It really gets the crud off my clothes." Even making the unlikely assumption that the whole demonstration was not rigged, observers should know better than to be convinced by such a small sample (one case). If the "experiment" were repeated honestly with a hundred women, would all of them pick Super Crud Remover? The advertiser tries to leave us with the impression that because this one woman prefers the product, everyone (the population) will. But we should be careful about assuming something to be true of the population at large from a sample of one.

Another problem is that a sample of individuals surveyed for such an ad might be deliberately biased. Advertisers are always surveying groups that are likely to be predisposed in their favor anyway, such as people who already own the product. Advertisers ask consumers, "How well do you like your Bass-o-matic?" and then show a small sample of interviews that went well from the manufacturer's point of view. It would be more convincing to sample people who had never used the product and to test the product against its main rivals. Since more advertising claims on television must now be based on facts, this type of commercial is becoming more widely used. In one interesting ad, owners of one type of luxury car are asked to test it against a competitor. Here is a case in which the sample tested is expected to be biased *against* the new product and for their old product, so if a preference is found for the new product, it seems to argue much more strongly for the new product.

Whenever you hear about preferences that people have exhibited, you should ask two questions about the sample: (1) How large was it? (2) How were people chosen to be in it?

The exaggerated graph.   A common way to show or hide differences in graphs is to exaggerate the results being plotted. This involves changing the scale on the graph in order to show off a difference, or (more rarely) to hide a difference. Suppose that the number of murders in a city increased from 72 to 80 to 91 over three years. The next year, the mayor is running for reelection and is eager to show that the city has been safe for the last three years under her administration. So her campaign workers draw up the graph shown in the left of figure B–5. By making the scale on the *y*-axis very long, they create the impression that the murder rate is fairly steady. In the same year, the city police are arguing that they need higher staffing levels. They want to show that the city is becoming more unsafe, so they depict the murder rate as increasing steeply by changing the scale, as in the right-hand graph of figure B–5.

The facts are shown accurately in both groups. However, the left graph gives the impression that the murder rate is increasing very gradually, hardly worth worrying about. (Hasn't the mayor done a good job leading the city?) The right graph, on the other hand, creates the impression that the murder rate is increasing dramatically. (Don't we need more police?)

FIGURE B–5.

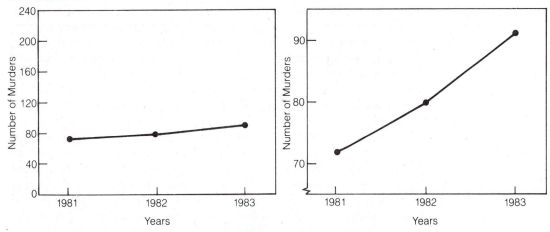

Variation in scales. The graph at the left seems to show the murder rate to be increasing only slightly, whereas the one at the right shows the rate going up dramatically. Yet, both graphs actually show the murder rate accurately—the difference is in the scale on the y-axis. It is important to examine a graph carefully and note the scale of measurement, since scale changes can make small differences look large and vice versa.

These graphing techniques are common. In fact, there are exaggerated scales used in some of the graphs in this book to show patterns of results more clearly. You should always look carefully to see what the scale is in a graph. With experimental data, it is more important to determine whether a difference is statistically reliable than to determine whether the difference appears "large" when graphed.

Absent or Inappropriate Comparisons

A common ploy used in advertising is to say that some product has x percent more of something good or y percent less of something bad. "Buy the new Thunderbolt, since it gives 27 percent better gas mileage." This sounds convincing until you stop to ask yourself, "27 percent better than what?" A missing comparison here makes the statistic completely meaningless. Perhaps the Thunderbolt gets 27 percent better mileage than a two-ton tank, which is hardly an argument for buying it.

Even when a specific comparison is made, it is often still inappropriate. The claim is often made in advertising that a product is better than last year's model. "Buy the new, improved, Thunderbolt. It gets 27 percent better mileage than last year's model." Of course, it could still be a real dog, even if it's better than last year's dog. What the consumer would really like is a comparison of the mileage efficiency of the new Thunderbolt with other new cars in roughly the same class, as is now provided by government testing.

Another problem in making comparisons is that often there is no information on the reliability of differences. In one commercial, two cars of the same make and year were filled with one gallon of gas, and test-driven at a constant speed around a track. The difference in the test was the type of gasoline used. One car stopped before the other, and the viewers were supposed to conclude that the sponsor's gasoline was superior to the other brand. But only after a long series of comparisons could a researcher statistically test for a reliable difference between the two types of gas. This is the same problem as occurs in the case of BAF versus Super Crud Remover; the sample of observations is too small.

In general, watch to make sure that in statements involving a comparison, the object of comparison is described and is appropriate. There should also be some statement about whether or not any differences are statistically reliable.

The Gambler's Fallacy

Statistical tests are based on probability theory: the theory of expectations about the likelihood of random events. It is interesting to note that people's perceptions of the randomness of events do not agree in some important respects with ideas from probability theory. People often draw conclusions that seem irrational when judged by the logic of probability theory. There is much interesting research on this phenomenon (for example, Tversky and Kahneman, 1971, 1974). Here we will examine one of the most common mistakes in judgments of probability.

Imagine a person flipping a coin 1,000 times. If it is a fair coin, it should come up heads about 500 times and tails about 500 times. The probability of its coming up heads over a large number of trials is 0.50, but of course even a fair coin will probably not come up heads exactly 500 times in 1,000 flips: it might come up 490 or 505. Yet the result is fairly close. Let us now take the case of a person betting on whether the coin will come up heads or tails. If the situation is truly random, a gambler has a probability of 0.50 of winning on any particular trial. Imagine that on five trials in a row, the gambler bets $5 that the coin will come up heads and each time it comes up tails. Of course, the fact that the coin comes up tails five times in a row is unusual, and the chances of such an event are quite low (.03). The gambler notes this odd occurrence. On the next bet, he doubles his bet to $10 and again bets on heads. Now he is more certain that the coin will come up heads.

The logic the gambler uses is as follows. "The coin is a fair coin. On the average, it will come up heads half the time and tails half the time. The coin has just come up tails five times in a row. Therefore, it is due to come up heads to even things up, because on the average it will come up heads half the time. So I should bet on heads, and even increase my bet." More generally, the logic is: "If the game is truly random and I am losing, then I should keep playing, because my luck is bound to change for the better." This kind of logic keeps gambling casinos at Las Vegas and Atlantic City humming and wipes out fortunes from otherwise intelligent people.

The fallacy of the argument is in applying the laws of probability—such as a fair coin coming up heads half the time—that hold only over tremendously large numbers of events. The laws cannot be applied to small runs. What the gambler overlooks is that the flips of the coin are independent events; what happened on previous flips does not influence what happens next. If the coin came up tails five times in a row, this does not increase the probability of heads on the next throw. It is still 0.50. The coin does not have a memory for previous trials, as the gambler seems to assume implicitly. The gambler should not feel any more certain on the sixth trial than he or she did on the first five. The probability of heads showing has not changed.

In some sense, the gambler's mistake is natural. There is a ring of truth to the argument, and it is based on true laws of probability. Over a very large series of throws, a fair coin will come up heads 50 percent of the time. The error comes in applying to a small series what is true over a very large series of events. The laws do not apply to small series of random events as well. With, say, 10,000,000 coin flips, heads will come up almost exactly 50 percent of the time. But if a gambler takes a small series of the larger number, say five flips, heads could come up either zero or five times with a probability of 0.06. These outcomes (all heads or all tails) are not terribly likely, but they are not vanishingly small, either.

SUMMARY

1. Understanding some elementary principles about statistics is crucial to the conduct of psychological research. There are two branches of statistics, descriptive and inferential.

2. Descriptive statistics are used to summarize and organize raw data. There are graphical methods for doing this, such as histograms and frequency polygons. However, the primary summary measures are those of central tendency of a distribution and dispersion of a distribution.

3. The primary measure of central tendency is the mean of the distribution, or what is usually called the average of the scores. The median (the middlemost score) is sometimes used, especially for distributions with extreme scores. The primary measures of dispersion are the standard deviation and variance. The standard deviation is used more often in descriptive statistics, and the variance is used primarily in inferential statistics. Most distributions in psychology are assumed to be normal, which means that the mean, median, and mode all fall in the same place; that the distribution is symmetrical; and that a certain proportion of scores falls under each part of the normal curve.

4. Inferential statistics allow us to make inferences about the reliability of differences among conditions. We want to infer from a sample of scores what the case is for the populations involved. A great variety of tests are used in inferential statistics. A similar

logic is applied in all. An alternative hypothesis is tested against the null hypothesis, which holds that there are no differences among groups in the experiment. Computations are performed that give rise to a value. This value is then compared with a distribution of values in a table that informs us as to what level of confidence we can have in rejecting the null hypothesis.

5. We use a z-score test for comparing a sample with a known population to see whether the sample comes from the same population. To determine whether two groups, an experimental and a control, differ from one another, we use the t test or Mann-Whitney U test, which apply when two independent groups of subjects are employed; and the sign test, t test, and Wilcoxon signed-ranks test, which apply when the measures in the two conditions are related (either by using a within-subjects design or by matching subjects). The Mann-Whitney and Wilcoxon tests are nonparametric statistical tests, since they do not make any assumptions about the population parameters underlying the sample observations that are actually used.

6. The analysis of variance is the important statistical procedure used in making comparisons among more than two groups. The simple analysis of variance is used in testing for reliability when one independent variable is manipulated. More complicated multifactor analyses are used when two or more independent variables are manipulated simultaneously. These multifactor designs are especially important in that they allow us to assess the interaction of factors that determine behavior.

7. Mark Twain wrote that "there are three kinds of lies—lies, damned lies, and statistics." Some ways in which statistics can be misused include drawing conclusions from small or biased samples; exaggerating the scales on graphs for effect; making inappropriate comparisons; and assuming that the laws of probability that hold for huge samples of observations can be generalized to small samples (as in the gambler's fallacy). Statistics themselves do not lie, but they can be used to give misleading impressions.

KEY TERMS

absolute mean deviation	dispersion
alpha level	distribution of sample means
analysis of variance	experimental hypothesis
arithmetic mean	F test
between-groups variance	frequency distribution
between-subjects design	frequency polygon
central tendency	histogram
correlation coefficient	homogeneity of variance
degrees of freedom	inferential statistics
descriptive statistics	inflection point
directional test	interaction effect

level of confidence (or level of significance)
main effect
Mann-Whitney U test
mean
median
multifactor analysis of variance
nondirectional test
nonparametric tests
normal curve
null hypothesis
one-tailed test
parameters
parametric tests
Pearson r
population
power of a statistical test
qualitative variation
quantitative variation

random sample
range
related measures design
reliability
robust tests
sample
sign test
simple (one-factor) analysis of variance
standard deviation
standard error of the mean
statistics
t test
two-tailed test
type I error
type II error
variance
Wilcoxon signed-ranks test
within-groups variance
z score (or standard score)

APPENDIX

Statistical Tables

TABLE A.   Proportions of Area Under the Normal Curve

How to Use Table A: The values in Table A represent the proportion of areas in the standard normal curve, which has a mean of 0, a standard deviation of 1.00, and a total area equal to 1.00. To use Table A, the raw score must first be transformed into a z score. Column A represents this z score; Column B represents the distance between the mean of the standard normal distribution (0) and the z score; and Column C represents the proportion of area beyond a given z.

Column A gives the positive z score.

Column B gives the area between the mean and z. Since the curve is symmetrical, areas for negative z scores are the same as for positive ones.

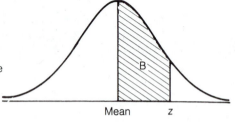

Column C gives the area which is beyond z.

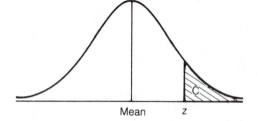

(A) z	(B) area between mean and z	(C) area beyond z	(A) z	(B) area between mean and z	(C) area beyond z	(A) z	(B) area between mean and z	(C) area beyond z
0.00	.0000	.5000	0.20	.0793	.4207	0.40	.1554	.3446
0.01	.0040	.4960	0.21	.0832	.4168	0.41	.1591	.3409
0.02	.0080	.4920	0.22	.0871	.4129	0.42	.1628	.3372
0.03	.0120	.4880	0.23	.0910	.4090	0.43	.1664	.3336
0.04	.0160	.4840	0.24	.0948	.4052	0.44	.1700	.3300
0.05	.0199	.4801	0.25	.0987	.4013	0.45	.1736	.3264
0.06	.0239	.4761	0.26	.1026	.3974	0.46	.1772	.3228
0.07	.0279	.4721	0.27	.1064	.3936	0.47	.1808	.3192
0.08	.0319	.4681	0.28	.1103	.3897	0.48	.1844	.3156
0.09	.0359	.4641	0.29	.1141	.3859	0.49	.1879	.3121
0.10	.0398	.4602	0.30	.1179	.3821	0.50	.1915	.3085
0.11	.0438	.4562	0.31	.1217	.3783	0.51	.1950	.3050
0.12	.0478	.4522	0.32	.1255	.3745	0.52	.1985	.3015
0.13	.0517	.4483	0.33	.1293	.3707	0.53	.2019	.2981
0.14	.0557	.4443	0.34	.1331	.3669	0.54	.2054	.2946
0.15	.0596	.4404	0.35	.1368	.3632	0.55	.2088	.2912
0.16	.0636	.4364	0.36	.1406	.3594	0.56	.2123	.2877
0.17	.0675	.4325	0.37	.1443	.3557	0.57	.2157	.2843
0.18	.0714	.4286	0.38	.1480	.3520	0.58	.2190	.2810
0.19	.0753	.4247	0.39	.1517	.3483	0.59	.2224	.2776

TABLE A *(Continued).*

(A) z	(B) area between mean and z	(C) area beyond z	(A) z	(B) area between mean and z	(C) area beyond z	(A) z	(B) area between mean and z	(C) area beyond z
0.60	.2257	.2743	1.08	.3599	.1401	1.56	.4406	.0594
0.61	.2291	.2709	1.09	.3621	.1379	1.57	.4418	.0582
0.62	.2324	.2676	1.10	.3643	.1357	1.58	.4429	.0571
0.63	.2357	.2643	1.11	.3665	.1335	1.59	.4441	.0559
0.64	.2389	.2611	1.12	.3686	.1314	1.60	.4452	.0548
0.65	.2422	.2578	1.13	.3708	.1292	1.61	.4463	.0537
0.66	.2454	.2546	1.14	.3729	.1271	1.62	.4474	.0526
0.67	.2486	.2514	1.15	.3749	.1251	1.63	.4484	.0516
0.68	.2517	.2483	1.16	.3770	.1230	1.64	.4495	.0505
0.69	.2549	.2451	1.17	.3790	.1210	1.65	.4505	.0495
0.70	.2580	.2420	1.18	.3810	.1190	1.66	.4515	.0485
0.71	.2611	.2389	1.19	.3830	.1170	1.67	.4525	.0475
0.72	.2642	.2358	1.20	.3849	.1151	1.68	.4535	.0465
0.73	.2673	.2327	1.21	.3869	.1131	1.69	.4545	.0455
0.74	.2704	.2296	1.22	.3888	.1112	1.70	.4554	.0446
0.75	.2734	.2266	1.23	.3907	.1093	1.71	.4564	.0436
0.76	.2764	.2236	1.24	.3925	.1075	1.72	.4573	.0427
0.77	.2794	.2206	1.25	.3944	.1056	1.73	.4582	.0418
0.78	.2823	.2177	1.26	.3962	.1038	1.74	.4591	.0409
0.79	.2852	.2148	1.27	.3980	.1020	1.75	.4599	.0401
0.80	.2881	.2119	1.28	.3997	.1003	1.76	.4608	.0392
0.81	.2910	.2090	1.29	.4015	.0985	1.77	.4616	.0384
0.82	.2939	.2061	1.30	.4032	.0968	1.78	.4625	.0375
0.83	.2967	.2033	1.31	.4049	.0951	1.79	.4633	.0367
0.84	.2995	.2005	1.32	.4066	.0934	1.80	.4641	.0359
0.85	.3023	.1977	1.33	.4082	.0918	1.81	.4649	.0351
0.86	.3051	.1949	1.34	.4099	.0901	1.82	.4656	.0344
0.87	.3078	.1922	1.35	.4115	.0885	1.83	.4664	.0336
0.88	.3106	.1894	1.36	.4131	.0869	1.84	.4671	.0329
0.89	.3133	.1867	1.37	.4147	.0853	1.85	.4678	.0322
0.90	.3159	.1841	1.38	.4162	.0838	1.86	.4686	.0314
0.91	.3186	.1814	1.39	.4177	.0823	1.87	.4693	.0307
0.92	.3212	.1788	1.40	.4192	.0808	1.88	.4699	.0301
0.93	.3238	.1762	1.41	.4207	.0793	1.89	.4706	.0294
0.94	.3264	.1736	1.42	.4222	.0778	1.90	.4713	.0287
0.95	.3289	.1711	1.43	.4236	.0764	1.91	.4719	.0281
0.96	.3315	.1685	1.44	.4251	.0749	1.92	.4726	.0274
0.97	.3340	.1660	1.45	.4265	.0735	1.93	.4732	.0268
0.98	.3365	.1635	1.46	.4279	.0721	1.94	.4738	.0262
0.99	.3389	.1611	1.47	.4292	.0708	1.95	.4744	.0256
1.00	.3413	.1587	1.48	.4306	.0694	1.96	.4750	.0250
1.01	.3438	.1562	1.49	.4319	.0681	1.97	.4756	.0244
1.02	.3461	.1539	1.50	.4332	.0668	1.98	.4761	.0239
1.03	.3485	.1515	1.51	.4345	.0655	1.99	.4767	.0233
1.04	.3508	.1492	1.52	.4357	.0643	2.00	.4772	.0228
1.05	.3531	.1469	1.53	.4370	.0630	2.01	.4778	.0222
1.06	.3554	.1446	1.54	.4382	.0618	2.02	.4783	.0217
1.07	.3577	.1423	1.55	.4394	.0606	2.03	.4788	.0212

TABLE A *(Continued)*.

(A) z	(B) area between mean and z	(C) area beyond z	(A) z	(B) area between mean and z	(C) area beyond z	(A) z	(B) area between mean and z	(C) area beyond z
2.04	.4793	.0207	2.50	.4938	.0062	2.96	.4985	.0015
2.05	.4798	.0202	2.51	.4940	.0060	2.97	.4985	.0015
2.06	.4803	.0197	2.52	.4941	.0059	2.98	.4986	.0014
2.07	.4808	.0192	2.53	.4943	.0057	2.99	.4986	.0014
2.08	.4812	.0188	2.54	.4945	.0055			
2.09	.4817	.0183				3.00	.4987	.0013
2.10	.4821	.0179	2.55	.4946	.0054	3.01	.4987	.0013
2.11	.4826	.0174	2.56	.4948	.0052	3.02	.4987	.0013
2.12	.4830	.0170	2.57	.4949	.0051	3.03	.4988	.0012
2.13	.4834	.0166	2.58	.4951	.0049	3.04	.4988	.0012
2.14	.4838	.0162	2.59	.4952	.0048			
2.15	.4842	.0158	2.60	.4953	.0047	3.05	.4989	.0011
2.16	.4846	.0154	2.61	.4955	.0045	3.06	.4989	.0011
2.17	.4850	.0150	2.62	.4956	.0044	3.07	.4989	.0011
2.18	.4854	.0146	2.63	.4957	.0043	3.08	.4990	.0010
2.19	.4857	.0143	2.64	.4959	.0041	3.09	.4990	.0010
2.20	.4861	.0139	2.65	.4960	.0040	3.10	.4990	.0010
2.21	.4864	.0136	2.66	.4961	.0039	3.11	.4991	.0009
2.22	.4868	.0132	2.67	.4962	.0038	3.12	.4991	.0009
2.23	.4871	.0129	2.68	.4963	.0037	3.13	.4991	.0009
2.24	.4875	.0125	2.69	.4964	.0036	3.14	.4992	.0008
2.25	.4878	.0122	2.70	.4965	.0035	3.15	.4992	.0008
2.26	.4881	.0119	2.71	.4966	.0034	3.16	.4992	.0008
2.27	.4884	.0116	2.72	.4967	.0033	3.17	.4992	.0008
2.28	.4887	.0113	2.73	.4968	.0032	3.18	.4993	.0007
2.29	.4890	.0110	2.74	.4969	.0031	3.19	.4993	.0007
2.30	.4893	.0107	2.75	.4970	.0030	3.20	.4993	.0007
2.31	.4896	.0104	2.76	.4971	.0029	3.21	.4993	.0007
2.32	.4898	.0102	2.77	.4972	.0028	3.22	.4994	.0006
2.33	.4901	.0099	2.78	.4973	.0027	3.23	.4994	.0006
2.34	.4904	.0096	2.79	.4974	.0026	3.24	.4994	.0006
2.35	.4906	.0094	2.80	.4974	.0026	3.25	.4994	.0006
2.36	.4909	.0091	2.81	.4975	.0025	3.30	.4995	.0005
2.37	.4911	.0089	2.82	.4976	.0024	3.35	.4996	.0004
2.38	.4913	.0087	2.83	.4977	.0023	3.40	.4997	.0003
2.39	.4916	.0084	2.84	.4977	.0023	3.45	.4997	.0003
2.40	.4918	.0082	2.85	.4978	.0022	3.50	.4998	.0002
2.41	.4920	.0080	2.86	.4979	.0021	3.60	.4998	.0002
2.42	.4922	.0078	2.87	.4979	.0021	3.70	.4999	.0001
2.43	.4925	.0075	2.88	.4980	.0020	3.80	.4999	.0001
2.44	.4927	.0073	2.89	.4981	.0019	3.90	.49995	.00005
2.45	.4929	.0071	2.90	.4981	.0019	4.00	.49997	.00003
2.46	.4931	.0069	2.91	.4982	.0018			
2.47	.4932	.0068	2.92	.4982	.0018			
2.48	.4934	.0066	2.93	.4983	.0017			
2.49	.4936	.0064	2.94	.4984	.0016			
			2.95	.4984	.0016			

TABLE B. **Critical Values of the *U* Statistic of the Mann-Whitney Test**

To use these tables, first decide what level of significance you want with either a one- or a two-tailed test. For example, if you want p = .05, two-tailed, use *(c)*. Then locate the number of cases or measures (n) in both groups in the particular subtable you have chosen. The U value you have calculated must be *less* than that at the appropriate place in the table. For example, if you had 18 subjects in each group of an experiment, and calculated U = 90, then you could conclude that the null hypothesis can be rejected, because the critical U value with groups of these sizes is 99 (see subtable (*c*)).

(a) Critical Values of *U* for a One-Tailed Test at .001 or for a Two-Tailed Test at .002

n_1 \ n_2	9	10	11	12	13	14	15	16	17	18	19	20
1												
2												
3									0	0	0	0
4		0	0	0	1	1	1	2	2	3	3	3
5	1	1	2	2	3	3	4	5	5	6	7	7
6	2	3	4	4	5	6	7	8	9	10	11	12
7	3	5	6	7	8	9	10	11	13	14	15	16
8	5	6	8	9	11	12	14	15	17	18	20	21
9	7	8	10	12	14	15	17	19	21	23	25	26
10	8	10	12	14	17	19	21	23	25	27	29	32
11	10	12	15	17	20	22	24	27	29	32	34	37
12	12	14	17	20	23	25	28	31	34	37	40	42
13	14	17	20	23	26	29	32	35	38	42	45	48
14	15	19	22	25	29	32	36	39	43	46	50	54
15	17	21	24	28	32	36	40	43	47	51	55	59
16	19	23	27	31	35	39	43	48	52	56	60	65
17	21	25	29	34	38	43	47	52	57	61	66	70
18	23	27	32	37	42	46	51	56	61	66	71	76
19	25	29	34	40	45	50	55	60	66	71	77	82
20	26	32	37	42	48	54	59	65	70	76	82	88

SOURCE: Adapted from Tables 1, 3, 5, and 7 of D. Aube, "Extended Tables for the Mann-Whitney Statistic," *Bulletin of the Institute of Educational Research at Indiana University*, 1953, 1, No. 2. From S. Siegel, *Nonparametric Statistics for the Behavior Sciences*. New York: McGraw-Hill Book Company, 1956. Reprinted by permission of the Institute of Educational Research and McGraw-Hill Book Company.

TABLE B *(Continued).*   *(b)* Critical Values of U for a One-Tailed Test at .01 or for a Two-Tailed Test at .02

n_1 \ n_2	9	10	11	12	13	14	15	16	17	18	19	20
1												
2					0	0	0	0	0	0	1	1
3	1	1	1	2	2	2	3	3	4	4	4	5
4	3	3	4	5	5	6	7	7	8	9	9	10
5	5	6	7	8	9	10	11	12	13	14	15	16
6	7	8	9	11	12	13	15	16	18	19	20	22
7	9	11	12	14	16	17	19	21	23	24	26	28
8	11	13	15	17	20	22	24	26	28	30	32	34
9	14	16	18	21	23	26	28	31	33	36	38	40
10	16	19	22	24	27	30	33	36	38	41	44	47
11	18	22	25	28	31	34	37	41	44	47	50	53
12	21	24	28	31	35	38	42	46	49	53	56	60
13	23	27	31	35	39	43	47	51	55	59	63	67
14	26	30	34	38	43	47	51	56	60	65	69	73
15	28	33	37	42	47	51	56	61	66	70	75	80
16	31	36	41	46	51	56	61	66	71	76	82	87
17	33	38	44	49	55	60	66	71	77	82	88	93
18	36	41	47	53	59	65	70	76	82	88	94	100
19	38	44	50	56	63	69	75	82	88	94	101	107
20	40	47	53	60	67	73	80	87	93	100	107	114

(c) Critical Values of U for a One-Tailed Test at .025 or for a Two-Tailed Test at .05

n_1 \ n_2	9	10	11	12	13	14	15	16	17	18	19	20
1												
2	0	0	1	1	1	1	1	1	2	2	2	2
3	2	3	3	4	4	5	5	6	6	7	7	8
4	4	5	6	7	8	9	10	11	11	12	13	13
5	7	8	9	11	12	13	14	15	17	18	19	20
6	10	11	13	14	16	17	19	21	22	24	25	27
7	12	14	16	18	20	22	24	26	28	30	32	34
8	15	17	19	22	24	26	29	31	34	36	38	41
9	17	20	23	26	28	31	34	37	39	42	45	48
10	20	23	26	29	33	36	39	42	45	48	52	55
11	23	26	30	33	37	40	44	47	51	55	58	62
12	26	29	33	37	41	45	49	53	57	61	65	69
13	28	33	37	41	45	50	54	59	63	67	72	76
14	31	36	40	45	50	55	59	64	67	74	78	83
15	34	39	44	49	54	59	64	70	75	80	85	90
16	37	42	47	53	59	64	70	75	81	86	92	98
17	39	45	51	57	63	67	75	81	87	93	99	105
18	42	48	55	61	67	74	80	86	93	99	106	112
19	45	52	58	65	72	78	85	92	99	106	113	119
20	48	55	62	69	76	83	90	98	105	112	119	127

TABLE B *(Continued).* (d) Critical Values of *U* for a One-Tailed Test at .05 or for a Two-Tailed Test at .10

n_1 \ n_2	9	10	11	12	13	14	15	16	17	18	19	20
1											0	0
2	1	1	1	2	2	2	3	3	3	4	4	4
3	3	4	5	5	6	7	7	8	9	9	10	11
4	6	7	8	9	10	11	12	14	15	16	17	18
5	9	11	12	13	15	16	18	19	20	22	23	25
6	12	14	16	17	19	21	23	25	26	28	30	32
7	15	17	19	21	24	26	28	30	33	35	37	39
8	18	20	23	26	28	31	33	36	39	41	44	47
9	21	24	27	30	33	36	39	42	45	48	51	54
10	24	27	31	34	37	41	44	48	51	55	58	62
11	27	31	34	38	42	46	50	54	57	61	65	69
12	30	34	38	42	47	51	55	60	64	68	72	77
13	33	37	42	47	51	56	61	65	70	75	80	84
14	36	41	46	51	56	61	66	71	77	82	87	92
15	39	44	50	55	61	66	72	77	83	88	94	100
16	42	48	54	60	65	71	77	83	89	95	101	107
17	45	51	57	64	70	77	83	89	96	102	109	115
18	48	55	61	68	75	82	88	95	102	109	116	123
19	51	58	65	72	80	87	94	101	109	116	123	130
20	54	62	69	77	84	92	100	107	115	123	130	138

TABLE C.   Distribution for the Sign Test

Alpha levels of the sign test for pairs of observations ranging from 3 to 41. x denotes the number of exceptions (the number of times the difference between conditions is in the unexpected direction), while the p level indicates the probability that that number of exceptions could occur by chance. If there are 28 paired observations and 20 are ordered in the expected direction, while only 8 are exceptions, the probability that this could occur by chance is .018.

x	p	x	p	x	p	x	p	x	p	x	p
n = 3		n = 12		n = 19		n = 25		n = 31		n = 37	
0	.125	1	.003	3	.002	5	.002	7	.002	10	.004
n = 4		2	.019	4	.010	6	.007	8	.005	11	.010
0	.062	3	.073	5	.032	7	.022	9	.015	12	.024
1	.312	4	.194	6	.084	8	.051	10	.035	13	.049
n = 5		n = 13		7	.180	9	.115	11	.075	14	.094
0	.031	1	.002			10	.212	12	.141	15	.162
1	.188	2	.011	n = 20				n = 32		n = 38	
n = 6		3	.016	3	.001	n = 26		8	.004	10	.003
0	.016	4	.133	4	.006	6	.005	9	.010	11	.007
1	.109	n = 14		5	.021	7	.014	10	.025	12	.017
2	.344	1	.001	6	.058	8	.038	11	.055	13	.036
n = 7		2	.006	7	.132	9	.084	12	.108	14	.072
0	.008	3	.029	n = 21		10	.163	13	.189	15	.128
1	.062	4	.090	4	.004	n = 27		n = 33		n = 39	
2	.227	5	.212	5	.013	6	.003	8	.002	11	.005
n = 8		n = 15		6	.039	7	.010	9	.007	12	.012
0	.004	1	.000	7	.095	8	.026	10	.018	13	.027
1	.035	2	.004	8	.192	9	.061	11	.040	14	.054
2	.145	3	.018	n = 22		10	.124	12	.081	15	.100
n = 9		4	.059	4	.002	11	.221	13	.148	16	.168
0	.002	5	.151	5	.008	n = 28		n = 34		n = 40	
1	.020	n = 16		6	.026	6	.002	9	.005	11	.003
2	.090	2	.002	7	.067	7	.006	10	.012	12	.008
3	.254	3	.011	8	.143	8	.018	11	.029	13	.019
n = 10		4	.038	n = 23		9	.044	12	.061	14	.040
0	.001	5	.105	4	.001	10	.092	13	.115	15	.077
1	.011	6	.227	5	.005	11	.172	14	.196	16	.134
2	.055	n = 17		6	.017	n = 29		n = 35		n = 41	
3	.172	2	.001	7	.047	7	.004	9	.003	11	.002
n = 11		3	.006	8	.105	8	.012	10	.008	12	.006
0	.000	4	.025	9	.202	9	.031	11	.020	13	.014
1	.006	5	.072	n = 24		10	.068	12	.045	14	.030
2	.033	6	.166	5	.008	11	.132	13	.088	15	.059
3	.113	n = 18		6	.011	n = 30		14	.155	16	.106
4	.274	3	.004	7	.032	7	.003	n = 36		17	.174
		4	.015	8	.076	8	.008	9	.002	n = 42	
		5	.048	9	.154	9	.021	10	.006	12	.004
		6	.119			10	.049	11	.014	13	.010
		7	.240			11	.100	12	.033	14	.022
						12	.181	13	.066	15	.044
								14	.121	16	.082
								15	.203	17	.140

TABLE D. **Critical Values of Wilcoxon's *T* Statistic for the Matched-Pairs Signed-Ranks Test**

In using this table, first locate the number of *pairs* of scores in the *n* column. The critical values for several levels of significance are listed in the columns to the right. For example, if *n* were 15 and the computed value 19, it would be concluded that since 19 is less than 25, the difference between conditions is significant beyond the .02 level of significance for a two-tailed test.

	Level of significance for one-tailed test		
	.025	.01	.005
	Level of significance for two-tailed test		
n	.05	.02	.01
6	1	—	—
7	2	0	—
8	4	2	0
9	6	3	2
10	8	5	3
11	11	7	5
12	14	10	7
13	17	13	10
14	21	16	13
15	25	20	16
16	30	24	19
17	35	28	23
18	40	33	28
19	46	38	32
20	52	43	37
21	59	49	43
22	66	56	49
23	73	62	55
24	81	69	61
25	90	77	68

Note that *n* is the number of matched pairs.

SOURCE: Adapted from Table I of F. Wilcoxon, *Some Rapid Approximate Statistical Procedures*, (Rev. ed.) New York: American Cyanamid Company, 1964. Taken from S. Siegel, *Nonparametric Statistics for the Behavioral Sciences*. New York: McGraw-Hill Book Company, 1956. Reprinted by permission of the American Cyanamid Company and McGraw-Hill Book Company.

TABLE E.   Critical Values of *t*

To find the appropriate value of *t*, read across the row that contains the number of degrees of freedom in your experiment. The columns are determined by the level of significance you have chosen. The value of *t* you obtain must be *greater* than that in the table in order to be significant. For example, with *df* = 15 and *p* = .05 (two-tailed test), your *t* value must be greater than 2.131.

	Level of significance for one-tailed test					
	.10	.05	.025	.01	.005	.0005
	Level of significance for two-tailed test					
df	.20	.10	.05	.02	.01	.001
1	3.078	6.314	12.706	31.821	63.657	636.619
2	1.886	2.920	4.303	6.965	9.925	31.598
3	1.638	2.353	3.182	4.541	5.841	12.941
4	1.533	2.132	2.776	3.747	4.604	8.610
5	1.476	2.015	2.571	3.365	4.032	6.859
6	1.440	1.943	2.447	3.143	3.707	5.959
7	1.415	1.895	2.365	2.998	3.449	5.405
8	1.397	1.860	2.306	2.896	3.355	5.041
9	1.383	1.833	2.262	2.821	3.250	4.781
10	1.372	1.812	2.228	2.764	3.169	4.587
11	1.363	1.796	2.201	2.718	3.106	4.437
12	1.356	1.782	2.179	2.681	3.055	4.318
13	1.350	1.771	2.160	2.650	3.012	4.221
14	1.345	1.761	2.145	2.624	2.977	4.140
15	1.341	1.753	2.131	2.602	2.947	4.073
16	1.337	1.746	2.120	2.583	2.921	4.015
17	1.333	1.740	2.110	2.567	2.898	3.965
18	1.330	1.734	2.101	2.552	2.878	3.922
19	1.328	1.729	2.093	2.539	2.861	3.883
20	1.325	1.725	2.086	2.528	2.845	3.850
21	1.323	1.721	2.080	2.518	2.831	3.819
22	1.321	1.717	2.074	2.508	2.819	3.792
23	1.319	1.714	2.069	2.500	2.807	3.767
24	1.318	1.711	2.064	2.492	2.797	3.745
25	1.316	1.708	2.060	2.485	2.787	3.725
26	1.315	1.706	2.056	2.479	2.779	3.707
27	1.314	1.703	2.052	2.473	2.771	3.690
28	1.313	1.701	2.048	2.467	2.763	3.674
29	1.311	1.699	2.045	2.462	2.756	3.659
30	1.310	1.697	2.042	2.457	2.750	3.646
40	1.303	1.684	2.021	2.423	2.704	3.551
60	1.296	1.671	2.000	2.390	2.660	3.460
120	1.289	1.658	1.980	2.358	2.617	3.373
∞	1.282	1.645	1.960	2.326	2.576	3.291

Table E is taken from Table III of Fisher & Yates: *Statistical Tables for Biological, Agricultural and Medical Research*, Published by Longman Group Ltd. London (previously published by Oliver & Boyd Ltd. Edinburgh) and by permission of the authors and publishers.

TABLE F. **Critical Values of the *F* Distribution**

Find the location appropriate values in the table by looking up the degrees of freedom in the numerator and denominator of the *F*-ratio. After you have decided on the level of significance desired, the obtained *F*-ratio must be *greater* than that in the table. For example, with $p = .05$ and 10 *df* in the numerator and 28 in the denominator, your *F* value must be greater than 2.19 to be reliable.

df for denom.	α	1	2	3	4	5	6	7	8	9
					df for numerator					
3	.25	2.02	2.28	2.36	2.39	2.41	2.42	2.43	2.44	2.44
	.10	5.54	5.46	5.39	5.34	5.31	5.28	5.27	5.25	5.24
	.05	10.1	9.55	9.28	9.12	9.01	8.94	8.89	8.85	8.81
	.025	17.4	16.0	15.4	15.1	14.9	14.7	14.6	14.5	14.5
	.01	34.1	30.8	29.5	28.7	28.2	27.9	27.7	27.5	27.4
	.001	167	148	141	137	135	133	132	131	130
4	.25	1.81	2.00	2.05	2.06	2.07	2.08	2.08	2.08	2.08
	.10	4.54	4.32	4.19	4.11	4.05	4.01	3.98	3.95	3.94
	.05	7.71	6.94	6.59	6.39	6.26	6.16	6.09	6.04	6.00
	.025	12.2	10.6	9.98	9.60	9.36	9.20	9.07	8.98	8.90
	.01	21.2	18.0	16.7	16.0	15.5	15.2	15.0	14.8	14.7
	.001	74.1	61.2	56.2	53.4	51.7	50.5	49.7	49.0	48.5
5	.25	1.69	1.85	1.88	1.89	1.89	1.89	1.89	1.89	1.89
	.10	4.06	3.78	3.62	3.52	3.45	3.40	3.37	3.34	3.32
	.05	6.61	5.79	5.41	5.19	5.05	4.95	4.88	4.82	4.77
	.025	10.0	8.43	7.76	7.39	7.15	6.98	6.85	6.76	6.68
	.01	16.3	13.3	12.1	11.4	11.0	10.7	10.5	10.3	10.2
	.001	47.2	37.1	33.2	31.1	29.8	28.8	28.2	27.6	27.2
6	.25	1.62	1.76	1.78	1.79	1.79	1.78	1.78	1.78	1.77
	.10	3.78	3.46	3.29	3.18	3.11	3.05	3.01	2.98	2.96
	.05	5.99	5.14	4.76	4.53	4.39	4.28	4.21	4.15	4.10
	.025	8.81	7.26	6.60	6.23	5.99	5.82	5.70	5.60	5.52
	.01	13.8	10.9	9.78	9.15	8.75	8.47	8.26	8.10	7.98
	.001	35.5	27.0	23.7	21.9	20.8	20.0	19.5	19.0	18.7
7	.25	1.57	1.70	1.72	1.72	1.71	1.71	1.70	1.70	1.69
	.10	3.59	3.26	3.07	2.96	2.88	2.83	2.78	2.75	2.72
	.05	5.59	4.74	4.35	4.12	3.97	3.87	3.79	3.73	3.68
	.025	8.07	6.54	5.89	5.52	5.29	5.12	4.99	4.90	4.82
	.01	12.2	9.55	8.45	7.85	7.46	7.19	6.99	6.84	6.72
	.001	29.2	21.7	18.8	17.2	16.2	15.5	15.0	14.6	14.3
8	.25	1.54	1.66	1.67	1.66	1.66	1.65	1.64	1.64	1.63
	.10	3.46	3.11	2.92	2.81	2.73	2.67	2.62	2.59	2.56
	.05	5.32	4.46	4.07	3.84	3.69	3.58	3.50	3.44	3.39
	.025	7.57	6.06	5.42	5.05	4.82	4.65	4.53	4.43	4.36
	.01	11.3	8.65	7.59	7.01	6.63	6.37	6.18	6.03	5.91
	.001	25.4	18.5	15.8	14.4	13.5	12.9	12.4	12.0	11.8
9	.25	1.51	1.62	1.63	1.63	1.62	1.61	1.60	1.60	1.59
	.10	3.36	3.01	2.81	2.69	2.61	2.55	2.51	2.47	2.44
	.05	5.12	4.26	3.86	3.63	3.48	3.37	3.29	3.23	3.18
	.025	7.21	5.71	5.08	4.72	4.48	4.32	4.20	4.10	4.03
	.01	10.6	8.02	6.99	6.42	6.06	5.80	5.61	5.47	5.35
	.001	22.9	16.4	13.9	12.6	11.7	11.1	10.7	10.4	10.1

TABLE F *(Continued).*

df for denom.	α	1	2	3	4	5	6	7	8	9
					df for numerator					
10	.25	1.49	1.60	1.60	1.59	1.59	1.58	1.57	1.56	1.56
	.10	3.29	2.92	2.73	2.61	2.52	2.46	2.41	2.38	2.35
	.05	4.96	4.10	3.71	3.48	3.33	3.22	3.14	3.07	3.02
	.025	6.94	5.46	4.83	4.47	4.24	4.07	3.95	3.85	3.78
	.01	10.0	7.56	6.55	5.99	5.64	5.39	5.20	5.06	4.94
	.001	21.0	14.9	12.6	11.3	10.5	9.92	9.52	9.20	8.96
11	.25	1.47	1.58	1.58	1.57	1.56	1.55	1.54	1.53	1.53
	.10	3.23	2.86	2.66	2.54	2.45	2.39	2.34	2.30	2.27
	.05	4.84	3.98	3.59	3.36	3.20	3.09	3.01	2.95	2.90
	.025	6.72	5.26	4.63	4.28	4.04	3.88	3.76	3.66	3.59
	.01	9.65	7.21	6.22	5.67	5.32	5.07	4.89	4.74	4.63
	.001	19.7	13.8	11.6	10.4	9.58	9.05	8.66	8.35	8.12
12	.25	1.46	1.56	1.56	1.55	1.54	1.53	1.52	1.51	1.51
	.10	3.18	2.81	2.61	2.48	2.39	2.33	2.28	2.24	2.21
	.05	4.75	3.89	3.49	3.26	3.11	3.00	2.91	2.85	2.80
	.025	6.55	5.10	4.47	4.12	3.89	3.73	3.61	3.51	3.44
	.01	9.33	6.93	5.95	5.41	5.06	4.82	4.64	4.50	4.39
	.001	18.6	13.0	10.8	9.63	8.89	8.38	8.00	7.71	7.48
13	.25	1.45	1.55	1.55	1.53	1.52	1.51	1.50	1.49	1.49
	.10	3.14	2.76	2.56	2.43	2.35	2.28	2.23	2.20	2.16
	.05	4.67	3.81	3.41	3.18	3.03	2.92	2.83	2.77	2.71
	.025	6.41	4.97	4.35	4.00	3.77	3.60	3.48	3.39	3.31
	.01	9.07	6.70	5.74	5.21	4.86	4.62	4.44	4.30	4.19
	.001	17.8	12.3	10.2	9.07	8.35	7.86	7.49	7.21	6.98
14	.25	1.44	1.53	1.53	1.52	1.51	1.50	1.49	1.48	1.47
	.10	3.10	2.73	2.52	2.39	2.31	2.24	2.19	2.15	2.12
	.05	4.60	3.74	3.34	3.11	2.96	2.85	2.76	2.70	2.65
	.025	6.30	4.86	4.24	3.89	3.66	3.50	3.38	3.29	3.21
	.01	8.86	6.51	5.56	5.04	4.69	4.46	4.28	4.14	4.03
	.001	17.1	11.8	9.73	8.62	7.92	7.43	7.08	6.80	6.58
15	.25	1.43	1.52	1.52	1.51	1.49	1.48	1.47	1.46	1.46
	.10	3.07	2.70	2.49	2.36	2.27	2.21	2.16	2.12	2.09
	.05	4.54	3.68	3.29	3.06	2.90	2.79	2.71	2.64	2.59
	.025	6.20	4.77	4.15	3.80	3.58	3.41	3.29	3.20	3.12
	.01	8.68	6.36	5.42	4.89	4.56	4.32	4.14	4.00	3.89
	.001	16.6	11.3	9.34	8.25	7.57	7.09	6.74	6.47	6.26
16	.25	1.42	1.51	1.51	1.50	1.48	1.47	1.46	1.45	1.44
	.10	3.05	2.67	2.46	2.33	2.24	2.18	2.13	2.09	2.06
	.05	4.49	3.63	3.24	3.01	2.85	2.74	2.66	2.59	2.54
	.025	6.12	4.69	4.08	3.73	3.50	3.34	3.22	3.12	3.05
	.01	8.53	6.23	5.29	4.77	4.44	4.20	4.03	3.89	3.78
	.001	16.1	11.0	9.00	7.94	7.27	6.81	6.46	6.19	5.98
17	.25	1.42	1.51	1.50	1.49	1.47	1.46	1.45	1.44	1.43
	.10	3.03	2.64	2.44	2.31	2.22	2.15	2.10	2.06	2.03
	.05	4.45	3.59	3.20	2.96	2.81	2.70	2.61	2.55	2.49
	.025	6.04	4.62	4.01	3.66	3.44	3.28	3.16	3.06	2.98
	.01	8.40	6.11	5.18	4.67	4.34	4.10	3.93	3.79	3.68
	.001	15.7	10.7	8.73	7.68	7.02	6.56	6.22	5.96	5.75

TABLE F *(Continued).*

df for denom.	α	1	2	3	4	5	6	7	8	9
						df for numerator				
18	.25	1.41	1.50	1.49	1.48	1.46	1.45	1.44	1.43	1.42
	.10	3.01	2.62	2.42	2.29	2.20	2.13	2.08	2.04	2.00
	.05	4.41	3.55	3.16	2.93	2.77	2.66	2.58	2.51	2.46
	.025	5.98	4.56	3.95	3.61	3.38	3.22	3.10	3.01	2.93
	.01	8.29	6.01	5.09	4.58	4.25	4.01	3.84	3.71	3.60
	.001	15.4	10.4	8.49	7.46	6.81	6.35	6.02	5.76	5.56
19	.25	1.41	1.49	1.49	1.47	1.46	1.44	1.43	1.42	1.41
	.10	2.99	2.61	2.40	2.27	2.18	2.11	2.06	2.02	1.98
	.05	4.38	3.52	3.13	2.90	2.74	2.63	2.54	2.48	2.42
	.025	5.92	4.51	3.90	3.56	3.33	3.17	3.05	2.96	2.88
	.01	8.18	5.93	5.01	4.50	4.17	3.94	3.77	3.63	3.52
	.001	15.1	10.2	8.28	7.26	6.62	6.18	5.85	5.59	5.39
20	.25	1.40	1.49	1.48	1.47	1.45	1.44	1.43	1.42	1.41
	.10	2.97	2.59	2.38	2.25	2.16	2.09	2.04	2.00	1.96
	.05	4.35	3.49	3.10	2.87	2.71	2.60	2.51	2.45	2.39
	.025	5.87	4.46	3.86	3.51	3.29	3.13	3.01	2.91	2.84
	.01	8.10	5.85	4.94	4.43	4.10	3.87	3.70	3.56	3.46
	.001	14.8	9.95	8.10	7.10	6.46	6.02	5.69	5.44	5.24
22	.25	1.40	1.48	1.47	1.45	1.44	1.42	1.41	1.40	1.39
	.10	2.95	2.56	2.35	2.22	2.13	2.06	2.01	1.97	1.93
	.05	4.30	3.44	3.05	2.82	2.66	2.55	2.46	2.40	2.34
	.025	5.79	4.38	3.78	3.44	3.22	3.05	2.93	2.84	2.76
	.01	7.95	5.72	4.82	4.31	3.99	3.76	3.59	3.45	3.35
	.001	14.4	9.61	7.80	6.81	6.19	5.76	5.44	5.19	4.99
24	.25	1.39	1.47	1.46	1.44	1.43	1.41	1.40	1.39	1.38
	.10	2.93	2.54	2.33	2.19	2.10	2.04	1.98	1.94	1.91
	.05	4.26	3.40	3.01	2.78	2.62	2.51	2.42	2.36	2.30
	.025	5.72	4.32	3.72	3.38	3.15	2.99	2.87	2.78	2.70
	.01	7.82	5.61	4.72	4.22	3.90	3.67	3.50	3.36	3.26
	.001	14.0	9.34	7.55	6.59	5.98	5.55	5.23	4.99	4.80
26	.25	1.38	1.46	1.45	1.44	1.42	1.41	1.39	1.38	1.37
	.10	2.91	2.52	2.31	2.17	2.08	2.01	1.96	1.92	1.88
	.05	4.23	3.37	2.98	2.74	2.59	2.47	2.39	2.32	2.27
	.025	5.66	4.27	3.67	3.33	3.10	2.94	2.82	2.73	2.65
	.01	7.72	5.53	4.64	4.14	3.82	3.59	3.42	3.29	3.18
	.001	13.7	9.12	7.36	6.41	5.80	5.38	5.07	4.83	4.64
28	.25	1.38	1.46	1.45	1.43	1.41	1.40	1.39	1.38	1.37
	.10	2.89	2.50	2.29	2.16	2.06	2.00	1.94	1.90	1.87
	.05	4.20	3.34	2.95	2.71	2.56	2.45	2.36	2.29	2.24
	.025	5.61	4.22	3.63	3.29	3.06	2.90	2.78	2.69	2.61
	.01	7.64	5.45	4.57	4.07	3.75	3.53	3.36	3.23	3.12
	.001	13.5	8.93	7.19	6.25	5.66	5.24	4.93	4.69	4.50
30	.25	1.38	1.45	1.44	1.42	1.41	1.39	1.38	1.37	1.36
	.10	2.88	2.49	2.28	2.14	2.05	1.98	1.93	1.88	1.85
	.05	4.17	3.32	2.92	2.69	2.53	2.42	2.33	2.27	2.21
	.025	5.57	4.18	3.59	3.25	3.03	2.87	2.75	2.65	2.57
	.01	7.56	5.39	4.51	4.02	3.70	3.47	3.30	3.17	3.07
	.001	13.3	8.77	7.05	6.12	5.53	5.12	4.82	4.58	4.39

TABLE F *(Continued)*.

df for denom.	α	df for numerator 1	2	3	4	5	6	7	8	9
40	.25	1.36	1.44	1.42	1.40	1.39	1.37	1.36	1.35	1.34
	.10	2.84	2.44	2.23	2.09	2.00	1.93	1.87	1.83	1.79
	.05	4.08	3.23	2.84	2.61	2.45	2.34	2.25	2.18	2.12
	.025	5.42	4.05	3.46	3.13	2.90	2.74	2.62	2.53	2.45
	.01	7.31	5.18	4.31	3.83	3.51	3.29	3.12	2.99	2.89
	.001	12.6	8.25	6.60	5.70	5.13	4.73	4.44	4.21	4.02
60	.25	1.35	1.42	1.41	1.38	1.37	1.35	1.33	1.32	1.31
	.10	2.79	2.39	2.18	2.04	1.95	1.87	1.82	1.77	1.74
	.05	4.00	3.15	2.76	2.53	2.37	2.25	2.17	2.10	2.04
	.025	5.29	3.93	3.34	3.01	2.79	2.63	2.51	2.41	2.33
	.01	7.08	4.98	4.13	3.65	3.34	3.12	2.95	2.82	2.72
	.001	12.0	7.76	6.17	5.31	4.76	4.37	4.09	3.87	3.69
120	.25	1.34	1.40	1.39	1.37	1.35	1.33	1.31	1.30	1.29
	.10	2.75	2.35	2.13	1.99	1.90	1.82	1.77	1.72	1.68
	.05	3.92	3.07	2.68	2.45	2.29	2.17	2.09	2.02	1.96
	.025	5.15	3.80	3.23	2.89	2.67	2.52	2.39	2.30	2.22
	.01	6.85	4.79	3.95	3.48	3.17	2.96	2.79	2.66	2.56
	.001	11.4	7.32	5.79	4.95	4.42	4.04	3.77	3.55	3.38
∞	.25	1.32	1.39	1.37	1.35	1.33	1.31	1.29	1.28	1.27
	.10	2.71	2.30	2.08	1.94	1.85	1.77	1.72	1.67	1.63
	.05	3.84	3.00	2.60	2.37	2.21	2.10	2.01	1.94	1.88
	.025	5.02	3.69	3.12	2.79	2.57	2.41	2.29	2.19	2.11
	.01	6.63	4.61	3.78	3.32	3.02	2.80	2.64	2.51	2.41
	.001	10.8	6.91	5.42	4.62	4.10	3.74	3.47	3.27	3.10

This table is adapted and abridged from Table 18 in *Biometrika tables for statisticians*, 2nd ed., vol. 1 (New York: Cambridge University Press, 1958), edited by E. S. Pearson and H. O. Hartley, by permission of the *Biometrika* Trustees.

TABLE G.   Random Numbers

	1	2	3	4	5	6	7	8	9
1	32942	95416	42339	59045	26693	49057	87496	20624	14819
2	07410	99859	83828	21409	29094	65114	36701	25762	12827
3	59981	68155	45673	76210	58219	45738	29550	24736	09574
4	46251	25437	69654	99716	11563	08803	86027	51867	12116
5	65558	51904	93123	27887	53138	21488	09095	78777	71240
6	99187	19258	86421	16401	19397	83297	40111	49326	81686
7	35641	00301	16096	34775	21562	97983	45040	19200	16383
8	14031	00936	81518	48440	02218	04756	19506	60695	88494
9	60677	15076	92554	26042	23472	69869	62877	19584	39576
10	66314	05212	67859	89356	20056	30648	87349	20389	53805
11	20416	87410	75646	64176	82752	63606	37011	57346	69512
12	28701	56992	70423	62415	40807	98086	58850	28968	45297
13	74579	33844	33426	07570	00728	07079	19322	56325	84819
14	62615	52342	82968	75540	80045	53069	20665	21282	07768
15	93945	06293	22879	08161	01442	75071	21427	94842	26210
16	75689	76131	96837	67450	44511	50424	82848	41975	71663
17	02921	16919	35424	93209	52133	87327	95897	65171	20376
18	14295	34969	14216	03191	61647	30296	66667	10101	63203
19	05303	91109	82403	40312	62191	67023	90073	83205	71344
20	57071	90357	12901	08899	91039	67251	28701	03846	94589
21	78471	57741	13599	84390	32146	00871	09354	22745	65806
22	89242	79337	59293	47481	07740	43345	25716	70020	54005
23	14955	59592	97035	80430	87220	06392	79028	57123	52872
24	42446	41880	37415	47472	04513	49494	08860	08038	43624
25	18534	22346	54556	17558	73689	14894	05030	19561	56517
26	39284	33737	42512	86411	23753	29690	26096	81361	93099
27	33922	37329	89911	55876	28379	81031	22058	21487	54613
28	78355	54013	50774	30666	61205	42574	47773	36027	27174
29	08845	99145	94316	88974	29828	97069	90327	61842	29604
30	01769	71825	55957	98271	02784	66731	40311	88495	18821
31	17639	38284	59478	90409	21997	56199	30068	82800	69692
32	05851	58653	99949	63505	40409	85551	90729	64938	52403
33	42396	40112	11469	03476	03328	84238	26570	51790	42122
34	13318	14192	98167	75631	74141	22369	36757	89117	54998
35	60571	54786	26281	01855	30706	66578	32019	65884	58485
36	09531	81853	59334	70929	03544	18510	89541	13555	21168
37	72865	16829	86542	00396	20363	13010	69645	49608	54738
38	56324	31093	77924	28622	83543	28912	15059	80192	83964
39	78192	21626	91399	07235	07104	73652	64425	85149	75409
40	64666	34767	97298	92708	01994	53188	78476	07804	62404
41	82201	75694	02808	65983	74373	66693	13094	74183	73020
42	15360	73776	40914	85190	54278	99054	62944	47351	89098
43	68142	67957	70896	37983	20487	95350	16371	03426	13895
44	19138	31200	30616	14639	44406	44236	57360	81644	94761
45	28155	03521	36415	78452	92359	81091	56513	88321	97910
46	87971	29031	51780	27376	81056	86155	55488	50590	74514
47	58147	68841	53625	02059	75223	16783	19272	61994	71090
48	18875	52809	70594	41649	32935	26430	82096	01605	65846
49	75109	56474	74111	31966	29969	70093	98901	84550	25769
50	35983	03742	76822	12073	59463	84420	15868	99505	11426

TABLE G *(Continued)*.

	1	2	3	4	5	6	7	8	9
51	12651	61646	11769	75109	86996	97669	25757	32535	07122
52	81769	74436	02630	72310	45049	18029	07469	42341	98173
53	36737	98863	77240	76251	00654	64688	09343	70278	67331
54	82861	54371	76610	94934	72748	44124	05610	53750	95938
55	21325	15732	24127	37431	09723	63529	73977	95218	96074
56	74146	47887	62463	23045	41490	07954	22597	60012	98866
57	90759	64410	54179	66075	61051	75385	51378	08360	95946
58	55683	98078	02238	91540	21219	17720	87817	41705	95785
59	79686	17969	76061	83748	55920	83612	41540	86492	06447
60	70333	00201	86201	69716	78185	62154	77930	67663	29529
61	14042	53536	07779	04157	41172	36473	42123	43929	50533
62	59911	08256	06596	48416	69770	68797	56080	14223	59199
63	62368	62623	62742	14891	39247	52242	98832	69533	91174
64	57529	97751	54976	48957	74599	08759	78494	52785	68526
65	15469	90574	78033	66885	13936	42117	71831	22961	94225
66	18625	23674	53850	32827	81647	80820	00420	63555	74489
67	74626	68394	88562	70745	23701	45630	65891	58220	35442
68	11119	16519	27384	90199	79210	76965	99546	30323	31664
69	41101	17336	48951	53674	17880	45260	08575	49321	36191
70	32123	91576	84221	78902	82010	30847	62329	63898	23268
71	26091	68409	69704	82267	14751	13151	93115	01437	56945
72	67680	79790	48462	59278	44185	29616	76531	19589	83139
73	15184	19260	14073	07026	25264	08388	27182	22557	61501
74	58010	45039	57181	10238	36874	28546	37444	80824	63981
75	56425	53996	86245	32623	78858	08143	60377	42925	42815
76	82630	84066	13592	60642	17904	99718	63432	88642	37858
77	14927	40909	23900	48761	44860	92467	31742	87142	03607
78	23740	22505	07489	85986	74420	21744	97711	36648	35620
79	32990	97446	03711	63824	07953	85965	87089	11687	92414
80	05310	24058	91946	78437	34365	82469	12430	84754	19354
81	21839	39937	27534	88913	49055	19218	47712	67677	51889
82	08833	42549	93981	94051	28382	83725	72643	64233	97252
83	58336	11139	47479	00931	91560	95372	97642	33856	54825
84	62032	91144	75478	47431	52726	30289	42411	91886	51818
85	45171	30557	53116	04118	58301	24375	65609	85810	18620
86	91611	62656	60128	35609	63698	78356	50682	22505	01692
87	55472	63819	86314	49174	93582	73604	78614	78849	23096
88	18573	09729	74091	53994	10970	86557	65661	41854	26037
89	60866	02955	90288	82136	83644	94455	06560	78029	98768
90	45043	55608	82767	60890	74646	79485	13619	98868	40857
91	17831	09737	79473	75945	28394	79334	70577	38048	03607
92	40137	03981	07585	18128	11178	32601	27994	05641	22600
93	77776	31343	14576	97706	16039	47517	43300	59080	80392
94	69605	44104	40103	95635	05635	81673	68657	09559	23510
95	19916	52934	26499	09821	87331	80993	61299	36979	73599
96	02606	58552	07678	56619	65325	30705	99582	53390	46357
97	65183	73160	87131	35530	47946	09854	18080	02321	05809
98	10740	98914	44916	11322	89717	88189	30143	52687	19420
99	98642	89822	71691	51573	83666	61642	46683	33761	47542
100	60139	25601	93663	25547	02654	94829	48672	28736	84994

REFERENCES

Adams, J. A. (1972). Research and the future of engineering psychology. *American Psychologist, 27*, 615–622.

Adamson, R. E. (1952). Functional fixedness as related to problem solving: A repetition of three experiments. *Journal of Experimental Psychology, 44*, 288–291.

American Psychological Association. (1972). Guidelines for psychologists for the use of drugs in research. *American Psychologist, 27*, 336.

American Psychological Association. (1973). *Ethical principles in the conduct of research with human participants*, Washington, DC.

American Psychological Association. (1981a). Ethical principles for psychologists. *American Psychologist, 36*, 633–638.

American Psychological Association. (1981b). Guidelines for the use of animals in school-science behavior projects. *American Psychologist, 36*, 686.

American Psychological Association. (1982). *Ethical principles in the conduct of research with human behavior*. Washington, DC.

American Psychological Association. (1987). *Casebook on ethical issues*. Washington, DC.

Amsel, A. (1962). Frustrative nonreward in partial reinforcement and discrimination learning: Some recent history and a theoretical extension. *Psychological Review, 69*, 306–328.

Amsel, A. (1971). Partial reinforcement: Effects on vigor and persistence. In K. W. Spence and J. T. Spence (Eds.), *The psychology of learning and motivation*, vol. 1. New York: Academic Press.

Angell, J. R. (1907). The province of functional psychology. *Psychological Review, 14*, 61–91.

Asch, S. E. (1951). Effect of group pressure upon the modification and distortion of judgment. In H. Guetzkow (Ed.), *Groups, leadership, and men*. Pittsburgh: Carnegie.

Asch, S. E. (1956). Studies of independence and conformity: I. A minority of one against a unanimous majority. *Psychological Monographs, 70, 9*. (Whole No. 416).

Asch, S. E. (1958). Effects of group pressure upon the modification and distortion of judgments. In E. E. Maccoby, T. M. Newcomb, and E. L. Hartley (Eds.), *Readings in social psychology*, 3rd ed., 174–183. New York: Holt.

Barber, T. X., & Silver, M. J. (1968). Fact, fiction, and the experimenter bias effect. *Psychological Bulletin Monograph Supplement, 70* (6, pt. 2), 1–29.

Barefoot, J. C., Hoople, H., & McClay, D. (1972). Avoidance of an act which would violate personal space. *Psychonomic Science, 28*, 205–206.

Barker, R. G. (1968). *Ecological psychology*. Stanford, CA: Stanford University Press.

Barker, R. G., & Wright, H. F. (1951). *One boy's day.* New York: Harper and Row.

Baron, R. A., & Bell, P. A. (1976). Aggression and heat: The influence of ambient temperature, negative affect, and a cooling drink on physical aggression. *Journal of Personality and Social Psychology, 33,* 245–255.

Baron, R. A., & Byrne D. (1977). *Social psychology: Understanding human interaction* (2d ed.). Boston: Allyn and Bacon.

Baron, R. A., Byrne, D., & Kantowitz, B. H. (1977). *Psychology: Understanding behavior.* Philadelphia: Saunders.

Bartley, H. (1958). *Principles of perception.* New York: Harper.

Baumrind, D. (1964). Some thoughts on ethics of research: After reading Milgram's "Behavioral study of obedience." *American Psychologist, 19,* 421–423.

Beck. S. B. (1963). Eyelid conditioning as a function of CS intensity, UCS intensity, and Manifest Anxiety Scale score. *Journal of Experimental Pschology, 66,* 429–438.

Bem, D. J. (1987). Writing the empirical journal article. In M. P. Zanna & J. M. Darley (Eds.), *The compleat academic: A practical guide for the beginning social scientist.* New York: Random House.

Benchley, R. W. (1937). The early worm. In R. W. Benchley, *Inside Benchley.* New York: Harper.

Bergin, A. E. (1971). The evaluation of therapeutic outcomes. In A. E. Bergin and S. L. Garfield, *Handbook of psychotherapy and behavior change.* New York: Wiley.

Berkeley, G. A. (1963). *A treatise concerning the principles of human knowledge.* New York: Bobbs-Merrill, (originally published 1710).

Bevan, W. (1976). The sound of the wind that's blowing. *American Psychologist, 31,* 481–491.

Beveridge, W. I. B. (1957). *The art of scientific investigation.* New York: Random House.

Biederman, I., & Kaplan,R. (1970). Stimulus discriminability and S-R compatability: Evidence for independent effects in choice reaction time. *Journal of Experimental Psychology, 86,* 434–439.

Blaney, R. H. (1986). Affect and memory: A review. *Psychological Bulletin, 99,* 229–246.

Blaxton, T. A. (1989). Investigating dissociations among memory measures: Support for a transfer appropriate processing framework. *Journal of Experimental Psychology: Learning, Memory, and Cognition, 15,* 657–668.

Blough, D. S. (1958). A method for obtaining psychophysical thresholds from pigeons. *Journal of the Experimental Analysis of Behavior, 1,* 31–43.

Blough, D. S. (1961). Experiments in animal psychophysics. *Scientific American, 205,* 32.

Boring, E. G. (1950). *A history of experimental psychology.* New York: Appleton-Century-Crofts.

Bornstein, M. H., & Sigman, M. D. (1986). Continuity in mental development from infancy. *Child Development, 57,* 251–274.

Bortolussi, M. R., Hart, S. G., & Kantowitz, B. H. (1986). Measuring pilot workload in a motion base trainer. *Applied Ergonomics, 17,* 278–283.

Bowd, A. D. (1980). Ethical reservations about psychological research with animals. *Psychological Record, 30,* 201–210.

Bower, G. (1961). A contrast effect in differential conditioning. *Journal of Experimental Psychology, 62,* 196–199.

Bower, G. H. (1972). Mental imagery and associative learning. In L. Gregg (Ed.), *Cognition in learning and memory*. New York; Wiley.

Bramel, D., & Friend, R. (1981). Hawthorne, the myth of the docile worker, and class bias in psychology. *American Psychologist, 36*, 867–878.

Breitmayer, B. J., & Ramey, C. T. (1986). Biological nonoptimality and quality of postnatal environment as codeterminants of intellectual development. *Child Development, 57*, 1151–1165.

Brickner, M. A., Harkins, S. G., & Ostrom, T. M. (1986). Effects of personal involvement: Thought-provoking implications for social loafing. *Journal of Personality and Social Psychology, 51*, 763–769.

Bridgman, P. W. (1945). Some general principles of operational analysis. *Psychological Review, 52*, 246–249.

Broad, W., & Wade, M. (1982). *Betrayer's of the truth: Fraud and deceit in the halls of science*. New York: Simon and Schuster.

Broadbent, D. E. (1971). *Decision and stress*. New York: Academic Press.

Broadbent, D. E., & Gregory, M. (1963). Division of attention and the decision theory of signal detection. *Proceedings of the Royal Society B, 158*, 222–231.

Brown, J. (1958). Some tests of the decay theory of immediate memory. *Quarterly Journal of Experimental Psychology, 10*, 12–21.

Brown, R. (1962). Models of attitude change. In R. Brown, E. Galanter, E. H. Hess, and G. Mandler (Eds.), *New directions in psychology*, vol. 1. New York: Holt, Rinehart, and Winston.

Brownell, K. D., & Stunkard, A. J. (1982). The double-blind in danger: Untoward consequences of informed consent. *American Journal of Psychiatry, 139*, 1487–1489.

Butters, N., & Cermak, L. S. (1986). A case study of the forgetting of autobiographical knowledge: Implications for the study of retrograde amnesia. In D. Rubin (Ed.), *Autobiographical memory*, 253–272. New York: Cambridge University Press.

Calhoun, J. B. (1962). Population density and social pathology. *Scientific American, 206*, 139–148.

Calhoun, J. B. (1966). The role of space in animal sociology. *Journal of Social Issues, 22*, 46–58.

Calhoun, J. B. (1971). Space and the strategy of life. In A. H. Esser (Ed.), *Environment and behavior: The use of space by animals and men*. New York: Plenum.

Campbell, D. T., & Erlebacher, A. (1970)(a). How regression artifacts in quasi-experimental evaluations can mistakenly make compensatory education look harmful. In J. Helmuth (Ed.), *Compensatory education: A national debate*, vol. 3, *Disadvantaged child*. New York: Brunner/Mazel.

Campbell, D. T., & Erlebacher, A. (1970)(b). Reply to the replies. In J. Helmuth (Ed.), *Compensatory education: A national debate*, vol. 3, *Disadvantaged child*. New York: Brunner/Mazel.

Campbell, D. T., & Stanley, J. C. (1966). *Experimental and quasi-experimental designs for research*. Chicago: Rand McNally.

Campion, J., Latto, R., & Smith, Y. M. (1983). Is blindsight an effect of scattered light, spared cortex, and near threshold vision? *Behavioral and Brain Sciences, 6*, 423–486.

Capaldi, E. J. (1964). Effect of N-length, number of different N-lengths, and number of reinforcements on resistance to extinction. *Journal of Experimental Psychology, 68*, 230–239.

Capaldi, E. J. (1966). Partial reinforcement: A hypothesis of sequential effects. *Psychological Review, 73,* 459–477.

Capaldi, E. J. (1971). Memory and learning: A sequential viewpoint. In W. K. Honig and P. H. R. James (Eds.), *Animal memory.* New York: Academic Press.

Carter, L. F. (1941). Intensity of conditioned stimulus and rate of conditioning. *Journal of Experimental Psychology, 28,* 481–490.

Cermak, L. S., & Craik, F. I. M. (Eds.). (1979). *Levels of processing in human memory.* Hillsdale, NJ: Erlbaum

Cermak, L. S., & Reale, L. (1978). Depth of processing and retention of words by alcoholic Korsakoff patients. *Journal of Experimental Psychology: Human Learning and Memory, 4,* 165–174.

Cheesman, J., & Merikle, P. M. (1984). Priming with and without awareness. *Perception & Psychophysics, 36,* 387–395.

Cheesman, J., & Merikle, P. M. (1986). Distinguishing conscious from unconscious perception. *Canadian Journal of Psychology, 40,* 343–367.

Childress, M. E., Hart, S. G., & Bortolussi, M. R. (1982). The reliability and validity of flight task workload ratings. *Proceedings of the Human Factors Society, 26,* 319–323.

Churchland, P. M., & Churchland, P. S. (1990, January). Could a machine think? *Scientific American,* 32–37.

Cicirelli, V. et al. (June 1969). The impact of Head Start: An evaluation of the effects of Head Start on children's cognitive and affective development. A report presented to the Office of Economic Opportunity pursuant to Contract B89–4536. Westinghouse Learning Corporation, Ohio University. (Distributed by Clearinghouse for Federal Scientific and Technical Information, U.S. Department of Commerce, National Bureau of Standards, Institute for Applied Technology, PB 184 328).

Cicirelli, V. G. (1970). The relevance of the regression artifact problem to the Westinghouse-Ohio evaluation of Head Start: A reply to Campbell and Erlebacher. In J. Helmuth (Ed.), *Compensatory education: A national debate,* vol. 3, *Disadvantaged child.* New York: Brunner/Mazel.

Clark, H. H. (1973). The language-as-fixed effect fallacy: A critique of language statistics in psychological research. *Journal of Verbal Learning and Verbal Behavior, 12,* 335–359.

Clark, W. C. (1969). Sensory-decision theory analysis of the placebo effect on the criterion for pain and thermal sensitivity (d'). *Journal of Abnormal Psychology, 74,* 363–371.

Clark, W. C., & Yang, J. C. (1974). Acupunctural analgesia: Evaluation by signal detection theory. *Science, 184,* 1096–1098.

Cohen, S., Glass, D. C., & Singer, J. E. (1973). Apartment noise, auditory discrimination and reading ability in children. *Journal of Experimental Social Psychology, 9,* 407–422.

Colasanto, D. (1989, October). Earthquake fails to shake composure of many Bay Area residents. *Gallup Report, 289,* 21–23.

Cook, T. D., & Campbell, D. T. (1979). *Quasi-experimentation: Design and analysis issues for field settings.* Chicago: Rand McNally.

Coren, S., & Girgus, J. S. (1978). *Seeing is deceiving: The psychology of visual illusions.* Hillsdale, NJ: Erlbaum.

Cornsweet, T. N. (1962). The staircase method in psychophysics. *American Journal of Psychology, 75,* 485–491.

Craik, F. I. M. (1977). Age differences in human memory. In J. E. Birren and W. Schaie (Eds.), *Handbook of the psychology of aging.* New York: Van Nostrand Reinhold.

Craik, F. I. M., & Lockhart, R. S. (1972). Levels of processing: A framework for memory research. *Journal of Verbal Learning and Verbal Behavior, 11*, 671–684.

Craik, F. I. M., & Tulving, E. (1975). Depth of processing and the retention of words in episodic memory. *Journal of Experimental Psychology: General, 104*, 671–684.

Cutler, B. L., & Penrod, S. D. (1989). Forensically relevant moderators of the relation between eyewitness identification accuracy and confidence. *Journal of Applied Psychology, 74*, 650–652.

D'Amato, M. R. (1970). *Experimental psychology: Methodology, psychophysics, and learning.* New York: McGraw-Hill.

Darley, J. M., & Latané, B. (1968). Bystander intervention in emergencies: Diffusion of responsibility. *Journal of Personality and Social Psychology, 8*, 377–383.

DeGreene, K. B. (Ed.). (1970). *Systems psychology.* New York: McGraw-Hill.

Dewey, J. (1896). The reflex arc concept in psychology. *Psychological Review, 3*, 357–370.

Doll, R. (1955). Etiology of lung cancer. *Advances in Cancer Research, 3*, 1–50.

Drickamer, L. C., & Vesey, S. H. (1982). *Animal behavior: Concepts, processes, and methods.* Boston: Willard Grant Press.

Duncker, K. (1945). On problem solving. *Psychological Monographs, 58(5)*, 1–112. Whole No. 270.

Dweck, C. S., & Bempechat, J. (1983). Children's theories of intelligence: Consequences for learning. In S. G. Paris, G. M. Olson, & H. W. Stevenson (Eds.), *Learning and motivation in the classroom*, 239–256. Hillsdale, NJ: Erlbaum.

Dweck, C. S., & Elliot, E. S. (1983). Achievement motivation. In E. M. Hetherington (Ed.), *Handbook of child psychology: Vol. IV. Socialization, personality, and development.* New York: Wiley.

Ebbinghaus, H. (1913). *Memory: A contribution to experimental psychology.* New York: Columbia University Press. (Reprinted by Dover, 1964).

Eibl-Eibesfeldt, I. (1970). *Ethology: The biology of behavior.* New York: Holt, Rinehart & Winston.

Eibl-Eibesfeldt, I. (1972). Similarities and differences between cultures in expressive movements. In R. A. Hinde (Ed.), *Non-verbal communication.* Cambridge, England: Cambridge University Press.

Elmes, D. G., Chapman, P. F., & Selig, C. W. (1984). Role of mood and connotation in the spacing effect. *Bulletin of the Psychonomic Society, 22*, 186–188.

Ericsson, K. A., & Simon, H. A. (1979). Verbal reports as data. *Psychological Review, 87*, 215–251.

Eriksen, C. W. (1960). Discrimination and learning without awareness: A methodological survey and evaluation. *Psychological Review, 67*, 279–300.

Eron, L. D. (1982). Parent-child interaction, television violence, and aggression in children. *American Psychologist, 37*, 197–211.

Eron, L. D., Huesmann, L. R., Lefkowitz, M. M., & Walder, L. O. (1972). Does television violence cause aggression? *American Psychologist, 27*, 253–263.

Evans, J. W., & Schiller, J. (1970). How preoccupation with possible regression artifacts can lead to a faulty strategy for the evaluation of social action programs: A reply to Campbell and Erlebacher. In J. Helmuth (ed.), *Compensatory education: A national debate*, vol. 3, *Disadvantaged child*. New York: Brunner/Mazel.

Eysenck, H. J. (1952). The effects of psychotherapy: An evaluation. *Journal of Consulting Psychology, 16*, 319–324.

Eysenck, H. J., & Eaves, L. J. (1981). *The cause and effects of smoking*. New York: Gage.

Fechner, G. (1860/1966). *Elements of psychophysics.* vol. 1. Trans. by H. E. Adler, D. H. Howes, and E. G. Boring (Eds.). New York: Holt, Rinehart and Winston.

Festinger, L. (1957). *A theory of cognitive dissonance*. Stanford, CA: Stanford University Press.

Festinger, L., Riecken, H. W., & Schachter, S. (1956). *When prophecy fails*. Minneapolis: University of Minnesota Press.

Ficken, M. S. (1990). Acoustic characteristics of alarm calls associated with predation risk in chickadees. *Animal Behaviour, 39*, 400–401.

Fischhoff, B., Slovic, P., & Lichtenstein, S. (1977). Knowing with certainty: The appropriateness of extreme confidence. *Journal of Experimental Psychology: Human Perception and Performance, 3*, 522–564.

Fisher, R. P., & Craik, F. I. M. (1977). Interaction between encoding and retrieval operations in cued recall. *Journal of Experimental Psychology: Human Learning and Memory, 3*, 701–711.

Fossey, D. (1972). Living with mountain gorillas. In T. B. Allen (Ed.), *The marvels of animal behavior*. Washington, DC: National Geographic Society.

Freedman, J. L., & Landauer, T. K. (1966). Retrieval of long-term memory: "Tip-of-the-tongue" phenomenon. *Psychonomic Science, 4*, 309–310.

Frisby, J. (1979). *Seeing: Illusion, mind, and brain*. Oxford: Oxford University Press.

Frost, R., Katz, L., & Bentin, S. (1987). Strategies for visual word recognition and orthographical depth: A multilingual comparison. *Journal of Experimental Psychology: Human Perception and Performance, 13*, 104–115.

Gabrenya, W. K., Latané, B., & Wang, Y. (1983). Social loafing in cross-cultural perspective: Chinese on Taiwan. *Journal of Cross-Cultural Psychology, 14*, 368–384.

Galle, O. R., Gove, W. R., & McPherson, J. M. (1972). Population density and pathology: What are the relations for man? *Science, 176*, 23–30.

Gallup, G. G., & Suarez, S. D. (1985). Alternatives to the use of animals in psychological research. *American Psychologist, 40*, 1104–1111.

Gardner, H. (1983). *Frames of mind: The theory of multiple intelligences*. New York: Basic Books.

Garner, W. R. (1974). *The processing of information and structure*. Hillsdale, NJ: Erlbaum.

Garner, W. R., Hake, H. W., & Eriksen, C. W. (1956). Operationism and the concept of perception. *Psychological Review, 63*, 149–159.

Gibson, J. J. (1979). *The ecological approach to perception*. Boston: Houghton Mifflin.

Gick, M. L., & Holyoak, K. J. (1980). Analogical problem solving. *Cognitive Psychology, 12*, 306–355.

Gick, M. L., & Holyoak, K. J. (1983). Schema induction and analogical transfer. *Cognitive Psychology, 15*, 1–38.

Glaser, M. O., & Glaser, W. R. (1982). Time course analysis of the Stroop phenomenon. *Journal of Experimental Psychology: Human Perception and Performance, 8,* 875–894.

Glucksberg, S. (1966). *Symbolic processes.* Dubuque, Iowa: William C. Brown.

Glucksberg, S., & Weisberg, R. W. (1966). Verbal behavior and problem solving: Some effects of labelling in a functional fixedness problem. *Journal of Experimental Psychology, 71,* 659–664.

Glucksberg, S., & Danks, J. H. (1967). Functional fixedness: Stimulus equivalence mediated by semantic-acoustic similarity. *Journal of Experimental Psychology, 74,* 400–405.

Glucksberg, S., & Danks, J. H. (1968). Effects of discriminative labels and nonsense labels upon availability of novel function. *Journal of Verbal Learning and Verbal Behavior, 7,* 72–76.

Gottsdanker, R., & Shragg, G. P. (1985). Verification of Donders' subtraction method. *Journal of Experimental Psychology: Human Perception and Performance, 11,* 765–776.

Graf, P., Mandler, G., & Haden, P. (1982). Simulating amnesic symptoms in normal subjects. *Science, 218,* 1243–1244.

Graf, P., & Schacter, D. L. (1985). Implicit and explicit memory for new associations in normal and amnesic subjects. *Journal of Experimental Psychology: Learning, Memory and Cognition, 11,* 501–518.

Grant, D. A., & Schneider, D. E. (1948). Intensity of the conditioned stimulus and strength of conditioning: I. The conditioned eyelid response to light. *Journal of Experimental Psychology, 38,* 690–696.

Green, D. M., & Swets, J. A. (1966). *Signal detection theory and psychophysics.* New York: Wiley.

Gregory, R. L. (1970). *The intelligent eye.* New York: McGraw-Hill.

Grice, G. R. (1966). Dependence of empirical laws upon the source of experimental variation. *Psychological Bulletin, 66,* 488–498.

Grice, G. R., & Hunter, J. J. (1964). Stimulus intensity effects depend upon the type of experimental design. *Psychological Review, 71,* 247–256.

Guilford, J. P. (1967). *The nature of human intelligence.* New York: McGraw-Hill.

Hadamard, J. (1945). *The psychology of invention in the mathematical field.* Princeton, NJ: Princeton University Press.

Hanson, N. R. (1958). *Patterns of discovery.* Cambridge: Cambridge University Press.

Hardy, J. D., Wolff, H. G., & Goodell, H. (1952). *Pain reactions and sensations.* Baltimore: Williams & Wilkins.

Harkins, S. G., Latané, B., & Williams, K. (1980). Social loafing: Allocating effort or taking it easy? *Journal of Experimental Social Psychology, 16,* 457–465.

Harlow, H. F. (1958). The nature of love. *American Psychologist, 13,* 673–685.

Harré, R. (1983). *Great scientific experiments.* Oxford: Oxford University Press.

Hart, B. M., Allen, K. E., Buell, J. S., Harris, F. R., & Wolf, M. M. (1964). Effects of social reinforcement on operant crying. *Journal of Experimental Child Psychology, 1,* 145–153.

Hart. J. T. (1965). Memory and the feeling-of-knowing experience. *Journal of Educational Psychology, 56,* 208–216.

Hart, S. G., Hauser, J. R., & Lester, P. T. (1984). Inflight evaluation of four measures of pilot workload. *Proceedings of the Human Factors Society, 28.*

Helmholtz, H. von (1962). *Treatise on physiological optics*, vol. 3. J. P. C. Southall (Ed.). New York: Dover.

Hetherington, E. M., & Parke, R. D. (1986). *Child psychology: A contemporary viewpoint*, 429–480. New York: McGraw-Hill.

Higbee, K. L. (1988). *Your memory: How it works and how to improve it* (2nd ed.). Englewood Cliffs, NJ: Prentice-Hall.

Hoff, C. (1980). Immoral and moral uses of animals. *New England Journal of Medicine, 302,* 115–118.

Holyoak, K. J. (1990). Problem solving. In D. N. Osherson & E. E. Smith (Eds.), *Thinking: An invitation to cognitive science*, vol. 3, 117–146. Cambridge, MA: MIT Press.

Holyoak, K. J., & Thagard, P. (1989). Analogical mapping by constraint satisfaction. *Cognitive Science, 13,* 295–355.

Horowitz, L. M. (1974). *Elements of Statistics for Psychology and Education.* New York: McGraw-Hill.

Huesmann, L. R., Eron, L. D., Lefkowitz, M. M., & Walder, L. O. (1973). Television violence and aggression: The causal effect remains. *American Psychologist. 28,* 617–620.

Huff, D. (1954). *How to lie with statistics.* New York: Norton.

Hull, C. L. (1943). *Principles of behavior.* New York: Appleton-Century-Crofts.

Hunt, E., & Lansman, M. (1975). Cognitive theory applied to individual differences. In W. K. Estes (Ed.), *Handbook of learning and cognitive processes*, vol. I. Hillsdale, NJ: Erlbaum.

Huxley, A. (1946). *Science, liberty and peace.* New York: Harper.

Hyde, T. S., & Jenkins, J. J. (1969). Differential effects of incidental tasks on the organization of recall of a list of highly associated words. *Journal of Experimental Psychology, 82,* 472–481.

Hyman, R. (1964). *The nature of psychological inquiry.* Englewood Cliffs, NJ: Prentice-Hall.

Imber, S. D., Glanz, I. M., Elkin, I., Sotsky, S. M., Boyer, J. L., & Leber, W. R. (1986). Ethical issues in psychotherapy research: Problems in collaborative clinical study. *American Psychologist, 41,* 137–146.

Intraub, H., & Nicklos, H. (1985). Levels of processing and picture memory: The physical superiority effect. *Journal of Experimental Psychology: Learning, Memory, and Cognition, 11,* 284–298.

Ittelson, W., & Kilpatrick, F. (1952). Experiments in perception. *Scientific American, 185,* 50–55.

Jacobs, J. (1961). *Death and life of great American cities.* New York: Random House.

Jacobson, E. (1978). *You Must Relax.* (5th ed.) New York: McGraw-Hill.

Jacoby, L. L., & Dallas, M. (1981). On the relationship between autobiographical memory and perceptual learning. *Journal of Experimental Psychology: General, 3,* 306–340.

Jacoby, L. L., & Witherspoon, D. (1982). Remembering without awareness. *Canadian Journal of Psychology, 32,* 300–324.

James, W. (1890). *Principles of psychology.* New York: Holt.

Jenkins, J. (1979). Four points to remember: A tetrahedral model of memory experiments. In L. S. Cermak & F. I. M. Craik (Eds.), *Levels of processing in human memory*, 429–446. Hillsdale, NJ: Erlbaum

Jensen, A. R. (1969). How much can we boost I.Q. and scholastic achievement? *Harvard Educational Review, 39,* 1–123.

Jones, R. F. (1982). *Ancients and moderns.* New York: Dover.

Kahneman, D. (1973). *Attention and effort.* Englewood Cliffs, NJ: Prentice-Hall.

Kamin, L. J. (1969). Predictability, surprise, attention, and conditioning. In B. A. Campbell & R. M. Church (Eds.), *Punishment and aversive behavior*. New York: Appleton-Century-Crofts.

Kangas, J., & Bradway, K. (1971). Intelligence at middle age: A thirty-eight year follow-up. *Developmental Psychology, 5*, 333–337.

Kantowitz, B. H. (1974). Double stimulation. In B. H. Kantowitz (Ed.), *Human information processing—Tutorials in performance and cognition*. Hillsdale, NJ: Erlbaum.

Kantowitz, B. H. (1982). Interfacing human information processing and engineering psychology. In W. C. Howell & E. A. Fleishman (Eds.), *Human Performance and Productivity*. Hillsdale, NJ: Erlbaum.

Kantowitz, B. H. (1985). Stages and channels in human information processing: A limited analysis of theory and methodology. *Journal of Mathematical Psychology, 29*, 135–174.

Kantowitz, B. H. (1989). Interfacing human and machine intelligence. In P. A. Hancock & M. H. Chignell (Eds.), *Intelligent interfaces: Theory, research and design*, 49–67. Amsterdam: Elsevier.

Kantowitz, B. H., & Casper, P. A. (1989). Human workload in aviation. In E. Wiener & D. Nagel (Eds.), *Human Factors in Aviation*. New York: Academic Press.

Kantowitz, B. H., Hart, S. G., & Bortolussi, M. R. (1983). Measuring pilot workload in a moving-base simulator: I. Asynchronous secondary choice-reaction task. *Proceedings of the Human Factors Society, 27*, 319–322.

Kantowitz, B. H., Hart, S. G., Bortolussi, M. R., Shively, R. J., & Kantowitz, S. C. (1984). Measuring pilot workload in a moving-base simulator: II. Building levels of workload. *Proceedings of the Annual Conference on Manual Control, 20*, 359–371.

Kantowitz, B. H., & Knight, J. L. (1976). Testing tapping timesharing: Auditory secondary task. *Acta Psychologica, 40*, 343–362.

Kantowitz, B. H., & Sanders, M. S. (1972). Partial advance information and stimulus dimensionality. *Journal of Experimental Psychology, 92*, 412–418.

Kantowitz, B. H., & Sorkin, R. D. (1983). *Human factors: Understanding people-system relationships*. New York: Wiley.

Kantowitz, B. H., Triggs, T. J., & Barnes, V. (1990). Stimulus-response compatibility and human factors. In R. Proctor and G. Reeves (Eds.), *Stimulus-response compatibility*. Amsterdam: North Holland.

Kaufman, L. (1974). *Sight and mind*. New York: Oxford.

Kaufman, L. (1979). *Perception: The world transformed*. New York: Oxford.

Kelman, H. (1966). Deception in social research. *Transaction, 3*, 20–24.

Keppel, G., & Underwood, B. J. (1962). Proactive inhibition in short term retention of single items. *Journal of Verbal Learning and Verbal Behavior, 1*, 153–161.

Kerlinger, F. (1973). *Foundations of behavioral research*. New York: Basic Books.

King, D. J. (1968). Retention of connected meaningful material as a function of presentation and recall. *Journal of Experimental Psychology, 77*, 676–683.

Kinsey, A., Pomeroy, W., & Martin, C. (1953). *Sexual behavior in the human female*. Philadelphia: Saunders.

Kintsch, W., & Kozminsky, E. (1977). Summarizing stories after reading and listening. *Journal of Educational Psychology, 69*, 491–499.

Kinzel, A. F. (1970). Body-buffer zone in violent prisoners. *The American Journal of Psychiatry, 127*, 59–64.

Knight, J. L., & Kantowitz, B. H. (1974). Speed-accuracy trade-off in double stimulation: Effects on the first reponse. *Memory & Cognition, 2,* 522–532.

Knight, J. L., & Kantowitz, B. H. (1975). Probing for semantic and acoustic intrusions in dichotic messages: Effects of presentation rate. Paper presented to Midwestern Psychological Association, Chicago.

Koestler, A. (1964). *The act of creation.* New York: Dell.

Köhler, W. (1927). *The mentality of apes.* London: Routledge and Kegan Paul.

Kravitz, D. A., & Martin, B. (1986). Ringelmann rediscovered: The original article. *Journal of Personality and Social Psychology, 50,* 936–941.

Lane, D. M., & Robertson, L. (1979). The generality of the levels of processing hypothesis: An application to memory for chess positions. *Memory & Cognition, 7,* 253–256.

Latané, B. (1981). The psychology of social impact. *American Psychologist, 36,* 343–356.

Latané, B., & Darley, J. M. (1970). *The unresponsive bystander: Why doesn't he help?* New York: Appleton-Century-Crofts.

Latané, B., Williams, K., & Harkins, S. (1979). Many hands make light the work: Causes and consequences of social loafing. *Journal of Personality and Social Psychology, 37,* 822–832.

Leon, G. R. (1990). *Case histories of psychopathology* (4th ed.). Boston: Allyn and Bacon.

Lester, B. M., & Brazelton, T. B. (1982). Cross-cultural assessment of neonatal behavior. In D. A. Wagner & H. W. Stevenson (Eds.), *Cultural perspectives on child development.* San Francisco: Freeman.

Lewin, K. (1948). *Resolving social conflicts.* New York: Harper.

Lichtenstein, S., & Fischhoff, B. (1977). Do those who know more also know more about how much they know? *Organizational Behavior and Human Performance, 20,* 159–183.

Locke, J. (1959). *An essay concerning human understanding.* New York: Dover. First published in 1690.

Lockhart, R. S., & Craik, F. I. M. (1990). Levels of processing: A retrospective comment on a framework for memory research. *Canadian Journal of Psychology, 44,* 87–112.

Long, G. M., & Garvey, P. M. (1988). The effects of target wavelength on dynamic visual acuity under photopic and scotopic viewing. *Human Factors, 30,* 3–14.

Lorayne, H., & Lucas, J. (1974). *The memory book.* New York: Ballantine Books.

Lovelace, E. A., & Twohig, P. T. (1990). Healthy older adult's perception of their memory function and use of mnemonics. *Bulletin of the Psychonomic Society, 28,* 115–118.

Lowe, D. G., & Mitterer, J. O. (1982). Selective and divided attention in a Stroop task. *Canadian Journal of Psychology, 36,* 684–700.

Luria, A. R. (1968). *The mind of a mnemonist.* New York: Basic Books.

MacLeod, C. M. (1988). Forgotton but not gone: Savings for pictures and words in long term memory. *Journal of Experimental Psychology: Learning, Memory, and Cognition, 14,* 195–212.

McClelland, J. L., & Rumelhart, D. E. (1981). An interactive activation model of context effects in letter perception: Part 1. An account of basic findings. *Psychological Review, 88,* 375–407.

McDaniel, M. A., Friedman, A., & Bourne, L. E. (1978). Remembering the levels of information in words. *Memory & Cognition, 6,* 156–164.

McDougall, W. (1908). *Introduction to social psychology.* London: Methuen.

Madigan, S. (1983). Picture memory. In J. C. Yuille (Ed.), *Imagery, memory, and cognition: Essays in honor of Allan Paivio.* Hillsdale, NJ: Erlbaum.

Marcel, A. J. (1983). Conscious and unconscious perception: Experiments on visual masking and word recognition. *Cognitive Psychology, 15,* 197–237.

Marks, L. E. (1974). *Sensory processes: The new psychophysics.* New York: Academic Press.

Marriott, P. (1949). Size of working groups and output. *Occupational Psychology, 23,* 4757.

Marshall, J. E., & Heslin, R. (1975). Boys and girls together: Sexual composition and the effect of density and group size on cohesiveness. *Journal of Personality and Social Psychology, 31,* 952–961.

Mason, W. A. & Lott, D. F. (1976). Ethology and comparative psychology. In M. R. Rosenweig and L. W. Porter (Eds.), *Annual Review of Psychology,* vol. 26. Palo Alto, CA. Annual Reviews Inc.

Massaro, D. W. (1975). *Experimental psychology and information processing:* Chicago: Rand McNally.

Mayer, R. E. (1983). *Thinking, problem solving, cognition.* New York: Freeman.

Medawar, P. B. (1969). *Induction and intuition in scientific thought.* London: Methuen.

Melton, G., & Gray, J. (1988). Ethical dilemmas in AIDS research: Individual privacy and public health. *American Psychologist, 43,* 60–64.

Metcalfe, J. (1986). Premonitions of insight predict impending error. *Journal of Experimental Psychology: Learning, Memory, and Cognition, 12,* 623–634.

Milgram, S. (1963). Behavioral study of obedience. *Journal of Abnormal and Social Psychology, 67,* 371–378.

Milgram, S. (1964a). Group pressure and action against a person. *Journal of Abnormal and Social Psychology, 69,* 137–143.

Milgram, S. (1964b). Issues in the study of obedience: A reply to Baumrind. *American Psychologist, 19,* 848–852.

Milgram, S. (1965). Some conditions of obedience and disobedience to authority. *Human Relations, 18,* 57–76.

Milgram, S. (1972). Interpreting obedience: Error and evidence: A reply to Orne and Holland. In A. G. Miller (ed.), *The social psychology of psychological research.* New York: Free Press.

Milgram, S. (1974). *Obedience to authority: An experimental view.* New York: Harper & Row.

Milgram, S. (1977). Ethical issues in the study of obedience. In S. Milgram (Ed.), *The individual in a social world,* 188–199. Reading, MA: Addison-Wesley.

Miller, D. B. (1977). Roles of naturalistic observation in comparative psychology. *American Psychologist, 32,* 211–219.

Miller, N. E. (1959). Liberalization of basic S-R concepts: Extensions to conflict behavior, motivation and social learning. In S. Koch (Ed.), *Psychology: A study of a science,* vol. 2, 196–292. New York: McGraw Hill.

Milner, P. M. (1970). *Physiological psychology.* New York: Holt, Rinehart and Winston.

Mook, D. G. (1983). In defense of external invalidity. *American Psychologist, 38,* 379–387.

Moriarity, T. (1975). Crime, commitment, and the responsive bystander: Two field studies. *Journal of Personality and Social Psychology, 31,* 370–376.

Morris, C. D., Bransford, J. D., & Franks, J. J. (1977). Levels of processing versus transfer appropriate processing. *Journal of Verbal Learning and Verbal Behavior, 16,* 519–533.

Moscovitch, M. (1982). Multiple dissociations of functions in the amnesic syndrome. In L. Cermak (Ed.), *Human memory and amnesia.* Hillsdale, NJ: Erlbaum.

Murphy, M. D., & Brown, A. L. (1975). Incidental learning in preschool children as a function of level of cognitive analysis. *Journal of Experimental Child Psychology, 19,* 509–523.

Natsoulas, T. (1967). What are perceptual reports about? *Psychological Bulletin, 67,* 249–272.

Nelson, T. O. (1977). Repetition and levels of processing. *Journal of Verbal Learning and Verbal Behavior, 16,* 151–171.

Newell, A., & Simon, H. A. (1972). *Human problem solving.* Englewood Cliffs, NJ: Prentice-Hall.

Nisbett, R. E., & Wilson, T. D. (1977). Telling more than we can know: Verbal reports on mental processes. *Psychological Review, 84,* 231–259.

Norman, D. A. (1969). Memory while shadowing. *Quarterly Journal of Experimental Psychology, 21,* 85–94.

Notterman, J. M., & Mintz, D. E. (1965). *Dynamics of response.* New York: Wiley.

Novick, L. R. (1990). Representational transfer in problem solving. *Psychological Science, 1,* 128–132.

Olton, R. M., & Johnson, D. M. (1976). Mechanisms of incubation in creative problem solving. *American Journal of Psychology, 89,* 617–630.

Orne, M. T. (1962). On the social psychology of the psychological experiment: With particular reference to demand characteristics and their implications. *American Psychologist, 17,* 776–783.

Orne, M. T. (1969). Demand characteristics and the concept of quasi-controls. In R. Rosnow and R. L. Rosenthal (Eds.), *Artifact in behavioral research.* New York: Academic Press.

Orne, M. T., & Evans, T. J. (1965). Social control in the psychological experiment: Antisocial behavior and hypnosis. *Journal of Personality and Social Psychology, 1,* 189–200.

Orne, M. T., & Holland, C. C. (1968). On the ecological validity of laboratory deceptions. *International Journal of Psychiatry, 6,* 282–293.

Pachella, R. G. (1974). The interpretation of reaction time in information-processing research. In B. H. Kantowitz (Ed.), *Human information processing—Tutorials in performance and cognition.* Hillsdale, NJ: Erlbaum.

Padilla, A. M. (1971). Analysis of incentive and behavioral contrast in the rat. *Journal of Comparative and Physiological Psychology, 45,* 464–470.

Paillard, J., Michel, F., & Stelmach, G. (1983). Localization without content: A tactile analogue of "blindsight." *Archives of Neurology, 40,* 548–551.

Paivio, A. (1969). Mental imagery in associative learning and memory. *Psychological Review, 76,* 241–263.

Parsons, H. M. (1970). Life and death. *Human Factors, 12,* 1–6.

Parsons, H. M. (1974). What happened at Hawthorne? *Science, 183,* 922–931.

Pavlov, I. P. (1963). *Lectures on conditioned reflexes.* New York: International Publishers.

Peirce, C. S. (1877). The fixation of belief. *Popular Science Monthly, 12,* 1–15. Reprinted in E. C. Moore (Ed.). (1972). *Charles Sanders Peirce: The essential writings.* New York: Harper & Row.

Peterson, L. R., & Peterson, M. J. (1959). Short term retention of individual items. *Journal of Experimental Psychology, 58,* 193–198.

Pfungst, O. (1911). *Clever Hans, the horse of Mr. Von Osten: A contribution to experimental, animal, and human psychology.* (Trans, by C. L. Rahn). New York: Holt.

Piaget, J. (1932). *The language and thought of the child,* (2nd ed.). London: Routledge & Kegan Paul.

Piliavin, I. M., Piliavin, J. A., & Rodin, J. (1975). Costs, diffusion, and the stigmatized victim. *Journal of Personality and Social Psychology, 32,* 429–438.

Piliavin, I. M., Rodin, J., & Piliavin, J. A. (1969). Good samaritanism: An underground phenomenon? *Journal of Personality and Social Psychology, 13,* 289–299.

Platt, J. R. (1964). Strong inference. *Science, 146,* 347–353.

Plotkin, W. B. (1979). The alpha experience revisited: Biofeedback in the transformation of psychological state. *Psychological Bulletin, 86,* 1132–1148.

Poincaré, H. (1929). *The foundations of science.* New York: Science House, Inc.

Popper, K. R. (1961). *The logic of scientific discovery.* New York: Basic Books.

Posner, M. I. (1973). *Cognition: An introduction.* Glenview, IL: Scott, Foresman.

Rapoport, A. (1975). Towards a redefinition of density. *Environment and Behavior, 7,* 133–158.

Rescorla, R. A. (1967). Pavlovian conditioning and its proper control procedures. *Psychological Review, 74,* 71–80.

Ringelmann, M. (1913). Recherches sur les moteurs animes: Travail de l'homme. *Annales de l'Institut National Agronomique,* 2e series-tome XII, 1–40.

Roberts, C. (1971). Debate I. Animal experimentation and evolution. *American Scholar, 40,* 497–503.

Roediger, H. L. (1980). The effectiveness of four mnemonics in ordering recall. *Journal of Experimental Psychology: Human Learning and Memory, 6,* 558–567.

Roediger, H. L. (1990). Implicit memory: Retention without remembering. *American Psychologist, 45,* 1043–1056.

Rogosa, D. (1980). A critique of the cross-lagged correlation. *Psychological Bulletin, 88,* 245–248.

Rollin, B. E. (1985). The moral status of research animals in psychology. *American Psychologist, 40,* 920–926.

Rosenthal, R. (1966). *Experimenter effects in behavioral research.* New York: Appleton-Century-Crofts.

Rosenthal, R. (1969). Interpersonal expectations: Effects of the experimenter's hypothesis. In R. Rosenthal and R. L. Rosnow (Eds.), *Artifact in behavioral research.* New York: Academic Press.

Rosenthal, R., & Fode, K. (1963). The effects of experimenter bias on the performance of the albino rat. *Behavioral Science, 8,* 183–189.

Ross, E. A. (1908). *Social psychology.* New York: Macmillan.

Rowland, L. W. (1939). Will hypnotized persons try to harm themselves or others? *Journal of Abnormal and Social Psychology, 34,* 114–117.

Rozin, P. (1986). One-trial acquired likes and dislikes in humans: Disgust as a US, food predominance, and negative learning predominance. *Learning and Motivation, 17,* 180–189.

Saegert, S., Mackintosh, E., & West, S. (1975). Two studies of crowding in urban public spaces. *Environment and Behavior, 7,* 159–184.

Scarborough, D. L. (1972). Stimulus modality effects on forgetting in short term memory. *Journal of Experimental Psychology, 95,* 285–289.

Scarr, S. (1988). Race and gender as psychological variables: Social and ethical issues. *American Psychologist, 43,* 56–59.

Schacter, D. L. (1983). Feeling of knowing in episodic memory. *Journal of Experimental Psychology, 9,* 39–54.

Schacter, D. L. (1987). Implicit memory: History and current status. *Journal of Experimental Psychology: Learning, Memory, and Cognition, 13,* 501–518.

Schacter, D. L. (1990). Introduction to implicit memory: Multiple perspectives. *Bulletin of the Psychonomic Society, 28,* 338–340.

Schaie, K. W. (1977). Quasi-experimental designs in the psychology of aging. In J. E. Birren and K. W. Schaie (Eds.), *Handbook of psychology and aging.* New York: Van Nostrand.

Schultz, D. P., & Schultz, S. E. (1987). *A history of modern psychology* (4th ed.). New York: Academic Press.

Scialfa, C. T., Garvey, P. M., Gish, K. W., Deering, L. M., Leibowitz, H. W., & Goebel, C. C. (1988). Relationships among measures of static and dynamic visual sensitivity. *Human Factors, 30,* 677–688.

Searle, J. R. (1980). Minds, brains, and programs. *Behavioral and brain sciences, 3,* 417–458.

Searle, J. R. (1990, January). Is the brain's mind a computer program? *Scientific American,* 26–31.

Seligman, M. E. P. (1975). *Helplessness.* San Francisco: Freeman.

Sherif, M. (1935). A study of some social factors in perception. *Archives of Psychology,* No. 187.

Shimamura, A. P. (1986). Priming effects in amnesia: Evidence for a dissociable memory function. *The Quarterly Journal of Experimental Psychology, 38A,* 619–644.

Sidman, M. (1960). *Tactics of scientific research.* New York: Basic Books.

Sieber, J. E., & Stanley, B. (1988). Ethical and professional dimensions of socially sensitive research. *American Psychologist, 43,* 49–55.

Silveira, T. (1971). Incubation: The effect of interruption timing and length on problem solution and quality of problem processing. Doctoral dissertation, University of Oregon.

Singer, P. (1978). Animal experimentation: Philosophical perspectives. In W. T. Reich (Ed.), *Encyclopedia of bioethics.* New York: Free Press.

Skinner, B. F. (1955). Freedom and the control of men. *American Scholar, 25,* 47–65.

Skinner, B. F. (1956). A case history in scientific method. *American Psychologist, 11,* 221–233.

Skinner, B. F. (1957). *Verbal behavior.* New York: Appleton-Century-Crofts.

Skinner, B. F. (1963). The flight from the laboratory. In M. Marx, (Ed.), *Theories in contemporary psychology.* New York: Macmillan.

Smith, A. D., & Winograd, E. (1978). Adult age differences in remembering faces. *Developmental Psychology, 14,* 443–444.

Smith, C. P. (1983). Ethical issues: Research on deception, informed consent, and debriefing. In L. Wheeler & P. Shaver (Eds.), *Review of personality and social psychology,* vol. 4, 297–328. Beverly Hills, CA: Sage.

Smith, E. R., & Miller, F. D. (1978). Limits on perceptions of cognitive processes: A reply to Nisbett and Wilson. *Psychological Review, 85,* 355–362.

Smith, S. L. (1981). Exploring compatability with words and pictures. *Human Factors*, 23, 305–315.

Spence, K. W. (1948). The postulates and methods of 'behaviorism.' *Psychological Review*, 55, 67–78.

Spencer, R. M., & Weisberg, R. W. (1986). Context-dependent effects on analogical transfer. *Memory & Cognition*, 14, 442–449.

Stanley, A. (1990, May 8). Pre-med student, 12, goes for record. *Roanoke Times & World-News*, 1, 10.

Sternberg, R. J. (1987). *The psychologist's companion: A guide to scientific writing for students and researchers*. Cambridge: Cambridge University Press.

Sternberg, R. J. (1988). *The triarchic mind: A new theory of human intelligence*. New York: Viking.

Sternberg, R. J., & Salter, W. (1982). Conceptions of intelligence. In R. J. Sternberg (Ed.), *Handbook of human intelligence*. Cambridge: Cambridge University Press.

Sternberg, S. (1969). Memory scanning: Mental processes revealed by reaction time experiments. *American Scientist*, 57, 421–457.

Stevens, S. S. (1961). The psychophysics of sensory functions. In W. A. Rosenblith, *Sensory communication*. Cambridge: M.I.T. Press.

Stroop, J. R. (1935). Studies of interference in serial verbal reactions. *Journal of Experimental Psychology*, 18, 643–662.

Suppes, P., & Zinnes, J. L. (1963). Basic measurement theory. In R. Luce, R. Brush, and E. Galanter (Eds.), *Handbook of mathematical psychology*, vol. 1. New York: Wiley.

Taylor, D. A. (1976). Stage analysis of reaction time. *Psychological Bulletin*, 83, 161–191.

Theios, J. (1975). Reaction time measurements in the study of memory processes: Theory and data. In G. Bower (Ed.), *The psychology of learning and motivation*, vol. 7. New York: Academic Press.

Thorndike, E. L. (1898). Animal intelligence: An experimental study of the associative processes in animals. *Psychological Review Monograph Supplement*, 2.

Tulving, E., & Pearlstone, Z. (1966). Availability versus accessibility of information in memory for words. *Journal of Verbal Learning and Verbal Behavior*, 5, 381–391.

Turing, A. M. (1950). Computing machinery and intelligence. *Mind*, 59, 433–460.

Tversky, A., & Kahneman, D. (1971). Belief in the law of small numbers. *Psychological Bulletin*, 76, 105–110.

Tversky, A., & Kahneman, D. (1974). Judgments under uncertainty: Heuristics and biases. *Science*, 185, 1124–1131.

Underwood, B. J. (1975). Individual differences as a crucible in theory construction. *American Psychologist*. 30, 128–134.

Velten, E. A. (1968). A laboratory task for the induction of mood states. *Behavior Research and Therapy*, 6, 473–478.

Warren, R. M. (1963). Are loudness judgments based on distance estimates? *Journal of the Acoustical Society of America*, 35, 613–614.

Warrington, E. K., & Weiskrantz, L. (1970). Amnesic syndrome: Consolidation or retrieval? *Nature*, 228, 628–630.

Watson, J. B. (1913). Psychology as the behaviorist views it. *Psychological Review*, 20, 158–177.

Watson, J. B. (1919). *Psychology from the standpoint of a behaviorist*. Philadelphia: Lippincott.

Watson, J. B. (1925). *Behaviorism*. New York: Norton.

Waugh, N. C., & Norman, D. A. (1965). Primary memory. *Psychological Review, 72*, 89–104.

Webb, E. J., Campbell, D. T., Schwartz, R. D., & Sechrest, L. (1966). *Unobtrusive measures: Nonreactive research in the social sciences*. Chicago: Rand McNally.

Weiskrantz, L. (1977). Trying to bridge some neuropsychological gaps between monkey and man. *British Journal of Psychology, 68*, 431–445.

Weiskrantz, L. (1986). *Blindsight: A case study and implications*. Oxford: Clarendon Press.

Weizenbaum, J. (1976). *Computer power and human reason*. San Francisco: W. H. Freeman.

Weldon, M. S., & Roediger, H. L. (1987). Altering retrieval demands reverses the picture superiority effect. *Memory & Cognition, 15*, 269–280.

Welker, R. L. (1976). Acquisition of a free-operant-appetitive response in pigeons as a function of prior experience with response-independent food. *Learning and Motivation, 7*, 394–405.

White, R. J. (1971). Debate II. Antivivisection: The reluctant hydra. *American Scholar, 40*, 503–512.

Wickelgren, W. A. (1977). *Learning and memory*. Englewood Cliffs, NJ: Prentice-Hall.

Williams, K., Harkins, S., & Latané, B. (1981). Identifiability as a deterrent to social loafing: Two cheering experiments. *Journal of Personality and Social Psychology, 40*, 303–311.

Wolf, M. M., & Risley, T. R. (1971). Reinforcement: Applied research. In R. Glaser (Ed.), *The nature of reinforcement*. New York: Academic Press.

Wrightsman L. S., & Deaux, K. K. (1981). *Social psychology in the 80's* (2d ed.). Monterey, CA: Brooks-Cole.

Wundt, W. (1874). *Principles of physiological psychology*. Leipzig: Engelmann.

Young, P. C. (1952). Antisocial uses of hypnosis. In L. M. LeCron (Ed.), *Experimental hypnosis*. New York: Macmillan.

Zajonc, R. B. (1962). Response suppression in perceptual defense. *Journal of Experimental Psychology, 64*, 206–214.

GLOSSARY

AB design a frequently used design in therapy in which a therapy (B) is instituted after measuring a particular behavior (A), a poor research design

ABA design see reversal design

ABAB design a completed reversal design often used in therapy such that the therapeutic procedure (B) is reintroduced

Abscissa the horizontal axis (or x-axis) in a graph

Absolute threshold in psychophysics, a hypothetical barrier which incoming stimuli must cross before they can be perceived

Aftercare the need for experimenters to guard the welfare of their subjects subsequent to the research manipulation; especially important in drug research

AI (artificial intelligence) the notion that computer programs can execute actions thought to require intelligence when done by people

Amnesia a memory disorder, usually caused by some injury to the brain, characterized by either total or partial memory loss

Analysis of variance a statistical test appropriate for analyzing reliability from experiments with any number of levels on one or more independent variables

Anthropomorphizing attributing human characteristics or emotions, such as happiness, to animals

Aphasic a person who has a disorder of language; usually associated with damage to the left hemisphere of the brain

A priori method according to Peirce, a way of fixing belief according to the reasonableness of the event

Arithmetic mean see mean

Autokinetic phenomenon the perception by a person in a dark room that a single, stationary spot of light appears to move

Awareness an issue in perception as to whether an individual can respond perceptually to an event in the absence of conscious awareness

Balanced Latin square a counterbalancing scheme in which each condition is preceded and followed equally often by every other condition

Behaviorism the school of psychology, originated by John Watson, that directed psychologists' attention to the study of overt behavior, not mind nor mental events

Behavior modification therapy that involves the use of operant conditioning procedures, emphasizing observation of behavior, its controlling variables, and contingent reinforcement

Beta a statistic in signal detection theory related to the criterion adopted by the observer

Between-group variance a measure of the dispersion among groups in an experiment

Between-subject design an experimental design in which each subject is tested under only one level of each independent variable

Bit the basic unit of information measured in binary digits

Blindsight according to Weiskrantz, the effect of certain kinds of brain damage, in which the subject has an inability to recognize objects, but retains the ability to detect the presence and movement of objects

Bottom-up processing cognitive processes involving feature extraction that begin with sensory stimulation

Brown-Peterson technique a way of studying short-term memory that involves first presenting a to-be-remembered item and then presenting material that limits rehearsal for a retention interval prior to a retention test

Carry-over effect the relatively permanent effect that testing subjects in one condition has on their later behavior in another condition

Case study the intensive investigation of a particular instance, or case, of some behavior; does not allow inferences of cause and effect, but is merely descriptive

Categorized list words used in memory experiments that are related by being members of the same category; e.g., articles of furniture: chair, bed, sofa, table

Ceiling effect see scale attenuation effects

Central tendency the center of a distribution of scores; descriptive statistics indicating the center of a distribution of scores; see mean and median

Chinese room a thought experiment developed by Searle that supposedly shows that AI is impossible

Classical conditioning a basic form of learning, in which stimuli initially incapable of evoking certain responses acquire the ability to do so through repeated pairing with other stimuli (unconditioned stimuli) that are able to elicit such responses; also called respondent conditioning

Cognitive psychology the study of how people acquire, store, and use information

Cohort effects a potential confounding when age is a variable, attributable to the effects of the people living at a time when a given individual is developing

Conceptual replication the attempt to demonstrate an experimental phenomenon with an entirely new paradigm or set of experimental conditions (see converging operations)

Conceptually-driven processing see top-down processing

Conditioned response (CR) the learned response to a conditioned stimulus

Conditioned stimulus (CS) an originally neutral stimulus that, through repeated pairings with an unconditioned stimulus, acquires the ability to elicit the response originally produced only by the unconditioned stimulus

Confidentiality information obtained about subjects should remain confidential unless otherwise agreed

Confounding the simultaneous variation of a second variable with an independent variable of interest, so that any effect on the dependent variable cannot be attributed with certainty to the independent variable; inherent in correlational research

Contingency the relationship between a response and its outcome in operant conditioning or the CS-UCS relationship in classical conditioning

Continuous reinforcement a schedule of reinforcement in which a reward follows every time the appropriate behavior is emitted

Control variable a potential independent variable that is held constant in an experiment

Converging operations a set of related lines of investigation that all bolster a common conclusion

Correlation a measure of the extent to which two variables are related, not necessarily causally

Correlation coefficient a number that can vary from -1.00 to $+1.00$, and indicates the degree of relation between two variables

Counterbalancing a term describing any technique used to vary systematically the order of conditions in an experiment to distribute the effects of time of testing (e.g., practice and fatigue), so they are not confounded with conditions

Criterion validity see predictive validity

Crossover interaction the reversal of the effect of one independent variable on a dependent variable at a certain level of a second independent variable

Cross-sectional studies the use of a large sample of the population of various ages at one time for testing purposes (contrast with longitudinal studies)

Cross-sequential studies are experiments that combine the cross-sectional and longitudinal procedures

d′ a statistic in signal detection theory related to the sensitivity of the observer

Data the scores obtained on a dependent variable

Data-driven processing see bottom-up processing

Debriefing when subjects are told all details of an experiment after they have participated; an ethical obligation of the researcher

Deception a research technique in which the participant is misled about some aspect of the project; may be unethical (see double blind)

Decision threshold the stimulus that elicits a response resulting from both the criterion and the strength of the stimulus (see beta and d′)

Deduction reasoning from the general to the particular

Degrees of freedom the number of values free to vary if the total number of values and their sum are fixed

Delimiting observations especially in naturalistic observation, the necessity to limit or choose the classes of behaviors to be observed

Demand characteristics those cues available to subjects in an experiment that may enable them to determine the purpose of the experiment, or what is expected by the experimenter

Dependent variable the variable measured and recorded by the experimenter

Descriptive statistics methods of organizing and summarizing data

Deviant case analysis investigation of similar cases that differ in outcome, in an attempt to specify the reasons for the different outcomes

Dichotic listening a test of attention in which two separate messages are delivered simultaneously, one to each ear

Difference threshold the average point at which two stimuli are judged to be different

Diffusion ($I = N^{-t}$) the power law showing that impact (I) of other people decreases as a function of the number (N) of other people

Direct perception Gibson's idea that we directly pick up and use the information afforded by the environment

Direct replication the repetition of an experiment as identically as possible to the first performance, to determine whether or not the same results will be obtained

Discriminative stimulus a stimulus that indicates whether or not a response will be reinforced

Dispersion the amount of spread in a distribution of scores

Distribution a set of values on a variable

Dizygotic developing from two different fertilized eggs

Double blind an experimental technique in which neither the subject nor the experimenter knows which subjects are in which treatment conditions

Double dissociation of function a technique in which opposite behaviors are elicited by two different tasks from different areas of functioning (see converging operations)

Dualism the idea that the mind and the body are separate entities

Dynamic perimetry a procedure, used to measure the visual field, in which a small visual target is gradually brought into the field of vision

Dynamic visual acuity ability to perceive detail in moving objects

Einstellung see set

Empirical relying upon or derived from observation or experiment

Empirical theory of perception the argument that perceptions are determined entirely by past experience

Episodic memory memories that are autobiographical and personally dated

Ethical principles of the American Psychological Association principles established to suggest ethical guidelines to researchers

Experiment the systematic manipulation of some factors in the environment in order to observe the effect of this manipulation upon behavior

Experimenter bias the effect that an experimenter may unknowingly exert on results of an experiment, usually in a direction favoring the experimenter's hypothesis

Experimental control the holding constant of extraneous variables in an experiment, so that any effect on the dependent variable can be attributed to manipulation of the independent variable

Explicit memory test a memory test that requires a person to try consciously to remember specific events

Ex post facto literally, "from after the fact"; describes conditions in an experiment that are determined not prior to the experiment, but only after some manipulation has occurred naturally

Extinction the weakening or elimination of conditioned responses by the withholding of reinforcement

Face validity the condition in which a measuring instrument intuitively seems to measure what it is supposed to measure

Factorial design an experimental design in which each level of every independent variable occurs with all levels of the other independent variables

False alarm the incorrect reporting of the presence of a signal on a trial in which only noise occurrs

Falsifiability view the assertion by Popper that negative results of a test are more informative than positive results

Fechner's law the logarithmic relation, developed by Fechner, of sensation to stimulus intensity: $\psi = k\log(s)$

Field research research conducted in natural settings, where subjects typically do not know that they are in an experiment

Floor effect see scale attenuation effects

Freedom to withdraw experimenters are ethically obliged to allow their subjects to discontinue participation in the research project

Frequency distribution a set of scores arranged in order along a distribution, indicating the number of times each score occurs

Functional fixedness the inability to use an object in a new context if it has already served a different function

Functionalism the school of psychology concerned with the function of psychological processes

Generality of results the issue of whether or not a particular experimental result will be obtained under different circumstances, such as with a different subject population or in a different experimental setting

Gestalt psychology the school of psychology emphasizing whole patterns as important in perception, rather than the artificial analysis of experience into parts (as in structuralism)

Graphemic the letter level of perceptual analysis

Hawthorne effect the condition in which performance in an experiment is affected by the knowledge of participants that they are in an experiment; see demand characteristics

Heterogeneous dissimilar; varying from others

Higher order interaction interaction effects involving more than two independent variables in multifactor experiments

Histogram a frequency distribution in which the height of bars in the graph indicates the frequency of a class of scores; also called a bar graph

Hit the correct detection of a signal that has been presented

Homogeneous similar; of the same kind as others

Human factors the discipline that tries to optimize the relationship between technology and the human

Hypothesis a testable statement that offers a predicted relationship between dependent and independent variables

Impact $(I = N^t)$ the power law showing that the impact (I) of others increases with the number (N) of other people

Implicit memory test a "memory" test that does not require a person to explicitly remember specific experiences, but that spontaneously exhibits the effects of those experiences

Independent variable the variable manipulated by the experimenter

Indirect perception idea that perception results from the interpretation of sensations; see direct perception for the contrasting approach

Induction reasoning from the particular to the general

Inferential statistics procedures for determining the reliability and generality of a particular experimental finding

Informed consent potential subjects must be in a position to decide whether to participate in an experiment

Instrumental conditioning conditioning in which a subject learns to make a response that leads to a reward or prevents a punishment; in contrast to classical conditioning, no eliciting stimulus is presented

Intelligence mental age (as determined by a test) divided by chronological age × 100

Interaction an experimental result that occurs when the levels of one independent variable are differentially affected by the levels of other independent variables

Interpolated task a task used to fill the interval between the study of material and its recall in memory experiments

Interstimulus interval the time between two successive stimuli, usually (but not always) measured from the onset of the first to the onset of the second

Intervening variables abstract concepts that link independent variables to dependent variables

Landolt C a way of measuring visual acuity, in which the gap of the C is varied and the observer determines when the gap is no longer visible

Large-*n* design an experiment involving a large number of subjects; usually analyzed by complex statistical procedures

Levels of processing a framework for studying memory that predicts that semantic or "deeper" encoding tasks will produce better memory for the material than perceptual or "shallow" encoding tasks

Longitudinal studies the testing of one group of people repeatedly as they age (contrast with cross-sectional studies)

Long-term memory retrieval of memories that have disappeared from consciousness after their initial perception

Main effect the condition in which the effect of one independent variable is the same at all levels of another independent variable

Mapping in problem solving, the set of correspondences between a source and target problem; how the two problems "map" onto each other

Masking the technique of presenting a jumbled visual stimulus immediately after a target stimulus, in order to stop the visual persistence of the target

Matched groups design an experimental design in which subjects are matched on some variable assumed to be correlated with the dependent variable, and then randomly assigned to conditions

Mean a measure of central tendency; the sum of all the scores divided by the number of scores

Mean deviation difference between an individual score in a distribution and the mean of the distribution

Median a measure of central tendency; the middle score of a distribution, or the one that divides a distribution in half

Mental workload an intervening variable, similar to attention, that modulates the tuning between the demands of the environment and the capability of the organism

Method of authority a method of fixing belief in which an authority's word is taken on faith (contrast with empirical)

Method of limits a psychophysical procedure for determining thresholds in which ascending and descending sequences of stimuli are presented

Method of tenacity a method of fixing belief involving a steadfast adherence to a particular belief, regardless of contrary arguments or data (contrast with empirical)

Mnemonic device a technique or strategy used to improve memory, e.g., the method of loci and the peg-word method

Modality effects different effects on retention often produced by visual and auditory presentation; auditory presentation usually produces better memory for the last few items in a series than does visual presentation

Monitoring task a form of dichotic listening in which observers are not required to verbalize a message as it is presented

Monotonic relationship the relationship between two variables in which an increase on one variable is accompanied by a consistent increase or decrease on the other variable

Monozygotic developing from the same fertilized egg

Multiple intelligences the theory that intelligence is actually comprised of seven different intelligences

Nativistic theory of perception the theory that genetic "wired-in" mechanisms account for perceptual capabilities (see empirical theory of perception)

Naturalistic observation the description of naturally occurring events without intervention on the part of the investigator

Negative reinforcing stimulus a stimulus, which when removed, increases the likelihood of the response that removed it

Nonreactive a term used to describe observations that are not influenced by the presence of the investigator; nonreactive methods are also referred to as unobtrusive

Normal distribution a distribution producing a symmetric, bell-shaped curve

Null contingency a reinforcement contingency in which there is no relation between a response and reinforcing stimuli

Null hypothesis the prediction that the independent variable will have no effect on the dependent variable

Null result an experimental outcome in which the dependent variable is not influenced by the independent variable

Objective measures dependent variables such as reaction time that can be easily verified (contrast with subjective measures)

Objective threshold according to Cheesman and Merikle, the stimulus energy level that elicits truly random behavior (compare to subjective threshold)

Observational methods research techniques based on simply observing behavior, without trying to manipulate it experimentally

One-tailed test a test that places the rejection area at one end of a distribution

Operant conditioning see instrumental conditioning

Operational definition a definition of a concept in terms of the operations that must be performed to demonstrate the concept

Ordinate the vertical axis (or y-axis) in a graph

Organization one characteristic of a good theory is to organize existing knowledge

Paired-associate recall a memory task in which a pair of words is given (e.g., mongoose-elephant) and later the first word is provided and the task is to recall the second word

Parallel forms two alternative forms of a test

Partial reinforcement a schedule of reinforcement in which a reward follows a desired response only on some occasions

Partial reinforcement effect the greater resistance to extinction exhibited for responses learned under partial rather than continuous schedules of reinforcement

Participant observation an observation technique in which the observer participates with those being observed; e.g., living with gorillas in the wild

Payoff the explicit monetary costs and benefits associated with making a certain type of response to a stimulus

Perception the awareness process typically viewed as more complex than sensation, and usually involving an interpretation of sensation

Perceptual defense an unwillingness to report perceiving unpleasant material, in contrast to an inability to perceive such material

Personal space the physical area surrounding a person within which a person will experience discomfort if another person enters; measured by noting the person's defensive reactions

Phenomenological experience a person's awareness of his or her own state of mind

Phonemic (phonological) the sound level of the perceptual analysis of words

Photopic vision vision controlled by the cones in the retina, typically in day viewing conditions

Placebo effect the improvement often shown in drug effectiveness studies when patients believe they have received a drug, although they have actually received an inert substance

Population the total set of potential observations (from which a sample can be drawn)

Positive reinforcing stimulus a stimulus, which when presented, increases the likelihood of the response that produced it

Power (of a statistical test) the probability of rejecting the null hypothesis in a statistical test when it is in fact false

Predictive validity the ability of a test score to predict behavior on some criterion measure; also called criterion validity (e.g., a law school entrance exam correctly predicts success as a laywer)

Primacy effect the better retention of information occurring at the beginning of a list, relative to information in the middle

Priming a technique for eliciting related cognitions by presenting a stimulus that primes a person to think of the related event; e.g., the word "table" makes you think of "chair"

Proactive interference forgetting which is produced by prior learning

Probability an estimate of the likelihood that a particular event will occur

Problem a vague question that is too general to be tested without additional refinement; see hypothesis

Protection from harm ethical researchers protect their subjects from any harm

Pseudoconditioning a temporary elevation in the amplitude of the conditioned response that is not due to association between the conditioned stimulus and the unconditioned stimulus

Punishment a stimulus, which when presented, decreases the likelihood of the response that produced it

Qualitative variation manipulation of an independent variable along a dimension that is not easily quantified, such as providing people different types of instructions in an experiment

Quantitative variation manipulation of an independent variable along a measurable dimension, such as the number of food pellets given a rat as reinforcement

Quasi-experiment an experiment in which the independent variable occurs naturally, and is not under direct control of the experimenter

Random groups design the random assignment of subjects to conditions in a between-subjects design

Range a descriptive measure of dispersion; the difference between the largest and smallest scores in a distribution

Reaction time the time between the onset of a stimulus and the making of a response to that stimulus

Reactive a term used to describe observations that are influenced by (or may be, in part, a reaction to) the detected presence of the investigator

Recall a measure of retention in which reproduction of material is required

Recency effect the better retention of information at the end of a list, relative to information in the middle

Recognition a measure of retention in which familiarity of information is judged

Regression artifacts an artifact in the measurement of change on a variable when groups of subjects who scored at the extremes on the variable are tested again; see regression to the mean

Regression to the mean the tendency for extreme measures on some variable to be closer to the group mean when remeasured, due to unreliability of measurement

Related measures design one in which several measures are taken either on the same subject, or on subjects matched on important dimensions

Reliability the repeatability of an experimental result; inferential statistics provide an estimation of the likelihood that a finding is repeatable; also, the consistency of a test or measuring instrument, determined by computing a correlation between scores obtained by subjects taking the test twice (test-retest reliability), or by their taking two different parallel forms of the test, or by scores obtained on each half of the test (split-half reliability)

Removing harmful consequences ethical researchers remove any harmful consequences that their subjects may have incurred

Replication the repetition of an earlier experiment to duplicate (and perhaps extend) its findings (also see systematic replication)

Reproduceability see reliability

Respondent conditioning see classical conditioning

Retrieval cue information presented at the time of a memory test to aid recall

Retroactive interference the forgetting of material produced by learning of subsequent material

Reversal (ABA) design a small-*n* design in which a subject's behavior is measured under a baseline (A) condition, then an experimental treatment is applied during the B phase and any changes in behavior are observed; finally, the original baseline (A) conditions are reinstituted, to ensure that the experimental treatment was responsible for any observed change during the B phase.

ROC function (receiver operating characteristic) a plot graphing hits against false alarms

Sample observations selected from a population

Scale attenuation effects difficulties in interpreting results when performance on the dependent variable is either nearly perfect (a ceiling effect) or nearly lacking altogether (a floor effect)

Scatterplot a graphical relationship indicating the degree of correlation between two variables, made by plotting the scores of individuals on two variables

Scotoma a region of blindness in the visual field, caused by a physical defect in the visual system

Scotopic vision night vision that is controlled by the rods in the retina

Secondary task an extra task on which performance is an index of attention

Semantic meaningful analysis of a word

Sensation the basic and elemental intake of stimulus information

Serial position the order in which information appears when studied for a later memory test

Serial position curve the graphical representation of retention as a function of the input position of the information; usually, memory is better for the first items (primacy effect) and the last items (recency effect) than for those in the middle; this typical finding is referred to as the serial position effect

Set the effect of expectancy of cognition; for example, if the people solve problems in one particular way, they will often approach new problems in the same set way, even when the original strategy is no longer effective; also called Einstellung, from the original German experiment

Shadowing task a form of dichotic listening in which the listener is required to repeat aloud (shadow) the message presented in one ear as it occurs

Shaping a technique for conditioning a desired response by rewarding successive approximations to that response

Short-term memory recovery of information shortly after it has been perceived before it has left conscious awareness

Significance level the probability that an experimental finding is due to chance, or random fluctuation, operating in the data

Skewed distribution a nonsymmetrical distribution

Small-*n* design research design utilizing a small number of subjects

Social loafing the decrease in individual effort that sometimes occurs when other people are present and when group performance is measured

Social facilitation the increase in individual effort produced by the presence of other people and when individual performance is measured

Speciesism a term used to describe the view that animal life is qualitatively different from human life and, therefore, the view is a form of bigotry

Speed-accuracy tradeoff in reaction time experiments, the ability of the responder to substitute changes in the percentage of correct responses for changes in speed of responding

Split-half reliability the determination of reliability of a test by dividing the test items into two arbitrary groups and correlating the scores obtained on the two halves of the test

Split-litter technique the random assignment of animals from the same litter to different groups; a type of matched groups design

Standard deviation a descriptive measure of dispersion; square root of the sum of squared deviations of each score from the mean, divided by the number of scores

Standard error of the mean the standard deviation of the distribution of sample means

Stevens' law the principle, stated by Stevens, that sensation grows as a power of stimulus intensity: $\psi = S^n$

Stress a psychological state of an organism when there is a disparity between its ability to cope with demands of the environment and the level of such demands

Strong AI the view that machines can possess intelligence of the sort possessed by humans

Strong inference Platt's view that scientific progress comes about through a series of tests of alternative theoretical outcomes

Structural consistency in problem solving, mapped elements in the source and target problems should play similar roles

Structuralism the school of psychology, originated by Wundt, in which the primary task of psychology was considered to be the analysis of the structure of conscious experience through introspection

Subjective measures introspective reports given on rating scales that usually cannot be objectively verified

Subjective report verbal report of a person's perceived mental state

Subjective threshold the stimulus energy level that yields claims of unawareness, but yields behavior indicating perception of the event (see objective threshold)

Subject representativeness the determination of generality of results across different subject populations

Subject variable a characteristic of people that can be measured or described, but cannot be varied experimentally (e.g. height, weight, sex, I.Q., etc.)

Subtractive method a technique originated by Donders to estimate the amount of time required for various mental operations by subtracting one component from another

Survey research the technique of obtaining a limited amount of information from a large number of people, usually through random sampling

Synergism another term for interaction, in which the joint effects of two variables combine in a way that is not a simple function of their individual effects

Systematic replication the repetition of an experiment while varying numerous factors considered to be irrelevant to the phenomenon, to see if it will survive these changes

Test-retest reliability the practice of giving the same test twice in succession over a short interval, to see if the scores are stable, or reliable; generally expressed as a correlation between scores on the tests

Tetrahedral model of memory Jenkins' four part analysis of memory experiments into type of subjects, orienting tasks, type of test, and type of materials

Token economy the technique of positive reinforcement, often employed by mental hospitals and other institutions, in which patients are rewarded for socially constructive behavior by tokens, which may later be exchanged for privileges

Tonal agnosia an inability to appreciate melody in music and speech; usually associated with damage to the right hemisphere of the brain

Top-down processing cognitive processes that begin with knowledge of concepts; contrast with bottom-up processing

Transfer appropriate processing the kind of memory test may determine the encoding activities that are useful for the test

Trials to criterion the number of study and test trials needed to recall material perfectly

Truncated range a problem in interpreting low correlations; the amount of dispersion (or range) of scores on one variable may be small, thus leading to the low correlation found

t-**test** a parametric statistical test for determining the significance of the difference between two groups, or between two treatments

Turing test the test devised by Turing in which a machine gives answers indistinguishable from humans; supposedly supports the strong AI position

Two-tailed test a test that places the rejection area at both ends of a distribution

Type-1 error the probability that the null hypothesis is rejected when it is in fact true; equals the significance level

Type-2 error the failure to reject the null hypothesis when it is in fact false

Unconditioned response (UCR) a response made to an unconditioned stimulus

Unconditioned stimulus (UCS) a stimulus that can elicit a response in the absence of conditioning

Unconscious inference Helmholtz's view that perception involves inferences about sensations, and the observer is unaware of making the inferences

Unobtrusive measures measures taken from the results of behavior, not from the behavior itself (see nonreactive)

Unobtrusive observations see nonreactive

Validity refers to whether a procedure or observation is sound or genuine

Variable representativeness the determination of generality of results across different manipulations of an independent variable, or different dependent variables

Variance a measure of dispersion; the standard deviation squared

Verbal report a subject's description of his or her phenomenological experience, often very difficult to verify

Weak AI the view that computer programs can be used to test theories of human intelligence

Weber's law a formula developed by Weber which states that the smallest perceptible difference (the just-noticeable difference) between two stimuli (e.g., weights) can be stated as a ratio between the stimuli that is independent of their magnitude, $\Delta I/I = K$

What-if experiment an experiment performed to see what might happen rather than to test a specific hypothesis

Within-group variance a measure of the dispersion among subjects in the same group in an experiment

Within-subject design an experimental design in which each subject is tested under more than one level of the independent variable

Word-fragment completion task an implicit memory test in which the subject has to fill in the missing letters of a fragmented word

Work load the amount of attention-demanding effort imposed on a person

NAME INDEX

Adams, J. A., 20
Adamson, R. E., 355–357
Allen, K. E., 281
American Psychological
    Association, 89, 90, 95, 99,
    100–104, 108, 113, 124–126,
    147, 149, 461, A-8, A-13–A-15
Amsel, A., 284
Angell, J. R., A-8
Aristotle, A-1, A-3
Asch, S. E., 412–413
Bacon, F., 9
Barber, T. X., 425
Barefoot, J. C., 460, 467
Barker, R. G., 31
Barnes, V., 492
Baron, R. A., 193, 420–422, 449
Bartley, H. R., 195
Baumrind, D., 424
Beck, S. B., 267
Bell, P. A., 449
Bem, D. J., 124, 149
Bempechat, J., 399, 401
Benchley, R. W., 293–294, 296
Bentin, S., 110, 111
Bergin, A. E., 279
Berkeley, G. A., A-2
Bernard, C., 158
Bevan, W., 474
Beveridge, W. I. B., 54, 109
Biederman, I., 231
Binet, A., 375, 390
Blaney, R. H., 90

Blaxton, T. A., 314
Blough, D. S., 184, 205–206
Boring, E. G., 159, A-1, A-6
Bornstein, M. H., 383
Bortulussi, M. R., 482–483, 485–486
Bourne, L. E., 313
Bowd, A. D., 97, 105
Bower, G. H., 270–275, 334
Boyer, J. L., 105
Bradway, K. C., 381, 383–385
Bramel, D., 73
Bransford, J. D., 313–314
Brazelton, T. B., 31–32, 77–78, 397
Breitmayer, B. J., 397–398
Brickner, M. A., 65–66
Bridgman, P., 214
Broad, W., 424
Broadbent, D. E., 235–238
Brown, A. L., 311–312
Brown, J., 300
Brown, R., 362
Brownell, K. D., 93–94
Buell, J. S., 281
Butters, N., 35
Byrne, D., 193, 420, 422
Calhoun, J., 451–452, 454
Campbell, D. T., 32, 48, 278, 393, 395–396, 430
Campion, J., 201
Capaldi, E. J., 284, 286
Carroll, L., 107

SUBJECT INDEX

Photo/Figure Credits continued from page iv

author. **Fig. 3–4.** Brincker, Harkins, and Ostrom. *Effects of Personal Involvement: Thought-Provoking Implications of Social Loafing,* Journal of Personality and Social Psychology, 51, 1986. Copyright © 1975 by The American Psychological Association. Reprinted by Permission. **Fig. 6–1.** Reprinted with the permission of Historical Pictures Service, Inc. **Fig. 6–2.** By permission of Johnny Hart and NAS, Inc. **Table 6–4.** Kantowitz & Sorkin *Human Factors: Understanding People-Systems Relationships.* Copyright © 1983. Reprinted with permission of John Wiley & Sons, Inc., **Fig. 7–1.** Copyright © 1983 B. Kantowitz, Text-Eye. **Fig. 7–2.** Copyright © M. C. Escher Heirs/Cordon Art—Baarn—Holland. **Fig. 7–3.** Copyright © 1983 B. Kantowitz, Text-Eye. **Fig. 7–4.** Copyright © 1980 Robert A. Baron, Psychology: Understanding Behavior. **Fig. 7–5.** Copyright © 1983 B. Kantowitz, Text-Eye. **Fig. 7–6.** From Ittelson and Kilpatrick *Experiments in Perception.* Copyright © 1951 by Scientific American, Inc. All rights reserved. **Fig. 7–7.** Copyright © 1958 by S. Howard Bartley, Ph.D. **Figs. 7–8 and 7–9.** From Ittelson and Kilpatrick *Experiments in Perception.* Copyright © 1951 by Scientific American, Inc. All rights reserved. **Fig. 7–15.** Cheeseman and Merikle. *Priming With and Without Awareness,* Perception and Psychophysics, 36, 1984. Copyright © 1984 Psychonomic Society Inc. **Fig. 7–17.** Cheeseman and Merikle. *Distinguishing Conscious, Unconscious Perceptual Processes.* Copyright © 1986 Canadian Psychological Association. **Fig. 8–12.** Pachella. *The Interpretation of Reaction Time in Information Processing Research.* Human Information Processing-Tutorials in Performance and Condition, 1974. Copyright © 1974. Reprinted with author's permission. **Fig. 9–1.** Reprinted with the permission of The Bettmann Archive, Inc. **Fig. 9–3.** Courtesy of the Neuropsychology Laboratory, Northeastern University. Photo by Shelley Gordon-Unnerstull. **Fig. 9–7.** Bower *A Contrast Effect in Differential Conditioning* Journal of Experimental Psychology, 62, 1961. © Copyright by The American Psychological Association. Reprinted by permission of the author. **Fig. 9–8.** Wolf and Risley. *Reinforcement: Applied Research.* In R. Glosser (ed.) The Nature of Reinforcement. Copyright © 1975. Used by permission of M. M. Wolf. **Fig. 10–1.** Reprinted with the permission of the Bettmann Archive, Inc. **Fig. 11–3.** Spencer & Weisberg from *Memory & Cognition,* 14, 1986, p. 446. Reprinted by permission of Psychonomic Society, Inc. **Figs. 13–2 and 13–5.** From S. Milgram, *Obedience to Authority An Experimental View.* Copyright © 1974 by Stanley Milgram. Reprinted with the permission of Harper & Row Publishers, Inc. **Table 13–1.** From *Social Psychology* (2nd ed.) by L. S. Wrightsman. Copyright © 1977 by Wadsworth Publishing Company, Inc. Reprinted by permission of the publisher, Brooks/Cole Publishing Company, Monterey, California. **Fig. 14–1.** Courtesy of Freelance Photographers. **Fig. 14–3.** Copyright © 1972 by United Press International. **Fig. 14–4.** From S. Milgram, *Obedience to Authority An Experimental View.* Copyright © 1974 by Stanley Milgram. Reprinted with the permission of Harper & Row Publishers, Inc. **Fig. 14–5.** Reprinted with the permission of Freelance Photographer's Guild. Copyright © 1981 by Mike Valeri, photographer. **Fig. 14–6.** From *Population Density and Social Pathology* by John B. Calhoun. Copyright © 1962 by Scientific American, Inc. All rights reserved. **Fig. 15–4 and 15–5.** Kantowitz et al. *Measuring Pilot Workload in a Moving-Base Simulator: I. Asynchronous Secondary Choice-Reaction Task.* Proceedings of the Human Factors Society, 27, 1983. Copyright © 1983. Reprinted by permission. **Figs. 15–6 and 15–7.** Kantowitz et al. *Measuring Pilot Workload in a Moving-Base Simulator: II. Building Levels of Workload.* Proceedings of the Annual Conference on Manual Control, 20, 1984. Copyright © 1984. Reprinted by permission. **Fig. 15–8.** NASA. **Tables B–4 and B–5.** From *Elements of Statistics for Psychology and Education* by L. M. Horowitz. Copyright © 1974 by L. M. Horowitz. Used with permission of McGraw-Hill Book Company.